Proliferating Talent

Proliferating Talent

Essays on Politics, Thought, and Education in the Meiji Era

Motoyama Yukihiko

EDITED BY
J. S. A. Elisonas
and Richard Rubinger

University of Hawai'i Press
Honolulu

02 01 00 99 98 97   5 4 3 2 1

Library of Congress Cataloging-in-Publication Data
Motoyama, Yukihiko, 1924–
  Proliferating talent : essays on politics, thought, and education
in the Meiji era / Motoyama Yukihiko ; edited by J. S. A. Elisonas and
Richard Rubinger.
    p.   cm.
  Includes index.
  ISBN 0-8248-1846-6 (alk. paper)
    1. Education—Japan—History—1868– 2. Politics and education—
Japan.   3. Education and state—Japan.   4. Japan—Intellectual
life—1868-1912. I. Elisonas, J. S. A., 1937–   . II. Rubinger,
Richard, 1943–   . III. Title.
LA1311.7.M68   1997
370'.952—dc21
                                              97-779
                                              CIP

Designed by Josie Herr

文濟維王生
王濟周國此
以多之克王
寧士楨生國

Born and bred in this kingly land
As pillars of the state they stand:
Talented gentlemen in glittering array
Ease King Wen's spirit,
Facilitate Chou's sway.

[THE BOOK OF SONGS, 235]

Contents

Editors' Preface

This volume is the outcome of an international symposium on the work of Professor Motoyama Yukihiko held in March 1994 in Bloomington under the auspices of Indiana University's Center for Research in the History of Japanese Education. We should first of all like to thank the Japan Foundation for the grant that made this project possible.

Much of the work of preparing the manuscript of this book was done while the editors were on sabbatical leave, and we are grateful for the opportunity Indiana University gave us to devote ourselves fully to this work. Both of us, in different years, were research associates at the Institute for Research in Humanities of Kyoto University. The generous support of the Isaac Ailion Foundation has, moreover, enabled Elisonas to take up a year's visiting appointment at the Centre for Japanese and Korean Studies of Leiden University. We are most appreciative of the splendid facilities made available to us at these two outstanding institutions. In particular we wish to thank Murakami Setsuko and Nakanishi Sachiko of the Kyoto institute's library for the extraordinary efforts they made in locating rare source materials for our use. Fukui Kyōko of the Faculty of Education and Umemura Chieko of the Faculty of Humanistic Studies at Kyoto University were also extremely helpful with bibliographical information and to them, too, we are most grateful.

Colleagues who were generous with their advice and assistance include Ishizuki Minoru, James L. McClain, Umihara Tōru, and Yokoyama Toshio. We thank them for their many valuable suggestions. Thanks also to Sue Tuohy of the East Asian Studies Center of Indiana University for providing administrative support and to Amy Miller for her help in making conference arrangements.

The makeup of this book owes much to the efforts of two groups of graduate students in the Department of East Asian Languages and Cultures of Indiana University. The members of one, the Yama no Sachi Ren, are listed by name in the table of contents: chapter 1 is the result of their translation project in a course on academic Japanese. The second group, called the Honzankai of Indiana University, played an equally important role in the background: in pursuing a course on research methods in Japanese, they were assigned such editorial duties as checking facts and preparing indexes and, above all, they compiled the book's glossary. The members of the Honzankai were Charles Andrews, Fukagawa Harumichi, Margaret Key, Jennifer Koch-Weser, Sara Langer, Mary Miller, Murakami Hideo, Dawn Ollila, and R. Keith Roeller. The excellent evaluations they all received for their class work assuredly were not the result of any sort of grade inflation.

The book's title was suggested by the material of chapter 6. The descriptive element *seisei* in the name of the school discussed by Professor Motoyama in that chapter, Seiseikō, undoubtedly refers to the well-known phrase *seisei taru tashi* (Chinese: *chi-chi tuo-shih*), found in a poem in the classic *Book of Songs* (Mao 235). Originally the phrase may have signified something akin to "a steady stream of officials." In the definitive gloss of Cheng Hsüan, however, *seisei* was attributed the nuance of proper comportment, so the phrase came to mean "many gentlemen of eminent worth," and the strophe in which it occurs may therefore be translated as it is in this book's epigraph. Just as Seiseikō suggests a School of Proliferating Talent that will contribute to the state's proper governance, *seisei taru tashi* expresses Professor Motoyama's central theme, the subordination of education to political concerns in Meiji Japan. This book delves extensively into the events of the Bakumatsu and Restoration era, so it is a most felicitous accident that Mao 235 should also happen to be the locus classicus of the term *ishin*, "restoration." We are indebted to our colleague Ignotus X. Niemendal for his learned comments on this poem and for help in its translation.

As this book is meant for a wide audience—ranging from undergraduates as yet unfamiliar with Japan to advanced specialists in Japanese educational history—readability has been one of the editors' principal concerns. Translators were asked to be faithful to the author's meaning but were also encouraged not to be bound by a literal approach to the Japanese of the original. The editors made some additional adjustments to the translated chapters.

Quotation *in extenso* is no doubt more easily (or, in any event, more frequently) accommodated in Japanese academic writing than in English. All lengthy extracts have therefore been scrutinized by the editors: some have been trimmed at the edges, others diminished to simple quotes. Many shorter quotations have in turn been reduced by paraphrasing. The objective throughout has been to ease the passage of meaning originally expressed in Japanese into the flow of English rhetoric. The editors have also let the principle of "less is more" prevail in dealing with another recurrent feature of Japanese scholarly style, the summations of an argument just concluded or just about to be made. Moreover, the occasional list of names without attributes has been demoted from the text to the endnotes. In the process the text has been cut minimally and, we trust, unobtrusively. We are confident that nothing of significance has been sacrificed to rhetorical expediency.

The translators and editors have also made some additions to the text. As far as possible, vital dates have been supplied for persons who appear in the narrative. The assumption that "everyone knows" a certain historical term, personage, or event has been strenuously avoided. Japanese terms that do not appear in the *Concise Oxford Dictionary* or the *American Heritage Dictionary* have in general been defined on first occurrence, even if they are commonplace to the specialist—as is the case, for instance, with "the old feudal domains, called *han*." Notes have been added wherever explaining an event (e.g., the Tripartite Intervention or the Kōtoku Incident) requires detail that would intrude unduly into the text. To cite an example of a different kind of elaboration: Addressing an audience that was already familiar with Japanese intellectual history, Professor Motoyama needed only to mention his source by name when he quoted Suehiro Tetchō on the government's reasons for enacting the restrictive press laws of 1875. To ease matters for the less expert reader, the translation identifies that source as "Suehiro Tetchō (1849–1896)—himself a newspaper editor who had been imprisoned for attacking the restrictive ordinances." On a few, rare occasions—when reference to an original source suggested that to add, not to cut, would enhance the author's point—the rule calling for abstemiousness in quotation has been violated. Thus the Yama no Sachi Ren could not resist the impulse to restore two strophes of doggerel that Professor Motoyama had omitted from his citation of "A Pretty Kettle of Fish" in chapter 1.

The editors assume responsibility for the book's annotation. A number of misprints were discovered in the original during the editorial process, but we saw no need to call attention to them individually. Hence the discerning reader who checks chapter 1 against the original and finds that whereas Professor Motoyama mentioned a list of twenty-one demands presented by the peasants in the Miuchi Uprising of 1867, the English version speaks of twenty-six is asked not to question the accuracy of those responsible for the translation—who looked up the source used by the author—and to blame instead the typesetter of the Japanese edition. Dates in the lunar calendar used in Japan until almost the end of the fifth year of Meiji have been converted into their Western equivalents throughout. In the example just cited, that means an adjustment of the date Keiō 2 (1866) found in the original, as the Miuchi Uprising occurred toward the end of that year, at a time corresponding to the first days of 1867 by the Gregorian calendar. Similarly, the Ansei era, which the usual dictionary definition places within 1854–1859, is put between the years 1855 and 1860 in this work, as it succeeded the Kaei period on a date corresponding to 15 January 1855 and was itself not followed by Man'en until 8 April 1860. The effort to convert vital dates has inevitably led to apparent discrepancies with Japanese reference works (e.g., as far as this book is concerned, Tokugawa Ieyasu was born in 1543, not in 1542).

Wherever possible, the translations of Japanese terms and names (e.g., Self-Help Society for Risshisha) adhere to the *Kodansha Encyclopedia of Japan*. Other standard works of first reference include *Kokushi daijiten, Nihon kokugo daijiten,* and *Kadokawa Nihon chimei daijiten*. The editors' most valuable scholarly resource, however, has been the author, Professor Motoyama Yukihiko, who constantly made himself available for questions regarding interpretation, annotation, and the location of important but rare sources. Once again, we find ourselves indebted to him.

J.S.A.E. and R.R.
Leiden and Kyoto
31 May 1995

Introduction

Richard Rubinger

Japanese educational history—educational history in general, some would say—has until recently not been a very fertile field. For many years the uninspiring, narrowly professional, and in-house nature of scholarship on educational history in the United States did not present a good model to follow. Not for nothing did Bernard Bailyn assume a harsh tone in his critique of nineteenth- and twentieth-century American historians of education. The concerns of those authors had been too narrow, Bailyn argued; there were serious limitations and deficiencies in their approach. They had glorified the public schools and neglected almost everything else. As a result, the role of education in history was trivialized and the field of educational history isolated from the main currents of historical scholarship; the fruits it bore were the "typical results of sustained inbreeding."[1]

In the three and a half decades that have passed since Bailyn published this critique, the field has become more open, and its recent products are more substantial than was the case before. Nevertheless, it would be fair to say that cross-national studies of education are still not as vigorously pursued as perhaps they ought to be; comparative education, especially if it involves the study of non-Western countries, apparently is not considered a viable professional enterprise by many Western scholars. There is a reason for that, as the problem of language imposes a formidable obstacle to research. No doubt for that reason, the serious study of Japanese educational history was first taken up by specialists in other disciplines who did, however, have the requisite language skills. Naturally, at first they constituted a relatively small group.

Western scholars had recognized the important role of education in Japanese history by the 1960s, when Ronald Dore and Herbert Passin drew attention to the educational legacy of the Edo period (1600–1868) in Japan's modern transformation and John Whitney Hall discussed the role of schools and teachers in historical perspective.[2] Notable works of the 1970s are Henry Smith's investigation of the student movement in the early twentieth century and Ivan Hall's biography of Mori Arinori, Japan's first minister of education, which examines the formulation of educational policy during the early Meiji era (1868–1912) in great detail. More recently, Carol Gluck has described the ideological uses of public education during the latter part of that era. Other studies that incorporate a view of Japanese educational history within a wider topical frame include Earl Kinmonth's book on the ethos of self-advancement among elites and Donald Roden's monograph on prewar student culture.[3]

The recent surge of research in Edo-period thought has also helped to illuminate problems related to education. Noteworthy in this regard are Tetsuo Najita's study of the ideas emanating from a merchant school in Osaka, Peter Nosco's book on nativism, Mary Evelyn Tucker's monograph on the seventeenth-century educator Kaibara Ekken, and Janine Sawada's analysis of the popular educational movement known as Shingaku.[4] A growing number of studies focus directly on issues of modern Japanese educational history. As early as 1973, Donald Thurston and Benjamin Duke published books on Japanese teachers and their political involvements. Problems of academic freedom and educational reform have been the main concern of studies that have come out in the last ten years. Horio Teruhisa, for instance, takes a critical look at the role of the state in limiting intellectual freedom in Japan. Byron Marshall addresses the question of academic freedom in prewar imperial universities in one book and treats the topic of political discourse on education in another. Leonard Schoppa deals with the political constraints that have inhibited educational reform in the postwar period, and Mark Lincicome devotes great care and detail to treating the classroom methods and ideas of Western-inspired innovators who made long-lasting reforms in education during the Meiji era.[5] In short, more and more Western scholars have developed an interest in Japanese educational history, and the field has expanded notably as a result.

In Japan, too, the field has been revitalized in recent years by the work of social, cultural, and economic historians who have examined education as they investigated the spread of popular culture in their country.[6] There the problem was not a lack of coverage but the excessive cultivation of exhausted soil. A proliferation of studies on Tokugawa and Meiji education published in the postwar period yielded more and more information but approached it along well-trodden paths and organized it within conventional frameworks. Japanese educational historians appeared to be fixated on such topics as the expansion of schooling, the extension of public policy and legislation, the rise of a centrally controlled national school system, and the schools' premodern roots.

Undoubtedly, much of those scholars' reluctance to experiment and hesitancy to pose new questions for research was prompted by the disturbing memory of their profession's collaboration with the militarist government during World War II. That regime valued historians of education as vehicles for propagating wartime ideology. Located as so many of them were in teacher-training institutions, they were isolated from their historian colleagues in the universities. They did, however, wield considerable influence over public-school teachers, their former students, to whom they continued to have broad access. Historians of education exerted themselves in tracing the diffusion of *kokutai* ideology (the faith in the unique, even mystical aspects of Japan's emperor-centered polity) among the people and in culling ideas that might support wartime superpatriotism from the thought of Kaibara Ekken, Yoshida Shōin, Nishimura Shigeki, and other prominent educators of the past.

Indeed, the field flourished as never before during the war. Its first professional society, Nihon Kyōikushi Gakkai (History of Japanese Education Society), was founded in April 1943, and the first issue of its journal, *Nihon Kyōikushi Gakkai kiyō,* was published in February 1945, half a year before the war's end. Publications on educational history multiplied as never before. According to one authority, 239 books and 225 articles on educational history were published between 1941 and 1944.[7]

Naturally, this field was devastated by the sudden shift in values brought about by Japan's surrender on 15 August 1945 and the country's occupation by the Allied powers. For some years it stagnated, as courses in educational history were forbidden at teacher-training colleges and the academic pursuit of Japanese tradition, a sensitive area under the occupation, was abandoned in favor of studies of the role that schools had played in Japan's adoption of modernity. Prompted by American insistence on more pragmatic studies, historians of education in Japan turned toward empirically based critical analysis, seeking to get away from the ideological biases that had so plagued the field in the wartime period. Emphasis veered sharply away from ideas, philosophy, and ethics into the safer waters of the collection of data and compilation of reference sources.

This shift had some highly beneficial consequences, as it set the foundations for future study. Particularly noteworthy in this regard was the compilation of a thirty-five-volume series of "Documents on the Modern Japanese Educational System," published in the 1950s, which contains all educational laws and ordinances issued from 1933 to 1952.[8] Similar efforts were put into publishing collections of data on local history. Works such as the four-volume "History of Education in Aichi Prefecture" and the eighteen-volume "History of Education in Nagano Prefecture" reached high standards.[9] Edited by professionally trained scholars, these works moved away from the amateurish and propagandistic local histories typical of the prewar and wartime periods and set new standards for comprehensive data collection and critical scholarly commentary.

Indeed, the early postwar work of scholars such as Ishikawa Ken (1891–1969) and Kaigo Tokiomi (1901–1987) was so impressive that Japanese educational history has had difficulty moving beyond the contours they delineated.[10] Ishikawa's stress on the quantitative aspects of schooling—numbers of schools and school attendance data—has apparently inhibited the equally important investigation of the quality and the broader social and political contexts of education. Kaigo's focus on government policy and legislation, important features as they are, has led generations of scholars to view education in Japan as predominantly a state enterprise, directed from the top down and devoid of significant social, intellectual, or cultural contexts.

Thus the main stream of educational history in Japan has followed the direction set by one or two major postwar figures, has remained fixed within boundaries largely defined by them, and has been confined to subject matter determined by existing sources, such as school data and government legislation. By and large, educational historians have been content with "picking up the droppings of others," as one scholar has colorfully described the redundancy of so much postwar scholarship.[11] It is understandable that an academic specialty seeking to distance itself from unfortunate aberrations of the past would hold fast to reliable source materials and cling to established interpretative frameworks. Caution, however, led to another kind of stagnation. During much of the postwar period, the field of Japanese educational history has been characterized by the constant reworking of territory that has been heavily tilled already and by factional bickering over arcane and trivial matters.

But at least one scholar associated with the Faculty of Education of a major Japanese university did develop an independent line of inquiry into educational history, one that owed little to the mainstream legacies outlined above. His is a provocative and original thesis that links educational development to broad aspects of culture, thought, and politics in Japan. This book seeks to present a sample of his scholarship before an international audience.

The Scholarship of Motoyama Yukihiko

Motoyama Yukihiko, who was born in 1924, was graduated from the Faculty of Letters of Kyoto University in 1949 after having pursued a course of studies in philosophy with a concentration in ethics. Given the changing tides of scholarship and the drift away from traditional subjects in Japan under the Allied Occupation, this was an academic choice that clearly ran against the grain of the times. His training was grounded in intellectual and cultural history as well as in moral philosophy, areas in which Kyoto University has long been noted; in short, it was unlike the narrower professional training of scholars in education. For thirty years from April 1958, Motoyama taught in Kyoto University's Faculty of Education, where he occupied the chair in the History of Japanese Education. In addition to courses in his own faculty, he gave a popular course in Japanese intellectual history in that university's Faculty of Law. Upon his retirement from Kyoto in April 1988, he joined the faculty of Kansai University.

Motoyama has inspired numerous undergraduates, has guided the graduate work of an international cadre of students, and has been extraordinarily helpful in furthering the academic endeavors of colleagues not only from Japan but also from North America, Europe, China, Southeast Asia, and Africa. Anyone who seeks to comprehend the ambivalences and complexities of Japanese education from the middle of the nineteenth century to the end of the Taishō era (1912–1926) will find his scholarship an invaluable resource.

This book consists of translations of representative pieces from the extensive corpus of Motoyama's writings. Five of the eight chapters are taken from a single source, the author's own collection of essays on the major theme of his work.[12] Three other essays were added to illustrate the diversity of his interests. The chapters are arranged in roughly chronological order and overlap in their subject matter. Although single essays may be read separately with profit, the complexity of Motoyama's ideas is revealed more fully to one who moves through varying perspectives from one chapter to the next.

The limitations of space and the breadth of Motoyama's work have forced the editors to make selections. We have generally restricted the period under consideration to the Meiji era, but several chapters deal with the transition from earlier times, and chapter 1, "Patterns of Thought and Action of the Common People during the Bakumatsu and Restoration Epoch,"[13] treats the period immediately before the Meiji Restoration of 1868. Other periods and topics that have occupied Motoyama's attention have regretfully been omitted. Samples of his work on the late Taishō era, mass media and public opinion, imperial and local educational assemblies, the historical lineages of political parties, and nativist thought could unfortunately not be included in this collection.[14]

The major theme linking Motoyama's diverse interests is that a basic premise of Japan's modernization was the preeminence of state power— a lesson the Meiji oligarchs learned and a policy they derived from their study of conditions in the West. The idea of state control was applied across the board—to politics and economics, to society in general and education in particular. Since the goal of the state was to make the country rich and strong, all aspects of education—its aims, content, system, and method—were made subservient to that end. Put another way, a persistent and defining characteristic of Japanese education has been its sensitivity to political interests and political ideas. This sensitivity or, rather, subservience of education to politics persisted from the late Tokugawa epoch, when plans to tie education to a new state form emerged, through the Meiji era, when linkages between nationalist political thought and education matured. (Indeed, according to Motoyama, the dependence upon politics is the hallmark of Japanese education even today.)

Not only the central government but also those out of power sought to subordinate education to politics. The state used public education to reinforce its political agenda; opposition groups used private schools to further their political aims. To appreciate how education functioned in Meiji society, Motoyama believes, it is therefore essential to understand the political programs of the government, of the opposition, and of various private groups. His work is pervaded by an interest in how educational ideas, policies, institutions, and practices resonated within the changing intellectual and political landscapes of the Bakumatsu and Meiji Restoration epoch (the 1850s and 1860s), the Meiji era, and the Taishō period.

Half the chapters of this collection (1, 4, 5, and 8) describe broadly the world of ideas in which concerns about political developments, education, and morality were played out. The others (2, 3, 6, and 7) look directly at the linkages between political programs and schooling.

Motoyama's writings on intellectual and political history are characterized by challenges to orthodoxy. Indeed, he appears to court academic confrontations, defying standard interpretations, accepted dogma, and conventional wisdom. He persistently questions generalizations about categories and designations such as "enlightenment," "conservative," "liberal," "traditional," and "nationalist," revealing nuances of contradiction, conflict, and complexity at every turn. In Motoyama's opinion, the ideas that formed the nation's moral framework at the time of Japan's emergence as a modern state were never uniform; rather, they were in flux and depended upon evolving national circumstances. Much the same applies to the ideological influences that shaped educational thought and practice; they, too, were heterogeneous and variegated. Through this type of analysis Motoyama projects an unusually clear view of the rich intellectual climate of the Meiji era.

Motoyama's intellectual feistiness is on display from the outset, in chapter 1, which deals with the critical two decades of Bakumatsu and the Meiji Restoration. In arguing that political rather than economic motives drove prominent members of the "common people," both rural and urban, to active engagement in the events of the restoration, he directly confronts the economic determinism of Marxist historians and establishes a central place for political motivations, the major theme in all his work. Ordinary commoners, Motoyama insists, were not people in the abstract, an undifferentiated mass; rather, they were living human beings with complex sensibilities. Severely tested by the unwanted intrusion of the West, they remained committed to their traditional ways. Motivated primarily by fear of change and driven into a corner as the very framework of their lives was shaken by foreign pressures, they wanted nothing so much as to maintain and reinforce the familiar structures of their existence. They were characterized, Motoyama says, by the desperate desire to cling to the shattering walls that enclosed their minds and their lives.

Here Motoyama takes a stand against restoration historians such as Hani Gorō and Hattori Shisō, who sought conscious revolutionary motivations in rural uprisings and the riots of the urban poor and found there the seedbed of an "energy" that spawned Japan's modern transformation. Scholars of this persuasion believed that a revolutionary consciousness sustained the behavior of the common people in the eventful epoch under review. Motoyama, however, is decidedly unromantic in this respect. Exactly what, viewed historically and objectively, was the ordinary consciousness of the common people? When and under what circumstances did they revolt, take part in uprisings, engage in riots? In what sense can it be said that their activities influenced the great changes of the restoration period? These are the questions he puts to the test, and he concludes that the commoners' motivations, far from being revolutionary, were in fact remarkably conservative. Whether farmers or townspeople, ordinary folk (as distinguished from the wealthier leaders among the commoners) did not play the heroic role attributed to them by proponents of the view of history as class conflict and the advocates of "people's history."[15] They appear in chapter 1 without revolutionary energies. Mundane matters of survival are their main concern.

Motoyama's nuanced historical analysis is most prominently on display in his essays on Meiji thinkers. In his discussion of the political thought of Tani Tateki (by his origins a Tosa samurai, later a conservative politician) in chapter 4, "The Confucian Ideal of Rule by Virtue and the Creation of National Politics,"[16] Motoyama analyzes "traditional" attitudes in the early Meiji decades and provides an important corrective to conventional views of the role of Confucian ideas in Japan's modern transformation. He argues that early Meiji conservatism as represented by Tani Tateki was a reasoned response to the wave of European Enlightenment ideas that swept over Japan in the early 1870s, promoted by the Japanese devotees of the movement for "civilization and enlightenment" (discussed in chapter 5). By describing the transmutation of conservative thought as it shifted focus over time, Motoyama suggests that traditional ideas could function constructively as a guide to the new circumstances of Meiji and did not necessarily represent the dead weight of the past. As an example, Motoyama contrasts Tani's thought with that of Motoda Nagazane and Nishimura Shigeki, who stood at the far end of the conservative spectrum in calling for the preservation of "customary ways" and the revival of Confucian morality as the primary goal of public education. Tani, on the other hand, refused to remain content with such stale traditionalism and injected a healthier form of conservatism into the public debates of the 1880s.

Tani's thought blended ideas on nationalism derived from a journey to Europe with ethical concerns regarding the lives of ordinary people. He espoused a Confucian political ideal, Humane Government by a True King, and took up its root imperative, Loving the People, to combat what he saw as the Meiji government's despotic policies of Westernization. As is shown by his example, Confucianism did not function simply as an ideology of the emperor system and of state power, as is often alleged; on the contrary, it could and did serve to create constraints on autocracy by obligating the government to serve the people. This conservative response to despotism was not articulated in terms of modern, Western ideas of popular rights; it was rather from a platform of Humane Government established by the ancient Chinese sages Confucius and Mencius that such a man as Tani attacked governmental arbitrariness and called for the "voice of the people" to be heard. In addition to stressing the primacy of the people, Tani pointed out that among the "things Western" which the government was so busily, uncritically, and unselectively importing was a lot of baggage that was inapplicable to Japan. Thus he took upon himself the role of critic, one that historians do not often assign to Confucians in Japan.

Presented in this more sympathetic way, Confucian notions of Rule by Virtue and the Kingly Way lose some of the negative emotionalism associated with them in much Western writing. The nature of the "conservative" appeal as a counterforce to Westernization and its by-products, bureaucratic despotism and insensitivity to the welfare of ordinary people, also becomes easier to understand as a result of Motoyama's analysis. Tani's thought and career, little known in the West or indeed in Japan, provide a needed corrective to the conventional view of Japan as a bureaucratic state supported by a uniform conservative mind-set. The conservative intellectual strain Tani represented transcended mere traditionalism; indeed, it was a species that bore fruit by mediating the adaptation of traditional thought to Japan's modernization. Insofar as it stimulated Japan to greater selectivity in the adoption of Western spiritual and material culture, Tani Tateki's type of conservatism performed a constructive and significant historical role.

In chapter 5, "Meirokusha Thinkers and Early Meiji Enlightenment Thought,"[17] Motoyama engages in the critique of a group of Western-influenced intellectuals who played a prominent part in the realm of Japanese thought and education during the 1870s, the "enlighteners" whose denunciations of Japanese tradition and culture in favor of universal law and Western models provoked conservatives to respond. He shows how the "rationalists" of the Meiji era, the men of "cool reason" with deeper and more extensive exposure to Western thought than the bureaucrats who ran the state, moved away from a concern for individual rights and adopted the emphasis on national needs. Although they used the Western notion of natural law to criticize the traditional social hierarchies of feudalism, they bypassed individual rights—the crux of the argument in the West. Even for thinkers whose ideas were carefully differentiated on other points—such as Fukuzawa Yukichi, Katō Hiroyuki, Tsuda Mamichi, and Nishi Amane—national independence uniformly took precedence. Hence the rights of the individual faded away from discussions of politics and education in the Meiji era, even among those who were most enthusiastic about borrowing the ideas of the European Enlightenment.

By the late 1880s the glow of Japanese enlightenment thought had dimmed in favor of cultural nationalism. The reasons, Motoyama suggests, were not only the absence of broad public support and the changing circumstances of international politics (increased competition with Western powers made them appear more like adversaries than models for reform; Japan's failure to obtain the revision of unequal treaties engendered frustration and much bitterness) but also the fundamental flaws in the thought of the "enlighteners" themselves. Their preference for national over individual rights, demonstrated by Motoyama, helps explain why the patriotic frenzy that swept over Japan in the course of the Sino-Japanese War of 1894–1895 engulfed some of the most ardent among them, such as Fukuzawa and Tokutomi Sohō.

Showing no favorites, Motoyama in chapters 4 and 5 subjects the liberalism of the conservatives and the conservatism of the liberals to a critical view. In the process he makes it difficult to adhere to the simple, conventional schema that posits a "liberal" ideological dominance over thought and education in the 1870s followed by a "conservative" counterattack in the 1880s. In chapter 8, "Thought and Education in the Late Meiji Era,"[18] Motoyama continues his attack on standard interpretations of Meiji thought, carefully applying the method of textual analysis to take apart the meanings of conventional political labels. He corrects the widely held view that the issuance of the Imperial Rescript on Education in 1890 imposed a uniform state ideology on Japan and thereby brought closure to debates among state authorities and groups out of power over the ethical content of national education. Far from bringing an end to ideological disputes about the role of national education, Motoyama argues, the rescript stirred up more debate.

In this final chapter of the book, Motoyama looks at the various meanings of "nationalism," "globalism," and "individualism" articulated by men like Tokutomi Sohō, Kuga Katsunan, and Miyake Setsurei from about 1890 to the end of the Meiji era. He finds that although the Imperial Rescript on Education offered protection for certain traditional ideas, other views contended against the rigidities of the bureaucratic state. Global perspectives, ideas of humanistic education and individual values, and notions of a citizen-centered society vied for attention, resulting in measures of reform even as authoritarian education was asserting itself and Japan was moving toward war, first with China and then with Russia. Major schools of late Meiji thought saw their mission as restraining the more xenophobic currents of nationalism. In this they were partly successful, as they had the ear of officials in the Ministry of Education—who are, somewhat surprisingly, portrayed here as more moderate than many elements of the public, schoolteachers, and the far more conservative Home Ministry.

In Motoyama's view, modern education became linked to political goals when compulsory schooling was used to provide ideological cohesion for a new imperial state shortly after the Meiji Restoration. The links were forged even before the restoration had run its course, as key leaders came to consider a national educational system indispensable to building support for the new government and maintaining an independent state. As chapter 2, "The Political Background of Early Meiji Educational Policy: The Central Government," makes clear in elaborate detail, however, they could not be applied until political and military centralization was completed.[19] Ideas about what sort of education was required and which sectors of the population ought to receive highest priority varied considerably over the course of political consolidation. While Confucianists and Shintoists were looking backward to their own representations of a virtuous past to be used as a moral guide to the future, more pragmatic political leaders had a different, forward vision. They saw modern education as the means to train the Japanese people in the practical skills they would need if they were to contribute to the defense of national security in a predatory international environment.

The ruling group demonstrated a remarkable pragmatism and capacity for change as political consolidation continued through the civil war fought against opponents of the imperial restoration, the transfer of the capital from Kyoto to Tokyo, and the rendition of domanial registers, culminating in the abolition of domains and the establishment of central control over the entire country. Iwakura Tomomi, the early Meiji government's paramount leader, first held the view that a reinvigorated but tradition-based institution of higher learning for court nobles was essential, but then moved closer to the ideas of Itō Hirobumi and Kido Takayoshi, who envisioned a more pragmatically oriented, Western-style university. Notions of the purpose of popular education also changed along with political circumstances. The training of elites for leadership was the initial objective; the eventual redefinition, however, was universal public schooling that would strengthen the nation as a whole. Central to Motoyama's argument throughout is the view that educational policy was intimately tied to changing political conditions. The process required for the emergence of a national policy in early Meiji was tortuous. For Japanese education, the transition from Tokugawa to Meiji was not smooth or easy.

To be sure, the leaders of Japan's central government were not alone in trying to subordinate education to political interests. Motoyama insists that political associations and their educational counterparts on the peripheries of power shared that tendency. Those out of power, no less than the leaders of local political factions, contributed to the educational ferment by establishing schools expressly to disseminate their own political ideologies. In short, political rivalry led to the establishment of educational institutions as various groups saw the need to cultivate talent that would propagate their ideas and pursue their alternative political programs. Three examples of Motoyama's interest in the interplay between center and periphery and his concern with the educational contributions of out-of-power political groups are included in this book.

The case treated in chapter 3, "Local Politics and the Development of Secondary Education in the Early Meiji Period,"[20] is Kōchi Prefecture, a provincial region famed as the birthplace of the popular-rights movement. The period examined extends from the Bakumatsu era of the 1850s and 1860s to the end of the 1880s. The central issue is the often antagonistic relationship between the provincial authorities imposed on Kōchi by the central government in Tokyo and groups carrying on political traditions current in the prefecture since those days when it was still called Tosa Province and was a feudal domain under the Tokugawa regime. Under discussion in this chapter are the activities of officialdom, political cliques of the old domain, and newer political associations that emerged in the early Meiji era—each with its own middle school promoting its own political program.

In general, the Meiji leadership's highest priorities in the 1870s were higher education to replenish the governing elite and primary education to provide the populace with basic skills (see chapter 2). Middle schools therefore represented the last link to be put in place in the chain of a centrally controlled modern school system. Consequently, local and private political interests remained influential longest at the secondary level, persisting well into the 1880s, when central policy intervened decisively and the middle schools were incorporated into the national educational system. Until then, the middle schools' relative independence from central control made them susceptible to patronage by local political factions. Motoyama uses the case of Kōchi to describe the details of this process as it worked itself out among the contending factions in one prefecture. He takes a comprehensive view, delineating the important role played by various political cliques in the Tosa domain before the restoration and describing their educational functions during the transition from Bakumatsu to Meiji. He points out that many of the pre-Meiji secondary schools were already engaged in training leadership based on talent in the old domain and shows that the open and progressive nature of early Meiji education in Kōchi reflected a carry-over from the past, not an imposition from above.

In this prefecture, the reformist tradition of the Tosa domain's political associations formed the backdrop for the development of groups that advocated self-reliance and opposed the central government's despotic pursuit of "civilization and enlightenment." An especially interesting example is presented by the well-known political party called Risshisha (Self-Help Society) and the private middle school attached to it as its educational arm, Risshi Gakusha. The political thought informing the society—and the ideology propagated by its school—was popular rights. The Risshisha emerged from the provincial environment of Kōchi to become a prominent political group on the national stage. It posed a significant challenge to the Meiji government throughout the 1870s.

Provincial educational traditions, however, were as diverse as the political interactions between center and periphery were complex. In Kōchi, a reformist tradition in prerestoration domain politics led to the foundation of schools that sought to propagate the doctrine of popular rights; in Kumamoto, similarly strong ties to the feudal past produced different results. Motoyama uses the example of the political association called Shimeikai and its school, the Seiseikō (School of Proliferating Talent)—the subject of chapter 6, "The Statist Movement and Its Educational Activities"[21]—to suggest that nationalist ideas centered on the interests of the state were as likely to develop in the provinces as at the center, generating educational offshoots. In Kumamoto, statist ideas developed out of local samurai experience. The men who fostered those ideas were by no means inspired by the central government's concerns; indeed, the founder of the Seiseikō, Sassa Tomofusa, and some of his closest collaborators had participated in the Satsuma Rebellion of 1877 and thus were by definition members of an antigovernment faction. Nonetheless, they were led to endeavors that would provide a model for the national educational system of the 1880s. Indeed, as Motoyama points out, military training, commonly thought to have been introduced into the school curriculum by Minister of Education Mori Arinori in 1886, was two years earlier already a part of the program of the School of Proliferating Talent. In the case of this Kumamoto private institution—in contrast to Kōchi—a correspondence in educational philosophy between center and periphery helped ensure support for the central government's objectives at the local level.

In this chapter Motoyama poses one of the most important questions one can ask about the Meiji era: Why did people so readily accept the policies of the new government? His answer moves away from the notion of coercion from above, a view prominent in standard treatments of the subject, and focuses instead on the manner in which individuals and local groups came to favor strong central government and statist policies on their own initiative and in pursuit of their own political interests. It will be noted that in this case, too, the subordination of education to politics is evident.

A different kind of private educational institution is treated in chapter 7, where the intellectuals associated with the Tōkyō Senmon Gakkō —Tokyo Specialist School, later to become Waseda University—are presented as the example of the "Spirit of Political Opposition in the Meiji Period."[22] When this group's leader, Ōkuma Shigenobu, was ousted from the ruling oligarchy in 1881 and the parliamentary model contemplated by the government shifted from England to Prussia, English "liberal" thought became the guiding philosophy of the opposition. In this chapter Motoyama explores how English thought defined the curriculum, methods, and goals of the Tokyo Specialist School. He contrasts these with the far less "liberal" models preferred by Tokyo University, which was supported by the government and in turn supported it, proclaiming its educational function to be the training of bureaucrats for the state. As circumstances changed—particularly after Ōkuma moved back into the government in 1896—opposition ideology shifted from political to economic concerns, and the Tokyo Specialist School's mission was transformed from inspiring its students to civic action by fostering a spirit of the "independence of learning" to training model citizens who would act in harmony with the state. The educational ideas of parties out of power on the national stage apparently were as dependent upon the changing fortunes of their political patrons as were those of educational leaders at the center and the peripheries of power.

As has been seen, Motoyama has constructed a broad political framework for his analysis of educational issues. Whereas he views the transfer of the capital to Tokyo and the abolition of feudal domains as the crucial events of early Meiji, for Motoyama the Political Crisis of 1881 marks the critical divide between early and later Meiji. After Ōkuma Shigenobu, the champion of the modernizers, was forced out of the government in 1881, the Japanese political spectacle took an interesting turn. On the right side of the stage, the ideas of the "conservative" Tani Tateki came to represent one kind of opposition thought. At the same time, Ōkuma, the darling of the "liberals," was thrust into opposition on the other side. At the center, despotic power was given a constitutional base under the hallowed authority of the emperor. The role played by education increasingly turned to building support for a state planned and controlled from above.

In an international conference that discussed aspects of Motoyama's work, Albert Craig suggested that academic writing styles may be compared to university campuses: Some are broad and expansive, with lawns and even woods encircling widely spaced buildings—the rural type. Others are crowded, with buildings huddled closely upon one another and little room to move about—the urban type. Motoyama's style resembles the latter. It is dense and tightly packed. The contents of his scholarship are rich with information that one will find nowhere else. The interpretative substance of his work has much to offer not only to specialists in educational history but also to readers whose main interests are political and intellectual history.

In the essays that follow, those interested in school history will find detailed discussions of the early development of the university and national plans for elementary schools (chapter 2), the emergence of middle schools (chapters 3 and 6), and the distinct academic styles of Waseda and Tokyo University in the late Meiji era (chapter 7). Those with other interests will find that considerable attention is also devoted to political developments: There are analyses of popular unrest in the restoration period (chapter 1), the restoration wars and the steps leading to national consolidation under the Meiji government (chapter 2), the popular-rights movement (chapter 3), regional repercussions from the Satsuma Rebellion of 1877 (chapter 6), the Political Crisis of 1881 (chapters 4 and 7), and public opinion at the turn of the century, during the time of the Sino-Japanese and Russo-Japanese wars (chapter 8).

Characteristic of all of Motoyama's work is a scrupulous attention to primary sources. Political actors, thinkers, the public, and special interests speak for themselves through their writings in newspapers, journals, and professional publications. Motoyama subtly and carefully analyzes their words to produce original theses with little reliance on the interpretative frameworks of other scholars. The enormous variety of his sources runs from expressions of popular discontent found in graffiti, posters, and popular songs of the period immediately before the Meiji Restoration (chapter 1) to the discourses, letters, and diaries of intellectual and political figures. Included among the latter are major figures at the center, such as Iwakura Tomomi, Itō Hirobumi, and Kido Takayoshi (chapter 2), no less than their local counterparts (chapters 3 and 6); among the former are Confucianists such as Nishimura Shigeki and Tani Tateki (chapter 4), the "enlighteners" of the Meirokusha (chapter 5), "statists" like Sassa Tomofusa and Tsuda Seiichi (chapter 6), "liberals" like Ono Azusa and Takata Sanae (chapter 7), and "nationalists" such as Tokutomi Sohō, Kuga Katsunan, and Miyake Setsurei (chapter 8). Chapter 8, which reveals extensive research in professional educational journals, traces the patterns of educational opinion both inside and outside official circles during the late Meiji period.

Education is a central concern for Motoyama, but his subject is education writ large. Schools are seen as institutions for the dissemination of ideas. He shies away from the analysis of textbooks, the study of curricula, and the compilation of attendance figures for their own sake; insofar as he discusses the histories of schools, it is not for their institutional glorification. His framework is broad, and the issues are central to the history of modern Japan—the consolidation of the centralized state, the relations between central authority and local power, the rise of nationalism, the relationship between individuals and the state, the limits of public and private interests, and the linkages among power, ideas, and practical policy. Motoyama has set the history of education in Japan within the broad political, intellectual, and historical contexts of which the professional proponents of school history would have deprived it. In so doing he has fixed Meiji education in its "elaborate, intricate involvement with the rest of society" and mapped its "shifting functions, meanings, and purposes," thus coming closer to Bailyn's "broader definition of education"[23] than any other Japanese scholar of his generation.

1

Patterns of Thought and Action of the Common People during the Bakumatsu and Restoration Epoch

Translated by
The Yama no Sachi Ren of Indiana University:
 William J. Farge
 Jennifer Koch-Weser
 Christopher Robins
 R. Keith Roeller

The term "common people" *(shomin)* will be used in this chapter in a completely conventional way, denoting those who did not have samurai status—people outside the ruling stratum of Japan's feudal society.

Great importance has been attributed to the role played by the common people in the Bakumatsu era and the period of the Meiji Restoration. Indeed, the study of their thought and actions is the cornerstone of an influential interpretation of this epoch. The pioneers of that interpretation, one developed from the standpoint of historical materialism, were Hani Gorō and Hattori Shisō. Hani posited the intensification of peasant uprisings and riots of the urban poor in the Bakumatsu era as the source of energy for Japan's modernization. Here he found the class struggle that was the driving force of history, a force seeking to do away with the opposition between the domanial lord and the peasant that was the fundamental contradiction in feudal society. Hani evaluated these upheavals highly as the manifestations of democratic and revolutionary energies. Hattori, on his part, identified the commercial economy's developmental stage in the Bakumatsu era with the "stage of manufacture." The bourgeois development of a commercial economy shook the feudal system; and that, he thought, was the cause of the intensified uprisings and riots. Accordingly, Hattori sought the basic line of Meiji Restoration history not only in the revolutionary qualities of the peasant uprisings but also in the political practice of the prime movers of commercial production, the so-called grass-roots *(sōmō)* bourgeoisie. These rural bourgeois, he found, had entered into an alliance—assuming the leadership role—with the lordless samurai activists whose political program was expressed in the slogan *sonnō jōi,* "Revere the emperor and repel the barbarians!"

To be sure, there were some differences between Hani and Hattori, but they did hold one preconception in common. Both thought that the actions and consciousness of the common people during the Bakumatsu and Restoration epoch ought to be evaluated as progressive. Subsequent studies of this topic have basically followed their line. Those studies, it would appear, share a few assumptions, which may be summarized roughly as follows: The economic base that sustained the political processes of that epoch was an antagonistic relationship between the commercial economy of the lord of the domain and the commercial economy of the farmers. The latter may be equated with capitalist production in the bud. The contradiction between these two economies resulted in intensified uprisings and riots. Those disturbances, in turn, determined political developments.

What about those works on the epoch's history that harbor doubts concerning the common people's progressive nature or even ignore the commoners altogether? Naturally, they are to be rejected as undeserving of the name "historical science."

Yet were the patterns of thought and action of the common people during the Bakumatsu and Restoration epoch indeed endowed with a progressive energy that sufficed to create a modern Japan? How would it be if, rather than rushing to apply the laws of human development taught by historical materialism to those three or four short decades of Japan's internal experience, one were to analyze the major causative factors of that period's history objectively, that is, in a manner befitting historians? One would conclude that the common people's attitudes and actions were only one of those causative factors. Moreover, they were objective conditions, rather than subjective causes. Should such a way of thinking be ignored as unscientific? I doubt it.

To adjudge the common people's role in the Meiji Restoration progressive and then permit no other approach to elucidating it can scarcely be called a humble attitude toward historical science. Surely, the special qualities of Japan's modernization would be understood all the better if a greater variety of concrete, historical analyses of the common people's attitudes and actions were encouraged. The people in question were indeed confronted with a historical contradiction, one that was unprecedented for them—an accident, so to speak, that befell late Tokugawa Japan, caused by external forces. How did they try to cope with the crisis? One wonders whether previous interpretations have done the commoners justice. Have they been appreciated as historical personages, as men and women who had to live through an extraordinarily tense and exciting period of social and political change?

The common people figure in those previous interpretations simply as "the masses" *(jinmin taishū)*. They are people in the abstract. They are scarcely looked upon as living human beings. The way they appraised and reacted to the challenges of the epoch is not put to a genuine inquiry. Had their motivations and actions been grasped objectively, the story would be different. It would be clear that they were not so simple as to be defined unequivocally as progressive; that, indeed, the commoners' patterns of thought and action were made up of various shadings.

If one truly wants to elucidate those patterns, it is not enough simply to stand on a "progressive" historical platform and direct "the masses" up a one-way street. It will not do merely to declare unhesitatingly that the historical role of the common people's riots and uprisings was progressive. Above all, it is necessary to analyze their behavior and consciousness in relation to their traditional attitudes toward life and to the changes that took place in their environment.

Changes in the Circumstances of the Common People's Lives

Urban riots and peasant uprisings increased and intensified in an unprecedented way after the unwanted visit of Commodore Matthew Perry's squadron to Japan in 1853, especially as the Meiji Restoration drew closer. Our reference shall be an authoritative chronological table of peasant uprisings prepared at Kyoto University.[1] If we compare the two eight-year periods 1852–1859 and 1860–1867, we will find 75 incidents listed in the first period—a yearly average of 9.4—and discover 132 in the second, an average of 16.5. The rate of incidence increases by more than 75 percent. Moreover, if that second period is divided into two four-year segments, the figures are 52 in the first phase and 80 in the second phase. Again, the yearly average rises dramatically.

Next, let us look at the causes of the uprisings. Apart from the standard causes, those common throughout the Tokugawa era—the high-handedness of village headmen, their violations of the law, disputes between villages, and so forth—this epoch's incidents most notably originated in price increases and in intensified exactions, that is, heavy taxes, special monetary levies, and restraints put on the peasants' commercial production in the form of expanded lists of objects liable to taxation and the like. Of the seventy-five uprisings in the period before 1860, six (8 percent) were due to price increases and fourteen (18.7 percent) to taxes, levies, and restraints on production. Of the 132 in the period 1860–1867, twenty-two (16.7 percent) arose from price increases and thirty-nine (29.5 percent) from intensified exactions. Not only did the total figure almost double in the second period, the number of incidents that broke out because of intensified exactions almost tripled and of those brought on by price increases almost quadrupled. It is of great importance to appreciate these facts. In particular, note that uprisings attributable to price increases, which occupy one-sixth of the total number in the years between 1860 and 1867, are a phenomenon peculiar to this eight-year period and are not seen in any other similar period of the Tokugawa era.

Did this peculiar phenomenon signify, however, that the domanial lords' regime had been overcome by a commercial economy which had developed spontaneously within the matrix of the feudal system or, more to the point, by the common people, who drove that economy? Definitely not. What, in that case, accounts for the eruption of the uprisings? Pressures from the outside—that is, from the Western powers and Russia—and from above, in the form of political changes initiated within Japan in the effort to resist those outside powers, had exacerbated the feudal system's internal contradictions. The common people's standpoint had not been considered, and their consciousness was not a factor in this process. Their traditional environment, however, was seriously disturbed by it and had degenerated. That was the reason for their violent expressions of discontent.

The opening of Japan's ports to trade in the Ansei era (January 1855–April 1860)[2] as a result of foreign pressures tied the country's feudal economy willy-nilly into the vast world market, hastened the dismantling of feudal commercial distribution structures, caused rapid price rises, and brought on hard times for lower samurai and for the common masses. These were the years when foreign pressures were converted to internal pressures. The so-called five commodities—that is, raw silk, cloth, grains (including rice), lamp oil, and wax, the principal export goods—came to flow directly from their production sites to the trade ports, bypassing established wholesaler networks. The Tokugawa shogunate feared that this dislocation would cause a shortage of daily necessities in Edo and that prices would increase. In 1860 it sought to forestall that possibility by issuing the Order to Forward the Five Commodities through Edo (Gohin Edo Mawashi Rei), and began to regulate trade in a peremptory manner. This regulatory policy, however, had little effect in the face of pressures from the outside, and prices continued to climb steadily under the direct or indirect influence of foreign trade.

The year 1860 marked a turning point. In addition to the burning

political question of the day—should Japan be opened to the outside
world or remain a closed country?—the Tokugawa regime confronted
the problems of the shogunal succession and of attempts on the part of
powerful domains to reform the country's governing system. These problems became extraordinarily complicated because the imperial court intervened in them. Just as they appeared to have been settled by the
oppressive dictatorship of Great Elder (Tairō) Ii Naosuke (1815–1860),
men opposed to the despotism of the Tokugawa regime set off the violence of the *sonnō jōi* movement in earnest, and Ii was assassinated at
the Sakurada Gate of Edo Castle by *rōnin*—lordless samurai—from
Mito. The shogunate and the domains had been forced to undertake
vast expenditures to bolster Japan's defenses after Perry's arrival, and
that brought on an intensified exploitation of the common people. After
1860, however, the financial quandary grew more profound as the
political situation deteriorated.

The conventional guiding principle of the domanial fisc had been
"calculate income and adjust expenditures accordingly" *(iru o hakarite
idasu o nasu)*. How to respond to the development of the commercial
economy—to adapt to it or to resist it—while remaining faithful to that
principle had been the recurrent problem of the feudal ruler. On its
solution depended the success or failure of the reforms undertaken from
time to time by the shogunate and the domains during the Edo period.
After 1860, however, the shogunate's and the major domains' brisk
engagement in political ventures transformed the nature of their financial organs, which became conduits for securing and dispensing funds
to be used in the arena of politics. Moreover, the perceived need for
armaments rose day by day—whether they were intended for resisting
foreign powers or for securing a strong say in Japanese affairs. Hence
the fiscal policies of the shogunate and the domains were completely
subordinated to their military policies, to the point where settling financial problems under the time-honored principle of a balanced budget
became impossible. Consequently, the shogunate and the domains not
only expanded their lists of taxable objects but also frequently began
ordering emergency levies. They even organized the common people
militarily and inflicted compulsory service on them by forming peasant
militias. To be sure, these measures in the end undermined the feudal
rulers' economic base and shook their authority. Popular uprisings broke
out in the breaches thus created in the feudal system.

The greatest reasons for the startling increase in the number of peasant uprisings and urban riots during the Bakumatsu and Restoration
epoch were the opening of foreign trade and the ensuing economic disorder, coupled with the social disjunction that accompanied the deterio-

rating political situation. The economic burden carried by the common people grew heavier. They were suddenly weighed down by unthought-of pressures from above and abroad; their traditional form of life broke down, and their habitual worldview disintegrated as a result of these external forces. These changes were more instrumental in hastening the feudal system's destruction than was the growth of a domestic commercial economy.

Nothing illustrates the powerful blow suffered by the common people more strikingly than the following list of the price increases they endured. In Edo, during the nine-year period from 1859 through 1867, rice went up by 270 percent, lamp oil by 300 percent, ginned cotton by 330 percent, tiles by 150 percent, wax by 140 percent, dried sardines by 200 percent, oil cakes by 300 percent, lumber by 150 percent, paper by 240 percent, green tea by 30 percent, Japanese sugar by 220 percent, and the cost of shipping by 40 percent.[3] These figures represent wholesale prices; it can be assumed that retail prices rose even more dramatically. Note that 1859 prices already represent a tremendous rise over the level of the 1830s and early 1840s, and it becomes all the more apparent that these price increases were abnormal. They had far exceeded the autogenous growth of a domestic commercial economy.

Extraordinary price increases hit Kyoto and Osaka as well. In 1864, the greater part of Kyoto burned to the ground in the Hamaguri Gate Incident (Hamaguri Gomon no Hen). This fire caused price rises even more severe than those in Edo. Between 1864 and 1867 rice prices increased eightfold, grain ninefold, *sake* sixfold; the price of soy sauce quintupled and that of sugar quadrupled.[4] Strangely enough, however, not a single riot broke out within Kyoto in 1866, even as revolts were on the rise in Edo and the Musashi region, no less than in Osaka and the Hyōgo region. The reason for Kyoto's relative calm was that moralists of the Shingaku school, in particular Kumagai Renshin (1783–1859) and Shibata Yūō (also known as Shibata Gaiken; 1809–1874), persuaded Mitsui, Shimada, Ono, and other merchant houses to provide relief to the poor; moreover, the offices of the two town magistrates *(machi bugyō)* of Kyoto, East and West, released emergency rice. In all, 4,953 ryō in gold, 1,389 ryō in silver, over 3,610 kan in cash coinage, in excess of 119 *koku* of rice and 11 *koku* of rice cake, more than 2,100 bundles of split firewood, and 740 bundles of brushwood were made available. This large amount of relief funds and goods mollified the poor, who were on the verge of rioting.[5]

Commodity prices in Osaka increased between 1859 and 1867 just as they did in Edo. Barley rose by 300 percent, wheat by 800 percent, soybeans by 700 percent. Salt became ten times more expensive, soy sauce four times, and rapeseed oil six times.[6] Rice does not appear in these Osaka statistics, but a chart of the history of that city's Dōjima rice market set out by Tōyama Shigeki makes it apparent that its price increased eightfold in those nine years.[7] In 1866 and 1867, when the forces mobilized for the shogunate's second campaign against Chōshū were stationed in Osaka, consumption increased dramatically. Consequently, prices soared. The inflation spread from the Three Metropolises throughout the country.

If these price rises had been balanced with comparable increases in the townspeople's cash incomes, there would have been no problem. That was not the case, however, and the steep jump in prices far exceeded the people's ability to cope. Let us examine, for instance, the wage increases of artisans in Edo during the period 1859–1867. Calculating from a base of 100 in the year 1859, the wages of a carpenter in 1867 amounted to 170. The earnings of a stonemason, a thatcher, and a cabinetmaker were 160; a woodcutter made 140 and a mat maker 110. The average figure is 150. How does it compare with commodity prices? Using an index of 100 for 1859, consumer costs in 1867 can be calculated as 297. In other words, while wages rose by an average of 50 percent in Edo, prices rose by almost 200 percent, four times as much.[8] The same was no doubt true in Kyoto and Osaka as well. This great incongruity between wages and prices inevitably broke down the stability of the common people's traditional way of life.

It is important to keep in mind here the phenomenal development of foreign trade. No doubt there were instances of extraeconomic coercion and sharp practice on the part of the foreigners, who took advantage of the ignorance of shogunal officials and Japanese merchants alike, but in the last four or five years of the Tokugawa period export trade nearly doubled and import trade increased more than five times. (To be sure, these are only the official figures. If contraband were also considered, the figures would be even higher.) In 1863 total exports amounted to 6,859,000 dollars; in 1867 the sum had risen to 12,133,000 dollars. The total volume of the import trade was 3,580,000 dollars in 1863. That figure jumped to 18,476,000 dollars in 1867.[9] Such an increase in trade in only four years was truly extraordinary and would not reoccur even in the Meiji period. These figures show with what vehemence Japan's feudal economy was sucked into the whirlpool of international market capitalism. That is what swept away the feudal system.

The production of almost all the chief export goods—raw silk, tea, raw cotton, silkworm egg–cards, marine products, oil, copper, wax, and so forth—had at least in part reached the stage of manufacture or the stage of household industry within a wholesale distribution system. For all that, output was limited, as it depended on a feudal mode of production that could not escape its essential limitation—to produce the goods was merely the subsidiary occupation of farm families. Together with the opening of international trade, a marked decrease in domestic consumption became apparent. Although the shogunate attempted to put the situation under control, it was in the end unable to overcome the demands of international capitalism, and the established mechanisms of the regulation and distribution of commercial goods broke down. Moreover, a tremendous outflow of specie from Japan accompanied the advances of international trade into the country. Without a doubt, that outflow was a major cause of the rise in prices.

The drain of specie arose because Japanese gold, which was disproportionately cheap in comparison with the parity of gold and silver on the international market, was being traded for the dollar at a fixed rate of exchange. As a protective measure, the shogunate reminted its gold and silver currency and debased its quality, but this step merely led to a loss of confidence in the coinage, and copper cash was left the only trustworthy means of exchange. To make matters worse, large amounts of copper were exported in disregard of the official limits, and it became scarce. Inflation was the result. But it was not only by causing a collapse of confidence in the currency or by disrupting the familiar flow patterns of goods that foreign trade shook the foundations of the feudal system. It also attacked those foundations by striking a blow against the commercial production that had begun to emerge autogenously from within the matrix of the feudal system. The limited capacity of Japanese commercial production during the Bakumatsu period could not but be exposed by that blow. It was the common people—the very ones whom one might expect, by rights, to constitute the productive stratum that would uphold the emergence of a new society—who were caught between the rock of the feudal system and the hard place of world capitalism.

The negative impact of foreign trade on commercial production had notable effects on both imports and exports. In exports, the silk goods industry was the most seriously affected. To be sure, the output of raw silk doubled in response to the rapidly expanding demand, and its production techniques were improved—but not to the extent that the stage of manufacture was achieved nationwide. In northernmost Honshū as well as in Kōzuke Province (now Gunma Prefecture), Shinano Province (now Nagano Prefecture), and in other regions, hand-reeling instruments *(zaguri)* became widespread, and there were even some places where elementary power-driven devices were used, but traditional techniques of spinning silk by hand prevailed on the national level until the early years of the Meiji period. Production may have doubled, but it was still unable to cover the demands of the foreign market; all too often, inferior products were produced to make up for the shortfall. No surplus remained, and the demands of domestic consumption could not be met.

The centers of silk cloth production, such as Kiryū in Kōzuke, the Nishijin district of Kyoto, and Hakata (now a part of Fukuoka) were dealt a devastating blow when the export of raw materials generated shortages and inflated prices. Kiryū evidently faced a crisis by 1859.7, just two months after Kanagawa (Yokohama), Nagasaki, and Hakodate were fully opened to foreign trade; that month, representatives of the villages of the area petitioned the shogunate's inspector general *(ōmetsuke)* for a ban on exports. They followed up this petition with other appeals to the shogunate, even daring to make a direct plea to Great Elder Ii Naosuke. Not only the textile manufacturers of Kiryū but also the small-scale farmers and artisans who depended on them ardently wished to put a stop to the exports. The extent of the disruption suffered by the economy of their region may be gauged from a petition that the representatives of the "new town" of Kiryū submitted to the Edo town magistrates in 1859.10: "At length our stock of raw silk has run out. We have had no choice but to lay idle our looms, and many people have lost their jobs. . . . Every night, bills complaining about the difficult situation are left posted at the residences of town officials and other important persons in the community, leaving all of us consumed with worry. If matters continue developing this way, there is no telling what sort of disaster may occur. As it is, all the villages face imminent decline and destruction; in the end, they may riot, as survival becomes ever more difficult."[10]

This situation on the eve of the Kiryū uprising was brought about by the crumbling of productive capacity as a result of pressure from the outside. The conditions in Nishijin were no different. As early as the spring of 1859, even before foreign trade had been formally opened, the weavers and raw silk merchants of Kyoto were already suffering from shortages and high prices of raw silk. They expressed their plight in a petition to the authorities: "The four foreign countries of America, England, Russia, and France have recently been permitted to trade. From last year into this spring, however, foreign traders have been coming one after another to Nagasaki desiring various goods to exchange commercially. Japanese raw silk is among those goods, leading to inflated prices in this locality compared with Nagasaki or Osaka. Hence the local weavers of Nishijin and those engaged in the silk trade are facing dire straits. . . . If even a small quantity of Japanese raw silk is permitted to be sold abroad now, then before long the entire country's stock will be depleted. That is a prospect we truly lament."[11]

By 1860 Kyoto's weavers found themselves in such a predicament that they asked their East town magistrate for a loan of 6,000 *koku* of rice from the government supply. They managed to get over the worst of their difficulty with the 1,000 *koku* that they were granted. The shogunate could not help becoming directly involved, and provided Nishijin with an emergency loan of 30,000 ryō. Other textile-producing areas, such as Hakata, Tango, Hachiōji, and Chichibu, faced the same trials as Kiryū and Nishijin. In Hakata, it is said, eight or nine out of ten weavers quit their trade. In the face of pressures from world capitalism, the Japanese silk-weaving industry of the Bakumatsu period had been dealt a devastating blow.

The cotton textile industry suffered similar distress. Let us look at the situation in some of its weaving centers. Before the opening of the Japanese market to foreign competition, the area of Mooka in Shimotsuke Province (now Tochigi Prefecture) was riding a wave of prosperity. In the favorable climate of economic development that prevailed from the Bunka through the Tenpō period (1804–January 1845), this area produced more than 380,000 *tan* [1 *tan* = about 12 yards] of cotton cloth a year. Then Mooka was overwhelmed and ruined by cheap imported cotton. By 1872, no more than 40,000 *tan* per year were being produced there. The areas of Ashikaga (on the border of what are now Tochigi and Gunma prefectures) and Tsukagoshi in Musashi Province (now Warabi City, Saitama Prefecture) had had ample reason to boast of their prosperity during the century's first half, but nearly every business in both these regions went under with the opening of Japan. The effects of foreign trade were also felt outside the Kantō region: the cotton-weaving centers of Matsusaka in Ise, of Aichi, and of Gifu went into decline as well. These districts were able to recover later by using cheap imported cotton yarn, but their adaptiveness only meant that the demand for domestic cotton for industrial use was gradually reduced. The cotton-weaving trade, which had reached the stage of household industry within a wholesale distribution system, lost important clients; until the adoption of spinning machinery, it was headed straight down the road to disaster.

It is clear that Japanese commercial manufacture—the weaving industry, in any event—was destroyed by the pressures of world capitalism long before it had attained the capacity for self-sustained growth that would have enabled it to pose a challenge to the feudal system. The silk-weaving trade, in particular, had grown up in a close symbiotic relationship with privileged wholesalers in the Three Metropolises; hence the very fact that traditional distribution networks were disturbed by foreign pressures dealt it a direct and devastating blow. Much the same could be said of other export merchandise, but it is time now to leave the survey of the effects of foreign trade and move on to another question: What pressures were brought to bear on the common people by the shogunate and the domains as political developments unfolded in the Bakumatsu period?

After the coming of the foreign ships, to "calculate income and adjust expenditures accordingly" became impossible. The cost of foreign relations and domestic political emergencies—not to speak of armaments—was immense. The shogunate's regular income was limited; there was, however, practically no limit to its expenditures. The deficit had to be made up, at least in part, with the lifeblood of the common people.

Let us look at military expenditures first. In 1853, the year of Perry's intrusion, the shogunate ordered that coastal fortifications be bolstered and a firearms factory established at Yushima. In addition, Mito *han* was ordered to construct a shipyard at Ishikawajima. A naval training school with Dutch instructors was opened in Nagasaki in 1854. A shipyard called the Nagasaki Ironworks (Seitetsusho) was constructed between 1855 and 1861. Plans were drawn up for the Tategami Warship Dockyard in 1863 and for the Yokosuka Ironworks (the predecessor of the Imperial Navy's famed Yokosuka Arsenal) in 1865; construction began in earnest the following year. These undertakings alone cost the shogunate nearly 20 million ryō, and that was only a part of the costs of military preparedness. The purchase of foreign warships and weapons required considerable outlays, representing more than 20 percent of the combined shogunate and *han* import aggregate. In the fourteen years from 1854 through 1867, the shogunate bought forty-four naval vessels for 3.3 million dollars, and the domains procured ninety-four warships for 4.5 million dollars. The imported weapons were mostly small arms; 480,000 pieces were acquired by the shogunate and the domains for a combined sum of 6.6 million dollars. The total cost of the weapons and warships was approximately 14.4 million ryō. This figure includes only imports that followed formal procedures. If contraband were added, the total would become even greater.

The cost of international relations included paying compensation for diplomatic incidents, dispatching missions abroad, opening the ports of Yokohama and Hakodate, and providing security for foreign envoys. Further domestic examples of extraordinary financial demands that had to be met by the shogunate are bribes to the imperial court, the costs of the two Chōshū expeditions, and the expenses of military reorganization. In any event, after the appearance of the foreigners' "black ships" at Uraga, millions of ryō vanished unproductively. The shogunate and domanial governments inflicted repeated levies on wealthy townspeople on top of the standard tax. This practice ultimately resulted in price increases and rebounded on the common people in general.

In 1853.6, the month of Perry's intrusion, the shogunate's senior councillors *(rōjū)* ordered shogunal intendants *(daikan)* in the provinces to collect a special levy; moreover, contributions were to be exacted from the wealthy of Edo and Osaka. In the Eleventh Month of the same year, the shogunate demanded payments from the common people of Edo and outlying districts. A month later, Osaka townsmen were given notice that they, too, would have to pay. In 1854.6 the town magistrates ordered a levy on Edo townspeople; next, the townspeople of Osaka, Hyōgo, Nishinomiya, and Sakai were made to contribute a total of 80,000 ryō. Payments were demanded one after another—in 1860 from the common people of Edo across the board, in 1865 in Edo and Osaka, and again in 1866 in Osaka, Hyōgo, and Nishinomiya. Many domains imposed the same sort of levies on their populace. For example, in Kanazawa they were collected in 1844, 1852, 1856, 1860, 1865, and 1866.

The sacrifices demanded of the common people did not stop at this increased economic oppression. Some commoners were even compelled to leave their traditional, peaceful lives and be inducted into the shogunate's infantry troops and the militias of the domains. The argument for raising units of farmer-soldiers had been generally accepted among intellectuals by the late 1830s, but it was not adopted by the shogunate until the early 1860s. Some of the domains, however, were beginning to put the idea into effect at midcentury.

The shogunate first ordered its bannermen *(hatamoto)* and direct vassals *(gokenin)* with allocated stipends between 100 *hyō* and 10,000 *koku* to provide infantry troops at the beginning of 1863 (in Bunkyū 2.12). The wealthier retainers, those with stipends over five hundred *koku,* were required to send able-bodied youth from their fiefs. Those with less income were made to contribute fixed amounts of cash. Later, in the course of the great reforms undertaken by the shogunate during the Keiō era (1865–1868), farmers under the rule of shogunal intendants in the Kantō region were also taken as foot soldiers, and farmers in shogunal domains in western Japan were organized into militias under their intendants and county magistrates. Uprisings erupted in opposition to this draft.

In the domains, the earliest example of the institution of farmer-soldiers, although they were not fully organized into units, can be found in Chōshū in 1849. That year artillery emplacements were constructed on Mishima, and the farmers and fishermen of that island were told to stand by and be prepared to guard the guns. Next was Obama. The defense policy adopted by this domain in 1851 envisioned using the resources of the entire *han* to ward off any foreign ships that might appear off its shores, and posts of duty were designated for farmers and townsmen, but these measures did not constitute a standing army. In 1854 Mito *han* decided to conscript farmer-soldiers for maritime defense. As many as fifteen hundred men among farmers of former samurai status, village chiefs, and peasants with prime land who had donated more than the fixed amount were permitted in 1856 to bear swords and surnames. These men were organized into militia units and made to study Arms and Arts during the agricultural idle season. Under the Regulations for the Militia promulgated in 1854, the Kōchi domain also organized and trained militarily some one thousand lordless samurai, farmers, sailors, and hunters between the ages of seventeen and fifty.

In 1863 Matsue *han* formed a militia of selected commoners from age seventeen or eighteen to age fifty. Three years later, this domain created a new militia for the defense of the Oki Islands, selecting from the upper stratum of commoners. Kokura *han*, too, in 1863.3 decided to build a rural army from the domain's wealthy farmers. In the same year, militias were organized in country districts by the Hiroshima domain.[12] Samurai were dispatched to teach fencing and Western gunnery techniques to recruits who were to be employed in the defense of the Inland Sea. In Saeki County alone these recruits numbered a thousand men; the total number, more than three thousand, was greater than that of any other domain's militia. In the Hiroshima domain, farmer-soldiers were given equal treatment with village chiefs and were allowed to bear one sword.

Other domains that had militias included Tsuwano, Wakayama, Tsu, Ōgaki, Ueda, Fukui, Kawagoe, and Sendai. Even in domains without organized militias, the commoners were apt to be kept under tight control. The villages maintained strict discipline, and the comings and goings of the villagers were restricted. The militias organized under domanial and shogunal authority were not the only such groups; village headmen and other village leaders also created military units. Among them were even outfits that took part in the Boshin Civil War of 1868–1869. Thus there were two kinds of militias, those under the authority of the domain and those under local village leadership. Regardless of the type of unit, however, the farmers' traditional way of life and thought was severely shaken wherever rural troops were organized. Becoming a soldier was a greater sacrifice for the farmer than any he had known previously. Conscription, new in the Bakumatsu period, consequently caused great anxiety among the farming population.

The opening of foreign trade no less than the period's political developments adversely affected the circumstances of the common people's lives, and in particular their economic situation. That was reason enough for them to be aroused; they were entirely conscious of having been forced into a struggle to combat starvation. But there was another side to the coin. Rewards, such as the right to bear a sword and a surname, could be gained for serving in the militia units. A commoner could raise his family status. To be sure, in some domains it had been possible to obtain the status of a country samurai *(gōshi)* for a financial contribution even before the 1830s; in the 1850s, however, similar policies were instituted throughout Japan. The opportunity for commoners, especially for the upper stratum of commoners, to raise their status was one of the most dramatic changes of this period of change. The way to social advancement was opened to them; they saw in their own minds that it was possible for them to take a step closer to the samurai. It goes without saying that the petite bourgeoisie and the poor peasants, for whom such an opportunity was remote, felt the weight of the changes in their living conditions as a heavy weight indeed. Hence it is only natural that the wealthy farmers and merchants should have been the first ones to respond positively to those changes.

The Political Activities and Perceptions of the Social Stratum of Wealthy Farmers and Merchants

Many wealthy farmers and merchants became involved in politics during the Bakumatsu and Restoration epoch. Yet was it their own sense of being the prime movers of commodity production and of the commercial economy that made them determined to engage in political activities? Did Hattori Shisō's "manufacture bourgeoisie" really exist, and is Naramoto Tatsuya's equation of country samurai with a productive middle-farmer stratum valid?

There surely is no need to delve again into Hattori's argument. There have been quite a few appraisals of the wealthy farmer-merchant stratum, and some of them develop perspectives critical of Hattori's line of reasoning. Hani Gorō, for instance, refused to attribute any revolutionary qualities to this group and consistently identified its members as feudalistic, privileged, intermediary exploiters who took advantage of their compatriots. To be sure, the Hattori theory itself originated as a rebuttal of Hani; but Hani was not alone in entertaining doubts about the revolutionary nature of the wealthy farmer-merchants. Many scholars have subsequently expressed the same skepticism.

Horie Hideichi is representative of the latter group of historians. His "Class Struggle in the Bakumatsu Period" discusses the reasons for the alliance formed between village officials and radical samurai *(shishi)* in the Tenchūgumi (Heavenly Retribution Band) and Ikuno rebellions of 1863.[13] According to Horie, the village officials were actually engaged in an effort to maintain their own traditional authority vis-à-vis the peasants. Seeking to deflect the attacks of ordinary peasants—and especially of poor peasants—from themselves, they diverted the peasants' antifeudal, revolutionary energy into the imperial loyalist, xenophobic, antishogunate movement. The village officials took the lead in utilizing the peasants' energy for the *sonnō jōi* movement because they felt the need to fortify their own position; moreover, economic conditions still permitted them to take such an initiative. In short, they did not decide to become involved in politics out of any sense of identity as the upholders of the commercial economy. It was rather the fear of losing their prestige and power in the village that motivated them; their conservative mentality made them cling tenaciously to their traditional authority. This fear, Horie asserts, was the root of their failure: they were betrayed by the peasants they had once organized.

According to Horie, there were two types of wealthy farmer-merchant: the old type, those ensconced in village leadership by tradition; and the new type, those involved in peasant commercial production, represented by merchants who were residents of the villages *(zaigō shōnin)*. The latter type of rural merchant—a new stratum of village leaders—mobilized the ordinary peasants, stood at the forefront of village democratization, and censured the injustice and lawlessness of the old type. The wealthy farmer-merchants who participated in the Tenchūgumi Rebellion and the Ikuno Disturbance belonged to the old type. In contrast, those who supported the new-style auxiliary militia *(shotai)* in Chōshū and those who organized the "grass-roots companies" *(sōmōtai)* of Echigo Province (now a part of Niigata Prefecture) belonged to the new type, and that was the reason for their success. In projecting this extreme class view of history, Horie developed an interpretation completely different from Hattori's.

Had Horie's *zaigō shōnin*, however, really reached such a stage of bourgeois maturation that they could disdain accommodations with networks of feudal commercial distribution and feudal privilege? If we look at the dispute between the Koroku-ha and the Shinroku-ha of Kurashiki, the answer is clearly no. In that case, the newly risen merchants of middle-farmer origins, who had grown with rural markets as their base, gave themselves privileges as soon as they came to occupy positions of village leadership.[14] Another example comes from the cotton-growing region of Settsu Province (now divided between Osaka and Hyōgo prefectures), where the upper level of "merchants resident in the villages" affiliated themselves with the *kabunakama* (a monopolistic trade association sanctioned by the shogunate) as soon as the shogunate ordered its restoration in 1854. These merchants obviously sought special prerogatives.[15] Evidently, the commercial economy of the time was not at a stage that would have encouraged them to reject coexistence with feudal privilege. Horie is correct to criticize the Hattori grass-roots bourgeois theory, but his argument is too formulistic when it comes to explaining the reasons for the wealthy farmer-merchants' involvement in politics.

In contrast to these critics of Hattori, Naramoto Tatsuya took up Hattori's theory and developed it farther.[16] He claimed that given the village merchants' hostility to foreign trade, it was natural for them to support the zealots of *sonnō jōi*. It was because of their support, according to Naramoto, that the feudalistic aspects of the jingoist faction faded rapidly. Therein he recognized the development of nationalism; he gave the grass-roots participants in the Tenchūgumi Rebellion and the Ikuno Disturbance as his concrete example. In the village merchants' resistance to Western capitalism Naramoto discovered a type of nationalist capitalism. But he presented no corroborative evidence regarding their way of thinking, so his theory remains confined within the bounds of hypothesis.

These are some of the past opinions that have to do with Hattori's theory. All of them explain the commoners' motivations for participating in grass-roots political movements strictly from the standpoint of class. It would be difficult to call them concrete, substantive studies of the common people's intentions and ideals. But they do deserve further examination and reflection.

What strengthened the rural merchants' resolve to act in the Bakumatsu and Restoration epoch was above all their political self-awareness. This was not a general or an inevitable sensibility, nor one formed by their affiliation with a class and connected to their concern for its interests. It arose only among those people who were in some form able to identify the Bakumatsu crisis from the perspective of the Confucianism and National Learning (Kokugaku) they had studied as children of a class with money to spare. The genesis of their political self-awareness presupposed that they had broken with the notions relating to their traditional status as farmers or merchants. Their ideas were clearly different from those of their fathers and grandfathers—men who had lived in the nineteenth century's early decades, the period of the commercial economy's development, and who had been proud of that status.

Let us look at a few examples. Takai Kōzan (1806–1883), a wealthy farmer and landlord of Saku County in Shinano Province, was also known as a wealthy merchant. The aristocratic Kujō family of Kyoto and the domains in northern Shinano were among his patrons. He came to Kyoto as a youth and studied with the imperial loyalist poet Yanagawa Seigan (1789–1858). After 1860, when the Kujō family was caught up in a political whirlpool as leaders of the court nobles within the collaborationist "union of court and military" *(kōbu gattai)* movement, Takai also worked for the realization of that union, campaigning for it alongside Sakuma Shōzan (personal name also read Zōzan; 1811–1864) of the Matsushiro domain and others. Overcoming the opposition of his wealthy farmer-merchant relatives, he made frequent, large donations to the shogunate; he dissipated the family fortune in his political involvements. He had of course been allowed to bear sword and surname from early on, and he was even granted ceremonial treatment appropriate to a senior councillor by the Suzaka domain, the recipient of his donations. He thought exactly like a samurai.

In contrast, his grandfather, who had amassed almost the entire family fortune in his lifetime, thought in exactly the opposite way. He responded positively to the heavy levies ordered by the shogunate during the Tenmei famine of the 1780s, but when he was offered permission to bear sword and surname in return for his contributions, he refused the honor point-blank: "Why would a commoner need to bear a sword?"[17] The grandfather's awareness of himself as a farmer-merchant was absent from the grandchild. Indeed, the lack of a sense of identity as a wealthy farmer was the precondition for a consciousness that ventured into political practice.

The same was the case with Shibusawa Eiichi (1840–1931), the son of a wealthy indigo merchant of Chiaraijima, Musashi Province. "Not for an instant," he said of his youth, "could I forget my hopes of making a career in the world as a samurai, rather than ending my life as a country peasant." Hence he was forced to tell his father, who tried to make him the successor to the family business, "My thoughts and yours are greatly different." Embracing strong opposition to the tyrannical attitudes of the shogunal intendants who ordered tax levies in 1856, he "concluded that after all the orientation of shogunal politics is not correct."[18] That realization led him to study in Edo and became his motive for joining the zealots. Here, too, we see a vivid gap between the generations.

The case of Hara Rokurō (original name Shindō Shunzaburō; 1842–

1933) was similar. He was born the last child of the senior headman of Sanaka Village, Asago County, Tajima Province (now part of Hyōgo Prefecture). His father was a wealthy farmer who managed a large-scale silk production business along with forestry interests. For five years from 1855, Hara associated with the hot-blooded youths of the Seikei Shoin, an academy run by Ikeda Sōan (1813–1878). He then studied under the Kokugaku scholar Ōkuni Takamasa (1792–1871) in the domain school of Ono *han*. Hara was led to political activity because of a longing to be a provincial samurai of Tajima in the tradition of his ancestors. Patriotic emotions sprang up within him. Overcoming not only his father, the wealthy farmer and entrepreneur, but also the opposition of the entire family, who begged him to continue the thriving business, he participated in the Ikuno Disturbance, as good as disinherited.

Having thus become an Ikuno *rōnin,* he left to procure weapons in Kyoto. On the way he encountered a cousin who was employed by his family as a clerk. "Shun, stop pretending to be a lordless samurai," the cousin remonstrated with him; Hara huffed in reply, "I am a completely different person from the likes of you."[19] His way of thinking certainly was unlike that of the clerk who exemplified the attitude of the family business. Hara's samurai pretensions are evident.

These are only two or three examples, but in fact almost all of the wealthy farmer-merchants who took up politics in the Bakumatsu period had overcome the consciousness of farmer and merchant status that informed their fathers. What distinguishes their ideas from those of former generations is their striking passion for political action and their longing to be samurai. The more intense their ardor for politics, the greater was their desire to approach the status of samurai, the sole proper leaders of feudal society. In the end, this ardor and desire turned them into antishogunate radicals. To be sure, there are exceptions, such as Takai Kōzan, but almost all the wealthy farmers and merchants who were motivated in this manner became involved as activists in the movement to revere the emperor and repel the barbarians.

The internal impulse of their actions was generated by the academic training they had received in former days, while the external push, which they so strongly felt, was provided by the changes in their living conditions, which had deteriorated as a result of external pressures. Thus they bid farewell to the status consciousness of their fathers. It was primarily the Kokugaku school of Hirata Atsutane (1776–1843), which had permeated to the level of the upper commoners in the Bakumatsu period, that inspired rural merchants with a political awareness and impelled them to become active in politics just like samurai. At least, it cannot be denied that the ideology of the leaders of the

Heavenly Retribution Band, the Ikuno Disturbance, and the "grass-roots companies" of Echigo was nourished either by National Learning or by political thought related to National Learning. In the case of the zealots of samurai birth, who had been the political leaders of feudal society all along, the consciousness of crisis trumpeted by the Mito School was accepted frankly and in an unadulterated form; when they committed themselves to political action, they were being faithful to their tradition. In the case of the wealthy farmer-merchants, who had traditionally been kept out of politics, it was first necessary to awaken a sense of political responsibility. If one recalls that the majority of those who launched themselves into political activism were at the same time village leaders—headmen and village chiefs—it appears entirely appropriate that the Hirata School of National Learning, a term practically synonymous with headman political education, should have been the seedbed of their self-awareness.

Let us look at some concrete examples of the relationship between National Learning and village leadership. Village officials in the Tokugawa period, while belonging to the upper level of commoners, were positioned between the daimyo and the farmers as an integral part of the structure of domanial authority. Even as they lost the character that, properly speaking, they should have maintained as leaders of the farmers, they were guaranteed a position of privilege by their loyalty to the *han*. Their awareness of their prerogatives as agents of the prevailing authority was strong, but their personal sense of responsibility for the governance of the village gradually weakened. The political ideology of National Learning instilled in such officials the notion that their political responsibility was equal to that of the daimyo; it inspired them with an enthusiasm for governing the village. The concept of "the sacred trust" *(miyosashi)* that Hirata Atsutane inherited from Motoori Norinaga (1730–1801)—that is, the principle of the government's being a trust derived from the sacred authority with which the emperor is endowed—spread widely among village leaders as the commercial economy permeated the countryside in the nineteenth century's first three decades and initiated a gradual breakdown of the peasant social stratum. It was the ideology that brought them to a resolve to rebuild the farming community.

A classical example of this ideology will be found in a book to which Itō Tasaburō has attracted attention—"Crafts Essential to the People's Households" *(Minka yōjutsu)* by Miyaoi Yasuo (name sometimes read as Miyahiro Sadao; 1797–1858). Miyaoi, the village headman of Matsuzawa in Katori County, Shimōsa Province (now Chiba Prefecture), was Hirata Atsutane's direct disciple and assisted in the publication of his works. He was also a close associate of the agricultural reformer Ōhara Yūgaku (1797–1858) and other scholars. In part two, section fifteen of "Crafts," entitled "The Village Chief," Miyaoi writes that the village official's political responsibility is ultimately based on the mandate of the emperor: "The village chief seems to be a person of humble position, but he is indispensable. When the origin of this office is examined, we find that it is the village chief who governs the locality as the representative of the domanial lord who governs provinces and districts as the agent of the Barbarian-Quelling Generalissimo who governs these Four Seas by investiture from His Gracious Majesty the Emperor. Keeping that in mind, the village chief takes loving care of the farmers who are below him. The obligation to devote himself to governing is his customary duty."[20]

Those village officials who have only a conceited awareness of their special power at the delivery end of domain authority, conspire with the intendants to oppress the villagers, and line their own pockets must therefore be condemned as "extravagant," "thieving," "criminal," and "blind" masters. Characteristically, this author who based the office of the village official on "investiture from the emperor" called himself "Miyaoi Yasuo, subject of the emperor in Katori County, Shimōsa Province."[21] As a subject of the emperor, he is not simply a village official answerable to a domanial lord, not a blind follower of the abuse of authority that emanates from the selfish ambitions of the lord or of his intendant. Miyaoi's political self-awareness and his sense of responsibility toward his position are as evident as is his enthusiasm for governing in a way proper to the village leader.

These qualities were not unique to Miyaoi Yasuo. The village officials who had received the baptism of the Hirata School of National Learning all thought more or less in the same way. Men who imbibed of the same, Kokugaku type of political ideology as Miyaoi in the final years of the Tenpō period (January 1831–January 1845) are to be found among the village headmen of Takaoka County in Tosa Province (now Kōchi Prefecture), the soil and the social stratum that gave birth to such prominent members of the Heavenly Retribution Band as Yoshimura Toratarō (1837–1863), Nasu Shingo (1829–1863), and Maeda Shigema (also known as Maeda Masatane; 1838–1863). In 1841 village headmen of that area formed a secret alliance to oppose the tyrannical rule of the Tosa domain's intendant. Their compact, entitled "Articles of Confederation," reveals how these village chiefs conceived of their station in life: "As far as this office is concerned, it is recorded in 'The Age of the Gods,' part 1, of the *Nihongi* (Ancient Chronicles of Japan) that Amaterasu Ōmikami scattered the seeds of the five representative grains, and at the time of the planting of the young rice shoots in the paddy, she ordained the Heavenly Village Chief (Ame no Muragimi). This truly applies to village headmen for all posterity. That being so, the duties even of lower officials have been legitimized by direct descent from this divine decree." Furthermore, this self-awareness expands into an ideal of responsibility in which the headman's duties are in essence no different from those of the domanial lord: he is a royal minister entrusted with the governance of the emperor's land and people. "This is the greatest secret, one that cannot be told to anyone outside of our group. As a rule, all the realm within the Four Seas has only one central pillar, but at this time there is a threefold extension. Provisionally, we shall take them all together and call them the four categories. His Gracious Majesty, the Sacred Emperor, is the sovereign; the shogun is his vicar general; the domanial lords are the captains; the village heads are the lieutenants. It is they who have been entrusted with the governance of the realm and its people. It is as if the domanial lord was a medicinal bolus of village headmen, and the village headman a little tablet of the domanial lord."[22]

The attitude that the village headmen ought by rights adopt as the farmers' leaders is expressed in a truly striking way in the compact of the alliance: When a samurai insists that a farmer be delivered to him, intending to cut him down, the village headman is to be mindful that "this is an imperial subject who has been entrusted to provincial governments by the imperial court. It is absolutely impossible for such an extradition to be made as a private matter." If he tries to force the farmer's being handed over, then the samurai "ought himself to be put to the sword on the spot," because he is then an "enemy of the court."

Yoshimura and the others who participated in the Heavenly Retribution Band inherited the traditions of the political self-awareness exemplified in this alliance formed by village headmen at a time before the political situation became aggravated during the Bakumatsu and Restoration epoch. Senior headmen or headmen themselves, they strove to realize the virtue of Loving the People. In due time, as the political crisis intensified, their sense of political responsibility, based on their self-awareness as lieutenants of the emperor, expanded from a view of politics centered on their individual villages to a nationwide political perspective. They committed themselves to the *sonnō jōi* movement with the intention of chastising the shogunate for the wrongs it had perpetrated—for violating the imperial decree, opening the country, yielding before the barbarians, and driving the people into untold pain and misery. That their political activism was tied up with the political self-awareness of the village headman class is clearly seen in a letter of farewell which Yoshimura wrote to his parents from Osaka after he had left his country home to join the zealots:[23]

> The truth is that the shogunate has become more and more tyrannical in recent years. It has humiliated the imperial court. The treatment it has universally visited on patriots who have sprung up all over the country, burning with righteous indignation, has been decapitation or imprisonment. Already the Japanologist Hanawa Jirō has been made to look into the ancient procedures and precedents for dethroning an emperor. The emperor's younger sister, Kazu no Miya [Princess Kazu], has been abducted. All of this is outrageous beyond words. To be sure, there is no one within the Four Seas who is not the emperor's subject, but it is the obligation of the princes and the village headmen to provide leadership. I have therefore decided to show in my own small way what a loyal man is capable of. To be sure, since people have basked in three hundred years of peaceful rule, they have lost the fighting spirit, and there appears to be no one who could stand up to the party of our opponents. My purpose has been to mingle in with the indignant patriots and, little by little, to exchange information with comrades from various domains. Over the past two months, I have been in direct communication with the patriots of Chōshū and Kyushu. I have now determined my plans and go into exile. I ought to have expressed my intentions to you at the proper time, but since the empire is in a crisis, I could not help telling you a lie. He who gives his all in loyalty, however, reaches the highest form of filial piety, so I am sure that you will not be angry with me. Having been burdened with village affairs from my youth, I am unskilled in Arms and Arts. That is my only regret.

One who had been "burdened with village affairs" from his youth naturally stood true to the "obligation of the princes and the village headmen to provide leadership." This "obligation," however, was nothing other than the one that nativistic political ideology had instilled in him. It was the village headman's political responsibility during a time of crisis.

The case of Ikuno is similar. Hara Rokurō and his friend Kitagaki Kunimichi (1836–1916) both had studied under the nativist Ōkuni Takamasa. Their predecessor, the senior headman Nakajima Tarobei of Takada Village, Yabu County, Tajima Province—one of the central figures in organizing the peasant militia of this area—had also been influenced by nativist thought. In 1843, at the age of eighteen, he had become a disciple of Ajiro Hironori (1784–1856), a Kokugaku scholar from Ise Yamada.[24] An additional illustrative case is provided by the Echigo village headmen who organized the "grass-roots companies" and fought in the Boshin Civil War. Their ideological foundations were built on the teachings of Suzuki Shigetane (1812–1863), a proponent of Hirata Kokugaku. (Suzuki also traveled to Chōshū and exerted an influence on a segment of the wealthy farmer-merchant stratum there.)

The representative personages of the Echigo region were the headman of Kuzutsuka in Kita Kanbara County, Endō Shichirō (1839–1892), who later became the leader of the Hokushintai (Pole Star Company), and Katsura Takahiro (1838–1881), senior headman of Niitsu, who formed a peasant militia and took charge of reconnaissance for the Meiji government's antishogunate army. Both of these men had received instruction from Shigetane, as had their fathers. Both came from families who had been living in the area since it was first settled; in other words, they were not any sort of newly risen "merchants resident in the villages" or parvenu landlords. Suzuki Shigetane first came through Echigo in 1843 on his way to seek out Hirata Atsutane in Akita. On this occasion, Shigetane visited the Katsura household, whose members became his disciples. The Endō family did the same a little later, in 1851, when Shigetane passed through the area a second time and stayed with them.

The nativistic political ideology Shigetane taught these wealthy Echigo farmers was the same as that absorbed by their fellows in Shimōsa and Tosa—to be aware, above all, of their position as village officials. An examination of the "Commentary on 'The Heirs of Heaven' " *(Yotsugigusa tsumiwake)* by Katsura Takahiro's father Takashige (1817–1871) makes this clear. This commentary on Shigetane's well-known treatise was widely read by the wealthy farmers of the region. "What is meant by the Great Way of our Imperial Deities?" it asks. "It is to give reverent service to the Divine Grandson of the Great Deity Illuminating Heaven, the recipient of the Sacred Trust of the Heavenly Progenitors. So that this chaotic, unordered realm might become a tranquil and perfected one—for it is written, 'Complete and solidify this drifting land'— each man in each household shall in the pursuit of his calling and of his ordained occupation Produce that which is given as his lot, Fulfill his duty to it, Adhere to its ways, and Execute it faithfully." For this reason, "the Great August Intention shall be internalized and transmitted from persons in authority on down to provincial governor, county administrator, district chief, and village headman; it shall be taught to the Imperial Treasures, the peasants; and the Imperial Treasures shall take it up and teach it to their households, wives, children, servants, and slaves, seeking to fathom the Intentions of the Gods."[25] In short, the duty of a village headman is to take the reign of ancient times as his model. If the likes of Endō Shichirō and Katsura Takahiro were to be faithful to this ideology, they could not help regarding the shogunate's rule as a tyrannical failure to internalize and transmit the "Great August Intention." Indeed, they burned with the political fever to correct that tyranny. The natural result of their ideology was that they became zealot activists.

Endō Shichirō succeeded his deeply trusted father as headman in 1864, when the Bakumatsu political crisis had already turned vehement. While his father was still alive, Shichirō had longed to be a samurai and had established a school of swordsmanship in his house, working hard at the warrior arts along with other youths in the vicinity. Wandering through various provinces in the early 1860s to explore the political situation, he came in contact with superpatriot samurai. Upon taking over the position of headman, however, he fulfilled his responsibilities admirably. On the occasion of the great flood of 1865 and the famine of 1866, which were accompanied by increases in the price of rice, he contributed his personal funds to help the needy. He formed the Pole Star Company in 1868.7, after Meiji government forces had landed from naval vessels at Matsugasaki and Shichirō had won the confidence of their staff officer, Maebara Issei (1834–1876) of Chōshū.

The intense changes in the political situation that enveloped these Echigo people in the Bakumatsu and Restoration epoch created the precondition for setting their actions apart from those of their predecessors who shared the same ideology. Their political horizons, too, expanded from a single village to the entire country. Their consciousness was no longer that of simple village leaders; it was one they shared with those elements of the samurai class who had committed themselves to the *sonnō jōi* movement.

Thus far we have considered the nativistic ideology that sustained the political activities of wealthy farmers, the main source of village leadership. Let us now look at two wealthy merchants, Miyake Jōtarō (1818–1882) and Shiraishi Shōichirō (1812–1880). It is known that Shiraishi received his baptism in nativist ideology, but Miyake's case is not clear on this point. Since the farmer-merchants' road to participation in politics presupposed their disavowing the status they actually held, and since it is an indisputable fact that Miyake became involved in politics because of a sense of self-importance at having had famous samurai for his ancestors, he would be worth examining as an exemplary case of the wealthy rural merchant even if it turned out that he had no connection with Kokugaku.

Miyake was a shipping agent from Tsurajima in Bitchū Province (now a part of Okayama Prefecture) and owned a large amount of land. Shiraishi was the senior headman of Takezaki (now a part of the city of

Shimonoseki) and ran a rice wholesaler and receiving agency. Hattori Shisō regards these two men as powerful constituents of a "new domestic commercial network that stretched from the coast of the Inland Sea as far as Kyushu in the west, and from San'in and Hokuriku to Ezo [Hokkaidō] in the north."[26] He calls them typical personages of the grass-roots bourgeoisie that led the zealots. According to Naramoto Tatsuya, Shiraishi developed contacts with the rural samurai of the Chōshū domain, whom he equates with a middle-level-farmer reformist faction *(chūnōsōteki kaikakuha),* and became a kind of third-party commercial capitalist, one independent of *han* authority.[27]

As befitted their wealthy merchant background, these two super-patriots did not wield a sword. Rather, they invested their capital in the political movement, as indeed Hattori and Naramoto assert. Is it really true, however, that their political goals amounted to the bourgeois design to exploit a nationwide market, as Hattori and Naramoto also maintain? Was it an economic ambition that caused them to form ties with the zealots and with the country samurai, that is, a "middle-level-farmer reformist faction"? In short, do those assertions amount to anything more than hasty speculation? It certainly appears that they do not, especially as they ignore Miyake's and Shiraishi's longing for samurai status. In any event, they deserve closer examination.

It is fact that Miyake Jōtarō and Shiraishi Shōichirō were links in the trade route connecting the Kinai region with Chōshū, Chikuzen, and Satsuma that was opened up by the Confucian teacher Umeda Unpin (1815–1859), a samurai expelled from his native Obama domain in 1852 for his antishogunate leanings, and further exploited after his death by Hirano Kuniomi (1828–1864), an imperial loyalist who deserted the service of Fukuoka *han* in 1858. But Umeda and his associates did not create and conduct their mercantile strategy in response to the bourgeois initiatives of Miyake and Shiraishi, the two grass-roots patriots. Rather, the plan was developed by *rōnin* for *rōnin;* Umeda and Hirano conceived of it as a device for securing finances for the *sonnō jōi* movement.

Observing the state of confusion that enveloped the shogunate after the arrival of Commodore Perry's squadron, Umeda worried about protecting Kyoto in the face of a foreign invasion: "No one knows when an unexpected calamity may strike, and it is hard to measure what might occur in the area of the capital. I am in great despair, as the imperial court's defenses are so meager."[28] Umeda's eye lit on the country samurai of Totsugawa in Yamato Province (now Nara Prefecture), who had nourished a tradition of reverence for the emperor since the fourteenth century, the days of the Southern Court. They could, he thought, be formed into an imperial guard that would repel the barbarians. Umeda made inroads into Totsugawa through wealthy Yamato merchants and physicians who were his disciples. At the same time, he thought that the prominent imperial loyalist domains might be turned into bulwarks safeguarding the court. Confronting the shogunate from behind those bulwarks, the court could then pressure it into obeying the imperial decree to close the harbors and expel the barbarians. Umeda first presented this plan to Mito *han,* but failed to persuade it. Then in 1856 he turned to Chōshū. To ease the way toward a political rapprochement between the imperial court and that domain, Umeda sought to establish a trade that would exchange Chōshū products for the Kinai products marketed by his wealthy merchant followers; not incidentally, the business would amass funds to support the creation of an imperial guard. The Chōshū domanial authorities were conceived of as the sole trading partner; there was no intention whatsoever to establish a direct, free trading relationship with Chōshū merchants. At the time, those domanial authorities belonged not to the autarkist party of the reformers Murata Kiyokaze (personal name often read as Seifū; 1783–1855) and Sufu Masanosuke (1823–1864)—that is, to what Naramoto Tatsuya would call the "middle-level-farmer reformist faction" of country samurai—but rather to the so-called Party of the Pedestrian View (Zokuron-ha) of Tsuboi Kuemon (1800–1863), a faction that advocated the policy of promoting private business by working in concert with privileged commercial capital. That is the reason Umeda's trading scheme could be arranged in the first place. As it happens, his journey to Chōshū was financed by 30 ryō advanced to him by none other than Miyake Jōtarō.

Umeda first met Miyake in 1856.4, but he was already intimately acquainted with Miyake's father. What created the bond between the two was their common loyalist ideology, and nothing else. In other words, it was not Miyake Jōtarō's sense of identity as a merchant that led him to take part in Umeda's Chōshū trading scheme. That much appears undeniable upon a consideration of Miyake's personal philosophy and his political activities.

Three factors nurtured Miyake's loyalism. The first was the pride he took in the story of his descent from the legendary general Kojima Takanori, who figures in the mediaeval romance *Taiheiki* as one of the most intrepid stalwarts of the Southern Court. The second was the influence of his grandfather Izaemon and his father Tatsuzō. His grandfather loved classical Japanese poetry and often went up to the capital to pursue his avocation with the experts resident there. During his stays in Kyoto he became impressed with the imperial loyalist theories of the Shintoist and Kokugaku scholar Takenouchi Shikibu (1712–1767). On returning to his home province, Izaemon gathered like-minded persons to plot the overthrow of the shogunate, only to incur the wrath of his domanial lord. He departed this world with a sense of anguish and frustration embedded in his heart. Izaemon's infatuation with the imperial cause appears to have been inherited by Tatsuzō, who was also somewhat of a literatus. As a youth, he studied Chinese-style painting *(nanga)* in Nagasaki with a Chinese from the Ch'ing empire, and his last years were spent in Kyoto, where he mixed with court nobility, littérateurs, and other men of leisure. He studied calligraphy under the Prince Abbot of the Shōren'in (also known as Nakagawa no Miya Asahiko Shinnō; 1824–1891), a notorious dabbler in politics, and had frequent close contact with Umeda Unpin, whom Tatsuzō taught painting. A family heritage of imperial loyalism was at work in Jōtarō from an early age.

Third, Jōtarō was a disciple of Morita Sessai (1811–1868). Sessai, a *rōnin* Confucian scholar from Gojō in Yamato Province, was in turn a disciple of the historian Rai San'yō (1780–1832), whose legitimist philosophy, expressed in the imperative "Revere the king, reject the hegemon" *(sonnō sekiha)*, he had embraced from early on. He was, moreover, an old friend of Umeda's and played a part in Umeda's effort to cultivate supporters in Totsugawa. The scholar responsible for inspiring so much patriotic zeal, Yoshida Shōin (1830–1859) himself, called on Sessai during a visit to Yamato and apparently extended him the courtesies ordinarily shown by the disciple to his master. It is not strange at all that Miyake Jōtarō, who studied under Sessai, should also have espoused his philosophy. Thus Jōtarō was drawn to imperial loyalism not so much by nativist influences as by the Confucian injunction to "revere the king, reject the hegemon," by his family tradition, and by his proud identification with ancestors who were adherents of the Southern Court.

By the time he met Umeda Unpin, Miyake Jōtarō had matured intellectually. He became excited by the opportunity he perceived in the intensifying crisis. Unlike his grandfather, who looked on the political situation with anguish and despair, and his father, who viewed it with the detachment of a littérateur, Jōtarō could not rest content with assuming a contemplative perspective. Violating the daimyo's strict prohibition of such travel, he made one trip after another to Kyoto. Finally, he came to share a close affinity with Umeda and committed himself to the cause of revering the emperor and expelling the barbarians. Upon resolving to join the movement, he pledged his sincere devotion to *sonnō jōi* by offering a pedigreed sword—a family heirloom—to his ancestral deities, and prayed for enduring fortune in war. As we can see, his sense of identity was scarcely that of a wealthy merchant.

Miyake's contribution to the movement was largely one of providing funds for the activities of Umeda and Hirano Kuniomi. After Umeda's death, he and Hirano joined with Shiraishi Shōichirō and, in carrying on with Umeda's last wish, moved toward establishing trade relations linking Chōshū, Chikuzen, Satsuma, and Bitchū. But Miyake had little business acumen and proved an utter failure. In just two trade ventures to Satsuma, he lost the better part of his assets, said to have consisted of more than 10 *chō* of land (about 25 acres or 10 hectares), dozens of ships, and tens of thousands in ready cash. On top of that, he was chastised by the daimyo for his relationship with Satsuma and was placed under house arrest. The Miyake family did not appreciate his imperial loyalism. Witnessing his failure, they were disgusted with his political activities and warned him again and again to sever his ties with the *rōnin*. Jōtarō, however, scorned their opposition and refused to quit the cause of *sonnō jōi*. Not only did he continue to associate with Hirano and other radicals, he invested more of his family's fortune in the movement. In 1867 he gathered fellow loyalists with the intention of starting an insurrection in Tanba but was dissuaded from pursuing this plan by Ōhara Shigetomi (1801–1879), Iwakura Tomomi (1825–1883), and other court nobles of the antishogunate party whom he consulted. Through and through, Miyake's political activities were projected from a samurai type of perspective grounded in his imperial loyalism.[29]

Let us next consider Shiraishi Shōichirō. Like Miyake, Shiraishi took part in Umeda's trading scheme for political purposes. Eventually, he obtained samurai status as a member of one of Chōshū's mixed militia units, the Kiheitai. In 1854, at the age of forty-two, he became a disciple of Suzuki Shigetane, the nativist scholar whose teachings had stirred the village headmen of Echigo, and his political consciousness was awakened. His contacts with imperial loyalist zealots influenced Shiraishi's thinking so much, however, that his ideological bent came to exceed his teacher's. Whereas Shigetane's broadly conceived antiforeign ideology had acquiesced on the point of opening the country, Shiraishi embraced a strict, hard xenophobia. His sentiments are most clearly shown in the following two poems, declaimed in Shimonoseki as part of a toast when he and Hirano heard the news of Great Elder Ii Naosuke's assassination in 1860:[30]

Kuni no uchi	When the whole country
mina Ōmikokoro o	embraces the Imperial Will
kokoro nite	in their hearts and minds,
emishi o utsu wa	is it such a mighty deed
mono no kazu ka wa	to crush the barbarians?

Ametsuchi no	We swear to the gods
kami ni chikaite	of heaven and of the earth:
emishibune	We shall not waver
utan to iishi	in our stated resolve—smash
kokoro kaemeya	the ships of the barbarians!

Now then, in what spirit did Shiraishi embark on the trade activities planned by Umeda, Hirano, and Miyake? It was nothing else but this. As the 1850s were drawing to a close, Shiraishi found out through his fellow Shigetane disciples Katsuragi Hikoichi (1818–1880) and Sagara Fujitsugu (1816–1883), Satsuma reformists who had taken up exile in Chikuzen, that Satsuma's so-called true-blue loyalists *(seichūshi)* entertained a plan to rouse their *han* to intervene in Kyoto. Shiraishi, deeply moved by this news, decided to help financially to turn that plan into reality. That was the eminently political motivation behind his trading activities.

Satsuma's plan for intervention in the central arena of politics had been formulated by the daimyo Shimazu Nariakira (1809–1858), interrupted by his death, inherited by his brother Shimazu Hisamitsu (1817–1887), and deferred by the son of the latter and successor of the former, the daimyo Shimazu Tadayoshi (1840–1897). One of the principal advocates of a march on Kyoto was Hisamitsu's close associate Ōkubo Toshimichi (1830–1878), the leader of the true-blue party. Ōkubo not only sought to advance this plan but formulated alternatives to be used in case of emergency. That is why he took up contacts with the Chikuzen exiles, through whom he proposed the idea of an alliance between Satsuma and Chikuzen and from whom he learned of Shiraishi and his political sentiments. Ōkubo proposed that commercial relations be initiated between the two *han* to create the preconditions for a Satsuma-Chikuzen military alliance. He chose Shiraishi to act as the intermediary of that trade and had him engaged by Satsuma as an official purveyor to the domain. During the march on the capital, Shiraishi was to be entrusted with the supply of military provisions. Shiraishi happily agreed to play the role designated for him.

That is how Shiraishi became involved in Bakumatsu politics. In early 1862, as word of Hisamitsu's impending march on Kyoto spread, Maki Izumi (1813–1864) and other zealots from various domains gathered at Shimonoseki, and Shiraishi, spurred by his inbred *sonnō jōi* ideology, took the opportunity to solidify his relationship with the radicals. In particular, he became close friends with Kusaka Genzui (1840–1864), Takasugi Shinsaku (1839–1867), and Matsushima Gōzō (1825–1865) of Chōshū as well as with Yoshimura Toratarō of Tosa.

Shiraishi's trading endeavors, however, ended in the same failure that had marked Miyake's. He incurred Hisamitsu's fury for his close ties with the radicals and as a result lost the appointment as official purveyor to the Satsuma domain that Ōkubo had arranged for him. Forced to repay the money he had borrowed from Satsuma to stockpile provisions for its army, Shiraishi fell into economic difficulties. Moreover, he could not help observing that Satsuma had adopted a policy of reconciliation between the imperial court and the shogunate. It was here that Shiraishi's political sentiments came to converge entirely with those of the Chōshū radicals.

The Chikuzen exiles sympathized with the impoverished state in which Shiraishi found himself as a result of being dismissed by Satsuma and tried to help him in any way they could. One of them, Fujii Ryōsetsu, consulted with Chōshū friends in Kyoto and at the beginning of 1863 arranged for a loan of 1,500 ryō to be made on Shiraishi's behalf, an event clearly described in Shiraishi's diary.[31] Naramoto Tatsuya, however, interprets this financial transaction by saying that Shiraishi, "operating from an independent position, approached the reformist elements in the domain and arranged for a colossal loan to be made on behalf of the Satsuma samurai from Chōshū's official residence in Kyoto."[32] This is clearly mistaken; the reverse is true.

On 1863.5.10, the day Chōshū *han* opened fire upon the foreign ships at Shimonoseki, observing the imperial order to expel the barbarians, Shiraishi—senior headman that he was—was ordered, much to his dismay, to provide protection for the daimyo's women. He envied his younger brother Rensaku, who had entered the fray of the battle with a banner that proclaimed, "Takezaki, first to fight for the country with utmost loyalty." (Rensaku would participate in the Ikuno Disturbance in the Tenth Month of this year and was destined to lose his life there.) A month later, on 6.8, Takasugi formed the Kiheitai militia, and Shiraishi joined straight away. On 7.4, he finally became the samurai he had always longed to be when he was appointed a retainer (even if a low-ranking one) of the Chōshū domain on Takasugi's recommendation. On 9.25 he was given the position of acting corporal. Those must have been the happiest days of his life.[33]

Once he had joined the militia, Shiraishi postured entirely as a samurai. His family fortune was reduced to nothing. His thorough devotion to the superpatriotic movement and the enormous sacrifices he sustained for it are realistically portrayed in a letter that Takasugi sent in 1865.8 to his fellow loyalist Kido Takayoshi (1833–1877), possibly the Chōshū domain's most prominent political personage of the time, concerning Shiraishi's need for financial assistance:[34]

I should ask you to please consider the case of Shiraishi Shōichirō that I put before you recently. As you well know, Shōichirō has long been a true patriot. He has been performing various services since before the three domains' intervention in the capital, and went to extraordinary efforts at the time of the formation of the Kiheitai. Accordingly, he was made a samurai some years ago. Even after that, however, he continued to involve himself in providing lodging to patriots, and as a result the small amount of gold that he had managed to save has been exhausted in loans and drained dry by his guests' demands for food and drink. This, I am told, has left him in extremely difficult straits. I am also told, however, that he has been ordered to provide a loan of 1,500 ryō and has consequently been forced to mortgage his house. On top of everything else, his brother Rensaku, on whose support he counted, was killed in battle at Tajima, and his spirits are very low. Since his prospects for the future are desolate, I beg you to use your good offices on his behalf.

There was no necessary link between the wealthy merchants' political activism and their class identity, perhaps least of all in the case of Shiraishi and Miyake. On the contrary, these two rejected their merchant identity; they were driven by the samurai aspirations that they embraced instead. They turned themselves into zealots of *sonnō jōi* and risked not only their personal fortunes but also their lives in the eager pursuit of their radical goals. A political consciousness motivated them, just as it did the village leaders. Nativist influences, as has been shown, were prominent in the political thought both of wealthy farmers and of wealthy merchants, but cases such as that of Miyake Jōtarō, whose approach to samurai sensibilities followed from his appreciation of the Confucian theory of duties and designations, were by no means rare. For instance, Ōhashi Totsuan (1816–1862), one of the patriots involved in the plot to assassinate Senior Councillor Andō Nobumasa (1819–1871) outside the Sakashita Gate of Edo Castle in 1862, was also a wealthy merchant, but it was as a Confucian that he first made his mark in the world. In the case of the village leaders, however, it is undeniable that National Learning exerted the greatest influence. Kokugaku led them to reflect on the nature of civil administration and eventually to adopt a critical attitude toward the way the shogunate and the domanial governments conducted affairs.

For all that, patriotic activists of wealthy farmer-merchant provenance developed only a limited political consciousness. At most, their political vision approached the level of sophistication attained by the radical samurai, but it lacked the capacity to reach one step further and to form a conception of the future state based on a broad international perspective. That is to say, the kind of imagination that could compass the prospect of Japan's modern transformation—of what the Meiji Restoration was to bring about—was practically nonexistent among them. That is why their movement was sporadic, ephemeral, and unsystematic, and why it was by and large a failure. Their drift after the restoration clearly reveals their shortcomings. Most of them held fast to ideals derived from Kokugaku and Shinto, ideals such as the restoration of the ancient norms of imperial government *(ōsei fukko)*, direct rule by the emperor *(tennō shinsei)*, and the unity of rites and regimen *(saisei itchi)*. They could not reconcile themselves with the Meiji regime's policies of Westernization. Shiraishi Shōichirō fled political and economic life altogether, becoming the head priest of the Akama Shrine in Shimonoseki. Endō Shichirō was implicated in Maebara Issei's Hagi Insurrection of October 1876 and lived out the rest of his days under a cloud. Miyake Jōtarō took part in the antigovernment conspiracy of the disgruntled court nobles Otagi Michiteru and Toyama Mitsusuke in 1871, escaped the death sentence that was passed over them in January 1872, but faced life imprisonment until he was amnestied in 1880.

Men such as Shibusawa Eiichi, Hara Rokurō, and Kitagaki Kunimichi, on the other hand, made the most of the Meiji environment. Shibusawa became the grand old man of the business world, Hara prospered as a middle-level entrepreneur, and Kitagaki flourished as a well-established bureaucrat. Each in his own way became the bearer of the new age. Ridding themselves of their antiforeignism, they all deepened their perception of the international order as it existed at the end of the Tokugawa era and during the early years of the Meiji period and responded to a new national consciousness. Abandoning their former jingoistic ideology, they were awakened to the new spirit of nationalism. When they embarked for Europe, Shibusawa and Hara bid a final farewell to their former selves. Their changed mentality differentiated them from the unreflective antiforeign fanatics. It must be pointed out that this transformation of consciousness did not necessarily have anything to do with their social position. Rather, it had a lot to do both with their outstanding temperament, which permitted them to become samurai and then to act as such, and with their good fortune, which allowed them to go abroad—Shibusawa as a retainer of the Hitotsubashi house, Hara as a result of the distinguished military service he had rendered after the Ikuno fiasco as a samurai of the Tottori domain, one who marched from Ueno to Tōhoku in the war for the imperial restoration.

So much for the wealthy farmers and merchants. We now turn to the ordinary farmers.

Peasant Uprisings and the Peasants' Mentality

Peasant uprisings increased in number and intensity during the Bakumatsu and Restoration epoch, primarily because of the dramatic change brought on in the countrymen's lives by political and economic pressures from above and from the outside. The peasants were unlike the wealthy farmers and merchants who have just been discussed. The peasants rioted not because they had suddenly awakened to a political self-consciousness and become fired up with revolutionary fervor against the feudal system, but because the psychological and economic stability of their traditional way of life was being destroyed. To look for a growing political maturity or a germinating modern bourgeois mentality behind this period's outbreaks of violence among the peasants would be fruitless. The cause of the violence was nothing else but this—the peasants' ability to eke out even a meager living was being threatened.

This is not meant to deny that the uprisings exerted a certain material, destructive force which shook the feudal system—regardless of what the peasants' motivation might have been. Let us take them for what they are worth. "There is no intention to belittle the effect of peasant insurrections," Kokushō Iwao wrote once. "Apart from causing considerable economic damage to the farmers themselves, they also had a lot to do, in the end, with reducing not only the finances but also the august status of the samurai. But it would be fallacious—consequentialism, a *circulus in probando*—to maintain on this basis that the peasant uprisings had the same significance in the social history of the Meiji Restoration as the *shishi* zealots' movement to overthrow the shogunate."[35] The point to be kept in mind above all is that the uprisings must be evaluated as the consequences of external motive forces. To put it another way, those consequences were not induced by the consciousness the peasants nourished or the goals they embraced.

Certainly it would be a mistake to underestimate the destructive force of the peasant uprisings in the Bakumatsu and Restoration epoch. If that energy had been methodically channeled with a sustained momentum—one powered by definite motivations—in a revolutionary direction, its potential to change the social order would have been considerable. In the uprisings of that period, however, there was no such revolutionary awareness. That is why in the end they represent nothing more than the recurrence of a localized, sporadic, and temporary phenomenon.

What, then, was the nature of the energy behind the uprisings? To answer that question correctly, we must pose another: What connection existed between the peasants' motivations and their actions?

By nature, farmers want to continue their traditional, conservative way of life. As a rule, they try to endure, not to resist, the exactions of authority and power. As Motoori Norinaga said, peasants may grow "sullen and ill-tempered," but they will not band together in an uprising "unless life becomes utterly unbearable." Even if someone sought to arouse one, he commented, "it would be difficult for the villages to get together."[36] Buyō Inshi, the pseudonymous author of "A Record of Personal Observations of Society" (*Seji kenbunroku;* 1816), was of much the same opinion: "Even if a great amount of extra tax is demanded, those who have something to spare are not going to make much of a fuss. It is rather the poor peasant forever teetering on the edge of misery who resorts to desperate conspiracies when burdened with an extraordinary levy—because he sees no other way out."[37]

Unless pushed to the wall, the peasants would not rise up. To be sure, a succession of "utterly unbearable" situations and one "extraordinary levy" after another became their daily environment in the Bakumatsu and Restoration epoch. Even then, if one looks at the whole picture, more peasants and villages stayed quiet than rose in insurrection. Indeed, the lack of outbreaks indicates the state of the peasants' daily consciousness and reflects their typical way of thinking better than anything else.

Yanagita Kunio has stated, "Peasant disturbances, which may have occurred only once in some villages and in others not at all in the three centuries of the Tokugawa era, no doubt were great events, but . . . they represent nothing more than an index, so to speak, to the agitation and excitement of the people of the time. When we consider them now, the peaceful progression of the remaining two centuries and several decades appears far more important."[38] These words may sound odd to someone who evaluates the mentality of those peasants who rose in revolt as something distinct from the farmers' ordinary outlook on life. But one who takes a comprehensive historical view of the uprisings and the peasants' state of mind cannot help nodding in agreement.

What distinguished the mentality of the peasants who played a part in the period's uprisings from the mentality of the wealthy farmers and townsmen who committed themselves to the superpatriotic *sonnō jōi* movement? It was above all the apolitical orientation of the former. The latter, who acted on the basis of a definite political ideology, made a sharp distinction between the character of their own endeavor and the nature of peasant uprisings. For example, in the fall of 1863 Shibusawa Eiichi abandoned his project for an action against the shogunate when his comrade Odaka Chōshichirō (1836–1868) cautioned him about its recklessness. Had his planned rebellion had a genuine chance of becoming the first step to toppling the shogunate, Shibusawa reasoned, "we would have died in honorable sacrifice" even if it had failed. "But in the end it was apt to be seen as identical to a peasant uprising—people would laugh at it as a light-headed venture akin to juvenile playacting. There were no loyalists to succeed us, so we would have died a dog's death."[39] In other words, Shibusawa feared that his project would end without a political effect—just like a peasant uprising. His appreciation of the nature of such uprisings was on the mark.

An apolitical orientation characterized even those peasants who participated in clearly political actions, such as the Ikuno Disturbance of 1863.10. Their motives for taking part can be divided into the following three: Some were blindly obedient to the traditional authority of village leaders. Some were incited by thought of profit, that is, by the promise of an improvement in their living conditions after the success of the undertaking. And some were forced to join; their motive was fear.

The first case is exemplified by an elderly survivor of this uprising, the peasant Kichibei. When asked about his motives during an on-site historical investigation, Kichibei answered, "The master, Nishimura Shōbei, said go, so I went." In this supposedly imperial loyalist venture, it appears that "apart from the leaders, no one had any idea of what loyalty to the emperor was all about."[40] The second case is illustrated in the report of an inquiry conducted into this uprising by the Tottori domain. According to this report, the lordless samurai who had infiltrated the Tajima region in the summer of 1863 incited the peasants with the following type of propaganda:[41]

> Inasmuch as there has been discord in the relations between the court and the military in recent years, a call to arms will be proclaimed in Kyoto in the near future. Then the provinces of Japan will be divided into two camps, East and West. The farmers of the Western camp, that is, of Kyoto, will be exempt from taxes this year; and in following years, it is the intention to exempt them from three-tenths of their taxes and require them to pay only seven-tenths. . . . Those who were quick to rally round the flag and take up the cause will be allowed to bear sword and surname, or they will receive a stipend or other appropriate rewards, according to the degree of their meritorious exploits.

The third case can be understood from a similar official report: "On the eleventh inst., an unknown number of lordless samurai came to the farm houses of the villages in the vicinity of Ikuno. They told the peasants to follow their orders even if they did not understand them; anyone who did not consent would be put to the sword. The *rōnin* succeeded in making an unknown number of peasants join their group and then took them away, making them carry a drum and fire bell. Report had it that they posted lookouts against pursuers at the Tajima, Tanba, and Harima exits."[42] Naturally, when it became evident that the Ikuno uprising was a failure, the peasants turned against the *rōnin,* who were holed up at Myōkenzan in the village of Yamaguchi. "Things having come to such a pass, the peasants drove out and scattered the lordless samurai and rang the alarm bell of Sainenji temple, so the village would not be blamed. . . . The peasants from nearby villages and hamlets, guns and bamboo spears in hand, gathered in Yamaguchi. Trusting their numerical superiority, they lined up their guns and opened fire on Minami Hachirō and others who were coming down the mountain."[43]

The main force of the Tenchūgumi was also composed of farmer-soldiers, but they scarcely flocked spontaneously to arms. The importunate manifesto issued by Yoshimura Toratarō when he was seeking recruits in Totsugawa certainly makes the peasants' participation appear coerced: "Because of burning need, all men between the ages of fifteen and fifty shall without exception report to headquarters on the twenty-fourth. Come early, bearing in mind that reasons for tardiness will be investigated and that anyone late without cause will be sentenced to severe punishment, according to the degree of his negligence."[44] In this way, the zealots raised as many as a thousand men, a force superior to their enemy's. At the attack on Takatori Castle (1863.8.26), however, the forced conscripts showed their true worth. As soon as the battle began and they were being fired upon, the peasants bolted and ran, deserting the superpatriots.

As seen at Ikuno and in the Heavenly Retribution Band, an almost irreconcilable distance separated the mentality even of those farmer-soldiers who supposedly rose up in response to the summons of the *rōnin*—insofar as they did not as individuals abandon their peasant way of thinking—from the political mentality of the wealthy farmers and merchants who positively supported the samurai. Needless to say, the mentality of those peasants who rose in insurrection on their own completely lacked a political character.

The double impact of external pressures and internal political developments drove some peasants to acts of violence in the Bakumatsu and Restoration epoch. One example, the case of Kiryū in 1859, has already been presented. Another significant case where external pressure led directly to a disturbance occurred as early as 1853.8 in Tochio, a village in Koshi County of Echigo Province:[45]

A mysterious event occurred here on the first day of the Eighth Month, when Myōjin, our gracious deity, emitted a light that illuminated a foot area. People were worried and said such things as, "Portents from Heaven are signs of disturbance in the realm." Just then, word came that dozens of foreign ships had been sighted off Uraga in Sagami Province, and there was great excitement throughout Japan. Accordingly, all the daimyo down to all the bannermen have had military duties levied on them. In all the provinces—not to mention the Three Metropolises—all the businesses are suffering and cannot make ends meet in these recessionary times. In our village group, in particular, the sole means of support is striped *tsumugi* fabrics. Retailers and middlemen have suffered great losses under the harsh economic conditions that prevail this autumn, and their destitution is so severe that they are unable to take care of their parents, wives, and children. The costs of farmers' refinancing the payment of this year's coal levies are double what they were before. The village headmen and tax collectors have become more willful than ever. Under such conditions, the farmers of this group of villages have reached a dead end. Even if they could take on another job, they would still be in desperate straits. Just when people were beginning to talk about bringing a petition before the shogun this autumn—how strange it was!—like a wind arising all of a sudden, with no leadership, on 8.23 paper placards appeared on the outskirts of Nishitani village and Higashitani village, calling for a consultation of all the farmers to discuss the economic plight of the *tsumugi* fabrics business. . . . In all, three thousand farmers assembled at eight o'clock in the evening. . . . They pressed down on Komukai village and from there moved on to Tochibori village and brought to naught the residence of the tax collector, Uemura Kakuzaemon.

The cause of this uprising is patent. Upon Commodore Perry's intrusion, constraints on consumption were initiated in the warrior society out of the sudden need for military preparedness. Even before foreign trade had begun, this belt-tightening was impeding the circulation of goods. As foreign pressure aggravated the situation, it became a foregone conclusion that politics would switch gears and convert to military demands. The consequent increase in the domanial lords' military expenses not only constricted the commercial market but led to the inevitable absorption of the peasants' surplus, to the point where their minimal level of sustenance was threatened.

Especially during the Keiō era (1865–1868), when the antishogunate trend had at length gathered enough impetus to be translated into concrete political action, domanial lords—in particular the daimyo and bannermen of the party that was on its way out, not to speak of the intendants of the shogunate's immediate domains—at best retained the means to exploit the peasants, but they had lost all ability to extend assistance or protection to them. That is why peasant uprisings increased so during the Keiō years.

The case of the peasants of eighteen villages of Kawabe County who rose up in 1866 as part of the large-scale rioting in the Hyōgo region is a graphic example.[46] Kawabe was bannerman territory. The land was inferior, with many undrained fields. Because the irrigation was poor and the farmers could not grow enough rice to live on, they had no choice but to cultivate rapeseed and cotton. For one reason or another —if not droughts then rainstorms, floods, and insect damage—poor harvests followed one after the other in the Bakumatsu period. But the storm of political activity at the end of the shogunate was more fierce and caused greater harm to the peasants in these unfortunate farming villages than the natural disasters.

In the Sixth Month of 1854, the year following Perry's arrival, the domanial lord ordered a special levy of 300 ryō to be apportioned among seven villages in his jurisdiction, ostensibly to assist with shogunal construction projects. In the Ninth Month there followed an additional levy of 300 ryō, supposedly to cover expenses incurred because of the presence of foreign ships. In 1856 there was an assessment of 400 ryō for the repair of the lord's residence, which had been damaged in the Great Edo Earthquake. In the spring of 1863 foreign ships appeared off the shore of Hyōgo, the domains were mobilized for the defense of Osaka Bay, and a large number of corvée laborers were conscripted from this area. The next year, the shogunate launched its first punitive campaign against Chōshū, and the expeditionary force marched through the Hyōgo region; accordingly, there was a draft of laborers for military purposes from the Kawabe area, and some of them were to die in battle. In 1865 the shogunate demanded a large amount of money for the war chest of its second Chōshū expedition. As if all that were not enough, there was a terrible rise in commodity prices.

One can see how the burden on the peasants grew heavier and heavier; clearly, they would be crushed if they stood idly by. To be sure, they did not merely wait for death with their hands folded, but until 1866 they did not riot once. They did nothing more than ask for easement of the tax assessments and issue repeated requests for relief in the form of rice loans from the lord of the domain. True to their traditional approach to life, they endured in silence. They finally rose up in 1866 because their lord, a bannerman of the shogunate, was unable to provide relief, his resources having been exhausted as a result of the second Chōshū expedition. With no means of survival other than demand that the wealthy hand over rice and cash, the poor peasants threw themselves into a "world renewal" uprising *(yonaoshi ikki).*

The example of Kawabe County is not exceptional. The peasants of immediate shogunal domains *(tenryō)* and of bannerman domains were in general treated more harshly than the peasants of outside vassal *(tozama)* domains. Those who labored in a remote countryside received worse treatment than those who lived closer to the daimyo's castle town. In such disadvantaged places, the peasants were crowded into a corner; if they wanted to survive, they had no other recourse but to attack the wealthy. Almost all the large-scale peasant uprisings of the Keiō era took place in this kind of deprived area. What was the reason? As the shogunate's political power declined, so did that of the shogunal intendants, the bannermen, and the hereditary vassals *(fudai)* of the Tokugawa. In the end, with their economic power destroyed, they had nothing left to patch over their deficiencies. Such lords did not have the time to attend to local government.

The neglect of the civil administration reached its nadir when the ravages of war reduced it to a complete abandonment of governance. Even before the outbreak of the Boshin Civil War in 1868, this condition was already at hand in those domains that participated in the shogunate's campaigns against Chōshū. The fierce, unprecedented, large-scale uprisings and riots that erupted in the Tōhoku domains attacked by Meiji government troops in the civil war are attributable to no other reason than this. The people lost sight of authority they could depend on, and the disturbances grew larger. Let us look at one or two examples from Echigo.

The first is a riot that took place in 1868 in Nishi Kanbara County, in the area surrounding Yoshida (a part of the Nagaoka domain), where two or three thousand farmers attacked the village headmen and wealthy farmers. The Tokugawa shogunate "was already near the hour of its destruction," and Nagaoka *han,* "the stalwart among the shogunate's Tōhoku adherents," was too engaged in the struggle for its own survival to attend properly to local government. The agitated populace seized this opportunity to "bring down the village headmen and officials, seeking revenge for the many years of extortion and oppression." Nevertheless, the account of this incident concludes, there was "not the trace of an ideological or political backdrop to this revolt, which took place at a time of momentous upheaval."[47]

The second example is a riot that took place in the same year in Shitada Village, Minami Kanbara County. This uprising had a certain political nature in that the peasants, in addition to opposing the heavy taxes, demanded the replacement of village headmen and officials by public election. On reading that "one hears it said that Mr. Nishigata Tamezō drafted the petition," it is difficult to avoid the suspicion that members of the wealthy farmer stratum directed this uprising from behind the scenes. That suspicion notwithstanding, it is apparent that the underlying cause of this riot, too, was the people's agitation and the peasants' destitution at a time of chaos:[48]

> In our hamlet, from around the third year of Keiō [1867] the requisition of laborers and provisions by the soldiery of various domains made the people's hearts tremble with fear. Every morning and evening there are new proclamations from the daimyo and new reforms initiated by the government army, bringing on changes in their policies. That good folk should abide in tranquility is now a buried custom of the past; disturbances have mounted and uprisings spread everywhere. Some, frightened by the noise of bullets, dare not take up their plow; others pocket the White Army's wages today, tomorrow go to work for the Reds. It is impossible to sort out the present situation. These days the habit of moderation has been destroyed, and the hearts of the people have changed for the worse. Has there been progress or not, has or has there not been regression during this time? In this day and age the holders of power in the provinces exercise their authority as they will upon the people of the lower classes. They levy taxes here and impose duties there, never thinking twice about the cruelty of those exactions. Thus the disparity between high and low grows extreme, and the lower classes are forced into absolute submission. But when they subject themselves to this inordinate extortion and apply themselves tirelessly to their duties, it then turns out that they are not paid for their labor! That is the cause of our anger. Our grievances have accumulated, as have our frustrations. How is it possible to put up with this rotten government beyond what we have already endured? On Meiji 1.8.29 [14 October 1868], men of high purpose who are roused to action by their bitter indignation send every village this letter with multiple endorsements, urging the people of the lower classes in every village to arise.

It would appear that the peasants were being used by someone or other. It is unlikely that the average countryman who participated in this uprising had a clear set of political demands. Rather, the peasants "moved with a blind recklessness, as if trying to catch the wind or capture the shadow. Without reflecting on what they were doing, folk from the thirty-seven villages of the Katōge and Nagasawa group rallied here or gathered there, following the herd instinct. 'Look at the state of the people! Reform the tyrannical government!' they echoed each other. They formed a league that is infecting the Katōge area with insurrectionary activities."[49]

To reiterate, the farmers who rioted were not motivated by an antifeudalistic or indeed by any sort of political consciousness but rather by fear for their very survival. When the civil war shook traditional authority, their anxieties grew even worse, and there may even have been those who, hating the oppressive government that had prevailed until then, looked forward to new rulers. But they did not desire a new political order or a new social system. Even if the peasants held a griev-ance against a cruel lord and even if that lord lost their affections com-pletely, those were no more than passive feelings. An active intention to overthrow the lord himself is nowhere to be seen. The peasants turned to one of two courses of action: either they demanded that the lord restore the security of their everyday lives, or they attacked the wealthy who had prospered by tormenting them and demanded rice and cash to help them get through their crisis. Where the wealthy and the authori-ties took the initiative to help the needy, as they did in Kyoto in 1866, everything ended peacefully. Even when an uprising did occur, if the lord responded to the peasants' demands to some extent, then, by and large, violence ceased.

For example, in the first days of 1867 a fairly large riot broke out in the Miuchi region of eastern Mimasaka (now a part of Okayama Pre-fecture), a detached domain of Toki Yoriyuki (1820–1873), the daimyo of Numata in Kōzuke Province (now Gunma Prefecture). The "Diary of an Appeal by Force" *(Gōso nikki),* an account left behind by Yura Nis-shō (1817–1886), a priest of the Nichiren sect who was one of those responsible for quieting this uprising, deserves to be introduced here, as it goes into detail concerning the peasants' consciousness.

Numata was a small *fudai* domain, and at the time it was bankrupt. It had fallen into such a fiscal crisis that it could pay no more than 10 or 20 percent of the nominal stipends of its retainers. No wonder the taxes imposed on the Miuchi region grew more severe every year. In 1866, moreover, the price of rice rose sharply in the entire Chūgoku region as a result of the shogunate's campaign against Chōshū. Ordinary farmers had been driven into such straits that they had no paddy fields left to mortgage. That is why some thirty villages and several thousand poor farmers of the region rose in revolt. The main targets of their attacks were rice traders, *sake* merchants, and wealthy farmers serving as vil-lage officials (here called *sewayaku,* "mediators"). Through the inter-cession of Yura Nisshō and three other priests, the farmers received 5,000 ryō in cash and 1,500 *hyō* of rice from the domain, and the riot died down in four or five days, a short time given its large scale.

According to Nisshō's diary, at the outbreak of the uprising the masterminds, their faces wrapped in black hoods or hidden under deep sedge hats, circulated through the villages and appealed for participation. Those who failed to join, they threatened, would have their houses broken down. First, they gathered as many as six hundred poor farmers and attacked the establishments of *sake* merchants. Then, bolstered by the *sake* they drank there, they spurred the ordinary farmers to violent action. This behavior fed upon itself, and before long the rioters' number had swelled to three thousand. For all the violent, combative emotions excited by the riot, the peasants did not lose their traditional reverence for the authority of the lord of the domain. Even as they wrecked storehouses and homes, showering jeers on the wealthy farmer "mediators," they "carefully protected the government warehouses, where the lord's rice was stored."[50] Nisshō was impressed by the thoughtfulness he witnessed in the midst of the disturbance. "We bear no grudge against the government office," one of the peasants told him, appealing for the discontinuation of the strict guard posted there (which could only stimulate the mob and incite more violence). Nisshō trusted those words and had the guard lifted.[51]

There was no clear purpose or self-awareness to the behavior of most of the rioters. When a certain headman who was generally trusted tried to calm one group by saying, "If the 'mediators' are bad, we should try to square things by requesting an investigation—so quiet down, quiet down!" the rioters replied, "All right, let's talk it over. We joined simply because we were asked to. No one knows what this is all about." And when Nisshō, eager to hear what "grave matter" could have set off the disturbance, stood in the way of a bamboo-spear-wielding farmer to ask him about the reasons for the riot, the man answered, "There's no reason, nothing serious. No, there is, there is, there is something. But I don't know what it is." "Then who knows?" asked Nisshō, but the man could only tell him, "I don't know who. Someone's got to know. Or maybe not." It was all completely "mixed up."[52]

When domain officials came from Osaka to investigate, the peasants submitted a petition containing twenty-six demands, including remission of half the taxes for the year and return of fields and paddies lost to foreclosure over the past fifty years. Under the condition that their twenty-six demands be withdrawn, the officials granted the relief mentioned earlier. Nisshō interceded with them to commute the masterminds' punishment, maintaining that the villagers "were just whooping it up, according to their custom; they didn't mean anything by it. The very ones who presented the petition will wake up tomorrow thinking, 'How could I ever have said such a thing?' I hope this may be of some help to you in reaching a decision."[53] In short, as Nisshō tried to explain, the peasants' actions were not hostile to the domain.

The carpenters' "world renewal" uprising that erupted the same year in Kawagoe *han* was also calmed through domain relief measures before it could become serious. In this domain, too, the economic burden on the townspeople of the castle town grew ever heavier as the political situation deteriorated and social conditions worsened. When construction declined, the carpenters who consequently lost their jobs gathered at the Hikawa Shrine and demanded that the price of rice be reduced: currently, 100 mon fetched 2 *gō* of rice; they wanted 5 *gō* for the same money. Before they could start a destructive riot, the domain government announced that it was in the middle of discussing how to put cheap rice on the market, and the gathering dispersed before this show of authority. The disturbance was calmed entirely when 3 *gō* of rice began selling for 100 mon immediately afterward—"the poor of Kawagoe were soothed when 100 coppers bought an extra *gō* of rice."[54]

It was more or less the same with the large gatherings of the Edo poor in 1867.11, as reported by Fukuchi Gen'ichirō (1841–1906):[55]

> About that time there were riots and rallies of the indigent poor throughout the city of Edo. Because of the failure of the previous year's crop, the price of rice kept rising. This autumn's harvest, too, was poor, and so prices rose more and more, until for one ryō one could get no more than 1.1 *to* [not quite 20 liters] of inferior rice. Toward the end of the Eleventh Month, the poor gathered here and there throughout the city and pressed the well-to-do for money to buy rice with. They prepared rice gruel in kettles set up on cooking fires that they built in the open areas of town and divided it up among the poor of the neighborhood. Those who did not come to these public kitchens were presumed to be wealthy and were pressed for contributions. As I lived in Shitaya, while walking through the neighboring areas I witnessed the gatherings in Ueno Hirokōji, Onarimichi, Kikuyabashi, in front of the Kōtokuji temple, and on the Sakuma riverside. The rallies, it was said, had become the fashion all over Edo, but these poor people were not so violent as to tear down the houses of the wealthy or to pillage and plunder for rice money. Actually it was no more than a cry for help exhibiting itself in a show of force, and so the crowds dispersed peaceably as soon as the office of the town magistrate issued a declaration promising assistance. As I remember, the longer of these rallies lasted no more than four or five days and the shorter ones two or three days at the most.

Because the shogunate took quick action—having learned from its experience with large-scale rioting during the Fifth Month of the previous year—these incidents did not get out of hand. Without a doubt, the peasants and the urban poor who rose up in revolt were almost all on the verge of starvation, as Fukuchi points out. In many cases the effectiveness of the shogunate's policy toward the starving determined the scale of their activities.

As is evident from these examples, commoners rioted when they had been pushed to extremes—when they had reached the limits of their endurance. Their uprisings, however, were not indications of any conscious ideological awakening. The traditional mentality always lay just under the surface of the rioters' passions. Many of them might indeed have reflected, "I woke up the next morning thinking, 'How could I ever have said such a thing?' "

Not surprisingly, even as rioting was taking place in some domains, in others where the civil administrations were attentive the peasants not only refrained from uprisings but took solace in their traditional lives and remained deeply thankful to their lord for his benevolent government. Sōma *han* is such an example. A report written in 1864 by a certain Sendai samurai evaluates the domanial administration of Sōma as "extremely good." Noted with particular approval is the progress of the domain's agricultural reclamation projects: waste land brought under cultivation has increased tenfold in the seven or eight years since the observer's last visit, "so there is no more land to be cleared, neither moor nor hill." This (presumably neutral) observer exalts Sōma's reputation: "The principle of Loving the People is put into practice effectively; the seasons of planting in the spring and reaping in the autumn are observed carefully; diseases and afflictions are looked into attentively; and the poor are given relief from their want and their weakness."[56]

In Chōshū, too, there was not a single disturbance after the great Tenpō Uprising of 1831. That was because "there was a great abundance of money and grain, and the government frequently made rice available to the lower classes at moderate prices." Attentive to civil government, the *han* administration gained the confidence of the common people. Not surprisingly—not, in any event, to the author of this report, the shogunal official Katsu Kaishū (1823–1899)—they responded in the domain's time of need. "Men in the prime of life all aspired to bearing two swords and handling a gun. For the most part, only the old were left working the fields."[57] The results were apparent in the shogunate's second Chōshū campaign: "Of great disadvantage to us in the government forces' present struggle with the Chōshū outlaws is that harmony and unity prevail everywhere in that domain. Even among the indigent poor, down to the lowest beggar, each wishes to sacrifice his life for his lord. Now if something were to happen in Edo, would any citizens of the capital be willing to face danger for the government?"[58] Thus observed a shogunal retainer, looking jealously at the cooperation between commoners and the domain authorities in Chōshū.

Amidst the great social changes of the Bakumatsu and Restoration epoch, the peasants, far from wanting to destroy feudal, traditional authority, retained their habitual attitude of submission to it. To be sure, that attitude now manifested itself in the form of a desire to improve their social status in accordance with the traditional hierarchy of values. In other words, they sought success within the framework of the old value system. It was on the presupposition of the existence of this peasant mentality that the shogunate and various domains allowed farmers to raise their status and social standing as recompense for ordering them to contribute money and for conscripting them. As noted previously, it was usual for farmers who had even a little extra to try to buy an improvement in their social standing by contributing money rather than by volunteering for the dangerous service in the militia. Depending on the domain, people competed with one another in giving contributions even when uprisings were intensifying.

Matsumoto *han* in 1868 is one example. This domain had already fallen on desperate times at the time of the 1866 Chōshū campaign. During the Boshin Civil War the Meiji government questioned its intentions, and Matsumoto made a contribution of 30,000 ryō to demonstrate its loyalty and insure its security. To make assurance double sure, it lost no time in marching an expeditionary force off to the Tōhoku front and assumed the responsibility for providing logistical support to the government's Tōsandō Army. All that required vast outlays of funds, and the domain's fisc could not possibly meet such great demands through ordinary means. The *han* tried to obtain additional funds by issuing domain bonds (*gosaikaku-kin,* literally "smart-money") in the Second and the Third Month of 1868, and it did manage to raise the sum of 90,000 ryō from the commoners of the castle town. That still was not enough, however, and in the Sixth Month a decree requiring "contributions for increasing official personnel" was issued in the farming villages of the domain. The blatancy of this attempt to sell the peasants long-coveted feudal privileges and social status was as remarkable as its success. When this order was issued, "barnyard plutocrats, dissatisfied with the strictness of class customs, competed to contribute. A great many won an official position or rank. One source reports that the domain collected 140,000 ryō by this device."[59] Evidently, the domain's calculations had taken adequate account of one aspect of the peasant mentality.

These examples ought to show that no matter how agitated farmers became in the Bakumatsu and Restoration epoch, their mentality remained squarely within the framework of feudal values, which they certainly had no inclination to reject. The peasants' stubborn adherence to their traditional way of thinking was made even more obvious when the young Meiji government set forth its new policies, especially at the time of the abolition of the *han* and the establishment of prefectures in 1871. When the daimyo were ordered to move from their old domains and take up residence in Tokyo, the peasants became anxious about the removal of familiar authority figures and their replacement with new and unknown rulers. Their demand that the old domanial lord remain in office as prefectural governor was the cause of a fair number of riots. Among the twenty-four uprisings in the fourth year of Meiji (1871), eight—a third of the total—had that aim.[60] One such uprising occurred in each of Shimane, Kagawa, Okayama, and Kōchi prefectures, and two each in Hiroshima and Ehime prefectures.

In particular, the "Taking Our Body Fat" (Aburatori) uprising, which took place in Takaoka, Agawa, and Tosa counties of Kōchi Prefecture at the beginning of 1872 (Meiji 4.12), deserves a closer look. According to the manifesto of the ringleader, a peasant called Takemoto Chōjūrō (d. 1872), the cause of these riots was that "the government has chased out the lord of the domain; instead, a wicked, barbarian-loving official has been installed in the prefectural office. It's really hard to take, but they intend to sell us Japanese to the foreigners, who will take our body fat to feed themselves. Not a day is to be lost. If we do not restore the prince our lord, kill the wicked official, and chase out the barbarian dogs right away, in five years there will be no Japanese people left. All as one, we must get ready for the showdown."[61]

The petition presented by the peasants to the prefectural office maintained that "if His Honor the Governor is made to go to Tokyo, the farmers will no longer enjoy their labors, and chaos will result. Unless Their Two Lordships keep faith with us and stay here in the province, it will be difficult for the farmers to continue with their labors." On view here is the farmers' ingenuous, deep affection for their former domanial lords, and simultaneously expressed is their fear that their traditional way of life would be destroyed by the new leadership. To understand the peasants' mentality more fully, however, one should take note of the existence of another item in the petition: "If the *eta* are made 'new commoners' and mixed in with the peasants, what are we faithful to? What purpose is there in making peasants into *eta?*"[62] This shows beyond a doubt that the peasants were bound to feudal, traditional notions of status. The terms *eta* (pariah) and *hinin* (unperson) were abolished on 1871.8.28, but there were outbreaks of rioting against their abolition in Hyōgo and Okayama prefectures, among other places. Whether such uprisings demanded the retention of former governors or of traditional discriminatory terminology, they expressed the peasants' deep-rooted opposition to anything that would destroy long-familiar concepts of authority and status. They were manifestations of the great anxieties regarding the new Meiji government that afflicted the peasants.

The peasants were not the driving force that toppled and destroyed the feudal system. Rather, the shocks that caused it to crack were induced by pressures from above and from the outside. The feudal system changed irreversibly, and the process of change overrode the farmers' traditional lives, taking no account of their consciousness. In the event, they were denied that system's protection, something they had taken for granted and expected to continue enjoying. The peasants sought stability; they wanted to secure the system from the shocks and to restore it; but, ready or not, they were cast loose from it. They lost the traditional basis of their existence, but they were unable to free themselves from a traditional consciousness. That is why they were anxious and dissatisfied with the new age. Their desire to maintain a traditional, stable way of life was at the root of their opposition to the currents that were swiftly eroding its base.

The Urban Commoners

No doubt it was the commoners of the Three Metropolises—particularly the commoners of Edo and Kyoto, the two focal points of politics—who felt the severe changes in the circumstances of their lives the most intensely. They had been cast into the very center of the political and social upheavals of the Bakumatsu and Restoration epoch. How did they view the various activities of the samurai and how did they respond to the incidents that drastically shook the peaceful, traditional lives they had led until then? To put it differently, what sort of awareness of the situation did the urban commoners express in their encounters with politics?

Apart from two or three petitions, there are almost no historical sources that would permit one to size up their frame of mind firsthand, and there is no other way to approach this problem than through indirect evidence. The contemporary materials in question are graffiti, posters, popular songs, and *chobokure* (a type of street performance: doggerel, often containing political and social commentary, sung to the accompaniment of a small drum), which express the emotions of the commoners, even if they were composed by people of various strata—including commoners, to be sure. Also useful are the letters in which domanial samurai who resided in Edo and Kyoto reported on the condition of the people and the political situation in those cities. Of course one should not expect accuracy from such sources, but even so they provide some idea of the general state of mind of city people, their hopes, and their dissatisfactions.

Three general conclusions may be drawn from this type of evidence. First, even city-dwellers, inasmuch as they were commoners in a feudal society, had never once been given the official opportunity to play an active role in the political arena. They led their lives in a private, confined society. Accordingly, the measure of their political awareness was a reflection of the eye they kept on their highly circumscribed interests. Their tendency to concentrate on their own problems was constantly reinforced and regulated by feelings of hatred, uneasiness, and even fear toward anything that would shatter the peace of their lives; by their dissatisfaction with political leaders who could not prevent the destruction of their livelihood; and by the mood of despair born from these disturbing feelings.

Second, unlike the samurai and the rural merchants, the urban commoners did not embrace "revering the emperor" or "expelling the barbarian" as political ideals, nor were they stirred by a feeling of national crisis. It was a sense of crisis regarding their individual lives that afflicted them. *Sonnō* and *jōi* made sense to them only as extensions of that concern. They did not comprehend the contemporary situation with any sort of awakened political consciousness, and in this regard they were similar to the peasants.

Third, the common people wanted their traditional way of life restored. In the case of Edo, they hoped that matters could be resolved through traditional channels of power and authority, and specifically through the resurrection of the ancestral law of the shogunate. In the case of Kyoto, the commoners could not help being affected by policies adopted by the imperial loyalists and the large, powerful domains, the dominant political influences in the imperial capital. Neither in Kyoto nor in Edo, however, did the common people engage in any kind of positive political action aimed at remedying their situation.

Tossed about in the storms of the Bakumatsu and Restoration epoch, they remained politically passive. They pinned their hopes on various political powers, including the shogunate, but were betrayed. Apprehension turned to fear, and then to a sense of utter despair. In the end, political changes initiated from above confronted them with a tragedy: they were made to break away from the structure to which their lives had been so closely attached.

In what form did the commoners' sentiments find their historic expression? Let us look from their point of view at three problem areas: the opening of the country to foreigners during the 1850s, the contention for influence in Kyoto during the 1860s, and the changes in the leadership of the shogunate that were occurring in Edo at roughly the same time.

The arrival of Commodore Perry in 1853.6 set off an intensification of military preparations and a tightening of consumption on the part of the shogunate and the domains. Even before the end of that year, the resulting paralysis of commercial trading was taking its toll on the people. As we have already seen, even the silk-weaving districts far removed from Edo had begun to feel the pressure. In the metropolis itself, an oppressive and gloomy air prevailed as the New Year of 1854 began. A *chobokure* complained:[63]

> Since autumn of last year not a diversion sets us free;
> the plum trees are in bloom, yet no one comes to see;
> no springtime mood is to be felt, though the new year has begun;
> the vernal rites are held, but no one comes for fun.

The fear of a foreign intrusion brought on an economic downturn, but the price of rice jumped as a result of military procurements undertaken as part of the buildup of coastal defenses. Anxieties began to affect the accustomed pattern of life:[64]

> No customers come to Yoshiwara today;
> the audience is scarce at the kabuki play;
> without ironclad credit the pawnshops will not pay;
> the price of rice has gone sky-high, and there it seems to stay.

No wonder the common people of Edo hated the shogunate's entry into relations with foreign countries. After the conclusion of the Treaty of Kanagawa in 1854.3, they became more and more discontented with its leadership, as is indicated in a comic poem *(senryū)* that derides Senior Councillor Abe Masahiro (1819–1857):[65]

> | *Abekawa wa* | Abekawa cakes |
> | *kinako o yamete* | without sugarcoating; spread |
> | *miso o tsuke* | with *miso* instead. |

["Abekawa," an obvious reference to Senior Councillor Abe, is an abbreviation for *Abekawa mochi,* a kind of rice cake dusted with sugared soybean flour. *Miso* paste, another soybean derivative, occurs in the idiomatic expression *miso o tsukeru,* "to spread *miso*," meaning to lose face making a mess of things.] The era name was changed to Ansei—"Stable Government"—on 11.27 (15 January 1855), but people felt that true stability could not be achieved unless there was a return to the closed country system, maintained strictly before but broken now:[66]

> | *Ansei o* | A-n-se-i read |
> | *shita kara yomeba* | from the right is i-se-n, |
> | *isen nite* | ships from foreign lands. |
> | *nokoru ichiji wa* | The letter A's left over: |
> | *Amerika no kuni* | for America it stands. |

The phrase "read from the right" [the Japanese original's *shita kara yomeba*, the vertical line "read from below"] referred to the proper standpoint, meaning that of the common people.

On 1857.10.28, U.S. Consul General Townsend Harris was received by the shogun in Edo Castle. To the common people, the breaking of the centuries-old ancestral law of the Tokugawa was a world-shaking event. Popular that year was the following *chobokure*:[67]

> Townspeople starve as time goes by
> and grow to hate the samurai.
> Even if they have some gold,
> all the lenders leave you cold,
> not like the pawnshops of old. . . .
>
> Never before has such a beast barged in,
> and no one stops this mortal sin;
> weak-willed daimyo, all done in. . . .
>
> The brothel houses of clients are bare;
> there are no buyers to buy any wares;
> about cherry blossoms no one seems to care. . . .
>
> Why has the world grown so dull and so plain?
> Just thinking about it addles the brain.

Just when they thought that their hopes had been dashed by Harris' reception at the shogunal castle, the common people breathed a sigh of relief when the imperial court refused to affix its seal to the Harris Treaty. Senior Councillor Hotta Masayoshi (1810–1864) became the target of ridicule for his failure to secure Kyoto's approval:

> In this trial of strength, the East has lost the test;
> the referee raises his fan to the victorious West.

America, England, Russia, France, and "the Germans and other vermin will all be laid to rest," this song continued, to conclude with the ringing phrase, "Peace in the realm forever!"[68] But the commoners could not envision this state of ideal peace coming about other than through Japan's isolation. When the imperial court ordered the ending of foreign contacts, its stature therefore suddenly increased in their eyes. In contrast to this, the *bushi* powers-that-be of Edo had been unable to block the foreigners' demands by force, and their failure led to expressions of scorn from the commoners:[69]

> Basking in extravagance,
> casting the Art of War askance,
> the samurai will rue the day
> they let the Americans come our way.

At a time when the commoners of Edo first began to voice these feelings of distrust for the shogunate and its supporting samurai caste, Ii Kamon no Kami Naosuke, the daimyo of Hikone, was unexpectedly elevated to the position of great elder by the shogunate and assumed dictatorial powers over the management of national policy. The commoners hoped that the man who was given this extraordinary office in the time of crisis would restore stability to their lives. "So bIi it," an anonymous broadside insisted:[70]

> Stop foreign trade, say we, and so be it. Honor the emperor, say we, and so be it. Block off the West, say we, and so be it. Get rid of Hotta, say we, and so be it. Lower the prices, say we, and so be it. Stop debasing the coinage, say we, and so be it. Restore people's spirits, say we, and so be it.

Obviously, the commoners expected much of the dictator. Hence they were all the more incensed when he rammed through the decision to open Japan, affixing his seal to the treaty in violation of the imperial decree. When Ii Kamon was assassinated on 1860.3.3, the commoners applauded:[71]

> Everyone shouts with glee
> on hearing of the end of Ii.
> Born and bred a Nipponese,
> he ate our rice without surcease.

> Come on, you fool, a coward from the first,
> of all the greedy bastards, you were the worst.
> Admitting the foreign dogs with your seal,
> did you not break the law in this deal?
> And bring the greatest shame on our land
> since heaven and earth apart came to stand. . . .

> The loss of his head and his grotesque demise . . .
> show Heaven's punishment realized,
> a boon Our Lord Ieyasu ordained
> to protect his descendants' integral domain
> and keep out the polluting Christian stain.
> People of the realm feel a sense of release
> that now will come an age of great peace.

When the era name was changed fifteen days after Ii's untimely death, the commoners voiced their hopes for the coming age:[72]

> The dictator has fallen, and so has the price
> of our daily sustenance, good old rice.
> The spirits of lowly folk are cheered,

and lately even the weather has cleared.
It is the dawning of the age of Man'en,
the age of Man'en—world renewal for all men.

These pasquinades criticized Ii for having broken the ancestral law of the shogunate. The traditional attitudes that reached to the core of the commoners' political mentality clearly resonate in all of these satirical songs. This nostalgia for things traditional was a wistful longing for ye olde Edo of times forlorn. The townspeople of Edo, these examples show, discussed the serious political problem of the country's opening in light of the effect it would have on their lives; and from that point of view they rejected it outright.

What was the thinking of the commoners of Kyoto at the time? The excitement caused in Kyoto political circles by Senior Councillor Hotta Masayoshi's journey to the city for the purpose of requesting imperial consent to a treaty with the foreigners, followed by the uproar aroused when Ii Naosuke concluded such an agreement contrary to the imperial will, awakened the Kyoto townspeople to the reality that they could do nothing about the opening of the ports. Like the Edoites, they lamented that their way of life would be constricted by the country's opening— perhaps none more so than the people of Nishijin, who had already suffered the first harsh blows of foreign trade. A broadside "From the Townspeople of Kyoto" makes it apparent that as early as 1858, commoners recognized the incompatibility between foreign trade and the security of their lives. Pinning their increasingly desperate hopes on the imperial court to forbid the opening of the country, they begged to be permitted to live their daily lives in safety:[73]

> The news that an accord has been reached in Edo to conduct commerce with the American barbarians has spread even to the lower classes. Things being what they are, the policy adopted more and more by the shogunate will be to take mercilessly from the farmers until they have nothing left to live on. . . . If in the end there is commerce with foreign countries, the price of rice will go higher and higher. Since middle- and lower-income townsmen and farmers will be in dire straits, we humbly request that the emperor graciously formulate a plan which will enable the common people to make a living. If no appropriate directives are issued from the imperial palace, the common people of Kyoto are certain to become even more despondent than they are now.

In the early 1860s, the problem of foreign relations turned into a domestic issue that gradually exposed the contradictions of feudalism to all levels and all corners of Japanese society. For all that, there was no fundamental change in the commoners' thinking on domestic issues.

After the death of Ii Naosuke, Senior Councillor Andō Nobumasa became the central figure in the shogunate and took over the reins of government. His demand for the marriage of the emperor's sister, Princess Kazu (1846–1877), to the shogun earned Andō the enmity of the radical faction. On 1862.1.15 a group of *rōnin* from Mito tried to assassinate him outside the Sakashita Gate of Edo Castle. Wounded in this attack, the senior councillor was forced to withdraw from his position. Immediately after this incident, prominent domains such as Satsuma, Chōshū, and Tosa established a presence in Kyoto, and many of the lordless samurai who had sprung up all over the country in the cause of *sonnō jōi* also flocked to the imperial capital. They all sought reforms in the government or even the overthrow of the shogunate. Consequently, senior officials of the shogunate and even the shogun himself found it necessary to undertake the journey to Kyoto. The scramble for political hegemony that was enacted there resulted in the coup d'état of 1863. 8.18, brought on the Hamaguri Gate Incident (a bloody encounter fought between the forces of Chōshū and the Kyoto contingents of Aizu and Satsuma) and the ensuing Great Kyoto Fire of 1864.7, and escalated into the shogunate's first punitive expedition against Chōshū later that year. Kyoto had become the veritable burning point of politics and for that reason will be examined first.

Though it may be stretching the point somewhat, it could be said that as far as the common people were concerned, Kyoto was caught up in a spiral of terror. In 1862.4, when Shimazu Hisamitsu, the powerful patriarch of the daimyo family of Satsuma, marched to Kyoto at the head of an armed contingent, the townsmen were convinced that combat between his forces and troops at the disposal of the shogunate's Kyoto deputy *(shoshidai)* was sure to follow. "The townsmen who lived in the neighborhood of the *shoshidai* mansion deposited their wives, their children, and all their household goods in the countryside, leaving nothing except cooking utensils in their homes. Those of few possessions all moved to such places as the area east of the Sanjō Bridge."[74] Satsuma, however, was clever enough to win over the people's hearts and minds. The Satsuma troops paid double the market value when buying townspeople's homes for use as their quarters. Realizing that the price of rice was on the rise, they did not as much as touch a single cup of it in Kyoto and the surrounding area. On the contrary, part of the supply they had brought along from their domain was released onto the local market, thereby making rice less expensive. Satsuma's purchasing agents stimulated the economy by buying other local commodities at high prices with the copper currency that was becoming scarce. Moreover, Satsuma samurai were enjoined to maintain strict military discipline when dealing with the populace. In these ways, Satsuma sought and gained the common people's trust and gratitude: "Not just in the capital and its surroundings but in the entire Kinai region and nearby provinces, they are saying that world renewal will be realized, the foreign ships driven away, and the price of goods lowered thanks to the Prince of Satsuma. The spirits of the people in Kyoto and in the countryside have been raised. For the Prince of Satsuma, it is being said, the people would gladly give their lives."[75]

Unlike Satsuma, the Kyoto deputy—so to speak the head of the shogunate's branch office in the imperial capital—was unable to take the initiative in establishing any policy toward the people. This deputy was Sakai Tadayoshi (1813–1873), the lord of Obama in Wakasa Province (now a part of Fukui Prefecture). He was so out of favor with the people that he could only be pitied, and they made fun of him mercilessly:[76]

Mina hito ga	We've all been poisoned
Wakasa kodai ni	by that Wakasa small fry;
aterarete	we'll welcome the sight
Ōhara kudari	of his back when he heads for
ato ga yokarō	home down the Ōhara road.

[The Ōhara road is indeed the direct route from Kyoto to Wakasa, but there is a scatological double entendre in the strophe *Ōhara kudari ato ga yokarō*, which can be understood as "Nothing like a big dump to make you feel good."] When he was relieved of his position by Matsudaira Hōki no Kami Munehide (1811–1873)—the broom *(hōki)* that sweeps clean—on 1862.6.30, Sakai was ushered out with ridicule: "Wakasa, what are you hanging around for? The Broom's been elevated, so scat! Go home!"[77]

In that same Sixth Month, Shimazu Hisamitsu left Kyoto to accompany the imperial envoy Ōhara Shigetomi to Edo, where they would seek a reform of the shogunate. After Hisamitsu's departure, Maki Izumi (1813–1864), Hirano Kuniomi, and other jingoist *rōnin,* along with their fellow enthusiasts of the *sonnō jōi* movement among the Chōshū domain's samurai, became the central figures of the Kyoto political world. They were permitted to take a hand (or, rather, they intruded) in court politics, acting in the capacity of chargés of state affairs *(kokuji goyōgakari).* Hot bloods among the court nobility, Sanjō Sanetomi (1837–1891) and Anegakōji Kintomo (1839–1863) in particular, assumed the role of the group's leaders. Their plans for the overthrow of the shogunate were conducted under the slogan of the "barbarians'" immediate expulsion, *sokkon jōi.*

These radicals were a menace and at the same time an anchor of stability to the townspeople. This was because the radicals, too, sought to win over the minds and hearts of the commoners, and their means for doing so included threatening the city's "corrupt merchants" not to think of driving up prices. A fragmentary report dated Bunkyū 2.12.12 (31 January 1863) describes their tactics as follows: "The *rōnin* wield a terrific power here. To start with, they have set down the exchange rates of gold and silver. A gold coin is to be exchanged for such and such a sum and the market price of rice is to be such and such; they have even determined what price is to be paid for coal and firewood. Any transgressor is to be summarily executed, and his head put on display down by the river bank. There are graffiti and posters to this effect here and there. I hear that since they appeared, everyone has been so afraid that prices have in fact been lowered."[78] Consequently the radicals, whose core element was composed of Chōshū *sonnō jōi* activists, reaped the gratitude of the commoners just as Satsuma had. "That Kyoto flourishes is due entirely to these *rōnin*," people were saying. "The majority in the city admire them."[79] Evidently the people did not concern themselves with the political antagonism that existed between Satsuma and Chōshū. According to a confidential informant of the shogunate, they spoke of both those domains "as if they were some sort of divine entities." Naturally, the shogunal authorities were "dumbfounded."[80]

In the course of the year 1863, the radicals for a time attained dominance over the imperial court. They persuaded the emperor to proclaim a campaign against the "barbarians" that he would lead in person, had orders issued to the shogun to present himself in Kyoto, and pressed the shogunate to fix a specific date for the expulsion of the foreigners. They developed the self-conceit that they could manipulate the direction of politics as they pleased and abandoned their former strategy of seeking to win the hearts of the people. As a result, the commoners began to fear rather than respect and support them.

Indeed, the townspeople were exposed to night after night of terror as bands of radicals and phony samurai pretending to be radicals carried out assassinations: "This morning a samurai was cut down by the Takasegawa, just south of Sanjō. . . . On the night of the twenty-sixth, one was killed on Sanjō or Shijō a bit west of Senbon-dōri. Townsmen were cut down on the evening of the twenty-fifth at Shinmachi-dōri and around Tachiuri."[81] In the meantime the shogunal authorities had forfeited any claim to authority over the commoners, who showed their contempt with jibes such as this: "When there's an unnatural death these days, the Kyoto deputy and the town magistrates only clean up the mess; so the Office of the Town Magistrate is called the Corpse Removal Office by all the world."[82]

The coup d'état of 1863.8.18—when proponents of the "union of court and military" occupied the imperial palace and seized power at the imperial court—broke out in this kind of atmosphere, and the anxiety of the Kyoto populace was rekindled. They lived in terror until the Chōshū radicals had abandoned their city. To be sure, just when the townspeople thought they had lost sight of any political authority that would guarantee their safety, one materialized. This new power was Aizu, a domain antagonistic toward the Chōshū radicals; its daimyo, Matsudaira Katamori (1835–1893), was charged with the office of the imperial capital's military governor *(Kyōto shugoshoku)*. The commoners' level of concern for the political situation rose, but certainly not out of any interest in politics itself. Commoners were interested in politics only insofar as it affected their daily lives. In the current situation, they put their trust in Aizu. Aizu owed its popularity in part to the discipline of its samurai, but more than that to its consumer spending, which prospered Kyoto. "The lord of Aizu," it was reported, "has visited the Charity Hospital (Seyakuin) and has been received at the imperial palace. As before, his reputation is truly impeccable. They say that by last month he had spent eight hundred thousand ryō. Apparently he spends one thousand ryō a day for box lunches, candles, and other miscellaneous items alone."[83]

The commoners' confidence in Aizu did not last very long. Around the time of the Hamaguri Gate Incident in 1864.7, it began to totter again. Security had not improved in the city after the coup d'état of the previous year, and Kyoto remained an arena of fear where murder and robbery in the streets were everyday occurrences. "According to a story I was told at Keage," a letter reported, "a man and the three-year-old child he was carrying were cut down before sunset last night here on the east side of town as they were returning from prayers at the Kōbō Temple. Still showing signs of life, they were immediately taken home in a palanquin, as they were locals. This morning, however, father and son both died. There are many fake *rōnin* about these days. They say that someone else was cut down a bit later last night on the east side. There is also much talk of burglars, robbers, and intruders."[84] Another letter related similar news: "Just when kabuki performances have started up again at Shijō, two low-lifes were cut down today in front of the theater. I, too, went to have a look. The performances, after all, continued without interruption."[85] The mood in Kyoto was grave, wrote an Aizu samurai: "What feeds the insecurity and keeps the minds of the people on edge is that every day there is another, novel kind of killing. One can never tell what tomorrow will bring. They stop at nothing, sparing neither man nor beast."[86] Under these circumstances, people came to doubt the ability of the military governor's office to control things. Indeed, it was on Aizu—not on the Chōshū troops, which had invaded their city—that they laid the blame for the fire and destruction caused in Kyoto by the Hamaguri Gate Incident. "The hearts of the people of the city are not with Aizu. In any case, they seem constrained to revile it. It is really a shame how unjust they are. No one could excel the Aizu domain in its exertions for the sake of the capital city; but by the same token, it would be difficult to exceed the degree of the people's disaffection with Aizu. For reasons I am unable to understand, not only the patriots but the entire city loves Chōshū."[87] (No doubt the reason the public's sympathies began to lean again toward Chōshū was that on the day set for the implementation of *jōi* in 1863, it had been the only domain that actually fired on the foreigners—the "barbarians" who were forcibly trying to foist on Japan the foreign trade loathed by the common people. On 1864.8.5 Chōshū then had to face the consequences, as a fleet composed of seventeen vessels from four nations—Britain, France, the Netherlands, and the United States—bombarded Shimonoseki, landed marines, destroyed Chōshū's forts on the Shimonoseki Strait, and reopened that important passageway to Western shipping.)

When all is said and done, what determined the way the common people of Kyoto sized up the situation was their concern for their lives and their livelihood. As long as a genuine stabilizing force failed to appear, they had no escape from fear and insecurity. Their hopes for preserving a traditional style of life alternated with despair when those hopes were betrayed. In due time they could not but fall into the psychological condition of the proverbial drowning man. Seen in this light, the *Ee ja nai ka!*—"Ain't it OK!"—dance craze of 1867, far from revealing a liberated mental state, represented the psychology of people who had nothing left to hold on to. In the end, people sought salvation in superstition. They followed the blind impulse to clutch at straws.

Let us now turn to the common people of Edo. In 1862.7, Shimazu Hisamitsu arrived in that city with the intention of effecting reforms in the shogunate. Hisamitsu succeeded in giving concrete shape to the *kōbu gattai* movement. Largely as a result of his efforts, Hitotsubashi Yoshinobu (the future shogun Tokugawa Yoshinobu; 1837–1913) was designated shogunal regent *(shōgun kōkenshoku)* and the daimyo Matsudaira Yoshinaga (Matsudaira Shungaku; 1828–1890) of Fukui in Echizen Province appointed shogunal chancellor *(seiji sōsaishoku)*. Just as had been the case when Ii first took center stage, Matsudaira was expected by the common people to fix all that was wrong with their world. One poetaster declaimed as follows:[88]

Kashikoshi na	It's a fair wind that
Koshiji no kaze no	blows from Fukui across
Fukui yori	the Koshiji Trail.
osamarinabiku	Content, the people bend as
shihō no tamikusa	grass before the soothing breeze.

At least one of the measures taken by the new chancellor certainly had a formidable effect. Because of his relaxation of the alternate attendance *(sankin kōtai)* system, the tradesmen of Edo lost their biggest customers—the daimyo, the samurai, and their families—all at once. Inevitably, the common people detested this policy. "What was once called the Flowering Edo is now a desolate countryside, the strangest thing ever," a letter complained.[89] "The townspeople are all withering away," stated another report. "Whatever township one passes through, all one hears is sighs and lamentations."[90] Needless to say, Matsudaira's popularity declined instantly. His sobriquet Shungaku, which included the character for "summit," attracted the thunderbolt of a destructive wit:

His High Exalted Loftiness is about to take a tumble,
and his top will be exposed as his whole peak crumbles.

Another *senryū* engaged in wordplay on his provenance and title:

Zōsai de	You can't fill your gut
ichizen meshi mo	on a bowl of the pap that's
kuwarenei	being dished out here.

[*Zōsai* (a rice gruel boiled with vegetables) puns on *sōsai* (chancellor), and *ichizen* (a bowl of food) on Echizen. Hence the extended meaning is "You can't fill your gut on a bowl of the pap dished out by this chancellor from Echizen."][91]

As though suffering hard times were not enough, the people were in addition terrified by a foreign threat. In 1863.1 Shogun Tokugawa Iemochi (1846–1866; r. 1858–1866), accompanied by Hitotsubashi Yoshinobu and a large suite, left Edo for Kyoto. The problems with the foreigners that came to a head while the shogun was away from his capital caused the common people's anxieties to mount. This particular crisis was the result of an incident that had occurred in the Eighth Month of the previous year, when samurai in the retinue of Shimazu Hisamitsu, who was on his way back to Kyoto from Edo, killed an Englishman and wounded two others in the village of Namamugi, on the outskirts of Yokohama. In 1863.2 England in the strongest of terms demanded the arrest of the perpetrators and the payment of indemnities.

The shogunate quickly sent word to all township officials in Edo:

"Advise the people that no matter what happens, there is no need to panic or become excited."[92] As if to corroborate the ominous tone of this proclamation, the wives and children of retainers of the Owari domain, which was entrusted with taking care of affairs in Edo during the shogun's absence, were suddenly told to go home. The families began to dispose of the more cumbersome of their luxury goods. "They sell their doll collections even as they are on display [for the Hina Matsuri, sc. Girls' Day, 3.3]. Even if they get only two or three ryō for something worth a hundred, they sell without objection." Now the townspeople were convinced that the British would attack and burn Edo, and a flight from the city ensued. The roads leading to the countryside "in every direction" were packed "by night and by day with the luggage of samurai, artisans, and merchants alike being carried away on carts, on horseback, and on the shoulders of bearers. Especially around Shiba and Takanawa, there is such a commotion as people try to sell off their household goods that one would think the fires are already burning toward us."[93]

Edo fell into a lawless condition as criminals took advantage of the citizens' confusion. "Throughout the city, robbery is rampant. The feeling is of being on thin ice."[94] As a result of diplomatic negotiations in the Third Month, the commoners' fear of a foreign attack was relieved for the time being, and the refugees returned to Edo. Yet people's fear of being robbed intensified, if anything, and they could not help doubting the shogunate's ability to keep the public peace. "Lordless samurai prowl about the city, muscling their way into the houses of the wealthy to demand money. There have been cases of violence. Although this is scandalous, there are no investigations, no judgments. At this the previous hubbub and bewilderment have been forgotten, as the rampancy of the *rōnin* appears even more terrifying than the rapacity of the barbarian swine."[95] The common people of course recognized only too well that the passing of their fears regarding the "barbarians" was not due to any positive efforts on the part of the shogunate but rather to its succumbing before the foreigners' demands.

Pressed by the radical faction of the imperial loyalists, the shogunate determined a date on which to "expel the barbarians"—1863.5.10. But the commoners knew that the shogunate no longer had the power to carry out this decision. When the shogunate sent notices throughout the city that ten cannon shots would be fired as a signal in case of an emergency, no one took this announcement seriously, and some even ridiculed it. "To the sound of cannon the battle commences" *(hyōtan no hirakihajime wa hiya de yari),* as one punning wag put it, fully intending to convey the homonymous meaning, "When you tap a new keg you drink the *sake* cold."[96] The Edo commoners' mistrust of the shogunate increased when they saw the disorder of the infantry units composed of farmers of bannerman territories, who had been recruited as a result of the military reforms that began in early 1863. These farmer-soldiers, who had gained a foothold on the lowest rung of the samurai class by virtue of their enlistment, showed their appreciation of this privilege by engaging in acts of wanton violence in the brothels of Yoshiwara, kabuki theaters, and restaurants. Naturally, the impression that the shogunate could not even keep troops from its own domains under control spread among the commoners. "A fading authority"[97] and similar expressions used to describe the Tokugawa regime are often seen in letters of this period.

In 1864 the shogunate issued an order intended to ensure the safety of people who had to be out after dark—all should carry a lantern. Immediately, a song ridiculing the government was heard: "Carry a lantern? Thanks a lot! Who'll dispel the political darkness?"[98] Yet the common people's mistrust of the regime was, more precisely put, not so much a lack of confidence in the institution as in its current leadership. Their feelings of hostility were directed against Matsudaira Shungaku and his staff, who had permitted themselves to be pressured by Satsuma into reforming the shogunate by breaking its ancestral law. The commoners' mistrust was not directed at the House of Tokugawa itself. On the contrary, when they heard that Chōshū had been forced to retreat as a result of the Hamaguri Gate Incident, they again embraced the fanciful expectation that the Tokugawa family would regain its traditional authority. There is something akin to an air of gloating self-satisfaction in a *chobokure* that describes how Chōshū's house elders Fukuhara Echigo (1815–1864) and Masuda Uemon no Suke (1833–1864) were "given secret orders to go to Kyoto, grab the imperial palace, and raise their flag" over the capital city. But this "ambitious plot" was foiled, and the ensuing fight resulted in a famous victory for the forces of justice:[99]

> The Chōshū troops lost; like puny weaklings, they fled.
> Some fell in battle, some fell over one another—dead.
>
> What a tremendous uproar, what a terrific shock!
> But still the Kantō stands, solid as a rock.
>
> The shogunate's military fortunes shall endure forever.
> Are the likes of Satsuma a match for us? Never!
>
> At this rate, bringing about prosperity and peace
> Should not be a difficult task in the least.

It's too bad some among the old and the young have no ken:
They're like wooden statues that pretend to be men.

Even to their cowardice there's a limit, you know:
The infantry can escort them to and fro.

In this pasquinade, the culprits are "the old and the young." To spell it out, the shogunate's senior and junior councillors—*rōjū* and *waka-doshiyori*—are the ones who cloud the Kantō's military fortunes. The Tokugawa family is not a target. The commoners' suspicion and criticism are directed, it is clear, at those "seniors" and "juniors" in the leadership who have broken the shogunate's ancestral law.

Only the revival of that law, as far as the commoners were concerned, could bring back their trust of the government, banish the terror that haunted the streets, and restore the "Flowering Edo" of old. A set of punning couplets called *Kenjō-taru tai*—"A Pretty Kettle of Fish" would be perhaps too loose a translation of the title—sums up their desires quite nicely:[100]

The imperial will is paralyzed
by desperate lordless samurais—
fix it; that's what we want.

The Divine Ancestor set down the law,
government's model formula—
stick to it; that's what we want.

Those who disregard Ieyasu's instructions,
officials guilty of obstruction—
sack them; that's what we want.

The traitors whose plots overwhelm
what used to be a peaceful realm—
whack them; that's what we want.

The *rōnin* cutthroats, whom all detest
for slaughtering the innocent populace—
wipe them all out; that's what we want.

The foreign trade by which we all
feel driven up against the wall—
stop it; that's what we want.

The various daimyos' families,
allowed to go home as they please—
bring back the hostages; that's what we want.

... and so forth. These same hopes are expressed in a somewhat ponderous *chobokure*:[101]

> By the law fixed by Ieyasu, the Ancestor Divine,
> the Radiance of the Sun that in Nikkō shines,
> if government that is humane, righteous, proper, and wise
> is carried out correctly, we can then surmise
> that all the people their allegiance will render,
> that the five grains will be harvested in abundant splendor,
> and that litanies of praise will be sung in refrain
> for the peace and prosperity that bless the reign.

When the shogunate followed up its victory in the Hamaguri Gate Incident with the apparent triumph of the first Chōshū expedition five months later, the feelings of crisis that had pursued the commoners of Edo for years were dispelled, and they came to anticipate the return of their traditional, peaceful lives. "This blessed realm!"—they sang—"This blessed realm that sheathes the sword and encases the spear!" Peace and traditional Japanese harmony were about to return, they thought: "A zither of honest Japanese wood [*waboku*, a pun on the homophonous word for peace] suits me better than the shamisen made with foreign craft."[102] These hopes, however, were transitory. They were betrayed with the commencement of the second Chōshū expedition.

The common people may have desired the revival of the ancestral law of the Tokugawa, but they were not at all pleased with the idea of a war's being fought for that purpose. Unconcerned with what they wanted, the shogunate in 1865.4 issued orders to prepare a second campaign against Chōshū and the next month imposed a large extraordinary levy on the townspeople of Edo "for the vast necessities of the shogun's march."[103] Along with the call to war, terrible price rises hit the commoners of Edo, who were already burdened with a high cost of living. Even the price of barley, which had been "unusually low" before the Sixth Month, soared out of sight. Price increases were so extreme that "the common people are left destitute; there is talk of cases of suicide."[104] The levy became the target of the commoners' resentment, as the following *chobokure* shows:[105]

> Why do prices go up
> when they ought to come down?
> "It's the tax, stupid!"
> is the only answer in town.
> "The government keeps high the prices
> by using strict tax-collection devices."

Your heart sinks when you hear this;
there's nothing you can say
except "It's time for tax relief!"
There's got to be a way
to shake up the wholesalers:
"Lower prices or rue the day!"

A change of the era name had immediately preceded the issuance of the hated order for the march on Chōshū, and the common people turned their contempt on both:[106]

Keiō to	Advance! it's ordered,
nengō kaete	and change the era name
goshinpatsu	to Keiō—
shita kara yomeba	OK, now stop right there! is
oke to iu koto	how it looks read from the right.

Here again, it is clear that the "right" view is the one from below, the commoners' perspective.

The 1866 riots of the Edo poor erupted from the rising resentment at the special tax and the rapid price increases brought on by the second Chōshū expedition. In the Sixth Month of the previous year, Edo rice merchants, who feared that the city's rice reserves were about to disappear, had petitioned the shogunate: "Currently there are no more than 60,000 *koku* of standard-grade rice in the government warehouses in Asakusa. Rice scattered in other warehouses throughout the city amounts to no more than 60,000 or 70,000 *koku*. In sum, there are only 120,000 or 130,000 *koku* of rice in Edo. If all of this is used up at one time, and not even the government rice is left, it will not be possible to do anything. It would be highly desirable to take measures now to purchase rice."[107] This dearth of rice increased the anxiety of the poor still further. With the exception of some of the extreme poor who had to suffer through those dark days, however, not one person emerged to put up positive resistance against the shogunal regime that had caused the suffering. As we have seen, some drove away their gloom and despair through *chobokure, kyōka* (inelegant verse), and *senryū*. Others, who had a little extra money in their wallets, tried to forget tomorrow by setting out for the amusement centers in search of sensuous pleasures.

The closer the shogunate came to its doom, the more this popular pleasure-seeking trend accelerated. A letter dated [1866].10.23 described "this strange state of affairs" where sensuous pursuits increased daily "in the midst of the people's suffering due to high prices" and the amusement quarters enjoyed great prosperity, with "an uninterrupted stream of palanquins *(hoi-kago)* passing all night to and from the brothel houses of Shinjuku."[108] Another, written in 1867.6, reiterated: "In the midst of these rising prices and the impoverishment of the people, every night the noise of the palanquin bearers plying the road to and from the brothels of Shinjuku never stops. Kabuki and *jōruri* theaters are packed. Sumo bouts and recitals of military romances or edifying tales draw large crowds. Geishas rush about from the east to the west of the city." This writer found the prosperity of the prostitute quarters and the theaters "an incredible thing."[109]

This attitude of the commoners can scarcely be called wholesome. Rather, it was a fin-de-siècle decadence that sought but failed to capture the dreams of the past. The popular writer Ryūtei Senka (also known as Ryūtei Tanehiko II; 1806–1868) caught the pulse of contemporary society accurately when he wrote on 1865.9.27, "The Eastern Capital is replete with extravagance and luxury, and yet it is filled with anxiety, worrying about the future as though about a dormant disease."[110] An "inelegant verse," composed that year by someone else whose observations were right on the mark, reveals the other side of the escutcheon of those same Edo commoners who loved extravagance and luxury:[111]

Yorokobi no	Joy shall come our way,
ō-zuru toshi ni	promised the designation
kawaredomo	of the new era;
yo o ushi to koso	this Year of the Ox, however,
kurasu konogoro	brings us the yoke of sorrow.

[*Yorokobi no ō-zuru toshi* (the year when joy shall come our way) is a wordplay on the Keiō era: the character used for *kei* may also be read *yorokobi*. Keiō 1 (1865) was the Year of Wood Junior and the Ox *(kinoto ushi)* in the sexagenary cycle.]

The commoners had grown weary of waiting for the revival of the ancestral law of the Tokugawa and the accordant restitution of their traditional, peaceful lives. Whatever hopes they retained were crushed as the shogunate embarked on its last reforms, carried out with French assistance by Iemochi's successor as shogun, Hitotsubashi Yoshinobu (r. 10 January 1867–3 January 1868). After Yoshinobu's adoption of a Western military system, the streets of Edo were flooded with the figures of samurai wearing a bizarre costume—*haori* with trimmed sleeves and *hakama* with narrow trousers. European-style drill, performed under the direction of French officers, became a daily sight. These novelties undoubtedly made a strong impression on the commoners. They were estranged from the world around them as the feudal system was disrupted. Even so, there were no signs of any spirit of resistance on their part, as is pointed out in this parody of a famous poem:[112]

Kuge wa tori	Nobles grasp at a
bushi wa kuni uru	land the *bushi* have sold out—
yo no naka ni	in such a world as this,
nani tote shimo ga	why do the lower classes
shizuka naruran	alone stay placid and still?

Conclusion

No revolutionary tendencies can be found in the actions and attitudes of the common people of the Bakumatsu and Restoration epoch. Even those who did take an active part in politics, such as the wealthy farmers and merchants discussed above, did so not because they viewed themselves as any sort of emergent bourgeoisie but rather because Kokugaku thought or other media had awakened in them a political self-awareness akin to that of the samurai, the ruling stratum of Japan's feudal society. Even if it did have a reformist character, their political consciousness was based on the traditional notion of duties and designations. No grass-roots bourgeois sense of identity (as Hattori Shisō would have it) and no class standpoint can be found in these people.

Contact with modern capitalist nations abruptly created the conditions for social change in the case of the backward country, Japan, long before the maturation of internal class conflicts could have brought them about. The formation of a modern national consciousness was mediated not so much by the rise of a revolutionary ideology as by the quantitative and qualitative increase of Japan's awareness of the outside world, that is, by the expansion of the country's international horizon. The models of progress, of society, and of the future Japanese state were to be found on that horizon. Not all recognized those models. Indeed, there were those who denied them outright and committed themselves heart and soul to the politics of xenophobia and jingoism. The mentality of such types stayed closed; it was shut up in a tight, traditionalist trap and could not be unblocked. Those who stuck to a xenophobic, exclusive vision of "my country above all" in the name of achieving national union were to find it impossible to open up a pathway to life in the modern world without at least a smattering of knowledge about foreign countries. The postrestoration fates of the political activists among the wealthy farmers and merchants graphically tell that story.

The average commoner of the Bakumatsu and Restoration epoch remained enclosed within thick and ancient walls. As long as they were not demolished by some superior or outside force, they would continue denying the commoners access to the wider world; but the commoners themselves neither saw a need for those walls to be broken down nor had the wish to contribute to their destruction. Thus the average commoner's mind, too, stayed closed—it had not yet been given the opportunity to open. What we observe in the peasants who took part in the uprisings of the Bakumatsu period, no less than in the urban commoners who were swept along powerlessly by the tide of events, is the desperate desire to cling to the shattered walls of their lives.

2

The Political Background of Early Meiji Educational Policy
The Central Government

Translated by Richard Rubinger

E ven as the drama of the Meiji Restoration was unfolding, some of its leading figures—men such as Iwakura Tomomi, Ōkubo Toshimichi, and Kido Takayoshi—were considering what forms education ought to assume in the new Japan. These men understood that a merit-based educational system which would train capable leaders was essential for a centralized state. They recognized that public education which would cultivate the minds and enhance the economic prospects of every citizen was indispensable to building a broad base of support for the new government. They knew that a national educational policy had to be put into effect if the goals of unity, centralization, and independence were to be achieved.

To implement such a policy was, however, not possible before 1871, when the Meiji government attained effective authority over the entire country by abolishing the old feudal domains, called *han,* and establishing prefectures in their place. To be sure, there had been an important preliminary step in laying down a centrally controlled political structure. The rendition of the domanial registers to the throne in 1869 put an end to the system of feudal rule and integrated the *han* into the new state as units of local government. But as long as the former daimyo remained governors of their old domains, and as long as the domains retained their military forces, the influence of the *han* could not be negated. Indeed, the domains remained formidable obstacles in the path of the central government's efforts, blocking it from intruding in their own policies. While they continued to exist, no national educational system could be created.

For all that, the Meiji government began educational planning early on, even while it was still engaged in a punitive campaign against the diehards of the Tokugawa shogunate in 1868. Compelled by political realities, it first started an educational program for the court aristocracy in Kyoto. When the political center was moved to Edo upon the defeat of the Tokugawa sympathizers, schooling was made available in that city to former retainers of the shogunate and to samurai of the various domains. But the emphasis rested on training capable leaders, that is, strengthening the government. Education for ordinary people was left up to regional offices. The central government itself was as yet unable to pursue a uniform policy.

Its educational initiatives from the time of the Restoration Edict of 3 January 1868 until the abolition of the *han* on 1871.7.14 were conditioned by changes in the relationship between the national leadership and the domains.[1] At the same time, the leadership's goals changed in accordance with shifts within the government, as authority was transferred from court aristocrats and daimyo to officials who had risen to power from the ranks of the samurai class. The Meiji government developed its ideas on popular schooling and merit-based training while consolidating its authority in the course of the complex political evolution that followed the restoration.

Political influences shaped Meiji education. Indeed, they have permeated modern Japanese education. Few of its aspects can be said to have achieved independence from politics and from the centralized authority of the state. This fact undoubtedly hastened the development and diffusion of a modern school system, but at the same time it created an educational structure that was particularly susceptible to political intrusions. Linkages between politics and education were close; economic factors had very limited influence. An intimate relationship existed between educational policy and the formation of state power.

The Meiji Restoration and Educational Policy

The new political authorities that were brought into being by the Restoration Edict first indicated their plan to establish educational institutions—more precisely, schools for developing "talent" among members of the imperial court aristocracy, the *kuge*—two and a half months later, on 1868.2.22. That day, the Meiji government's presidium *(sōsaikyoku)* appointed three superintendents of schools *(gakkō-gakari)*, directing them to "examine structures and regulations" suitable for the schools that the government intended to establish.[2] These three men were Hirata Kanetane (1799–1880) from the Office of Shinto Affairs, Tamamatsu Misao (1810–1872) from the Office of Home Affairs, and Yano Harumichi (1823–1887). "The times are not easy," they were reminded. "We cannot tell what influences may come to us from foreign lands. Whatever they may be, we should strive to establish rigorous procedures on a large scale so as not to be overwhelmed by them."[3]

The three superintendents were all Shintoists and scholars of National Learning (Kokugaku) who had close ties to the court aristocracy. Hirata was a member of the founding family of the Hirata school of Shinto; Tamamatsu was close to the prominent courtier Iwakura Tomomi (1825–1883) and had taken part with him in restoration planning; Yano, a teacher of the aristocratic Shirakawa family, had from the 1850s worked for a revival of the ancient Office of Shinto Affairs, cooperating with aristocratic families such as the Gojō and the Sawa. Yano, who was knowledgeable not only in Kokugaku but also in sinology, in 1868.2 submitted to the Gojō family a proposal for the establishment of schools based on the traditional concept of the unity of rites and regimen *(saisei itchi)*. The new government put these three men in charge of ceremonial observances and governmental rites. Not unexpectedly, the philosophy that underlay the educational structure they devised was imperial restorationist Shinto.

Most likely, the motive force behind a Shinto-based education for the courtiers was Iwakura Tomomi, who held the office of a deputy chief executive officer *(fuku-sōsai)* and was the government's most powerful figure. That the initiative was Iwakura's may be surmised because, as will be seen presently, the leading samurai officials—Ōkubo Toshimichi (1830–1878), Kido Takayoshi (1833–1877), and Gotō Shōjirō (1838–1897)—were opposed to a Shintoist educational policy.[4] The immediate postrestoration period was beset with uncertainties. The government's base was still extremely unstable. The success of its punitive campaign against the party of Shogun Tokugawa Yoshinobu (1837–1913; r. 10 January 1867–3 January 1868) was by no means assured; what attitude the *han* throughout the country would adopt toward it was not at all clear. In short, this was no time for optimism in undertaking new ventures. Nevertheless, there were political reasons—both domestic and foreign—for Iwakura to push ahead with Shintoist educational policies even though schooling was not as critical a concern as other problems faced by the government.

Iwakura was convinced that a true restoration required a return to the ancient imperial polity that had existed before the ascendency of the military class—of samurai or *bushi*. In those days, the emperor had ruled with the assistance of court aristocrats, who exercised government in his stead. If that polity was indeed to be restored, then it was essential to train the nobles to be as capable of leadership as samurai, and to do so as soon as possible. Even as he planned the imperial restoration in his country retreat during the last years of the Tokugawa era, Iwakura feared that if the shogunate were to be toppled through the initiative of samurai, the *bushi* would remain entrenched and another regime run by military aristocrats similar to the mediaeval Hōjō or Ashikaga would emerge. Civil aristocrats, he thought, must therefore assume leadership of the restoration, and the imperial court must take command militarily. Unfortunately, the courtiers were unaware of their responsibilities. In "Admonition to Court Nobles" written in 1866.3, Iwakura tried to stir them to action:[5]

> Court nobles have contempt for samurai, consider them the same as menials, and do not know what military affairs are all about. When a crisis occurs, however, they are dependent on those very same "menials" and are happy or sad depending upon the look on the faces of the *bushi*. So the nobility is incapable of reclaiming the authority granted it by emperors in times past. . . . The reason our Imperial Land lost its martial vigor is because the imperial court abandoned its military prerogative, and that happened because the nobility was arrogant and lazy. The responsibility for the failure to restore the country's former glory therefore cannot but be shouldered by the nobles themselves. How then can we blame the samurai alone? In this time of crisis, it is of utmost importance for the court to take the initiative in putting the country in order and external pressures under control. If that is to be achieved, above all the nobility must cooperate wholeheartedly and participate in the Imperial Design, thus setting an example for the *bushi*.

The advent of the Meiji Restoration was exactly the opportunity Iwakura needed to realize his hopes for the *kuge*. But the courtiers, witnessing the overthrow of the shogunal regime and believing that their time had come, became more arrogant and idle than ever. On 1868.1.16, the day after the imperial edict to subjugate Tokugawa Yoshinobu and his party was issued, Iwakura again admonished the Kyoto aristocracy, urging on them the necessity for education. The "orders to pursue and smite the bandits," the aristocrats were told, "shall at length make imperial authority flourish." At such a juncture, "all the nobility—from imperial princes and the highest nobles on down to titular officials not ranked as chamberlains—should be inspired to the most strenuous

efforts, ready to give their lives in loyal service to the cause of the imperial court." There are some, however, who—far from rising to the occasion—"remain uninvolved spectators to events and expect to receive
stipends for doing nothing." There are even the greedy who "speculate
about getting raises in the future." Iwakura had news for them: "The
times demand that hereditary stipends be decreased, not increased. If
someone performs distinguished service, he may then be given an individual, not a heritable, increase in stipend. Insofar as offices and ranks
are concerned, the traditional social hierarchy will also be reformed:
instead of hereditary family status, appointments will be made on the
basis of talent. Keeping this in mind, all should earnestly devote themselves to the study of Arms and Arts," beginning with reading and
swordsmanship. "It is intended that those who, exerting themselves in
study night and day, reach a level of accomplishment, shall be rewarded
with an official appointment commensurate to their talents. Do not be
remiss; persist in your endeavor!"[6]

One must appreciate the concerns of the government's most powerful
figure to understand why the government viewed the education of court
aristocrats as a priority in the restoration's immediate aftermath, at a
time when politics was in turmoil. Iwakura did not pick three Shintoists
to draft an education program merely because they had enjoyed close
ties with him since the 1850s. Rather, he picked them because he thought
that the Shinto values incorporated in their design not only could compete successfully with the Confucian value system—which had provided
ideological support for the *bakuhan* structure (the Tokugawa-era conglomerate of the shogunate and the feudal domains)—but would undermine that ideology. The Shintoists' advocacy of the "unity of rites and
regimen" as the intellectual basis for the new state solidified a patrician
way of thinking that interpreted the restoration to mean a return to the
ancient imperial order—as, indeed, the term itself suggested.

But it was not simply because Iwakura wanted it that an educational
program for court nobles was instituted. Its necessity was recognized
even by the samurai officials who did not support Iwakura's Shintoist
plan. Political realities demanded capable leaders from the imperial aristocracy. Behind Tokugawa Yoshinobu's formal surrender of sovereignty
to the emperor on 1867.10.14 there had been a scheme devised by the
shogun and collaborationist daimyo to retain power. Iwakura had seen
through that stratagem and had himself led the coup d'état that foiled
it; but two other architects of the coup, Ōkubo Toshimichi and Saigō
Takamori (1827–1877)—both of them samurai of the prominent
Satsuma domain—had then pushed him to mount a punitive campaign
against Yoshinobu. Not only the dispossessed leaders of the shogunate

but ordinary domains criticized this policy of force, claiming that it did not accord with the emperor's will. Given such a lack of support, the new government was compelled to justify its policies as actions undertaken on the emperor's behalf. Its expedient was to devise a political edifice where the authority derived from the emperor was made to appear superordinate to that of the domains. To populate its façade, the new government appointed imperial courtiers to important positions. As a first step, members of the imperial family and of the Kyoto aristocracy were placed along with daimyo and samurai in the highest posts— chief executive officer *(sōsai)*, senior councillor *(gijō)*, and junior councillor *(san'yo)*—of the so-called Three Offices *(sanshoku)*, a governmental structure established immediately after the restoration and intended to create a balance of power between court nobles and *bushi*.

The government then carried out a reorganization meant to unify its goals and improve its efficiency. Both in the Seven Departments System *(shichikasei)* that was created on 1868.1.17 and in the Eight Bureaus System *(hakkyokusei)* that succeeded it two weeks later, on 2.3, a Department and a Bureau of Shinto Affairs, meant to implement the ideals of the restoration, were placed at the top of their respective hierarchies. The government sought thereby to show the public its intent to return to the ancient imperial order. *Kuge* clearly predominated over samurai in the Seven Departments System, where no fewer than fifteen of the twenty-one most responsible positions, including chief executive officer, deputy chief executive officer, and department head, were filled by members of the imperial family and court aristocrats, compared to only six occupied by daimyo. Under the Eight Bureaus System, the equivalent posts all came to be filled by imperial nobles; those daimyo who had been department heads were lowered one rank to assistant head of bureau. The further advance of court aristocrats into the top echelons of the government when the Seven Departments metamorphosed into the Eight Bureaus after fourteen days is striking. Even men of the "great families," such as Konoe Tadahiro (1808–1898) and Takatsukasa Sukehiro (1807–1878), previously shunned by the restoration leaders, re-emerged in the political limelight. Courtiers, their retainers, and their close associates were hired in every office of the new bureaucracy. Their promotion indicated the great effort made to establish the imperial aristocracy's ascendency over domanial samurai and to manifest the reality of imperial rule in the personnel organization of the government. But the courtiers enjoyed only the appearance of superiority. In both tables of organization, the reins of actual authority were in the hands of talented samurai from the domains of Satsuma, Chōshū, Tosa, and Hizen.

In the desire to expedite its campaign against the remnants of the shogunate, which had escalated into a war with several domains in the Tōhoku region (northeastern Honshū), the government made great efforts to avoid being seen narrowly as a force run by Satsuma and Chōshū and to establish the public image of an imperial regime. Court nobles were employed as an essential part of this stratagem. Not only were they appointed to government offices, they were commissioned as military officers under the command of General Arisugawa—that is, the imperial prince Arisugawa no Miya Taruhito (1835–1895)—and sent to the field in Tōhoku. Civil aristocrats commanded troops and took the responsibility for controlling the populations of conquered areas. Not many of them, however, had the skills to resolve the mounting political, financial, and administrative problems of an expanded war and the occupation of conquered territory. Capable samurai had to be included in the government to make it effective; but that exacerbated the public's worries about Satsuma and Chōshū's growing influence. Here the government was ensnared in a trap of its own making. How could it avoid a decline in efficiency if it stuck to its policy of appointing courtiers to top posts? To train them in administrative and political skills—in other words, to educate them—was the only apparent solution.

"With two or three exceptions, the courtiers are like women dwelling secluded in some back room," Ōkubo Toshimichi complained to Kido Takayoshi. "It would be dangerous to give them any say over the realm at all."[7] For all that, they had to be endowed with authority befitting the restoration of rule by the imperial court; else it would be impossible to put the domains under control. That much was undeniable, and Ōkubo was the first to admit it. As he put it to Iwakura toward the end of the Meiji regime's first year of existence, "The imperial government has not yet been stabilized. The situation, it has been said, is as fragile as a stack of eggs; certainly, it is a matter of great concern. I respectfully submit that it will be difficult to replace chief ministers of state *(hoshō-kyō)* from among the court aristocracy; nor is there anyone suitable among the daimyo. This matter merits your attention. . . . In any event, imperial courtiers occupying the position of chief minister must control the domains of this realm, since no daimyo—no matter how wise or intelligent he may be—can possibly fill that role."[8] From this standpoint, he saw no reason to oppose the *kuge*-centered educational policy advocated by Iwakura.

Domestic conditions made educating the imperial aristocracy essential; the foreign situation, too, was such that the samurai members of the leadership group could not reject Shintoist education out of hand. From the First Month of 1868, the government clearly set forth an open-country *(kaikoku)* policy. On 1.15 friendship was proclaimed with various foreign countries. On 2.7, as a result of Ōkubo's maneuvers, the six daimyo of Satsuma, Chōshū, Tosa, Hizen, Echizen, and Aki issued a memorial on the importance of the emperor's formally receiving foreign envoys. The Kyoto aristocracy had persistently opposed foreign demands for such an audience; armed with this memorial, however, the government prevailed upon the court officials to agree to one, and it was held on 2.29.

The public announcement of the audience, dated 2.17 and drafted by Iwakura, makes clear his basic diplomatic position: the historical and particularistic values of Japan were to coexist with global and universalistic values. "Now that we have friendly relations with foreign nations, we cannot avoid taking to heart and into use both the unique national polity of the Imperial Land and the universal law of the rest of the world."[9] Japan's "national polity" *(kokutai)* was included as an essential component in Iwakura's concept of foreign relations because he believed that the new government should take a positive and independent diplomatic stance, in contrast with the old shogunate's passive policy of yielding to foreign pressures. In Iwakura's view, the intellectual basis of an autonomous diplomacy lay in *kokutai* theory, but restorationism and an internationalist policy were not contradictory. Rather, the more actively the country's opening was pursued, the more deeply an awareness of the Shinto-inspired notion of the national polity would be felt.

That awareness, however, must not be undermined by foreign ideas, in particular by Christianity. Thus the traditional policy banning Christianity was upheld not just by Iwakura but by samurai officials as well. Their dilemma was how to keep Christian ideas from infiltrating a country that was being opened to the world. An educational policy that idealized the restorationist Shinto of the Hirata school, permitting no compromise with alien influences, seemed an appropriate defense against the spiritual crisis brought on by foreign policy. Even samurai officials had to recognize the suitability of using Shinto to resist the influx of the foreign religion.

Thus it was no accident that a superintendency of schools should have been created at just the time when the government had clearly set forth its open-country policy, immediately after the announcement of the emperor's audience with foreign envoys; and it was entirely logical for the presidium to insist on "rigorous procedures" to govern education at the time of that appointment. The intention was to keep out the influence of Christianity at all costs. The superintendents, led by Yano Harumichi, moved ahead energetically with their inquiries into the design of an educational structure; Iwakura, urged on by political demands, was eager to begin educating the nobility without delay and did not wait for a report of their findings. On 1868.3.12 he announced that the Gakushūin, the court aristocracy's school, would reopen seven days later.[10] This institution, established in 1845, was known for a Confucian educational philosophy that was strictly opposed to Shintoism. In 1862–1863, when the jingoist *sonnō jōi*—"Revere the emperor, repel the barbarians!"—movement was at its height in Kyoto, its zealots had made the Gakushūin the base of their activities, and the school's educational functions had been suspended as a result. Now Iwakura was seeking to revive them.

He was influenced in doing so by Gakushūin Confucianists (that is, former shogunal educational officials), including Nakanuma Ryōzō (Kien; 1830–1896), Nukina Ukon, Toyooka Ayasuke (1814–1886), and others. Among this circle were some merited activists in the cause of imperial restoration; Nakanuma, in particular, is well known for having joined in the plans of country samurai of Totsugawa in Yamato Province to demonstrate their reverence for the emperor by repelling the "barbarians."[11] Toyooka and Nukina had been urging the necessity of providing education for the aristocracy upon the imperial court for some time. On 1867.11.21, Toyooka submitted a reform plan that called for a revival of the Dajōkan (Grand Council of State; set up as the supreme administrative body in the eighth century, but in abeyance since the twelfth), the abolition of Tokugawa feudal customs, and the promotion of men of talent. Included in his twenty-nine-article draft was a proposal to revive the Daigakuryō (Court College; institutionalized as a Confucian academy for training court officials in the eighth century, but in decline from the eleventh). Another article sought the regeneration of classical traditions among the aristocracy: "From those permitted access to the inner palace on down to those who are not, all should return to the customs of ancient times. It is desirable that they become proficient in the martial arts of our Imperial Land and train themselves in the use of bow and arrow, sword and spear, horsemanship and artillery."[12] Following the restoration, Nukina wrote to Iwakura with a proposal to raise the status of the Gakushūin to that of a proxy Court College (Daigakuryō-dai).[13] There is no doubt that such influences weighed heavily in preparing the way for the subsequent revival of the Gakushūin.

Soon after the Gakushūin was reopened, a document called the "College Statutes" *(Gakushasei)* was prepared by the superintendency of schools.[14] On 1868.3.28, the presidium sent the draft to each government department for opinions. The ancient Daigakuryō may have been the model for the college envisioned by these statutes, but Shinto was to provide its educational philosophy. The first item mentioned was the edifice meant to be the symbolic center of education at this school, a Shrine to the Heavenly Progenitors. The head of the college would also serve as the head priest of the shrine, and the entire faculty and student body were required to participate in its rite of worship "once in each of the four seasons of the year." In other words, Shinto ritual would take the place of the spring and autumn *sekiten* ceremony, a rite in honor of Confucius and his disciples that had been observed at the old Daigakuryō. Indeed, Confucianism was to be dislodged from its traditional preeminence in the curriculum. Academic substance would instead be derived from Shinto, in particular from a branch of learning called Fundamentalism (Honkyōgaku, a variant of Kokugaku), which "reveres the Great Way of the Gods Above and teaches students personal and family ethics, the profound mystery of the duality of this world and the other world, and the Grand Obligation [of loyalty to the emperor] imposed by Heaven and Earth." The other offerings were to be statecraft, rhetoric, "alchemical-medical sciences" (*hōgigaku,* also called "applied sciences"), and "barbarian" (that is, foreign) studies or *gaibangaku.* Confucianism, which had been the highest ideological authority in the Tokugawa period, was not included under statecraft, the most essential course for the training of government leaders. Rather, it was reduced to a part of the study of China, merely another one of the foreign areas treated along with Russia, England, France, Holland, India, and "the Three Koreas (inclusive of Ryūkyū)." Including "barbarian studies" and "alchemical-medical sciences" (i.e., divination, astronomy, medicine, and mathematics) in the "College Statutes" was the response devised by the school superintendency to the conditions brought on by the open-country policy.

The problem was that setting up a dual track in the curriculum, with courses in Fundamentalism set off against courses in "barbarian studies," created an ideological hierarchy with a clear bias. The core of the curriculum was restricted within limits defined by the particularistic values of Shinto and Kokugaku; Confucianism and Western studies were marginalized. This division was seen as absolute. It did not even go as far as Iwakura's basic diplomatic position, which espoused a coexistence of dual values, comprehending both the national polity and global law.

The officials who were asked for their opinions showed little interest in the draft. The only response came from Akizuki Tanetatsu (1833–1904) of the Office of Home Affairs, and it was adversely critical. The second son of the daimyo of Takanabe in Hyūga Province, Akizuki had been an educational magistrate under the shogunate and continued to be interested in problems of education. Two points in his critique are worth noting—that the "College Statutes" restricted education to court aristocrats and that they neglected Confucianism. According to Aki-zuki, a course on statecraft could ignore neither Western nor Chinese studies; in the crucial area of rhetoric, moreover, Chinese learning was all-important. He therefore opposed putting Confucianism under the rubric of foreign studies. Although he did not state it directly, Akizuki made it clear that he placed greater importance on statecraft than on Fundamentalism in the curriculum.[15]

Government departments ignored the draft document primarily because of its avoidance of practical learning and its Shintoism, which was seen as too particularistic. All in all, this educational scheme was adjudged unsuitable for a nation seeking unity at home and independence in international affairs. Meant to address important domestic and foreign concerns, it was actually out of step with the times. The political situation at the time the "College Statutes" were drawn up was different from that of the immediate postrestoration period. The indirect path to unification—subjecting the domains by that ancient ideology, the unity of Shinto rites and regimen—was no longer in favor, and government leaders consequently no longer felt the strategic necessity to demonstrate the courtiers' preeminence by appointing them to the highest positions. The court aristocracy's ideological, value-oriented view of politics was being set aside as Ōkubo and Kido sought a more real, political form of authority for the emperor. Keenly aware of the need to control the domains through the exercise of imperial sovereignty, these influential leaders made it a matter of their immediate attention to cultivate a Japanese emperor after the model of West European absolute monarchs.

A proposal to move the capital to Osaka that he submitted to Iwa-kura on 1868.1.23 is the clearest expression of Ōkubo's intentions. If Japan is to be unified rapidly and equipped to deal positively with the international situation, Ōkubo argues, then the emperor, heretofore the embodiment of a religious mystique "that had assumed human form," a monarch who still dwelt in the traditional world of the ancient court, must be educated to become a political ruler who could properly be called "the master of the realm." He would then become a sovereign in whom all the people, down to the lowest born, put their trust, one whose "deeds are such that the aspirations of high and low are fulfilled and all the myriad people are moved to shed tears" of gratitude. The emperor should be the focal point of political power and the pillar of a structure in which all the people's loyalties were tied to the one ruler. To bring this about, Ōkubo insisted, the emperor must be removed from his palace in Kyoto and the capital relocated in another city; there was no alternative. Exhibiting no trace of the influence of Shinto ideas, Ōkubo believed that the emperor should not be a religious figure in the traditional mold of the unity of rites and regimen. Rather, he should be an enlightened despot on the model of the West, where "at this very moment kings walk their lands with only one or two retainers and nourish millions of people, thus putting the Princely Way into practice."[16]

The idea of moving the capital was an expression of Ōkubo and Kido's resolve to reject the ancient imperial model and to create one anew. In a letter to Itō Hirobumi (1841–1909), who at the time was a junior councillor, Kido makes it clear that he agreed with Ōkubo entirely: "We must quickly smash the nest of the opposition [Edo], set up rules for dealing with foreigners, and arrange for the move of the Highest to Naniwa [Osaka]. This is top secret."[17] Because of strong resistance from court circles, no action was taken. Strenuous efforts by Ōkubo and Kido did, however, bring about the emperor's triumphal expedition to Osaka on 1868.3.21, the first step toward realizing the idea of transferring the capital from Kyoto. The emperor's entry into the shogunate's former stronghold in western Japan was meant as a demonstration of his sovereign prestige and as a way of rallying support for the punitive action against Tokugawa Yoshinobu, but it also involved more profound considerations on the part of Ōkubo, Kido, and others. It was part of their plans to reorganize the imperial institution, and its success encouraged them to reject the Shintoist form of the state and to continue their trial-and-error approach to restructuring based on Western models.

In regard to foreign affairs, the principles of an open country policy were clearly established in the Charter Oath (Gokajō no Seimon) that was promulgated on 1868.3.14 at Kido's request. In its opening lines the emperor declared that "base customs of the past shall be abolished" and proclaimed the determination to "seek knowledge throughout the world." These statements went as far in articulating internationalist and universalist values as was possible then. But the philosophy represented in the "College Statutes," which gave priority to particularistic, Shinto values, had clearly become an anachronism that had to give way to the demands of practical politics. The vaguely defined goal of a resuscitated imperial order, proposed early in the restoration, had been replaced by the political objective of a Western-style enlightened despotism. International and universal values were becoming dominant. An open-country policy was being actively pursued. When one considers all that, it is not surprising that the educational goals of Ōkubo, Kido, and other samurai leaders should have favored Western studies and sought the training of capable men who had a knowledge of the West.

The active pursuit of *kaikoku*—"Open the country!"—brought forth a xenophobic reaction from a group that advocated *jōi*—"Drive away the barbarians!" There were recurrent incidents, including murders of foreigners. The new government, already burdened with various difficulties that had been exacerbated by foreign commerce, was forced to take upon itself the even more treacherous problems of international relations. In a letter to Kido, Ōkubo discoursed on the current dearth of and urgent need for men with the modern knowledge required to solve such problems: "The two capable men I mentioned the other day, Fukuzawa Yukichi and Nishi Shūsuke, are busy with other important work. So I asked Ōmura [Masujirō] for advice. I suggest you consult him as well. As you know, [Guido Fridolin] Verbeck, an American residing in Nagasaki, is a knowledgeable and virtuous man and is well acquainted with our Imperial Land; I have felt for some time that he could be quite useful. I have also heard Soejima [Taneomi] say that Verbeck is learned in law and would be particularly useful in questions regarding diplomacy with foreign countries. If you hire him and take him under your wing, others will surely want to learn from him at once. Would that not be an excellent outcome? New schools are about to be founded. One like the shogunate's old Kaiseisho ought, I think, to be opened immediately. When that happens you are apt to find him of great use indeed."[18] In this letter Ōkubo disparages Iwakura's Shintoist educational project as useless and urges that Western-style educational institutions be quickly established instead.

Kido was even more insistent than Ōkubo on an enlightened approach to politics. He was concerned about the revitalized influence of the advocates of *jōi*, their opposition to the *kaikoku* policy, and the pressures they were placing on the government. He suspected that the xenophobic party's opposition and the activities of Hirata Shintoists within the government were not unrelated. "Expulsionist views are growing stronger," Kido wrote to Itō Hirobumi. "Some are very dissatisfied because foreigners have since last year been visiting the imperial palace, which places Japan on the same footing with other countries. These xenophobes are circulating pamphlets among the masses. At the heart of this movement are people involved in the agitation in the Kurume and Higo domains, along with followers of the Hirata school. I believe these people are organizing *rōnin*."[19] One would not expect Kido, who viewed Hirata Shintoists and Kokugaku scholars as a significant opposition force, to support a document such as the "College Statutes," one written by their leaders, Hirata and Yano.

Kido and Ōkubo were, however, not the only critics of the particularistic educational ideal. Nagaoka Moriyoshi (1843–1906), a younger brother of the daimyo of Kumamoto (i.e., Higo *han*), was another samurai junior councillor who had definite opinions on education, even if he was employed in the Office of Military Affairs. "The Imperial Land becomes more and more open," he wrote to a senior vassal of his *han*. "Western studies and Western lifestyles flourish in each domain. I, too, mainly read Western books and appreciate their enormous significance. They represent reason. People who study in the Japanese schools and the military schools that I see arising in the near future will, I imagine, develop the Western kind of vision. If our home domain does not reform itself, how can we maintain our pride?"[20] As the letter makes clear, at least this junior councillor wanted a Western spirit to inhabit the new educational structure being planned by the superintendents of schools, something the latter never considered.

Knowing that the views of Ōkubo and Kido—that is, of the government's actual leaders—were adversely critical (not to speak of the other samurai councillors' opinions), even such supporters of Shinto-based educational policy as Iwakura came to reconsider the implementation of the policies called for in the "College Statutes." The adoption of that document had become increasingly problematic by the Fourth Month of 1868, as the political situation continued to develop advantageously for the government. Victory in the punitive war against the Tokugawa could be realistically forecast by the middle of the Third Month. The victorious march on Edo fortified the government's authority over the domains, and it was quick to take advantage. On 4.5 the *han* were ordered to initiate reforms in the spirit of the Charter Oath; on the fourteenth, restrictions were placed on military forces maintained by them in Kyoto; and on the twentieth, domanial military forces were limited to fifty men per 10,000 *koku* of assessed yield. On the twenty-first, the commander of imperial forces, Prince Taruhito, entered Edo Castle and assumed administrative control over the shogunal capital.

The government used its new authority effectively in reducing the threat it faced from the domains, but it had yet to achieve national stability. A recalcitrant portion of the shogunate's forces in Edo, calling themselves the Shōgitai, refused to submit and made a last stand on the heights of Ueno. Most of the rest of the Tokugawa supporters escaped from Edo and ran off to the Kantō countryside and the Tōhoku region. On 5.3 various northeastern domains, led by Aizu, formed an alliance against the government, and the flames of war spread to Tōhoku. For several months the military situation fluctuated.

To be sure, the government controlled Edo. That very fact made it a stronger force—not inherently but because the army acting at its behest had occupied the home base of the Tokugawa regime. That army was led by Satsuma, Chōshū, and Tosa. As long as the Tōhoku war progressed successfully, those three domains remained united and the government's authority expanded. What, however, would happen once the war ended? There was the danger that the domains' unity would break up, that they would adopt independent positions, and that the central government would again be weakened. The leadership group knew that they must build a firmer political structure if they were to assure themselves of real power. Hence they began a program of reforms.

On the twenty-seventh day of the Fourth Intercalary Month, after the emperor had returned from Osaka to Kyoto, the so-called Constitution of 1868 *(Seitaisho)* made public the aims and the substance of those reforms.[21] The governing apparatus set out in this document, which adopted the Charter Oath as its political ideal, is remarkable in several respects. The Constitution of 1868 revived the Dajōkan, where all state authority would be concentrated, "thereby eliminating the affliction of the divergent issuance of governmental ordinances." The Grand Council's prerogatives were, however, to be divided into distinct legislative, administrative, and judicial functions, "thereby eliminating the affliction of overbearing authority." The internal balance of powers (along with sensitivity toward the outside, that is, to the intentions of the *han*) would, it was hoped, ensure the central regime's stability.

The reforms also included a new table of ranks, extending the path to government office to a wider pool of talent. As before, the top positions of chief minister *(hoshō)* and senior councillor, were reserved for members of the imperial family, court aristocrats, and daimyo; but lower-level appointments, such as junior councillor or department head, were to be made solely on the basis of merit, without regard to rank or social status, and were opened to commoners. A direct result was that it became difficult for the less capable courtiers to be promoted. Evidently, the growth of the government's authority after the takeover of Edo had reduced the need for placing nobles in key positions for purely political reasons.

The Constitution of 1868 divided the Dajōkan into seven departments: first, a deliberative body, the Giseikan, with upper and lower divisions; then, Shinto Affairs, Administration, Finance, Military Affairs, Foreign Affairs, and Justice. Regionally, the country was organized into metropolitan districts *(fu)*, domains *(han)*, and prefectures *(ken)*. The lower house of the Giseikan was made responsible for dealing with the needs of the domains. Government officials were to serve four-year terms and would be selected by ballot. The most powerful leaders were Iwakura Tomomi and Sanjō Sanetomi (1837–1891), both of whom held the office of senior councillor in the upper house of the Giseikan concurrently with that of chief minister in the Department of Administration (Gyōseikan). Appointed as junior councillors in the upper house of the legislature were Komatsu Tatewaki (1835–1870) and Ōkubo Toshimichi of Satsuma; Kido Takayoshi and Hirosawa Saneomi (1833–1871) of Chōshū; Gotō Shōjirō and Fukuoka Takachika (1835–1919) of Tosa; as well as Soejima Taneomi (1828–1905) of Hizen, Yokoi Shōnan (1809–1869) of Higo, and Yuri Kimimasa (1829–1909) of Echizen. Remarkable is the balancing of two each from Satsuma, Chōshū, and Tosa. The head of each department was an imperial courtier or a daimyo, as was the vice-chairman; the positions of deputy *(hanji)* and below were filled by samurai.

Despite the reformers' best intentions, the new institutions could not create a strong central government. In the first place, the samurai junior councillors who held real power were emplaced in the government's legislative branch without being given legislative authority; second, the Department of Administration did not exercise adequate control over the other departments; third, the number of senior and junior councillors was not fixed, so their numbers grew (as private deals were made) to the point where the government practically could not function. Finally, delegates sent by the domains to represent them in the lower house of the deliberative body were unable to put aside their narrow local interests and adapt the agenda of their *han* to the national interest.

Another important set of problems faced by the new regime was the disposition of the Tokugawa family and the restoration of peace and order in Edo. The government's ability to sustain its authority depended on the solution of this issue. Assigned to cope with it was Sanjō Sanetomi, who was appointed inspector general *(dai kansatsushi)* for the Kantō region on 1868.intercalary4.10. Equipped with plenary powers to deal with the Tokugawa, he left Kyoto for Edo without awaiting the results of the governmental reform. To assist Sanjō, Ōkubo also went off to Edo on 5.23. He had big plans for that city. Its name, he proposed to Iwakura, should be changed to "Tōkyō"—Eastern Capital—in preparation for the emperor's journey there. The domains should be set astir and troops got ready to make it a truly triumphal progress.[22]

Control of Edo and progress in the Tōhoku war had increased the government's strength, but in fact this only meant expanded influence for Satsuma, Chōshū, and Tosa—commonly known by the acronym Sat-Chō-Do—whose troops formed the bulk of the victorious army. Although the government was now able to control the other domains, the prepotent three became increasingly difficult to handle. Iwakura, who had become the most powerful figure in the new government by taking over both judicial and administrative leadership, additionally sought a military role for himself as a way of counteracting the predominance of these three domains. In 1868.6, he requested that the emperor grant him permission to take command of the Hizen forces and go to the front.[23] By risking his life, Iwakura thought, he would enhance the court aristocracy's prestige; Sat-Chō-Do, moreover, would become more manageable if made to share military honors with Hizen.

Iwakura labored to find other ways to control that formidable trio by further energizing the *kuge*, and his eagerness to promote the court nobility's interests was reflected in his educational policy. Abandoning the unpopular Shintoist "College Statutes" as soon as their defects became clear, he transferred his support to the familiar and less controversial Confucianist Gakushūin, which was suddenly promoted to the status of a proxy Court College on 1868.4.15 even though it had only just reopened on the nineteenth of the previous month. The evident motive for the Gakushūin's elevation to its new status was to provide leadership training for the Kyoto aristocracy.

Iwakura's impatience to establish educational institutions for the courtiers was also related to the progress of governmental reform. He believed that the new personnel organization that was about to be given legal form in the new "constitution" should first be applied to the lower ranks of the aristocracy. On the twenty-first of the Intercalary Fourth Month, the nobles were greatly encouraged when the government told them as a group that talent would be rewarded by promotion to leadership. "Do your duty," they were exhorted. "Be quick to rise to the occasion. Perform great deeds in service to the state. Be diligent, be industrious, exert yourselves to the uttermost to build the foundations of a nation where the people's security is ensured. Thus set the emperor's mind at ease."[24] On the same day, a notice promoting learning was sent to young courtiers: "The most urgent task now is the development of talent. Accordingly, those less than thirty years old are excused from attendance at court in order to devote themselves to studies and pursue practical training. As promotion will depend on accomplishment, it is ordered that you work diligently, in strict conformity with that intention. An institution for training in Arms and Arts is to be founded presently, but for the time being you shall attend the proxy Court College."[25]

A letter sent by Iwakura to Sanjō in Edo makes it clear that those two were behind these appeals to the court aristocracy and shows that Iwakura was so eager to train talented younger courtiers (with an eye to taming the three dominant domains) that he was willing to incur the antipathy of the *kuge* class itself. "I am resigned to have a hard time of it," he said, "for the sake of reform."[26] At a time when he was requesting to be put in command of field troops to check the growing preeminence of Sat-Chō-Do, Iwakura was unwilling to limit his demands for the court aristocracy's education to civil affairs: he wanted it extended to military skills. As a result of the authorities' "preoccupation with other matters," the inauguration of a university was delayed. Instead, the opening of a military school for the imperial aristocracy was announced on 1868.7.28. "All courtiers, including those permitted access to the inner palace as well as titular officials not ranked as chamberlains, may enter the school if they wish. It is, however, ordered that those among them who are below the age of thirty, and who shall be excused from attendance at court, make every effort to concentrate as much as possible on studies."[27] It will be noted that the curriculum of this school was not confined to military matters but was to include mathematics and other areas of Western studies.

Even as he was moving away from his earlier restorationist vision, Iwakura Tomomi could not give up the dream of the development of a court aristocracy that would establish an imperial government standing above the domains it commanded. As he considered the courtiers' education within the broader political context, his tactics changed from Shintoist to Confucianist, and his teaching plan came to include military studies. His pragmatic views did not meet with universal approval. The greatest dissatisfaction with his policy of subordinating educational concerns to politics came from the superintendents of schools—Tamamatsu, Hirata, and Yano—in whom Iwakura had first placed his trust, only to push them aside later. To them, the restoration of imperial rule meant the political realization of their Shinto ideals. Naturally, they reacted strongly when they discovered that their Shintoist model was discarded, that a Confucian educational policy was being urged, that the plan for a university had been deferred, and that a military school had been established instead. Angry that matters had proceeded without regard to his and his two colleagues' views, Tamamatsu in 1868.7 asked Iwakura to implement the "College Statutes" immediately. He and his colleagues had been working, Tamamatsu said, on the design of a university "in compliance with the Imperial Court's order issued in the Second Month." Their plans were "all but completed," and they were looking forward to that institution's opening in the near future, when the Gakushūin was "unexpectedly, and without our being notified" designated a proxy Court College. "The original purpose has been altered, and now we confront the uncomfortable situation of a tripartite conflict between a School of Advanced Studies deprived of its advanced studies [sc., a university that has lost its raison d'être], a proxy Court College, and an Academy of Arms and Arts. I consulted with my colleagues, and we pointed out repeatedly that this contravened the emperor's original intention"—evidently to no avail, as the only result was that "a certain Iwashita from Satsuma," appointed to act as mediator, informed Tamamatsu that the person in charge of school matters was away in the eastern part of the country and nothing could be decided until he returned to Kyoto. Bristling at what he considered the patent disregard of an urgent imperial order, and professing concern lest people coming from near and far to the capital to attend the proposed university be disappointed, Tamamatsu begged Iwakura to "consider the situation and work for a quick resolution, although I know you are busy."[28]

That same Seventh Month, Tamamatsu, Hirata, and Yano followed up this demand with a joint letter to Iwakura that criticized the government's educational policy. Their first objection was that the government had tried to appease them by appointing them to an Office of Education (Daigakkan) which was one in name only: "It is called an office but does not have the substance of an office; it is not ranked with the other offices; it does not have control over educational policy. That being so, a post in it is the same as the military titles borne by civil aristocrats and the civil administrative ranks held pro forma by military men." In the second—and most important—section of their four-part critique, they argued that their office could be made meaningful only if the Gakushūin were put under its authority. It was illogical, they maintained, to establish a separate, independent government-sponsored institution; hence the proxy Court College should be no more than a subordinate entity for teaching the Chinese classics. "Originally, it was intended that after the inauguration of the school, the Gakushūin would combine with us so that the Confucianists would learn the fundamentals of the Imperial Way." By failing to follow that plan and permitting the Gakushūin to maintain a separate status, the government had, in effect, "created factions among educators." The disputes that were sure to result would cause "unceasing damage" to the entire educational program. "Since these are unreasonable dispositions, we request you to have the situation examined again at a meeting of the court council."[29]

As Tamamatsu noted, Iwakura had sought to solve the problem by having Iwashita Masahira (1827–1900), a junior councillor from Satsuma, assigned the responsibility of an educational liaison officer; but Iwashita, too, failed to implement an educational policy that would have satisfied Tamamatsu and his group. It was not just that the provisions of the "College Statutes" were anachronistic. The men's hopes were frustrated because one or two of the samurai *san'yo* were strongly opposed to the plans for a university, as is indicated in a memorandum sent to Iwakura by Ogawa Kazutoshi (1813–1886), who had himself been a junior councillor while serving as a deputy in the Bureau of Internal Affairs under the Eight Bureaus System. Telling Iwakura not to be overly concerned about that opposition, Ogawa urged Iwashita's appointment as a regular school commissioner *(gakkō goyōgakari)*, and if possible Kido Takayoshi's as well. He also recommended that one of two court nobles, Nakayama Tadayasu (1809–1888) or Ōgimachi-Sanjō Sanenaru (also known as Saga Sanenaru; 1820–1909), be appointed head of the Office of Education, and urged the immediate establishment of a university.[30]

The identities of those alleged by Ogawa to have been the university's opponents are not known, but it is clear that Ōkubo was not a supporter. Immediately following the restoration, Ōkubo took the position that *kuge* education was indispensable but should have a content that emphasized Western studies; he was against the establishment of a Shintoist academy. From a letter he wrote to Iwakura at the end of the first year of Meiji, we also know that Ōkubo thought it was not yet the time to set up permanent structures. This view pertained to the entire polity, not just the projected university, as his letter makes clear: "It is true that the governmental organism and the administrative structure have already been formed. However, society is still being renewed day by day and month by month. We can expect today's actuality to have changed by tomorrow and this year's reality to be different by next year." Ōkubo, who was exceptionally astute, viewed the political situation as too fluid to permit fixed structures to be erected. No doubt his perception of conditions affecting education was the same. He anticipated the consolidation of a sound polity some years hence. Now was the time, he was convinced, to prepare for that future and develop new talent by sending outstanding court nobles, daimyo, and samurai to the West for study. From that experience, he believed, "paragons will emerge. Blending Japanese, Chinese, and Western learning, gauging the present and surveying the past, they will lay open the foundations of an indomitable Imperial Way." Only then, he thought, could the edifice of imperial rule be raised and the restoration's work completed.[31]

It is clear that Ōkubo could not support a university based on a rigid doctrine which disregarded the needs of the day, and it is as apparent that he believed study abroad to be the most effective means of training talented leaders. Hence the Imperial Way (Kōdō), too, was for Ōkubo something to be created by combining the best of native and foreign thought. Its substance could not be based on existing Shinto ideology.

The Transfer of the Capital

After Ōkubo's close friend Iwashita Masahira became educational liaison officer, the government's educational program developed with the

Imperial Way as its central ideology. Iwashita designed a policy that resisted the demands of the Shintoists and sought to implement it by mollifying them on the one hand while placating the Gakushūin group on the other. This was a difficult course to steer, but he had both Iwakura's and Ōkubo's support in doing so. His solution was an educational design based not on Shintoism or Confucianism per se but rather on an eclectic notion of Kōdō—his Emperorism incorporated a mix of Shinto, Confucian, and Western thought.

Helping Iwashita to formulate this ideology was Hasegawa Akimichi (1815–1897) of the Matsushiro domain, an assistant deputy in the Office of Military Affairs who was simultaneously assistant to the head of the military school. During 1868 he had written Iwakura twice (once in the Seventh Month concerning organizational reform and again in the Eighth Month on school governance), and Iwakura knew that Hasegawa supported the Kōdō ideology before appointing him educational liaison officer on 1868.8.25, following his submission of a proposal on educational policy.

Hasegawa's thought was influenced by the Late Mito School. He took the ultranationalist position that Japan was the sovereign of all countries and that the Japanese emperor was the most sacred personage in all the world. He explained this political theory on the basis of a cosmology devised by himself. According to Hasegawa, the universe and everything in it emanated from the Three Energies *(sansai)*—the sun, the earth, and man. Japan was the country governed by generations of emperors directly descended from Kunitokotachi no Mikoto, a god born of the sun as father and the earth as mother, and Kōdō was the way of the divine sovereigns who were the "emperors of ancient times" and who "inspected the forms of the sun and the earth, perceived the moral nature of the sun and the earth, and established the acme of humanity according to the great natural law and order of the sun and the earth."[32] Hasegawa's Emperorism was an individualistic value, one that posited the "divine sovereigns" as creators. At the same time, referring as it did to the "natural law and order," it was firmly anchored in a universalistic principle. His Way, Hasegawa stated, "is the Way of the Divine Sovereigns," and that "is the Great Way of the Three Energies."[33] According to him, it "exemplified ethics and clarified phenomena," hence incorporated both physical and metaphysical elements. That was its special feature.

What Hasegawa called the Great Learning (Taigaku) meant illuminating this Way of the Divine Sovereigns and "studying the great natural law and order of the sun, the earth, and man, taking them to heart, and putting them into practice." His thought, as already noted, was characterized by a universalism that was sustained by Hasegawa's own peculiar cosmology. Hence his Kōdō, unlike Hirata's Shinto, was not exclusionary or xenophobic. "Whatever ethics and science the Four Savage and the Eight Barbarian nations possess is all comprised in the philosophy of the Three Energies, forming a part of the Imperial Way and Imperial Studies (Kōgaku)," Hasegawa maintained. "In the ethics and science of the Four Savage and the Eight Barbarian nations there is accordingly nothing that originated in a source other than the Imperial Way and Imperial Studies."[34] It followed that there was positive value in studying Confucianism, Buddhism, and Western learning—they were all part of Kōdō and Kōgaku.

For these reasons, Hasegawa made a sharp distinction between other schools of thought and his own: "The Great Learning of the Imperial Way is not what is commonly known as Shinto, labeled Kokugaku, or called by the names of Japanology (Wagaku), Ancient Studies (Kogaku), Fundamental Studies (Hongaku), and so forth. Those schools present only one facet of the Imperial Way and then stick to it, perversely distorting it; or they mix in trivialities from Confucianism, Buddhism, and Taoism; or they recklessly malign and abominate Confucianism and Buddhism; but always they cleave single-mindedly to their own particular doctrines and private fabrications. These are vices that narrow the Imperial Way and subvert the Imperial Doctrine."[35]

Iwashita introduced Hasegawa to Ōkubo, who was impressed with Hasegawa's "lofty argument" and found him an "irreplaceable talent."[36] Conditions were ripe for Iwashita to start implementing a school policy that used Hasegawa's syncretist philosophy. The successful progress of the Tōhoku campaign had increased the importance of samurai leaders within the government. Beginning in the summer of 1868, the views of samurai officials such as Ōkubo, Iwashita, and Hasegawa came to be reflected even in educational policy toward the imperial aristocracy, a matter previously pursued by Iwakura and the Shintoists or Iwakura and the Confucianists.

Iwashita began his educational reform by announcing on 1868.8.17 that the proxy Court College would be moved to a new location at the residence of Prince Kajii (that is, the Imperial Abbot of the Sanzen'in) and would be reopened soon with new regulations. (It had been closed temporarily to quiet the objections of Tamamatsu and the Shintoists.) All concerned were ordered to "attend without fail" when the school reopened. A month later, on 9.16, a notice designed to preclude further conflict between the Shintoists and the Gakushūin group announced the creation of two schools, one for each party. These were the Kangakusho (Chinese Studies Institute), which was set up on 9.18, and the Kōgakusho (Imperial Studies Institute), which was to follow three months later. The notice stated that there were plans to found a university where "men of talent would be prepared in Arms and Arts," but admitted that those plans were incomplete. In the meantime, an institute for Imperial —that is, Japanese, or more precisely, Shinto—studies would be located at the residence of the high court noble Kujō Michitaka (1839–1906); one for Chinese studies would be opened at the Kajii residence. "As previously announced, all courtiers from those permitted access to the inner palace on down to titular officials not ranked as chamberlains may enter these schools as they wish. It is, however, ordered that those among them who are below the age of thirty, and who shall be excused from attendance at court, make every effort to concentrate as much as possible on studies."[37]

The Japanists and the sinologists were meant to cooperate with each other, as is clearly indicated in the regulations of these two institutes:[38]

Item. The national polity shall be clarified; duties and designations shall be rectified.

Item. Western science and Chinese classics are the two wings of the Imperial Way. Since the middle ages, when the military usurped sovereignty, duties and designations have been deranged in many ways. Be keenly aware of this.

Item. Frivolous rhetoric and empty theory are forbidden. Training shall be practical. Instruction shall combine Arms and Arts.

Item. Kōgaku and Kangaku shall not engage in doctrinal conflicts or contests of prestige.

Item. Entrance is limited to those between the ages of eight and thirty. Exceptions will be made, however, for older persons who show promise.

Item. Progress in studies shall be tested twice each year.

Item. The first five days of each month are designated for admission to studies. Entrants shall wear formal dress on the day of their admission to studies.

. . .

Iwashita's and Hasegawa's influence is obvious in the comprehension of Japanese, Chinese, and Western learning within the "Imperial Way," no less than in the prohibition of infighting between the two rival groups.

In essence, the Chinese Studies Institute was the successor of the Daigakuryō-dai, and its teachers came from the faculty of the old Gakushūin. The Imperial Studies Institute was the result of a compromise between Hasegawa's Kōdō and the ideology reflected in the "College Statutes"; on 9.24, Yano Harumichi was put in charge of the school, and it is not surprising that Hirata and Tamamatsu also became central figures on its faculty. Because their Fundamentalism (Honkyōgaku) differed substantially from Hasegawa's Kōgaku, however, they strongly objected to the name of the institution. The Kōgakusho came into being somewhat later than the Kangakusho because Yano insisted on constructing a Shrine to the Heavenly Progenitors as tutelary deities of learning, and the school's opening was delayed until the shrine was completed. On 22 January 1869, it was officially announced that lectures would commence four days later. All courtiers, "from those permitted access to the inner palace on down to titular officials not ranked as chamberlains," were encouraged to enter the institute and study diligently. "As previously announced," this encouragement of learning applied especially to "those under thirty, who are excused from attendance at court in order to concentrate entirely on studies." It was pointed out that "learning has of recent been in decline in the Imperial Land, so we are at a disadvantage with respect to foreign countries." The courtiers were exhorted to make learning flourish again, for a well-defined purpose: "All must embrace the intent of the Imperial Restoration and pursue studies vigorously in order someday to make a contribution to the state."[39]

The spirit of compromise behind the establishment of the two institutes is apparent in the incorporation of both Kōdō and the ideas of the "College Statutes" in the educational policy described in the regulations of the Imperial Studies Institute. The notion that "one should observe the Imperial Way and also seek to penetrate Confucian and Western learning to the extent of one's ability" was Hasegawa's. The idea that the nativist thinkers Hakura Azumamaro (i.e., Kada no Azumamaro; 1669–1736), Okabe Mabuchi (i.e., Kamo no Mabuchi; 1697–1769), Motoori Norinaga (1730–1801), and Hirata Atsutane (1776–1843) "shall be the main doctrinal source, but apart from them, a wide selection shall be made from the miscellaneous works of other schools" was the position of Hirata Shinto followers.[40] This eclectic bill of fare, obviously compiled with political considerations in mind, satisfied neither Hasegawa nor the Shintoists. Hasegawa expressed his distaste for its half-baked Japanism, complained that his views had not been followed, and submitted his resignation "due to illness."[41] Yano, too, was angry: "What passes for schooling here is like child's play."[42] Without going into the content of their thought, one may grant both Yano and Hasegawa loyalty to their convictions. Being faithful to their beliefs, both were understandably hostile to Iwashita's giving priority to politics without respecting their scholarly positions.

The Kangakusho and the Kōgakusho—both of them outgrowths of a spirit of political compromise—were from the start unlikely to achieve their promise. But the actual cause of their downfall was accidental, not inherent. The schools had been set up close to the end of the Tōhoku war, at a time when plans were being made for the emperor's triumphal progress to Edo and, indeed, for transferring the center of politics to that city. Naturally, the educational center could not stay behind. As part of the restoration of peace and order in the old shogunal capital after the fall of Edo Castle, the new government absorbed and revived the shogunate's educational institutions; educational activities were already being made available to former shogunal vassals and to domanial samurai. It was essential for the Meiji regime to develop a structure with uniform regulations governing educational institutions both in the new eastern center of government and in Kyoto. The court-centered Kyoto schools posed a problem: they were vulnerable to the charge of being politically behind the times.

As early as 1868.4.10, a pacification decree had been proclaimed for Edo, which was to be administered by a Commandery for the Conquered East (Seitō Dai-Sōtokufu). The proclamation informed samurai and townspeople alike that Tokugawa Yoshinobu's death penalty had been withdrawn, that measures were being taken for the employ of capable shogunal vassals, and that the security of the townspeople's lives and businesses was guaranteed. Apparently, the commandery feared popular unrest. A city that had long submitted to the stern justice of the Tokugawa was not eager to obey the new regime. Indeed, maintaining public order in Edo proved a difficult task for the government, which had to depend on Satsuma, Chōshū, and Tosa to provide the occupation forces. When the conflict between the government's army and the shogunate's supporters spread from the Kantō area to the Tōhoku region, the commandery was burdened with yet another grave problem. It found it far from easy to concentrate simultaneously on fighting a war in Tōhoku and maintaining civil order in Edo.

How to deal with Yoshinobu's surrender was a question with serious implications to the success or failure of the latter effort. Opinion within the commandery was divided between Saigō Takamori, who favored leniency, and Ōmura Masujirō (1825–1869), who insisted on severe punishment. On the fourth of the Intercalary Fourth Month, Saigō went to Edo, where he advocated a demonstration of mercy; it was, he thought, essential to the government's maintaining control over the city. In the event, full authority for dealing with the Tokugawa family and for the administration of Edo was at Ōkubo's insistence given to Sanjō Sanetomi, who was appointed inspector general of the Kantō and left to take up his duties there on the tenth of that month. Immediately after arriving in Edo two weeks later, Sanjō announced that the House of Tokugawa would be maintained in the person of Tayasu Kamenosuke, the scion of a collateral family, who became its head under the name of Tokugawa Iesato (1863–1940). This alone did not suffice to quiet the fears of Edoites, who rested uneasy as long as the issue of how much land and income would be retained by the Tokugawa remained unclear.

Influenced by the views of the commandery's military superintendent, Etō Shinpei (1834–1874), Sanjō on 5.12 established the metropolitan district of Edo-fu as a mechanism for the city's civil governance. Three days later, the diehard Shōgitai of Ueno were brought under control. On 5.19 Sanjō created a Military Government (Chindai) for the eight provinces of the Kantō, with Prince Arisugawa Taruhito in command. Five days after that, Sanjō himself took control of these facilities. On 5.24 the government, respecting Sanjō's advice, vested the lands of Sunpu and Fuchū, assessed at 700,000 *koku,* in the Tokugawa family, temporarily dispelling the anxieties of old shogunal retainers.

Sanjō and the commandery's leadership viewed the emperor's personal presence in Edo as the best means of restoring order to the city and the Kantō region. This question was of course also being discussed in Kyoto, as Ōkubo indicated in his diary on 1868.5.24, the day after he was ordered to Edo as Sanjō's assistant: "Today Iwakura visited the imperial palace and made an unofficial decision on an important matter. I am extremely pleased at this happy turn of events."[43] There is no doubt that the "important matter" was the imperial journey. Ōkubo left Kyoto on 6.5 and spent some time in Osaka before going off to Edo, where he arrived on 6.21. Kido and another insider, Ōki Takatō (1832–1899), also received orders to go to Edo to prepare for the emperor's journey.[44] They left Osaka on 6.23 and arrived in Edo two days later. Sanjō brought Ōkubo, Kido, and Ōki together with Ōmura and Etō from the commandery, and they held meetings on successive days at Edo Castle. A corollary to their plans for the emperor's reception in the East was the formulation of policies to ensure a strong governmental structure. These policies were put together in a short time, and Kido and Ōki went back to Kyoto on 6.29 to report to Iwakura, who was in agreement with the conclusions reached. On 7.17 he obtained the issuance of an imperial edict in which the emperor's intentions were made public: "We have now taken personal control over all state affairs so as to take care of the concerns of Our untold millions of subjects and to relieve their hearts of anxiety. Inasmuch as Edo is the premier stronghold of the Eastland and the central place where goods converge from the four directions, We shall travel there in person and see to government there. Accordingly let Edo from now on be called Tōkyō, the Eastern Capital. That is because We look upon all within the seas as one family and treat East and West alike. Commoners, heed these intentions!"[45]

On the same day, the government abolished the Military Government in Edo, and its commander, Prince Taruhito, was left in charge of purely military affairs. Instead, a Chinshōfu or Government-General was set up under Sanjō Sanetomi. This new governmental organism, which had a structure analogous to that of the Grand Council of State in Kyoto, was given administrative and tax-collecting authority over all regions east of Shizuoka. It helped pave the way for the emperor's journey by taking control of conquered territory that expanded as the Tōhoku war progressed and by strengthening the central government's hold over these lands.

In the "Eastern Capital" preparations for the imperial progress went smoothly, but in Kyoto there was strong resistance from courtiers, self-proclaimed imperial loyalists, and ordinary citizens. When news of the government army's defeats on the Echigo front, where proshogunate forces recaptured Nagaoka Castle on 7.24, became known, the opinion that the emperor's journey should be either postponed or abandoned altogether became the overwhelming view at court. Were it to be postponed, however, "rumors would circulate," as Kido observed. Hence it was decided merely to announce that the journey would take place, "without going into detail on just when."[46] To show that the vision of "all within the seas as one family" and the intention to "treat East and West alike" were about to become reality, it was further announced on 8.4 that the emperor would leave for Tokyo soon.[47] Because of the influence of those opposed to the move, no specific date was set, and this announcement made their opposition all the stronger. Iwakura was concerned because "some courtiers advised the emperor that the timing was inappropriate, as the domains in Tōhoku are still up in arms. Some discontents, members of the 'grass-roots' *(sōmō)* patriotic movement, rushed to checkpoint gates on main roads to stop the journey. Towns-people are worried that the imperial journey will be followed by an order to move the capital from Kyoto, so the situation is troubled. Some senior and junior councillors accordingly argue that the visit should be postponed."[48] His own view was that a postponement was out of the question.

Sanjō and Ōkubo, who were in Tokyo but were aware of the situation in Kyoto, urged Iwakura and Kido to set a date for the imperial journey right away. Etō Shinpei also objected vehemently to its delay. He insisted that the plan be put into effect rapidly in the interests of firming public opinion in the "thirteen provinces east of Suruga," not visited by an emperor "since heaven and earth were opened up," where proshogunate sentiment was still strong.[49] Iwakura was afraid of stirring up more opposition by setting a day for the journey, but he was unable to ignore the intensity of demands from Tokyo. On 8.28 he issued a general itinerary for "the middle of the Ninth Month," again without setting a specific date.[50] That same day, the government announced that on the eighth of the Ninth Month the era name would be changed to Meiji. Its intention was to restore public confidence, but, this action did not placate the Tokyoites.

Observing Kyoto's noncommittal attitude, Ōkubo wrote Kido that there was no time to lose. In his letter of 1868.9.6—the second in two days—he argued that an imperial journey to Tokyo was the only way to change the fact that people were entirely familiar with the shogunate but unaware even of the emperor's existence. Ōkubo questioned how the government could gain national support unless public opinion in the Kantō were united behind the emperor. He urged a decision on Kyoto in the strongest terms: "Even if the government should lose the West of Japan, it must maintain control of the East. All should keep their eyes open, realizing that today's temporizing causes tomorrow's irreparable calamity. If the Lord Chief Minister (Hoshō Denka, i.e., Iwakura) and three or four of the other wise men in government were now to exert themselves and put up a resolute, indomitable effort, then the grand enterprise of the restoration shall be accomplished on a permanent, imperishable foundation. I prostrate myself, begging that this be done. May I be sentenced to death, and may my blood be shed to expunge my guilt if I am wrong."[51]

Ōkubo's eager anticipation of the emperor's departure for Tokyo was no doubt related to signs that the Tōhoku war was about to reach a successful conclusion. On 9.4, the Yonezawa domain surrendered; on the fifteenth, the fortress of Sendai fell; on the twenty-seventh, the Aizu domain capitulated after a month-long siege of its castle. For all that, the new government could not expect to rule the Kantō and Tōhoku regions until it consolidated popular support there; and it was apparent to Sanjō, Ōkubo, and Etō, the administrators of the northeastern territories, that the only means to do that was to manifest the emperor's authority throughout those regions. Ōkubo, for one, believed that the imperial journey should precede the war's conclusion. Not satisfied merely to write to Kido, he decided to put his arguments before the leadership in person, left Tokyo by ship on 9.9, and four days later arrived in Kyoto, where he presented himself at the Grand Council of State and gave a detailed account of the situation in the Kantō. He swayed the hesitant courtiers, and 9.20 was fixed as the date for the emperor's departure for the East. To crown Ōkubo's efforts, the emperor left Kyoto on the appointed day and followed the Tōkaidō highway to Tokyo, attended by Iwakura, Kido, and others. They arrived in Shinagawa on 10.12, and the emperor entered Tokyo Castle on the following day. This was a triumph of major symbolic importance. It was a giant step taken by the Meiji government toward the country's unification.

After seeing the emperor off in Kyoto, Ōkubo returned to Tokyo by ship and was present to welcome him to the former castle of the shoguns. The event is recorded in an uncharacteristically emotional entry in his diary: "It is a fine day with no hint of clouds in the sky. I went to headquarters at 9 A.M. and began the conference. Then I went out to the west side of the castle to await the appearance of His Majesty's Phoenix Carriage, which arrived at 2 P.M. The procession was magnificent. It was as if its grandeur reached to the heavens. . . . The ceremony was truly the most splendid in a thousand years. I cannot express how pleased I am. At the same moment, thousands of imperial army soldiers came back to Tokyo in triumph from the subjugation of [the northern provinces of] Ōu. What a happy coincidence!"[52]

On 10.17 the emperor issued his first statement to government offices as the ruler of a unified Japan: "The Imperial Land is one unified body; East and West are treated alike. On this Our visit to Tokyo, We shall personally inquire into problems both domestic and foreign. Ye hundred officials and holders of authority, with one heart unify your energies to achieve great ends. Hesitate not to inform Us with righteousness and frankness about the merits and demerits, rights and wrongs of each issue."[53] On the next day, the Government-General, having accomplished its mission, was abolished. In its place, regional offices of the Grand Council were established in Tokyo as a visible sign of a unified government and of direct imperial rule. The emperor remained in Tokyo until 20 January 1869, when he went back to Kyoto, promising to return.

On 10.23, with the Tōhoku war over, Prince Taruhito reported to the emperor in Tokyo Castle that the Northeast had been pacified. He was accordingly relieved of his responsibilities as commander of the army of occupation. The central government's control now extended throughout Japan except for Hokkaidō. The country's political center was transferred to Tokyo, and the government went about establishing nationally unified political, financial, military, and educational systems, beginning this task in the Tōhoku region.

The transfer of the seat of government also meant the transfer of educational policy from its former center to the new imperial city.

When Tokyo became the capital in the spring of 1869, the Kyoto schools fell into neglect, but a university was newly established in Tokyo. As part of the political reforms that followed the rendition of the domanial registers to the throne *(hanseki hōkan)* in the summer of 1869, the university was formally made a government institution. The schools that formed its basis were not the Imperial Studies Institute and Chinese Studies Institute of Kyoto, which were considered out of tune with the requirements of unification, but educational institutions of the old shogunate in Edo, which were restored under the auspices of the new government.

The Military Government (Chindai) had adopted the expedient of using the old regime's remaining apparatus to govern the city. The shogunate's administrative offices for temples and shrines, for the towns-people's dwelling quarters, and for finances were simply renamed. Officials of the imperial Military Government were made responsible for them, but shogunal magistrates and lower officials were retained and used to administer the city. On 5.28 the Chindai additionally announced that those Tokugawa bannermen *(hatamoto)* and protocol officers *(kōke)* who pledged allegiance to the imperial government would be divided into three new ranks—intermediate court officers *(chūdaifu)*, lower court officers *(gedaifu)*, and upper samurai *(jōshi)*—and that their new status as direct retainers of the emperor (in other words, imperial courtiers) would be guaranteed. The appointment of erstwhile officials of the shogunate to responsible positions and the grant of new status to former shogunal vassals were policies intended to win over adherents of the old regime. As a result, many new officials and courtiers were suddenly created in Edo. Inasmuch as the Grand Council of State had instituted instruction for the aristocracy in Kyoto, the Military Government could hardly ignore the education of these new courtiers and their children in Tokyo. To take care of their needs, it first took over the main shogunal college, Shōheikō, on 6.11 and then successively absorbed the shogunate's medical institute, Igakusho, and its institute of Western studies, Kaiseisho. On 6.26 the Medical Institute became the first school actually revived by the Military Government, because of the need for a hospital to treat sick and wounded soldiers from the Tōhoku war.[54]

The Shōheikō was restored on 6.29. Put in charge as chief school administrator was Katagiri Seisuke (1837–1873), the head of civil administration in the Military Government. Ishimaru Sanzaburō (Sekisen; 1813–1899), a teacher at the old Shōheikō, and two others were made department heads. Nineteen instructors were appointed to serve under them.[55] The school's name was changed to Shōhei Gakkō, but most of the teachers came from the old Confucian college of the shogunate. Thus there was none of the conflict between Shintoists and Confucianists here that had characterized the Kyoto institution. From the start, a Confucian education was provided. On the opening day, the Military Government made the following announcement: "Government has undergone a great renewal. Duties and designations shall be clarified; talent shall be fostered. Hence the Chindai-fu has been ordered to revive the Shōhei Gakkō. All those wishing to enroll should submit applications to the school."[56] The phrase that "duties and designations *(taigi meibun)* shall be clarified"—that is, reoriented to the emperor—was especially included because it was expected that much of the school's constituency would be retainers of the old shogunate.

In the Seventh Month, after the Military Government was abolished and the Government-General established, the Shōhei Gakkō and the Medical Institute came under the administrative jurisdiction of the Tokyo metropolitan government (Tōkyō-fu), where Katagiri Seisuke assumed the office of deputy magistrate *(hanji)* with no change in his official responsibilities as head of the Shōhei Gakkō. On 8.22 the metropolitan government issued an edict intended mainly for former shogunal retainers: "The most essential task now, at the moment of reform, is nourishing human talent. A university must therefore be established as soon as possible, but this cannot be done immediately because of various problems. For the time being, students from the age of seven to twenty should attend the Shōhei Gakkō daily. Those with incomes of less than 300 *hyō* will receive stipends sufficient for one person. You must take this matter seriously. Rather than flutter about like butterflies in the useless composition of poetry, study practical knowledge that is immediately useful. Study hard day and night."[57]

On the day this scholarship edict was issued, preparations were already under way to receive the emperor in Tokyo. Three days earlier, however, Enomoto Takeaki (1836–1908) had escaped with the defunct shogunate's warships from Tokyo, heading for the North. Obviously, the Government-General did not yet enjoy complete authority. That the Tokyo metropolitan government should have been trying at such a time to impart hope and reassurance to the children of minor retainers of the fallen shogunate by encouraging their school attendance (and providing scholarships, however limited) demonstrates what an important part education played in the authorities' effort to restore peace and order to the city in preparation for the emperor's visit.

On 1868.8.30 the Shōhei Gakkō made provisions for children to obtain practice in reading off elementary texts, but only six made an appearance.[58] Under the circumstances this poor attendance is understandable. The former shogunal vassals remained in financial straits and mental distress; no matter what Tōkyō-fu tried to do for them, it seemed, nothing was satisfactory. Nevertheless, pursuant to the Government-General's intent, the metropolitan government kept generating educational plans. Its draft for a school system envisioned that the highest post would be occupied by a court aristocrat or a daimyo; two deputies would assist with the administration; two professors of doctoral rank *(hakase)* and a number of academic assistants *(jokyō)* were to form the instructional cadre. The scale was not large, but it is noteworthy in itself that such educational plans were drawn up despite the pressure of other affairs.

The professors were given the sterling official responsibilities to "explicate the Supreme Duty, extend enlightenment, cultivate talent, and establish a probationary category to test the suitability of recommended candidates."[59] As in the earlier announcement of the Military Government, the emphasis here was on expounding moral obligations. This educational strategy reflected an ideological policy that laid stress on teaching the "Supreme Duty" of reverence for the emperor. Evidently, former vassals of the shogunate and domanial samurai who had entered the service of the Chinshōfu upon surrendering to the imperial government in the course of the Tōhoku war were in special need of that type of instruction. Authorities in Tokyo made education in *taigi meibun* as essential for these samurai as it was for the new courtiers.

The Kaiseisho, the shogunate's distinguished center for Western learning, was taken over by the new authorities on 1868.6.18, and the Government-General put Mitsukuri Rinshō (1846–1897) in charge of the institution. Although preparations for starting instruction went ahead, the school's formal opening was delayed until 9.12, when educational activities began under the direction of Kawakatsu Hiromichi (b. 1830) and Yanagawa Shunsan (1832–1870). It appears, however, that the Kaiseisho was unable to carry out its mission satisfactorily in 1868, and that requires some explanation.

When the Kaiseisho reopened, the decision had been made and the schedule already set for an imperial progress to Tokyo. The Government-General exercised considerable power in the Kantō, so much so that it rivaled the Grand Council of State, which was still located in Kyoto. Sanjō Sanetomi, who was deeply troubled by this division of authority, thought of using the occasion of the imperial journey to abolish the Chinshōfu. First, however, the Government-General would take charge of the three educational institutions in Tokyo; upon the abolition of that office, they would be taken over by the Grand Council. Accordingly, the Chinshōfu took the Medical Institute out of the metropolitan government's control and placed it under its own jurisdiction. On 9.14, it did the same with the Shōhei Gakkō. On 1868.10.13, the emperor entered Tokyo Castle, and the regional offices of the Grand Council were set up. Five days later, the Government-General was abolished, and the three schools were put under the authority of the Grand Council's Department of Administration (Gyōseikan). But the regional office of the Gyōseikan was temporary and not capable of administering the three schools. Hence the Igakusho and the Kaiseisho were again temporarily transferred to the authority of the Tokyo metropolitan government. The Kaiseisho was brought back under the control of the Department of Administration on 11.13.

The presumption behind these changes of jurisdiction, which coincided with the emperor's progress to Tokyo, was that an educational system with uniform regulations, one controlled by the government, would eventually be established. When authority over the Shōhei Gakkō was transferred to the Department of Administration, the office of chief school administrator in the Tokyo metropolitan government was abolished, and educational activities were suspended. Jurisdiction over the Kaiseisho continued to change for a time, and the school was moved from Hitotsubashi to Tsukiji and then to the Western studies institute's old grounds at Kanda Nishiki-chō. During that time, regular educational activities could not be conducted.

Educational policy in Tokyo developed on the assumption that order was about to return, and a serious attempt was made to cope with the spiritual malaise of the shogunate's old retainers at the Shōhei Gakkō. But there was little hope that the disestablished vassals of the Tokugawa, reduced to despair by the changes that had overcome them, would have the heart for learning, and efforts to educate them proved unsuccessful. The Kaiseisho was naturally expected to impart new Western knowledge, but its opening was delayed. The timing of the emperor's visit complicated things; administrations shifted; the school was moved; and in the end it never began educational activities. The Medical Institute, alone of the three institutions, was able to carry out its responsibilities.

Once the day for the emperor's journey was set, the Chinshōfu, which controlled the eastern half of Japan in place of the Dajōkan, decided to turn back all its administrative authority to the Grand Council of State. As its jurisdiction over educational institutions was to be turned over also, the Government-General had no intention of carrying out a full-scale educational policy of its own from that time onward. The Grand Council, however, came to grapple seriously with the question of the entire country's unification upon incorporating the Government-

General's powers. In the spring of 1869, the capital was transferred to Tokyo; during the summer of that year, the domains would surrender their documents of enfeoffment to the throne. While rendition per se did not amount to unification, at the very least it constituted a formal acknowledgment of that goal. In the midst of these changes, educational policy, too, was compelled to take a new path.

The Rendition of the Domanial Registers

The imperial government's victory in the Tōhoku war and the destruction of the recalcitrant domains in the eastern part of Japan meant that the Meiji leadership could for the first time plan a centrally controlled political structure. The emperor's journey, however brief, to the former seat of shogunal power and his assumption of direct rule over a united country further encouraged the leadership to believe that they were within reach of their goals. The institution of a national, unified, bureaucratic system of governance had, they felt, at length become feasible. This awareness of new political possibilities led some of them in the fall of 1868 to begin advocating reformist views in education. Their proposals were fundamentally different from educational policies in force until then, which were directed at a privileged segment of the population—the court aristocracy in Kyoto and the samurai in Edo. It is significant to note that new educational concepts developed in close connection with new ideas on how to bring about changes in Japan's feudal social structure.

On 1868.10.21, while the emperor was still in Tokyo, Iwakura Tomomi put before the Dajōkan a number of proposals on various areas of concern, such as military, financial, judicial, and legislative affairs. A section on education was included in these proposals. Indeed, Iwakura emphasized the special importance of education, which he viewed as "fundamental to the country's future"; accordingly, he thought it "desirable that someone be appointed immediately to look into the matter."[60] This perception of the political role of education was a departure from Iwakura's previous focus on the schooling of imperial courtiers. His vision expanded to encompass the entire population—a change of attitude that reflected developments in the political arena, most notably the pacification of Tōhoku.

Iwakura's educational initiative evidently encouraged others to come out with their own opinions. Thus Kido Takayoshi in January 1869 submitted a proposal urging "the immediate promotion of universal education." In the interests of coping with the "rich and powerful countries of the West," Kido maintained, it ought to be recognized that "the strength and prosperity of a country lie in the strength and prosperity of its people. If ordinary people are held back by ignorance and poverty, the beautiful phrase 'imperial restoration' has no meaning and the effort of keeping up with the leading countries of the world must fail."[61] Arguing that the intellectual enlightenment of every individual was as fundamental as economic development to building true national strength, Kido urged that a program of schooling be implemented for the entire population. Consequently, his educational views must be distinguished from others current until then, such as proposals for the development of *jinzai* or "talent" (i.e., the training of bureaucrats) and the feudal period's schemes for the indoctrination of commoners.

A month after Kido had submitted his proposal, a more reformist view was put forward by Itō Hirobumi, who at the time was governor of Hyōgo Prefecture. Itō's suggestions on educational policy were included in the "Principles of National Policy" that he drafted after having seen the petition made by the daimyo of Satsuma, Chōshū, Tosa, and Hizen to surrender their domanial registers to the emperor. Itō thought that rendition would soon be an accomplished fact throughout Japan, and his "Principles" offered advice to government leaders on how to manage national unification and foreign diplomacy after the completion of that process. In Itō's mind, education was closely related to those two concerns.

Itō was convinced that education played an important role in securing the foundations of a modern state, and he believed that developing every person's intellectual ability would naturally lead to Western-type "civilization and enlightenment" *(bunmei kaika)*. In the conventional view, the educational purposes of universities and elementary schools were connected directly to the goals of national strength and prosperity. Itō, however, linked education to the activation and expansion of a person's natural capacity for knowledge:[62]

> The human body is endowed with eyes, ears, nose and mouth, and each of these must be used in accordance with its function. If, while knowing how the nose and mouth perform their functions, we then fail to realize how to apply the eyes and ears to theirs, that would be the same as not having eyes or ears. Today, the world situation has changed dramatically. Engaged in intercourse with all the world, men vie with each other to keep their ears and eyes open, gaining information that spreads from one person to another and eventually reaches ten thousand. Accordingly, we have initiated a policy of civilization and enlightenment. Now is our millennial opportunity to reform the bad old habits that have been followed in our Imperial Land for centuries, and to open up the eyes and ears of

the people of our realm. If, at this juncture, we fail to act quickly and make our people broadly pursue useful knowledge from throughout the world, we will in the end reduce them to a backward folk without eyes and ears. We must therefore establish new universities and change our old, conventional style of learning. A university should be founded in each of the capital cities, Kyoto and Tokyo, and elementary schools should be opened in every locality, from metropolitan districts, domains, and prefectures on down to every district and village. Pursuant to each university's charter, people of city and country alike shall be brought to the light and to knowledge.

Itō's innovative ideas transcended the dualism that had characterized the feudal age, when one type of education was provided for the ruling classes and another for the ruled. Instead, he appears to have envisioned a single-track educational system in which universities and elementary schools would be articulated parts of a unitary structure, one built on the principle of universal schooling. At the bottom of his argument are truly "enlightened" concerns: "Grounded upon the virtue of charity, we should value human life and look upon people without discriminating among them as to their high or low status. People should be permitted to enjoy the rights of freedom and independence." And he specifically rejected the feudal class structure: "People should not be made to keep their place as samurai, farmers, artisans, or merchants. Samurai should not be prevented from becoming farmers, and farmers from becoming merchants or artisans."[63]

Kido's and Itō's educational concepts were products of the new political climate that developed after the pacification of Tōhoku. Both viewed educational policy in the context of their efforts to do away with the surviving elements of daimyo and domanial power, and both linked educational reforms to the abolition of feudalism (or at least to the return of registers of enfeoffment). When Iwakura made his proposals before the Grand Council of State, however, the government leaders were as yet unprepared to entertain views of the type put forward by Kido and Itō; to be more precise, they were as yet unable to turn such views into binding policies. Even if national unity had become a real possibility with the successful conclusion of the Tōhoku campaign, the government's triumph had been brought about by the military forces of Satsuma, Chōshū, and Tosa; its own forces were all but nonexistent. The Tokugawa and the domains that had supported their lost cause were defeated, but the Meiji government remained impotent before its own three great allies, Sat-Chō-Do. It could not force a unified school system on them, let alone on all of the domains.

For all that, the leadership group as a whole evidently shared the belief that education was an area deserving urgent attention. In any event, on 1868.10.27—less than a week after the submission of Iwakura's proposal to the Dajōkan—Mitsukuri Rinshō was appointed to an office to be called the Gakkō Torishirabe Goyōgakari (Inspectorate of Schools). The president and vice-president of this office were designated on 11.2; they were the former daimyo of Tosa, Yamanouchi Yōdō (Yamanouchi Toyoshige; 1827–1872), the president of the planning board for a deliberative assembly, and the board member Akizuki Tanetatsu, respectively. On 11.3–4 Hishida Bunzō, Matsuoka Tokitoshi (1814–1877), Mori Arinori (1847–1889), Kanda Takahira (1830–1898), and Uchida Tsunejirō (Uchida Masao; 1838–1876) were all appointed school inspectors. It is noteworthy that four of the inspectorate's top personnel—Mitsukuri, Mori, Kanda, and Uchida—were scholars of Western studies, the first time such specialists had participated in the government's educational planning. The educational policies of Iwakura and the rest of the leadership group were no longer completely biased in favor of Shinto, Confucianism, and Kōdō; their scope had been extended to include Western models. The new ideas were initially to be tested in Tokyo.

The Inspectorate of Schools established basic procedures for the Shōhei Gakkō and the Kaiseisho with the aim of restoring both institutions' educational activities, which had been temporarily suspended in the Tenth Month of 1868, when the Government-General was abolished. On 22 January 1869, the basis for a table of organization at the two institutions was established by the new official ranking procedures stipulated by the so-called Constitution of 1868.[64] On the same day, Uchida Masao was named the new principal of the Kaiseisho and Matsuoka Tokitoshi was appointed head of the Shōhei Gakkō. Yoshino Kinryō (1802–1878) became a professor of the second rank, Ōhashi Terutsugu (Ōhashi Masateru; 1836–1881) and one other were named professors of the third rank, and Kawasaki Rosuke (1805–1876) and one other were appointed to probationary status as junior professors at the Shōhei Gakkō. No appointments were made to the instructional staff of the Kaiseisho—renamed Kaisei Gakkō—until 1869.3.9, when Irie Bunrō (1834–1878) and one other were made professors of the second rank, Sahara Junkichi and three others became professors of the third rank, and Ōtsuki Hikogorō was appointed to probationary status.[65]

On 25 January 1869 a new Education Department (Gakkōkan) was established under the Department of Administration (Gyōseikan). Yamanouchi Yōdō was made secretary of education *(chigakuji)*; Akizuki Tanetatsu was appointed his deputy; Matsuoka Tokitoshi and Uchida Masao were made assistant deputy secretaries of education but kept their teaching responsibilities. Twelve days later, the Education Department announced that the Tōkyō Shōhei Gakkō and Kaisei Gakkō would open on 1869.1.17 (27 February); that entry would be permitted only on the twenty-seventh of each month; that both schools required a formal application; and that it must include details of the applicant's place of birth, address, age, name, and employer or superior.[66]

The Shōhei Gakkō and Kaisei Gakkō were not part of a system of universal education. Rather, they were institutions that trained "talent" for government service. No restrictions, however, were placed on qualifications for entrance to them; and that is the most notable point in the Education Department's announcement. Recall that in the Kyoto schools, entrance was restricted to courtiers, and that even in the old Shōhei Gakkō—when it was revived by the Chindai and taken over by Tōkyō-fu—it was limited to former shogunal retainers and samurai seconded to the central government by the Tōhoku domains. In this context, the action taken by the Education Department appears as an epochal event. Its Inspectorate of Schools had, it would appear, at least to some extent taken upon itself the task of carrying out the aims of Iwakura's educational plan, which had the establishment of a mass-based national school system as its main principle.

Most of the entrants to the Tōkyō Shōhei Gakkō at its reopening were not old retainers of the shogunate but samurai from various domains. Among them were many rough and ragged returnees from war. Naitō Meisetsu (1847–1926), who entered the school at this time, vividly describes what the atmosphere there was like:[67]

> These days, with the opening of the Shōhei Gakkō, dormitory students from all the domains increase steadily. New dormitories have been built in addition to the old ones from shogunate days, and I have heard estimates that there are more than four hundred students. There may be lots of them, but they don't study much. . . . I and some others were asked to take charge of questions on Confucian philosophy, but the times being what they are, no one came with a question, so the job was purely titular. . . . Quite a few [of the students] were war veterans. Many were from Satsuma, and all of these had their hair cut in the Western style and were quite conspicuous. What's his name had lost an arm. To cultivate a "tough guy" image was the fashion among the war veterans, so anyone who wanted to study was scorned as a shilly-shallying fogy. Many students would go off in the afternoons and, depending upon how much money they had, go to a large or small restaurant, drink *sake,* and summon a geisha, although some went to the brothels in Yoshiwara, Fuka-

gawa, or Shinagawa. Upon returning they would tell tall stories and boast of their triumphs.

As suggested here, conditions at the Shōhei Gakkō were a carry-over from the rowdiness for which academies of the Edo period were notorious. The number of students had increased, but their mores had not improved. The atmosphere became completely dissolute because of the samurai returning from the Tōhoku war. Unfortunately, we do not have similar records describing the day-to-day atmosphere at the Kaisei Gakkō.

Befitting a school that would impart new knowledge from the West, two Europeans—the Frenchman Pousset and the Englishman Parley—were invited in the Eighth Month of 1869. Classes to be taught in foreign languages by foreigners were constituted regular courses of instruction, and those taught by Japanese using translated texts were designated supplementary courses. Verbeck came from Nagasaki and was made vice-principal of the Kaisei Gakkō in the Fourth Month of 1869. According to Kido, however, the situation there was far from ideal: "There are a great many students, and they are totally undisciplined. Even though they seem to be respecting the rules a little better from about the Ninth Month, this cannot be called significant improvement."[68] The Shōhei Gakkō and the Kaisei Gakkō had been reopened and formalized, but they were not performing up to expectations. And the Inspectorate of Schools had other problems on its hands beside higher education. From the beginning of 1869, it had to grapple earnestly with the task of drawing up comprehensive plans for a national school system that could provide an adequate foundation for the country's future development.

The principal items on the agenda of the government's leadership at the beginning of 1869 were sending the emperor again to Tokyo and transferring the capital there, completing the country's unification, and building centralized authority. It was recognized that an educational system was among the unified national structures that had to be created as soon as possible. The importance attributed to educational policy by Iwakura and other top leaders is indicated by the fact that such influential men as Yuri Kimimasa, Kido Takayoshi, and Ōkubo Toshimichi were put in charge of school governance on 1869.1.18, when the government issued two new documents: "Regulations for Legislation and Administration" and "Organization and Management of Gijō and San'yo Offices."[69] These new mechanisms were created because the political situation in Kyoto was insecure. Seeking to prevent the emperor's second journey to Tokyo, the old jingoist clique was intimidating the leadership group both covertly and overtly. On 1869.1.5, they assassinated Junior Councillor Yokoi Shōnan. This terrorist attack filled the remaining *san'yo* with fear. It was a clear sign of political crisis.

As noted earlier, the leader most troubled by the conspiracies of the "imperial loyalist" xenophobes was Kido. Ōkubo, too, was concerned about the agitation that afflicted the political leadership. "Now that the power over life and death is in the hands of rank outsiders," he worried, the realm "cannot but collapse in a landslide."[70] Unable to ignore the government's loss of authority, Iwakura inquired whether Ōkubo could find a way out of the crisis. Ōkubo's response was an appeal for unity and responsibility: "As there is government, so there are rules and regulations. The hundred officials and holders of authority should unify their hearts and efforts. Even while in different locations, they should be of the same mind. . . . Men charged with an office under government should consider it their self-appointed duty to improve their capabilities, to put aside the private and embrace the public interest, and to translate their actions into evident accomplishments. Once that happens, a part of government's central purpose will have begun to unfold."[71] This was the ideological basis of the new "Regulations for Legislation and Administration" and "Organization and Management of Gijō and San'yo Offices." Anticipating the day when those two offices would indeed be reorganized, Iwakura wrote to Ōkubo that great efforts had gone into dividing work between senior and junior councillors and allocating specific responsibilities among them so that "we can accomplish hundreds of matters efficiently."[72]

In the agenda prepared by Iwakura for discussion at a Dajōkan conference on 1869.1.24 was an item of considerable importance for the future establishment of a national school structure. Iwakura noted that investigations were being pursued in Kyoto on schools of "Imperial" (i.e., Japanese) as well as of Chinese studies, and that the same was being done in the Kantō. In the desire to make sure that "East and West are treated alike," he proposed that the three Kyoto school superintendents be dispatched to Tokyo to facilitate coordination.[73] Iwakura's proposal received unanimous support and was approved. As a result, the nativist Hirata Kanetane and the sinologist Nakanuma Ryōzō were sent to Tokyo on 2.2 and 3.9 respectively. They cooperated with members of the inspectorate in Tokyo in drawing up plans for a comprehensive national school system. The policy they developed was to establish a university in each of the two capital cities, Tokyo and Kyoto, and to divide the country into eastern and western regions, which were to be subject to uniform school rules. "Imperial studies" would be the primary material at the university level, but the study of classical Chinese texts would also be made available.[74]

The pacification of Tōhoku was the precondition for determining the government's policy to establish universities in Kyoto and Tokyo and adopt a unified national system of education. But a precondition is just that and no more. The leadership could not foresee how political conditions would develop. The crucial question—how to control Satsuma, Chōshū, and the other domains that had come to the fore by defeating the allies of the Tokugawa—was never out of their minds. To be sure, the government had acted promptly on the proposal Iwakura submitted on 1868.10.21, in which he pointed out the patent need to institute uniform regional administration throughout the realm; a week later, an ordinance titled "Administrative Rules for Domain Governance" was issued.[75] Getting the various domains to accept that plan and then to implement it was, however, a problem.

After the Tōhoku campaign, real power in the prominent southwestern domains shifted from the daimyo and a few highly placed families into the hands of ordinary samurai, who were opposed both to dominance by a daimyo and to control by a central government. They reformed domain governance with an eye toward creating a new feudal structure that would serve their interests. As a result, the tendency toward going it alone grew in the domains, and the central government found it increasingly difficult to extend its authority over them. This was particularly the case in Satsuma. Ōkubo drafted a reform plan for Satsuma based on the government's new "Administrative Rules," but veterans of the Tōhoku war opposed it, and his effort failed.

Because of the unrest generated there by his proposals, Ōkubo was asked by the daimyo of Satsuma to return to his home province and provide personal leadership for his plan. On 1869.2.16, while he was in Satsuma, Ōkubo recorded the failure of his mission in his diary: "The most pressing need of political reform at this time, I maintained, is to choose men of talent, putting aside private interests and making appointments impartially on the basis of the widest possible selection. That occasioned some heated discussion on the part of Kawamura, Ijūin, Nozu, and other unit commanders. This evening we did come to an agreement, as they adopted a broad-minded, magnanimous attitude. Indeed, they criticized adversely the policy pursued by the ordinary samurai. The ordinary samurai, however, remained unpersuaded, and so no conclusive agreement could be reached."[76] Evidently, Satsuma samurai were not about to submit meekly to the central government, even when it was Ōkubo himself who sought to prevail upon them.

Satsuma's strength was indeed considerable, but it could afford an independent posture only because of the government's weakness. And it was not the only domain to which the central government's authority failed to extend. The two other true victors of the Tōhoku war, Chōshū and Tosa, also adopted the position of defending their separate interests. Itagaki Taisuke (1837–1919), who joined the government as a junior councillor in 1869.4, described the conditions of those days trenchantly if somewhat dyspeptically: "Almost all matters, large and small, were left to the discretion of the domains, in the name of the common weal or of public opinion. In actuality, there was no united government. Unable to act on their own, officials merely stood by helplessly, noses out for every breath of air from the powerful domains. . . . Even as the domains grew ever bolder and more formidable, the central government lost all its ability to restrain them. The government ordered whatever the domains requested, and it did so without emendation. Thereby it brought about a great deal of inequity among the people of the various domains"—because the people of the weaker *han,* it was left unsaid, were left holding the short end of the stick.[77]

The man who most clearly recognized the dangers of the particularistic trend that followed the conquest of the Northeast was Kido Takayoshi. How much he worried about this obstacle to national unity may be observed in two letters that he wrote to Ōmura Masujirō in the First Month of 1869. The first of these was caustic: "The lords of the realm may be all right—as far as they themselves are concerned, anyhow—but when it comes to their domains it is a different matter. The *han* are consumed with a burning ambition, and each is so intent on claiming credit for itself that they argue about nothing except how they should be rewarded. They have become immensely arrogant, far worse than in the days of the old shogunate. They make willful demands on the imperial government, commensurably with their power. One hears them talk glibly about 'duty' and 'obligation,' but for the most part it turns out to be lip service. As I size up the world situation, I see not the slightest inclination on the domains' part to make even a gesture toward contributing to the Imperial Land's preservation through all ages to come."[78] The second letter, written a week or two later, made the same point: "The Shogunate has fallen, but any number of petty shogunates have arisen in its place. Things being what they are, Japan cannot achieve its objective of standing tall in the world."[79] Unless the domains' pretensions to autonomy were broken, Kido believed, it would not matter what kind of system the government tried to institute nationwide. To build a unified, comprehensive structure would be close to impossible.

The method Kido devised for breaking the political deadlock was the rendition of the domanial registers. Kido knew that this by itself was not the ultimate remedy for the central government's weakness; the only true solution, he realized full well, was to abolish the domains entirely. But the government as yet lacked the power to do that. Accordingly, his plan was to carry out rendition as a temporary measure, reorganize the *han* into parts of a regional administration under the national government, and then try to attack the roots of domanial autonomy. Kido had conceived this strategy as early as the Second Month of 1868, when the punitive campaign against Yoshinobu was just getting under way and when government leaders still had a great fear of making any public statements about the questions affecting the domains. Even at this early date, however, Kido anticipated what would happen after the defeat of the Tokugawa and their allies: "It will not be long before the campaign in the Eastland is over and the troops are withdrawn. But once the army of each domain goes back home and the domains secure their foundations, exercising administrative and judicial powers in their regions, it will be difficult to undo the damage."[80] Rendition, he thought, was an absolutely essential expedient.

First, Kido made his intentions clear to the daimyo of Chōshū, Mōri Tadamasa (Takachika; 1819–1871), and obtained his agreement on 1868.7.23. He then revealed his plans to Ōkubo, whom he asked to persuade the daimyo of Satsuma. On 1868.9.18, Kido recorded in his diary: "Today I talked to Ōkubo Ichizō about a secret matter. He agreed with me and promised to do his best. How I lament having been unable to act on something that has been on my mind for such a long time! As this concerns the very future of the Imperial Land, I seek no glory for myself but shall be satisfied to see my aspirations accomplished at the hands of others, if only I can contribute in some small way to my lord, my father, and my Imperial Land. I only regret that as yet I could not share my innermost thoughts with Ōkubo but had to be content with an outline of the surface."[81] At this stage, Kido did not dare breathe a word about the abolition of the domains even to Ōkubo. He spoke with similar restraint to Gotō Shōjirō on the same day and asked for Tosa's cooperation.

Working together, Kido, Ōkubo, and Gotō gradually developed a detailed plan for rendition. In the meantime—in the Eleventh Month of 1868—the daimyo of Himeji on his own initiative petitioned the government to be permitted to surrender his documents of enfeoffment. His petition was rejected, because the insider group of Kido, Ōkubo, and Gotō thought that it would be more efficacious for their domains to make the offer first. (It so happened that Itō Hirobumi, unaware of the group's intention, expressed the view that the petition should be granted and a reward bestowed.) By the Twelfth Month, Iwakura,

Sanjō, and other top leaders were made aware of the insiders' designs. On 1869.1.14, Ōkubo met Hirosawa Saneomi of Chōshū and Itagaki Taisuke of Tosa along with other representatives of those two *han*, and they reached agreement that their domains' registers should be rendered to the throne. Satsuma, Chōshū, and Tosa accepted this plan "without question"; Tosa was "particularly enthusiastic," Ōkubo reported to Iwakura. "Rest assured, all is well."[82] Hizen also agreed to the plan and joined it at about the same time.

On 1869.1.23, the daimyo of Satsuma, Chōshū, Tosa, and Hizen jointly signed a petition offering to render their domanial registers to the throne. Their offer was received with assurances of the high regard the emperor had for their loyal intention; a determination would be made in the matter after the emperor's next visit to Tokyo, when a national assembly seeking an expression of "public opinion" was to be held. Similar overtures from the daimyo of Tottori, Okayama, Higo, Hiroshima, and Uwajima followed. Rendition was about to become a reality. Government leaders were resolved to send the emperor again to Tokyo regardless of the criticism they might draw from the Kyoto aristocracy, the superpatriots of the *sonnō jōi* clique, or "grass-roots" discontents. Now they had to grapple with the problems of bringing together the daimyo in a national assembly as soon as possible. Once that was done, the process could be completed smoothly with the emperor's approval of the domains' petitions to render their registers to him.

The emperor left Kyoto on 3.7, despite strong opposition from court nobles, and arrived in Tokyo on 3.28. The political situation that greeted him upon arrival was far from reassuring, as may be surmised from Ōkubo's plaint to Iwakura:[83]

> Now is a time of domestic and foreign crisis. The life or death of the Imperial Land is at stake. Dangers impend on all sides; we are, it seems, perpetually within a hair's breadth of disaster. Since last year the civil war has at length been put down, and we seem to be enjoying a moment of peace. But the great and the lesser barons harbor suspicions against one another, and the people of the realm are troubled. Their hearts are in a flux, and that is more dangerous than the mobilization of a million soldiers. If we think it is peaceful today, that is merely because the terrible fire under the floor has yet to burst into the open. How can we ignore this, how can we ignore this? After my arrival in Tokyo, I paid careful attention to conditions. The British envoy humiliates important officials and treats them like children. Low-ranking outsiders insult government officials and treat them like servants. The foreigners despise and ridicule

us; our own compatriots act loose and slipshod with us; no place is free
of this shame. Naturally, the people do not have any confidence in the
government. The clamor of dissatisfaction is heard on every street corner.
In fact, the people are beginning to feel nostalgic for the old shogunal
regime.

Ōkubo appealed for a strengthened central government, one that could
overwhelm the daimyo, gain the people's trust, and thus reduce the danger. Neither Iwakura nor Sanjō dissented from his entreaty. Both feared
the situation in Tokyo, deplored the government's weakness, and were
resolved on fortifying it prior to the national assembly.

A step taken toward that end was a sorting out of personnel by
ballot. This selection procedure, which was carried out on 1869.5.13–
14, was applied to chief ministers as well as senior and junior councillors, no less than to heads and assistant heads of departments. Until
then, there had been no set number of senior or of junior councillors,
and their numbers had expanded to eighteen *gijō* and eleven *san'yo*
through various forms of patronage. The intent of the ballot was to
weed out incapable high officials and to put affairs in the hands of a
select few; it was hoped that cohesion in the government bureaucracy
and unity in policy determination could be achieved thereby. There was
strong opposition from some, like Ōmura Masujirō and Yamanouchi
Yōdō, who rejected what they called republican principles. The ballot
was carried out nonetheless, at Ōkubo's insistence, in order to present
the national assembly with a unified voice, all special interests apparently swept aside.

The long-anticipated national assembly was held from 5.21 to 5.25.
In attendance were officials of the fifth rank and above from the several
offices of the Grand Council of State, the Education Department, the
Office of Petitions (Taishōkyoku; instituted in 1869.3 and known as
Taishōin from 1869.7), and metropolitan and prefectural governments,
as well as imperial princes, high courtiers, and lords of domains. At the
assembly, the emperor inquired about three matters: the "means to
prosper the Imperial Way," the "new institution of domanial governors," and the "opening up of the Ezo territory" (i.e., Hokkaidō). The
second of these inquiries concerned the rendition of the domanial registers, and almost all the daimyo responded that they agreed with the
plan. The emperor honored their responses. On 1869.6.17 he authorized the rendition volunteered by Satsuma, Chōshū and other domains,
ordered all the rest of the *han* to surrender their registers, and appointed all the daimyo as domanial governors *(chihanji)*. Thus the
daimyo were divested of their legal status as feudal lords, one they had

held since the foundation of the Tokugawa shogunate at the beginning of the seventeenth century; and their domains were redefined as units of regional administration in the Meiji state, along with the metropolitan districts and prefectures. To be sure, only the form of a centralized nation-state had been put together. But the new domanial governorships—unlike the old domanial lordships—would not be heritable. This decision, taken at Kido's particularly strong insistence shortly before the rendition took place, sharply underlined the growing difference between the Tokugawa era's conglomerate realm and the Meiji state.

Having obtained the surrender of the domanial registers, the central government next worked on refining its table of organization. In 1869.7 it adopted the so-called two-council, six-ministry structure *(nikan roku-shōsei)*. This was the first centralizing reform of government departments since the imperial restoration. The designations of offices and the titles of their personnel were adapted from the Taihō Code of the eighth century (there were nine official ranks, from first to ninth). As had been the case then, the Office of Shinto Affairs (Jingikan) was placed above the Grand Council of State, if only symbolically. The Jingikan supervised Shinto ceremonies and promoted the "means to prosper the Imperial Way," but it had no administrative authority. Hence the Dajōkan was in fact the more powerful institution. It contained the highest policy-making organs, namely, the offices of a minister of the left and a minister of the right, who counseled the emperor; three major counselors *(dainagon)*, who participated in national administration and provided political advice; and three imperial advisers *(sangi)*. These officials were assisted by a staff of major comptrollers *(daiben)* and their subordinate bureaucrats. Under the Grand Council were six ministries with specific responsibilities: Civil Affairs (Minbushō), Finance (Ōkurashō), Military Affairs (Hyōbushō), Justice (Gyōbushō), Imperial Household (Kunaishō), and Foreign Affairs (Gaimushō). The head of each ministry was given the title of *kyō*, or "lord" (à la "first lord of foreign affairs," and so forth); immediately under him was a vice-minister called *taifu*. As before, imperial courtiers were named heads of ministries; but samurai bureaucrats, appointed to offices below that level, held real authority.

With this reform, the Dajōkan in fact became the highest state organ, one that had the power to control each ministry. This was a significant change from the previous state of affairs, when "Grand Council of State" did not refer to an organism with specific powers or functions but amounted to no more than a general term for the various government offices. That such bodies as the Taishōin (the new name for the Office of Petitions), the Shūgiin (the new name for the Kōgisho, the legislative body that had been opened on 1869.3.7), the Daigakkō (University), and the Danjōdai (Board of Censors) should have been directly subordinated to the Grand Council was a clear indication of the effort to strengthen central authority. From the standpoint of the history of education, it should be noted that this reform first established the University as the institution which would administer education under the centralized authority of the state.

In reforms at the regional level, domains *(han)* were made regional administrative units under the same administrative rules as metropolitan districts *(fu)* and prefectures *(ken)*. The personnel consisted of a governor; regular and provisional, upper and lower counselors; senior and junior local administrative officials; and scriveners. The duties of the *han* governors were somewhat different from those of the governors of *fu* and *ken*, who were to "administer the registers of Shinto shrines and of the population; nourish the people; spread enlightenment; inculcate proper habits; collect taxes; supervise labor on public works; determine rewards and punishments; and keep the registers of Buddhist priests and nuns" throughout their areas of responsibility. The *han* governors in addition had military authority in their areas of administration; rendition had not deprived the domains of their military forces. All the regional governors in effect ruled over the people, as administrative control over religion, education, taxation, and jurisdiction was concentrated in their hands.[84]

This table of organization established the University as the state's paramount educational institution and at the same time its highest agency for the management of education. Its administration consisted of a curator *(bettō)*, a senior and a junior deputy, three regular senior assistants and three regular junior assistants as well as an unspecified number of probationary appointees to those posts, and three senior and nine junior clerks. The professoriate was made up of eight professors at full rank, ten at intermediate rank, and junior professors of no set number. There were also academic assistants, dormitory prefects, and interns; each of these positions had higher, intermediate, and lower grades. In addition, there was a whole hierarchy of scriveners, copyists, and other school functionaries and factotums.[85]

Along with serving as the head of the Daigakkō, the curator also functioned as a minister of education. His duties were to "supervise the University and the two institutions of higher learning, the Medical School (Igakkō) with its attached hospital and the Kaisei Gakkō; oversee the preparation of a national history; and administer all educational policies of the metropolitan districts, domains, and prefectures." He was, in short, endowed with the highest responsibility for educational administration in the country's major subdivisions. After rendition, however, the daimyo were made governors of their former domains; and as long as their military authority was recognized, the nation could not be said to be under centralized rule. Similarly, the Daigakkō was formally charged with the oversight of education in a centralized administrative system, but its actual authority did not extend to the domains or even to the metropolitan districts and the prefectures. Real authority over education and culture was in the hands of regional administrators, who carried out educational policies from independent positions that they considered appropriate to their respective constituencies. The University was unable to intercede or to override them.

Because the members of the Inspectorate of Schools from Kyoto and Tokyo worked on completing "University Regulations" *(Daigakkō kisoku)* at about the same time as the rendition process was moving forward, they were able to envision a nationally unified social structure.[86] For this reason, their "University Regulations" would establish a concept of university education that was very different from the educational assumptions of the "College Statutes," the proxy Court College, the Imperial Studies Institute, the Chinese Studies Institute, the Shōhei Gakkō, and so on. That is, rather than the particularistic values of Shintoism or Confucianism, they were able to implant more universalistic values at the core of the concept of a university.

The idea of a national education that was incorporated in "University Regulations" rested on universal principles asserted on the authority of the emperor, as is apparent from the ringing final phrases of the document's preamble: "We shall not deviate from the principles of the Charter Oath, which has called forth a grand Imperial foundation. Base customs of the past shall be abandoned. Universal justice will be followed. Knowledge shall be sought throughout the world. This shall be the scope of the university."[87] The underlying rationale accorded with political agenda, in particular with the pursuit of national unification (which had led to the rendition of the domanial registers) and with the promotion of the state's interest in overseas developments (for which national unification provided the essential platform). More specifically, it involved overcoming the conflict between traditional and Western values, facilitating the acceptance of Western learning and technology, and nurturing men of talent regardless of their social origins. Consequently, this idea of a university, although it invoked universal values, did not imply that education would be depoliticized; rather, it meant that education would be subordinated to the new political realities of the postrendition period.

The Way was the organizing principle adopted by the Inspectorate of

Schools in response to these agenda. This educational concept was based on the Confucian—in particular, the Chu Hsi Neo-Confucian—notion of principle *(ri)*. The school superintendents sought, however, to render the idea of the Way as expansive and as abstract as possible, in the process linking it with Western values. "University Regulations" had the following to say about this concept:[88]

> The Way is Substance. Omnipresent in matter, it is everlasting in time. It is so great that nothing is beyond its bounds, so minuscule that it contains nothing within. It is the natural principle of heaven and earth, and human beings are all endowed with it. Its essentials are manifest in the Three Principal Relationships and the Five Abiding Virtues. Its workings are evident in government, in jurisprudence, and in education. Its details are recorded in Japanese, in Chinese, and in Western books. Schools expound upon the Way, spread knowledge, and cultivate talent and virtue in order to present its practical application to the nation. The import of the Shinto scriptures and the national classics is reverence for the Imperial Way and elucidation of the national polity, and these ought to be considered the goal of the Imperial Land and the first duty of the scholar. The Chinese way of ruling the nation and pacifying the realm through the ethics of filial piety and fraternal affection, as also Western teachings of progress and enlightenment through study based on rational investigation—these, too, are informed with the Way. They shall be culled assiduously and taught in our school.

The Way was not any particular set of values singled out as an absolute, whether it be the nativism of Shinto or Kokugaku, the ethics of Confucianism, or Western scientific rationalism. Rather, it was "the natural principle of heaven and earth," an essential value that inhered in each of these three distinct ideologies. The goals of the University were to clarify this Way that permeated the realms of nature, ethics, and politics; to analyze it through an inquiry into various distinct value systems; to master it; and to establish it as the foundation for knowledge, virtue, and talent. That was the purport of "University Regulations."

On the basis of this traditional yet comprehensive view of education, the Inspectorate was able to organize a university structure with the Shōhei Gakkō as the Main University College (Daigaku Honkō) and the Kaisei Gakkō and the Medical School as the branches. Despite the universalist principles enunciated in "University Regulations," however, studies in "the Shinto scriptures and the native classics"—"the first duty of the scholar"—were given priority over Confucianism and Western learning. Symbolically, the Confucian *sekiten* ceremony was done away with; instead, the Shinto gods of learning enshrined by the "College Statutes" were to be worshiped. The strong insistence of the school superintendents from Kyoto was not the only cause of the primacy allotted Shinto. An even weightier reason was the University's inability to conduct itself freely within the official structure that confined it. We must not forget that it was not only the country's paramount educational institution but also the head office of educational administration in an imperial state where an Office of Shinto Affairs occupied the apex of the governmental structure.

From 1869.7.4, the University was closed while a detailed schedule of courses was worked out. On 7.18 a conference was held on the syllabus of instruction, and here, too, the influence of nativist scholars was great. Shinto and nativist classics were given prominence in the basic reading classes that were to precede the specialized curriculum. The sinologists remained strongly dissatisfied, but it was decided to open the school on 8.5. Not unexpectedly, the antagonisms between Shinto and nativist scholars on the one hand and scholars of Chinese studies on the other not only intensified with the school's opening but came to involve students of sinology. The dormitory prefect, supporting the views of the students under his charge, went so far as announcing his resignation. Shintoists and nativists formed a solid block, uniting behind the University commissioner *(Daigakkō goyōgakari)*, Maruyama Sakura (1840–1899). Attacks on the Chinese faction intensified. It became difficult to conduct educational activities.[89]

The curator—no longer Yamanouchi Yōdō but the former daimyo of Fukui, Matsudaira Yoshinaga (1828–1880)—knew that his own authority did not suffice to resolve the matter. Hence Yoshinaga sought refuge in "public opinion." On 1869.9.12 he submitted a brief, four-item syllabus to the consideration of the Shūgiin. The syllabus contained the following three Shintoist-nativist propositions: "*Item.* Reverence for the gods of learning of the Imperial Land; abolition of the *sekiten* ceremony at the temple of Confucius. *Item.* Abolition of the reading of Chinese texts; sole use of Japanese books. . . . *Item.* Mencius' theory of status and moral obligations contradicts our national polity, and will not be permitted in the regular curriculum. There is no objection to the private study of Mencius."[90] Of the 197 representatives from the various domains in the Shūgiin, only the representative from Karatsu supported Yoshinaga's proposals, undermining any authority the curator might have had for persuading the Chinese faction of the justice of the nativist view.

That same month Katō Yūrin (1809–1884), the head of the Chinese Studies Institute in Kyoto, submitted his "Memorial on Higher and Lower Schools" to the curator. It criticized "University Regulations" on three points. First was the provision of rudimentary reading classes within the university. "The mix of higher and lower learning in one place would create utter confusion," Katō observed, and would jeopardize the university's future. He saw much of positive value in the educational institutions of feudal times, where members of elite families were trained for leadership from childhood, on the basis of their highborn pedigree. The place of those institutions, he thought, should be taken by another type of elite educational system, an integrated structure where the talented would progress from primary school to university. He wanted such a system established quickly. Katō's second complaint was only natural for a Confucianist: he objected to the special place allotted Shinto and opposed the abolition of Confucian ceremonies. His third criticism was the lack of entrance criteria based on birth. In Katō's view, the "mixture of samurai and commoners" would prevent a real leadership class from being formed.[91]

Matsudaira Yoshinaga was now confronted with a difficult set of circumstances. In view of his inability to resolve the great hostility between the Shinto-nativists and the Chinese studies faction, educational activities at the University had become impossible. His resort to public opinion through the Shūgiin as a means of settling the conflict had merely elicited opposition to the nativist proposals. He could not ignore Katō's view that an articulated sequence from lower to higher education was needed. The curator had no choice but to close down the University temporarily.

More than ever, there was a need to emphasize universalistic approaches to education and to direct serious attention to Western studies. This fundamental reform would be undertaken under the direction of the Grand Council of State from 1869.9 to 1870.2. On 15 January 1870, the Dajōkan decreed that the name of the Daigakkō would be changed to Daigaku, effective immediately. The rudimentary reading course was closed; "the metropolitan government will provide elementary schools" instead. Externs would no longer be permitted; regular students who were in lodgings would be transferred to dormitories on campus currently occupied by the auditors. Naturally, "enrollment will decrease, as no new students will be admitted to the dormitories."[92] The order was couched in general terms to avoid angering either the nativist clique or the sinologist faction, but the intent to reduce the scale of the institution was clear. The real objective was to move away from the Main College of the Daigakkō with its traditional Sino-Japanese curriculum and give priority to institutions that offered Western studies, that is, the Kaisei Gakkō and the Medical School.

When the Grand Council three days later amplified its previous order

regarding the transformation of the Daigakkō into the Daigaku by spec-
ifying that the Kaisei Gakkō "will be called Daigaku Nankō and the
Medical Institute will be called Daigaku Tōkō," that was not merely a
change in nomenclature. Rather, it meant that the two institutions were
elevated from their former status of branch schools to that of constituent faculties—South University College and East University College, respectively. The very next day, the council ordered the Daigaku to weed
out teachers of Shinto, Kokugaku, and Chinese studies by a student
vote.[93] The Dajōkan was trying to apply to the University a policy that
had succeeded in reducing the number of superfluous officials through a
vote taken by selected upper-echelon leaders in 1869.5.

The university reacted to these initiatives of the Grand Council of
State by revising its statutes. In 1870.2, it issued a document called
"University Regulations and Intermediate and Elementary School Regulations" *(Daigaku kisoku oyobi chūshōgaku kisoku)*.[94] The active participation of Western studies scholars in drawing up this new statute is
apparent. The document is composed of sections on substance, structure, recruitment, examinations, fees, and curriculum. Substance *(gakutai)* refers to the university's philosophy of education. Its organizing
principle, while heir to the universalistic concept of the Way from the
earlier *Daigakkō kisoku,* differed from it in two important ways. First,
the priority given to studies of Shinto and the native classics, which had
generated hostility among teachers and students of sinology, was eliminated. Second, some basic distinctions were adjusted. In the earlier
"University Regulations," learning for the purpose of clarifying the
Way had been separated by country of origin into Chinese "ethics of
filial piety and fraternal affection" and Western "teachings of progress
and enlightenment through study based on rational investigation."
Subjective opinions regarding those countries were therefore likely to
determine the value attributed to a field of learning. The new statute,
however, would have distinctions to be made solely according to the
category of learning, whether it be "filial piety and fraternal affection,"
"ruling the nation and pacifying the realm," or "study based on rational investigation." Through the "study of both domestic and foreign
knowledge, the one supplementing the other," learning would be freed
from irrational and emotional national biases; it would achieve the
Charter Oath's ideal to seek knowledge throughout the world. Clearly
manifested here is the University's intention to expand the concept of
the Way to its limits. Shown also is the desire to shed Shinto ideology,
no longer a political essential in the training of officials.

The section entitled "Structure" prescribed that "one university shall
be established in the imperial capital, and intermediate and elementary

schools founded in each metropolitan district, domain, and prefecture. All the intermediate and elementary schools shall follow the regulations set out by the University. Their duty is to nourish talent, diffuse knowledge, and serve the needs of the state." Clearly, elementary, intermediate, and higher schools were to be organized into a single-track sequence designed for training officials. It is also clear from this section of the new regulations that the elementary schools were not intended to be part of a scheme of universal education, as envisioned by Kido and others, but rather as the entry level to an elite educational sequence. "Methods of Recruitment" described how the government would attract the nation's best talent to the University from throughout the country. Because the institution's goal was the training of officials and the cultivation of talent for the state, the tuition would of course be paid from public funds. Under "School Fees," it was explained that the necessary revenues would be raised by assessing the metropolitan districts, domains, and prefectures according to their annual tax base measured by putative rice yield.

The final section, "Curriculum," contained noteworthy innovations. Whereas the *Daigakkō kisoku* had addressed only the Main College, the new regulations not only treated the Honkō, South College, and East College together but structured their curriculum with reference to the educational programs of Western universities. Prepared by scholars of Western studies, the program of studies was divided into five areas: religion, law, science, medicine, and literature. These were known as the Five University Courses. Religion (made up of two sections, Shinto studies and moral training) and most of the literary course (Chinese classical texts and composition) were located in the Main University College. Literature's philosophy section was at the South University College, as were law and science. Instruction in medicine took place at the East University College.

The collateral "Intermediate and Elementary School Regulations" set out guidelines for institutions established for advancing students to the University. The subjects to be covered in elementary schools (for ages 8–15) included reading, penmanship, arithmetic, and geography, as well as material introductory to that covered in the Five University Courses. The curriculum of the intermediate schools (for ages 16–22) consisted of more specialized study of the material taught in those courses. These regulations put the basic goals of the educational sequence discussed above into concrete form.

Since the new regulations provided for a single University, which would be located in Tokyo, plans for similar facilities in Kyoto were abandoned. In 1869.9 the Grand Council used the pretext of preparations for the foundation of a university in Kyoto to order the Rusukan (the Caretaker Office that looked after the emperor's affairs in Kyoto while he himself was away) to close down both of Kyoto's institutes of higher studies, the Kōgakusho and the Kangakusho. Toward the end of the year, on 11.22, there followed orders to stop work on the Kyoto college until school regulations were issued. Opposition from the two Kyoto schools was so fierce, however, that even the Rusukan could not ignore it. Taking advantage of its special position as an imperial agency, the Caretaker Office at the beginning of 1870 (in Meiji 2.12) merged the two schools, creating Kyōto Daigakkō. The Grand Council of State in Tokyo, which had supported scaling down the traditionalist Main University College as a goal of its reform program, was not pleased with the establishment of a similar institution in Kyoto and repeatedly directed that control over it be transferred to the Kyoto metropolitan government. The Rusukan's head official, Nakamikado Tsuneyuki (1821–1891), warned Sanjō and Iwakura that agitation by extremist groups was practically unavoidable, now that the emperor was not expected to return to Kyoto. Matters would only be made worse if, on top of that, a university were not maintained in that city. For that reason, the Caretaker Office would continue to support the school. In the end, however, control over the institution was transferred to the Kyoto metropolitan government—leading to a fate that resembled the closing of the Daigaku Honkō in Tokyo, to be discussed below.

The government, in short, abandoned the idea of setting up two universities, one in the East and another in the West. As the sole agency for the central regulation of educational authority, the University in Tokyo by itself came to guide educational policy for regional administrations throughout the country. The "University Regulations and Intermediate and Elementary School Regulations" had been written with this intent, as noted previously. The goal, clearly spelled out under "Structure," was training elites and cultivating officials for government service.

These goals conflicted with those of elementary schools already established by the metropolitan and prefectural governments, which were primarily institutions for training the children of commoners. Their objectives were set out in the "Administrative Procedures for Metropolitan Districts and Prefectures" of 1869.2.5 as follows: "The main task is to have the pupils learn reading, writing, and arithmetic. They shall be equipped to write petitions and letters, to keep records, and to use the abacus. In occasional lectures they shall also be informed about the national polity and contemporary conditions, teaching them loyalty to the emperor and filial piety and inculcating proper habits."[95]

Although the "University Regulations and Intermediate and Elemen-

ns" went beyond the traditional educational prac-
s' social status, they did not fully transcend the
f samurai and commoner, and thus they differed
niversal education conceived by Itō and others.
iversity requested the Grand Council of State to
ns" printed and distributed to the metropolitan
prefectures as soon as possible. The University's
h a request was its interest in assuming control
y nationwide. The Dajōkan, however, decided
inting out that the new statutes were not yet in
self. A copy would, however, be kept on file and
one interested.[96] It is possible that the Grand
by concern about whether or not the "Regula-
amural disputes, but the real reason for its
ere. Although rendition had formally united the
at as yet lacked effective control over the
hey would ignore the "Regulations."
dered the registers of their domains, they saw
ad wielded as feudal lords diminish even
d domanial governors. In their place, their
ji) attained preponderance in the domains,
gaining the trust of the lower-pedigreed segment of the samurai class
and taking control of *han* politics as, indeed, they controlled the *han*
military. In the prominent southwestern domains, this trend was evident
early on; it was one of the things that made rendition appear feasible in
the first instance. After the surrender of the domanial registers, the
trend gained strength and spread nationwide. In the *han,* reforms were
spearheaded by samurai who took full advantage of the central government's calls for change, using them in the pursuit of their own local
interests while at the same time resisting the government's centralist initiatives. In such domains pressures to create an educational system to
train talent for the central government were defied.

Consequently, the "University Regulations and Intermediate and Elementary School Regulations" were implemented only at the University.
As the Grand Council had feared, they not only proved ineffective in
resolving intercollegial disputes but aggravated the conflict between
university authorities on the one hand and the nativist and Chinese
studies groups on the other. Paradoxically, this exacerbation was caused
by the attempt to reconcile the nativists and the sinologists by sur-
mounting their differences with a newly articulated philosophy of the
Way and a curriculum that stressed learning based on Western humanism, social models, and natural science. But the attack on the "Regula-

tions" was not just an internal university matter. Outsiders such as Tamamatsu Misao and Yano Harumichi were dissatisfied at the rejection of plans for a nativist-Shintoist college in Kyoto and were critical of the University's treatment of what to them were fundamentals. "The Way is Substance, et cetera, is all that the Regulations have to say," they complained to the Dajōkan in 1870.4. "There is nothing in them about the provenance of the Grand Principle of the Imperial Way."[97] Tamamatsu and Yano objected to a concept of university education unrelated to Shinto and nativist ideas; they maintained that the "Regulations" ran counter to the emperor's originally expressed "sacred intentions" regarding the establishment of a university. Such assaults by Shintoists from the outside, however, no longer posed serious difficulties for government and university authorities.

The real problem was the combined attack from within the University by both the nativist and the sinologist groups. On 5.4 they submitted a jointly signed criticism of the "Regulations" to the curator. Rather than state directly that Western studies were overemphasized, they intimated that the curriculum was too formalistic, too regulated, and too piecemeal in its approach as a result of its reliance on Western models. These defects would dampen the students' ardor for learning, they complained; and they blamed school officials for cooperating with Western studies scholars in the organization of such a curriculum. They insisted that such officials be dismissed and that teachers who could organize a curriculum on the basis of specialized educational expertise be authorized to revise the *Daigaku kisoku oyobi chūshōgaku kisoku*.[98]

Ideological opposition was not the only issue confronting university authorities. They had no means to resolve the bitter disputes between the bureaucrats who ran school offices and the teachers who opposed bureaucratic management of education. Students joined with faculty to criticize the authorities; one difficulty was piled upon another at the Main University College. As a result, university officers requested that the Dajōkan take appropriate action, but the response was that the council would not change the regulations because it could not countenance pressure from either faculty or students. Then, on 1870.7.12, the Grand Council announced that the Main College "will be temporarily closed for purposes of reform" and followed that announcement up the next day by informing all the institution's employees below the rank of *hannin* (junior official) that they were discharged. The students were told to leave the dormitories.[99] Curator Matsudaira Yoshinaga submitted his resignation.

A memorial drafted by Fujino Kainan (1826–1888) on behalf of numerous faculty and students blamed the crisis on school officials such as Senior Assistant Kusuda Hideyo (1830–1906), who had conspired, it was alleged, with Western studies scholars in the South University College and tried to establish school regulations based on Western models. According to Fujino, Matsudaira Yoshinaga as well as his senior deputy, Akizuki Tanetatsu, and University Commissioner Tanaka Fujimaro (1845–1909) agreed with those officials; Junior Deputy Shima Yoshitake (1822–1874) and Junior Councillor Soejima Taneomi agreed with the Japanists and the sinologists. When the latter group sought to impeach the curator, orders were suddenly given to close the Daigaku Honkō.[100]

The school's closing had broader implications. Since the restoration of imperial sovereignty, the Meiji government had been involved in a struggle with the remnants of the old *bakuhan* conglomerate's political power structure. As it sought to strengthen its own power vis-à-vis the domains, the government insistently emphasized that its role in bringing about the imperial restoration gave it transcendent authority over the *han*. To translate that claim into actual ascendency was the government's prime task, and its educational policy was subordinated to that political requirement.

Until the time of the rendition of the domanial registers, however, the government pursued its goal in an inconsistent manner. On the one hand, it sought to check the inimical relics of the old order by establishing metropolitan districts and prefectures under the central government's direct control. On the other, it scarcely laid a finger on the domains of the hereditary feudal lords, thereby not only confirming their existence but leaving them free to develop their particularistic local interests. After rendition, the Meiji government reorganized the feudal system, denied the hereditary lords their ability to pursue particularistic policies, integrated the domains into a network of regional administration under central control, and at least in form created a system of centralized authority. But the social structure remained essentially feudalistic, as though the *han* of the Tokugawa period had remained in existence. Whatever the Meiji government's ultimate objective may have been, it had yet to alter the essence of the old feudal structure. Even as the government sought to negate the political power of the remnants of the old regime by abstracting their authority to itself, it was compromising with them. It sought their dissolution on the installment plan.

That was the basic political posture adopted by the Meiji government down to the time when the Main University College was closed.

As the government's educational policy was determined by its political stance, the educational system of this period was formed within the wider context of two contradictory forces intermingling—the drive toward centralized political authority on the one hand, and the inertia of the feudal social structure on the other. The period's guiding educational principle did nothing to resolve such contradictions but sought to rationalize them, reflecting the government's intention of compromising with the domains. In the shifts from Shintoism to Confucianism and then to the Imperial Way, it was not so much traditional Confucian values per se as their inherent universality that mattered. A process of trial and error marked the approaches to the Way and led to the adoption of a universalistic value system. But no matter how universalistic the adopted principle was, tradition could not be completely denied—learning that was entirely free from traditional values could not be tolerated, and foreign values could not be accepted fully. That much is apparent from the fierce hostility between the nativist and Chinese scholars on the one hand and university officials and Western scholars on the other, the immediate cause of the closing of the Daigaku Honkō.

Education at the Main College sought to embrace new values while holding on to the traditional value system. Even as it attempted to rationalize the contradictions of this heterogeneity, it could not divorce itself from its old feudal roots. Although status limitations were removed from the entrance criteria of the Daigaku Honkō, it remained confined within the traditional limits of a school that nourished members of the ruling class. Abolishing status merely meant enlarging the pool from which bureaucrats would be pumped into government offices. The prevalent idea of education was quite different from the notion of universal education conceived early on by Kido and Itō. That is why the image of the moral character of the feudal leader remained so firmly entrenched as the paragon of talent and virtue in both sets of university regulations, the earlier *Daigakkō kisoku* and the later *Daigaku kisoku oyobi chūshōgaku kisoku*.

If the Meiji government had wanted to continue supporting the development of a centralized polity on the social foundations of feudalism, it would have been unnecessary to close the Main College because of "internal disputes." Regardless of the reasons given, the Grand Council of State took this measure because a desire to change the government's previous political posture had by then clearly evolved among the leadership. They were newly determined to pursue centralization without any longer compromising with the remnants of feudalism. In that

ıe Daigaku Honkō symbolized the end of a distinct
e Meiji state.

and the Road to the Abolition of the Domains

ıe government's equipping itself with the means to
er control had at length developed by 1870.7, and
ed the leadership's resolve to act. Two of the sev-
visioned may be considered of prime importance.
ıng the two most powerful domains, Satsuma and
e actively with the government. The second postu-
were ripe for the Dajōkan to be strengthened and
ɔ be reformed. A plan for the fundamental restruc-
ʻalled "National Foundation Policy,"[101] was pre-
ʌ the aid of Etō Shinpei and was submitted to the
ıte in 1870.8. The leadership's intent to establish a
authority was concretely manifested in this plan,
the abolition of the domains.

ins under control, a problem that had long plagued
ɛs, did not necessarily involve dealing with each and
han. The heart of the matter was the refractoriness
of Satsuma and Chōshū. Particularly nettlesome was the hostility of
Satsuma. Satsuma's war hero, Saigō Takamori, refused the official rank
the government sought to confer upon him and explained his motive to
Ōkubo by saying that he wanted to spare the government some embarrassment: "If someone from our domain who does not hold an official
position is bestowed a title by the imperial government, he becomes the
government's man. Now it is plain to see that should such a thing happen, some muddlehead is sure to complain, 'Satsuma men don't take
orders from the central government!' and the like. It would be inexcus-
able on my part to start something like that."[102] One may infer from
this the degree of antipathy toward the government shared by most
Satsuma samurai. It is important to note that the other domains paid
close attention to Satsuma and were greatly influenced by events there.
Even Chōshū, where anti-Satsuma sensibilities were intense, could not
afford to ignore its rival. But if the cooperation of these two great
domains could be secured, it would not be so difficult for the government to gain ascendency over all the others. Ōkubo and Kido directed
their close attention to the pursuit of this goal. Sizing up the postrendition state of affairs, they concluded that they could bolster the government's ability to deal with the domains by prevailing on the daimyo of

Satsuma and Chōshū and on Saigō Takamori not only to support the government but to take part in its highest councils. Among other things, that would secure the backing of Sat-Chō's military might for the government. The real problem remained Satsuma. If only Satsuma could be won over, Chōshū—they knew—was sure to follow.

In January 1870, having worked out their plans in detail, Ōkubo and Kido returned to their respective domains to carry them out. Kido, however, found his hands full with the problem of settling a military mutiny that had broken out in Chōshū and had no time for anything else, no matter how important. His plans opposed by Shimazu Hisamitsu (1817–1887), the patriarch of the Satsuma daimyo family, Ōkubo, too, was unsuccessful. Kido returned to Tokyo in 1870.3, Ōkubo two months later. Having failed to maneuver either Satsuma or Chōshū into compliance with their designs, they temporarily abandoned the policy of reliance upon those two domains; instead, they redoubled their efforts to strengthen the government internally, not an easy task. In 1870.7, however, Ōkubo was presented with another opportunity to stage the Satsuma scenario. Saigō Takamori had been appointed senior councillor of the Satsuma domain, thereby being put in a position to control policy making in that *han*. The next month, his younger brother, Saigō Tsugumichi (1843–1902), returned from Europe. If Takamori's influence sufficed to sway opinion in Satsuma (and Ōkubo was well aware that it did), and if Tsugumichi's influence could in turn be used to align Takamori behind the central government, then there was a chance that Ōkubo's plan might yet succeed. With Iwakura's and Kido's agreement, Ōkubo met with Tokyo's Satsuma contingent, entered into negotiations, and was rewarded with success when Satsuma, Chōshū, and Tosa dispatched troops to Tokyo, propping up the central government and creating a precondition for abolishing the domains.

Ōkubo took a major step toward dealing with the second main issue, that of uniting the leadership and strengthening the Dajōkan, when he carried out the separation of the Ministries of Civil Affairs and Finance. This action, taken by Ōkubo upon consulting with Iwakura and obtaining Kido's as well as Ōkuma Shigenobu's agreement, forestalled the danger of a serious split in the leadership group.

The Ministry of Civil Affairs had been established in the administrative reform of 1869.7.8. On the principle that there was a close if not inseparable relationship between civil administration and financial affairs, appointments of its top personnel were conflated with those of the Ministry of Finance, so that on 8.12 the offices of first lord or minister *(kyō)*, vice-minister *(taifu)*, and deputy vice-minister *(shō)* came to be held concurrently in the two ministries. As a result, Civil Affairs and

Finance were in effect consubstantiated and turned into an extremely strong organism that overwhelmed other ministries and put the Grand Council of State into disarray. In the interest of fortifying the government's unity and the Dajōkan's authority, it became necessary to separate the two ministries.

Matsudaira Yoshinaga was first lord of civil affairs and of finance throughout the time the two ministries were united, but Vice-Minister Ōkuma Shigenobu (1838–1922) actually ran them. With the collaboration of Deputy Vice-Minister Itō Hirobumi, Ōkuma recruited intellectuals into government service and created a new bureaucratic cadre to staff offices, such as the Revision Bureau (Kaiseikyoku), that he set up within the Ministry of Civil Affairs. Wide-ranging new policies were drafted in this bureau, which laid down a radically capitalist line in civil administration, finance, transportation, trade, industry, communications, and public works. The new cadre of intellectuals constituted the most progressive group in the government. Not even the Dajōkan could restrain them or regulate the unified financial policy that they pushed forward in their zeal to build a methodical foundation for their vision of a "prosperous country"; and they themselves paid no heed to the conflict they provoked with those in other ministries or regional administrations who held more realistic or conservative views.

Kido backed the aggressive policies of these "new intellectuals." Ōkubo, however, was anxious lest they cause the government to split and the Grand Council to lose its authority; he thought of ways to bridle the group. Behind Ōkubo was Iwakura; Sanjō stood behind Kido. The situation clearly had the makings of a crisis that might lead to conflict at the Dajōkan's topmost level. In short, the government was threatened with disintegration.

On his way back to Satsuma at the beginning of 1870, Ōkubo encountered complaints from regional administrators in the Kansai area about the high-handedness of the Civil Affairs–Finance bureaucrats. Anguishing over the best means to settle the problem, Ōkubo shared his concerns with Imperial Adviser Soejima Taneomi: "None of the actions of the Ministry of Finance, in particular, expresses the people's will. . . . Hence Civil Affairs and Finance are sure to lose the confidence of the public. Without the people's trust, they cannot function. I find this lamentable and reprehensible in the extreme."[103] Little wonder that after the failure of his maneuvers in Satsuma, Ōkubo made strengthening the government's internal cohesion his highest priority. "It is essential to make Civil Affairs and Finance clearly separate and distinct from each other," he wrote in his 1870.3 memorandum on reforming governmental institutions.[104] Iwakura, needless to say, was of the same opinion. The problem was taken up several times by the Grand Council of State, but was difficult to resolve as long as Sanjō and Kido were against the proposal. Finally, Ōkubo and like-minded imperial advisers used the tactic of mass resignations to force a decision on Iwakura, who persuaded Kido and Ōkuma to go along. The two ministries were successfully separated on 1870.7.10, reinforcing the leadership's expectations that the Dajōkan could be reformed and the government strengthened.

In 1870.8, now that the conditions essential for reform were satisfied, Iwakura put his "National Foundation Policy" before the Dajōkan with a certain degree of confidence. Iwakura's vision of a national political structure clearly encompassed the abolition of the domains. *To establish a county-prefecture system, the policy should be revealed gradually* was the heading of one section of his argument. The advantages of such a system over the feudal order were patent: "With the realm's strength consolidated and with authority equalized in the realm, imperial prestige will flourish and the untold millions enjoy the blessings of security. The county-prefecture system is the means for bringing about this desired end, as it shall concentrate a multitude of forces and a multitude of energies into one. As we seek to compete with the overseas powers, we have no better choice than to rely on this system."[105] Its adoption, Iwakura noted, would make it possible to unify and standardize not only administration, finance, and the military but also education.

How did these political changes and proposals affect educational policy? The Grand Council's order postponing the circulation of the "University Regulations and Intermediate and Elementary School Regulations" came at a time when the government was beset by the problems that have just been described. The decision to close the Main University College on 1870.7.12 came immediately after the resolution of the thorny issue of the two ministries and was carried out because the Dajōkan did not want to jeopardize its newly restored authority by yielding to the faculty's and the students' pressure for revised regulations.

The "National Foundation Policy" that Iwakura presented the very next month before the Grand Council contained important educational provisions, ones more concrete and elaborate than the brief proposal he had submitted to the Dajōkan on 1868.10.21; and it ought to be reiterated that this elaboration was made possible by his placing the abolition of the domains on the agenda. *Middle and primary schools should be established throughout the realm and put under the control of the University* was the heading of another section. "To make sure that none of the people in the realm is left uneducated, two or three middle schools and several dozen or a hundred primary schools must be built in each metropolitan district, domain, and prefecture. The development of human wisdom is unquestionably the way to lead the nation to civilization, wealth, and power. The elimination of ignorance among the people of the realm cannot, however, be accomplished in one day. If we do not build now, we shall regret it later. Hence we should have an education ordinance distributed quickly throughout the metropolitan districts, domains, and prefectures and should place schooling under the University's supervision."[106]

The educational views advanced by Kido and Itō immediately after the pacification of Tōhoku and premised on the domains' rendition of their registers—that is, the notion of a school system with universal education at its base—now came to be uttered by the government's topmost leadership, who had targeted those same domains for abolition. The "University Regulations and Intermediate and Elementary School Regulations," drawn up on the framework of an elite education based on talent and suffused with the moralistic ideology of the leadership class, had clearly become a thing of the past, as far as the government was concerned. But the government still had to recruit talent into its service. For all its unremitting pursuit of centralization and its rejection of compromise with the domains, the government nonetheless faced considerable difficulties in planning to construct schools on a scale sufficient for universal education; more to the point, it was not in the position to wait until talented leaders were trained under such a design. But the talent that was wanted now was completely different from the former model of a leader firmly grounded in the Way. Rather, the government sought the bureaucrat armed with the Western knowledge and the technician equipped with the Western skills needed to build a modern nation. For that reason, the South University College and East University College remained open under the Grand Council's direct supervision, and educational activities continued there even after the Main College was closed.

Regulations were issued for the Daigaku Nankō in the Intercalary Tenth Month of 1870. The educational goals set out in their preamble show that a pragmatism bearing no relation to the concept of the Way was the school's guiding spirit: "Beginning with [foreign-language] pronunciation and conversation, students shall gradually expand their studies to diverse areas. A broad range of subjects shall be taught comprehensively and accurately, so that practical skills can be fully developed." Even so, paragraph 3 of the regulations insisted that "since it is essential for students to devote themselves to Japanese and Chinese

studies in their early years, no one who has not reached the age of sixteen shall be admitted."[107] That the formation of character through
Japanese and Chinese studies should have been included among the pre-
requisites for entrance to the South University College attenuated its air
of rigid pragmatism. Immediately after the abolition of the domains,
however, a Ministry of Education (Monbushō) was created, the official
names of the Daigaku Nankō and Daigaku Tōkō were changed to
Nankō and Tōkō—South College and East College—respectively, the
schools were placed under the new ministry's jurisdiction, and the statutes of South College were revised again soon after (on 1871.10.18).
This time, no educational goals were set down, and entrance requirements were reduced to the statement "Those seeking admission to studies
will be rejected if they lack a general ability to read ordinary official
and private documents."[108] Moral formation was no longer mentioned.

What the Ministry of Education expected of South College immediately after the abolition of the domains was the cultivation of talent useful for building an industrial nation and a state governed by laws. That
is why the ministry wanted above all to do away with Confucian education and why it put all its efforts into law, science, and technology. Its
rationale is presented with a flourish in the proposal submitted to the
Grand Council of State in 1871.11 by Senior Assistant of Education
Tanaka Fujimaro:[109]

> What clarifies the law and details regulations? That is the canonical duty
> of the state. Who prospers the industrial arts and masters rational knowl-
> edge? That is the all-important obligation of mankind. In our Imperial
> Land, however, studies remain afflicted by the lingering bad habits of
> sinology, whose essence is rhetorical flourish on the outside and sophistry
> inside. Time that should be utilized profitably is squandered frivolously,
> and the self-indulgent, far from wasting only their own lives, even seduce
> others into imitating them. . . . The harmful influence released thereby
> upon the public is by no means small. Unless this very day they are res-
> cued from their evil ways, these good-for-nothings are sure to disgrace the
> nation. And there is no means to effect this rescue other than hiring many
> teachers of specialized subjects and vigorously supporting specialist
> schools.

As politics progressed from the latter half of 1870 toward the abolition of the domains, the goals of the University were freed from a concept of the Way that had been accommodated to the feudal structure.
Whatever learning, knowledge, or technology best suited the purpose of
building a new nation could henceforth be introduced into the curriculum. In a sense, that was progress. But the reverse of the coin was that

the idea of the university was never brought into question at all, and that utilitarianism and a belief in science for the sake of technology—divested of any ideal character—came to be considered the totality of a university education. As a result, the University's subordination to politics was made even more definite.

To reject Confucian values may have been natural, as the goal was the formation of a modern state. The consequence, however, was a rejection of ideology in general, and higher education was accordingly deprived of a platform for criticizing contemporary politics. On display here is the precipitate nature of the priority that the government habitually gave to political considerations in matters relating to education, a practice it pursued not only in the period of policy changes during the early Meiji years but throughout the process of educational modernization in Japan. This was the origin of the continuing dominance of value-neutral science and technology in Japanese universities.

As soon as the political commitment to abolish the domains was made clear, a movement against any compromise with feudalism became apparent in the educational policy of the University, which had made the cultivation of talent its mission. The education of the populace, however, was left to the administrations of metropolitan districts, domains, and prefectures and neglected by the central government. Even though the road to the abolition of the domains had already been laid down, the *han* still remained in existence. The government had little choice but to defer intervention in their educational policies. Hence the plan of providing universal education for the sake of the intellectual advancement of the nation's entire populace was not realized until the enactment of the Education Order (Gakusei) by the Ministry of Education in the Eighth Month of 1872.

3

Local Politics and the Development of Secondary Education in the Early Meiji Period
The Case of Kōchi Prefecture

Translated by Albert Craig

The most prominent characteristic of secondary education in Kōchi Prefecture during the early Meiji period was that it developed in close conjunction with prefectural politics. Kōchi was distinguished neither by economic nor by cultural conditions conducive to modern progress in education, and politics therefore became the principal factor that fostered its growth there. Indeed, it is possible, although no doubt extreme, to say that the early history of secondary education in this prefecture cannot be fully understood without taking into account the vicissitudes of a broad configuration of political forces.

The mention of politics in Kōchi in the early Meiji decades immediately brings to mind the popular-rights movement led by the Risshisha (Self-Help Society); what was truly important, however, was not so much that movement per se as its confrontation with the advocates of the prerogatives of the state. A careful view further reveals that the situation in Kōchi, a prefecture made up exclusively of the former Tosa domain *(han)*,[1] was shaped by that domain's political conflicts. That is to say, rivalries which had existed among various factions of Tosa *han* were renewed in Kōchi Prefecture; they were carried forward, virtually unchanged, from the late Tokugawa into the early Meiji period. Significantly, those revived factions not only formed separate political associations but also founded their own educational facilities. The associations viewed education as part and parcel of political activity, a way of inculcating the young men gathered under their aegis with a particular set of political ideas. But it is also true that the associations greatly advanced the cause of education in Kōchi. Indeed, they remained so active in this field until the late 1870s that the prefecture could neither disregard them nor develop an independent secondary school policy without them. Only after about 1879 would the prefectural authorities be able to put forward educational programs that transcended the influence of these political groups.

Until the 1880s, in other words, secondary education in Kōchi Prefecture remained directly tied to the history of the Tosa domain, in particular to the period of reform at the end of the Tokugawa era. It was unable to sever its links with politics. Yet education's very inability to separate itself from its past led to its future development. To trace the course of that evolution is the aim of this essay, which will pursue its inquiry from two viewpoints—official policy and the educational programs of nongovernmental political associations.

Educational Policy in the Tosa Domain at the End of the Tokugawa Period and the Beginning of the Meiji Era

Although Japan's central government promulgated an Education Order (Gakusei) in the Eighth Month of 1872, Kōchi Prefecture followed an independent course, one based on schooling programs initiated by Tosa *han*, until new official and private educational organizations were established in 1874. Kōchi could afford to do so because Tosa's educational policy had been modernized in response to the political and social changes of the Meiji Restoration. By the time the domains were abolished in 1871, Tosa was already pursuing the cultivation of talent appropriate to a new era.

To understand secondary education in Kōchi during the early Meiji period, it is therefore necessary to go back to the prerestoration years. Until they were abolished in July 1873, institutions founded under the Tosa domain continued to provide education to young men in Kōchi Prefecture.[2] These institutions included the Chidōkan (the domain school that was to become central to secondary education in the prefecture) as well as the Kyōritsu Gakkō and Gyūkō Gakkō (which taught the foreign languages then much in demand) and their antecedents, the Translation Bureau and the Medicine Bureau of the Kaiseikan, the central office that governed domain enterprises. Why were these schools able to respond so well to the new age? To start with the conclusion, it was because among the factions that competed for leadership in Tosa *han* during the tumultuous prerestoration years—the Reformists (Kaimeiha), the Imperial Loyalists (Kinnōha), and the Conservatives (Shukyūha)—

the Reformist group was the one that took the lead in formulating the domain's educational policy. The Imperial Loyalist and Conservative factions did not play important roles. The progressive, open nature of education in the prefecture in the early Meiji period was, so to speak, a legacy of the enlightened aspects of domain politics.

What political forces encouraged the establishment of educational institutions in Tosa in the late Tokugawa era, and under what circumstances did those institutions come into being? In seeking answers to these questions, let us first look at the domain school called Chidōkan and the schools created as subordinate parts of county governments in the course of the Ansei Reform. This reform was undertaken by the Tokugawa shogunate and the various domains in reaction to the foreign threat that was brought home when a U.S. Navy squadron commanded by Commodore Matthew Perry intruded on Japan in 1853.6. Unlike the Tenpō Reform of the previous decade, which had been conservative in nature, the Ansei Reform in Tosa took shape as a positive policy to enrich the domain and strengthen its military. Under its fifteenth daimyo, Yamanouchi Yōdō (Yamanouchi Toyoshige; 1827–1872; r. 1849–1859), the domain had become more open and progressive, not least because it had obtained graphic information about the West from Nakahama Manjirō (1827–1898), a native of Tosa who had been cast away at sea and taken to America after his rescue. Made aware of the urgent need for maritime defense, the daimyo responded by seeking to strengthen his domain's military preparedness. The necessary first step, he determined, would be to reform its finances and its political system. Accordingly, Yōdō promoted Yoshida Tōyō (1816–1862) to the office of inspector general *(ōmetsuke)* in 1853.7, appointed him to the post of chief administrator *(shiokiyaku)* four months later, and proceeded to carry out a series of changes based on Yoshida's counsel.

In terms of Yoshida Tōyō's career, the Ansei Reform in Tosa can be divided into two periods: from his appointment as the domain's chief administrator in 1853.11 to 1854.6, when he was dismissed for some reason; and from his reinstatement in 1858.1 to 1862.4, when he came to a violent end. During the first period, the reform was decidedly military in character. It sought to meet such objectives as the establishment of a maritime defense system within Tosa and the encouragement of cannon production; its main feature, however, was the effort to centralize power as a precondition for putting the domain's other reform policies into effect. During the second period, the reform became more open and enlightened. It came to involve such projects as studies of the feasibility of overseas trade, the purchase of naval vessels, and plans for maritime exploration and colonization; in addition, the domain undertook the overhaul of the administrative system that was needed if those positive measures were to be realized. Schools were appended to county governments as an expression of the domain's centralizing policy in the first phase of reform. The Chidōkan was founded in the effort to link education with the reform of the administrative structure during the second phase.

The effort to centralize power in the domain began with reform on the county level at the very end of 1853 and the beginning of 1854.[3] Six of Tosa's seven counties had hitherto been under the office of the magistrate of counties *(kōri bugyō)* in the domain's capital, Kōchi (Hata County was the sole exception). If direct control over distant provincial areas was its objective, that office had clearly failed to serve its purpose. To repair the apparent deficiencies of this organizational design, county government offices were newly created to strengthen the domain's control over the more remote districts of Aki, Kagami, and Takaoka; only the three counties of Tosa, Agawa, and Nagaoka were left under the magistrate in the castle town. At the same time, each county government was made responsible for maritime defense in its area. With these measures, Yoshida Tōyō intended to effect a more consolidated military system throughout the domain. Next, he sought to institute a draft, planning to make commoners under the jurisdiction of each county administrator subject to military service. To ensure that the rural samurai *(gōshi)* and soldiers from the common classes would be properly educated, moreover, schools attached to the county offices were to be created in Aki, Kagami, Takaoka, and Hata. These plans were implemented by 1854.9.

The purpose of these new county schools is evident from their curriculum: they were intended to give military training and to inculcate their students with an awareness of the need for the domain to be prepared militarily. For example, Tano Gakkō, the school of Aki County, taught classical Chinese, calligraphy, archery, gunnery, jujitsu, and military drill; four of the six classes listed in its lesson plan were devoted to military instruction.[4] Enrollment was restricted to soldiers drawn from the rural samurai and the common classes, groups that had previously been denied entrance into domain schools. In other words, these new institutions were not open to commoners in general. Nevertheless, the very fact of their being brought into existence, even if it was done in the face of a foreign threat, is an indication of the progressive nature of Yoshida Tōyō's reform program. (Under the Education Order of 1872, they would become public primary schools.)

Yoshida's measures were put into effect one after the other, but he himself was dismissed from his position in 1854.6. For three and a half years, he would be denied any part in formulating policy. This did not mean, however, that the domain's reforms were suspended altogether. On the contrary, a great earthquake that hit Tosa in 1854.11 strengthened the daimyo's resolve to push ahead. At the time of the earthquake, Yamanouchi Yōdō was in Edo, fulfilling his alternate year residence requirement in the shogunal capital; in 1855.2, having received the shogunate's permission to cut short his stay, he returned to his home province to deliver an address to his vassals. He exhorted them to repay their debt to previous generations of daimyo, stressed the need for strict standards in selecting men for office, and dwelt on the question of what kind of learning nourished talent. According to an endorsement signed jointly by the house elders, Yōdō also spelled out his reform policy in specific terms: seven years of retrenchment, the simplification of the samurai rank and status system during that period, and permission for samurai to live on their fiefs so that they would become self-sufficient.[5] The views on learning expressed in the daimyo's lecture were later incorporated in the educational philosophy of the domain school:[6]

> Learning is indispensable. Without it, even a person of ability will accomplish little. I have neither ability nor learning, so I am always at a loss. Because of this I wish all the more for you to study. But if your interests are solely belletristic, if all you do is concentrate on stylistic refinements and curlicues and think that is learning—then, even if you memorize a thousand books, it will be of no avail. In any event, I want you to study bearing in mind the domain's well-being and policies that may help it. In the martial arts, until now, you have each boasted of your own school and spoken ill of the others, the tendency being most pronounced in the case of schools of firearms. This is because you have not properly understood the Way of Arms. Henceforth all of you, the spearman and the swordsman alike, must stop trying to ferret out the esoteric secrets of one school alone and start devoting yourselves to schools other than your own. You must pursue the military arts for the sake of their practical use.

Yōdō, who held firmly to his views, for a while personally took the lead in domain reform. In 1858.1, however, he decided to enter the arena of national politics by intervening in the controversy over the shogunal succession. It was at this juncture that he reappointed Yoshida Tōyō and put him in charge of the reform program in Tosa.

Yoshida's second term in office was marked by manifold reforms in the realms of financial affairs and of politics. He sought to foster enterprises and drew up plans for overseas trade under domain management. In 1861.9 he proposed the purchase of warships, with an eye to increasing not only the domain's military preparedness but also its commercial strength through navigational training and voyages to distant waters. These farsighted schemes laid the ground for the future enterprises of the Kaiseikan (a central office to be discussed shortly, established in 1865).[7] Yoshida reformed the samurai rank and status system over the opposition of members of the Yamanouchi house and of highly placed samurai families. He simplified its complicated structure by reducing it to five ranks, with the intention of opening the way for the promotion of talent from a wider pool of samurai. Linked to his plans for promoting talent was a series of educational reforms, which included the equalization of educational opportunities for all samurai and the abolition of the system under which the headships of families specializing in the various civil and martial arts were inherited.

One of Yoshida Tōyō's most noteworthy achievements after he was put back in office was the foundation of a new domain school, brought about with Yōdō's full approval in the face of opposition from the entrenched conservative faction. This school, which was opened on 1862.4.5 under the name of Bunbukan—it was renamed the Chidōkan in 1865.7—was a great improvement over the institution that it replaced. The former domain school, called Kōjukan, had been founded in 1759 by the eighth daimyo of Tosa, Yamanouchi Toyonobu (1709–1768; r. from 1725). Only the civil arts were taught there; the martial arts were left to specialist families. In the Kōjukan, moreover, learning essentially meant the study of Chu Hsi Confucianism; in particular, the Nangaku school of Yamazaki Ansai (1618–1682) alone was considered orthodox, while other interpretations were eschewed. To be sure, history and national studies (Kokugaku) were offered as well.[8] The school adhered to the old feudal custom of admitting only the sons of upper samurai but allowed the students to study with individual experts as they wished; attendance was not obligatory.

In comparison to this conservative establishment, the new Bunbukan was markedly progressive. As its name implies, it taught both the civil *(bun)* and the martial arts *(bu)*. Its doors were open to lower samurai and to soldiers who were commoners; indeed, attendance was obligatory for all samurai from ages sixteen to thirty-nine. The curriculum was divided into Chinese studies, medicine, military studies, Western studies, and astronomy. "No equipment was lacking," and there were target ranges, riding grounds, and practice halls for the martial arts. In a departure from the former practice, both upper and lower samurai were admitted "without any distinction, as education was considered obligatory and encompassing all the people." This new policy "ensured the future of those who completed the course of studies; it cleared the way for appointment to office on the basis of talent." The instructional staff was chosen "from superior scholars at large," without regard for the old system of inherited family headships. "For its time it was a bold step."[9]

The objective of the Bunbukan was to educate the domain's future leaders in keeping with the daimyo's injunction to "study bearing in mind the domain's well-being and policies that may help it." No doubt Yoshida Tōyō hoped to stand at the head of a leadership group educated at the school in a reformist spirit; but only three days after the school's opening, on the evening of 1862.4.8, he was assassinated by rural samurai belonging to the Imperial Loyalist faction.

At the time, as noted earlier, three main political factions existed in Tosa. They had emerged, according to Tani Tateki (given name sometimes read as Kanjō; 1837–1911), in response to the forced retirement of the daimyo, Yamanouchi Yōdō, at the time of the Great Ansei Purge in 1859.[10] The proshogunate, conservative Shukyūha, composed of upper-ranking samurai families, was one such party. Another was the progressive and reformist Kaimeiha led by Yoshida Tōyō. The third, the proemperor Kinnōha, was further divided into a rural samurai group and a castle town samurai faction. The rural group, headed by Takechi Zuizan (1829–1865), was formed in 1861.8 to protest the shogunate's punishment of Yōdō; linking up with extremist samurai in Satsuma and Chōshū, it hoped to overturn the shogunate by force. The castle town group, which was led by Konami Gorō (1812–1882), Hirai Zennojō (1803–1865), and Itagaki Taisuke (1837–1919), called for "expelling the foreigners" but did not yet, in the early 1860s, advocate the shogunate's overthrow. Until the restoration of imperial rule, the Loyalist party remained hampered by the tensions between castle town samurai and rural samurai.

In terms of the changing fortunes of these three factions, the six years from 1862, when Yoshida Tōyō was assassinated, to 1868, when Tosa troops fought on the imperial government's side in the Boshin Civil War, can be divided into three periods. The first period lasted until the suppression of Takechi Zuizan's faction about the Ninth Month of 1863. During this time, Takechi's group extended its activities to Kyoto, where it consorted with extremists from Satsuma and Chōshū. As a consequence of this group's participation in national politics, the Imperial Loyalists' power in the domain increased. Their growing influence became evident in the educational sphere when Yamanouchi Toyoyoshi (1815–1863), on whom the faction pinned its hopes, was named head of the Bunbukan three weeks after its opening; Toyoyoshi, an uncle to Yōdō and to the regnant daimyo Yamanouchi Toyonori (1846–1886; r. 1859–1869), was known for his proimperial intellectual sympathies.

The Loyalists' plans for the domain school were outlined in a memorial titled "A Decision regarding the Unification of Politics and Education" and presented to the inspector general of Tosa on 1862.8.28; the document proposed that the propagation of proemperor and antiforeign thought was of the essence in education.[11]

The second period lasted from the fall of 1863 until about the Sixth or Seventh Month of 1867, when Itagaki Taisuke, Tani Tateki, and other Imperial Loyalists signed a secret pact with Satsuma with the objective of forming an alignment of forces to overthrow the shogunate. During this period, the domain's government was in the main run by members of the Conservative and the Reformist factions. Yamanouchi Yōdō (ostensibly retired from affairs, but still the power to be reckoned with in the domain) consistently supported the latter group. His sympathies were revealed clearly in the Intercalary Fifth Month of 1865, when he had one of Yoshida Tōyō's followers, Gotō Shōjirō (1838–1897), named to the post of councillor *(sansei)* and charged with the continuation of Yoshida's policies. Five months later, Gotō was appointed the founding director of an office to be called the Kaiseikan and entrusted with the management of its enterprises. Unhappy over this move, the Conservative and Imperial Loyalist factions argued that the project was not so pressing. Yōdō, however, refused to heed their criticism and insisted that it proceed.

The Kaiseikan, which was opened in 1866.2, gave instruction in naval science, including navigation and gunnery. That was, however, far from its sole purpose. Rather, it was made up of eleven bureaus: the Kashokkyoku or Commodities Bureau, which supervised the sale of domain products and the purchase of ships; the Gunkankyoku, which oversaw the domain's naval and commercial vessels; the Kangyōkyoku, which guided and controlled domain enterprises; the Chūhōkyoku, which controlled the manufacture of firearms; Hogeikyoku (whaling); Zeikakyoku (customs); Kōzankyoku (mining); Chūsenkyoku (mint); Kayakkyoku (gunpowder); Ikyoku (medicine); and Yakkyoku (translation). Agencies of the Commodities Bureau were, moreover, established in Osaka and Nagasaki.[12]

The Kaiseikan's multiple mission was intended to strengthen the domain's naval power, develop Tosa's natural resources, promote trade, adopt new knowledge, and foster education. In short, as Yōdō stressed in a talk that he gave in 1866.4 to enlighten the opposition, it was designed to put a policy of enriching the country and strengthening the military *(fukoku kyōhei)* in effect in Tosa. Yōdō spoke passionately on the need for his project to succeed. Scorning the very notion of "mere profit," he maintained that his policies were not "calculated for the enrichment and power of my own house" but were rather "the way for the protection of our Imperial Land." In one breath, he threatened the elite of Tosa with punishment if they failed in the work of the Kaiseikan; in the next, he entreated them to expand their vision and "think of new ideas."[13]

The Translation Bureau and the Medicine Bureau of the Kaiseikan were among the Reformists' more enduring contributions to education. Although the two bureaus underwent several changes, they and their successor institutions served until the beginning of 1874 as the center for instruction in foreign languages in Tosa. Their heritage provided the basis for a foreign language school attached to the prefectural teachers' training institution, Tōya Gakkō, which was founded in February 1874. The returned castaway Nakahama Manjirō and his students served along with Hosokawa Junjirō (1834–1923) as instructors at the Translation Bureau, which was assigned the mission "to teach the learning of the countries of the West." Appointed to the Medicine Bureau "for those who wished to study Western medicine" were Yokoyama Kaoru, Yamakawa Tomomasu, and others. The Nagasaki agency of the commercially oriented Commodities Bureau is said to have made purchases of Western-language books and European printing type for these institutes. Any Tosa samurai seeking entrance was admitted, and students at the Kaiseikan were excused from study at the Chidōkan.[14] Given this choice, those from lower-ranking samurai families apparently tended to prefer the Western-oriented course, while those from the upper ranks chose the Chidōkan.[15]

The third distinct period in the history of the three factions was the half year from 1867.6 to 1868.1, when Tosa troops left to join the campaign against the shogunate. During this phase two large political movements stood in opposition to one another. One, led by the Reformist Gotō Shōjirō, advocated the return of sovereignty to the emperor. The other was composed of the more vehement Imperial Loyalists, led by Itagaki Taisuke and Tani Tateki, who sought the overthrow of the shogunate by military force. In contrast to the former group, which mainly plotted in Kyoto and looked to Yōdō for guidance, Itagaki's party mustered followers in Tosa and had the regnant daimyo Yamanouchi Toyonori for their titular head. The latter group sought, with considerable success, to dominate the domain's military affairs. Itagaki was appointed chief inspector and superintendent general of the Tosa military, while Tani was made a military commissioner, appointed officer in charge of training in Arms and Arts, and concurrently assigned to the Chidōkan; together, the two succeeded in getting the daimyo himself to write a directive concerning military reform, which was promulgated in

1867.7. The Imperial Loyalists may have taken the initiative in military matters, but their rivals for influence in Tosa appeared to win the day when Gotō was singled out for promotion to the office of intendant (*bugyōshoku*), assuming this high ministerial post in the domain on 1867.10.11, three days before the shogun formally returned sovereignty to the emperor. The changes that Gotō decided to carry out in the domain government with Yōdō's support included military reform, which accordingly became the joint concern of both the Reformists and the Imperial Loyalists. Itagaki was named the troop commander and entrusted with the training of the military.

Military reform impinged on the educational sphere as drill came to take precedence over studies at the Chidōkan. In 1867.10 it was proclaimed that "the present course of studies is to be dissolved. The students will be permitted to pursue either the civil or the martial arts, but all are required to undergo military drill." According to new rules announced two months later, academic studies were to be confined to part of the morning; the rest of the school day was for military training. Military science, martial arts, and horsemanship occupied the even days; odd days were devoted almost entirely to drills. When the Boshin Civil War began and Tosa troops left for the front on 1868.1.13, it was decided that "in view of the crisis at hand, all studies in the civil and the martial arts are to be suspended and the students made to pursue drill exclusively." By the Fourth or Fifth Month of the same year, however, the schedule was amended to include some classes with an academic content in the morning.[16]

Apart from this third period—that is, the months immediately before and after the return of sovereignty to the emperor—educational policy in Tosa was determined almost exclusively by the Reformist faction, accurately reflecting the openness of politics at the time. But the movement to strengthen the domain's military continued even after the beginning of the Meiji era, and formal educational activity was forced to remain in abeyance until about 1870.10, when the Reformists again took control.

With the end of the civil war in the autumn of 1868, political leadership in Tosa had reverted to the Imperial Loyalist faction, which had distinguished itself in battle. In recognition of his military valor, Itagaki was appointed house elder and commander in chief of the army; Tani was made a councillor. In 1869.1, the four domains of Satsuma, Chōshū, Tosa, and Hizen submitted a joint petition requesting permission to render their domanial registers to the throne, in other words, turn over administrative control over the *han* to the new central government. As Tani was to write later, however, even the four domains that took the initiative in petitioning to surrender their domain registers "seemed in doubt" whether rendition could be effected.[17] In private, he says, all felt that the country would once again be swept in turmoil. Anticipating further disturbances, government leaders in Tosa held firm to their policy of a strong military and formed a league of all the domains in Shikoku—with Tosa at its head—against the day of renewed conflict.

Tosa sought to lay the ground for the expansion of its military forces by carrying out several reforms meant to replenish the domain's coffers, which had been depleted by the civil war of 1868. In 1869.3 the domain reduced the rank stipends of samurai across the board, forbade the three house elders to live on their fiefs, and reorganized the system of offices. At the time the Office for Military Affairs was dominated by Imperial Loyalists, such as Executive Officer Fukao Tanba, Councillor Tani Tateki, and Councillor Kataoka Kenkichi (1843–1903). Officials in Tosa, however, had to contend with the fact that since Gotō and Itagaki were already employed at the central government as co-opted officials *(chōshi)*—Itagaki in addition acted as the supervisor general of Tosa's military affairs—domain policy on the highest level was being determined in Tokyo. In 1869.4 Tani was therefore sent to Tokyo as liaison officer for the domain's military. There he conferred with Itagaki on a basic policy for military reform, and the two decided to adopt the French model. They invited Numa Morikazu (1844–1890), who had been the commander of the defunct shogunate's training unit, to come to Tosa as instructor in charge of military training. Numa declined the invitation, recommending in his place three officers formerly under his command, but agreed instead to become an English-language instructor at the Kan'yō Gakkō (School of Sinology and Western Studies), which was opened in 1869.10 at the Tosa domain's estate in Tokyo.

Accompanied by the three officers, Tani returned to Tosa in 1869.10 and immediately set to work by ordering drill grounds and barracks to be enlarged. The next month, a local militia *(gōhei)* system was laid down and a Naval Bureau (Kaigunkyoku) established. Organized in 1870 were eight infantry battalions, one artillery battalion, one troop of cavalry, and one company of engineers; this constituted a standing force of 6,600 regulars and 2,400 reserves. (A foreign military specialist, the French officer Fréderic Emile Antoine, was hired on a one-year contract in 1870.6 with a view to improving the artillery.) Maintaining such an epoch-making modern military establishment required a corresponding reorganization of the domain. Above all, the domain's financial base had to be strengthened. The domain's leadership group, headed by Itagaki and Gotō, accordingly decided to enact reforms of the system of samurai rankings and hereditary stipends. The reforms, which were in line with policies adopted by the central government upon the rendition of the domanial registers, took place in the last two months of 1869; in this regard, as in others, Tosa was ahead of other domains. The traditional, minutely graded order was abolished, and a system with three upper samurai (or "gentry," *shizoku*) and three lower samurai (or "soldier," *sotsuzoku*) ranks took its place. Hereditary stipends were eliminated in favor of salaried offices, thus creating a modern bureaucracy. In January 1870 (Meiji 2.12), the domain office made the following official announcement:[18]

> 1. In accord with the principle of human equality, the exclusive right of samurai to civil and military posts is dissolved, and they shall revert to the same status as everyone else in the domain.
>
> 2. Both samurai and commoners shall be appointed to official and military posts and remunerated with salaries.
>
> 3. Hereditary samurai stipends shall be commuted to bonds, such bonds being regarded as family property which may be divided, bought, and sold; over the years, they may also be redeemed by the government.

In keeping with these decisions, Tosa *han* in 1870.1 promulgated a Government Charter (Seitaisho) that not only established a new domain bureaucracy but also expressed some noteworthy intentions regarding public opinion and education. The charter stipulated that a Planning and Accounting Bureau (Takushikyoku) and a Military Affairs Bureau (Gunmukyoku) be placed directly under the Governor's Office (Chijifu). It also provided for a Legislative Bureau (Gikyoku) and the establishment of schools, "in order that public opinion be widely considered and the way opened for education."[19] It was at this juncture that the Chidōkan was given both educational and administrative functions, being placed, along with the Legislative Bureau, under the Governor's Office. All officials staffing the school were, however, given concurrent appointments in the Military Affairs Bureau, thus ensuring the continued dominance of that bureau over education.

As noted earlier, Tosa embarked on its large-scale program of armament and administrative reform in anticipation of renewed warfare on the national level. Its administrative reforms look as though they were carried out in cooperation with the government in Tokyo. Its military effort, however, was in complete disregard of the directive issued by the central government in 1870.3, which restricted each domain's forces to one platoon (sixty men) per 10,000 *koku* of productive capacity.[20] When one considers that Tosa's nine thousand men exceeded this legal limit more than six times, it becomes obvious that the spirit that moved the domain's reforms was not so much the desire to accommodate the government as the ambition to achieve autonomy through military self-strengthening. In 1869 and 1870, the domain's leaders—the Reformists Gotō Shōjirō and Fukuoka Takachika (1835–1919), no less than Itagaki, Kataoka, and Tani of the Imperial Loyalist faction—were united in their determination to strengthen Tosa against all foreseeable developments. But whereas the Reformists thought in terms of the domain as a whole and wanted to build hospitals, bring schools up to date, and form a popular assembly, the Loyalists stressed military strength. The two factions inevitably came into conflict, particularly on financial questions.

The Reformists thought that the domain's finances could be based on the various enterprises of the Kaiseikan and that the Osaka branch of the Commodities Bureau should be used as an agency for expanding trade. In tune with their policy, the domain issued paper notes as its resource for buying up local products, paying the salaries of bureaucrats and military officers, building hospitals, and defraying the costs of other projects. To issue paper notes was no doubt unavoidable if the domain was to cope with the exploding costs of armament and to finance the commutation of fiefs and stipends. Despite the vigor of the Kaiseikan's commercial enterprises, however, there was not enough income to cover these expenses. The domain's response was to print more money, leading to inflation and hardship for its people.

Tani, Kataoka, and other Imperial Loyalists at the Military Affairs Bureau opposed the mercantilist policies of the Reformist faction and called for greater military funding; at the same time, however, they advocated self-sufficiency through retrenchment. They wanted to dismiss superfluous officials, abolish paper money, and prohibit the sale of the domain's products outside its borders; they were against salaried offices (that is, they were for hereditary stipends); and they opposed all projects that did not fill a pressing need (defined by them). In 1870.8 Tani drew up an eighteen-article memorandum on reform and submitted it to the domain's government in the name of the Military Affairs Bureau. In the reaction that followed, the domain dissolved the rural militia, reinstituted the stipend system, and suspended the construction of a new official residence for the retired daimyo, not to speak of work on a Western-style, brick hospital on a hill overlooking the Gyūkō River.[21] The Reformist administration had allotted 3,000,000 ryō in newly issued paper notes to the pursuit of such plans—wastrel schemes that had to be stopped, in Loyalist eyes.

On hearing of these developments, Gotō and Itagaki hurried back to Tosa. Itagaki's stay in Tokyo had made him cognizant of the national political situation. He had abandoned his earlier, narrowly promilitary outlook and had become critical of the reactionary policies of the Military Affairs Bureau. From about the time of the rendition of the domanial registers in 1869.6, he had come to agree with Gotō's progressive views. He, too, had become a Reformist.

In 1870.10, Itagaki and his group succeeded in getting Tani dismissed from his post at the Military Affairs Bureau and put a stop to his policies. Appointing himself grand councillor (*daisanji*, the highest position in the domain under the daimyo-governor), Itagaki named his sympathizers Fukuoka Takachika, Kataoka Kenkichi, and Hayashi Yūzō (1842–1921) to the next highest post (provisional grand councillor), packing the domain office with men belonging to the Reformist faction. Over the next three months, he carried out a reform that was even more thoroughgoing than its predecessor in seeking to institutionalize and extend socially the "principle of human equality" enunciated in the proclamation of January 1870. Ranks within the samurai class were abolished, and samurai were permitted to enter any occupation, a right not given them previously. The unicameral Legislative Bureau, with a membership made up of *shizoku,* was changed to a bicameral institution with an upper chamber of gentry and a lower chamber of commoners.[22] The cooperation of samurai and commoners, who were now legally equal, was meant to ensure greater wealth and power for the domain. A declaration issued by the domain government at the beginning of 1871 (in Meiji 3.12) describes the reforms' guiding principles as follows:[23]

> In truth, a human being is the most precious of all living things in this world. A human being is endowed with a mysterious and wondrous nature, possessing both knowledge and skill. For one who is the lord of creation, it goes without saying, there can be no such distinctions as those between samurai, farmer, artisan or merchant, rich or poor, higher or lower classes. . . . It is to be hoped, therefore, that the civil and military functions which have principally been the responsibility of the samurai will now be extended to all of the populace; that the truth will be disseminated that humans, regardless of class, are precious beings; that everyone will strive for the acquisition of knowledge and skills; that the right to freedom and independence will be granted to all; and that all will be allowed to achieve their goals and objectives. . . . To instruct the people in the way of civilization and enlightenment, to build schools everywhere and foster education, to seek wealth and power, to urge samurai and commoner alike to vie with one another in exerting themselves, to change the old customs profoundly, and to engage in new enterprises—are these not truly the great and pressing tasks at hand?

Initiated with such a display of enlightened principles, the reforms were in actuality conceived as preconditions for the domain's military strengthening. A mere month after this declaration was issued, however, the military policy of the *han* changed completely, from expansion to reduction. In 1871.1, the Tosa leaders were informed of the central government's decision to form an Imperial Guard (Shinpei) and decided to contribute troops to that unit, taking this step in anticipation of the eventual abolition of the domains. Tani was recalled to the Military Affairs Bureau in 1871.4, this time not to expand the military but to disband regular domain troops and organize a contingent to serve in the Imperial Guard. A month later, he established the Tosa Military School (Tosa Heigakkō) to train officers for that unit. The school continued to operate even after the domains were in fact abolished in 1871.7, but as Tani began working at the central government's Ministry of Military Affairs (Hyōbushō) and realized that his fears about a renewed outbreak of civil strife were unfounded, he closed it down at the beginning of 1872 (in Meiji 4.12). He then saw to it that its students were admitted to the Military Academy (Heigakuryō) in Tokyo or to the Kainan Shijuku, a private school of the Yamanouchi family that will be discussed presently. From the Fourth Month of 1871, in short, armament was abandoned and enlightenment made the domain's primary concern. That meant a reform of the educational system.

Educational reform began with the Chidōkan, the domain school that had been turned into an institution for military training at the time of the civil war of 1868. In 1870.10 all required courses were temporarily abolished, and the students were told to study whatever they wished. On 10.23 the domain set down the guidelines for a basic curriculum of six courses—writing, arithmetic, reading, Confucian classics, outline of history, and elementary Western studies—and issued the following statement urging the establishment of private schools: "Since the education of the people cannot be put off for even a day, both samurai and commoners alike are to apply themselves daily to studies, and private schools may teach what they wish."[24] This encouragement of private schools was merely a temporary measure for the period during which the Chidōkan was preparing to reopen.

When the domain school did reopen three months later, in 1871.1, its curriculum included four important innovations. The parallel pursuit of Arms and Arts was abolished, the school being redefined as a place for academic concerns. The course of studies was divided into two: a combination of Japanese or, rather, "Imperial" and Chinese studies *(kōkangaku)* was one sequence and Western studies *(yōgaku)* the other —the choice being left to the student. Third, and most important, commoners were admitted for the first time. Finally, the section that taught reading was detached from the domain school proper, with a view to setting up primary schools in the near future, and admission to the Chidōkan was "limited to those who had completed the basic reading course." This measure in effect constituted the Chidōkan as a secondary school that would teach specialized subjects.

Of the courses taught there, Western studies merit special attention, as their content was not simply language study. As stated in the official pronouncement of 1871.1.24, "a translation section has been established" so that students could study Western learning through translations and works by Japanese authors.[25] Ueki Emori (1857–1892), who studied in this section about 1872, listed the following in the journal of the books he had read: *Yochishi ryaku* and *Kon'yo zushiki,* two works on world geography; *Bankoku gaishi* (An Outline of the Histories of the Myriad Nations); *Enkakushi ryaku,* another historical work; *Eishi* (A History of England); *Seiyō jijō* (Conditions in the West) by Fukuzawa Yukichi (1835–1901); and *Seiyō kakkoku seisui kyōjaku ichiran-hyō* (A Look at the Rise and Fall and Relative Strength of Western Nations) by Katō Hiroyuki (1836–1916).[26] When one considers that the seeds of Ueki's later intellectual activities were sown here, one senses how effective the course of Western studies in the Chidōkan's translation section must have been in opening the eyes of young men to the outer world.

The educational objective set down in the school regulations of the Chidōkan was to "foster talent for the nation and maintain social morals."[27] The school's aim was to train the future elite of both domain and nation, but it offered everyone in the domain, whether samurai or commoner, the opportunity to obtain that elite education. Hence it may be said that it carried out the ideology expressed in the declaration on reform, rights, and responsibilities issued by the domain in Meiji 3.12.

Another notable aspect of the domain's enlightened educational policies was the emphasis placed on language study. Foreign languages continued to be taught even while the Chidōkan was temporarily closed; indeed, the domain stepped up its efforts to hire foreign instructors, offering handsome salaries. In 1870.4, the Englishman Thomas Hellyer was given a three-year contract as a language teacher (Hellyer was accompanied by his wife, who also participated in instruction "zealously"); three months later, Frederick Adrian Meyer, another Englishman, accepted a year's contract as "Head Instructor for Languages and European Education" at 200 dollars a month.[28] In the Intercalary Tenth Month of 1870, instruction was begun for samurai sons from ages twelve to seventeen. The classes were given at two schools that had no connections with the Chidōkan but had grown out of the Translation Bureau and the Medicine Bureau of the Kaiseikan. One of the schools was called the Inhinkan, the new name given to the Kaiseikan in 1870.1. The other was the Yōgakkō (School of Western Studies); it was originally intended to be a preparatory school for the medical course of the Gyūkō Hospital, one of the "inessential" projects temporarily halted by Tani's retrenchment policy. The latter school was established at a Zen temple on the banks of the Gyūkō River.[29] Specific information about the Inhinkan is unavailable, but it is known that the Gyūkō Yōgakkō employed Yokoyama Kaoru (a former instructor at the old Medicine Bureau), Kume Hiroyuki, and Mori Shunkichi (a Keiō graduate), along with the Hellyers. Among the students were Toyokawa Ryōhei (1852–1920), Sengoku Mitsugu (1857–1931), Yamamoto Yukihiko (1844–1913), Chigami Kiyoomi (1856–1916), and Fukutomi Takasue. It is unclear whether or not the two schools were like the Chidōkan and admitted commoners.

The effects of the vigorous effort made by Tosa *han* from the end of 1870 to foster secondary education continued even after the abolition of the domains and the institution of the prefectural system in 1871.7. Schools operated by the former regime were neither reduced in size nor abolished altogether in Kōchi, as they were in many of the defunct domains. As a result of the efforts of members of the Itagaki faction, such as Hayashi Yūzō, who became prefectural councillor *(sanji)* in 1871.11, and Iwasaki Nagatake, who was to become provisional governor *(gonrei)* of the prefecture in 1872.11, the Chidōkan remained in operation until 1872.7 and the language schools until February 1874.

To be sure, the prefectural authorities developed a new educational policy of their own. Under Kōchi Prefecture, the emphasis shifted to the establishment of primary schools. This change, too, was related to the old domain's policies, which had envisioned the establishment of primary schools that would prepare students to enter the Chidōkan (constituted a secondary school) and the language schools. In line with that vision, the domain school's former reading section was in 1871.8 reopened as the Kōchi Primary School Attached to the Chidōkan.[30] On 1871.4.18, shortly before it was to go out of existence, Tosa *han* had issued an official notice concerning village schools *(gōgakkō)*, ordering cooperatives to be formed and village schools to be established in "areas where people can assemble easily." In 1872.2, Kōchi Prefecture promulgated new regulations for primary schools, establishing regular *(seisoku)* and simplified *(hensoku)* Western language courses in primary schools and forming an elementary section *(yōnenka)* at the Kōchi Primary

School. The village schools were also designated elementary sections. In this manner, education within the prefecture was put on a single track: village school, primary school, and Chidōkan. It was a matter of individual choice whether one went on from the elementary to the primary course, but entrance from the primary course into the Chidōkan was by examination. Thus Kōchi Prefecture went about developing a modern educational system, one that would encompass the entire populace, on the basis of the old Tosa domain's educational system and from the standpoint of its own educational plan.

In 1872.7, however, financial problems and pressure from the central government forced the prefecture to close the Chidōkan, and its unique school system crumbled. Earlier, in 1871.11, the Finance Ministry had issued a statement to all prefectures: "Now that the edict establishing prefectural governments has been promulgated, regulations regarding schools in each jurisdiction shall be forthcoming. In the meantime, educational facilities are to be managed not with government funds but with moneys raised from interested parties." The prefectural authorities of Kōchi responded that they were reluctant to close down schools, however temporarily; educational fund-raising, moreover, took time, and so they wanted to "continue as before until prospects are clearer." Resisting the central government's pressure, the prefecture continued to support the Chidōkan, but it could not prevail against superior power. After several fruitless exchanges of letters with Tokyo, Kōchi closed the old domain school.[31]

Although the Chidōkan was forced to shut its doors, the prefecture did its utmost to continue the foreign-language program, however reduced in scale. It combined the two extant language schools into an institution called the Kyōritsu Gakkō and asked the two English teachers to stay on. Soon enough, the central government interfered with this new school, too. The policy pursued by the Ministry of Education after the promulgation of the Education Order of 1872 disavowed secondary schools founded by the former domains. Hence the ministry ordered the Kyōritsu Gakkō abolished, on the pretext that its course of studies was "neither that of a university nor that of a secondary school," and the school was temporarily closed in May 1873. Even then, the prefecture tried to resuscitate it. Although the Hellyers were let go, Meyer was retained, and the school—renamed the Kyōritsu Gakusha in the desire to comply with the ministry's "Regulations concerning Foreign Language Schools" of April 1873—continued its educational activities, though on a reduced scale. In January 1874, the Ministry of Education ordered Kōchi Prefecture to close the institution once and for all, since its "willful opening was improper."[32] Thus the educational institutions developed in the Tosa domain's enlightened and progressive tradition since the Ansei Reforms were at last condemned to extinction.

The Formation of Political Associations and Secondary Education

With the closing of the Kyōritsu Gakusha in 1874, the secondary schools that traced their history to Tosa *han* disappeared from Kōchi Prefecture. The institutions that replaced them were founded either by the prefecture or by former samurai, but it was not until 1879 that the prefecture finally began an active program of educational development. Until then, the initiative rested in the main with private parties. Of this period's five middle schools, two were prefectural, namely the Tōya Gakkō, which was meant for teacher training, and its affiliated "simplified middle school," Hensoku Chūgaku. The other three—Risshi Gakusha (1874–1879), Seiken Gakusha (1874–?1879), and the Tosa Branch School of the Kainan Shijuku (founded 1876)—were private institutions. The role of private schools appears all the more substantial if the educational activities of associations affiliated with the Risshisha are also seen as a kind of secondary education. Such activities grew out of the *sakangumi,* or traditional youth training groups for samurai sons.

In late 1873 and early 1874, following the split in the central government over whether Japan should invade Korea, those among the civil and military bureaucrats from Tosa who had favored invasion returned from Tokyo, and a revival of the configuration of political forces dating from domain days resulted. Among these civil officials were Itagaki Taisuke and Fukuoka Takachika, who had carried out enlightened political reforms in the Tosa domain before going to work for the central government. The military men included Kataoka Kenkichi, Tani Shigeki, Kitamura Shigeyori (1845–1878), and others who had previously formed the nucleus of the antishogunate movement in Tosa; after the Meiji Restoration, these advocates of military expansion had served in Tokyo as officers and noncommissioned officers in the Imperial Guard and its successor, the Konoe Guard.

In November 1873, immediately after quitting the Konoe Guard, the military bureaucrats—together with Hayashi Yūzō, who was then at the Foreign Ministry—gathered in front of Yamanouchi Yōdō's grave and founded a society called the Kainan Gisha. The civil bureaucrats from Tosa, who were joined by the Hizen natives Etō Shinpei (1834–1874) and Soejima Taneomi (1828–1905), in January 1874 formed the Aikoku Kōtō (Patriotic Public party), Japan's first "modern" political party. Declaring their opposition to exclusive rule by the domain cliques (that is, to the ascendency of men from the former Chōshū and Satsuma domains over the central government), they presented a memorial "On Establishing a Popular Assembly" to the Sain, a quasi-legislative body of the central government. They then left Tokyo for home. In February 1874, Etō raised an armed disturbance—the Saga Rebellion—in Hizen.[33] Stirred by this turn of events, some of the Tosa military men began speaking of rising in arms themselves, and a wave of unrest swept Kōchi Prefecture. Moreover, since many of the advocates of a Korean invasion, both civil and military officials, were originally members of the Imperial Loyalist faction, their activities led to a revival of traditional factional animosities.

"The prefecture is generally divided into three factions," reported a secret agent sent out by the central government. "One is the imperial loyalist, antiforeign faction, which has been exerting itself since about 1863. The members of this faction proclaim their determination to rush forthwith to the aid of the throne, should there be any talk of a republican form of government, the introduction of Christianity, or any other threat to the imperial government. They dislike the recent dissolution of domain troops and continually talk about moral duty." The second faction, he said, "is composed of those still loyal to the shogunate. Even now its members refuse to recognize the imperial government and speak only of the debt owed to their former lord. They harbor a grudge against Itagaki and Gotō." The third "supports the dissolution of troops."[34]

As this report makes clear, the three main factions were identified with the proinvasion civil and military bureaucrats, who opposed the Tokyo government; the old rural-samurai-based faction of the Imperial Loyalist party, which stood in opposition to the bureaucrats; and the unregenerate, proshogunate Conservative party, the Shukyūha, which discountenanced the new imperial government while at the same time opposing civil bureaucrats like Itagaki and Gotō. Apart from these three, there was also a Neutral faction, which was unaligned with any of the others and tried to adapt to the changing times. From 1874 on, prefectural politics developed in the context of these factional conflicts. So did education, as the factions went about founding their own private schools with the aim of furthering their respective political objectives. Thus the Risshisha (Self-Help Society), an association whose leadership was composed of civil officials as well as of military men, brought into being an educational institution called Risshi Gakusha; the Seikensha (Self-Restraint Society), a group of shogunate loyalists, started a school by the name of Seiken Gakusha; and military bureaucrats founded an academy called Kainan Shijuku. Let us first have a look at the educational activities of the latter three groups and of the Neutral faction. For reasons of chronology, an inquiry into the links between the old Imperial Loyalists and education should be left for later.

The Risshisha was formed in April 1874. Its founding fathers included Itagaki Taisuke, the leader of the civil bureaucrats; the military bureaucrats Kataoka Kenkichi and Tani Shigeki; and Hayashi Yūzō. It was to become the strategic base of the popular-rights movement in Tosa as well as the precursor of other regional political associations in Japan. The historical role played by this organization is well known, and it is therefore unnecessary to go into detail about its activities. Several points should be raised, however, regarding the relationship between the Self-Help Society's original purpose and the political ideals of the Reformist faction in prerestoration days.

The Reformists' idea of basing the domain on the principle of the equality of the four classes was expanded by the Self-Help Society into the notion of founding a nation-state on the realization of political freedom and popular rights. The slogan of domain independence, used by the Reformists as a means of gaining political leadership during the restoration years, was translated by their successors into the ambition to establish the preeminence of Kōchi Prefecture in the popular-rights movement across the nation; it served also as the intellectual foundation for the advocacy of local autonomy in the draft constitution *(shigi kenpō)* prepared by the Jiyūtō (Party of Liberty). It was this sense of the importance of local autonomy that gave rise to the Self-Help Society's criticism of the centralizing and standardizing policies pursued by the central government and to its insistence on respect for local self-government. And it was precisely because of the traditional emphasis on domain autonomy in Tosa that the heirs to the Reformist faction's ideals in Kōchi—unlike Saigō Takamori (1827–1877) and Etō Shinpei, who had similarly lost out in the debate over Korea—were able to make the transition to the popular-rights movement.

The Risshi Gakusha was founded, along with the Hōritsu Kenkyūjo (Legal Studies Institute), as the educational arm of the Risshisha. For this purpose the Self-Help Society borrowed some 20,000 yen and the building of the old Kaiseikan from the former Tosa daimyo. The school's educational objectives were defined by the society's political ideals, expressed memorably in its founding charter: "A people's self-cultivation, its self-rule, and the independence arising from these are the foundation of a nation's well-being." They had nothing to do with the ideas embodied in the central government's Education Order, which stressed the need to acquire new knowledge for the sake of advancing "civilization and enlightenment." In contrast, the founding charter of the school stated that "a multitude of scholarly disciplines exist, but it is people who determine the use to which they are put." Placing its primary emphasis on educating people who would make practical use of their new knowledge, the Risshi Gakusha set the cultivation of good conduct as its first goal. By a person of "good conduct," the school did not mean a passive paragon of virtue or follower of the Way, but rather someone "with drive, who can face up to difficulties. Without these qualities, little can be accomplished. A person with drive is energetic, and that energy is nourished by loyalty and honor."[35] In the eyes of the school's founders, such a one "worked with self-cultivation and self-reliance to extend the rights of the people." As the charter suggests, the educational goal of the Risshi Gakusha was the formation of character.

The school's first principal was Ikeda Ōsuke (1849–1920), a member of the Self-Help Society. His staff included Fukuoka Seima, the older brother of Fukuoka Takachika and former instructor of history at the Chidōkan, and six other teachers.[36] True to the spirit of the founding charter, moral education was based mainly on Confucian teachings. For physical education, horsemanship was required. According to the Ministry of Education's annual report for 1874, the school had three hundred students; in the following year's report, however, the number is listed as seventy.[37] The Risshisha helped with the school's support, supplementing the monthly tuition paid by the students with a sum of 300 yen each month. The society's president, Kataoka Kenkichi, showed a deep personal concern with the school's progress, donated 50 yen toward the purchase of books, and gave scholarships to ten students to further their studies at the Hiroshima Normal School.[38]

From about the middle of 1875, the Risshisha's leaders became acutely aware that new knowledge was needed if their goal of popular participation in government was to be achieved, and they decided to add courses in the English language. In October, Yamada Heizaemon and Ikeda Ōsuke traveled to Tokyo to seek English teachers. Eguchi Takakuni and Fukakado Fuchimoto, graduates of Keiō Gijuku, were hired at a salary of about 150 yen, and the organization of the Risshi Gakusha was thereby put on a more solid footing. As a result, the number of students rose; on 10 August 1877, the *Tōkyō Nichinichi shinbun* reported that three hundred were enrolled. More Keiō alumni came to teach English at the school;[39] some of them also took part in political discussions sponsored by the Self-Help Society and helped in its other activities. They are, however, perhaps best known for a pedagogical innovation: rather than teaching by rote, they sought to instill a spirit of independence by "having the students first study the text on their own, and offering explanations only when a problem was encountered."[40] Some of the books used at the school were Spencer's *Principles of Soci-*

ology, Bentham's *Introduction to the Principles of Morals and Legislation,* and the *Napoleonic Code.*[41] As the sole school offering English instruction in Tosa, the Risshi Gakusha became known as the Keiō of Western Japan.[42]

The Risshi Gakusha's novel stress on English attracted many young men who wished to study the language, unmindful of the school's original purpose. At the same time, however, this emphasis on language dissatisfied those who had been attracted by the political ideals of the Risshisha and drawn to the school by the appeal of its founding charter. For instance, the 1876 entrant Yokoyama Matakichi found "not a single flaw" in the founding principles of the school, but he complained about its tendency to emphasize mathematics and English and to slight "Chinese classics and history, subjects that stir the blood of young men." Some of the students, he notes, nearly staged "a strike of sorts," demanding that the courses be changed.[43] Thus a school founded for the purpose of training men of action who would contribute to the popular-rights movement gradually took on the character of a *yōgakkō,* or school for Western studies. To be sure, by seeking to satisfy the need for new political knowledge, the Risshi Gakusha performed an important educational function. Many of its students—men like Sakamoto Namio and Ōishi Masami (1855–1935)—were later to make their mark in the political world. The school's fate was sealed, however, when it was discovered in August 1877 that some members of the Self-Help Society had plotted to raise troops in response to the Satsuma Rebellion. The society's leaders were arrested and imprisoned, and it fell into financial difficulties; its school, too, found it increasingly difficult to sustain operations and was finally closed in 1879. Even after the imprisonment of its leaders, however, the Self-Help Society sought to recover its fortunes by taking various youth groups under its wing. Throughout the decade beginning in the late 1870s, it expanded its political power in the prefecture and carried out educational activities through these groups.

During the Edo period, many groups called *sakangumi* were formed in the Kōchi castle town by the sons of samurai families "for the purpose of study, the pursuit of knowledge, and the cultivation of moral character," that is, the inculcation of the samurai spirit.[44] After the domain's abolition, however, the samurai class not only suffered severe social and economic blows, but also experienced a relaxation of its customary feudal code of behavior. The development of pleasure quarters—not permitted in the days of the old domain—and the emergence of sharp commercial practices further contributed to the deterioration of the character of samurai youth to "what one would nowadays call a complete state of depravity." Filled with apprehension at this state of affairs but "hopeful of reviving the spirit of the *sakangumi,*" Itagaki and others among the Self-Help Society's founding members accordingly sought to instill "progressive political ideas that would lead the way to a second restoration" among the youth of Tosa.[45] Liberal-minded youth groups responded with enthusiasm, and political associations were founded one after the other.

These associations, which were made up of youths who had reached the age of fifteen or sixteen, were in character very much like private academies *(shijuku)*. At the Hōensha, for instance, Yokoyama Matakichi taught the Chinese classics and Chinese poetry,[46] while the Hatsuyōsha's young men pursued learning under a sinologist by the name of Kurohara. All the students of Kondō Arata's private academy entered the Shōyōsha as a group; the members of the Yūshinsha "encouraged one another in their studies."[47] A regular study section set up at the Shūritsusha admitted not only association members but also other young men of the area to a course of studies divided into six classes; four hours of classroom instruction were given daily. There was also a special night section, meant "to encourage the pursuit of learning among the populace," for youths employed in shops in the city.[48] For all their inadequacies, these associations served as informal institutions of secondary education. From about 1879 and 1880, the education they offered became increasingly political, as they began to participate in political activities under the Risshisha's guidance.

Next, let us turn to the Seikensha and its school, the Seiken Gakusha, although not much is known about them. This association was formed by the men described in the previously cited investigative report as "still loyal to the shogunate." It was headed by Hara Shigetane, a former instructor of military science at the Chidōkan. The political objectives of the Self-Restraint Society remain unclear, but it may be imagined that it was not so much a formally organized party with well-defined political views as a group of reactionaries who banded together at the time of the political schism set off by the question of a Korean invasion, seeking to counter the growing power of the Imperial Loyalist faction, their erstwhile foe, in Kōchi Prefecture. The slogan of loyalty to their former daimyo was nothing more than a political prop for these disgruntled elements. "The Seikensha is a thoroughly feudal party," asserted an article that appeared in the *Tōkyō Nichinichi shinbun* of 10 August 1877. "It claims to have 1,500 members; in fact, however, there are no more than 800, the rest being mere sympathizers. Its headquarters is within the precincts of the old castle. It has opened a school for Chinese studies with a student body of some 400. Recently, all the students have been hard at work on land reclamation." It is unclear when the Self-Restraint Society went out of existence, but it was probably dissolved around 1878 or 1879, when the old Imperial Loyalists, the Neutral faction, and other political groups tried to form a grand alliance directed against the Self-Help Society.

As to the Seiken Gakusha, the educational arm of the "thoroughly feudal party," the Ministry of Education's annual report for 1874 reports that its founding principal was Shimomoto Toshiyoshi and states that it had 290 students. In 1875, their number is given as 270.[49] What happened later is not known, nor is there any information about the school's curriculum, apart from the fact that it emphasized Chinese studies. An anecdote found in an article by Mori Matakichirō and Kondō Arata gives us an idea, however, of the spirit that prevailed at the Seiken Gakusha: apparently, it was nicknamed Hachi Gakkō, the Bee School, because its students continued to bear their "stingers"— that is, swords—in defiance of the government's abolition of that old samurai privilege.[50] The school is not mentioned in the annual report for 1879. Judging from that absence, we may assume that it closed sometime that year or in 1878, that is, about the time the Self-Restraint Society itself was dissolved.

A more enduring institution was the Tosa Branch School (Bunkō) of the Kainan Shijuku, which came into being in February 1876. It was the only one of the private secondary schools founded during this period that continued in existence after the Secondary School Act of 1886, when it was reorganized as the Kenritsu Chūgakkō (Prefectural Middle School). It was a unique establishment, proud of its scholarly character. The origins of this school derived from the activities of military officials who belonged to the faction favoring the invasion of Korea. Its parent institution, the Tokyo or main branch of the Kainan Shijuku, had been founded in 1873 by Tani Shigeki, Kitamura Shigeyori, Yamaji Motoharu, Tsuchiya Yoshiya, and other guard officers, who had formed a society called the Kainan Gisha soon after the split in the government over the Korean issue. With the exception of Tani Shigeki, they refused to join the Risshisha on their return to Tosa; eventually, Tani Tateki persuaded them to rejoin the Konoe Guard. In short, they were military men who remained faithful to the martial traditions of the old Tosa domain.

The establishment of the Kainan Shijuku in Tokyo in 1873 was a consequence of the dissolution of the Imperial Guard and the formation of the Konoe Guard in the Third Month of 1872. Relieved of the expense of contributing to the Imperial Guard, the domain decided to give the surplus moneys of 30,000 yen to the men who had served in the unit. They in turn determined in January 1873 that the most meaningful way of using the funds would be to found a private school, which would be situated at the An'yōin temple in Shiba. A short time later, they presented the school to their former daimyo family, the Yamanouchi, who merged it with the School of Sinology and Western Studies that had been opened in the Tosa domain's Tokyo residence in 1869. The Kainan Shijuku began its work in September 1873. Its educational objective was to serve as a preparatory school for entrance into the government military academy, Heigakuryō.[51]

French studies and military studies were the mainstays of the Kainan Shijuku. Chinese classics, mathematics, history, and calligraphy were also taught. When the school was founded, the Tosa domain's sometime military instructor Antoine was asked to teach French; Nojima Tanzō would later become his successor. An English course was also established, and Mori Shunkichi, the former instructor in Western studies at the Gyūkō Gakkō, was put in charge of it. The enrollment was about twenty. Half of them were alumni of the former domain military school who had been unable to get into the government military academy. Among these were Kusunose Sachihiko (1858–1927), who later became a lieutenant general in the army, the future admiral Shimamura Hayao (1858–1923), and others who became high military officers. Ueki Emori also studied at the school for a while.

The Kainan Shijuku's Kōchi branch was the creation of Yoshida Kazuma (1846–1910), a rural samurai from Nagaoka County who had fought in the Boshin Civil War and moved from the Imperial Guard to the Konoe Guard after the restoration. A childhood friend of Takechi Kumakichi (1840–1874), the would-be assassin of Iwakura Tomomi, Yoshida had been nurtured in the Tosa domain's military traditions and was a strong advocate of invading Korea. After the defeat of the pro-invasion faction, he returned to Tosa. He was dissatisfied with Tosa's lack of power in the central government vis-à-vis Satsuma and Chōshū, and keenly felt the need for educating men of talent who would be no whit inferior to those from the rival domains. "I am deeply convinced," he wrote, "that the task at hand for the men of Tosa is not to rush about founding contentious factions in search of empty fame but rather to nurture talent slowly and steadily, planning for the long-term good of the nation."[52] In 1876, Yoshida obtained an audience with the former daimyo, proposed the establishment of a branch school in Tosa, and was given permission to proceed. Although its principal was to change several times during the years before 1882, in practice Yoshida Kazuma remained firmly in control of this school.

In contrast to the Risshi Gakusha, a school generated by the spirit of local autonomy and dedicated to the education of men who would contribute toward its development, the Tosa Branch School of the Kainan Shijuku was inspired by a domain clique consciousness that was a variation on the earlier theme of domanial independence. Its purpose was to cultivate talent of a national caliber, that is, to educate men who would expand Tosa's influence in the central government. Nothing less than an increase of Tosa's power in Japan's military would satisfy Yoshida Kazuma's militarism or fulfill the traditionalist ambitions of the Kainan Shijuku. It was only natural that Yoshida gradually redirected the school's approach toward the goal of educating military men.

After 1880 the Kainan Shijuku was classified as a "miscellaneous school" *(kakushu gakkō),* that is, a school outside the government's formal ranking system. Although the main school in Tokyo closed in 1881, the Tosa branch continued to flourish under the leadership of Tani Tateki, its secretary general, and with the help of Yamanouchi Toyonori, the former daimyo. In 1882, it was renamed the Kainan Gakkō, and Yoshida Kazuma was appointed principal. The next year, encouraged by Toyonori's wishes that it "devote itself exclusively to the education of military men in conformance with His Majesty's sacred intention to expand the army and navy,"[53] the school defined its educational objective as the systematic training of military men and forced all those students who did not wish to become professional soldiers to quit. Thus the school took upon itself the task of continuing the former Tosa domain's martial heritage and embarked, with the former daimyo Toyonori's full support, on a peculiar type of educational activity motivated by the aim of augmenting Tosa's role in the nation's military. Staying aloof of prefectural politics, the school went its own way through the decade beginning in 1877, but it changed direction and was reorganized upon the promulgation of the Secondary School Act in 1886 and Toyonori's death that year. In 1888, it became an "ordinary secondary school" *(jinjō chūgakkō)* in conformance with the act. The Yamanouchi family continued to bear its operational costs.

The so-called Neutral faction (Chūritsuha) also had its school. This group, which was unaligned with any of the three main factions found in the prefecture in 1874, set up its own political association, the Chūritsusha (Neutral Society) two years later. Whereas the Self-Help Society and the Self-Restraint Society had been formed on their own, the Neutral Society was, so to speak, created from above, under the guidance of Sasaki Takayuki (1830–1910), a high official in the central government who was a native of Tosa. In the background, according to the distinguished scholar of Tosa politics and personalities Hirao Michio, was the wave of unrest that swept Kōchi Prefecture in the autumn of 1876 in the wake of the turmoil caused in southwestern Japan by the Akizuki and Hagi rebellions. "Hoping to rescue the people from this crisis," Hara Tetsu, Imahashi Iwao (a Justice Ministry bureaucrat who was Sasaki's trusted follower), and others in the prefecture decided to form a moderate political association, one that would "stand in the middle between the Risshisha and the Seikensha." This was the Chūritsusha. Its members, originally adverse to constitutional monarchy, "would of course comply with the wishes His Majesty expressed on the matter," Sasaki himself noted. "The reckless argument for popular rights is, however, bound to cause public disorder and defile the national polity. This we find abhorrent, and thus we stand in opposition to its partisans [the Risshisha]. Others will therefore view us as a progovernment party."[54] Indeed, that was only to be expected.

In October 1876, Sasaki was secretly ordered by the government to go back to Kōchi to soothe popular emotions. Ideally, he wanted to merge the Self-Help Society and the Self-Restraint Society with the Neutral Society and put the new organization under government control, but his designs were unsuccessful. Next, he sought the support of Tani Tateki and other prominent natives of the prefecture for his scheme to establish a Neutralist-affiliated school that would educate moderate, apolitical men; the foundation of a publishing company was also discussed. Tani was ambivalent about the enterprise. In the end, he refused his assistance to the political activities of the Neutral Society (indeed, he believed it should be abolished because its existence would only exacerbate factional tensions in the prefecture). He did, however, agree with the plans for the press and the school and gave Sasaki a firm pledge of support for the latter: "As soon as the school's regulations are drawn up, I shall ask like-minded men to contribute money. If you think it appropriate, I should also like to offer a modest sum myself according to my means."[55] As the school is not even mentioned in the annual reports of the Ministry of Education, it remains unclear what it taught. The *Chōya shinbun* did mention on 21 March 1877 that "the Chūritsu Gakusha prospers ever more by the day," and the *Tōkyō Nichinichi* reported on 10 August of that year that "the Chūritsusha has opened a school of Chinese studies, where more than sixty students are being educated." Hence one may assume that this was a small school with many of the characteristics of a traditional private academy for Chinese studies.

As noted above, the Neutral Society was formed in the hope of reducing the tensions raised in Kōchi Prefecture by the autumn 1876 uprisings in southwestern Japan. With the imminent prospect of another rebellion, one led by Saigō Takamori, Imahashi became anxious lest efforts on the part of Imperial Loyalist elements to join with the Self-Help Society and go to Saigō's aid embroil the entire old Kinnōha. To prevent this, he worked to enlarge the Chūritsusha, formed an alliance with members of the Yūkōsha, an Imperial Loyalist group in Takaoka County, and published a written pledge that they would not ally themselves with the rebel Saigō. In bringing about this coalition of anti-Risshisha forces in the prefecture, Imahashi had—if minimally—fulfilled the objectives that Sasaki hoped to achieve. In October 1878, however, the Neutral Society dissolved itself in deference to Tani's stated wishes, obtained funds from the central government through Tani's good offices, and was reincarnated as the Hyakusasha—literally, "Hundred Works Society"—an association to help samurai set up new enterprises. On 16 October 1878, the *Tōkyō Nichinichi* cited the motives behind the dissolution of the Neutral Society as follows:

> The people's hearts have been calmed at last, and day by day they advance in enlightenment. It is to be hoped that the barbarous custom of jealousy and mutual recrimination will soon disappear. Compared to the days when the association was first founded, the situation has greatly changed. At present, we should strive and work solely for the acquisition of knowledge and the provision of employment. Indeed, learning and jobs depend on one another and are only possible together. Rather than indulge in empty words and futile arguments, we ought henceforth turn our attention to the pursuit of knowledge and jobs. We should emphasize practical learning that will make it possible for us to obtain profits and make ourselves and our families independent. Only then can we extend our efforts to other matters. Hence we shall put our hearts into becoming ever more open and large-minded, drop the restrictive name Chūritsu ["stand in the middle"], pursue learning as we see fit, and work for productive industry and greater prosperity. We trust that this direction is not inconsistent with the original purpose of our association.

Not only was the name of the Chūritsusha changed, its character was transformed. From a political association with educational goals, it changed to a group that had the practical objective of job training for samurai who had lost their livelihood. The new Hyakusasha established its main office in Kōchi and found employment for former samurai in its tea-cultivation and match-manufacturing enterprises. It also opened branch offices as well as schools in Kagami, Takaoka, and Hata counties.[56] The *Doyō shinbun* reported on 6 November 1882 that the expenses of the Yūkō Gakkō in Takaoka County were covered from a special payment of 10,000 yen which the county had received from the Hyakusasha. As will shortly be described in detail, the school consid-

ered worthy of such support was affiliated with the old Imperial Loyalist faction.

All of these private schools had links to political associations. Each
had its own unique and separate educational aim. How, then, did Kōchi
Prefecture deal with them? The prefecture's policy on secondary education and the line adopted by prefectural governors toward various
political forces in Kōchi were of necessity closely related matters. The
governors during the period that most concerns us were Iwasaki Nagatake, who succeeded Hayashi Yūzō and served from November 1872 to
August 1876, and Koike Kunitake (1846–1919; he later changed his
family name to Watanabe), who followed Iwasaki and served until June
1879. As Iwasaki belonged to the Itagaki clique, the prefecture during
his tenure was lenient, even compromising toward the Risshisha. Moreover, it did not ignore the old domain's educational policies but showed
them great consideration in setting its own plans. In essence, Iwasaki
adhered to the "principle of the equality of the people," the guiding
philosophy of the Reformist faction in former days, and followed
the ideal of the equalization of educational opportunity proclaimed by
the central government's Education Order of 1872. Even before that
order was promulgated, the prefecture (as noted previously) had developed its own unique policy for the expansion of primary schooling.
Iwasaki's goal was to consolidate that policy in the sense of the central
government's decree. Thus, in developing secondary education, the
prefecture quite naturally began by founding schools for teacher training. The Tōya Gakkō, which opened in February 1874, was the first of
these.

The "Prefectural Gazette" *(Ken kōhō)* of 30 January 1874 notes that
this institution was modeled along the lines of a normal school *(shihan
gakkō)* and intended to train future teachers as a first step toward realizing a proper educational system for Tosa. Entering students had to be
fourteen or older, and their term of study was set for six months. Initially, there were few applicants, so in December 1874 the school began
recruiting students with the promise of tuition loans. To qualify for
those, one had to be between twenty and forty and have some background in "Imperial" (i.e., Japanese) and Chinese studies as well as in
history, grammar, and mathematics; presumably, insistence on these pre-
requisites accelerated the process of teacher training. In October 1875,
the school's purpose was more clearly defined: "The main objective will
be training in classroom instruction."[57] Other than lowering the age
requirement to between eighteen and thirty-five and extending the term
of study to one year, however, no major changes were made. In January
1876, centers for training primary school teachers were established in

Aki, Sagawa, Suzaki, and Nakamura. Their programs lacked unique characteristics.

Governor Iwasaki not only tried to put teacher training on a solid footing but also sought to resuscitate the Kyōritsu Gakusha, which had been forced to close under orders from the Ministry of Education in January 1874. As a result of his efforts, that school got a new lease on life as an institution for teaching foreign languages, and again began giving instruction—with the ministry's permission—on 7 February 1874. No sooner revived, however, the Kyōritsu Gakusha lost its individuality and was renamed the Attached Simplified Middle School (Fuzoku Hensoku Chūgakkō) of the Tōya Gakkō. On the principle of the division of responsibilities, Japanese and Chinese studies were reserved for the latter school, which was set up on the grounds of the old Chidōkan.[58] After Iwasaki was dismissed from office in August 1876, another reorganization would follow.

Iwasaki's dismissal was instigated by elements of the Neutral faction. He was succeeded on 26 August 1876 by Koike Kunitake, an official from the tax bureau in Tokyo. Seeking to carry out the central government's policies, Koike bent all his efforts toward purging the Self-Help Society from the prefectural office and extirpating the old Tosa domain's lingering influence from Kōchi.

Koike's efforts were reflected clearly in two aspects of his policy toward secondary education. The first was the reform of the Tōya Gakkō, beginning in October 1876. That school, too, lost its individual name, being renamed the Kōchi Prefectural Normal School (Kōchi-ken Shihan Gakkō) in line with the general designation specified for all such schools by the Ministry of Education. Its regulations were also changed: "Since the students of this school will one day serve as models for young children, admission will not [any longer] be based on intelligence and academic skills alone. Applicants will be chosen on the basis of their moral rectitude and docility."[59] Even if the Tōya Gakkō's stated purpose was nothing more than "training in classroom instruction," it would appear that it had retained traces of the old domain's emphasis on the samurai ethos. If the reminiscences of an instructor, Ibaraki Sadaoki, are to be trusted, its atmosphere was marked by "arguments that at times could become fierce, or even violent."[60] The new Normal School professed a more profound aim, one directed at the development of inner qualities, but what did that mean? There is little doubt that its objective was to sweep away all vestiges of the old domanial ethos and train teachers who would put the precepts of the Education Order of 1872 into practice. To that end, it sought to create a new man, one completely divorced from the traditions of the Tosa domain.

Koike next reorganized the prefecture's foreign language school in accordance with the secondary school regulations of the Education Order. In February 1877, it became the Simplified Middle School Attached to the Kōchi Prefectural Normal School (Kōchi-ken Shihan Gakkō Fuzoku Hensoku Chūgaku; the names of the old Kyōritsu Gakkō became more unwieldy with each successive reincarnation). Its new purpose was to "give instruction to those older than primary school age and provide preparation for those who may go on later to middle school or normal school."[61] The study of foreign languages was eliminated from the curriculum, and an educational tradition of the old Tosa domain was finally brought to an end.

In November 1878, Koike separated the Simplified Middle School from the prefectural normal school and renamed it the Kōchi Middle School (Kōchi Chūgakkō). Courses were divided into two sections: a four-year ordinary section and a four-year higher section. The first four years were for "ordinary upper-level instruction."[62] The study of foreign languages was not required; the purpose was nurturing local talent. The next four years were to be a "step leading to an advanced specialized school" *(senmon gakkō)*. English was taught to facilitate entry into such schools; admission was not restricted to graduates of the ordinary section but was open to "those of suitable academic ability." In their scale and conception, the reforms went beyond the ministry regulations issued earlier in 1878; indeed, they approximated closely the guidelines that would be set forth in the "General Rules concerning Secondary Schools" issued by the Ministry of Education in 1881. This was clearly a noteworthy initiative on the part of the prefecture, one free of any vestige of the old domain's tradition. It may well be imagined that the underlying intent of these reforms was to channel the political ambitions of the young men associated with the Risshisha into aspirations to higher education.

Although Kōchi Prefecture's policy toward secondary education from 1874 to 1878 was determined by the political position of its governing officials, it was still centered on the private schools that were closely tied to the political factions of the old domain. Beginning in 1878, however, the prefecture gradually turned its energies to building secondary schools that were new both in form and in substance, that is to say, schools that transcended prefectural politics and showed no trace of the old domanial tradition. In contrast, two of the three private schools that had been mainstays of secondary education closed down by 1879 —the Risshi Gakusha after the arrest of the Self-Help Society's leaders and the Seiken Gakusha when its parent organization was absorbed in a coalition of anti-Risshisha forces. The Kainan Gakkō alone remained open, having stayed away from political infighting.

New secondary schools were founded, however, not only by the prefecture but also by the old Imperial Loyalist faction, which reemerged under the new political conditions created by the establishment of a prefectural assembly in 1879. Eventually, associations affiliated with the Self-Help Society also revived their own educational institutions. In the tradition of their predecessors, these private schools alternately opposed or conformed to the prefecture's educational policies. As we are about to see, however, they too would become less politically directed.

The Consolidation of Prefectural Government and Secondary Education

From 1879 until 1884 Kōchi Prefecture took positive steps to increase the number of prefectural secondary schools. Thereafter, it shifted its attention to integrating the teaching programs of these schools and strengthening their curricula. As has just been pointed out, what prompted this shift was a desire on the part of the Kōchi authorities to separate secondary education from the old domain's tradition and isolate it from prefectural politics. The authorities hoped to depoliticize education in the prefecture and make it conform to policies set down by the central government. This was not so easily done, however, either before or after 1879. Without paying careful heed to the changing political circumstances, the prefecture could not realize its educational plans.

In the earlier phase, the formation of the Self-Help Society in 1874 had led to the revival of the old Tosa domain's factions, and contentious political associations proliferated. In the period following the opening of the prefectural assembly in 1879, these factions sorted themselves into pro- and anti-Risshisha groups, adopting clear-cut positions either against or for the central government. The emergence of an anti-Risshisha coalition may in part be attributed to the success, however tentative, of Sasaki and Imahashi's efforts. A more direct reason, however, was that their rival's power had increased. The Self-Help Society had played the lead role in the formation of the Tosa Provincial Council, the precursor of the Kōchi Prefectural Assembly, in August 1878. Even after the council was reorganized under pressure to make it fit into the framework laid down by the central government's Prefectural Assembly Regulations, the Risshisha retained so much power in the new assembly that it was difficult for other factions to exert an influence in prefectural politics. This forced them to form a coalition—known as the Kokumintō or Kokumin-ha, the Nationalist faction—which became active in prefectural politics from about 1879.

The memoirs of the important bureaucrat, businessman, and politician Kataoka Naoharu (1859–1934) contain an interesting paragraph in which the contrast between the Kokumin-ha and what he calls the Jiyūha or Liberal faction (that is, the Risshisha-related associations) is described from the standpoint of an old Takaoka County Imperial Loyalist. Unlike the Liberals, he says, the Nationalists did not use mass politics in seeking to gain power in the national government, but this did not mean they failed to raise a following:[63]

> The Nationalists asserted that self-cultivation and domestic harmony were the foundations of a nation's peace and tranquility. They eschewed shrill and arrogant political activity. Instead, they focused on training the people of the prefecture in practical skills and instructing them in ways of increasing production. They opened private schools for the young in various places, seeking to disseminate knowledge and instill ideas of constitutional government. By these measures, the Nationalists hoped to awaken a healthy national consciousness in the people of the prefecture. If all applied themselves to production, they believed, the temptations of foreign thought would be dispelled and the extremist Liberals driven out of the prefecture; at the same time, subversive elements from outside the prefecture would lose the base of their activities here and be intimidated into inaction. The Chūritsusha in Tosa County, the Kōyōsha and Shūdōsha in Hata County, the Shigakkō in Kagami County, and the Yūkōsha and Yūkō Gakkō in Takaoka County had all been established in line with the principles of the Nationalist party. They formed an alliance that was directed, needless to say, against associations affiliated with the Risshisha.

In April 1881, the Nationalist coalition founded a formal political association with headquarters in Kōchi City. This association, called the Kōyōkai, openly declared its opposition to popular rights and its support for an increase in state rights. In contrast with the Self-Help Society's advocacy of a constitution determined by the people themselves, it called for one granted by the emperor. It marched in step with the central government.

The Self-Help Society did not react passively to this opposition. Rather, it worked hard to reverse the decline it had suffered after the arrest of its leaders and continued its efforts to guide the political and educational activities of a fair number of affiliated societies. Concentrating on the city and the environs of Kōchi, it sought to increase popular support by helping city workers in commercial and other enterprises to form associations. The societies gathered under its aegis opposed the ascendency of Satsuma and Chōshū and were vocal in their advocacy of political freedom and popular rights, causes espoused by Itagaki Taisuke. Prominent among these groups were the Gakuyōsha,

Kaitensha, Hatsuyōsha, Shūritsusha, and Yūshinsha, which "prospered until about 1887, laboring persistently and mightily for their country in great endeavors." They strove for the establishment of a national assembly and exerted themselves for the "three petitions"—for freedom of speech, reduction of the land tax, and revision of the unequal treaties. Many other groups were founded between 1880 and 1883 "on a temporary basis as night schools for young boys or associations for laborers, lasting only half a year or a few years at most. Besides devoting themselves to national affairs, their members also worked hard at their studies." Apparently, they read Spencer, Bentham, John Stuart Mill, Adam Smith, and Rousseau; the history of the French Revolution was also a favorite topic. "Through these readings, they tried to advance their knowledge of politics."[64]

The Self-Help Society thus sought to regain its power by enlarging its organizational base. To disseminate its political ideas, it also sponsored public lectures, which were regularly attended by more than a thousand. Within the prefectural assembly, it pressed for an expansion of the franchise and greater powers for the assembly itself. The society was also active outside the prefecture. From about October 1879, when Kataoka Kenkichi and other leaders were released from prison, it stepped up its efforts to guide the national popular-rights movement, forming the Kokkai Kisei Dōmei (League for Establishing a National Assembly) and the Jiyūtō (Party of Liberty).

In short, political forces in Kōchi Prefecture were split into two distinct factions. Each tried to influence prefectural politics, at the same time becoming more deeply involved in education. Standing between the Self-Help Society and the Nationalists, as it were, how did the prefectural government go about formulating policy, and in particular its policy toward secondary schools? The prefectural authorities were as yet unable to stand above factional infighting. At least until Tanabe Yoshiaki's appointment in March 1883, successive governors were forced to rely on—that is, compromise with—the factions representing the right and left, and their policy on secondary education was circumscribed by this necessity. For the prefectural governors, to put it more concretely, depoliticizing secondary education meant freeing it from any influence by the antigovernment Risshisha. To do this, they were obliged to compromise with the Kokumin-ha.

Kōchi Prefecture's secondary education policy began to take effect with the establishment of prefectural middle schools at Suzaki, Nakamura, and Aki (in Takaoka, Hata, and Aki counties, respectively). These schools were a response to an expected nationwide increase in primary school graduates, as is clear from the prefecture's report to the

Ministry of Education.[65] But they were also meant to prevent the infiltration of the Self-Help Society's influence on young men in the prefecture, and this goal was taken into consideration in selecting staff. The principal appointed at the Kōchi Chūgakkō in January 1879, for example, was Hirota Masao, who had studied at the Daigaku Nankō and Nishō Gakusha. This was one "new intellectual" who had old Imperial Loyalist credentials; he would later become an instructor at the Loyalists' Kachō Gakusha and serve as a Nationalist representative in the prefectural assembly. Ueda Enzō (d. 1906), who served as the principal of the new Nakamura Middle School from April 1879 to February 1880, and Nishimura Tsukuda, the principal of the Aki Middle School from September 1879 to September 1882, had both been Confucian scholars at the old domain school; they were affiliated either with the Self-Restraint Society or with the Imperial Loyalist party. Ueda's successor Kuwabara Kaihei (in office February 1880 to February 1882) was the headman of Hata County and a key figure in the Meidōkai, an old Imperial Loyalist association in that county. Ibaraki Sadaoki, the principal at the Suzaki Middle School from January 1879 to May 1884, was likewise a conservative Confucian scholar. The choice of the principals for the new prefectural middle schools, together with the June 1879 and March 1880 decrees forbidding public servants and prefectural schoolteachers to participate in political debates and lectures, would appear to indicate that the prefecture was determined to separate civil servants and teachers—no less than the young men of school age in the prefecture—from politics.

The foundation of new, "apolitical" middle schools progressed apace during the tenures of Governor Koike and his successor Kitagaki Kunimichi (1835–1916; in office June 1879–January 1881). In February 1881, the Akaoka Middle School was opened in Kagami County, on the grounds that although there were several secondary schools to the west of Kōchi City, there was only one to the east, resulting in an imbalance.[66] The Risshisha opposed these moves consistently. "As to our views on education," it maintained, "we desire not interference but freedom."[67] Or again, it asserted, "Those who are independent must study independently. There are independent-minded persons in every village and town in Kōchi. Are they not capable of studying on their own?"[68]

At the extraordinary session of the prefectural assembly in February 1881, the Self-Help Society became more aggressive in its opposition. This was a result, most probably, of the conciliatory policy adopted toward the group by Governor Tanabe Terumi (also known as Tanabe Teruzane; 1841–1924), who was named prefectural governor in January 1881. Having served as first secretary under Kitagaki and learned from his experience, Tanabe hoped to govern smoothly by making good use of the Risshisha's political influence. He reshuffled personnel, appointing men affiliated with the Self-Help Society to positions at the prefectural office and as county chiefs in Takaoka, Agawa, Nagaoka, and Kagami. As a result, the society's power quickly spread at the county level.

The Risshisha's members can be found everywhere, complains a letter written by Kataoka Naoharu. Nakajima Nobuyuki (1846–1899), a former member of the Chamber of Elder Statesmen (Genrōin), has been lecturing "in every county and every village" since his return to Kōchi on 27 January 1881; he has been "holding parties" to entertain "the rich and powerful as well as school teachers" and has been successful in obtaining their pledges to join the Self-Help Society. "Indeed, the situation is such that nine out of ten in the prefecture toady to the Risshisha."[69] Kataoka was incensed by the governor's personnel changes, which he was to recall with renewed indignation in his memoirs: "His mode of operation put the interests of the Liberals first and foremost. Anyone with even a whiff of Nationalist leanings was dismissed. No one was spared, from experienced prefectural officials—section and subsection heads with long years of devoted service—on down to county chiefs; all were fired. . . . Because the Nationalist party, which had hitherto acted as a counterforce, suddenly was destroyed without reason, the Liberals could no longer be held in check, no matter how wild or insolent their behavior."[70]

The personnel changes affected the Kōchi Chūgakkō, too, as the Risshisha member Yamamoto Yukihiko was appointed to succeed Hirota Masao as principal in January 1881. The spread of popular-rights ideas among the students expanded even further. Nakauchi Genma, an 1880 entrant, remembered this as an exciting period when "youth associations were established in every part of the city. Middle school students joined in droves, and political ideas percolated into their brains. The famous words uttered by Patrick Henry on the eve of the American declaration of independence, 'Give me liberty or give me death,' were on every whippersnapper's lips."[71]

Quick to take advantage of Governor Tanabe's attempt to win it over, the Self-Help Society used the extraordinary session of the prefectural assembly in February 1881 to demand the abolition of the four prefectural middle schools; reduction of the tax burden was its reason. Although there are no materials documenting this debate, one can glean much of what took place from the editorial "Should Prefectural Secondary Schools Stay or Be Abolished?" in the 20 March 1881 issue of the *Kōchi shinbun*:

It is reported that the honorable members of the assembly, worried lest the forthcoming increase in local taxes place an intolerable burden on the people, have discussed which expenses to cut and are now inclined to eliminate funds for middle schools. . . . Alas, should so drastic a measure be passed, what will happen to our ambitious youths, who have their sleeves rolled up, as it were, in their eagerness to get to work! . . . Are the members of the assembly so cold-hearted that they can put up with this? . . . Is it because they have something else on their minds that they think of doing this? Only when the people have severed themselves from the spirit of dependence, only when they develop such resilience that they are willing to seek death in order to gain life, then for the first time will it be possible to substitute private for public schools. It is a rash argument that clutches at a superficial conception of 'liberal education' and fails to inquire into its real advantages and disadvantages. The effect of such a precipitous change [as the abolition of the schools] would be incalculable. Why, it might interrupt our progress toward civilization!

One should note that until August 1881, when the *Kōchi shinbun* became the organ of the Self-Help Society, both its president, Fukao Shigeyuki, and its chief editor, Sakazaki Sakan, belonged to the Neutral faction. Although the newspaper's policy was to let all political persuasions be heard, it is not surprising—considering the views of its head officers—that it published such an editorial, which goes out of its way to support the prefectural authorities' policy on secondary schools and their opposition to education carried on outside the auspices of the state.[72] This view, however, was rebutted in the 11 April 1881 issue of the same newspaper by someone calling himself Komatsuzaki Bunko; he proclaimed himself a long-time supporter of "liberal education" and justified his opposition to state schools with pithy reasoning: "When private schools are established, each kind of school flourishes because teachers teach what they wish and students study what they desire. It does not take any particular intelligence to realize this. This being the case, it follows that the reason private schools do not flourish today is because prefectural secondary schools stand in their way."

Tanabe, however, overrode the opposition. He not only kept the four prefectural schools operating but pressed on with plans to increase their number. In February 1881 he founded the previously mentioned Aka-oka Middle School. Then, in June 1882, he changed the program at the Kōchi Chūgakkō in accordance with the Guideline Regulations for Secondary Schools issued by the government in July 1881. Instead of a four-year ordinary and four-year higher course system, which was unique to Kōchi in that it permitted "those of suitable academic ability" to enter the higher level, a four-year elementary section and two-year higher course were instituted, and entry to the higher level was restricted to those who had completed the lower. By compromising with the Self-Help Society on personnel matters, Tanabe had succeeded in separating the educational system from politics. That is to say, he brought it into line with the government.

Tanabe may have used the Self-Help Society for his own purposes in Tosa, but he was basically a bureaucrat faithful to Tokyo. At the very time he was staffing the Kōchi Chūgakkō and county offices with men sympathetic to popular rights, he was also forbidding schoolteachers to engage in public political discussions (29 July 1882) and students to participate even in academic lecture meetings (17 August 1882). The Nationalists, however, continued to oppose his policy of compromise with the Risshisha. A delegation that included Minami Ryōsuke and Kataoka Naoharu was sent to protest in Tokyo, where they obtained Sasaki Takayuki's assistance. Their appeal to Itō Hirobumi to dismiss Tanabe was successful. In November 1882 Tanabe was named a provisional first secretary at the Home Ministry and replaced as the governor of Kōchi by Ijūin Kaneyoshi.[73]

Ijūin's term as governor was cut short by his death in Kōchi in March 1883. During his brief tenure, however, he managed to purge men with Risshisha affiliations from the prefectural and county offices and to dismiss the school principals and teachers appointed by his predecessor. In their place, he appointed Nationalists or those unaffiliated with any faction. Such changes were particularly noticeable at the Kōchi Chūgakkō, where Principal Yamamoto Yukihiko, Supervisor Sawamura Katsushi, and five other teachers were dismissed in one fell swoop. The school secretary, Ōishi Kanji, was made principal, and the Nationalist Nishimori Shintarō was appointed an instructor. The change in personnel was so drastic that it was duly reported in the *Doyō shinbun* of 4 January 1883. A committee of four students, elected by some forty of their peers at the school, demanded a meeting with the governor and presented a petition which pointed out that all the teachers who had been newly dismissed were men who believed in freedom and inquired pointedly, "Does this mean, by any chance, that all who hold such views will no longer be hired by the government?" At the Aki Middle School, too, the principal, Fukui Jun'ichirō, and a teacher, Aoki Yoshimasa, were dismissed. "Deprived of Mr. Aoki, the students were like crabs that had lost their claws, and pleaded for his reinstatement."[74]

By compromising with the Self-Help Society in matters of personnel, Tanabe had been able to depoliticize the system of secondary education. Now, by compromising with the Nationalists, Ijūin had depoliticized it in terms of personnel—a task his predecessor should have carried out but could not. Ijūin's actions had great repercussions in secondary education in Kōchi, but he died before developing any constructive policy and was succeeded in March 1883 by Tanabe Yoshiaki (1834–1897), a provisional first secretary in the Home Ministry in Tokyo (not to be confused with Tanabe Terumi, governor in 1881–1882). His predecessors had pursued the depoliticization of schools from two different directions; the new governor inherited that task from them and sought to accomplish it in conformity with the policies of the central government in Tokyo. Soon after his arrival in Kōchi, at the ordinary session of the prefectural assembly in April 1883, the Risshisha again proposed abolishing the five prefectural middle schools, but the proposal was defeated. One of its opponents, who voiced the sentiments of the Nationalist party, piously invoked the emperor as his buttress against the forces of "Liberalism." To him, the public secondary schools, which taught courses prescribed in regulations "promulgated in the form of a Decree from His Gracious Imperial Majesty," were "splendid and upstanding institutions," and the "school abolitionists" were at once "guilty of disrespect to His Majesty the Emperor and of bringing misfortune to the people." He believed that the times called for an expansion of the prefectural secondary school system.[75]

Tanabe Yoshiaki's administration was above politics in the sense that unlike his predecessors he sided with neither faction but chose to govern by using his own powers of leadership. This stance was reflected in his secondary school policy. He realized that the issue of expansion was a bone of contention in factional struggles and believed that the schools themselves, departing from their original intent, had become hotbeds for politically inclined youth. Instead of expanding the school system, he therefore thought that he should concentrate on developing practical education. What persuaded him of the urgent need to do that, Tanabe wrote the Ministry of Education, was "the prevalence of a peculiar affection among the people under my jurisdiction (and this is true even of ordinary students), the tendency to theorize. They seem to take pride in debating politics and law on the slightest provocation, and look down on practical learning. In the end, this bad habit will produce, if not villains and ruffians, then bankrupts and scoundrels. If one wishes to reform them and turn them all into good people who practice self-cultivation and domestic harmony, it is imperative that priority be given to developing practical schools for agriculture and the trades."[76]

In January 1884 the Ministry of Education issued instructions for middle schools to be consolidated. In deference to those instructions, Tanabe Yoshiaki submitted to the ministry a plan to concentrate in one place all the funds hitherto required for the operation of the prefecture's middle schools by abolishing four of them—Sagawa, Nakamura, Aki, and Akaoka—and leaving only the Kōchi Chūgakkō. His first step was taken in June 1884, when—without consulting the prefectural assembly —he suddenly decreed that the four institutions would become branch schools of the Kōchi Chūgakkō as of the end of the month. In June of the following year, he abolished the branch schools altogether and merged them with the Kōchi Chūgakkō. In effect, he had carried out the ministry's one-prefecture, one-middle-school plan even before its announcement in the Secondary School Act of April 1886.

From a national perspective, the elimination of the four schools accorded with plans to standardize secondary education in Japan. In Kōchi terms, Tanabe Yoshiaki's measures (for all his resolve to stand above politics) amounted to a rejection of the Nationalist view that the times called for an expansion of the prefecture's secondary school system and the acceptance of the Self-Help Society's belief that prefectural middle schools should be abolished. Considering that the standardization pursued by the Ministry of Education was the diametric opposite of the Risshisha's ideal of freedom of education, it was ironic that the society's demands were met in this manner. The goal of "depoliticizing" secondary education—a longtime concern of the prefecture—had, however, at length been attained.

In any event, it is doubtful that the four abolished schools were, as has been asserted, "in a hopeless situation by about 1883"[77] and that their elimination and merger were simply a matter of course. According to the report of Isawa Shūji (1851–1917), a Ministry of Education official who made an inspection of the prefecture in October 1882, the schools at Akaoka and Nakamura were "unworthy of being called secondary schools," but those at Aki and Sagawa were "well supervised" and had "truly remarkable" school spirit; the classroom instruction and the students' academic ability were "superior to any I have seen."[78] Isawa also noted with admiration that "although the building was not well equipped, the work done there was most praiseworthy. Not a fault could be found with mathematics or with other subjects."[79] It is therefore hard to believe that all four schools were already in decline. The Aki school, in particular, would on the contrary appear to have been flourishing. According to an unpublished local history of Aki, it had an enrollment of 150 and boasted a staff of one principal, two teachers of classical Chinese, four of English, three of mathematics, and one of science.[80] If these sources can be trusted, then two of the four schools were conscientiously fulfilling their functions, factional strife notwithstanding. The elimination of all four meant that they had been sacrificed to the political goals of the prefectural authorities.

How did private schools fare in the face of these policies and these changes? Aside from the Kainan Gakkō, they continued to be sponsored by various political associations in the prefecture. Three developments, however, distinguish this period from the preceding one. First, secondary schools were founded by Imperial Loyalist associations with the backing of the Nationalists, something that had not happened before. Second, though established by political groups, the schools began drifting away from factional infighting and became less political in their aims. Third, the people themselves began showing a greater interest in education and called for secondary schools.

Middle schools established by associations affiliated with the Imperial Loyalists included the Kachō Gakusha, founded in Kagami County in June 1879 by the Reinansha; the Yūkō Gakusha, opened in Takaoka County that November by the Yūkōsha; and the Meidō Gakusha, started in Hata County in 1882 by the Meidōkai. The first of these was formed when Mori Shintarō, an old Imperial Loyalist who had founded the Reinansha in Kagami County in 1874, merged a school that he and Ōishi Madoka operated with one in Nagaoka County that was run by Ikeji Taizō.[81] The resultant Kachō Gakusha, situated in Tatsuta Village in Kagami, was recognized by the prefecture as a secondary school. In addition to a classroom building, it had a dormitory and a practice hall for the martial arts. The Confucian scholar Nakanuma Ryōzō (also known as Nakanuma Kien; 1830–1896) and his son Seizō were invited from Kyoto to teach Chinese studies. Hirota Masao, the former principal of the Kōchi Chūgakkō, was hired in 1880; he lectured on Bentham's *Introduction to the Principles of Morals and Legislation* and Spencer's *Social Statics*. With the further addition of teachers in mathematics, English, and law from the Kōchi Chūgakkō and other prefectural schools, the Kachō Gakusha gradually took shape as a full-fledged secondary school. The number of students ranged from several dozen to about a hundred, some coming from as far away as Tokushima Prefecture. Indeed, the school's reputation was such that it was known for a while as the "fount of learning east of the castle."[82] In 1886, however, the school was abolished.

Little is known about the Yūkō Gakusha except that it was approved as a secondary school by the prefecture in 1879, that it was situated in Ōnogō Village in Takaoka County and later moved to Suzaki, and that Kataoka Naoharu was involved in its establishment. Some inkling of its character is given in Isawa Shūji's "Inspection Diary" of October 1882, three years before the school closed: "This school was built by men belonging to the old 'Imperial Loyalist' faction with the aim of educating their sons, but its rules and curriculum are solid and it is a middle school in every sense of the term. Many of its students come from farming families."[83] Not much is known about the Meidō Gakusha, either. It was established in 1880 or 1881, when some members of the old Kinnōha formed the Meidōkai by merging two Loyalist associations, the Gyōyosha and the Shūdōsha, in Hata County. Classified by the prefectural authorities as a "miscellaneous school," the Meidō Gakusha had the character of a private academy and mainly gave instruction in Chinese studies and the martial arts.[84]

These schools are representative of the private academies affiliated with the old Imperial Loyalist party. All were funded by the county branches of the Hundred Works Society. Ikeji Taizō, the principal of the Kachō Gakusha, served concurrently as the head of the Kagami branch of the Hyakusasha; Mori Shintarō was a committee member; and their school shared the objective spelled out in the public announcement of the dissolution of the Neutral Society, cited above: "We ought henceforth turn our attention to the pursuit of knowledge and jobs. We should emphasize practical learning in order to obtain profits and make ourselves and our families independent." Recalling Isawa's comment that the Yūkō Gakusha's "rules and curriculum are solid," one may conclude that the Loyalist-affiliated schools were in fact apolitical and that they functioned in the spirit of Tani Tateki's desire to see the political associations dissolve. The depoliticization of the Loyalist party's schools did not mean, however, that education had become genuinely independent of state authority. As seen earlier, when Nationalist representatives opposed the proposal to abolish prefectural middle schools at the 1883 assembly session, they invoked loyalty to the imperial government to justify their support of the prefecture's policy. In this sense, it may be considered symbolic that the Imperial Loyalist schools were disbanded just as prefectural schools were being merged in 1885 and 1886.

In parallel with the Loyalist party's activity, associations affiliated with the Self-Help Society also founded secondary schools. These were the Kōchi Kyōritsu Gakkō, planned in February 1881 and opened in May 1882, and the Gakkakyoku (Academic Bureau) of the Gakuyōsha, established in January 1884. The Kyōritsu Gakkō, which was classified as a "miscellaneous school" by the prefecture, had a two-year regular course and a two-year higher course, each with English, Japanese and Chinese, and mathematics sections. Standards in the English sections were high. History, physics, zoology, and economics were taught in English in the regular course, as were mechanics, law, social studies, psychology, astronomy, political science, and chemistry in the higher course.[85] In February 1886 (by which time the four prefectural middle schools had been abolished), the Kyōritsu Gakkō further strengthened its program by hiring two American teachers, Glennan and MacAlpin.[86] Other than this, nothing is known about the staff or the student body except that Kataoka Kenkichi served as principal. Needless to say, the school was established by leaders of the Risshisha in hopes of resuscitating the old Risshi Gakusha. Its funding, however, did not come from the Self-Help Society. The Yamanouchi family donated 15,000 yen in response to the society's overtures, and 450 donors from Kōchi and elsewhere gave another 11,000 yen. The dual nature of the school's funding is reflected in its name, Kyōritsu, which means "built together." The new school was distinctly apolitical; in this respect, it differed completely from the Risshi Gakusha, which was no more than the educational organ of a political party.

In the *Kōchi shinbun* of 30 July 1881, Ueki Emori made a fervent appeal for help in collecting funds for the Kyōritsu Gakkō: "O compatriots five hundred thousand strong in this land of Tosa! Join forces to accomplish this task. Come forth with your available resources and help us to succeed. It is for your sake, for the sake of our Tosa, and for the sake of the nation that we sincerely desire this. We beg of you, exert yourselves to the utmost, strive with all your might!" His appeal to everyone in Tosa was no doubt one reason why the institution, unlike those founded by the prefecture or the old Imperial Loyalist faction, was able to approximate the ideal of a school independent of politics.

Another reason why the Kyōritsu Gakkō became apolitical in the true sense of the word was the initiative taken by its principal, Kataoka Kenkichi. It is described by the entrepreneur Ōishi Tamotsu (1870–1924), a sometime Christian minister, as follows: "Associations by this or that name had sprung up in every part of the prefecture. By day, the members would practice swordsmanship, and by night, half drunk, they would mount the podium and give vent to extremist political views. Seeing this, Kataoka restructured the [Risshi Gakusha], making it over into the Kyōritsu Gakkō. He raised its academic standards and turned it into a purely educational institution."[87] Moreover, in November 1884 Kataoka became a Christian. As he incorporated Christian precepts into the school's educational philosophy, the apolitical character of the school became even more pronounced, and it came to differ qualitatively from those that based their education on loyalty to the state.

The third and most important reason for the school's apolitical nature was that the Self-Help Society's educational views had changed. In March and then again in April of 1880, the society took a lead role in forming the League for Establishing a National Assembly. It thus became the matrix from which the Party of Liberty would arise. In the process the Risshisha gradually lost the character of a regional political association motivated by traditional antipathies to the old domain and was transformed into a regional base for a nationwide political party. Furthermore, it found it necessary to draw up a draft constitution as a theoretical guide to future action; Ueki Emori set to work on this draft in August 1881. The Self-Help Society's educational views were derived from this document, which was permeated by a firm commitment to the doctrine of human rights, as well as by a belief in regional self-government that had developed out of the earlier assertion of domain autonomy. Hence the emphasis on an education free of government interference was at the core of those views: "The Japanese people are free to teach and study whatever they wish. . . . Schools must not bend before the authority of the central government." Regional self-government, however, had an important role to play, and local education had to be respected: "Education should be strongly encouraged in local areas. Both public and private primary, secondary, and Western studies schools should be founded and made to flourish."[88] The educational philosophy expressed in the draft constitution was the intellectual basis for the apolitical nature of the Kyōritsu Gakkō, and it was only natural for its author to compose a manifesto that sought to rally support for the school.

The Kyōritsu Gakkō continued in existence until May 1903, when it merged with the Tosa Jogakkō (Tosa Girls' School) and stopped admitting boys. The other educational organ affiliated with the Self-Help Society was the Academic Bureau of the Gakuyōsha, opened in January 1884. Strictly speaking, this was not the kind of formal educational institution that could be called a school, but it did offer instruction at the secondary school level. On its staff were Maeda Mototoshi and Inoue Ton as English instructors; Shimomoto Enzō, who taught the Chinese classics; and Yokoyama Matakichi, who taught poetry and prose. Maeda also taught mathematics.[89]

The educational activities of the political associations also led to a growing demand for schools on the part of the populace. In response to lectures by members of various political associations touring the prefecture, night schools sprang up both in the city of Kōchi and in the outlying counties in 1882 and 1883. At least two illustrative cases of the popular demand for secondary education ought to be cited.

The first is an instance in Nagaoka County that was reported in the *Doyō shinbun* on 20 April 1883: "On the twelfth of this month, several dozen people from Nagaoka County, represented by Yamamoto Seishin, submitted a petition to the prefectural government. Claiming that inequities exist in the use of their local taxes, and giving as a reason the not inconsiderable inconvenience suffered by the children of the county in obtaining an education, they asked that the outlay for other items be reduced and the money used for the construction of a middle school in the county." Their petition was rejected, but the report indicates the extent to which the people in the area desired secondary education. The second case concerns the private Geiyō Gakusha in Aki County, which was founded in March 1886, after the prefecture had closed down the Aki Middle School. Deploring the closure, interested parties borrowed the building of the defunct school to form a new one of their own. Kondō Shitchū, Nomura Morinobu, and Hirota Masao were hired as teachers. The three-year course of studies consisted of Japanese and Chinese classics, English, and mathematics. In 1888 it was extended to five years, and its curriculum was expanded to approximate that of an ordinary prefectural middle school; in 1892, however, financial difficulties forced the Geiyō Gakusha to close. These are but two cases, yet they should not be taken lightly. Not only do they illustrate the growing popular demand for secondary education, they also show that the people themselves were willing to act to obtain it.

Until about 1884, secondary education in Kōchi Prefecture was closely linked to the changing political situation. On the one hand, its development centered on the five prefectural schools and accorded with the prefecture's political interests. On the other hand, it was fostered by two political factions that differed in the stance they took toward the central government and established "apolitical" educational institutions in keeping with their respective educational views. Ideologically, the schools affiliated with Imperial Loyalist groups played an ancillary role to the prefectural schools, while those associated with the Self-Help Society carried out their educational activities from the standpoint of an advocacy of popular rights and sought to nurture free and independent human beings. After July 1884, however, the prefecture changed its course of action. In 1885, it merged the prefectural middle schools with the Kōchi Chūgakkō and subordinated its educational policy to that of the central government. As if in agreement, the schools affiliated with the old Imperial Loyalist faction also disappeared about the same time. The two private schools that survived were the Kyōritsu Gakkō and the Kainan Gakkō. Both received aid from the Yamanouchi family, but their ideological orientations were diametrical opposites. The former school upheld modern liberal ideas, while the latter (which was reorganized as an ordinary middle school in 1888) remained promilitary in the traditional sense.

Ironically, popular demand for secondary education rose just as the prefectural schools were being merged and reduced in number. When the prefecture failed to respond, the people formed schools on their own. The Geiyō Gakusha is a prime example of such schools, which increased rapidly in number from 1887.[90] Indeed, one could almost say that from the middle 1880s onward, private schools again became the mainstream of secondary education in Kōchi Prefecture. Moreover, there had been immense progress, because the motive for founding such schools had changed. They were no longer meant to accommodate political interests but rather to meet the demands of the people.

4

The Confucian Ideal of Rule by Virtue and the Creation of National Politics
The Political Thought of Tani Tateki

Translated by W. J. Boot

The object of inquiry in this chapter is the thought and the actions of one man, Tani Tateki. The purpose of this close look at Tani is to elucidate the criticism directed at the Meiji government by adherents of conservative political thought that reflected the traditional moral vision of Confucianism. The analysis, which covers the first half of the Meiji period, also seeks to clarify the role played by that conservative political persuasion in the creation of "Meiji thought."

The Meiji Government and Conservative Thought

Not many people will have heard of Tani Tateki (1837–1911). Even someone who happens to know his name (which is sometimes read as Tani Kanjō) will not remember much more than that Tani was the courageous general who held Kumamoto Castle at the time of the Satsuma Rebellion, withstanding the siege laid by the army of Saigō Takamori (1827–1877). The siege of Kumamoto in 1877, however, was only a small part of Tani's long life. Far more important, both to Tani as an individual and to the history of political thought in the Meiji period, was his political career. Tani took his stand on the Confucian moral ideal of the Kingly Way. Accordingly, he discountenanced the bureaucratic, Europeanizing, despotic notions of the Meiji government, preached the virtue of Loving the People, and advocated for Japan an independence based on assuring the people's livelihood. Never one to shrink from criticizing the government, he could justly be called the "voice of the people that has no voice."

Tani's was not the only conservative voice to make itself heard in early Meiji Japan. Various strands of conservative thought existed in the period, but they may broadly be distinguished into two types. Inspected in greater detail or from a different point of view, they could probably be divided in all kinds of other ways, but choosing the following two is the easiest way to bring the problem into focus.

Type I comprises the thought and practice of members of the former samurai class, who demanded the revival of the feudal privileges they had once enjoyed; of the former court aristocracy, who dreamed of the glorious times of the ancient imperial court and expected to recreate that age through the restoration of direct imperial rule; and of Shinto priests and scholars, who counted on the growing political influence of the court aristocracy to revive the power of the shrines and the prosperity of the Shinto world. It comprehends, in general, the thought and practice of all those who felt a revulsion against the whole of the Westernizing policies of the Meiji government. Their demand, concrete and reactionary, was for the government to give up those policies. This is the type of people one discovers in declining classes that cannot adapt themselves to the times and whose intention it is to restore what could be called their traditional pattern of behavior.

Type II, in contrast, comprises those people who understood the historical meaning of the revival of direct imperial rule and of the Meiji Restoration. They were straightforward in acknowledging the defects of the old pattern of behavior; for all that, however, they had no doubts at all about the Confucian system of ideas. Indeed, they tried to bring some method into their political activities by using those traditional moral ideals as their standard of reference.

This second type is related to the well-known way of thinking that is summed up by the watchword "Eastern ethics, Western arts" (*Tōyō dōtoku, Seiyō geijutsu*). At the core of their political thought stood Rule by Virtue. Those who belonged to this second type consequently opposed policies that ignored the immediate interests of the people's livelihood; they censured the government's modernizing élan and its authoritarian tendencies; they condemned it for infringing the ideals of the Kingly Way and of Loving the People, that is, for being a despotism that negated what they regarded as ultimate values. Conscious as they were of the rule that a humane government "listened to the voice of the people," they urged a more gradual modernization, one that would keep pace with the conditions that actually governed the people's lives. Among those endowed with such a sensibility are to be found thinkers and politicians who had studied under the foremost political theorists of the Bakumatsu period (1854–1867). Type II, then, includes those whose intentions were, so to speak, oriented toward the traditional value system.

To be sure, the Meiji government, too, was conservative in its political ideas. That much is evident—to cite only the most obvious example —from its rejection of the revolutionary demands made by the popular-rights movement *(jiyū minken undō)*. But does the government's conservatism truly compare with the two types that have just been described? Both of those types aimed at traditional goals; both clearly belonged in the traditionalist camp, either because of the ideas they espoused or because of their pattern of behavior. That could not be asserted of the early Meiji government, which was characterized by a strong urge to destroy tradition, coupled with as strong a tendency to exploit tradition as a means to an end. In short, the government's ideas and actions set it apart from the conservatism that is at issue here, which was bound to tradition ideologically. For all that, the first of the two types of conservatism outlined above could amount to nothing more than the driving power of reactionary social disturbances; it had no positive significance within the history of Meiji political thought. Hence it may as well be omitted from consideration, with attention concentrated on Type II, which manifested itself characteristically in Tani Tateki.

Insofar as Tani's conservatism was bolstered by Confucian moral ideals, it was of course essentially different from modern, democratic political thought. He appealed to a logic of gradual social improvement, but that was something he had taken over from elsewhere to make good a deficiency in his own conservative way of thinking. The young Tokutomi Sohō (1863–1957), who preached his own brand of democracy, *heiminshugi*, showed how sharply he had discerned the character of that way of thinking when he wrote about Tani Tateki's political movement in 1887: "This New Conservative party, however elusive and protean its arguments and however unfathomable its gospel may be, in the final analysis is nothing but the one word—eclecticism." It was only natural for Sohō to criticize Tani's logic as fraudulent. In however progressive a robe it might be dressed, Sohō maintained, it showed a lack of comprehension of the principles of social structure and of the laws of social progress "that link everything and cannot be untied."[1]

Sohō was correct, and his comment clearly marks the limits that applied in general to the logic of early Meiji conservatism, intent as it was on following a traditional system of ideas. This is, however, precisely the place where the problems begin, for once one has recognized the limitations of this logic, the issue becomes: What *in concreto* were the angle and the contents of this eclecticism? In other words, what did the conservatives take from others, and for what purpose? These questions are important in seeking to determine the level of political significance attained by conservatism in the early Meiji era.

When the major conservatives of that era are considered from this point of view, the one closest to the traditional ideology turns out to be Motoda Nagazane (also known as Motoda Eifu; 1818–1891), who had special political influence as a palace adviser in immediate proximity to the emperor. Next comes Nishimura Shigeki (1828–1902), who generated a movement for educating the people on his own, without relying on the government, and who censured the government for the contradictions that inhered in its modernizing cultural policies. Third comes a man who had gained a deep understanding of modern nationalism through his travels in Europe and was therefore all the more able to speak for the concrete interests of the people—Tani Tateki.

All these thinkers or politicians were able to deliver criticisms pertinent to the contemporary situation. Their political significance and the role played by each, however, depended on changes in the character and the social sensibility of the Meiji government, the object of their censure. Only through an analysis of this point can one come to understand why their critical activities had objective importance.

Motoda and Nishimura preached a National Doctrine and a National Ethic that amounted to a revised form of Confucianism. They developed their ideas as a criticism of the government, maintaining that the government's bad policies made such an educational movement necessary. This criticism was most pertinent and appropriate in the period before the Political Crisis of 1881, that is, in the days when the government did not yet consider putting itself on a constitutional basis. Once it did, however, their complaints more or less lost their pertinence; Tani's, on the other hand, became objectively more significant. In part, this significance can be attributed to new elements that had entered Tani's conservatism but were not to be found in the thought of people like Nishimura. Primarily, however, Nishimura's criticisms lost their positive significance after the crisis because of changes undergone by their object, the government. This point needs some further clarification.

Ever since the Meiji government had come to power, it had exerted all its strength to free itself from the treaties of the Ansei era (January 1855–1860), which had placed Japan in a subordinate position with respect to the United States, Russia, and Europe. Its objective was to secure Japan's complete independence internationally. With that end in view, it had set itself the task of achieving a unified Japanese people by wiping away the feudal demarcations that divided the country into localized power bases and by freeing the populace from the fetters of the feudal status system. This aspiration was not limited to the government authorities. It was shared by the champions of people's rights, who were opposed to the government; by the traditionalists; and by the Western-minded intellectuals represented by the Society of Meiji Six (Meirokusha).[2] Japan's independence was a categorical imperative imposed on all Meiji Japanese.

As its first step toward this goal, the Meiji government embarked on a daring campaign of domestic reform. At its core were the young bureaucrats gathered in the Ministry of Finance, who had acquired the necessary new knowledge from the West. With their help the government set about overthrowing feudalism, creating a modern, centralized national system of authority, and propagating the Western ideas essential to its objectives. The government wanted urgently to create a Japanese capitalist structure that could resist the pressures of the European and American powers, and in particular the immense strength of the capitalist economy that drove them. It also wanted to establish a social system that would promote developments in that direction. No one, however, could expect the modernization of such a backward country as Japan to follow a natural process of maturation or the building of capitalism to arise out of existing domestic circumstances; the proper conditions had to be created. What had to be done first, the Meiji leadership felt, was to found a strong regime and to foster the growth of an enlightened social layer, one that would support the government in the exercise of its authority. Afterwards there would be time to decide on a political setup and a distribution of power conducive to modern economic strength and appropriate to its social foundations.

The historical events of this period are generally known, so there is no need to go into them. Put in a few words, they had a twofold significance. First, the government created a *regime*—a centralized bureaucratic structure—that raised feudal Japan to the level of a modern unified state and at the same time brought into being a homogeneous *nation*—one without status discrimination—that actually managed the economy and society of this unified state. Second, to facilitate the introduction of capitalism, the government rapidly implemented the policy of "civilization and enlightenment" *(bunmei kaika),* one that sought its models in Europe and America. It thereby made it possible for the energies of the nation to cooperate fully in achieving the goals of the state. During the short epoch that is identified by that slogan, flowers from foreign countries were with feverish haste transplanted into the feudal soil of Japan.

The government itself was not a capitalist regime, and yet it demolished the foundations of the old society in its hurry to bring about the preconditions for fostering capitalism. To accomplish that, the government needed strong powers. Put another way, its ability to make Japan into a modern nation—its capacity for "enlightenment"—rested on two premises: the despotism inherent in the *hanbatsu,* the cliques from the old domains in which feudal power had been concentrated and which ran the new regime; and the means to legitimize this despotism, namely, the government's monopoly of the traditional authority of the emperor.

Thus the single body of the government was simultaneously inhabited by two contradictory qualities, modernity and despotism. This contradiction caused frequent dissension within the ruling group, whose internal antagonisms immediately spread outward in the form of political contention and social disturbance. The conservatives, not opposed to despotism as such ideologically, nonetheless criticized the government because of this internal inconsistency: "The recent reforms in our country take no account of the people's convenience; reforms are made solely according to the government's convenience. . . . Without thinking in the least of the people's convenience, they suddenly reform the ancient laws that have been in force for hundreds or thousands of years, and they think they do it right."[3] A perception of reality peculiar to them underlay the conservatives' judgment. Nishimura Shigeki phrased it thus: "Of itself, the realm is at peace; it is only that stupid people intentionally throw it into disorder."[4] But the contradiction within the government was not criticized only from a conservative point of view. It was also pointed out by the intellectuals banded together in the Meirokusha, the most prominent of whom was Fukuzawa Yukichi (1835–1901); Nishimura, incidentally, was also a member of that society. To be sure, the idea of a civil society espoused by those intellectuals was the opposite of the conservatives' cherished notion.

That was not all. The abolition of the feudal system, abruptly forced by the government, had given rise to a wave of sensual liberation and indulgence in carnal desires that swept all the way from the bureaucratic stratum, through the former samurai, down to the ordinary people; it had brought about an era of moral vacuum, one devoid of any consciousness of social norms. Modern, Western thought as it was propagated at the time contained no idealistic appeals that might have filled this vacuum—another reason why it failed to satisfy the idealism of the traditional conservatives and gave an impression of insufficiency to the earnest young men who were in search of new moral ideals. In the event, some of them turned toward Christianity. The observations Yamaji Aizan (1864–1917) makes in his "Historical Essay on the Church in Modern Japan" go some way to explain why conservatism became prominent and Christianity popular:[5]

I believe that the conservative trend of those days may to some extent have been propelled merely by "love for the old," but when I turn back to its roots and inquire deeply into its origins, I also see that it had greater and more serious causes than that simple feeling. Shall I try to describe them? First, the new learning from the West did not give satisfaction to the people. Even though the Japanese people had grown tired of Neo-Confucian pantheism, nevertheless, to seek the original source of morals in an unshakable authority is a need that in all ages lies secluded at the bottom of men's hearts—and neither empiricism nor skepticism, and certainly not a Theory of Rights will ever be able to satisfy this need. Second, the propagators themselves could not but recognize that their preachments totally lacked the authority to rectify the immorality and bad customs of those days, which were a reflection of materialistic tendencies. Looking back, I cannot help being amazed at the extraordinary weakness of the authority that was meant to suppress the animal desires of the Japanese people. Let us just cast a glance at the things that were printed in those days. . . . Is it not true that there were books no different from obscene prints or pornography? But the government did not forbid them, and the schools did not exclude them from their premises. Even youngsters and children read them, and did not know enough to be ashamed. . . . This is why a conservative reaction was born in one part of society.

The government did, in fact, have such a character. The social consciousness really was as it is described here. That is why Nishimura Shigeki's traditional, conservative criticism was so meaningful. To him, there were no reasons why new social elements that were qualitatively different from Japanese society as it had existed until then should suddenly be transplanted to Japan, as the bureaucrats of the modernizing faction were planning to do. He saw no necessity, moreover, either to deny the continuity that existed between the society of the Meiji period and the society that had preceded it or to deny the existence of all kinds of beneficial sensibilities that connected the two societies. He was therefore opposed to the notion that the government, ignoring the way in which the people ran their daily lives, could self-righteously effect changes—changes to which the people would be unable to adapt smoothly. Inspired by what ultimately was the idea of the Kingly Way, he proclaimed the unity of moral cultivation and statecraft. From the government authorities he expected an ethical attitude and sympathy with the people; a gradual reform, one adapted to the conditions and realities of the life of the people, would be best, he thought. Instead of a bureaucratic, unfeeling despotism, he wanted a kinder, gentler despotism that ruled through virtue.

Before 1877 Nishimura refrained from criticizing the government directly and did not openly express himself, even within the Ministry of Education where he worked. That year, however, the intrinsic discord that had been brought to a head within the government by the 1873 proposal to invade Korea finally exploded in the form of the Satsuma Rebellion; the antigovernment agitation conducted by the popular-rights movement also came to a climax about that time. Nishimura now made the most of the traditional values and feelings, which remained strong and influential in the people's actual lives; he attempted to arouse the people's ethical consciousness, challenging the nation to become aware that it was part of the body politic. Asserting that "many of the powerful and the rich are people whose moral conduct is improper," he drew the natural conclusion: "One who seeks to practice the Way in the present age must first propagate things that do not agree with the intentions of the powerful or the rich."[6] He gathered enthusiasts around his own banner, founded societies for moral activism, and through them developed a movement on a national scale for the education of the people. This movement evolved from the Tokyo Society for the Study of Moral Training (Tōkyō Shūshin Gakusha) of 1876, through the Japanese Association for Expounding the Way (Nihon Kōdōkai) of 1884, into the Japanese Association for Spreading the Way (the homophonous Nihon Kōdōkai) of 1887.

In the government's pursuit of modernization, Nishimura had discerned elements destructive of the national ethic and had accordingly found himself unable to trust it any longer. This was at the root of his criticism of the government, and that criticism was certainly pertinent. To be sure, after 1881 Nishimura's ethical movement rather lost the critical pertinence in regard to the government that it had possessed earlier. But his idea that the fundament of the state's prosperity rested on the morals of the nation had at least one important effect: it underlay the development of a sentiment that Tani Tateki was later to exploit and transform into a national political movement. Or, rather, it may be more accurate to say that the concrete manifestation of Nishimura's idea, the national movement that developed through the medium of his societies for moral education, laid the foundations of that sentiment. In any event, when we compare Nishimura's moral activism with Motoda Nagazane's scheme of formulating a National Doctrine, we must conclude that Nishimura's fully qualifies as a national movement—unlike Motoda's design, which was likewise meant to buttress the national ethic. All the steps toward the implementation of the latter scheme were taken under the aegis of the emperor's authority.

The Government after the Crisis of 1881
and Traditional Conservative Thought

Both Nishimura and Motoda attributed the rise of social unrest to the contradictory manner in which the government pursued modernity while embracing despotism, the two principles that determined its policies. They thought that the cause of unrest lay in the government's failure to introduce modernization systematically in accordance with traditional moral ideals and believed that systematizing policy in that manner would, by the same token, mean stabilizing society. Had they wanted to criticize the government's despotic character as such, they would have had to question the nature of despotism; as far as they were concerned, however, the most urgent task of the moment was the adjustment of modernity, and to that they turned. This was only a natural priority for those who attached importance to the continuities between the society of the Meiji period and the preceding society. Those who stressed the social discontinuity, as did the Western-minded intellectuals of Fukuzawa's party, criticized despotism for what it was; so did the activists of the popular-rights movement, who opposed the government directly in the political arena. To stretch a point, the government's modernizing élan was too forceful for the traditional conservatives to focus on its despotic character; its despotism, on the other hand, was too flagrant for the champions of popular rights and the Western-minded intellectuals to size up the suitability of its modernizing policies from the standpoint of the people's real interests.

Another voice was added to the chorus of criticism when Tani Tateki, the commander in chief of the Eastern Area Army (Tōbu Kangun buchō),[7] spoke out against the pension regulations enacted by the Army Ministry in March 1879. His reason for doing so was that the regulations were modeled after the French system, the beneficiaries being limited to wives and children, the constituent members of the modern family. The Army Ministry, manifesting an attitude that was bound up with the government's notions of modernity, had at the very least ignored the existence of the traditional family system. Tani expressed his dissatisfaction in a memorial to the Grand Council of State (Dajōkan):[8]

> In our country, when we set up teachings, we make loyalty and filial piety their basis. This goes a long way back. Therefore, when somebody is loyal in serving his lord, the officials commend him and the people praise him. Loyalty, propriety, and filial piety are the exquisite virtues of the human race and the most famous product of the East. Since intercourse

with foreign nations began, the various systems and institutions have changed greatly; there are those that have gained and those that have lost as a consequence. They who fawn upon the fashions of the day, only imitating Western ways, denigrate and diminish even those sterling qualities of our mind and nature in which we excel and the foreigners fall short. . . . But even if the systems and institutions of our country have changed greatly, one thing remains unaltered from former days: loyalty and filial piety are obligations implied in the human condition. Therefore, when parents raise their children, there is not one who does not desire them to be loyal subjects and pious children. How much more does this apply to those who make soldiering their profession! Since from the beginning death is their lot—how loyal, how pious are they who die when they must die! Nowadays the surviving parents of someone who has died for the state cannot enjoy the same rights as his widow or his children. How then can we say that the balance is kept even? When privately I reflect on the Army Pension Regulations, I note that there is a statute regarding the support of the widow but provisions for the support of the parents are lacking. Thus I know for sure that the regulations are based on the Western system and that it is not a matter of their being carelessly composed. What to do, however, with the fact that they are not in accord with the teachings or the human feelings of our country?

There is no mistaking the underlying tone that runs through Tani's criticism. Neither in its intent nor in its contents does it depart an inch from the edifice of Nishimura's or Motoda's thought. Nevertheless, what he said was significant, because it addressed the real interests of the people in an objective way. It was unlikely, as Tani pointed out, that a modern family as stipulated in the pension regulations would really exist in contemporary society; and it was a fact, as he noted, that an awareness of loyalty and filial piety as norms for the people's daily life had not yet lost its value.

Once, however, their adversary had rid itself of its modern affectations—the center of their criticism—these critics' ideas, if unchanged, could not but lose their pertinence. And that was destined to happen when the government chose the new direction of constitutional reform while at the same time making full use of elements of tradition. The occasion for that was the Political Crisis of 1881. Principal imperial adviser *(sangi shuhan)* Ōkuma Shigenobu (1838–1922), the powerful figure who had forced through the policy of modernization, overriding all internal or external opposition, was with one stroke banished from the government. Purged along with him were the young bureaucrats, mainly graduates of Fukuzawa's school, who had helped Ōkuma to exe-

cute his policy as his staff. At one fell swoop, the government had severed the root of the conservatives' discontent. Ōkuma had used despotic
power to push forward his modernizing policies, which were fundamentally directed at establishing a capitalist society. Being precipitate,
rational, and uniform, they went against the immediate interests of the
people; and yet, ultimately, they were not unrelated to the realization of
a civil society.

In the course of this purge, the government threw off what could be
called its "raw" modernity. Quite a few good studies exist already, so
there is no need to go into detail on the problem of how the crisis broke
out. What, however, was its significance? After the death of Ōkubo
Toshimichi (1830–1878), the Meiji government had lost the center of its
internal cohesion and had become, as Miyake Setsurei (1860–1945) described it in his "Contemporary History," a "motley congregation" of
the Satsuma-Chōshū clique on the one hand, and Ōkuma's on the other.[9]
The government was not only confronted with the popular-rights movement and its agitation for the opening of a parliament, which reached
its highest peak in 1879–1880, but was also embarrassed by the polemics
about sovereignty that greatly enlivened the newspapers in 1880–1881.
If it was to maintain its dignity and prevent disturbances of the social
order, the government had to strengthen itself quickly. It did so by
excluding Ōkuma from its midst and reaffirming the solidarity between
Satsuma and Chōshū—all in the name of the unity and order of the
state. (A Saga man, Ōkuma was a foreign element as far as the Sat-Chō
clique was concerned.) That was the main point of the Political Crisis of
1881.

Even before this crisis, the government had been considering the
necessity of recasting itself in a constitutional mold. It had realized that
it would only be adding fuel to the flames if it sought to oppose the rising popular-rights movement with the methods laid down in the Public
Assembly Ordinance (Shūkai Jōrei) of April 1880, that is, if it tried simple suppression by force. The government had to choose a new direction if it was to get this movement under legal, rational control. In other
words, constitutional reform was unavoidable.

In December 1879 the sovereign consulted all the imperial advisers
(sangi) about their opinions regarding constitutionalism. The considerations shared by the government's animating spirit, Iwakura Tomomi
(1825–1883), with his fellow oligarchs Sanjō Sanetomi (1837–1891)
and Prince Arisugawa Taruhito (1835–1895), are worth noting:[10]

> These days, people who ardently desire the establishment of a parliament
> and clamorously debate it have sprung up on all sides. If we ignore them

and fail to heed this desire, I fear that the masses will be incited more and more by their riotous words and that the peace of the realm will be disturbed; in the end we should face an uncontrollable disaster. This thought fills me with distress. Therefore I wish that the government would speedily determine the time for the opening of a parliament and that it would draft a constitution on the firm basis of our own national polity but with selective reference also to the good institutions of the various European and American countries. Once the day comes when the draft is completed, His Majesty may graciously examine its merits and its disadvantages in detail, looking back on what has passed and pondering the future. If he were then to rule on it and manifest it to the countless millions of people, then—I earnestly hope—we shall be able to maintain the peace of the realm forever. This is something I urgently and unceasingly desire.

This is a clear exposition of the oligarchs' designs. The government's intention obviously was to modify its despotic character, not to abjure it—come what may.

One of the opinions solicited by the emperor did, however, signify a denial of despotism. The last response to be submitted, it was Ōkuma's request for an immediate implementation of a British system of parliamentary politics, written on his behalf by Yano Fumio (Ryūkei; 1850–1931). Point 7 ("General Principles") of this statement asserts the following: "Constitutional government is government by political parties. The struggle between political parties is a struggle between principles. Therefore, a political party should gain power when its principles come to be held by more than half the nation, and it should lose that political power when they go counter to the principles of the majority. This is true constitutional government, and herein lies its true advantage. If, having used its form as our model, we were to throw away its true spirit, that would not only be unfortunate for the country but, in my opinion, also disastrous for the rulers. Nor would it be a calamity to the rulers only in their own time; for they would bequeath to later generations a tainted reputation of love for power."[11]

As a result of expressing such an enlightened opinion, Ōkuma became the only member of the government whose popularity actually increased at a time when the government was under heavy popular attack because of its scandalous scheme to sell public property in Hokkaidō. This earned him the hostility of one of the elders of the Satsuma faction, Kuroda Kiyotaka (1840–1900), who had become the butt of public opprobrium for his role in devising that scheme of privatization, which would have brought great financial gain to a group of merchants headed by Godai Tomoatsu (1835–1885), another Satsuma man.[12] Ōkuma remained steadfastly against that plan even after it received the government's initial approval in July 1881, and it was dropped later that year as the voices of popular opposition mounted. In the interest of preserving the cohesion between Satsuma and Chōshū within the government, however, it was decided that Ōkuma must be cast out. On 12 October 1881, he was forced to leave office. On the same day, the government issued an imperial proclamation that designated 1890 as the year a parliament would be convened.

Thus the government robbed the popular-rights movement of its weapon, the petition for the opening of a parliament, while at the same time it rid the conservatives of their fears concerning the government's modernity. Thereafter the government chose Prussia as the advanced country on which to pattern itself, as that model accorded best with the constitutional metamorphosis it wanted to put itself through. Having rejected the political thought of England and France, it went full speed ahead along the road of what may be called a constitutionalization from above, that is, the bestowal of a constitution by the emperor upon his people. Inoue Kowashi (1843–1895), secretary of the Grand Council of State, mapped out this course of action.

In June 1881, as the government was still going through the process that would lead to its eventual transformation, Tani Tateki left its service. Tani resigned his position as commandant of the army's Military Academy out of dissatisfaction with the authorities that had failed to accept his request for a revision of the Army Pension Regulations and had chosen to ignore his exposure of the illegal dealings of the prefect of Nagasaki in connection with the removal of the army cemetery in that city. On 12 September, Tani and three other generals who had grown dissatisfied with the Army Ministry—Torio Koyata (1847–1905), Miura Kanju (Gorō; 1846–1926), and Soga Sukenori (1843–1935)— submitted a petition for the establishment of a constituent assembly. They appealed for the organization of the government—the root, in their view, of the social disturbances—to be firmed up; requested the enactment of an imperial constitution, so that "people's hearts would be given something to turn to"; and asked that equitable measures be taken to settle the matter of the sale of public property in Hokkaidō, the affair that had generated so much antigovernment sentiment.[13]

In October 1881, Tani and a friend from his home district, the conservative Sasaki Takayuki (1830–1910) who was a member of the emperor's entourage, organized a group called the Chūseitō (Fairness party): "We consult with like-minded people; we support the Imperial House; we have as our goal the establishment of a constitutional system; we maintain the peace of the realm with fair, unbiased principles, without running toward radicalism or drifting toward temporizing; and we expect in this way to safeguard the happiness of the people."[14] The actual aim of the Fairness party, however, was to persuade the government of the necessity to enact an imperial constitution that would define the conduct and the powers of a parliament before one was convened— as opposed to the popular-rights movement's radical demands for the opening of a parliament. The group's more concrete goals included devising measures to stop the sale of government property in Hokkaidō and to bring about the retirement of Ōkuma, in their eyes the extremist who was disturbing the government's unity. In other words, Tani played a part in the purge of the modernizers, even though he himself was in the opposition. He did so out of a desire for the government to pull together in the interest of stabilizing the order of the state. The stance that he assumed vis-à-vis the government in organizing the Chūseitō corresponds with the attitude he had adopted four or five years earlier, when he collaborated with the same Sasaki in setting up the Chūritsu-sha—Neutral Society—to counter the activities of the Risshisha (Self-Help Society; a political association that was at the forefront of the popular-rights movement) in his native province of Tosa. What, in sum, did Tani's political activities during these years amount to? He had formulated a practical criticism of the government's aspirations to modernity, no less than of the people's hopes for citizen-like political power. But his ideas and his criticism could no longer be pertinent to the government after the Political Crisis of 1881.

The Meiji government's resolution of that crisis—the expulsion of Ōkuma and his followers, undertaken concomitantly with the proclamation of an imperial rescript that set the date for the inauguration of a parliament—was a neatly turned trick to perpetuate its despotic power. Uematsu Kōshō (1876–1912), who had ties with Ōkuma's Kaishintō (Reform party), points this out almost as if he were praising the enemy's dexterity: "This was truly the cleverest of all the various political stratagems at which the clique government had tried its hand up till then. The fact that the feudal cliques still exist today, it is no exaggeration to say, is totally due to this."[15] It is hardly necessary to point out, however, that this particular stratagem was not an attempt of the Meiji government to maintain and preserve its former, "raw" despotism. Rather, the government used its despotic power as a means of ensuring the revisions that it had to undergo. In any event, through this political crisis the government did manage to rid itself of the "raw" modernity that was the other constituent element of its internal contradiction. Moreover, its plan was to go on and dissolve the whole contradiction by refining its "raw" despotism and transmuting it into a constitutional system after the Prussian model, one with an imperially bestowed constitution. (This was the design conceived by Inoue Kowashi.) The mélange of two contrary ideologies, the Restoration of Imperial Rule *(ōsei fukko)* and the Meiji Renewal *(Meiji ishin)*, in which "raw" despotism and "raw" modernity had been confusedly entangled, was now raised to the level of a new principle—the conception of an imperial state in which the emperor's authority, characterized by the ancient model of the Kingly Way, and his functioning in a modern constitutional system were mutually mediated and thus unified.

The Meiji government thought that the realization of this ideal would be the way to secure Japan's independence as a state. Now that it had a clear perception of its goal, the government was ready to use just about any means—despotic power, traditional authority, Western manners and customs—that might help to attain that objective. To the members of the ruling group, the ideal of the imperial state transcended everything. No matter how ardently they pursued this new ideal, however, their fervor did not mean that they had abjured despotism; and even if they intended to reform themselves as a constitutional government, they could not actually assume that constitutional character until the parliament opened in 1890. When in the intervening years the government made an expedient use of its power, it did so without any reference to its transcendent moral principle, and that use of power appeared utterly without disguise.

By way of preparing for the introduction of a constitutional system, the Meiji government in 1882 dispatched Itō Hirobumi (1849–1909) to Europe to conduct a survey of the fundamental principles of Western states. Later that same year, it regulated the finances of the imperial household. In 1884, it created the peerage system. In this way it constructed a substantial basis for an imperial regime not directly founded in the people. In 1885, it abolished the Grand Council of State, introducing a modern cabinet system, and reorganized the bureaucracy. The government also tried to placate the leaders of the Jiyūtō (Party of Liberty), which had revolutionary inclinations, and of the Reform party, which persisted in its demands for a system of parliamentary party politics to be put into effect. With these conciliatory tactics, the government sought to make these parties disband or in any event to weaken them and split them up; in short, it did its best to transform the popular political forces that opposed it into parliamentary parties that would assist it. Adopted on the educational front was the statist educational policy of Mori Arinori (1847–1889), which was intended to raise a nation of loyal subjects, one suited to the operation of the imperial constitution. All these things were possible only through the expedient use of despotic power.

Behind the policy of conciliating the political parties and behind the educational policy lurked the delicate calculations of Inoue Kowashi. Immediately after the imperial rescript on the establishment of a parliament was issued, he gave Itō the following counsel:[16]

> Of all the writings that nowadays circulate amongst the people, not one fails to preach the excellence of England. Of all the theories the young children learn, not one neglects to nurture the spirit of reform. All the people are exposed to these influences from morning until night, internalizing them as their nature. Ten years from now the old will be gone, the young will have grown, and these ideas will finally reach their strongest influence. It cannot be fathomed as yet whether they will not suddenly burst forth and give rise to a revolution. When one quietly thinks this over, his heart chills. I believe that the public feeling is able to change the political system, but the political system is not able to control the public feeling. A constitution may be the way to establish the nation, but the public feeling is what upholds a constitution. If a constitution completely goes against the public feeling, how could one hope for it to be definite and unchangeable!

It would appear, then, that although the government went about its preparations for the introduction of a constitutional system in a despotic and authoritarian fashion, there was some room to argue that its peremptoriness was unavoidable; after all, no concrete expression had as yet been given to the new conception of the state.

If the new state structure desired by the government truly was intended as the means of securing the unity of the nation and the independence of the Japanese people from foreign interference, the Meiji government should have waited until 1890 to settle at least such major diplomatic issues as the revision of the treaties. The government, however, chose not to wait. On the principle that diplomacy thrives best on secrecy and undivided responsibility, it sought to achieve the revision of the treaties and to prepare the ground diplomatically for the introduction of a constitutional system before the parliament was inaugurated. In short, the government did not in a true sense try to coordinate its domestic and foreign policies as parts of its progress toward the creation of a constitutional system.

As is shown by a declaration made by Minister of Foreign Affairs Inoue Kaoru (1835–1915) at a cabinet meeting in July 1887, treaty revision was approached from the point of view of transforming Japan into something "just like a European country" and making the Japanese people into something "just like a European people." In other words, it meant "creating a new European empire in the region of the Far East." Therefore Japan's interior should be opened to foreign access, the contacts between "them" and "us" should increase in frequency, and the government should in this way "make everybody not only feel the inconvenience and realize the unprofitability of his present way of life but also absorb the knowledge of the West, its vigor, and its energy."[17]

For several years from 1884–1885 on, the so-called policy of Europeanization was in force; this was the notorious Rokumeikan period. This new policy still ignored the realities of national life, so in this respect it did not bring a change; in its nature, however, it differed considerably from previous modernizing policies. These had been aimed at creating a capitalist economy that had never before existed in Japan. They may not have been very thorough, but they did signify an attempt to modernize the social structure as such—an attempt not unrelated to the concept of a modern civil society. "Europeanization," in contrast, was nothing but an external Westernization of Japan, one more stratagem for the revision of the treaties, meant to give collateral support to the secret diplomatic efforts of the imperial state. It strongly smacked of an attempt to curry favor with the foreign nations. This is clear from two humiliating provisions that were included in Inoue's draft for the treaty revision: "Our government will create a judicial organization and criminal law, a law on criminal procedures, civil law, commercial law, a law on trial procedures, etc., following the doctrines of the West" and "Our government will appoint judges and public prosecutors of foreign nationality."[18]

The policy of Europeanization drew some perceptive criticism. A Jiyūtō activist, Suehiro Tetchō (1849–1896), remarked in October 1887 that the government's apparent conviction that "priority should be given to foreign affairs rather than domestic matters" would mean the "unavoidable introduction of the material products of modernization." Hence luxury would naturally increase in society. In government, the emphasis on external matters would necessarily involve an expansion of the bureaucracy. How would the "necessary expenditures" be met? "Those who are among the people" have "advocated lower taxes until they were blue in the face," but all their pleas will have been in vain. And the unfortunate results of the policy "would not stop here." Since the general idea is "to let the foreigners know that the domestic government is well organized and the realm at peace," the government can obviously ill afford "to let the dissatisfied elements in the country wag their tongues to their hearts' content." Suppression of freedom of speech would be the inevitable result.[19]

Although he eagerly desired the Europeanization of the common people, the young Tokutomi Sohō, too, was dissatisfied with the government's policy:[20]

> Its sole purpose is to extract from the foreigners the sweet words "Japan has really modernized." Our people will not be able to add the least bit of happiness to their lives. It is as if the constitution and the laws come nearer and nearer to perfection while the people lose their rights more and more, as if society is improved while the people suffer more and more, as if religion spreads while ethics deteriorate more and more, as if education flourishes while ignoramuses increase more and more. Such is the society we are creating, a hypocritical kind of society scarcely imagined by social philosophers, and we must not be surprised. To make the foreigners happy and to buy their flattery in this way would be permissible, if it did not have its price. Since no politician is an alchemist or a sorcerer, however, one should know that the money to pay that price has all been found through shaking out the contents of our people's purses. Flattery from foreigners undoubtedly has some value, but is it so valuable that we should buy it at the price of bankrupting our fellow Japanese? That should be called a rather exorbitant price.

As these criticisms show, "to give priority to outside matters" in reality meant nothing but putting the interests of the foreign nations first. The policy increased the nation's economic burden and strongly injured its self-esteem. Europeanization, which had appeared as a substitute modernization policy, was a far cry from what had once been the main objective—the introduction of capitalism.

From the middle of the 1880s onward, the government tried in the ways described above to eliminate the contradictions inherent in "civilization and enlightenment," but in all this it acted despotically. However vehement their words might be, the traditional conservatism of Nishimura or of Tani—the Tani of those days—cannot be called an objective criticism of this government; already their criticisms did not mean much more than a subjective warning because the government no longer had the qualities needed to put up a fundamental resistance against anything traditional. Rather, it made full use of elements of tradition itself: behind the policy of Europeanization it held in readiness a special kind of statist education. Things had come to such a pass that Itō Hirobumi himself, who had resolutely opposed all of Motoda Nagazane's schemes for the formulation of a National Doctrine even in 1879 (when the popular-rights movement was at its peak), in 1890 no longer dared to oppose the same Motoda Nagazane's drive for the promulgation of an Imperial Rescript on Education. It might be true that people who lived under social relations carried over from the feudal period had been abruptly cast into a new social reality by modernizing policies which resulted in the destruction of their livelihood and that this dislocation had confused their moral sensibilities. For all that, with this new government it was no longer meaningful to try protecting the material interests of the people by correcting its moral confusion. The government had not reverted to an old, reactionary, feudalist policy; but it had adopted a new ideology of the state, the one described above.

We may therefore conclude that the ideas about the moral indoctrination of the people perfected in Nishimura Shigeki's "Principles of Japanese Morality"[21] had fulfilled their critical task, in that they made the Meiji government formulate the new idea of the imperial state and attuned people's sensibilities to cultural nationalism, which suddenly arose as the new political and intellectual issue about 1890. Traditional conservatism could no longer limit itself intellectually and practically to being a national ethical movement; in any event, it could not do so if it wanted to occupy a position of objective criticism vis-à-vis a government that was, so to speak, transitional from the middle of the 1880s until the inauguration of the parliament. If the conservatives did limit themselves in this way, now that the government had shed the elements that exposed it to criticism, what was the likely consequence? They might as a result pick off the tender buds of modernization that grew from seeds sown so recently, after the hard soil of feudalism had at last been broken by various forces emanating both from the government and from the people at large. Such a development in the advocacy of conservatism might even cause the government to equivocate regarding its intention to introduce a constitution. Tokutomi Sohō deplored this prospect. "One may abolish the aristocratic radical parties, but one must not abolish the mood of progress together with them," he pleaded. "If enthusiasm for maintaining our national polity leads to preserving even those customs that are troublesome and dangerous for the country and the emotion called 'Japan' is accordingly diminished, if the ideal called 'the state' is exalted and the ideal called 'the people' declines, if the spirit called 'conservatism' is born and the spirit called 'progress' dies, then our country will have lost all its vitality. . . . If this reactionary trend is permitted to rush ahead on its winding course, I am afraid that in 1889 society is apt to be like an exposition of the Antiquarian Association."[22]

Sohō's fear was not destined to be realized completely, for conservative political thought, supported by the traditional ideology, succeeded in formulating an appropriate objective criticism of the government's despotism and its Europeanizing policies. In this critique, modern European nationalism was blended with the traditional moral ideal of the Kingly Way, which considered the well-being of the people as the ultimate end of politics.[23] This new formulation was a souvenir brought home by Tani Tateki from his travels in Europe between March 1886 and June 1887.

After Tani resigned his commission in 1881, he took part for a while in the political activities of the Fairness party; but he gave that up also, returned to his home province of Tosa, and devoted himself to the administration of a school founded by the Yamanouchi family, the house of the former lord of his native domain. In May 1884 he was given a new official appointment, this time with the Imperial Household Ministry, becoming the rector of the Peers' School (Gakushūin). The government, which had made a clean sweep of the "modernizers," reformed its image, and taken a new road, came to regard him as a useful man. With the introduction of the cabinet system in 1885, he was appointed minister of agriculture and commerce—one of the two cabinet members who did not come from Satsuma or Chōshū.

In March of the following year he departed for Europe. According to Itō Hirobumi's official biography, it was actually Itō who first urged Tani to visit the West and whose good offices made the journey possible: "Prince [Itō] entertained high expectations of Tani's loyal character and his integrity. He wanted Tani to observe the situation in the various countries of the West, in the hope that he could cede the position of imperial household minister to Tani, were Tani to come back with the elementary attainments needed in a constitutional politician."[24] Tani, however, did not turn into the kind of fashionable bureaucrat that Itō hoped he would become, one consciously attuned to the policy of Europeanization. Instead, he returned an even greater champion of cultural nationalism than he had been when he left. Moreover, his journeys had considerably deepened his understanding of democratic nationalism, a political and ideological system that the government bureaucrats were anything but eager to adopt. He did not, however, reject the traditional Confucianist ideology.

An orderly sequence of exposition would at this point require describing the way in which Tani Tateki criticized the government and the kind of influence he exerted after his return from Europe. Some backtracking, however, is desirable if Tani's activities are to be more fully understood. Let us, then, first have a general look at the way in which his political consciousness grew and developed.

An Inquiry into the Development of Tani Tateki's Political Consciousness

The Kingly Way, it need hardly be reiterated, was the ultimate normative criterion of Tani Tateki's political thought. When he censured the government in concrete terms, something he did for the first time when he took up the problem of the revision of the Army Pension Regulations, he based himself on this ideal; before that he had not consciously held any convictions that were critical of the government, such as those espoused by Nishimura Shigeki.

At the outset of the Meiji Restoration, Tani's mentality was that of a stolid feudal warrior, who rather belonged to Type I mentioned at the beginning of this chapter. He had distinguished himself in the Tōhoku Campaign[25] of 1868 as chief of staff (*daigunkan*) of the Tosa troops. When he was co-opted in 1869 by the central government and ordered to assume the duties of a junior secretary of the Board of Censors (Danjō no shōchū), he wrote to his teacher Yasui Sokken (1799–1876) that he was afraid he would be obliged to censure all current affairs if he joined that office, perhaps even "attaint the person of [his] aged Lord!"[26] After consultation with his teacher, he refused the appointment.

The full breadth of his notion of feudal duty and of his sense of loyalty as a daimyo vassal, the core concepts of his conservative thought at that time, is conveyed by a memorial he addressed in 1869 to Sanjō Sanetomi, who was then one of the two chief ministers of state (*hoshō*) at the head of the government's executive branch: "My ambition is that I wish to make my former lord a Nitta or a Kusunoki. I would not dare expect that I could ever become a Nitta or a Kusunoki myself. But how would even heroes like Nitta or Kusunoki have been able to hold out in isolated Chihaya Castle or slash through the strategic vitals of Kamakura without retainers like Funada or Onchi? There are greater and smaller positions in which one can serve the imperial cause. The minister should make it his goal to serve like a Nitta or a Kusunoki, and a lesser vassal such as I should make it his goal to serve like a Funada or an Onchi. This is my ambition."[27]

That being his attitude, Tani naturally did not approve of the proposed new social order, that is, the administrative division of the country into counties and prefectures. In a protest drafted in the same year 1869 and also intended for Sanjō, he wrote that this was a Western system which would delight jurists like Fukuzawa Yukichi but was definitely unsuited for Japan in its present condition. "Generally speaking," he maintained, "those daimyo vassals who say that the counties and prefectures should be established are either the rustic, the low, and the unsalaried or the unruly and the insubordinate, not the pure and the loyal."[28]

It seems probable, however, that his consciousness of being a feudal retainer—his preoccupation with his own domain—actually was bound up with his judgment of the prospects society had after the rendition of the domanial registers *(hanseki hōkan)* in 1869. This judgment was in turn conditioned by the narrowly feudal nature of his vision, which made him expect "another war before long"; the train of events, he feared, would "follow the old ruts of the Genkō and Kenmu eras,"[29] the heroic but ultimately tragic half-decade (1331–1336) of Go-Daigo's attempted imperial restoration. For that reason his feudal attitude was bound to change when he realized that his judgment of the situation had been erroneous. When feudal domains were abolished and prefectures established peacefully and quietly in 1871, that was an event of sufficient importance for Tani to discard his old convictions and enter the service of the central government as a provisional senior secretary *(gon no daijō)* in the Ministry of Military Affairs. He recalls the change in his state of mind as follows: "Why should I hide it! I was someone who for a long time held to his feudal convictions. I had expected that Satsuma and Chōshū would fight each other for supremacy and would occasion a major war. My goal was to nurture the strength of Tosa and, when the time came, to exhaust myself in deeds of loyalty to the imperial court. But Satsuma and Chōshū dealt with everything fairly and in the common interest—against my expectations, which turned out to have been empty fantasies. Thereupon I resolutely abandoned my former convictions."[30] Tani sympathized with the predominant place that the leaders of Satsuma and Chōshū, Ōkubo Toshimichi and Kido Taka-yoshi (1833–1877), allotted in their way of thinking to an impartial state that transcended the interests of their own domains. Moreover, he had to face the reality that Japanese society was moving continuously in the direction of a centralization of power. Hence his feudal conscious-ness crumbled easily, leaving as its only residue his concept of moral duty.

At the time Yamagata Aritomo (1838–1922) was vice-minister *(taifu)* in the Ministry of Military Affairs. Yamagata, the most progressive among the military bureaucrats after the death of Ōmura Masujirō (1825–1869), strove to introduce a unified military system functioning under the central regime and exerted himself to build a new army based on conscription. Through his collaboration with Yamagata, Tani gradu-ally developed the mental makeup of a military bureaucrat.

In 1873 Tani was appointed commander of the Kumamoto garrison, replacing Kirino Toshiaki (1838–1877), a Satsuma man who was a believer in the principle of a "tough" military, that is, a defender of the indispensability of samurai. As Tani was about to leave Tokyo to assume his new duties in Kumamoto, Kirino briefed him by "reviling Yamagata" and the conscription policy with the words, "Calling up dirt farmers and making them into puppets—what possible good can come of that?"[31] Tani, however, took a different approach; and as a result of the training he gave them, his men of commoners' extraction became the elite troops who were able to withstand the siege that was to follow at the time of the Satsuma Rebellion in 1877.

The military official in Tani was dissatisfied with the reality of local administration that he found in Kumamoto, where a clear division of duties between the civil and the military branches had not been brought about as yet and where the local governor also held military authority, as had the feudal lords of the past. He reported to the central government:[32]

> As I see it, the prefectural bureaucracy is the prefectural bureaucracy and the garrison is the garrison. Not only do they not seem to work together in harmony, it is almost as if they have nothing to do with each other. The soldiers have not yet rid themselves of their old habits, and the manners of the feudal days still linger with the prefectural bureaucrats. Amongst the latter there are those who have only a slight interest in making the recruits answer their call-up, fail to make a thoroughgoing effort to set the people to right, and maintain instead that commiseration with the people's plight is the way to be its good shepherd. There are also many who, not knowing the first thing about soldiering, argue that soldiers drafted from the four classes of the people are not suited for real service. When such officials have fallen short in the supervision of their jurisdiction and the people riot, they are flurried and at a loss what to do, and they forget their duties. At the least sign of trouble they call up the former samurai, line them up in formation, and recklessly let men who do not even know close order drill play with firearms. They seek to pacify the people by intimidation, but the rebellious elements do not fear them; on the contrary, they merely provoke the outlaws. Not only have they no success, they are more and more looked down upon. . . . This garrison may or may not have an abundance of men of talent; but all, in any event, are fulfilling their duties, even if unworthy of their posts. When my powers are arbitrarily infringed upon, how could I possibly pass it over in silence?

Again, it was the military official in Tani that was stirred in 1874 to demand that the government take decisive, military-style measures to rectify the corruption and depravity of the central bureaucracy; to brace up the morale of the people it should, moreover, display the strength of imperial autocracy, do away with the multifarious discussions, and resolutely pursue the plan to attack Taiwan that had been hanging fire since the previous year. At least one of those wishes was realized, and later on that year Tani proudly took part in the Japanese army's punitive expedition to Taiwan.[33] In 1877, during the Satsuma Rebellion, he was to experience the siege of Kumamoto. During these campaigns, he learned the strength of a commoners' army, and the correctness of his own beliefs was confirmed. Not the slightest trace, however, could as yet be seen in Tani of a political attitude critical of the government.

Tani engaged in political activities only after his bureaucratic sensibilities had been negated by the traditional ideology. This fact is of extreme importance in tracing how his political consciousness matured. His interest in politics grew more intense as he gradually drifted away from the center of power within the Ministry of Military Affairs: in 1878, the year after the Satsuma Rebellion, he was assigned to be commander in chief of the Eastern Area Army; but before long, in 1880, he was transferred from that important post and was instead appointed director of the army's military academy, the Rikugun Shikan Gakkō, and of the Toyama Gakkō, an institution for training noncommissioned officers. His immediate motive for throwing himself into political activism, however, was the political situation in his native land, Tosa.

At that time two major political factions confronted each other in Tosa: the Risshisha (Self-Help Society), a group of activists for popular rights led by Itagaki Taisuke (1837–1919), and the Seikensha (Self-Restraint Society), which drew its followers from those who had sided with the shogunate in the Bakumatsu period; each had a number of smaller political associations in its orbit. These two factions were engaged in continuous political strife. The Seikensha pushed the appointment of the former lord of the domain, Yamanouchi, as governor of Kōchi Prefecture, and turned to the lord's house for funds to support its maneuvers. This meant that a danger existed, not only that the Yamanouchi would be dragged into the maelstrom of political strife and would run afoul of the central government, but also that the family might fall into serious financial hardship. Out of a desire to save his liege lord's house from these difficulties and to curb the champions of popular rights, Tani helped Sasaki Takayuki, Hijikata Hisamoto (1833–1918), Nakamura Kōki (1838–1887), and others to organize the Neutral Society in Tosa. This was his first step into political activism. Coming to realize, however, that his involvement in founding one more political association where so many already existed might give the impression that he had done so just to make mischief, he did not engage himself too deeply in it.

Now that he had come to pay attention to the political conditions in his home province, however, Tani was distressed to see that political strife there was changing into something that someone of his sensibilities could only view as a confused, violent struggle. In a letter he addressed to Sasaki Takayuki in April 1878, he urged Sasaki to dissolve the Neutral Society, deplored the collapse of the ancient morals, and reviled the Self-Help Society: "When I size up the state of affairs in my homeland, it is really as if I see the eighteen tribes of the Taiwanese savages. All tribes hate and quarrel with all others. Force is what they rely on, fighting is what they exert themselves at, politeness and civility lie in the dust. But the group that lords it over all the others with artful trickery is the Risshisha. With their mouths they talk about civilization, but their actions match those of the Taiwanese savages. When they see an official, they are sure to bark. This must be because people's rights, wretched wights, perhaps even dogs' rights are all the rage. Ridiculous!"[34] He despised Itagaki Taisuke as an opportunistic renegade. The distrust of political parties stayed with him for the rest of his life.

Tani's political awareness originated from a thoroughly regional, conservative preoccupation, namely, the desire to protect his lord's house from the political strife within his old domain. What caused his political interest to expand so that it included the whole nation was his reaction to two previously mentioned problems, the revision of the Army Pension Regulations and the removal of the army cemetery in Nagasaki. These two problems concerned the parents and the ashes of the men who had faithfully fought and fallen in action under Tani's command in Kumamoto and on Taiwan. That is what inspired Tani with a strong antagonism against bureaucratic insensitivity and made him surrender to his yearning that the Kingly Way and Loving the People be made the basis of politics. At last, he had discovered a way to distance himself from the government and found an ideology that provided him with the basis to attack it.

As noted above, with the death of Ōkubo the government had lost the pivotal person who kept it together. Because it had become extremely unstable, it resorted to coercive measures toward the outside. Internally, however, the government found itself unable either to establish a rational bureaucratic structure or to maintain cohesion among its officialdom, and it was obliged to seek survival from one crisis to the next by utilizing networks of personal, sentimental connections. That was intolerable to someone with Tani's ethical views.

In 1881 the government conferred decorations for meritorious service at the time of the restoration, but it did this with a bias toward present bureaucrats rather than former domanial lords. Judged by the feudal concept of social duty, Tani thought, this conferral of honors was unjust. Under the slogan of Rectifying the Names, he delivered scathing criticisms of the whole complex of private connections that existed within the government. His next actions that were critical of the government were the petition for the establishment of a parliament and the organization of the Fairness party, but these have already been discussed.

At the approach of the 1880s, Tani lightly divested himself of the military and bureaucratic sensibilities he had once acquired, changing into a politician with a distinct tinge of the opposition about him. To be sure, his oppositional attitude differed from that assumed by the proponents of popular rights. The benevolent paternalism inherent in his idea of the Kingly Way inspired him with a distaste for the insensitivity of the bureaucracy, and his feudal concept of duty made him dissatisfied with the web of private relations that held the government together. Because these traditional ideas formed the intellectual basis of his criticism of the government, he never came to terms with the despotic power that the government used unabashedly after the Political Crisis of 1881. Tani's antigovernment attitude did not, however, turn into a purely subjective set of feelings akin to Nishimura's. Rather, his journey to Europe led him into objective criticism of the government. The maturing process of his political sensibilities during this period may be traced through his "Diary of My Journey to the West."[35]

Tani departed from Tokyo on 13 March 1886. His first stop outside his motherland was the port of Hong Kong. There, confronted directly with the imposing appearance of the British fortifications, he could verify with his own eyes that the evil clutches of Western imperialist aggression had reached to Japan's doorstep.[36] And he directed his thoughts to the parlous condition of Japan, a country that in the midst of such international tensions did not yet feel any strains or need for resistance.

On 3 April he met in Ceylon with the "defeated Egyptian general" ʿUrābī Pasha, who told Tani the "stirring tale" of his struggle against England for the liberty of his country.[37] Fifteen days later, Tani made the following diagnosis on the spot in Egypt: "The sovereignty has already fallen into the hands of England and France, and the people has become enslaved to the British. All of this came about because Saʿīd Pasha was envious of the civilization of Europe and incurred a greater foreign debt than the strength of his country allowed. He started all kinds of construction projects, and when he could not meet the obligations on his foreign loans, it was in the end all placed in the hands of the British and the French. After that the taxes became ever more cruel. It was because the people had fallen into this situation that ʿUrābī Pasha raised troops: an irrepressible passion to resist the foreigners moved him. So fearsome are foreign debts!"[38]

When he observed in Egypt a situation of colonial dependence in which all traces of the country's former prosperity had been erased,

Tani no doubt thought back to the policy of Europeanization in his own country. And we may also assume that he was distressed by the realization that such a policy, when unaccompanied by national power, could threaten a country's independence. Whether or not the policy's implementation relied on foreign loans, the enormous financial resources it required led directly to harsh taxation, sacrificing the people's vital energies. It was fully possible that Japan would follow in the footsteps of Egypt as a result of adopting Europeanization. Such feelings of distress burdened Tani more and more the farther he went on his journey to the West. Even before he had trod European soil, he was gripped by apprehension about the international environment in which Japan found itself and the governmental policies that were singularly ill adapted to coping with it. How could Japan's independence be secured?

Tani approached this question from the standpoint of a conservative with a traditional ideology. Rather than direct his attention toward the rapid social changes or the unnecessary imitations of foreign culture, he fixed his eyes on the continuities in society, sizing up the problem from the point of view of encouraging the natural development of Japan's agriculture and traditional industries. In June, while in France, he met the director of a certain agricultural school. Hearing him expand on the theme that "agriculture is the foundation of the state," Tani gained confidence in his own method of observation, noting, "This completely agrees with the traditional East Asian theory."[39]

That same month he traveled through Switzerland, where he concluded that "the modernization of Europe lies in the progress of agriculture and manufactures. Only when agriculture and manufactures are prospering can commerce also attain prosperity." He was especially impressed with the fact that Switzerland, though it lay in the midst of the European powers, nevertheless was able to maintain its neutrality and preserve its honor as an independent state. He recognized that Switzerland's strength lay in its governance; the country "has a republican system and the people itself governs. There are no harsh laws or onerous rituals, and the folk are friendly and simple. They diligently apply themselves to agriculture and manufactures. Here truly is the reality of freedom and independence." (Its young men, he noted, all rushed to arms to defend Switzerland's borders "whenever something happens in the neighboring countries";[40] hence it was impervious to invasion.) He could comprehend the solidity of the close internal links among the economy, the politics, and the patriotic spirit of independence in a modern nation-state, such as he had seen in Switzerland, without feeling any contradiction with his cherished ideals of the Kingly Way and Loving the People.

From Switzerland, however, Tani went on to the Kingdom of Bavaria in Germany, and there his attachment to the idea of Loving the People manifested itself in quite a different manner, as a sharp criticism of the Bavarian monarchy's despotism and the people's impoverishment. In his entry for 24 June, he writes as follows:[41]

> Many European politicians hate the royal or imperial form of government. I totally failed to understand their reasons, but now that I see Bavaria, I notice that although the country is small, I do not know how many hundreds of millions are spent on palaces, art, and so forth. This all is extracted from the flesh and blood of the people. When I look at the appearance of the countryside, it is poorer than France or Switzerland, and the fields are not cultivated. More than half the population lives in small wooden houses, and even in the cities more than half of the children go barefoot. The clothes, too, are utterly coarse. Even though nowadays the government is no longer as repressive and cruel as it used to be, when one compares the destitution of the people with the beauty of the palaces, one will be able to deduce how harmful luxury and waste are to the people. It is not by accident that the theory of popular rights arises, and it seems inevitable that the politicians hate the royal or imperial form of government and desire a republic. In a country like our Japan, Loving the People while showing kindness to all men is considered to be the fundamental responsibility of the monarch; hence there can be no government that harasses the people. . . . When one compares Japan with foreign lands, one will surely call ours a country in which high and low are truly happy.

Here Tani realizes that a monarchical government that is not informed with the moral ideal of the Kingly Way can easily lapse into authoritarian despotism and that such despotism will always force the people into poverty. But he does not yet criticize that form of government in general. On the contrary, he affirms the possibility for a monarchical government that does follow the Kingly Way, like that of Japan, to create a nation-state of the same solidity as Switzerland's—if it makes the most of the ideal of Loving the People and manages smoothly a constitutional system that "listens to the voice of the people." According to Tani, the best point of a republic was that it assured the people's solidarity and enriched their lives; in this respect, a republic corresponded with the Kingly Way and with Loving the People. Consequently, in his opinion, the Japanese government would have to give concrete shape to benevolent rule by the emperor according to the Kingly Way. A government that failed to do so must be censured.

One with his experiences naturally found it extremely dangerous that Japan, even as it considered securing national independence to be its most urgent task, should be seeking its models exclusively in Germany.

His views of that country were deductions that followed naturally from his theory of the Kingly Way. Whereas France, he thought, was handicapped by a weak government, Germany's weakness inhered in the country itself.[42] Prussia, he said, "puts authority first and generosity second; because of its deep feeling of distrust that the people might revolt, it increases its police force and intensifies its surveillance. The whole country is poor in the spirit of harmony."[43] He often called his friends' attention to the fragility of German national cohesion. One of his younger fellow-countrymen, Shimamura Tateo (1856–1910), was "especially impressed" by Tani's insistence on this point. The opinion that German policies amounted to "repression that cannot possibly last forever" was his greatest insight, according to Shimamura, who commented in his reply to Tani: "This is an idea that none of those gentlemen who used to be dazzled at a mere superficial glance at Europe ever dreamed of."[44]

In the summer and autumn of 1886, Tani visited Austria for extended stays on four occasions. There he met Lorenz Freiherr von Stein (1815–1890), who had often been recommended to him by Itō Hirobumi. When von Stein lectured him on constitutional law, Tani found that he could go along completely with his Austrian mentor's historicist ideas. In his diary entry for 26 July, he wrote that he found von Stein's argument extraordinarily impartial and very useful, since it was founded on a clear perception of the differences between Japan and Europe. "It seems quite different from the 'Germanism' that has been so popular of late."[45] In a lengthy recapitulation of his views on the West that he sent to "someone in [his] home province" in 1889, Tani attributed the following words to von Stein: "A nation's government should know that country's history by heart. Only after acquiring a detailed knowledge of its own nation's manners and customs should it seek to adopt the strong points of other countries. To apply what I have taught directly would therefore be extremely dangerous for you." Tani remembered this lesson until the end of his days. It strengthened his confidence in his own conservatism. Moreover, his understanding of von Stein's historicism added extra value to Tani's ideas about government according to the Kingly Way: "Rooted in the history of Japan's foundation; grounded upon a way of governing where the emperor regards the whole people as his children—having determined our basis, we take from the good laws of all countries those points that are not harmful to our national polity."[46]

Ideas formulated in this way were more than mere conservatism; they involved the history and the genius of the nation. It was natural, then, that Tani's faith in the Kingly Way was not at all shaken by this journey.

Rather, it was reaffirmed, as he appreciated anew its superiority to the various political ideologies of Europe. On 31 July, for instance, he wrote, "When I look back over the road that I have come, already five months have gone by; I cannot but lament how time has passed! I have heard things that I had not yet heard and have seen things that I had never yet seen; there has been much to admire. As regards political virtue, however, no subtle scheme seems to exist here. Fair and impartial methods that were in use in the Far East, like the well-field or the equal-field system, are not yet known to the scholars in Europe, not even in substance. The Socialists have grasped only one side of this principle of equity without being able to comprehend its full essence; instead, they threaten to disturb society. Their fault is not knowing the Kingly Way." More profoundly confident than ever in the doctrine of the Kingly Way, Tani regretted not having met the "ringleaders" of the Socialists to expound it to them.[47]

The net result of Tani's European journey, at least as far as his political awareness is concerned, was that he attempted to combine his new appreciation of a modern nation-state's political and economic solidity with his traditional commitment to the Kingly Way. It would be difficult to assert that he understood the historical essence of modern republicanism or of absolutist despotism, but it is beyond doubt that his political consciousness developed into something drastically different from what it had been in 1881–1882. Strengthened by that new awareness, Tani turned over in his mind the various concrete political problems Japan faced. In October, under von Stein's direction, he set about finishing the draft of a memorial that he wanted to submit to the Japanese government. Imbedded in this memorial was his dissatisfaction with the government's policies on treaty revision and Europeanization (a sentiment that he recorded in his diary under 13 November) as well as his aspiration for Japan to attain true independence (which may be observed in a letter he wrote from Rome to Soga Sukenori in January 1887). Let us first look at the diary:[48]

> Alas, Japan's present speedy progress almost seems like a sign of the country's ruin. All countries busy themselves with armaments and prepare for war with an intensity that increases day by day. But our country, from the sea in the east to the sea in the west, does not yet possess even one gateway! All we have is a navy that cost the treasury 17,000,000 yen, but not one of the main ports on our coasts has yet been fortified. Our army counts fewer than 50,000 men. With what could we defend our country? And yet, to take a look at our internal affairs, we undertake large-scale construction projects, we improve the city layout, we build

government offices, we reform the theater, we revise ladies' dresses, we spend our money on diamonds—all activities suited to times of peace and quiet. Thus the government, heedless of the welfare of the people, executes policies that suit only its own convenience. Above—one is awed to mention them—it restrains Their Imperial Majesties; below, it stops up the mouth of the people and seeks with all its might to oppress it. Although the government tries to wheedle the foreign powers into revising the treaties by giving an outward show of civilization and enlightenment, Western experts know that this enlightenment is not the real thing, but rather a flower wildly blooming in the wrong clime—before some years have passed, it will decline. It is therefore decidedly unreasonable to expect that completely equal treaties shall be concluded. If we make even more concessions than we already have and ram the revisions through by force, I cannot begin to tell the harm that will follow.

Lamenting any part he himself may have had in misguiding Japan, Tani concludes that the measures being undertaken to bring about treaty revision would in the end be counterproductive.

In the letter to Soga, he relates that he is plagued by grief for Japan and is "stabbed to the heart" every time he hears of the cosmetic measures being undertaken by the government, such as the introduction of new habits of dress and the reform of the traditional theater. If the government wants a "real" modernization, he says, it must base it on a "real" constitutional system. "Unless they grant freedom of speech and freedom of writing, and unless they stimulate the people's feelings of autonomy, whatever they do will be labor lost. I, too, have now greatly revised my former opinions. Japan is the Japan of His Majesty the Emperor, the Japan of thirty-seven million Japanese. How large it is, how great! It is dangerous to leave it to the small wisdom of a few bureaucrats. When we rejoice together with the masses and grieve together with the masses, not only will the country become peaceful but modernization, too, can be expected. . . . It is as if my emotions are boiling, but it is difficult to tell you with a writing brush for my tongue. I await a time after my return, when I can pour forth all the feelings that fill my heart."[49] One may observe here Tani's firm determination to impeach the government. Shortly after his return to Japan in June 1887, he was to fulfill that intention.

Tani Tateki in 1887

In April 1887 Inoue Kaoru's overbearing, secret draft for the revision of the treaties, which included the humiliating provisions mentioned above, had been accepted by all countries that were party to the negotiations. In June, however, the juristic adviser to the cabinet, Gustave Emile Boissonade de Fontarabie (1825–1910), came out in opposition to Inoue's draft and personally handed a memorial to that effect to Prime Minister Itō Hirobumi. His action provoked a vehement conflict of opinions among the cabinet ministers about whether the draft should be approved or rejected. There were reactions outside the government as well. In 1887 the diplomat Komura Jutarō (1855–1911) had got together with some of his Kaisei Gakkō classmates to organize the Kenkonsha (Heaven and Earth League) as a kind of institute for the study of politics and organ for discussion.[50] The league was professedly neutral. In July 1887, however, Komura protested to his like-minded friends against the wrongness of Inoue's draft, and they agreed to work together to get it revoked, either by inciting public opinion or through persuading individual members of the cabinet against it. Both within the government and without, agitation against treaty revision threatened to burst into flame that summer.

On 23 June that year, Tani Tateki returned to Japan. Ten days later, faithful to the vow he had made to himself in Europe, he proceeded with the impeachment of the government. He began by openly presenting to the government his "Essentials of the State," a document of more than ten thousand words that castigated the government's despotism and the precedence the government gave to considerations of foreign policy. Tani's next steps were to hand a memorial against the revision of the treaties to Itō, resign his position as minister of agriculture and commerce, and join the ranks of the opposition.

Deeply moved by his action, the opposition politicians welcomed Tani with open arms, and "young enthusiasts in the capital" who greatly admired his abrupt but principled resignation organized a "Convention to Honor and Commend Comrade Tani" on 1 August 1887. "By four o'clock in the afternoon, as many as three hundred enthusiasts had gathered in the precincts of the Yasukuni Shrine in Kudan. At the entrance to the shrine flew a large banner, on which was written in large characters *Kokka no Tateki* (literally, 'Shield and Bulwark of the State') and, next to this, 'Presented to Mr. Tani, a private citizen of the Empire.' They also put up small paper flags on which they had written things like 'Mr. Tani's daring resignation,' 'Long live Comrade Tani,' 'Oh how daring he is!' and 'General Tani leaves office: Heaven grieves for the state.'" Thence the group marched to Tani's house in Ichigaya, demonstrating along the way, and disbanded in a high state of enthusiasm.[51]

Although their thought was essentially incompatible with his, Tani could nevertheless exert such a strong appeal on the proponents of popular rights because of his patriotic sentiments and because of his proposal to establish the independence of Japan on the basis of modern nationalism. These two themes were woven with strong rhetorical emphasis into the contents of his two memorials, the fruits of his journey to the West. At the risk of excessive length, it is therefore necessary to introduce the contents of these memorials in their broad outlines.

Three partially overlapping elements together make up the criteria on which Tani based his "Essentials of the State." The first is his understanding of the solid national cohesion that is proper to modern nationalism. The next is his perception of the shortcomings of absolutism— for example extravagance, oppression, and the resulting impoverishment of the nation. The third, which unifies the preceding two, is his idea of the Kingly Way. These three criteria underlay the major points of Tani's criticism, which are divided into seven categories on the basis of their contents. He takes up the abuses of the age in the following order:

1. *The abuse of personal connections.* This time Tani did not criticize the corruptive influence of personal connections from the point of view of moral obligation, as he had done in 1881, but approached it from the angle of formulating political objectives. The point he stressed was that the government tried to justify its vacillating and inconsistent policies—the results of these personal connections—by having recourse to the emperor whom it monopolized. "They look on His Majesty the Emperor," he said, "precisely as on someone of their own party, and there is the danger of their trying to make the people forget that in truth he is the Sacred Ruler of all thirty-seven million." He argued that the emperor should be regarded as someone "totally outside political discussions."[52]

2. *The abuse of the cabinet.* A system of cabinet responsibility should be instituted, as befitted constitutional politics. "That cabinet," Tani maintained, "should bear responsibility, above, toward the sovereign and, below, toward the legislature."[53] No room must be left for favoritism.

3. *The abuse of frivolity.* Tani sharply censured the bureaucrats' and the nobility's luxurious way of living, an abuse brought about by Europeanization. He urged them to think over the fact that these expenses were "all paid with the sweat of the people."[54] The foreigners' contempt, he insisted, would be the sole result of such frivolous politics.

4. *The abuse of diplomacy.* Under this heading, Tani tore to pieces the humiliating foreign policy that sprang from the government's attitude that trouble abroad was to be avoided at all costs. This attitude, he

insisted, must be ended once and for all. "To raise up our country in the future, vie in prosperity with Europe and America, and maintain our independence in the Eastern Sea," he stressed, it was necessary above all to make plans for maximizing national strength and prepare to establish a substantial equality with the foreign countries.[55]

5. *The abuse of the executive.* This abuse stems from the bureaucrats' lack of a sense of responsibility. "They look on their official positions as if they were private possessions and on the state's taxes as if these were their private wealth."[56] As long as that is the case, it will be impossible to produce a disciplined, unified, efficient administration. Moreover, each ministry creates its own independent power base, and the cabinet has no real political power; on this point there is much to learn from the bureaucratic structures of Europe and America. Furthermore, local administration ignores the actualities of the particular region and forces uniform policies on the populace. The local clerks play at being officials, assume haughty airs, and are unkind to the people. It would be better to allow regional self-government to a much larger extent, to mitigate the centralist system, and to leave regional politics as an honorary function to men of good moral repute who are popular with the people. The police have forgotten that their proper task lies in being an arm of the administration and instead concentrate on being an arm of the judiciary. On top of that, they are even appointing "secret investigators" in imitation of Prussia. They should promptly return to their original duties.[57]

6. *Frugality.* "Europeanization," the corruptive influence of personal connections, and the luxurious customs of the nobility and the bureaucrats will, according to Tani, inevitably lead to higher taxes. As government spending increases year in, year out, the populace "are forced to abandon their homes and become increasingly debilitated." It is an insufferable spectacle, resembling that of Egypt at the time of its collapse. "In a country like ours, where industry and commerce have not yet developed, agriculture must truly be considered the foundation of the state, and industry and commerce will not prosper unless the farmers have first become wealthy." Note, however, that in present-day Japan "the taxes on the farming population are extremely cruel and do not have their like in any other country." It follows that "there is hardly another example in the world of a farming population that is as unhappy as ours." The enrichment and strengthening of the state cannot be achieved in this way. Tani's physiocratic message was that the government should retrench and should exert itself to "foster the great root of the state: the strength of the people."[58]

7. *The constitutional system.* The government has not made any kind

of serious preparation for the constitutional political system that will be introduced during the coming two or three years. It feels sure of itself, thinking, "We have the financial might; we have the military might; we shall be able to push through whatever irrational constitution we want to; we shall be able to kill off whatever unruly elements there may be." How should the government prepare for a real constitutional system? Surely not by decorating the façade, reinforcing its despotic powers, and thinking up ways to control the parliament! Rather, it should do so by permitting freedom of speech, abolishing the Public Assembly Ordinance, raising the level of public opinion, and taking cognizance of what the people want. The freedoms of speech, assembly, and association are the true strong points of the countries of Europe and America. If the government pursues "Europeanization" because it really wants a constitutional system, it can hardly be right for it to forget this; but as long as it did forget—and that, according to Tani, was the case—its policy of Europeanization was something where "words and actions were in conflict and prior and posterior reversed."[59] One who looks at this final passage will see that Tani's understanding of the constitutional system as such was much more accurate than that of Itō Hirobumi and his fellows.

When Tani met Motoda Nagazane in early 1889, Motoda was rejoicing that Itō had recently taken to advocating a "Japanese kind" of constitution, contrary to his original views. Tani's response laid bare the government's true intentions: "Personally, I think that Itō shows his usual cunning. . . . On the one hand, it is something he says because he is still waiting to see which way the cat will jump. On the other hand, he does not want to be out of countenance with those who are bound to express dissatisfaction with our coming constitution, which will not be the usual European thing and therefore will not work in that subtle way that makes a constitution a real constitution. Hence many people will be dissatisfied with it and will cite foreign laws, claiming that in England it is like this and in Germany like that. Itō obviously wants to be able to tell them that ours is a constitution 'Japanese-style.' It is really the height of impudence."[60]

This first memorial is an excellent argument. Ensconced in his moral ideals of the Kingly Way and of Loving the People, Tani points out the many instances of the Meiji government's misrule and proposes a solution: The abuses should be rectified by introducing the strong points of the modern nation-state. The memorial against the revision of the treaties that Tani offered to Itō complements that argument. The purport of this second document is as follows: To curry favor with the foreigners, the government promises to compile codes and statutes of the kind that they like. In that case, however, the spirit of national independence will eventually become unrecognizable. It stands to reason that the object of enacting codes and statutes can only be to "further the peace and happiness of the people of our own country." To forget this and enact codes and statutes with reference to the foreigners' point of view means permitting them to interfere in legislation, a sphere that is the main prerogative of independence. This is "a sign of the collapse of our country."[61] Therefore, a draft for treaty revision that contains this kind of promise must at all costs be stopped. These abuses all stem from the fact that the government does not consult with the people but pushes through its foreign policy in secret and on its own responsibility.

All that is needed to carry out treaty revision properly is for the government to stop being so secretive toward its own people and pusillanimous toward the foreigners. The government must first restructure itself and bring about the new constitutional politics of public debate, but that is something it can surely accomplish in two or three years. "Both high and low will then make it a point to restrain their behavior. His Majesty the Emperor above will make it his first principle to abide by the outcome of the people's public debate, and the people below will respectfully accept his Sacred Intentions. High and low will be united, and the will to hold together domestically and to compete with the foreign countries will be stimulated. Matters such as these revision drafts will all be discussed with the people of the realm. With the outcome of this public debate and with public opinion in hand, we will appeal to the fair judgment of the world and let the world decide on right or wrong; we will be firm and forthright, and may expect to execute resolutely what we have decided."[62] The countries of Europe and America do not fear the government's power, but they respect the nation's public opinion. Having obtained the strong support of the public, the diplomats will at length be able to assume a resolute attitude in their negotiations.

In this second memorial Tani is clearly arguing that treaty revision be postponed until after the inauguration of the parliament. Unlike the government authorities, Tani correctly perceived the domestic and the external concerns to be parts of one larger problem. The solution to that problem, he thought, could be found in strengthening national cohesion and enhancing national power through the mediation of constitutional politics.

Could it be that Tani was departing—however tentatively—from the Kingly Way and moving toward modern nationalism? At about this time he visited Itō, who had withdrawn to his country house in Natsushima to draft the constitution. In describing this visit to Kuroda Kiyotaka, Itō noted that Tani had talked about having become "a champion of popular rights." That much, it seemed to Itō, was obvious from Tani's memorial.[63] On Itō's evidence, one may conclude that Tani was in those days strongly aware of the necessity to create an internal connection between civil rights and sovereign rights that would protect both state and nation from the government's complacent policy of Europeanization and its humiliating approach to treaty revision.

On 1 August, Itagaki Taisuke followed up Tani's indictment of the government by attacking its despotism in a memorial that also ran to some eighteen thousand words. No sooner submitted, the memorials of Boissonade, Tani, and Itagaki were secretly printed; slipping through the meshes of the government's strict censorship, they circulated amongst political activists throughout the country. The *Doyō shinbun* relates the extent of the commotion they occasioned in the world of politics: "Ever since comrades Itagaki and Tani submitted their memorials, the young enthusiasts who had grown bored with the chronic lethargy of the times have roused themselves everywhere. Suddenly, they display a courage a thousand times stronger than was their wont. Of their own accord they knock on the gates of government ministers and attempt to hold earnest discussions about the abuses of the age, or they urge the ministers to resign. They compose memorials, petitions, and the like. The political world has become quite lively."[64] Political activists were not the only ones influenced, however; some bureaucrats, following Tani's example, resigned their positions. "How can he have created this great an excitement in people's minds?" asked the *Mezamashi shinbun*. "It is because of the appropriateness of his reaction to the abuses of the age and the utter sincerity, one that practically overflows from the paper, with which he deplores the state of the world. Hence it is not only readers in private life, angry and aroused, who are of course supporting him. Even among the officials there are many who concur and repent of their mistaken opinions."[65] Among those who left government service at this time were Kuga Katsunan (1857–1907) and Miyake Setsurei, who were both to become important publicists. Others who gathered about Tani after his dramatic resignation included members of the Heaven and Earth League and Shiga Shigetaka (1863–1927). They formed a force in the political world and in the press, and their banner was cultural nationalism.[66]

Thus the antigovernment agitation intensified. On 18 July 1887, it caused Minister of Foreign Affairs Inoue to halt treaty revision; on 17 September, Inoue handed in his resignation. Presently, in October, it developed into a large national political movement, led by the general representative of Kōchi Prefecture, Kataoka Kenkichi (1843–1903), that pressed the government with its demands for freedom of speech, the reduction of the land tax, and the reform of foreign policy; hence it is called the Movement of the Petition for Three Important Matters (San Daijiken Kenpaku Undō). It also inspired the organization of the nonpartisan Teigai Club,[67] which became the matrix of the Unified Political Movement (Daidō Danketsu Undō) of the following year. On 25 December 1887, the government finally issued the Peace Preservation Law (Hoan Jōrei) against this popular movement, even going so far as to banish several hundred activists simultaneously from Tokyo.

What conclusions may we draw from all this? In the middle of the 1880s, after the Party of Liberty had been disbanded, the popular political forces had become sluggish. Tani Tateki's impeachment of the government, however, showed them a new target and stimulated a new political struggle that was greater than any individual party. Even if Tani did not desire political conflict as such, he nevertheless was the plug that sparked off the struggle against the government, a struggle which lasted from 1887 until the inauguration of the parliament. This was the form in which Tani's oppositional attitude manifested itself in the political world of 1887.

The group that had gathered around Tani was generally called the New Conservative party (Shin Hoshutō). Tokutomi Sohō, who gave them this nickname, characterized them in the following way:[68]

> The present world of politics really is a disorderly, irregular world. Although the realm swarms with the armies of the world of politics, there are absolutely no grounds on which one can base a judgment as to who in this mêlée are true allies and who are true enemies. Nevertheless, there is in this mêlée one company of friends that raised its banners early on in secret, assembled its forces, and is ready to take its stand, now that it counts. I do not know whether the public knows it or not, but "New Conservative party" is what I call this company. . . . Present-day conservatism has changed its appearance; it no longer is the bigotry that it was in 1881–1882. At a time when the progressive mood inclines somewhat toward conservatism, the political ideas of conservatism show up somehow dressed in the clothes of progress. These two embrace each other as if they had arranged it beforehand. There is of course no room for doubt that the New Conservative party is here to stay. And who might be the leader of this New Conservative party? It is Mr. Tani Tateki. . . . The emergence of the New Conservative party today is something quite different from the emergence of the Constitutional Imperial Rule party (Rikken Teiseitō)[69] in 1881–1882. Today's New Conservative party, notwithstanding the fact that it reacts against the mood of progress, has been

excited especially by the activities of the aristocratic radicals. Therefore, although they will not become the enemies of the Meiji government, neither are they a company of supporters that will slavishly follow it in everything. That they are pusillanimous, narrow-minded, obstinate, and eccentric is not something for which they deserve special praise; but when one witnesses their righteous indignation, dauntless integrity and bounteous patriotic spirit, and when one sees them tuck up their sleeves, proud of being Japanese Men, they do become extremely appealing. Therefore I certainly do not regard the New Conservative party that is about to be born today as identical to the Imperial Rule party of old, that is to say to the Rikken Teiseitō which assembled for profit, disbanded for profit, and was organized by a majority of small men who knew no shame.

In these words this young champion of *heiminshugi,* Tokutomi, who hoped for the realization of party politics in the British way and felt discontented with the constant flux that swept Japan's political arena, described the growth process of his most worthy rivals, who banded together not for gain but because of their convictions and who were pioneering a new field in the world of politics.

The intellectual core of the New Conservative party consisted of the future members of the Seikyōsha (Society for Political Education), which was founded in 1888. The magazine *Nihonjin* (first published in April 1888) and the newspaper *Nihon* (first issued in February 1889) were to be the group's principal organs of opinion. The New Conservatives preached a Japanese cultural nationalism, formulating the leading principles of the resistance against the policy of Europeanization and the humiliating revision of the treaties. Contrary to what is often asserted, their cultural nationalism did not imply that they propagated the doctrine of the absolute rights of the state; and they had nothing to do with militarism, which would sacrifice the whole of the people's existence to establish national sovereignty, considering military aggression to be the aim of the state. Nor was it the case that the New Conservatives wanted to preserve the old Confucian ethics and feudal customs under the name of national characteristics. Indeed, they took a contrary view. They sought to maximize the power of the state by developing the economic strength of the entire nation. The state, they thought, would become strong if it was supported by citizens who were, each of them, endowed with political and national awareness. Through historical reflection on the nation's heritage, they wanted to create a peculiar Japanese culture that would make a contribution to the world's other cultures. All in all, their point of view was that of cultural historicism in a broad sense. It shared the character of modern nationalism.

The special feature of the New Conservatives' cultural nationalism was that it had developed under the stimulus of the nationalistic movements in nineteenth-century Europe. "Our nationalist movement has arisen in reaction to Europeanism," Kuga Katsunan (the editor of *Nihon*) maintained, "in the same way as European nationalism arose in reaction to the oppression of the European countries by France."[70] "To exhaust your strength for your own country is to exhaust yourself for the world," Miyake Setsurei asserted. "To exalt the special characteristics of your own race is to further the evolution of mankind. Why should the defense of the fatherland be in conflict with universal goodwill?"[71] The cultural nationalists judged that the necessary steps on Japan's road to independence were an autonomous national cohesion, the development of national economic strength, and the extension of the national individuality—not the government's emulation of Europe. The evaluation given them by Yamaji Aizan was by no means undeserved:[72]

> Here is something for which I must solicit the attention of the reader. The conservative reaction that arose in 1881–1882 was, concretely speaking, nothing more than the restoration of Chinese lore; the conservative reaction that began around 1887 was, however, nothing less than a manifestation of national self-awareness. It is, of course, a fact that quite a few abbots of mountain temples, old Shinto priests, and Confucian scholars nostalgic for the study of the classics gladly participated also in this second conservative reaction. But it is also a fact that the party leaders who caused this reaction were by no means people who lacked a knowledge of the culture of the West. They . . . had breathed the spirit of the nationalist movements in the European countries. . . . They were of the opinion that the existence of a tendency for Japan to become in its thought and its customs virtually a province of the West was a most dangerous phenomenon. They had seen that the European powers all did their best to maintain their national qualities in their languages, their literatures, their manners and customs. . . . They had finally reversed the intellectual fashion, and the so-called national spirit (those of their contemporaries who were not in sympathy with their contentions claimed that it was a conservative spirit) had finally come off victorious.

What was the effect of Tani's activities in 1887? Not only did he exert an influence on the world of politics, his traditional conservatism was the intellectual matrix from which healthy nationalist ideas were launched into the center of public discussion in the late 1880s. "If one had made the Mr. Tani of 1881–1882—or even of 1884–1885—listen to the contentions of the Mr. Tani of 1887, the former Mr. Tani no doubt would have looked at the present Mr. Tani and considered him a rebel and a traitor."[73] These words, with which Tokutomi Sohō criticized Tani in the previously quoted article, "The New Conservative Party," aptly describe the admirable development that Tani's political awareness underwent during and after his European tour.

Conclusion

A few additional remarks should be made about two other topics: how Tani's political thought developed *in concreto* through his personal political activities in the following years and how this previously unknown strain of conservative political thought, this cross developed by Tani between the Kingly Way and modern nationalism, related to the intellectual climate of the 1890s and especially to the cultural nationalism of the Seikyōsha, the Society for Political Education to which a brief allusion has just been made.

First, then, Tani's political activities. As befitted an advocate of the Kingly Way, Tani consistently took the standpoint of a public servant whose task it is to assist the virtue of his lord—the position that Tokutomi Sohō described as follows: "Although they will not become the enemies of the Meiji government, neither are they a company of supporters that will slavishly follow it in everything." Consequently, Tani thought that to assist the sovereign was the government's task as well; he himself could serve the emperor and the nation either by cooperating with the government or by admonishing it. He hated the campaigning by the political parties that was motivated only by the scramble for power and was personally averse to organizing a political party. For this reason he went so far as to defend himself against the name by which the general public called his group. He even gave instructions for a clarification to be put in the newspaper *Nihon:* "It would be good," he wrote, "if the baseless expression 'New Conservative party' could somehow be disposed of."[74] In 1889, as soon as it became clear that the plans for treaty revision drafted by Ōkuma Shigenobu, who had succeeded Inoue Kaoru as minister of foreign affairs in the Kuroda cabinet (30 April 1888–24 October 1889), contained humiliating conditions, just as Inoue's had, Tani assembled the comrades of the Heaven and Earth League and the Society for Political Education under his banner and founded the Nippon Club. He became the backbone of the so-called five groups against treaty revision, and his activities were the driving force that led to Ōkuma's downfall. Once he had succeeded in that objective, however, he immediately dissolved the club. On this point he differed appreciably from his fellow-conservative Torio Koyata, who organized the Conservative Fairness party (Hoshu Chūseitō) and did conduct party activities.

After he had become a member of the House of Peers when the Imperial Diet was opened in 1890, Tani was careful to explain: "When the popular parties oppose the government, they do so in order to replace it; when I oppose the government, I do so in order to correct its misrule."[75] It was characteristic of his political practice that he should thus set himself up as a kind of remonstrator general or custodian of public opinion—the interpreter, so to speak, of vox populi. Using *Nihon* as the organ for his own journalistic publications, he tried to carry through his political arguments against the background of national public opinion. Increasing the nation's economic strength remained the most important item on his political agenda. Because of his innate physiocratic bent, Tani was especially solicitous to further the cause of independent farming. Accordingly, he advocated the alleviation of the land tax and resisted its increase, seeking to restore the people's strength. When these demands became part of the party programs of the Jiyūtō and the Kaishintō, he was willing to cooperate with them in this regard.[76]

Tani opposed expansions of armament that did not bring about an increase in the nation's productive capacity and objected to protective measures that favored privileged capitalists at the expense of sacrificing the nation's livelihood. He called such policies "inflating the state with air" and predicted that before long such a bloated organism would burst like a balloon. From this standpoint he proposed in 1891 a motion called "Fostering the Military"; in 1893 he presented to the Privy Council the memorial "Strict Enforcement of Official Discipline"; and in 1898 he published the "Memorial against the Increase of the Land Tax," taking issue with the proposal for such an increase made by Taguchi Ukichi (1855–1905).

These were the most important political activities Tani undertook even as the nationalistic point of view on which he had pinned his hopes started to fade away. For instance, even his demand that the land tax should be alleviated to help the independent farmers—his central means of improving the nation's economic strength, an issue for which Tani had shouted himself hoarse—had lost its significance. It no longer meant supporting the independent farmer or raising the tenant to independent status. On the contrary, because from 1892–1893 on the parasitic landowner system became the basic structure of Japanese agriculture, it came to signify measures of protection for landlords who reaped without sowing. Tani's political activities could no longer fulfill the role of an objective criticism of the government. During the two or three years around the time of resistance to treaty revision, his critical activity was not only appropriate but effective; then it ceased being truly meaningful.

Finally, what was the relationship between Tani's political thought and that of the Society for Political Education? Kuga Katsunan discussed the rise of "our nationalist movement" in reference to European nationalism. Indeed, the political ideas that Tani had acquired on his tour of inspection through modern Europe were taken over by the young intellectuals of the society almost without modification and served to leaven their cultural nationalism. This was a valuable effect of their personal, practical participation under Tani's banner in the national movement against treaty revision. One should not assume, however, that the traditional conservative ideology that was the unifying factor in Tani's political consciousness was accepted by the members of the Seikyōsha. After all, even though they joined him in opposing Europeanization, they were mainly university graduates who had acquired the new learning; they were colored intellectually not so much by traditionalism and conservatism as by historicism. Whether they succeeded or not is a different matter, but what characterized their endeavors was the attempt to understand the problems of national peculiarities and national self-awareness not only in terms of the Kingly Way but more broadly, in terms of the many facets of national life, such as the arts, scholarship, thought, politics, and economy of Japan. At least the members of the Society for Political Education directed their intellectual efforts toward the new historicist way of thinking that had been born from the European disenchantment with the rationalism of the Enlightenment. They were not rooted in premodern ideas, as Tani was.

Real "Meiji thought" took its beginning from here. The essential characteristic of the new nationalism of the 1890s was precisely that it did depart from the Kingly Way, to which Tani adhered until the very end. Tani's political ideas and activities had more or less fulfilled their role in 1889–1890, when they nourished the early development of the Society for Political Education. In any event, the Seikyōsha was blessed with the healthiest understanding of the spirit of the new age. Even if Tani's ideas were not transmitted to the younger generation in unadulterated form, it is no doubt true that only the new wine which he had put into old wineskins flowed into those new wineskins which were suited to receive it. On the whole, this was a fortunate circumstance, one that made the cultural nationalism of the younger generation into something more sane and wholesome than it might otherwise have been.

5

Meirokusha Thinkers and Early Meiji Enlightenment Thought

Translated by George M. Wilson

The great social transformation that followed the Meiji Restoration of 1868 was designed to empower Japan to resist pressure from the advanced capitalist countries, adapt to that pressure, and turn it to use in getting rid of the forces of feudalism that still persisted in the country. The task required the nurturing of real independence in the eyes of the foreign powers, and that could only be done by destroying Japan's feudal foundations and equipping the country with a modern national administration. A new kind of bureaucrat accomplished this transformation. The archetype of this new breed, Ōkuma Shigenobu (1838–1922), said of Japan's progress: "All this is nothing but the result of adopting the superior features of Western institutions. That Japan has been enabled to do so is a boon conferred on her by foreign intercourse, and it may be said that the nation has succeeded in this grand metamorphosis through the promptings and the influence of foreign civilization."[1]

Even as the "new bureaucrats" who were conversant with the ways of the advanced capitalist countries managed the nation's course by using various foreign countries as models, "civilization and enlightenment" *(bunmei kaika)* appeared on the scene—a phenomenon that may be compared to an exotic flower hastily transplanted to feudal soil through efforts from above and pressure from outside. The *bunmei kaika* project was begun by the modern bureaucrats, but it was also betrayed by them. They are the ones who gave the era of "civilization and enlightenment" its historical character by formally implementing the modern legal codes. That legalism became the chief political feature of the modern Japanese state.

Even if the "boon" conferred on Japan resulted from contact with foreign civilization, however, the diplomatic effort that brought it about was no mere formality. The most famous of all the Meiji thinkers, Fukuzawa Yukichi (1835–1901), pointed out that "our national opening did not bring us only the foreigners themselves. It also brought us the conveniences of social activity that had been invented and devised in foreign countries." He added that "the ease of our national opening was not due solely to a change in relations between Japan and the foreign countries. It was also necessary to bring about self-induced change all over Japan. Hereafter our country will at last be able to share in operating and advancing these [modern] conveniences."[2] A substantial improvement in the people's social and economic life should have resulted. In the decade of "civilization and enlightenment" that came after 1872, however, the formal restructuring of Japanese society from above was given priority over any sort of material improvement in the people's lives.

"Civilization and enlightenment" is a label that marks the unavoidable metamorphosis of the old Japan, a country compelled by its opening to establish direct links with the world capitalist market. But the era called by that name was also a product of the "enlightenment" policies undertaken by the new bureaucrats who set the nation's course, looking all the while to the advanced countries for models. Hence the real trend of the times produced undeniable excesses and an unnatural quality; yet at this very moment the judgment of "cool reason" made its appearance. Who were the bearers of "cool reason" to Japan in the decade after the restoration? They are not to be sought among men still imbued with the old consciousness and ipso facto opposed to what the new bureaucrats stood for. The real "rationalists" had to possess a more profoundly modern consciousness—a deeper Western consciousness—than that which motivated the new bureaucrats. These were the famous figures who belonged to the Meirokusha (Society of Meiji Six), and they are the topic of this chapter. The focus will be on a debate that engaged some of that society's leading members and revolved about an essay written by Fukuzawa Yukichi in 1874, "On a Scholar's Calling," that is perhaps the most straightforward expression of the "enlightenment" argument put forward in those days.[3]

The new bureaucrats were in a hurry to have Japan assimilate Western civilization as the material basis for achieving a "wealthy country with a strong military" *(fukoku kyōhei)*. Their view was that Japan should supplement its civilization from the outside—what might be called an exterior approach to civilization. In contrast to them, the Meiroku-sha thinkers were engaged in enlightenment activity requiring the production of a critique of the realities that Japan faced at the time. They preferred to proceed from within, approaching Western civilization from an interior standpoint in order to improve popular life. These thinkers were unique in that they were fully attuned to the European Enlightenment's notion of Reason. Most had the Kaiseisho, the old shogunate's institute of Western studies, in their academic background. As a result they were directly in touch with Western knowledge and could read "letters running sideways." Many of them had studied in Europe or America even before the Meiji Restoration.

The new intellectuals of "civilization and enlightenment" held natural-law ideas such as those expressed by Fukuzawa at the beginning of his "Encouragement of Learning" *(Gakumon no susume):* "Heaven never made a person above others and never made one below others; so everyone stands the same as others in the eyes of heaven, for at birth there is no distinction between rich and poor, or between high and low."[4] These thinkers came onto the scene in an era when feudal morality, especially the rigorous denial of the passions demanded by the status ethics of Tokugawa Japan, was undermined by the Meiji Restoration. With the old prescriptions of virtuous conduct under attack, European natural-law thought acted as an additional wedge against the long-dominant value system by allowing vent for the senses and emotions, so long denied by feudal discipline.

An essay called "The Passions Must Prevail" asked, "What is the object in giving birth to human life?" and answered, "It is for the self to gratify its desires, to rejoice in the extreme, nothing else.... When things are put in the world, such as money or food and clothing, their reason for being is that heaven put them here for people to enjoy, and those who use them are to have their own way, to be free and unrestrained."[5] This is the attitude of a well-known champion of popular rights, Seki Shingo (1854?–1915), toward the meaning of human life. As a sensual expression of the natural rights theory, it had a vital mediating role. It is true that the worship of passion was already prominent in townspeople's society during the Tokugawa period, but the intellectuals had reduced that urban world to something standing outside contemporary morality. From their perspective, the feelings could never serve as the basis of a system of moral values. The very fact that Seki Shingo could express the meaning of life in the dictum The Passions Must Prevail and advocate liberating desire throughout society is an indication of how much the Japanese value system was changing after its long domination by feudalism.

Given this sort of support for feelings and emotions at the heart of "civilization and enlightenment," it is not surprising that popular equality, the basic human right, was taken to refer to the gratification of desire. The new unit of value was ability, and merit ruled supreme. The old status system thus gave way to a new type of merit system; a new morality was opened up. The very idea of "a high official and a plutocrat in cotton clothes, eating their rice gruel . . . is bizarre," one up-to-date author contended; he found nothing wrong with "spending lavishly, if you have a lavish income."[6] The creed of the "civilization and enlightenment person"—to encourage enjoyment to the extent of one's ability —became the gist of the whole movement. This creed involved paying attention to "carpets and clocks and superficial ornamentation, such as putting on a chapeau, wearing a Western suit, and spending money pointlessly." Another author observed that "civilization is generally misunderstood as a process that refers to going to prostitutes and geisha, behaving without manners, and affecting a luxurious lifestyle like the British, or one of dissipation à la the French."[7]

Thinking such as this was deeply rooted, especially among samurai who had overthrown the feudal regime with their own hands—in other words, the very people who occupied seats of power in the new government. As seen through the eyes of a moralist such as Nishimura Shigeki (1828–1902), it was something to be deplored. Writing in the pages of *Meiroku zasshi,* the journal of the Meirokusha, he condemned it as the conceit held in common by "the set that runs to utility, staining and defaming the Way of Confucius and Mencius." Not only did the new governing class fail to promote "ethical and proper scholarship," Nishimura complained, but their behavior fell "beneath that of the public they outrank."[8] It would appear that the praise of passion had left its murky venues in the townspeople's world of the old shogunate and entered the new milieu of "enlightenment." The vocabulary of natural law was borrowed to promote the self on a grand scale. The merit-first attitude of the "might is right" type of samurai—those who had come out victorious in the Meiji Restoration and, being on top, were enjoying a life of luxury—was set off starkly against this background by the envy, jealousy, and unceasing agitation of the malcontents who had been displaced from their seats of power and now awaited the chance to regain prominence.

Torio Koyata (also known as Torio Tokuan; 1847–1905) questioned the meaning of the Meiji Restoration, taking the point of view of the déraciné samurai. It seemed to him that the despotism of the shogunate had been left behind only to be replaced by a dictatorship of three of its former feudatories, Satsuma, Chōshū, and Tosa. "Those who bear the virtue of the restoration and who advance down its road to power are lifting their own spirits by oppressing others," Torio complained.[9] Here we encounter the sense of inequality that the former samurai felt, imbued as they were with the notion of a merit-based career but finding themselves unable to make it on merit. This change of consciousness on the part of the former samurai was a visible truth that gradually spread to all the people, who were liberated from a way of life based on feudal status. It was bound up with two big events, the Boshin Civil War of 1868, which may be called a general settling of the shogunate's political accounts, and the decision to move the capital from Kyoto, which was put into effect the following year. The modern bureaucrats had to pass through this basic process to establish a strong regime before they could implement a positive policy of Europeanization. Samurai consciousness changed in the process, and the two big events formed a direct medium conveying their thought to the next stage, that of linking up with Western ideas and accepting Europeanization.

The feudal value system began to break down during the Boshin Civil War, which drove a wedge in the lord-vassal nexus. Ōkubo Toshimichi (1830–1878) and Kido Takayoshi (1833–1877) stood at the head of the modern bureaucrats and steadily promoted the policy of building a rich country and a strong military. They had sought the military overthrow of the shogunate and opposed the arrangements whereby the Tokugawa formally turned over sovereignty in the fall of 1867, as planned by Saigō Takamori (1827–1877) and Iwakura Tomomi (1825–1883), who were the real leaders of the Meiji Restoration. Then the imperial army and its emblem, the Brocade Banner, exhibited such charismatic energy when fighting did start at Toba and Fushimi early in 1868 that the domains still backing the shogunate elected to change sides in favor of the imperial court as the civil war progressed. Ōkubo even conveyed the impression that "the Japanese will follow anyone who shouts about the imperial court. They will even turn against their lords. . . . This is a sign of a really weak country."[10] Evidently, the classic nexus of feudalism was coming undone because of the politically transformative quality of the idea of *sonnō*—"Revere the emperor!"

As Yoshida Shōin (1830–1859) clearly set forth in his logic of "throne and multitude," however, the *sonnō* idea might disqualify the Tokugawa feudal conglomerate from ruling Japan, but it could not achieve the constructive effect of bringing about national unity. Nor could it check the disorder of the lord-vassal consciousness, cultivated under the feudal system for almost three centuries, even though it became the basis for political change. If the Meiji Restoration were to fulfill the mission of a social revolution, it could not adhere to the old morality.

Nobody knew this better than the Meiji leaders. During the final phase of the civil war in 1869, as government forces were about to attack proshogunate diehards led by Enomoto Takeaki (1836–1908), who held out at the Goryōkaku fortress in Hakodate, Ōkubo and Kido developed a scheme to suppress Enomoto by making use of the abdicated last shogun, Tokugawa Yoshinobu (1837–1913; r. 10 January 1867–3 January 1868), and of the man who had taken his place as head of the House of Tokugawa, Tayasu Kamenosuke (also known as Tokugawa Iesato; 1863–1940). Another Meiji oligarch, the powerful court noble Sanjō Sanetomi (1837–1891), opposed that plan, so it was dropped. This episode suggests that the old morality was still useful for purposes of intrigue but had lost its authority over the new bureaucrats who would direct the Meiji state.

The destruction of feudal morality in the Boshin Civil War prompted the appearance of triumphant (that is, arrogant) soldiers who sought to capitalize on their wartime exploits. Most of the daimyo were fine, but it was different with the samurai who actually administered their domains, Kido complained. "They act haughty and willful, using their domain's strength egotistically. They talk endlessly about duty and right, but mostly it is just talk," he was moved to lament to Ōmura Masujirō (1824–1869). "This is eroding the Great Way."[11] How to control this warrior consciousness was a problem. The old status ethic had begun to collapse and needed to be finished off. In this letter to Ōmura, Kido raised the prospect of invading Korea. The idea was to use an external problem to manipulate internal affairs, something that would expose the inability of feudal ethics to control a warrior society at just the time when Japan's political transformation was ending.

Another sure way of furthering the ambitions of the restoration's commanders would be to propose moving the capital away from Kyoto. Such a move would go a long way toward dissociating the new leadership from those members of the Kyoto aristocracy who still hid in the shadows of what they defined (more hopefully than realistically) as the restoration of the ancient norms of imperial rule. The new leaders were determined to convert the ideal-type of emperor, one who personified the traditional concept of the unity of rites and regimen *(saisei itchi)*, into a political ruler, one who would separate rites from regimen and distinguish between religion and rule. They wanted to place the emperor at the core of the new political mechanism, thereby establishing the foundation of a centralized and unified state.

Ōkubo's idea of moving the capital away from Kyoto, first broached in early 1868, became the germ of this plan. One of the new intellectuals from Hizen, Ōki Takatō (also known as Ōki Minpei; 1832–1899), and the sometime farmer polymath Maeshima Hisoka (family name often read as Maejima; 1835–1919), planned the move despite intense opposition from the Kyoto courtiers.[12] On 1869.3.7 the Phoenix Carriage finally left Kyoto for "Tōkyō," the new Eastern Capital. In its train, a multitude of military and civil officials, great and petty lords, and samurai of all ranks fought to migrate and congregate in the city previously called Edo. In a few years, the new capital doubled the prosperity of the Great Edo of old, and those who had thronged there began to cultivate the exotic flower of "civilization and enlightenment." The impetus that moving the capital gave to the destruction of the old sense of ethics was anything but temporary, to hear Ōkuma Shigenobu tell it:[13]

> Those who had been envious of the profligacy of the feudal lords and rich merchants unexpectedly came into their own as a result of the abrupt change in circumstances; they took profit from deposits, came to live a life of ease, called themselves gentlemen, and were addressed as sir by others. It was as if the hungry had been fed and the thirsty given drink. But then they fell into profligacy themselves, competing to be the first to dance for joy. The officials who were to be the standard for the people remained convinced that Edo meant a pleasure trip and were sunk in perpetual dissipation. . . . Day by day and month by month, the customs of our country were being destroyed by the restoration reforms and the eastward move of the imperial capital. Samurai morale declined, morality fell to the ground; things tended to fly out of control.

To be sure, the people who gathered in this city, especially the officials in seats of power who were driven to an insatiable pursuit of gratification, contributed greatly to making Tokyo the capital of "civilization and enlightenment."

Hagiwara Otohiko (1826–1886) expressed the contemporary Tokyoite's pride in this new cultural capital: "The restoration is grand forever. Tokyo is so enlightened, prosperous, and elegant when compared with any place in the world. You can stop counting on five fingers when you mention Tokyo along with Peking in China, Paris in France, London in England, and Russia and America."[14] In truth, the city's prosperity was born of the change in the lifestyle of the highborn classes, including the samurai. It is no doubt also true that the deeper sources of this prosperity were the emperor's journey to his new capital and the attendant influx of the bureaucrats, the former daimyo, and the former samurai, as a writer named Takamizawa Shigeru noted at the time.[15]

The "prevalence of a sense of energy," according to Miyake Setsurei (1860–1945), drove the changes that accompanied the restoration. "Those who were highest in government" filed into the prostitute quarters "and not only enjoyed themselves but were actually afraid of being considered incompetent unless they indulged in wild merrymaking."[16] The departure from the feudal value system, keyed by liberation of the passions, engendered prosperity. The affirmation of sensual pleasure awakened a vigor in all aspects of life, greatly raising material desires. Takamizawa put it very well when he said that "without realizing it, the Tokyoite is always busy running to something—running to enlightenment, running to civilization, running to crabby script, running to salaries, running to newspapers, running to commerce, running to drink, running to love, running to fame, running to profit."[17]

The torrent of sensual liberation that was unleashed by the two great events—the Boshin Civil War and the move of the capital to Tokyo— simply swept around feudal strictures. To ignore or seek to evade change is a universal phenomenon, and it was a problem that confronted the feudal ethic from within, undermined it, and made it fall into disarray. The old value system was rejected in favor of privileging humanity through the liberation of the passions, thus signifying the construction of a new morality. In the eyes of some intellectuals, however, this kind of situation prevailed only when "the sun has set but the moon has not yet risen," as Nishimura Shigeki characterized it.[18] Or, as Fukuzawa put it, "It is as if we had cast off the burden inherited from our forebears and relaxed without shouldering any new baggage in its place."[19]

On the other hand, this consciousness offered possibilities to the new bureaucrats. In their drive to accomplish a social and economic transformation and in their confrontation with the West, they could appeal to the people's self-interest. This tactic may be seen in the preamble of the Education Order of 1872, which states that "an education is the basis of personal wealth." This is the kind of appeal that was used often, for instance when the Conscription Law, the granting of land certificates, and other "civilizing" policies of the Meiji government were put into practice. The "enlightenment" activities of the Meirokusha members were carried out with this social consciousness very much in mind.

The Meirokusha Program for Enlightenment

The era of "civilization and enlightenment" changed character between the early 1870s, the time of the initial destruction of feudalism, and the time when industrialization moved ahead later in that decade. This change took place as Ōkubo Toshimichi and other new bureaucrats such as Itō Hirobumi (1841–1909) and Ōkuma Shigenobu took charge of the government with the clear intent of building a modern state. After the change, the social consciousness that had served the purpose of destroying feudal values was simply no longer tolerated. Its sensual and spontaneous side was suppressed. The strong expectation was that this energy could be sublimated into the will to construct a modern Japan.

The Meirokusha, the topic of this chapter, appeared in the historical limelight at the very start of this change. Behind its emergence, however, was a shift in attitudes on the part of Japanese government leaders who had toured Europe and America between 1871 and 1873. This shift was important in that it revealed a division in the government over the idea of attacking Korea. Indeed, it in itself was more important than its by-product, the debate over Korea, insofar as setting off the change in the era's character was concerned.

For the sake of Japan's future, "something" had to be adopted from Western civilization; that much was clear. Ōkubo and Kido learned different lessons from going on the grand tour of the West, but both agreed that Japan had to reform in order to regain its external autonomy. Upon his return to Japan after observing the industrial prosperity that lay at the root of British wealth and strength, Ōkubo planned an economic policy designed to promote industry at home. After the defeat of the leaders who wanted Japan to attack Korea, Ōkubo became home minister and put that very policy into effect. In 1875–1876, ignoring political and social opposition, he carried out a land tax revision and restricted the stipends of former samurai, opening the way for capital accumulation as well as for creating modern industrialists out of the old soldiers.

By contrast, Kido Takayoshi saw the base of the wealth and strength of Western countries as a product of the steady development of the idea of nationhood and of a finished legal system able to provide rational support for national unity. He regarded the enlightenment policies of the early 1870s as unrelated to the real roots of Western power, considering them a form of playing to the gallery. Kido fretted that most of those policies proceeded from sheer expediency. "It is not that everything has to be based on law, but with people running this way and that, talking about autonomy and liberty while scheming for their own convenience, our sensibilities are changing frivolously. Compared with six or seven years ago, we are as different as heaven and earth."[20] Kido also worried that the rise of sensual liberation, an undercurrent of the enlightenment project, would threaten the ideological health required for national unity—the result of adopting only the bad aspects of Western thought. That is why, when he got back to Japan in 1873, his was the first voice in favor of a white paper calling for clear political rules and regulations.

Thus "civilization and enlightenment," which speeded up the requisite conditions for the modern state as symbolized by the railroads, telegraphs, and postal system of the first years of the decade, set off the transformation that brought industry and constitutional government as well as the idea of nationhood to prominence. The turning point was the Meiji leadership's tour of Europe and America between 1871 and 1873. A view based on existing social conditions would argue that this transformation, moved forward by the pioneering intent of the government leaders, nevertheless signified a sudden policy shift on their part. This shift became visible during Ōkubo's term as home minister, a time of enlightened despotism. Despite its justification as a matter of state, it meant real trouble for society. It was inevitable that an antigovernment movement, made up of former samurai and farmers, would rear its head.

Insofar as the modern bureaucracy enforced social change as a categorical imperative without regard for the real state of society, frictions unavoidably developed between the changes and the old ways. A sense of blind feudal obedience generally persisted throughout society, but the main reason for the lessening of frictions and the absence of a nationwide resistance movement was the tough stand taken by the administration—put another way, its arrogant high-handedness vis-à-vis the forces of resistance. But that was not all. The feudal value system, provoked by the affirmation of the passions, could be used by the government to appeal to the people's selfishness. Among those who had drunk of the torrent of emotional liberation, the old morality no longer functioned as a set of internal norms to guide personal feelings. "Social intercourse" was governed by what Fukuzawa referred to as Japan's inveterate "partiality to power"—authority still dominated the institutional structures of Japanese life, and everyone was inclined to curry favor with the powerful.[21] "Toadyism is abroad in the land," complained Fukuzawa; indeed, it was the atmosphere suffusing society. The "spirit of resistance," the samurai mettle that he had admired in Saigō Takamori during the Satsuma Rebellion of 1877, had fled the consciousness of the former samurai while their antipathy toward the government simply dissolved.[22]

Here lay the need for that "spirit of popular independence" on behalf of which Fukuzawa had raised his voice. He was concerned that Japan might not be able to attain true independence based on a national awakening if the government continued to impose policies dogmatically. "Unless this trend is changed, the government may raise the standard of civilization, but only the appearance of civilization will result, and the people will waste their energy while the civilized spirit declines."[23] Fukuzawa accurately pointed out the contradiction between policy and reality in the prevailing social consciousness. This concern was not limited to him but was common among the intellectuals who typified the Meirokusha. They already took a worldwide perspective that recognized both internal and external stimuli, and it was impossible for them to attack the government by taking the side of the people, who seemed to be perpetual bystanders, satisfied with the old material social relations that the intellectuals were trying to sever. The corollary is that they could never fully rely on the people vis-à-vis the government, which itself ignored social reality.

This concern of theirs became a powerful motive for the intellectuals to organize the Meirokusha, and it is evident in the enlightenment movement that centered on their society, its journal, and the lectures of its members. They possessed a self-consciousness represented by Fukuzawa's statement that "the country's independence is our goal, and our present civilization is the means to achieve this goal."[24] These thinkers sought to resolve the contradiction between policy and reality by teaching the people about Western civilization. They were not directly committed to the formation of a civic society but focused totally on securing national independence. Even for Fukuzawa, society was a strictly secondary concern; he trumpeted a doctrine of national power first, ahead of domestic considerations, in light of the Darwinian reality of the international order.

What, then, was the meaning of enlightenment at that time? Its advocates intended to use the theory of natural rights to make a people accustomed to a closed traditional society turn to the open modern world. They sought to cultivate a sense of nationhood capable of dealing with world conditions. In short, enlightenment meant encouraging a resolutely external attitude on the part of a blind and dumb people. The instrument of enlightenment was to be the Meirokusha.

The Society of Meiji Six was founded after the new bureaucrat Mori Arinori (1847–1889) returned from America in July 1873, bearing a message described by Nishimura Shigeki as follows: "In America every academic specialty is pursued, academic societies are formed to study the field, and lectures are given to benefit the people. Our country's scholars isolate themselves and do not interact, so society at large derives little advantage from their work. I want our scholars to do as scholars do in that country and form societies to engage in collective research. The country must be rescued from its recent moral decline by dispensing with the old scholarship. We therefore need to form a society, first to plan the elevation of scholarship, second to establish standards of morality."[25] Such a plan for Japanese scholars to organize an academic society was epochal. "This is the first time a scientific and literary society has been formed," Nishimura observes proudly. "All of those in the society are celebrated talents. People say that great ideas and unprecedented theories will surely issue forth from it. We pray that the eyes of the ignorant will be opened by the excellent thinking of the society's members and that they will establish a model for the whole realm and broaden the vision of all our intellectuals."[26]

The society's organ, the *Meiroku zasshi*, first came out in March 1874. Each issue had a press run of 3,200 copies, and success was piled on success. Cabinet ministers and young scholars alike sought the origins of knowledge in this journal. It accomplished a great deal in giving every stratum of society a sense of what the writers meant by "civilization and enlightenment." The purpose of establishing the Meirokusha, as stated in Article 1 of its bylaws, was for "people to congregate, exchange opinions, disseminate knowledge, and explain it"[27]—in other words, not to discuss political questions but to engage in academic discourse. To be sure, as Fukuzawa noted later, the members were determined "that the Japanese people be changed through an understanding of conditions in the West." He graphically described the nature of the enterprise: "We wanted to put people through the door of 'civilization and enlightenment,' and the sooner the better. In a manner of speaking, we were trying to serve as the import agent for the new ideas of the West on behalf of Japan, the master of the Eastern Way."[28]

It is necessary at this point to take up the argument for a popularly elected assembly put forward in January 1874 by Itagaki Taisuke (1837–1919) and others who had resigned their posts in the government. Their proposal so stirred up public opinion that it transcended their original intent, taking on a very practical coloration. Conservative nationalists such as Torio Koyata took umbrage at this liberal agitation: "Using the two characters *min* and *ken* ["people" and "rights"], these people want to destroy the country's order, violate political laws, and form parties and classes, as if dishing out food to the starving without concern for time or place. Racing blindly after one another, they will only make the country lose its independence and bring on disaster." Torio was convinced that "this idea of *minken* will be used to justify the mob violence of later ages."[29] For their part, the new intellectuals of the Meirokusha felt that they had to say something against both conservatives and radicals when their proposals allowed for such violent possibilities.

Meirokusha members thus preached the absolute necessity of a popularly elected assembly but also criticized the content of the Itagaki memorial. They scrutinized the government policies that had invited the dispute over a parliament and called for a popular awakening to the general ills of the time. One appraisal of the *Meiroku zasshi* suggested that at least for the time being, "unrestrained discussion of everything under the sun has become extremely respectable."[30] On the other hand, the society's head, Mori Arinori, stressed its fundamentally academic and educational character. He sought out the reflections of the members and issued a warning about fortuitous incidents and unforeseen consequences. Within the society, however, the members could not stay away from politics in their discussions.[31]

Then on 28 June 1875 the government suddenly proclaimed a new Libel Law (Zanbōritsu) and Press Ordinance (Shinbunshi Jōrei) and set about regulating radical populist ideas. Members of the Meirokusha wanted to turn speech into action at this restrictive moment. On 11 August of that year, the society voluntarily decided by a vote of nine to four to stop publishing the *Meiroku zasshi*. Fukuzawa agreed mainly for reasons of preserving scholarly conscience. Others voted because they could not resist suppression of speech or because they could no longer claim that words were unrelated to politics.

To be sure, the government did not have the *Meiroku zasshi* in mind when it issued the press laws. According to Suehiro Tetchō (1849–1896)—himself a newspaper editor who had been imprisoned for attacking the restrictive ordinances—the principal targets were periodicals "inclined to 'radicalism,' to use the terminology of those days." (It will be noted that such journals drew criticism from Meirokusha members.) In particular, Suehiro named the *Hyōron shinbun* under Ebihara Boku (1830–1901), which was noted for its vociferous advocacy of popular rights but was also linked to Saigō Takamori's party of samurai malcontents in Kagoshima. Suehiro called this journal a "veritable lair of rebels" against the Chōshū clique. "Every issue attacked the cabinet, sparing no effort—especially the issue on the Osarizawa Copper Mine Scandal, which exposed secrets about Inoue Kaoru and others involved. It was merciless. That sort of thing was sure to provoke the government in the most direct way. It was the time in our country's history when the Private School (Shigakkō) network [where young men were given military training] was active in Kagoshima, and no one could tell when an explosion might erupt there. The realm was full of disgruntled former samurai, and there were forces just waiting for a military disturbance to arise. Hence the government saw an acute danger in the growing increase of the power of the press, fearing its ability to agitate people's minds. So it happened that the press laws were enacted because of the memorials of a few scholars."[32]

Although the decision to stop publishing the *Meiroku zasshi* was occasioned by the press laws, the government was not to blame for it. The journal had not violated the press laws. Certainly it was noted for its bold contents, but that was no reason for it to go out of existence.

The society's members were the reason. As Fukuzawa recognized, the decision to terminate the journal arose from a lack of unanimity in their thinking, making it difficult for the Society of Meiji Six to attain the collective aims that Mori had advocated.

Why was this? Society, the object of their criticism, had become a complex problem. There was no question of delivering Western civilization to the "master of the Eastern Way" through the agency of the Meirokusha. In the early phase of "civilization and enlightenment," the concept of the Public Way of Heaven and Earth (a reference to Western natural-law thought) may have served as an ideological weapon in place of the ambiguous Confucian Way of the Ancient Kings, making possible a critique of the antiforeign exclusionist thought that had marked late Tokugawa history. By stressing the idea of international equality and thereby justifying relations with foreign countries, this critique was able to avoid the ideological obstacle of importing Western civilization. At this new stage, however, it would no longer do to preach the optimistic idea of international equality as a basic condition for Japan's independence. The issue had to be moved a step forward from ideas to concrete methods.

The Meirokusha's problem in this later period, therefore, was to reassess the terms of "civilization and enlightenment" adopted by the government and to ask how they could sensibly be established and nurtured in Japan. In the *Meiroku zasshi* the members took the practical step of looking at how the government was carrying out its policies, but the various authors fell into ideological conflicts and emphasized differing preferences. They had all set out to study modern thought, but they had strong individual traits and could not avoid disharmony. To be sure, the end of the *Meiroku zasshi* did not mark an end to their enlightenment activities. On the contrary, after the journal stopped publication they revived those activities in special ways. Good examples of this are Fukuzawa Yukichi, Nishimura Shigeki, and Katō Hiroyuki (1836–1916).

Consider 1874–1875, the moment of transition to the government's version of "civilization and enlightenment." The appearance of the *Meiroku zasshi* was a product of that very moment. The objective conditions drew the enlighteners into social activism involving the contradictions between policy and reality as these were revealed in the pages of the journal.

The Ideas of the Enlighteners

What was Western civilization, and how should it be adapted to Japan? That was the problem all the enlighteners had in common; its starting point lay in seeking to eliminate the tremendous difference between the government's policy standard and the people's consciousness of being the subject that had to live with Western civilization. What was the ideological basis on which the enlighteners stood, and what was it that precipitated their sense of the problem? The answers to these questions depend on an appreciation of what was required of them as people and as thinkers.

The enlighteners' ideas may be divided according to their approach to the relationship between government and people. The intellectuals depicted here were in agreement that they would not be driven passively just to the technical operation of Western civilization, what may be called the objective aspect of modernization. As an example of someone who proposed just that, take the famous oligarch Itō Hirobumi. He held that the people had no relation to politics; it would do for them to fulfill the objective function of modernization allotted them by government leaders. Even after the Meiji Constitution was promulgated "by" the emperor in 1889, Itō still argued that the national policy should be "to educate the people with a view to their becoming factors in the progress of the country."[33] The Meirokusha thinkers were dissatisfied with such formulations. They participated subjectively in the formation of modern Japan, not just as components that belonged to the state but as individuals who sought to cultivate the people through a desire to conceive of the state as something that acted together with themselves. They wanted to delineate the proper shape of the relationship between the state and the people. "A person lacking the spirit of independence will not be so considerate as to think about his country," was Fukuzawa's overarching rationale.[34]

Katō Hiroyuki's contribution to the Meirokusha's effort was to refute the thesis of reverence for the emperor propounded by the nativist thinkers of Kokugaku (National Learning). "The notion of achieving unity with the emperor's mind is a poor idea, revealing something of a mean spirit," Katō maintained. In Europe, he asserted, "such mean-spirited people would be accused of being slaves at heart." According to Katō, "if we give up liberty and simply follow the will of the emperor, acquiescing on that account in the loss of our right to freedom, then liberty and independence will be virtually impossible to attain for Japan."[35] Nishi Amane (1829–1897) wrote in his turn that the "national character" of the Japanese had always been "supremely well suited for despotic government." But now that Japan had embarked onto the "floating world" of international relations, bonds were being relaxed on the domestic scene, and intelligence was winning out over might; hence, Nishi pointed out, Fukuzawa was right to criticize the Japanese national character as one that makes for "a people without energy."[36]

Nishi's close associate, Tsuda Mamichi (1829–1903), commented that "in our country's present situation, those favoring private enterprise are very few—not just few but practically nonexistent." This "grave and lamentable" lack of initiative was the sole "cause of our inability to expand our national power," he concluded, stressing that it was essential "to equip our people with a spirit of independence and freedom."[37]

These authors all relied on natural-rights theory. Not even Nishimura Shigeki, who is generally considered a Confucianist, can be called an exception on this issue. Working from a Confucian ethical standpoint, Nishimura could not fully embrace the Western natural-rights theory, but he did contend that "as it was said of old, heaven's reason and human desire must clash."[38] He opposed the sensual view of natural rights, so commonly preached at the time, basing himself on the political thought of the Chinese classic known as *The Great Learning*: "To cultivate the self and manage the home will govern the country and pacify the realm."[39] This idea was originally expressed by government leaders, who took the people as the object of the moral good virtuously done by those who govern. Nishimura, however, construed the proper scope of this Confucian approach to extend from those who govern to the whole people, as if to imbue the entire populace with the rulers' virtue.

Nishimura saw the state as "something divided into the government and the people. Still it has been a single whole since its origin, the same as a person in whom spirit and body are fused." Furthermore, "the government's interest is the people's as well, while the people's interest is the government's." So the sublimation of conflict based on the private aspirations of government and people is to be found in the state. "Although it is to government's advantage to rule by force, expanding taxes will injure the state's wealth and strength as also its peace and its honor. The government must therefore overcome its own devices and suppress self-interest. To extend popular rights and decrease taxes is to the people's advantage, but to enact these policies would mean injuring the country's wealth and strength as well as its peace and honor. The people must therefore overcome their passions and restrict what they do for their own private gain."[40] This is the form of state-as-a-person theory he advocated, holding that for the public interest of the state to be realized, the people would have to superintend the state's self-interest while finding the meaning of popular rights through the public good of the entire country.

This version of popular rights may be seen as an expansion of the notion of Confucian virtue to the people. In trying to view the people and the state as self-consciously joined, however, Nishimura was no different from his fellow Meirokusha members. The person they wanted to find was one who could appeal to this kind of state. Nothing expresses this more clearly than their effort to overcome the contradiction between policy and reality through the "illumination" *(keimō)* of the people's consciousness. Since this view is the same as that of Confucianism, however, no hasty conclusion should be drawn about the character of their thinking.

A symposium on how to cultivate this new person, featuring Katō, Tsuda, Nishi, and Mori, appeared in the second issue of *Meiroku zasshi.*[41] This 1874 colloquy ultimately teaches us what Fukuzawa meant in his article "On a Scholar's Calling," where he spoke of the social utility of the scholar as a means of developing a new person in Meiji Japan. This debate may therefore be used as a key to the sort of relationship between government and people that these writers were depicting.

First to be considered is Fukuzawa, the one who brought up the issue. His aim was to show that the extreme misgivings held by intellectuals about the state of Japan's independence were justified: there was genuine cause for alarm. In the hour of peril, "we who were born in this country and call ourselves Japanese must do our part." According to Fukuzawa, the responsibility for any country's independence is borne equally by its government and its people. He proceeds on the assumption that the two have differing functions: "to the extent that something is involved with governing, it is the task of the government," but the many other matters that are unrelated to governance "remain the business of ordinary persons." When the workings of these two preserve a balance, "the whole country will run perfectly."

The metaphor at the core of the whole debate—external stimulus versus internal cultivation—was a means of explaining this point. In developing it, Fukuzawa was referring to a process "like that which the human body goes through, in which a balance of forces proves unachievable unless all systems are maintained." It is a "law of human physiology that survival is impossible in the absence of external stimulus." Applying this rule to the state, Fukuzawa held that the basis for maintaining its independence is to be found in a balance of internal (governmental) forces and external (popular) forces. "There must be a balance corresponding to internal and external; the government is like the life force and the people an outside stimulus."[42] The intent of this metaphor was to emphasize the reliance of both government and people on these internal and external relations, rather than on the status relations of the old feudal hierarchy, as an absolute condition of national independence.

When he speaks of government, Fukuzawa has more in mind than the narrow sense of the term—of government limited to "the" government. He points instead to the mutual interaction of the two key factors, external stimulus and internal cultivation, in arguing that "government refers to how a country works." Addressing this point in his essay "On a Scholar's Peace of Mind," Fukuzawa insisted that "the people have to be involved in governing the country." Government, he wrote, does not relate solely to the offices where bureaucrats sit carrying out decisions; in its broadest sense, it "includes even the governance of one's family." This broad interpretation was central to Fukuzawa's thought at the time. Government in the narrow sense—"the" government—is "just a part of human affairs," he said. Government does not drive society; on the contrary, it is society that prescribes government's form of existence. Fukuzawa therefore concluded that "government is not a cause of transformation in human affairs; it is rather the result of a human transformation." The old view of politics is thus deprived of its faith in government omnipotence—in government as an absolute value.[43]

Fukuzawa's understanding of Western civilization was enhanced by his view of civilization in general. For him, the significance of the West never lay exclusively in material technology, not even when he spoke of adopting Western civilization as an instrument for securing Japan's independence. "The unique duty of the Japanese," he said, "is to uphold our national polity *(kokutai)*; to uphold the *kokutai* requires us to preserve our national sovereignty; to preserve our sovereignty requires us to raise the people's intellect. The first thing to do on the road to intellectual advancement is to sweep away our indulgence of old habits and customs by confidently adopting the spirit of civilization as practiced in the West."[44] He elaborated on this "spirit" as follows: "In former days when activities and events were fewer and the people largely uninvolved, power necessarily prevailed, but as time passed this simple and placid world gave way to a complex and eventful one; it is as though a new sphere had been opened up for activities of the body and of the mind. Today it is the nations of the West that make up this complex world." By abandoning its indulgence of the stagnant ways of old, Japan could sustain the same level of spiritual activity as modern Europe, which had given birth to pluralistic culture. The very act of introducing this sort of spiritual activity into Japan would be the means of advancing Japanese civilization. That is why Fukuzawa loudly proclaimed that "the key to becoming civilized is to diversify and invigorate human activities."[45] In other words, the diversity of civic life in the West brought multiple forms of originality and value for human life; and Fukuzawa's idea of "popular government" was modeled on the principle that all the people are to manage their own affairs.

Subjectivity was the distinctive feature Fukuzawa identified in this spirit of diversity operating at the core of Western civilization. For him subjectivity was a natural law that enabled humanity to triumph over nature, despotism, and custom—in short, to become civilized. Japan had not yet reached this level, the third and highest type, that of a "civilized country" *(bunmeikoku)*. Fukuzawa contrasted the countries of Africa and Australia, which were "barbarous" *(yaban)*—a first-level type of society antithetical to subjectivity, in which life hinges on chance and nature's fury—with societies such as Japan and China, which were "semicivilized" *(hankai,* "half open"). Life in those second-level societies remained shackled by convention and borne down with the burden of the past, making them incapable of sustaining freedom of behavior. "We must not wallow in our old ways. We must not rely on the kindness of others. We must not remain content with the present as we cultivate our virtue and sharpen our knowledge," Fukuzawa exhorted his countrymen. He went on to affirm the limitless nature of human progress: "Do not be satisfied with minor matters, plan for future greatness. Advance without retreating, achieve without ceasing. The way of scholarship is not a vacuous path but the road to practical discoveries. Let the business of commerce and industry prosper day by day so as to deepen the sources of happiness. Let knowledge be put to use today and its fruits invested for the benefit of future generations." The limitless nature of progress would eliminate all natural and artificial restraints, allowing such progress to be gained through the development of basic human nature, which is "naturally adapted to civilization."[46] Fukuzawa's natural rights theory thus provided the basis for his view of civilization and progress and was the starting point of his enlightenment project.

Ultimately, his explanation of the spirit of civilization brought Fukuzawa to emphasize the role of *jitsugaku* (practical studies). By this he meant the pursuit of scientific knowledge in order to master nature, connoting a spirit of free inquiry based on subjectivity. "In a world of trust there is much falsehood; in a world of doubt there is much truth." It follows that in contrast to the blind credulity characteristic of feudalism, *jitsugaku* featured what he called a "spirit of doubt." Accordingly, "the progress of civilization in both material and spiritual matters consists in the discovery of reality by investigating the way things work. When we inquire into how the peoples of Western nations came to develop their present civilization, we find that it sprang from a single point—doubt." In saying this, Fukuzawa was thinking of the free subjective spirit that arises from doubt as the precondition of modern natural science. He criticized the vogue of worshiping foreigners for its lack of that very spirit of doubt—"trusting in the new with a trust that puts its trust in the old." Such unquestioning adulation could only block the growth of practical studies and would hardly reflect a "civilized spirit." It would be as if the old feudal spirit had been turned inside out.[47]

On Fukuzawa's reading of the road to Japan's independence, the goal certainly was beyond the government's reach. The government needed to base its actions on the spirit of practical studies, "to allow people to go about their business without hindrance, recognizing and safeguarding their ambitions." Thus government fulfills a partial function in human affairs. "Private citizens are the ones who carry out the tasks of civilization; the government's job is to protect that civilization."[48] The principle of the division of labor permeates both of them.

When Fukuzawa reflected on Japan's present condition, using the spirit of civilization as a standard, he saw the government's absolute supremacy and the people's utter lack of strength, something so abject that no balance could exist between them. The situation was so bad that "out of ten private enterprises, at least seven or eight have a government connection," he observed.[49] Fukuzawa allowed that "since the time of the restoration, government personnel have done all they could, and they are able people, qualified to carry out policies. Inevitably, however, there is much that they cannot accomplish." The cause of it all, he complained, "is the people's ignorance and folly."[50] Here he was referring not only to the people's irrationality, superstition, and lack of knowledge but to the very fact of their nonmodern consciousness.

The government's "civilizing" policy failed to take account of these points and therefore involved a fundamental perversion. "Down to the present we do not see an effective union, but only a government that is despotic as before and a people that is an ignorant, powerless mass, just as before."[51] The result was regrettable: "Today the government has a standing army, and the people could be expected to recognize that such an army is to defend their country. Far from celebrating its greatness and its energy, however, they consider it a tool for intimidating the people and are terrified of it. The government has schools and railroads, and the people could be expected to take pride in them as a sign of civilization in the country. On the contrary, however, the people see these things as redounding to the benefit of the government. . . . The people have embraced a feeling of fear and dread vis-à-vis their own government, so they have no incentive to compete with foreign countries and to struggle for civilization." Fukuzawa further regretted the people's inability to prevent the suppression of popular energy. He cautioned them that "a country's civilization cannot progress by the power of the government alone" and warned of the government's excesses.[52] It was unjust for the government to exceed its limits and intervene in the people's lives, just as it was impermissible for the people to rely unreservedly on the government. His critique goes beyond the rights and wrongs of particular policies and phenomena, focusing on the basic problem of how to revolutionize the spirit of a nation and people whose emblem seems to be "ignorance and folly."

Fukuzawa's proposed solution was to find leaders who would stick to the private spirit. "We require someone who will display reliable goals for the people by producing examples." With the possible exception of a few specialists in Western studies, however, no one like that was to be found. What is more, such scholars would require a uniquely modern consciousness to sustain their calling. The trouble was that they "know government but not the private sector, know the skills associated with standing on top of the government but not what it means to live under the government." They might call themselves Western scholars, but they were still afflicted with the evils of traditional sinology, "as if their body were Chinese and only their clothing Western"; they only pieced out a fragmentary knowledge of the West. Not one among them was qualified; hence Fukuzawa would have to accept this responsibility himself: "To advance civilization in our country and preserve its independence . . . is of course our task, and we must first open up the edge of the matter not only by giving guidance to the people but also by acting as pioneers for those who say they are Western scholars, showing them what their intentions should be."[53]

What Fukuzawa speaks of as "popular government" throughout "On a Scholar's Calling" does not stand apart from his popular-rights thesis. He advocates fulfilling private goals on behalf of the people and believes that "if we state our position without yielding, we can put a needle into the government on everything." The urgent need is "to get rid of the evils of old and restore popular rights." If the people reject the predominance of authority, if they destroy the prevailing climate of reverence for officials and contempt for the people, they will be aware of their own subjectivity. In this way "a real Japanese people would come into being for the first time, a people who would stimulate the government and not be its plaything. . . . The people's strength and the government's strength would balance each other, thereby maintaining the nation's independence."[54]

For Fukuzawa, popular rights did not mean the direct right to participate in government—government in the narrow sense. Popular rights referred to the fundamental condition, even precondition, of progress toward participation in government through establishing private life and liberating the people's spirit. "To spread the climate of liberty and independence throughout the country, to take the country for one's own without regard for rich or poor, high or low"—this would be the foundation of popular consciousness, and it would liberate the popular spirit from the bad habit of fearing and relying on the government.[55]

Fukuzawa criticized the popular-rights advocates for pursuing government in the narrow sense. Instead, he lauded the superiority of indirect politics, that is, of allowing people to manage their own lives. The popular-rights movement sought a narrow political transformation by going all out for an elective assembly, and this seemed to Fukuzawa no better than a game to divide the government's powers.[56] He repeatedly stressed that such a movement could not hope to achieve popular rights of any sort but would simply end up going back to the old spirit of "revering officials and despising the people" *(kanson minpi)*. A political movement that kept on this way could not so much as discriminate between democracy and monarchic authoritarianism; it might "just assume that conditions would improve and put too much faith in things as they are."[57]

What kind of social consciousness did Fukuzawa identify while this enlightenment movement was developing? In a letter to Baba Tatsui (1850–1888), written in 1874 while Baba was studying in London, Fukuzawa points to the liberation of the senses and the disturbance of feudal values arising from political crises such as the Boshin Civil War and the capital's transfer to Tokyo. Though military rebels have been put under control, he says, "our minds are confused, and this situation will only get worse. I would like us to take advantage of the present unprecedented opportunity to get rid of the indulgence of old habits, bring in new elements, and reform the people's way of thought."[58]

In his "Encouragement of Learning," Fukuzawa advocated natural-law thinking when he explained the principle of the rights of man: "What hurts the status of a farmer can also be expected to hurt the status of a land steward, while something sweet in the mouth of a land steward will taste sweet to a farmer. Everyone wants to avoid what is harmful and take what is sweet. It is a person's right to follow his heart without being hurt by others."[59] This puts desire at the foundation of personhood. Notwithstanding, Fukuzawa did not recognize the unconditional affirmation of sensuality, because he never simply accepted the trend of the times. He proposed a pluralistic social life, one whose main point was to develop a spirit of civilization that would extend the rights of man on the basis of personal progress. The wave of sensual liberation, Fukuzawa thought, brought people a chance to take advantage of the campaign for enlightenment.

It is time to consider the controversy over Fukuzawa's ideas and to compare them with those of his opponents. First comes Katō Hiroyuki, whose ideological position most sharply contrasts with Fukuzawa's. Katō's rebuttal of Fukuzawa in the *Meiroku zasshi* derived from his totally opposed view on the matter of outside stimulus and on the issue of scholars staying out of government. The crux of it lay in Katō's position on the state. Katō argued that "internal development and external stimulus are both essential. At the present time, however, internal development is more essential. Our specialists in Western studies therefore most certainly should not avoid entering government service as they seek to achieve their ambitions."[60]

At the time Katō was withdrawing from the natural-rights theory he had held and beginning to switch to a theory of the state as a person, analogous to a living organism. He shifted from a contract theory that took the individual as the crux of the state to a view of the state as primary. From the start there were internal motives for this change in his thinking about natural law. In this connection, it is also important to note that from 1872 on Katō was given the opportunity to tutor the Meiji emperor. As a textbook he used *Kokuhō hanron*, his own translation of *Allgemeines Staatsrecht* by the Swiss-German legal and constitutional scholar Johann Kaspar Bluntschli (1808–1881), who viewed the state as an organism.

Katō's view of the state as a person rejected both the theory of a natural-law contract and the theory of absolute monarchy. It sublimated the conflict of monarch and people by establishing state sovereignty instead of monarchic or popular sovereignty. It posited a personality of the state that expressed the public interest through existing mechanisms of state authority. It left the state independent of the monarch and of the people's individual goals and interests. Insofar as it was based on this idea, Katō's opposition to Fukuzawa could not have been more natural.

"Fukuzawa's thinking is too liberal," Katō argued. "Not that being liberal is unacceptable, but when it is too liberal, a liberal argument will weaken state authority, and if the state's authority is weak, it cannot stand." So he considered Fukuzawa's liberalism excessively political—too much on the side of popular rights. Liberalism in this sense was incompatible with Katō's idea of state sovereignty. He quoted the view of the pan-German thinker Konstantin Frantz (1817–1891), the advocate of a federalist Mitteleuropa, to the effect that "liberals always seek to broaden popular rights and reduce the authority of the state."[61]

Bluntschli's *Allgemeines Staatsrecht* took as its keynote the theory of society as an organism (as opposed to the social contract theory); its indispensable condition was that "social tranquility could not be maintained unless the right of sovereignty was unique by virtue of the state's being an organism." Bluntschli advocated "the independence of the state, the fulfillment of its might, its uniqueness, and its possession of the various powers to rule." Rousseau's social contract theory came in for criticism on the grounds that "the right of sovereignty would revert to the general will (that is, the will of the masses). It would mean throwing out supreme authority and replacing it with supreme will. This is terribly mistaken."[62] Because Katō construed Fukuzawa's liberalism politically, it made sense for him, following Bluntschli, to think of Fukuzawa's external stimulus as something dangerous that impinged on the supreme and unique sovereignty of the state.

Actually, Fukuzawa viewed the state as a collectivity of individuals. In principle he did not recognize a qualitative difference between the rights of the state and those of the individual; indeed, the way to strengthen the state was to strengthen individual rights. His theoretical foundation thus differed from that involved in Katō's view of the state. During this period, Fukuzawa did not advocate the political liberalism that frightened Katō, nor did he preach popular sovereignty. So Katō's critique of Fukuzawa must be called arbitrary.

That critique is also related to Katō's peculiar understanding of natural-law thought. His interest in Western institutions dates from his 1862 political essay in the form of a colloquy, "The Grass Next Door" *(Tonarigusa),* in which he speaks of a bicameral constitutional system as "the easiest way to carry out benevolent government and to secure human harmony." This form of government was "fair and open" *(kōmei seidai,* a criterion Katō invokes repeatedly); indeed, it was the only means of saving the state from downfall. The state's very basis, according to this essay, rests on "never forgetting that the realm belongs to all the people; it is not a vehicle for the monarch alone, but was meant chiefly for the people."[63] The quality of any particular form of government depends on the fate of the country it serves, Katō maintained. In constitutionalism he saw the institutionalization of the doctrine of benevolent government.

In "A Look at the Rise and Fall and Relative Strength of Western Nations" *(Seiyō kakkoku seisui kyōjaku ichiranhyō),* which he wrote in 1867, Katō pointed to constitutional government as the unique source of the wealth and strength of Europe and America. This form of government "unites officials and people, and cannot become the government's property. Constitutional government is the reason why Europe with its enlightened wealth and strength rules the world."[64] This was the source of Western wealth and strength that Katō had in view: total harmony of high and low, one mind and one body, between government and people. The constitutional system is the means to bring about such harmony. Katō's view contrasts with Fukuzawa's argument that the basis of Western wealth and strength lay in a balance of forces between the government and an independent and autonomous populace.

Katō's 1868 "Survey of Constitutional Systems" *(Rikken seitai ryaku)* and his 1870 "Outline of True Government" *(Shinsei taii)* also deal with national political strategies. He was quoted in a popular periodical to the effect that the 1868 essay, while different in appearance from "The Grass Next Door," is "entirely one with it in principle."[65] "True Government" shared a focus on the form of government with "The Grass Next Door" and the "Survey" of 1868, but it went one step further. Specifically, "True Government" no longer concentrated on what Katō called the legal and institutional "system of governance" *(chihō)*, that is, "the constitutional system that is the basis for keeping the peace," but juxtaposed it with the political and administrative "technique of governing" *(chijutsu)*, that is, "the art of keeping the peace here and now." If good order is to be maintained in a state, both must be present; one does not suffice: "they are like the wheels of a cart, the wings of a bird." The crux of this "technique of governing" lay in "keeping the people content."[66] In this 1870 book Katō put all his effort into fashioning a statesman's art that would harmonize high and low—the art that he called "true government."

The basis for this art, Katō said, is the statesman's knowledge of natural law concerning the origins of the people and the government. "Without this knowledge, the arbitrary execution of the art of governing would cause us to revert to the original state of nature . . . and on this account we would fall into tyranny." So his natural-law person is not one of the Hobbesian, antisocial type but rather one founded on the social instinct, à la Grotius. Aiming for that sort of natural rights, this person innately possesses natural-law constraints; and government originates not in a Hobbesian, rationalized form of absolutism, in which everybody cedes natural rights to the absolute power holder, but from the development of a Grotius-like impulse, from self-restraint based on a social contract that unites free persons. In speaking of the "original rise of state and government," Katō points to a time when "there was nothing to unite and homogenize the multitude, people did as they pleased, and there was no basis for the pursuit of happiness through a system of parallel rights and duties." Eventually, people came to accept an order of restraints and subjected themselves to being governed. Those restraints, however, were not intended to "enchain" people so they could be "manipulated by the government." Rather, they were entered into "for the sake of unity and harmony only."[67]

Katō touches concretely on the rights and duties of government and people revolving about this sort of natural-law thought. A little further on in his argument, he refers to the subjugation of the Indies by Britain and other Western powers. According to Katō, the native population was only too glad to exchange the willful tyranny of their indigenous rulers for the protective embrace of the Europeans. "The ignorant populace, who would not understand a word if one talked to them of 'duty' or 'principle,' could not care less about coming under a colonial regime or whatever, but will submit gratefully to any authority that enables them to live their lives in peace. Governments must know this principle very well, and take care not to lose the people's support." Here the statesman is chiefly addressed, and in a way Katō is proceeding on the idea of Confucian benevolent government. The ruler's "first duty is to use every exertion in pursuing the way of caring, and provide the basis for a peaceful life"[68]—as in the Chinese classics where discussions of benevolence and nurture appear. Yet the various points Katō makes are all designed to instruct the monarch. He never ventures to speak to the public, and his natural-law program is just a concoction prepared for statesmen, without relevance for the people. When he talks this way about natural law, the difference between him and Fukuzawa is huge: As far as Katō was concerned, natural law worked for the rulers, not the ruled.

Katō's "New Thesis on the National Polity" *(Kokutai shinron)*, published in 1875, is his last work based on natural-law thought, and in the 1880s he himself took it out of print. With this book he assumed the role of an enlightener. According to Katō, traditional political thought —Confucianism and nativism—"gave no evidence that the land and people were anything other than the monarch's private belongings." Having missed this point, even the most renowned sages of ancient China were liable to Katō's charge that they had preached a doctrine of "Revere the ruler, despise the people." The status ethic that underlay the traditionalists' argument was nothing but a defense of the state as a family despotism. The views of the Japanese nativists in particular were "terribly contrary to the truth." Finding this "really contemptible,"[69] he mounted a merciless critique of them.

Katō emphasized that the people's servility, typical of the system of family despotism—the condition cultivated by the old nativists and sinologists—was incompatible with constitutional government, which was the source of the West's wealth and strength. The technique of governing reserved for statesmen in "True Government" is set free and extended to the people in the "New Thesis" of 1875. One chapter, called "The Right of Popular Liberty and the Spirit of Liberty," contains his famous remark that the spirit of respect for the emperor is "a form of spiritual enslavement." Katō argued that "when the dictates of monarchic government violate ethics or obstruct the private rights of the people," it is "only proper to resist them."[70] He even recognized the right of resistance against undue infringement of natural rights, adapting natural-law thought to defend the subjectivity of the people.

Katō's "New Thesis" does not, however, involve a defense of popular sovereignty. He cites Frantz to the effect that "human rights *(jinken)*—that is, the rights that people have at birth—are the various inherent *(koyū)* rights held by each person. Apart from those, there are private rights *(shiken),* but they arise through everyday interaction with others and are known as acquired *(tokuyū)* rights. Such a thing as the right to take part in government cannot possibly be called a human right": it falls outside the category of natural rights and amounts to no more than a privilege. "Whether or not to grant this right depends on considerations of state security. Hence it must be considered only fitting not to permit such a right to those who appear likely to cause harm if they were granted it."[71] There are suggestions here of the state-as-a-person thesis.

It has been shown that Katō's natural-law thought stresses three points, all of which restrict the basic rights of the people. First comes a theory of the origin of state and government; second, the idea of personal harmony between government and people; and third, restraint of monarchical authority through the rejection of family despotism. By setting extrapolitical limits on basic popular rights, Katō aimed to sublimate government and people, and these three points denote his state-as-a-person thesis. Relations between government and people must always be morally harmonized in a personlike unified state. This was his fundamental intention; constitutional government was but the means to it.

The mark of Katō's thought lay in his effort to keep the people's subjectivity within tolerable limits by putting priority on the means of achieving a traditional political ideal—something akin to Confucian benevolent government. He was uninterested in a thoroughgoing revolution in the human spirit. This distinguished him from Fukuzawa, who found the source of Western civilization through a process of excavating the concrete foundation of civic social consciousness, thinking thereby to address the immediate issue of just such a spiritual revolution. Katō looked for the source of Western civilization in its attainment of harmony between high and low, facilitated by superior political institutions—not in some sort of civic consciousness.

Next to be considered is "A Critique of 'On a Scholar's Calling' " by Tsuda Mamichi. Tsuda and Katō both attended the academy started by Sakuma Shōzan (1811–1864; personal name also read as Zōzan), so there were intellectual affinities between them from the start. In many ways, Tsuda prefigured the work of Katō, who was seven years his junior. In particular, Katō's "Survey of Constitutional Systems" owed much to Tsuda's 1866 notes "On Western Public Law" *(Taisei koku-hōron)*, a Japanese synopsis of the tutorials that the Leiden legal scholar Simon Vissering had given him on the subject during Tsuda's years of study in the Netherlands between 1863 and 1865.[72] Tsuda's ideological position during the era of "civilization and enlightenment" is often considered to be in the same category as Katō's. On close inspection, however, it is clear that there are differences between them in the way they understood the connection linking government and people. These points of difference were already evident when Tsuda criticized Fuku-zawa's "On a Scholar's Calling." Unlike Katō, who did not have doubts about Fukuzawa's external-stimulus, internal-cultivation metaphor even though he stood it on its head, Tsuda took a good look at it, found it wanting, and brought up another metaphor in its place.

The procedure he used to criticize Fukuzawa offers a key to Tsuda's thought. Reading conflict between government and people in the metaphor of "external stimulus, internal cultivation," Katō had sought resolution by uniting them in a single personality—in contrast to Fukuzawa, who meant to make the most of the conflict itself. For his part, Tsuda drew an analogy between the state and the human body, but noted that it was "a mistake" to say that "the government is the life force and the people an external object." In particular, Tsuda found fault with Fuku-zawa's metaphor because "the people belong to the country and are therefore an internal entity"; moreover, "an external stimulus may be compared to foreign relations"—necessary but not decisive. He did not support the notion that a relationship of conflict existed between government and people, proposing instead the analogy that the "government is like the spirit, the people like the body."

Like Katō, Tsuda harbored an organic conception of the essence of the state, and he regarded the government-people relation as a matter of natural law: "Although we think of the body as something obedient to the call of the spirit, in reality the body follows the law of its own nature. If we use it to go beyond this law, we will weaken the spirit as well as the body; they will become exhausted and finally die. But if we use the body according to the law of its nature, it will become more and more healthy."[73] Tsuda explained that when he spoke of a law of nature, he did not mean a metaphysical law governing human existence but a law of nature concerning objective things—a physiological law of the body, as it were. Such a law was "nothing else but this—what [objective] things must correspond to; the systematic order that exists among them." It was "a law of nature; as such it is never subject to human control."[74]

By comparing the people to the carnal body—to nature—Tsuda could impute to them an objective existence that followed its own rules, outside the control of the arbitrary will of the government—the spirit. Relations between government and people could then be established as physiological relations between brain and body, following familiar sanitary precepts to avoid the ravages of the flesh and preserve physical health. By "the people" Tsuda accordingly meant an external entity that was quite independent of the government's will, and such a definition of the term approximated Fukuzawa's external object. Considering that Tsuda never acknowledged a relationship of conflict between government and people, however, he and Fukuzawa were very different in their understanding of that external entity.

When Fukuzawa spoke of the people as an external object, he always stressed their independence, their positive function vis-à-vis the government, and their subjectivity. In contrast, for Tsuda an external object was just an objective entity with fixed philosophical laws. He scarcely inquired about its role as a stimulus. In other words, Fukuzawa emphasized the people's subjectivity, whereas Tsuda stressed the condition of nature inhering in the people, who could not be compelled to endure government despotism. In expressing this as "the law of the body's nature," he was seeking to correct the government's traditional view of those it ruled.

Just what did Tsuda mean by the law of the body's nature? He was referring to passion, which originates in our human instincts. "On Passion," his *Meiroku zasshi* article, maintains that "passion is our most important innate feature, what makes us alive"; it is "the creator's grandest blessing on us, a wonderful gift bringing joy to our lives." Tsuda criticized the teachings of Confucianism and Buddhism, particularly stressing the point that the natural law posited by Sung Neo-Confucianism suppressed human nature, thereby negating passion, the true law of nature. "The Chu Hsi school's fixed view of reason as antithetical to passion is utterly ridiculous," Tsuda declared, and then asked rhetorically, "How can they claim that passion is opposed to the laws of nature?" On the contrary, it was the root cause of civilization! "We can hope that it suffuses our nature, for passion aspires to happiness and delights in liberty, which covets novelty. Is not passion the truest and most necessary part of our nature? It is why we act in concert with progress."[75]

Japan failed to expand its national power, according to Tsuda, because a "national style of unlimited monarchy since ancient times" had suppressed the laws of nature. Hence he looked forward to something that would bestow "a climate of autonomy and liberty" on the Japanese.[76] Autonomy and liberty meant respect for people's wants and the development of their latent abilities. Here Tsuda went beyond the bounds of Confucian political thought, but his version of "autonomy and liberty" differed from Fukuzawa's, which advocated stimulating the government from outside. Tsuda therefore approved of the establishment of a popularly elected assembly, regarding it as entirely appropriate to the times.[77] In regard to the prerogatives of the representatives, he did not recognize their right to legislate but would only give them the rights of deliberation and administrative supervision, holding that the "law of the people's nature," like the law of the body's nature, must be observed.

The disagreement between Tsuda and Fukuzawa appears to rest mainly on their differing views of "practical studies." If the spirit of civilization that emanated from the West was the true form of practical studies in Fukuzawa's view, then Tsuda's emphasis was on the workings of Western civilization: rather than the spiritual roots that had created it, he stressed the way it operated. His essay "On the Way to Promote Enlightenment" contains this insight: "On matters of substance, we speak of authentic reason chiefly in terms of phenomena. Practical studies include astronomy, physics, chemistry, medicine, economics, and the philosophy of the modern West. A society will be truly civilized when these practical studies are in vogue throughout the land, so that they reach everyone."[78] Tsuda encouraged the imitation of foreign cultural models as a means of disseminating practical studies. "On Rejecting Protective Tariffs" argued that before planning the unrestricted inflow of Western civilization, it was necessary to enlighten the Japanese, who "have not yet penetrated the inner sanctum of enlightenment, having only begun to knock at the good and beautiful door of Western culture."[79] The harm produced by discrepancies in the export and import trade was therefore a fitting burden, a form of tuition paid for the opportunity to study the West. (At the time, Japan was importing much more than it exported.) In another article, Tsuda praised the benefits of travel by foreigners in Japan's interior, because "seeing is believing and experience better than study"—hence interaction with foreigners would "increase knowledge and enlightenment among our general public."[80] Practical studies, for Tsuda at least, consisted of gleaning from the fruits of Western scholarship and the material side of civilization. He did not stress their subjective spirit.

Tsuda's critique of Fukuzawa is not confrontational, since it was born of Katō's view of the Fukuzawa line as a form of political liberalism. Tsuda did not go beyond the view he expressed in his "Critique of 'On a Scholar's Calling,'" where he praised Fukuzawa's liberalism as his own while criticizing Fukuzawa's thesis for arguing that "we should all leave government service and stay in private life. To do so would be much too radical."[81] Here, however, Tsuda displayed no quantitative difference between himself and Fukuzawa. (The qualitative difference between them in understanding Western civilization is clear.) Tsuda's enlightenment thinking is different in character from Fukuzawa's and from Katō's. Rather than transplant national subjectivity to the people through emphasis on their autonomy and liberty, Tsuda wanted to cultivate the faculty of popular membership in the modern state. To that end, he would check the government's self-righteous policy of authoritarian modernization, just as he would respect passion as a natural law promoting the people's growth.

Finally, Nishi Amane's turn comes. In his critique of Fukuzawa, Nishi differed from the others in that he did not focus on the question of whether a scholar should be inside or outside government. Rather than a scholar's political *location*, Nishi spoke of a scholar's *vocation*, in and of itself. He first asked whether Fukuzawa's ideas were appropriate to the realities of the day. Fukuzawa's anxiety about Japan's independence had a vague basis in the notion of an independent popular spirit—an "extremely uncertain foundation," one lacking verifiability, Nishi thought. Were not all of Fukuzawa's assertions "deceptive in logic even though not without a grain of truth"? Did not Fukuzawa commit the logical error of failing to marshal evidence? This appears to be an extremely positivistic and rationalistic pronouncement on his part, yet in refuting Fukuzawa, he himself concluded that "despite bad habits, our fortunes as a people since the restoration do seem to have improved in comparison with earlier days." However—and this is a key to exploring Nishi—we must note that his own vague comments about progress offer no hint as to the identity of the true prime mover of that progress.

Nishi did indicate what he meant by progress. "Such things are not man-made" and are "not subject to human or policy restraint, resulting instead from trends in the world itself"—that is, they are cut off from the subjective workings of man. Nishi developed his critique of Fukuzawa from this viewpoint. The gist of it was to deny Fukuzawa's personal plan to become the paragon of the people through activating their will for autonomy and independence: "It is suitable for the 'stimulus' to be applied gradually as the people progress toward civilization. If the stimulus is forcibly started, it is bound to become excessive." Such a stimulus could not stand by itself as the prime mover of progress, Nishi thought. If it were applied in ignorance of the trend of the times, then (far from leading to progress) it could only be a source of confusion. So he could not agree with Fukuzawa that the duty of a scholar was to serve as a stimulus, to activate the people. Instead, it must be to regulate the people's activities, to recognize the level of their culture and enlightenment, to determine "whether the temperature ought to be raised or lowered." Therefore it seemed inconsequential whether a scholar served in government or stayed in private life. One who surveyed the parameters of culture and enlightenment did have a role in government, however: it was to exert unerring guidance about the trend of the times and to act "like the quinine that makes the life force pulsate" in revitalizing government policy. If there was no one in government who could serve as such a guide, Nishi feared, the government's policies would end in futility or even do great harm. If scholars all stayed in private life—if they kept out of government, as Fukuzawa wished—that would be akin to "defying a cold and taking a fever that turns into the plague."[82]

What basis did Nishi adduce for this critique? This question is related to his idealistic manner of approaching Western civilization, unlike Fukuzawa's essentialist approach and the concrete and materialistic attitudes of Katō and Tsuda. Nishi's concern was not with the component parts of Western civilization but with its fundamentals. Fukuzawa followed this same tendency toward a comprehensive view of the spirit of civilization. What Nishi found there, however, was not Fukuzawa's pluralistic social consciousness but a metaphysical system based on a monistic and unified social existence. The way to achieve it in Japan was not through Fukuzawa's pursuit of human affairs, or Katō's constitutional system, or Tsuda's imitation of foreign lifestyles, but through a philosophy that would comprehend Western scholarship, and above all the system of thought informing it. Mori Ōgai (1862–1922) quotes a letter that Nishi wrote in 1862, just before he went to the Netherlands to study, in which he argued that "only by studying *hirosohi* can the principles of life be explained." This "philosophy," Nishi thought, was superior to Neo-Confucianism of the Ch'eng-Chu school. "In regard to building a proper political economy, it is superior also to the Mencian idea of the Kingly Way."[83] This comment shows just where Nishi's concern with Western civilization lay. His understanding of the West did not change much in the course of his life. He made his scholarship understood through philosophy, psychology, logic, and aesthetics, chiefly in their theoretical aspects. During the era of "civilization and enlightenment," he carried out his enlightenment activities on the basis of apprehending social existence through a philosophical method. For him this was the sole index of civilized progress, and at the time it made him a unique figure.

Nishi's conception of philosophy matured through contact with the thought of Comte and Kant while he was overseas. Nishi was particularly moved by the freshness of Comte's ideas. "Recent efforts to determine the truth through positive evidence and debate will help young scholars in the future. Auguste Comte is the leading advocate of these things, the like of which we have not yet seen in Asia."[84] In 1873 Nishi said in "Finding the Physical and the Spiritual" *(Seisei hatsuun)* that he had come to believe in "the positivism of Auguste Comte and the inductive method of the famous Englishman John Stuart Mill."[85] Nishi therefore adopted the empirical model of thought, opposed as it was to the Confucian deductive method of reasoning.

From this methodological position Nishi criticized Fukuzawa's idea of spirit or "character" *(kifū)* for having no concrete basis. To be sure, the system of rules that Nishi embraced was not based on empirical social law à la Comte but on "mental principle" or "psychology," as shown in his "New Thesis for Making Many into One" *(Hyakuichi shinron)*, which appeared in 1874. Nishi divided the Great Ultimate posited by Neo-Confucian cosmology—the system that unites human nature with the natural world—into two separate sets of rules: natural law as an a priori principle, that is, physics *(butsuri)*; and human nature as an a posteriori principle, that is, psychology *(shinri)*. At a stroke he liberated the criterion of human existence from nature's control by calling it "psychological." To Nishi, psychology was not something easily changed like fashion but basically immutable. That is, it was not an empirical law but a metaphysical system. That system required the criterion of an a priori order based on an innate human nature, close in substance to the Chu Hsi Neo-Confucian view of inherent traits: "Heaven does not issue orders individually, nor does it prescribe individual rewards and punishments. There is but one human nature, and everybody is endowed with it."[86]

Here it can be seen why Nishi dedicated himself to positivism and acknowledged empirical social laws, yet did not rationally plan for the construction of a new society based on them but was forced instead to leave progress to some ambiguous "trend of the times." This in turn explains why he did not recognize the subjective stimulus of the people as the prime mover of social progress, but on the contrary linked the criterion of an a priori order with social progress and spoke of humankind adapting to it.

The contradiction between Nishi's methods and his conclusions can be pointed out here and there in his works, and for that reason appraisals of his thought will vary. It would seem, however, that the essence of his thought inheres in this very contradiction. It might therefore be an interesting problem to make a thinker such as Nishi the object of inquiry, looking more closely into this contradiction to find the method in his particular mix of new and old thought. This kind of mix is something common among transitional thinkers. His pattern of receptivity to foreign ideas is also interesting. Here, however, it has sufficed to indicate the point within the contradiction that gave Nishi a basis for criticizing Fukuzawa.

Since philosophy was his weapon of enlightenment, Nishi believed that "it is vital to arrive at a unified view of the academic disciplines. If such a view is established, human enterprises and the social order will be settled as a matter of course." Only when practical knowledge is organized according to philosophical understanding will the universal "health and peace" of society finally be attainable. "If we add the element of hard work to this, the result will be the wealth and strength of the realm. The two elements of health-peace and wealth-strength will then prevail. People will become mild and cheerful and will be promoted to the domain of longevity, dwelling in a condition in which they can, as is said [in *Mencius*], 'nourish their living and bury their dead.' In short, they will enjoy prosperity, and prosperity in turn is humanity's ultimate achievement."[87] Thus he contemplated the prospect of a serene society, corresponding to an a priori order but far removed from human progress.

For Nishi, all doctrines—those involving politics, education, religion, scholarship—were obliged to serve a unified goal, as he argued in "Making Many into One." That goal was " 'harmony,' as it is called in the West."[88] Nishi understood natural law by way of philosophy as an expression of "mental principle," that is, psychology. Using psychology as his ideological weapon, he criticized Neo-Confucianism for its dependence on a feudal status society and on a changeless hierarchical nature.

Nishi deserves high marks for displaying the common qualification of enlighteners of the time—advocacy of human equality. Even if his natural law of psychology could fully demonstrate equality, however, it could not likewise substantiate subjectivity. Its main feature was the use of "natural reason" *(tenri)* to give stability to an unstable social reality. His intent was to dissolve the contradiction between policy and reality by teaching the necessity of orderly social activity and by warning the people about radical policies on the part of the government. On this point, however, Nishi differed not at all from the other thinkers.

Despite variations in their thinking, the intellectuals who debated Fukuzawa Yukichi's essay "On a Scholar's Calling" agreed on at least one thing. They were all unsympathetic to Fukuzawa's idea that "popular government" called for the people to be an external stimulus and for scholars to stay out of government. They disagreed among themselves—and with Fukuzawa—on how to interpret the modern spirit. Katō and Tsuda focused on Western civilization in its concrete particulars; Nishi stressed Western knowledge as a system of a priori principles. Compared to Fukuzawa, the others could not break with the conventional mode of responding to the West, illustrated by Sakuma Shōzan's notion of "Eastern ethics, Western science"—a response that would have Japan adapt by separating "civilization" from its social base as a way of holding onto Japanese tradition. It was not the spirit of Western civilization that inspired such thinkers; their approach derived from their reading of the modern West's actual accomplishments.

Conclusion

The new intellectuals of Meiji Japan's era of "civilization and enlightenment" cast a wide net. In intellectual history, their role was to nurture a New Person able to deal with the transformation wrought by the government's radical policy of modernization; they played the part of enlighteners who alerted Japan to the possibilities of a variety of models based on the European Enlightenment. They drew on the eighteenth-century ideology of natural law, the idea of natural rights, to break down feudalism's hierarchical status system and clear the way for constructing a new social order. Unlike the natural-rights concept in Europe, however, their concept of enlightenment failed to address the task of establishing the individual in Japanese society. Rather, it aimed at the formation of the people as a nation. Instead of focusing on individual persons as formative subjects of a new state order, the Meirokusha thinkers were caught up with the problem of how best to incorporate such persons into the state. In that respect, they differed little from Itō Hirobumi and the other Meiji oligarchs.

So it happened that in a Japan governed by the Darwinian international environment of the late nineteenth century, the theory of natural rights took on a twofold historical role. It liberated the feudal person fixed by status as a means of securing independence for the whole people in a nation-state. At the same time it made the people conscious only of belonging to a nation, not to a community of free individuals. To be sure, the sense of personal equality spread like wildfire, carried on the flames of the "liberation of the passions." Since this took place just as Japan's political transformation was coming to an end, such an attitude had to be grounded in a social consciousness capable of conflating natural rights and sensual satisfaction.

Natural-rights thinking was thus conditioned by the historical problem of Meiji Japan. The turn toward a modern civic consciousness was held in check by the very political forces that had set it in motion in the first place. Once the rational construction of the state order became their primary task, the new intellectuals lost their character as enlighteners. And so the enlightenment project went nowhere during the short era of "civilization and enlightenment" in the 1870s. These intellectuals were bound to focus on controlling passion, not on affirming it as a way of helping to bring down the feudal status system. Instead of fashioning an individual principle of control based on natural rights, they had to compromise with the state's power for keeping order. Even Fukuzawa, acting as a natural-law rationalist in his 1875 "Outline of a Theory of Civilization," began to voice a form of irrational patriotism, in effect circumscribing the historical role of natural-rights thought.

Perhaps it was to be expected that the Meirokusha thinkers would accept the attenuation of the idea of individual superiority—the proper first principle of any theory of natural rights. By adding the goal of immediate national independence to the natural rights agenda, they played into the hands of the radical popular-rights forces working for liberation of the senses. As a result the intellectuals of the Society of Meiji Six turned into critics of popular rights, thus managing ironically to undermine their own enlightenment activity. This is a major problem, but not a mystery. It helps to account for a further irony: why a revived Confucian ideology could become a full partner to these thinkers. While the new bureaucrats were exploiting Confucianism to cement state control over the entire populace, the Meirokusha intellectuals found themselves harking back to it even as they abandoned the rights of the individual in favor of the rights of society.

Meiji Japan did indeed empower itself to achieve national independence. In the process, however, the individual values at the heart of the *bunmei kaika* project were sacrificed on the altar of collective goals.

6

The Statist Movement and Its Educational Activities
The Shimeikai and the Seiseikō of Kumamoto

Translated by E. Patricia Tsurumi

The Meiji state expected all Japanese schools, and public schools in particular, to instill nationalist thought in the minds of the entire populace. The cultivation of nationalist ideology was made their objective by Education Minister Mori Arinori's school orders of 1886 and gradually became embedded in Japan's modern educational system thereafter. Why did nationalism take root in the Japanese people's education with such comparative ease? Educational history has so far dealt with only one side of the problem. We have been told about the penetration of the state's political will into educational policy—undeniably a pervasive phenomenon—but why the people themselves actively accepted nationalist education is a question that has scarcely been treated. Surely the state's educational policy could never have set down firm roots, no matter how much pressure the government applied, if the ground had not been prepared first. That much is amply illustrated by the government's inability to implement its Education Order of 1872 by coercion. To elucidate the conditions that promoted receptivity to the government's basic policy from below, among the people, is therefore of prime importance to Meiji educational history.

The general aim of this chapter is to clarify the relationship between politics and education in Meiji Japan. The particular objective is to provide evidence of popular support for nationalist education, illustrating the conditions for its active acceptance in Japanese society. Toward that end, the chapter discusses a nationalistic political movement pursued in the interests of the state and examines the related educational activities of samurai who sought to secure and safeguard the nation's independence during the early years of the Meiji period. The specific topic taken up here is the relationship between a statist political party known as the Shimeikai and a private academy called the Seiseikō (School of Proliferating Talent) in Kumamoto.[1] This is a good example of the nationalist links between politics and education, but it is far from being the only one. Others that come to mind immediately are the relationships between the political society called Gen'yōsha and the Kōyō Academy in Fukuoka or those between the disgruntled proponents of an invasion of Korea and the Kainan Shijuku in Tosa. All these schools sought to imbue their students with nationalism. Human cultivation was pursued there with the aim of ensuring the country's independence.

Nationalist indoctrination, the essence of Meiji public education, had its genesis in the political movements and educational activities of statist groups of the samurai elite. It was pursued in a way that strengthened education's dependence on politics. Educational goals took a back seat to political considerations among samurai activists of factions of the popular-rights movement as well, something that is exemplified clearly in the relationship between the Risshisha and the Risshi Gakusha of Tosa as well as in that between Ōkuma Shigenobu's Constitutional Reform party and the Tokyo Specialist School, discussed elsewhere in this book.[2] In other words, political action taken both by statists and by advocates of popular rights to control education was a distinctive feature of the Meiji scene from the beginning of the era right down to the time of Mori Arinori's stewardship. Their efforts represent the local incarnations of the Meiji period's central educational philosophy.

Under what conditions, then, did the relationship between the Shimeikai and the Seiseikō come to promote the subordination of education to politics in Kumamoto? The political agenda of the Shimeikai and the educational program of the School of Proliferating Talent both inherited the traditions of a political movement of Kumamoto samurai, and the activities of their members no doubt were a major factor in causing nationalist educational ideas to seize hold in that city. But how did these two groups come to support the fundamental designs of Meiji education, which they voluntarily—on their own initiative—propped up from below? A consideration of the thought of three individuals who played key roles in the foundation of the Shimeikai and the management of the Seiseikō—Sassa Tomofusa, Tsuda Seiichi, and Takahashi Nagaaki—will help in answering these questions and will in turn require a look at the samurai education that shaped the ideology of these three Kumamoto men.

Although it is not directly relevant to this chapter, we cannot forget that two important figures in the political and educational history of Meiji were born in Kumamoto—Motoda Nagazane and Inoue Kowashi. Both of them had a hand in drafting the Imperial Rescript on Education. Inoue, in particular, prodded the oligarch Itō Hirobumi, persuaded him to adopt a Prussian-style constitution and an educational system to go with it, and paved the way for the policies of Mori Arinori. The political, ideological, and educational soil of Kumamoto that produced these two was the same earth that nourished Sassa, Tsuda, Takahashi, and others of their ilk. Motoda Nagazane and Tsuda's father shared the same background in Kumamoto's Practical Learning party at the end of the Edo period. Inoue Kowashi received his political baptism in another faction of Kumamoto samurai, the Academy party, as did Sassa and Takahashi. These facts lead us to the headwaters of one stream of Meiji education in Kumamoto.

Politics and Nationalistic Education in Kumamoto

The Seiseikō, which held its opening ceremony on 11 February 1882, had a direct predecessor in the Dōshin Gakusha (School of Kindred Spirits). That predecessor had been founded on 11 February 1879 by fellow townsmen of Sassa Tomofusa (1854–1906), who was himself in prison on the charge of taking up arms in support of Saigō Takamori (1827–1877) in the Satsuma Rebellion of 1877. In his "History of the Seiseikō," Sassa gave four reasons why he was determined to found a school in Kumamoto despite being incarcerated. "There may be a multitude of ways to save the country, but education affects them all," Sassa first pointed out. "In these dangerous times, those who are devoted to the state should contribute to the wealth of the country by educating our youth and our children in order to invigorate the people." Next, he raised the specter of radicalism: "Profligate doctrines that are circulating in our country could spread to our youth. This is something to be dreaded. If we do not promote true education grounded in the ethics of our national polity *(kokutai)*, and if we do not foster the character and capabilities of our people as subjects of the Imperial Land, how is our empire to survive the tides now engulfing the world?" Third, he referred to the devastation with which war had visited Kumamoto in 1877: "The town was reduced to ashes. Voices reading and studying could no longer be heard. People passing by the town all grieved and lamented; there was not one who did not weep. At such a time as this, there was surely an urgent need for education!" Sassa's final point addressed the paradoxical opportunity presented to Kumamoto in the war's aftermath: "The situation was as after a flood, when everything has been washed away. Roads and bridges can be built freely then, in the emptiness left by the destruction. . . . This was the ideal time to reclaim education and to reform the world of the young."[3]

And just what kind of education was needed? Sassa's argument clearly subordinates education to political concerns, setting educational goals that are meant to serve nationalist priorities. His first reason for establishing a school was not to develop human character but to serve the state. His second reason was to counter the antistatist ideas of the advocates of popular rights. These objectives could best be approached by putting nationalistic ideology at the core of the educational program, the better to disseminate it among the people. (In this regard, Sassa anticipated the thrust of the Imperial Rescript on Education of 1890.) In his two last points, Sassa suggested that the time was ripe for action: the wartime destruction of feudalistic values was an opportunity that should be seized for the sake of beginning anew with nationalistic education.

A survivor of Saigō's defeated rebel army—accordingly branded a war criminal—Sassa was by definition a member of an antigovernment faction. As he and his followers involved themselves in education projects, those near them worried about the public perception of their "forming a party in the aftermath of the conflict" and withheld approval of what they were doing.[4] As a result, few contributed money to their endeavor. When the Dōshin Gakusha was reconstituted as the Seiseikō in 1882, this rebirth was denounced publicly as "Sassa hatching the egg of a rebellion."[5] In the midst of the difficulties caused by his notoriety as an opposition figure, Sassa relates, he happened by chance to pick up a copy of Samuel Smiles' *Self-Help* that was lying on a desk. "Over and over again I read the passage in Smiles' Introduction about the children of humble country folk learning reading and arithmetic in their dwelling or their front yard and later renting a room in a cholera hospital to set up a school that in time was to accomplish great things. It made me think that our situation is exactly like this."[6] Thus inspired, Sassa and his followers established a school.

In spite of his antigovernment stance, Sassa's approach to education was exactly the same as the Meiji government's. This becomes comprehensible when one realizes that the priority given to politics was not just a feature of the government's educational policy. During the early Meiji period, politics ruled in every realm—social policy, economics, culture, ideology—and the subordination of other interests to politics was the universal practice followed by both the government and its opponents. The differences between them were not determined by their educational views but derived from new images of the state that were projected from their political positions. Even before nationalistic education was imposed on the country by Mori Arinori (1847–1889; minister of education from 22 December 1885), it existed in the ideology emphasized by Sassa Tomofusa and his supporters, who were outsiders to state power. They opposed the Meiji government's policy of "civilization and enlightenment" and its experiments with Europeanization. They criticized its Education Order of 1872 (Gakusei) and the Western-style school system set up by it. The "Kindred Spirits" of the Dōshin Gakusha pushed for nationalist education from below. When their school turned into the Seiseikō, the educational program of Sassa and his cohorts became one of the tangible planks in the political platform of the Shimeikai, and their willingness to subordinate education to politics became even more apparent.

The Shimeikai was organized in September 1881. Tokutomi Sohō (1863–1957), then a member of the Sōaisha (Mutual Affection Guild), a group with an opposing ideology, identified the generative force behind the rival party by saying that the authorities favored the creation of the Shimeikai "at a time when appeals for a legislative assembly grew ever more numerous and the government was beset with many problems."[7] Indeed, this party was organized by the bureaucrat Yasuba Yasukazu (1835–1889), a native of Kumamoto, after consultation with the oligarch Iwakura Tomomi (1825–1883). But Tokutomi Sohō notwithstanding, the Shimeikai was not organized solely according to the intentions of those at the top.

According to Tsuda Seiichi (1852–1909), one of this political party's key figures, there were two pivotal moments in its formation.[8] The first, preliminary step was the foundation of the Society Lamenting the State of the Country (Jisei o Ureuru Kai). This event took place in Tokyo in the spring of 1880, when some government officials who were natives of Kumamoto held a meeting with "several gentlemen newly come from our prefecture to the capital," including Sassa, Takahashi Nagaaki (1858–1929), Kimura Tsuruo (d. 1897), and Shiraki Tamenao (1834–1887). "Lamenting the current state of politics, they decided that it was necessary to form a political party which would support the implementation of the Imperial Edict of 1875 and assist in creating constitutional government;[9] would work to eradicate the violence and radicalism spreading among the people; and would preserve order in society by promoting morality and learning. All this it would strive to accomplish so that our country could become the most developed and enlightened nation in the East." The society's membership increased with every meeting. That autumn they unanimously chose Yasuba and Furushō Kamon (1840–1915) to initiate the political party.

The second critical moment, according to Tsuda, came at the beginning of the summer of 1881, when Shiraki Tamenao returned to Kumamoto, where he founded the Constitutional Association (Kenpōkai) in consultation with representatives of various local political factions—the old Practical Learning party (Jitsugakutō or Jitsugakuha), the so-called Academy party (Gakkōtō), and the Mutual Affection Guild, an offshoot of the popular-rights movement. (Soon Sassa, Takahashi, and Kimura also returned to Kumamoto; eventually, so did Yasuba and Furushō.) Representatives of these diverse interests came together in the spirit of the Tokyo meetings to form a "grand coalition" that would overcome factionalism, and they called their united party the Shimeikai. Their unity foundered on the sovereignty issue. The adherents of popular rights, the progressive elements of the Mutual Affection Guild, and the Nuyama segment of the Practical Learning party broke away; the "grand coalition" split apart. As a result, the Shimeikai was reconstituted as a political party of statists, prominently including Sassa, Kimura, Takahashi, and Tsuda; according to Tsuda, essentially it was formed from below. If one considers that in 1880 Sassa and his circle thought of organizing their own political group, to be called the Public Unity Association (Kōdōsha), it is plain that the reconstituted Shimeikai was the realization of the Kōdōsha's professed ideal—emperor-centered statism —in a different form.

"Seek to achieve the united front of all your compatriots," the Kōdōsha urged its members. "Join your joys and fears in times of peace and in times of peril to preserve security and happiness. Domestically, respond to the benevolence of His Majesty the Emperor by endeavoring to maintain His Majesty's position as the empire's very foundation, keeping it as solid as Mount Fuji. Let us display our valor throughout the world with the Flag of the Rising Sun forever."[10] Little wonder that bureaucrats from Kumamoto—men like Yasuba Yasukazu, Furushō Kamon, and Inoue Kowashi (1843–1895)—gave full support to Public Unity. Naturally, they also supported its successor organization, the Shimeikai; indeed, they even helped to formulate its objectives. None other than Inoue Kowashi, who was to make quite a name for himself as a lawgiver, drafted the manifesto called the "Aims" *(Shushi)* of the Shimeikai, which sought to clarify the society's main political goals.

On 1 September 1881, the Shimeikai adopted a "Covenant" *(Kiyaku)* that pledged "(1) to extend the authority of the state by serving the Imperial House and supporting constitutional government, (2) to promote social enlightenment by advancing education and rectifying morals, and (3) to seek the strength and prosperity of the nation by working for public welfare and our own independence." The first point spelled out the basic political goals of the organization, and the other two identified activities directed to education and the common weal as the means of realizing those goals. There was a clear intention to subordinate education to political interests.

A supplement to the "Covenant," dated 5 May 1882, emphasized a crucial point: "It is evident that the sovereignty of the Japanese state inheres in the emperor. We shall not accept any different view."[11] This addendum was apparently considered necessary because of the tumultuous debate on sovereignty that shook the entire Japanese political world in the early 1880s. In the back rooms of the Shimeikai, too, a split occurred over the locus of sovereignty. To eradicate the radicalism that it believed to be spreading among the people remained, however, the society's priority as it continued to lament the state of the country. Its "Aims" highlighted that priority by pointing out how perilous the times had become since Japan, for so long isolated in a corner of East Asia, had opened its doors to a new era of international relations:[12]

> Radical political ideas from Europe have flowed into Japan in a single wave. In a few years they have spread throughout town and country with the speed of a calamity. To use medical terms, a nation that suffers an epidemic for the first time will inevitably become gravely ill, and then one cannot but be amazed at the destructive power of nature. Wherever that destructive force is felt, the disease spreads: radical thought thrives on its own virulence. Ordinary, everyday speech is not the kind of discourse that incites people. New, unusual arguments work best in gathering a crowd and organizing a party. All this we have witnessed before our eyes. Why, then, is it that in an age when people welcome radical arguments so readily, we go against the tenor of the times? Why is it that we take risks? Why do we advocate views that are unbiased? It is because we have no choice but to do so.

The political purpose of the Shimeikai was to prevent popular-rights ideas that had their origins in Europe from spreading to Japan; hence Europe was its target. The anti-Europeanism that had characterized the oppositionist stance of Sassa and his colleagues was focused on countering the inflow of the radicalism that they associated with European thought. They did not intend to support the government. Even if they remained in the opposition, however, their anti-Europeanism could not but reinforce the government's suppression of the popular-rights movement. That is how the Shimeikai came to play the role attributed to it by Tokutomi Sohō—that of a progovernment party.

According to Tsuda Seiichi, the Shimeikai was attacked in the newspapers not only in Kumamoto but also in Tokyo. It was called "a progovernment party, a supporter of bureaucratic authority, intellectually barren, and so on. There was no end to the slander and calumny. The worst of the criticisms was that the Shimeikai was an anarchist party that would destroy all probity." Yasuba and Furushō had returned to Kumamoto on orders, the newspapers alleged; to set up a group that would support the government and fight Western ideas of popular rights was their purpose. All that was false, Tsuda maintained. Unfortunately, the Shimeikai had "not yet had the chance to start a newspaper of its own," so it was "in no position to express its philosophy or to reveal the truth."[13] Tsuda's apologia was no mere self-justification. The attempts of Sohō and others to deny the oppositionist character of the group are wide of the mark, after all.

A sense of crisis concerning Japan's international position as a late developer also underlay the formulation of the Shimeikai's other priority, the effort to unify the Japanese people as the most expedient means of securing Japan's independence. Sassa Tomofusa's plaint graphically describes this second major point:[14]

> In the present emergency, we confront the most extreme peril and face the most extraordinary misfortune since heaven and earth were opened up. The general trend of the world over the last several hundred years has been changing daily. Getting the upper hand in so many ventures, the white races encircle East and West like a great snake. Our country may lose its opportunity and fall behind the changes. It is as though we were taking small coins to a market that deals only in gold bullion or confronting a great host with a handful of men. Our country is like raw meat cast before hungry tigers, like ice exposed to the hot sun. If we want to defend our national polity, develop our national strength, and turn danger into security, we must unite the minds and energies of our people. Radical views prosper at such times as these. If as a result the people is split into factions, the national polity will be torn apart, and our nation will fall victim to outsiders, just as India became a prey to the English. . . . Hence we must do our utmost to fulfill our duty to preserve our Imperial Throne for all eternity. Those who do nothing but use official positions to benefit themselves, obstruct public business, and foment internal dissension are not welcome in our party. Nor are promoters of tumult, subverters of public morals, and advocates of anarchic republicanism, who destroy the good order of society.

The emphasis upon excluding from the Shimeikai anyone who obstructed national unity—officials no less than private citizens—illustrates the society's character as an opposition group. The spiritual basis of that national unity lay in "the eternal nature of our Imperial Throne," which made Japan's sovereign unlike that of any foreign country.[15] Herein was rooted the Shimeikai's approach to nationalistic education: it was a necessary means to the goal of uniting the people, as the second article of the "Covenant" implied.

In the course of the consultations that took place around the time the Shimeikai "raised its banner of loyalty and patriotism," Sassa says, fears were expressed that "even united hearts and efforts might not suffice as power struggles dominated the international scene and the weak fell prey to the strong. With radicalism and profligacy rampant, how could we possibly succeed?" As long as radical views remained mere superficial imports from abroad, Sassa felt, there was no need to be concerned; if they were permitted to continue making inroads into society, however, the effect would be devastating. "What will the fate of the nation be?" he asked. "To save the situation, schools must be established and education spread throughout the land—schools that shall cultivate loyal and patriotic men for the well-being of the nation."[16] It was Sassa's hope that the Dōshin Gakusha was such a school, and "everyone agreed." Thus the decision was made to build on its foundations. In other words, the School of Kindred Spirits was to be used to achieve the political ends of the Shimeikai; and, in fact, the educational program of the Dōshin Gakusha and of its successor, the Seiseikō, never veered from the Shimeikai's political program.

Hence the educational ideology of the School of Kindred Spirits deserves some scrutiny. Its "Founding Prospectus" *(Kensetsu shuisho)* was written by Sassa. In it are three points that especially command attention.[17] The first argues that school is where people are molded: "From birth people have a wondrous nature. If that nature is not formed and reformed, however, there will exist only unenlightened, ignorant, simple, barbaric people. How then can we rise above other creatures? It is only through learning that human nature can be illumined." The second point highlights the gap between the Meiji government's educational policy and the people's actual living standard, seeking to make an argument for cheap, accessible, private schooling: "Official schools limit students by age, entrance examinations, school timetables, and fees. The young who have no money, free time, or learning skills are unable to enter school, even when they are keen to do so. Should we sacrifice the true souls of these lads? No, we cannot! This is why we must establish a private school." Neither of these two, however, was the real reason for establishing the Dōshin Gakusha. The overriding aim was the third one spelled out in the prospectus: "Fifty of us, with one mind, founded this school. Funds were insufficient, the building was small, facilities were lacking; for all that, we were determined to provide education in our eagerness to correct the evils of the past. Our great purpose was to promote respect for imperial authority and to increase our nation's strength. We wanted our youth to have opportunities for schooling and to study together so that they might contribute to the nation's welfare." This was their real intention. The wondrous nature of mankind was to be made manifest, the right to receive an education was to be guaranteed—but above all the national polity was to be served. The primary goal of the Dōshin Gakusha was political, the enhancement of imperial power. That was what the "Kindred Spirits" really sought.

These aims were inherited and elaborated by the School of Proliferating Talent, as the "Record of the Seiseikō," recited at school opening ceremonies on 11 February 1882, made clear:[18]

> Although it is said that the state's fortunes depend upon the Will of Heaven, in reality they repose in the actions of men. If it disposes over splendid human resources, even a weakened country can become a prosperous nation, guarded against dangers abroad and upheavals within. Thus will our country's setting sun be made to rise again. The nation's well-being is closely related to the talents of its people. Today it is claimed that our nation is secure, but that is certainly not true. At home, various rebel groups advocate extreme ideas; abroad, strong nations prey upon the weak, seeking to swallow up the world. Japan is on the brink. Something very small could push the country one way or the other, toward prosperity or decline. It is irresponsible people who say that whatever happens is the Will of Heaven, the trend of the times, beyond all human power to repair. Is that the proper way to think? If we had capable people, they would not only lament the state of affairs but would also do something to help save the nation. That is why the Dōshin Gakusha, School of Kindred Spirits, was founded in former days. Now we have gathered our ideas and combined our efforts to reform our task and broaden the scope of the school's activities. Accordingly, its name has been changed to Seiseikō, the School of Proliferating Talent. Our opening ceremonies are being held on 11 February, auspicious National Foundation Day, of the Fifteenth Year of Meiji. Our high purpose is to educate capable young people so that they can become useful contributors to the nation's future welfare. For those who have enrolled in our school, we have the following message. You shall develop all your virtues and talents, and free your intellect. Abandoning foolish, useless studies, you shall devise techniques useful in governance. Avoiding base, timid habits, you shall nurture a progressive resolve. Putting an end to the fashion of reckless frivolity, you shall work to implement warm-hearted sincerity.

> Breaking through limited, mean views, you shall build a lofty spirit. Never daunted, you shall not falter. You shall become the bulwark of the Imperial House and the foundation of the state.

The consciousness of a crisis involving late-developing Japan permeates this "Record of the Seiseikō" just as it did the "Aims" of the Shimeikai, but the essential educational goals of human cultivation, still emphasized in the "Founding Prospectus" of the Dōshin Gakusha, are no longer in evidence.

That personal development in the School of Proliferating Talent was meant to be no more than an avenue that led to manning the ramparts of the state can also be seen clearly in Sassa's exegesis of the school's "Three Main Principles," namely, "correct morals and clear responsibilities," a "strong sense of honor and display of vigor," and the "refinement of knowledge and promotion of enlightenment." Sassa explained why the Seiseikō stressed the first and the second of these principles by noting that the third "already has its place in Japan" whereas the others had yet to establish themselves. He was convinced that "we must first cultivate virtue, nurture spirit, and temper the body. Then we can refine our knowledge." Students trained according to this method would be "physically healthy and strong, capable of patience and endurance." The school would, he hoped, make them into "the most loyal and patriotic citizens of the state," men fully able to "fulfill their unique destiny" as subjects of the Japanese Empire.[19] The school's educational philosophy, it is patent, was thoroughly nationalistic.[20]

Nevertheless, just as the Shimeikai was not born as a progovernment party, the Seiseikō was not intended to follow the government's educational policy unquestioningly. Indeed, the school's own policy was generated by the spirit of resistance to the Education Order of 1872, as Sassa's disciple Noda Hiroshi (1866–1954) reported in reminiscing about his mentor:[21]

> Even now I vividly remember the day in the spring of 1884 when our Teacher showed me the "History of Japan since the Restoration" that he had written. Pointing to the section on the liberal and Western-influenced preamble to the Education Order that had been promulgated by the Grand Council of State in 1872, he commented that with a government educational policy like this, he could not help lamenting the future of Japan. Our Teacher's goal in setting up the Seiseikō in the educational sphere was fundamentally the same as the purpose behind establishing the Shimeikai in the sphere of politics. He intended to reveal the majesty of the national polity and (clarifying what is called the Greater Duty) to rectify people's hearts, thus shoring up the foundations of Imperial Rule.

The Mito School's philosophy of undifferentiated loyalty and filial piety was the root and trunk of his method. Not only was the thrust of his educational ideas directed against the current of the times, it was opposed to the government's policies. Hence the School of Proliferating Talent was subjected to hostility from society, oppression from the authorities, and antagonism from eminent Kumamoto seniors in Tokyo, who sent Viscount Komeda Torao to Kumamoto as their emissary to terminate the school. . . . I remember how terribly agitated our Teacher became when he spoke of this incident.

If the Education Order's pedagogy was knowledge-based, the Seiseikō cultivated virtue. According to Noda Hiroshi, Sassa liked to use the word *neru* (to train), so it became common among the students. In Sassa's "training" one can clearly discern a prototype of educational methods later implemented by Mori Arinori. It "put all its effort" into realizing "two major principles that we had discovered—that it was necessary to reintroduce the old methods of group education, and that it was most effective to keep the students in residence." This was the prototype of the "living education" later provided throughout the country in the dormitories of Mori's normal schools. Sassa himself assumed the role of a live-in supervisor and sought to revive the Kumamoto tradition of autonomous training *(jichiteki kyōiku)* for students of the samurai class. Moreover, Sassa rejected an emphasis on intellectual learning and stressed physical training, holding forced marches once a month to "strengthen comradeship and nurture endurance and energy."[22] In late 1882—before anyone else in the country—he made swordsmanship and judo a part of the school's program.

Then Sassa took the Seiseikō's training approach a step further and put infantry drill in the curriculum. This was the beginning of military training in Japanese schools. In February 1884 the Ministry of Education gave permission for military-style calisthenics to be conducted, and in April of that year—before any other school—the School of Proliferating Talent was employing officers and noncommissioned officers of the Thirteenth Regiment in Kumamoto to give its students military training. (Mori's experimental military-style calisthenics were not introduced in the Tokyo Normal School until February 1886, two years later.) How thoroughgoing the Seiseikō's infantry drill was may be judged from the memoirs of Adachi Kenzō (1864–1948), who reminisced about the so-called unscheduled exercise held in the dormitory on the model of a military alert: "An alarm bell rang madly late at night, the sleeping students leapt up all at once, put on leggings and straw sandals, and formed a line. Those who lined up fastest were praised. After that the night march began, more than a *ri* [about 4 kilometers or 2.5 miles] each way. Then everyone went back to sleep."[23]

In 1885 a Chinese-language program was instituted to prepare for Japan's future domination of Asia. The same year, a German language program was established. The reason given was that Germany was fashioned "very much like our own country," hence German studies could be "utilized for our country's benefit."[24] Sassa's pro-Prussian leanings were the result of the influence of his eminent countryman Inoue Kowashi and of Inoue's friend Furushō Kamon. Sassa's letters of 1885 or 1886 to Adachi Kenzō and others maintain that "the only way" for the Shimeikai to assist in building Japan was "to cultivate the spirit of loyalty to ruler and love of country," a spirit that was—he knew from Furushō's reports—"the essence of Germany's prosperity and progress." The Seiseikō must do its part in fostering that spirit by marches, excursions, and so forth. "German military music is essential," Sassa felt. Furushō had not only reported that "everyone, including women and children, sings songs of loyalty and patriotism on German festival days," but had gone to the trouble of translating them into Japanese. "Very pleased" that Japan and Germany shared the same fundamental values, the two agreed that Prussian marches would be ideal accompaniment to studies at the School of Proliferating Talent.[25]

Its educational philosophy no less than its actual training program would appear to qualify the Seiseikō as the very source and model of nationalistic education in Japan. The relationship that the school developed with the Meiji government reinforces that impression. On 21 May 1883 the emperor gave the school a gift of 500 yen. To those associated with the Seiseikō, this bounty arrived like a bolt out of the blue. It had come about as a result of a tour of Kyushu that House of Peers members Watanabe Noboru (1838–1913) and Ozaki Saburō (1842–1918), Vice-Minister of Agriculture and Commerce Maeda Masana (1850–1921), and Inspector Kawakami Hikoji of the Ministry of Education had undertaken in April of the previous year to assess living conditions. While in Kumamoto, they had visited the School of Proliferating Talent; back in Tokyo, Motoda Nagazane (personal name often read as Eifu; 1818–1891) and his colleagues acted on what these visitors reported about the institution. The emperor's official commendation had the effect of designating it a model school. Maeda Masana, who had studied in Germany during the Franco-Prussian War of 1870–1871, reputedly told Seiseikō students that their school reminded him of Germany.[26] Maeda's comment suggests that years before Itō Hirobumi (1841–1909) set Mori Arinori the task of fashioning a system of popular education which would support a Prussian-style constitutional order, the Seiseikō might already have met Itō's expectations.

After the imperial commendation, those connected with the school gained confidence. "When all Japan is rushing toward soft and insipid education, pursuing only the acquisition of knowledge, the School of Proliferating Talent alone is championing throne-centered thought," Uno Harukaze (d. 1938) boasted. "That this has been brought to His Majesty's attention is proof that our ideas are correct." As far as Adachi Kenzō was concerned, there were two reasons why Japan had become a first-rate nation. Not only was the country "blessed by the unity of its people and the loyalty and bravery of its army and navy," but it could also boast the Seiseikō, "which basks in unprecedented imperial favor and spreads its educational policy of loyalty and patriotism throughout the land." The School of Proliferating Talent, he concluded, was "not just Meiji Japan's treasure, but one for all the ages."[27]

Another connection with the government came about when Mori Arinori, the minister of education himself, inspected the Seiseikō in January 1887. According to Sassa, Mori "carefully examined everything about our school's foundation, history, philosophy, aims, morale, and curriculum. Afterward he favored us with frequent praise. It seems that the spirit taught over many years at our school sat well with the minister. Ah! What had long been broadcast as our opposition to mainstream education and as our arrogance in failing to change now gave us cause for great satisfaction." Noda Hiroshi remembered Mori's commenting, "I have visited many schools and have always been disappointed, but now for the first time I have seen one that is really a school."[28]

An even more telling exegesis of Mori Arinori's attitude can be found in the speech given by Inoue Kowashi at the Imperial Classics Research Institute (Kōten Kenkyūjo) on 9 March 1889, the month after Mori was cut down by an assassin. This speech sought to vindicate Mori's policies, which (Inoue feared) were becoming widely misunderstood:[29]

> I come from Kumamoto, and in Kumamoto there is a school called the Seiseikō, which was established to bring together former samurai and other interested persons. At first it was not in accord with the regulations, but it has recently been reformed and has come within ministry guidelines. From the beginning this school has been dedicated to the *kokutai* ideal and has stressed moral teachings and physical training. For example, the students marched in formation more than 11 *ri* [44 kilometers] one day to pay their respects at the grave of the Generalissimo of the West [Prince Kanenaga] in Yatsushiro. That shows what an unusual school this is. From the ordinary educator's perspective, it may not look like a school to praise. When Viscount Mori toured Kyushu, however, he visited the Seiseikō and lauded its philosophy. Schools should be like this, he said; even if intellectual accomplishment is not emphasized at the Seiseikō, its

goals are consistent with the most important principles of education. So he declared the school a model, and after his return to the capital he reported it as such to His Majesty. Since this is something that concerns my native place, I must respectfully thank Viscount Mori. This occurrence supports the claim that his educational philosophy was education for the national polity.

Illustrated here is the close match between the program of the School of Proliferating Talent and the ideals that governed Education Minister Mori Arinori's approach. Sassa reciprocated by abandoning the openly critical attitude he had hitherto shown toward the government's educational policy. Instead, he declared himself to be fully in accord with Mori, who had caused Sassa's educational ideas to be disseminated and implemented throughout the country. In Sassa's newly expressed opinion, Mori had "cleansed education of many of the harmful effects that had prevailed until his time. He instituted new principles in his ministry. As a first step he suppressed intellectual deviation and promoted moral education. He expanded physical training and made character formation central. He clarified the ultimate goals of education by articulating the tripartite functions of intellectual, moral, and physical training. This is a major reform in our country's education, one that we must welcome warmly."[30] But nationalistic schooling, shaped independently by former samurai of an oppositional statist persuasion, had been implemented in Kumamoto long before Mori formulated his educational policy.

Early Meiji Political Factions in Kumamoto

Feudal domains throughout Japan experienced controversy and unrest at the time of the Meiji Restoration. Intense confrontations were apparent everywhere, but emotional quarrels and struggles among political cliques were more common than conflicts over ideology or policy. As elsewhere, a variety of factions contended in Kumamoto. For all their acerbity, however, in Kumamoto such conflicts had characteristics that do not allow them to be categorized simply as emotional or irrational fights. There, apparently diverse factions discovered common ideological ground and gradually moved toward collaboration of the kind that brought about the formation of the Shimeikai as a union of conservative groups. Whereas in other domains factional infighting was ruled by emotion, in Kumamoto it had a certain substance to it. There, partisan struggle manifested rational elements derived from two traditions of samurai education rooted in the late feudal age.

One of these traditions was fostered at the Jishūkan, the Kumamoto domain school that had been set up in 1755 by the "enlightened lord," Hosokawa Shigekata (1720–1785), to promote learning and martial arts. Under its first director, the learned Akiyama Gyokuzan (1702–1763), and his successors, the school produced a number of outstanding scholars in various fields, including not only the officially sponsored Neo-Confucianism of Chu Hsi but also Yōmeigaku (Wang Yang-ming Neo-Confucianism), Kogaku (Ancient Learning, i.e., Classical Confucianism), Kokugaku (National Learning), and medical studies. The fundamental objective of the Jishūkan's educational policy was to enhance every student's personal qualities, unlocking and deploying the talents of each individual for the domain's benefit. That is the goal indicated in an anecdote regarding the instructions the lord supposedly gave the director. Akiyama was like a "carpenter building the state," Shigekata said, and he had only one request to make—that Akiyama, "leading the young people who are the domain's treasure, should not have them all cross to the far shore via the same bridge. If those who lived up the river were taken across on an up-river bridge and those who lived down the river were taken across on a down-river bridge, they would develop their talents directly, avoiding circuitous routes. Separate bridges ought to be built across the river, connected to the path of filial piety, brotherly love, loyalty, and devotion on the other side."[31] That is to say, individual differences ought to be respected in developing an educational program. This tradition of the domain school helped to instill confidence in their own beliefs among the Kumamoto samurai. It was one reason why the conflicts among the various factions had a rational nature.

The second tradition was what Sassa called *kyōtō kyōiku* (group education). This tradition involved socialization through membership in autonomous alliances called *kyōtō* or *ren*. These were small groups formed independently by the sons of samurai living in the several wards into which the castle town of Kumamoto was divided. There were about ten such groups, which derived their names from their localities. They closely resembled what in neighboring Kagoshima were called *gojū*, but differed from the latter in that they were organized only among the sons of middle and upper-ranking samurai. Uno Harukaze wrote about his experience as the member of one of these alliances as follows:[32]

> Avoiding people from other wards, we devoted ourselves to the Way of the Warrior, seeking perfection in Arms and Arts. Each month, on the Jishūkan holiday, we met at the home of one of us to read the *Analects* of Confucius. Then we scrutinized our progress in the literary and the mar-

tial arts and in the development of character. If someone was not living up to his pledge or was behaving improperly, an appropriate punishment would be meted out. If his misconduct was extreme and there was no prospect of rectification, he would be banished from our company. No other group would admit someone who had been ostracized, and he would have no hope of improving his position in the future. Thus the *kyōtō* greatly influenced an individual's career and his chance to demonstrate talent and virtue outside the Jishūkan. Samurai sons were admitted to the group from about the age of eight. They submitted themselves to its nurturing of scholarship and martial arts and its refinement of character. In this way, the group succeeded in developing outstanding people.

To strengthen group solidarity, each *ren* labeled all others *taren* (stranger groups). Another former member offers us a glimpse of the rivalry that was encouraged as part of the training process in the alliances:[33]

> We grew up under strict discipline. From an early age, we submitted to extremely severe restrictions for the good of the group. We were taught to act fearlessly in the face of hostilities from the outside. Should we be walking about the town with the older members of the *ren* and come upon a swaggering young stalwart with a great sword at his side, they would order us to "attack." Even though everyone knew full well that he was not really our enemy and understood the folly of all-out hostilities, we feared being censured as cowards. So, in high spirits, we instantly provoked a fight. The battle would commence and then come down to a hand-to-hand bout between our older members and the swaggerer. That is how our fighting spirit was nurtured. We were prepared to walk resolutely through fire and water and bravely explore the very brink of death.

The esprit de corps and combativeness produced by such training perhaps unavoidably added antagonistic features to the rivalry among the various factions in Kumamoto. In 1860 one of the Jishūkan teachers, Iguchi Teisuke, criticized the *ren* over the harmful effects of what he believed to be unnecessarily intense intergroup competition. In a memorial submitted to the daimyo and titled "An Opinion on Local Education" *(Gōgaku no shigi)*, Iguchi urged the reform of the domain's educational system: "Some say that if there were no quarrels among our parties, the samurai spirit would die, but this is not true. When our young hot bloods yield to their youthful ardor and fight, they think that they are raging with valor. That is an unconscionable error. Those who endeavor day by day to follow the Way of the Warrior never forget their mortality. They do not struggle mindlessly like this. It has, however, been the rule since ancient times that the rash and self-indulgent who insolently ignore the admonitions of fathers, elder brothers, teachers, and friends must suffer certain and ignominious defeat when it comes down to life and death."³⁴ Iguchi's criticism adheres to the rigorous view of order in society held by Chu Hsi Neo-Confucian scholars. To eliminate evil practices, Iguchi advocated the complete isolation of each *ren*, recommending that young men be forbidden to leave their wards without cause and that a school staffed with strict teachers be provided for each *ren*.

Iguchi did not fully understand the educational function of the groups, failing to realize that competition among them was the result not so much of a clash of ideas as of efforts to strengthen and maintain solidarity. As Uno Harukaze wrote, the competitive character of the *ren* did not remain imprinted on youth permanently. The groups' purpose was the pursuit of Arms and Arts, that is, nourishing faithful vassals of their lord. Their basis was geographical, and young members of one ward's group viewed those of other wards as enemies. Yet when those same youths grew up, became the heads of their families, and advanced to responsible positions in their lord's service, "their youthful feelings of animosity toward those of other alliances disappeared. They served in harmony with others, devoting themselves wholeheartedly to their duties."³⁵ The groups' educational traditions—that of conflict with other *ren*, in particular—demanded that combative feelings not be carried over into adulthood. That requirement had the positive effect of imparting a rational character to factional disputes. Intense, antagonistic conflict among the factions was consequently not the result of the educational programs pursued in the groups but rather of the combative spirit of individuals nurtured in the *ren*. Iguchi missed this point.

Respect for individuality, stressed in the domain school's policy, and the experience of rational argument over substantive issues, gained through training in the ward-based groups, were part of Kumamoto's educational heritage. These two traditions kept factional disputes in Kumamoto from becoming irrational fights of the sort that erupt from tangled emotional interests—from resembling, for instance, the intrigue-filled conflicts in which samurai cliques contended for control of a domain's administration *(oie sōdō)*. Kumamoto factional disputes had substance. They tended to be between organizations with different doctrines, different scholarly positions, or different political experiences. In other words, the character of the factions there was more like that of political associations. They were bound together by their aims.

Confrontations among these political factions of the early Meiji era were rooted in antagonisms among three schools of thought that arose in Kumamoto in the late Edo period. These three were known as the Practical Learning, Imperial Loyalist, and Academy parties.

The Practical Learning party (Jitsugakutō) was the school of Yokoi

Shōnan (1809–1869), who—inspired by the reformist ideology that emanated from Mito—led the reforms of the Tenpō era (1830–1843) in Kumamoto, and of his supporter Komeda Zeyō (1813–1859), a member of one of the domain's traditionally dominant families. The Jitsuga-kutō criticized the traditionalist methods of instruction which had by that time established themselves in the domain school, objecting to the Jishūkan's avoidance of practical methods of instruction and its penchant for formalism, textual exegesis, annotation, and rote recital. What was needed instead, the Practical Learning party proclaimed, was training in management, for such training would bring good government to the country and security to the people.

Komeda, in particular, was strongly influenced by the imperial loyalists of the Mito School, their spiritualism, and their professions of loyalty to the throne. In the 1850s, while he was in Edo (posted there in readiness for possible defense duties in Uraga, the entry to Edo Bay), Komeda maintained close contact with Fujita Tōko (1806–1855), a scholar who was one of Mito's more strident spirits. Komeda did not, however, adopt the Mito School's militant antiforeignism in its entirety; rather, he accepted Yokoi's advocacy of opening the country. Later, differences surfaced between Yokoi and Komeda concerning the interpretation of the important dictum "The Way of the Great Learning is to exemplify illustrious virtue *(meitoku)*, to love the people *(shinmin)*, and to rest in the highest good." To Yokoi, this first sentence of the Confucian classic, *The Great Learning*, meant that the enrichment of people's lives was the prime essence and first goal of politics; in Komeda's view, it taught that cultivating virtue among leaders was of primary importance. These differences led the Practical Learning party to split into two groups. One was called Nuyama Jitsugaku after the place where Yokoi Shōnan lived in seclusion; the other was known as Tsuboi Jitsugaku, bearing the name of Komeda Zeyō's domicile.

The Imperial Loyalist party (Kinnōtō) of Kumamoto also had two branches. One of them was an outgrowth of Higo Kokugaku, a school of thought that may be traced back to the late eighteenth century and the person of Ri Shimei (pseud. of Harada Jun; 1738–1814), professor of the Jishūkan, who was at the same time a scholar of Chu Hsi Neo-Confucianism and the principal exponent of National Learning in Higo Province. Ri Shimei corresponded with the great Kokugaku scholar Motoori Norinaga (1730–1801) and wrote myth-based essays on the national polity. The development of Higo Kokugaku culminated with Hayashi Ōen (1798–1870), renowned as Kumamoto's greatest National Learning scholar of the restoration period. It was Hayashi's followers who formed the ultratraditionalist God-Revering party (Keishintō) of the early Meiji years.

The other faction of the Kinnōtō originated in the early nineteenth century under the influence of the thought of Tomita Nichigaku (1762–1803), an instructor at the domain's medical school. Somewhat of an intimate of the famous imperial loyalist eccentric Takayama Hikokurō (1747–1793), Tomita was a fervent legitimist himself. An adherent of Kogaku, he wholeheartedly embraced the classical Confucian ideal "Revere the king, reject the hegemon" *(sonnō sekiha),* a political imperative subsequently given wide prominence in the work of the historian Rai San'yō (1780–1832). Tomita is known for his discourses on the subject's moral obligations to the sovereign, such as "On Hostility to the Enemy and True Loyalty" *(Tekigai chūgi-hen)* and "Policies for Reinvigorating the Kingly Way" *(Ōdō kōsui saku),* which exalted the legacy of Emperor Go-Daigo (1288–1339) and his Southern Court.[36] In short, the imperial loyalism nourished by Ri Shimei and by Tomita Nichigaku, the two patriarchs of the Kinnōtō of Kumamoto, grew from very different intellectual ground. The party's two factions, in turn, reflected their patriarchs' orientations.

The Academy party (Gakkōtō) was originally a label given graduates of the Jishūkan who belonged to neither of the other two schools, that is, to those adherents of Chu Hsi Neo-Confucianism who customarily entered the mainstream of domain administration. Later, it came to refer mainly to those who advocated administrative reforms with an eye both to supporting the Tokugawa shogunate and to repelling the "barbarians" (the Western powers and Russia). Unlike the Practical Learning and Imperial Loyalist parties, the Academy party had no conspicuous political ideals. It was more pragmatic than the other two, and much of its political effectiveness lay in its refusal to go to idealist extremes.

These three groups emerged as political parties in the 1850s as they clashed over the burning problems of the day—*sonnō* (reverence for the emperor) or *sabaku* (support for the shogunate), *jōi* (repelling the barbarians) or *kaikoku* (opening the country).[37] Both factions of Practical Learning advocated opening the country. The Imperial Loyalists, on the other hand, were fervent expulsionists and maintained contacts with superpatriotic groups all over Japan. A faction of young Academicians, too, demanded that foreigners be kept out and criticized domain administrations which supported the shogunate's strategy of opening ports to them. Apparently, those who took this position simply appropriated the Academy label.[38] Each of the three parties struggled from its own point of view to unite domain policy and deal with the political situation.

After Shogun Tokugawa Yoshinobu (1837–1913; r. 10 January 1867–3 January 1868) formally returned sovereignty to the emperor on 9 November 1867, the partisan character of the political differences among the factions became stronger, and their struggle for control of the domain administration intensified. Now that the proshogunate position had lost its meaning, something unprecedented happened: their common stand against the "barbarians" brought the Academicians and the Loyalists closer together. The latter took power from the Kumamoto domain's erstwhile proshogunate mainstream in the restoration's aftermath. Forming a coalition government with a segment of the Academy party, the Loyalists implemented a conservative policy in the interests of the samurai class. The coalition opposed both factions of the Practical Learning party, which were linked with progressive elements in the central government. In the summer of 1869, however, the domains surrendered their registers of enfeoffment to the new central government. One consequence was that in the spring of the following year, political power in Kumamoto was transferred to a new coalition made up of the two Practical Learning factions.

Now that the Jitsugakutō held political power, it set about sweeping away the symbols of the past. The demolition of Kumamoto Castle and the closing of the domain school were two conspicuous signs of its repudiation of the ancien régime. The Practical Learning administration undertook such modernizing measures as the public selection of officials, the establishment of a school of Western studies staffed by foreign teachers, and the introduction of Western-style reforms in the domain's military. It sought to "exemplify illustrious virtue" through a wide-ranging tax reduction and the abolition of the domain's monopoly on marketing. Practical Learning's hold on power, which lasted until 1873, was opposed by the Loyalists and the Academicians from a conservative position. These two opposition parties observed the central government's support of their rivals and of course opposed its progressive policies also.

Fearing an intensification of factional struggle, the central government in 1873 installed the Tosa man Yasuoka Ryōsuke (d. 1876) as governor *(gonrei)* of Kumamoto. Yasuoka swept away the Jitsugaku administration and tried to work with the Academy and the Loyalists. The reason for those developments was that the Practical Learning party had no military backing, whereas the Loyalists and Academicians were backed by the military establishment of Kumamoto even after it had officially become defunct upon the dissolution of the domain's army. After the central government took direct control of the Kumamoto administration, all three parties turned more or less into opposition groups. The three had to decide whether to approve or reject the Europeanization pursued by the central government and whether to accept or denounce the popular-rights movement that was gaining momentum throughout the country. The parties were thus compelled to make weighty political choices. The opportunity was created for a thorough rearrangement of Kumamoto's political scene into conservatives and reformers, a division that would transcend the party interests of the three traditional groups.

Then, in 1877, the Satsuma Rebellion broke out. From the ranks of both conservatives and reformers came supporters of Saigō Takamori, entrusting him with the realization of their political dreams. As a result, the hard-won opportunity for a major reform of Kumamoto politics was lost. When the rebellion ended in Saigō's defeat, disgruntled former samurai came to realize the futility of military opposition to the government. The Loyalist and Academy parties suddenly lost their strong warrior constituencies and heavy military coloring. They were substantially weakened, but that very fact encouraged them to integrate themselves into a broad alliance. The result was the formation of the Bōgokai (Self-Effacing Society) in 1880, a step forward in the evolution of the Shimeikai. Yet after the initial postrebellion period had passed, each faction's consciousness of its uniqueness, one nourished through traditional education, was reawakened. As we have already seen, the grand coalition split apart. The Sōaisha and the Nuyama faction of Practical Studies pulled out, insisting that sovereignty resided in an elected assembly. The remaining, conservative factions regrouped and reconstituted the Shimeikai.

Sassa Tomofusa tells us how the leading figures of those groups came together in the Shimeikai and the School of Proliferating Talent. First, he discusses those with an Academy affiliation, listing twenty-four by name, and noting in particular that during the last years of the Tokugawa era, "Ikebe Kichijūrō, Kamada Keisuke, Furushō, and Takezoe strongly advocated support for the shogunate and expulsion of the barbarians." After the return of sovereignty to the emperor, however, those two became moot issues, and the Academicians were certainly rational enough to give them up; indeed, "everyone preached loyalty to state and emperor." From 1868 to 1870, the Academicians linked up again with the Loyalists, with whom they had earlier been allied because of shared antiforeign convictions; Furushō, Kimura, and like-minded others were instrumental in making the connections. "Ikebe, Kamada, and Isawa took over the domain administration, along with the late Sumie Jinzaburō and others of the Loyalist ilk. They tended to view the Practical Learning party as the sole enemy."[39] Sassa also mentions the names of eight "young stalwarts" who followed Ikebe and Kamada and took an active part in the Academy party. Two of those eight died in the 1877 struggle. Of the twenty-four important Academy figures he listed, five were executed for participating in the Satsuma Rebellion. Eight of the remaining nineteen were connected with the Shimeikai and the School of Proliferating Talent. The executed five were ideologically close to Sassa and his colleagues and might have joined the political activities of that group had they lived. If this conjecture is acceptable, then thirteen of the twenty-four Academy leaders—the majority—probably shared the ideas fostered by the Shimeikai and the Seiseikō.

There is, in other words, no doubt that the early Meiji period's Academy party was the generative matrix of statism and nationalist education in Kumamoto. Why did this happen? In response to changing realities, the Academy party returned to the political realism it had cultivated earlier, when it had been in power, and transformed its "antibarbarian" doctrine into a statist theory. This party's philosophy contrasted clearly with the political idealism of the Imperial Loyalists, whom Sassa treats next.

He lists twenty-seven of the main members of the Kinnōtō, tracing their ideological lineage to the Kokugaku scholar Hayashi Ōen (fifteen younger affiliates are also mentioned by name). Of the twenty-seven leading figures, eight died for the superpatriotic cause before the restoration; six were either killed in action or by their own hands in the revolt raised in Kumamoto by the Shinpūren (Divine Wind Confederacy; also known as the Keishintō, "God-Revering party"), a band of disgruntled, antireformist samurai, in October 1876; and one, a convert to popular rights, died in prison. Sassa portrays the political evolution of the survivors: "Until about the time of the restoration, they were inimical to the Academy party. Since their faith in loyalty to the emperor coincided to some extent with that of the Practical Learning party, sometimes they united with that group. From about 1869 or 1870, however, the situation changed drastically. Western customs were widely adopted, and—since the Jitsugakutō advocated Western customs—a great gap opened between Practical Learning and the Loyalists, who linked up instead with Ikebe, Kamada, Furushō, Kimura, Sakurada, and others of the Academy party."[40] Of the twelve surviving leaders of the Kinnōtō listed by Sassa, only one had any connections with the Shimeikai or the Seiseikō. There is, moreover, no evidence that any of the fifteen who died would have joined the political endeavors of Sassa and his colleagues, had they lived. On the contrary, it is more likely that they would have opposed Sassa and company.

In contrast to leading Academy figures, no senior Imperial Loyalist leader appears among the founders of a statist party or progenitors of nationalist education. The senior Loyalists continued to cling unreflectively to the political ideals of the late Tokugawa period and were deeply dissatisfied with current realities. They took a hand in the Hagi and Akizuki uprisings[41] and were swept up in the Shinpūren eruption. They threw away their lives in armed antigovernment struggles that had less chance of success than even Saigō's rebellion. They sacrificed themselves for their ideals. Of those who survived, many became cynical and withdrew from politics, disappearing into obscurity. Their idealism kept their antiforeignism from being converted into support for a new statism, as happened in the case of the "repel the barbarian" ideology of the Academy party.

On the other hand, of the fifteen younger-generation Loyalists Sassa listed, four had connections with the Shimeikai and the Seiseikō. (Of eight junior Academicians he mentioned, three were so connected—a proportional disparity, to be sure, but not a significant one.) Those burdened with the heritage of the late Tokugawa era's Imperial Loyalist party may have lacked the capacity to adopt statist or nationalist ideologies. When some of its younger adherents confronted new realities, however, they managed to transpose their antiforeignism into statism and link up with Academy members.

Using Sassa's lineage of political parties, we can trace the ideology that supported the statist political movements and nationalist educational efforts of Academicians Furushō Kamon, Kimura Tsuruo, Ikebe Kichijūrō (1838–1877), and Sakurada Sōshirō (1829–1877), as well as of the younger Imperial Loyalists, the Sassa brothers, Uno Harukaze, Takahashi Nagaaki, and Takashima Yoshitaka (1853–1926). This new ideology arose out of the transformation that the political beliefs of the Imperial Loyalist and Academy parties had undergone during the turmoil of the Meiji Restoration. While its substance derived from those parties' traditional commitment to *jōi*—protecting Japan against "barbarian" incursions—it was by no means identical with the xenophobia of the late Tokugawa period. Rather, it addressed the new era and concerned itself with expanding the country's prestige, as may be seen in the two parties' support of Saigō Takamori's advocacy of invading Korea. Moreover, the imperial loyalism common to both during the early Meiji era was quite different from the Shintoist restorationism— the unity of rites and regimen—that Hayashi Ōen had preached; it was a new kind of political thought, which acknowledged the emperor as the absolute sovereign and the spiritual authority uniting the populace. Sassa, who remained as opposed to Europeanized central government as the "God Reverers" of the Keishintō, turned away from their Shinto ideology because they had no new political ideas to offer. The Keishintō's political program amounted to nothing more than anachronistic calls for a return to a mystical, fundamentalist Way of the Gods and complaints about the government's broken promises to keep Japan pristinely Japanese.

The newness of the ideology of Sassa and his comrades struck a chord with some members of both Practical Learning factions. When Tsuda Seiichi, one of the enthusiastic founders of the Shimeikai and the Seiseikō, was recruited from the Tsuboi Jitsugaku faction by Sassa and his group, he brought that party's *kaikoku* orientation—its readiness to allow Western influences into Japan—with him. Since the 1860s, he had been close to Motoda Nagazane, a drafter of the Imperial Rescript on Education who is not noted for progressive ideas. For all that, Tsuda remained an enlightened individual. As early as 1869, he went to study in America.

Apart from Tsuda, who came from Practical Learning to the Shimeikai and the Seiseikō? To reiterate, following Sassa's outline: Practical Learning was divided into two factions. One, the Komeda faction, was also called Tsuboi Jitsugaku or the Illustrious Virtue party (Meitokutō); Harada Sakusuke numbered among its leading figures. The other, the Yokoi faction, also bore the names Nuyama Jitsugaku and Loving the People party (Shinmintō); among its leaders, along with Yasuba Yasukazu, were Kaetsu Ujifusa (1833–1908) and Yamada Takeho (1831–1893). Although these two factions of Jitsugaku were "incompatible," according to Sassa, each had members interested in forming an alliance to oppose the Imperial Loyalists and Academicians. At the time of the restoration, Sassa says, the Komeda and Yokoi factions joined forces with the Loyalists to devote themselves to the imperial cause—clashing only with Ikebe, Kamada, and others of the Academy party. About 1869, however, a gap opened between the Yasuba-Kaetsu group and that of Harada Sakusuke, driving the Nuyama and Tsuboi factions even further apart. Among those active in the Tsuboi faction at that time, Sassa further specifies, were Tsuda Seiichi, Oka Jirotarō, and Sawamura Daihachi.[42]

Kaetsu Ujifusa and Yamada Takeho, two of the central figures of the Nuyama faction, joined the Shimeikai at the beginning. In the sovereignty debate, however, their advocacy of an elected assembly brought them into conflict with Sassa and comrades, who argued that all sovereignty resided with the emperor. So Kaetsu and Yamada quit the Shimeikai. Yasuba Yasukazu and Miyagawa Fusayuki—also from the Nuyama faction of Practical Learning—stayed with it to the end. No Tsuboi senior leader was connected with either the Shimeikai or the Seiseikō, but two younger members, Tsuda and Sawamura Daihachi, were involved in both. Of the nineteen members of the various factions of the Practical Learning party who are mentioned, including those of the younger generation, two were briefly involved with the Shimeikai and four—two seniors and two juniors—remained committed to the end. This total included four members of the Nuyama faction, including those only briefly involved. Evidently, the simple, idealistic moralism that characterized such groups as Tsuboi Jitsugaku during the last days of the shogunate did not breed statist and nationalist commitments.

As the Tokugawa regime was about to come to an end, the Practical Learning and Imperial Loyalist parties formed a temporary alliance to confront the Academy, but their basic ideological differences soon resulted in a rift. Furthermore, the temporarily allied main factions of the Practical Learning party also broke apart in short order. Durability was obviously not a notable characteristic of political alliances in Kumamoto. Nevertheless, a merger of conservative groups and a coalition culminating in the Shimeikai became possible because a new political mind-set—one absent from the traditional factions—emerged after the Meiji Restoration.

One might have expected survivors of the Divine Wind Confederacy to join the Shimeikai as members, but in fact not more than one did. No participant in the Shimeikai came from a group called the People's Rights party (Minkentō) that was formed about 1873 or 1874, chiefly by former Imperial Loyalists.[43] After 1877 these men organized the Mutual Affection Guild (Sōaisha), which opposed the Shimeikai and became the center of progressive political forces in Kumamoto.

It therefore becomes all the more important to direct attention to ideological developments within Kumamoto's three main political parties after the restoration. Of particular interest are the ideas of the younger members of Tsuboi Jitsugaku and of the Imperial Loyalist party. Conflict among the various political factions of the early Meiji era provided opportunities for the younger members of each group to reflect on the issues and attune themselves to new political purposes. All factions keenly felt the need of cultivating new kinds of human talent in the pursuit of their respective goals. The result was the establishment of institutions of learning that would cultivate ideas held in common within the political group. Thus the School of Proliferating Talent was set up so that the political goals of the Shimeikai could be realized. Its foundation did not happen by chance but was part of a broader process.

The young men who campaigned on behalf of statist politics and nationalist education in Kumamoto were not at all intent on keeping up old Academic and Loyalist thought. They sought to make up for deficiencies in the educational policies of the Kumamoto domain and Kumamoto Prefecture on their own. They allied themselves with older members of their respective political parties' local factions and exerted themselves in the pursuit of their own educational projects. In short, ignoring —and, indeed, opposing—the government's official educational policies, they worked tirelessly to implement the kind of character training they deemed essential to their political movement.

We now turn to the ideological development of those men who were to become the leading lights of the Shimeikai and the School of Proliferating Talent and look at the way their progress was linked to the broader context of education in Kumamoto.

Education in Kumamoto During the Early Meiji Period and the Formation of Samurai Statism

Immediately after the imperial restoration, Kumamoto's government was run by a coalition of the Loyalist and Academy parties. Extremely conservative, they focused their policies on the samurai class. Regarding education, they confined their interest to the traditional curriculum of the domain school that taught samurai from the middle ranks up. In the autumn of 1869, modest reforms were initiated. Elementary reading, writing, and other primary courses ceased to be taught at the domain school; instead, neighborhood schools *(gōkō)* were set up in six wards of the castle town, and instructors from the Jishūkan were sent there to offer primary schooling. Those changes, however, were no more than a reaction to Iguchi Teisuke's 1860 memorandum, which was cited above. They were not indications of any kind of progressive trend. As before, education for lower-ranking samurai and for commoners was largely left to private academies *(juku)* and writing schools *(terakoya)*. During the period from 1868 to 1872, there were 910 *terakoya* and 74 private academies in Kumamoto; 24 of the latter were not established until after the restoration.[44] At first glance these figures suggest a strong demand for education among lower samurai and commoners. As a result of the Jishūkan's abolition in 1870, however, sons of middle- and upper-ranking samurai also began to study in private schools. The young men connected with the Shimeikai and the Seiseikō were largely fellows who had been brought up in private schools. That, probably, is why they were able to move beyond traditional Academy party thinking.

Sassa Tomofusa, Tsuda Seiichi, and Takahashi Nagaaki were all sons of Kumamoto samurai above the middle rank. They were all members of the Uchi-Tsuboi ward *ren*. What kind of schooling did they receive?

Sassa Tomofusa, the son of the Academician Sassa Rikusuke, was born in 1854 in the Uchi-Tsuboi ward of the Kumamoto castle town. He entered the Jishūkan at an early age. At fifteen, he was selected to be a dormitory student supported by domain funds, a privilege granted only to the exceptionally gifted. Although he placed himself in the Loyalist lineage in his genealogy of the three parties, he had the typical schooling of an Academy adherent. He acquired his new nationalist consciousness and his role as a representative of the Loyalist party's younger generation after the abolition of the domain school.

Tsuda Seiichi was also born in Uchi-Tsuboi ward, two years before Sassa and in a family with different political affiliations. His father, Tsuda Nobuhiro (1824–1883), was a leader of Tsuboi Practical Learning. Nobuhiro, a man who had been granted promotion by the domain elder, Komeda Zeyō, naturally became a prominent figure in Jitsugaku's Komeda faction; as naturally—given the sympathies of his political patron—he formed an acquaintance with Fujita Tōko and became friendly with superpatriotic zealots *(shishi)* from Mito. In January 1868, at the time of the restoration, Nobuhiro was appointed a junior councillor *(san'yo)* by the Meiji government. According to Tokutomi Sohō, Seiichi was brought up by his father and by Komeda "from infancy" on the teachings of the Mito School, minus its militant antiforeign ideology; he also received instruction from another leader of Practical Learning, Motoda Nagazane. Seiichi entered the Jishūkan as a young boy, but his early familiarity with Practical Learning's open-door policy toward the foreigners made him discontented with the training he received at the domain school. Toward the end of 1869, at the age of seventeen, he left Japan for the United States, where he was to stay from January 1870 to August 1873. He had hoped to enter the U.S. Military Academy at West Point or the Naval Academy at Annapolis, but that plan was thwarted. Instead, he attended (and was graduated from) Monson Academy, a preparatory school in Massachusetts, and spent a year studying at Yale University. "Even though he was in America, he did not adopt American customs," if we can trust Tokutomi Sohō. "On the contrary, he resisted them, remaining a determined adherent of Japanism."[45] In short, when Tsuda Seiichi left for the United States, his way of thinking had already been moulded by Tsuboi Jitsugaku.

The youngest of the three, Takahashi Nagaaki, was born in Yatsushiro in 1858. He was the son of Takahashi Chōkan, an Academy samurai who had been posted to Yatsushiro to keep a lookout against the Satsuma domain. In 1866 Nagaaki moved back to Uchi-Tsuboi ward in Kumamoto with his parents and became a member of its samurai youth group. He entered the Jishūkan at the age of eight, but in 1869, when that academy was reorganized and ward schools founded, he transferred to the school opened in Tsuboi. Of the three, in other words, only Takahashi studied in a ward school. His bloodline was even more

Academic than Sassa's. He acquired the new way of thinking only after the Jishūkan's abolition in 1870 sent him to Sassa's private school.

In the spring of 1870, political power in Kumamoto passed from a Loyalist-Academic coalition to an alliance of Practical Learning factions. The former coalition had refused to cooperate with the central government's Europeanizing policies; indeed, Kumamoto Loyalists had linked up with conservatives in Tokyo in an effort to sweep away the supporters of Westernization. Moreover, Loyalist leaders had undertaken a reorganization of the domain troops who had participated on the central government's side in the 1868 Tōhoku Campaign against the diehards of the shogunate. All that was ample grounds for the central government to seek a change of administrations in the Kumamoto domain.

The new Practical Learning regime dissolved the conservative military forces and set about implementing the Europeanization pushed by Tokyo. Education was identified as one of the fundamental supports of the former regime's reactionary thought. Consequently, not only the Jishūkan and the ward schools but all the old educational institutions were done away with, in accord with plans to promote Western-style schooling. The statement of purpose of the Kumamoto School of Western Studies (Kumamoto Yōgakkō), established by the domain in early 1870, illustrates the spirit with which those reforms were pursued: "Those who seek Western learning increase day by day, . . . but there is no one who comprehends its true meaning. That is because no one knows the proper way to approach it. We must therefore build a new center for Western studies in the domain. We shall invite instructors from abroad who will be prepared to train children thoroughly from the beginning in so-called primary education. Once the proper foundations are established, the students will be placed in programs appropriate to their talents. Placement based on merit is the most important aspect of Western methods of instruction, and we shall follow the procedures of schools in the West. We shall set standards and follow the best practices, seeking to promote learning in all fields."[46]

The reforms carried out by the Practical Learning regime negated all the traditions of the domain's former administration. The reforms shocked many; according to Uno Harukaze, some said that they amounted to the disintegration of domain government.[47] In particular, the educational reforms seemed to be snatching away all the schools of the samurai class; hence the Uchi-Tsuboi *ren* of Sassa and Takahashi immediately opposed the Practical Learning party. They sought their own instructors and set up their own educational medium as a base for the promulgation of their ideas.

When the Jishūkan closed, Sassa Tomofusa entered the private school of the prominent Loyalist Hayashi Ōen, where he studied National Learning. His friend Shimizu Koichirō (1854–1932) states that this was a major event in Sassa's life, one that made him reject Practical Learning, scorn the Academy, and devote himself to the cause of loyalty to the emperor.[48] It was, however, the influence of his uncle Sassa Junjirō that prompted Tomofusa to enter Hayashi's school in the first place. A stalwart of the Imperial Loyalist party, Junjirō had been close to the prophet of imperial loyalist thought, Yoshida Shōin (1830–1859) of Chōshū, and had enthusiastically participated in the movement to "revere the emperor and repel the barbarians." Sassa acquired his political consciousness from this uncle and was inspired by it to adopt Hayashi Ōen's ideal of restoring the old imperial order. But Sassa's convictions were not the unrealistic, mystical beliefs of the God-Revering party, the main lineage of the Hayashi school. Academy pragmatism ran in his veins. He was not a fanatical idealist. Studying with Hayashi enabled Sassa to adapt imperial loyalist expulsionism—*sonnō jōi* thought—to the realities of the postrestoration world. He came closer to the Loyalist party, and his statist thinking became stronger.

After the Jishūkan was dissolved, Takahashi Nagaaki studied Confucianism at the private school of Kunitomo Shigemasa, a former teacher at the domain academy. He mixed with young comrades like Sassa Tomofusa and Takashima Yoshitaka, who had left the Academy party and were moving toward the Loyalists. He developed his own thought according to the traditions of ward school education.

While Sassa and Takahashi were gravitating toward the Loyalist party and becoming receptive to statist thought, what was in the mind of Tsuda, studying in America? From letters he exchanged with his father, it is apparent that—in the tradition of Tsuboi Practical Learning—he was also shifting toward statism, although from a different angle than that of Sassa and company. In America, Tsuda thought a great deal about Japan's crisis in foreign relations. He wrote his father that Japan should overcome its backwardness and secure its independence by colonizing Hokkaidō and dispatching aid to Korea. "We are following a fickle policy at a time of unceasing changes," he complained. Since Nabeshima Naomasa (1814–1871) had resigned as director of the Land Development Bureau in September 1869, plans to exploit the resources of Hokkaidō had turned into empty words. "Nothing has been done about the urgent need to develop the land and settle people there. With Russia taking advantage and pressing against our border, we have cause indeed to lament." Korea, too, was on Tsuda's mind. He had learned from newspapers that Korea was earnestly trying to stave off the "barbarians" and had "frequently asked Japan for troops" to support its own program of *jōi*. The Japanese government, however, "seems to be divided into two camps, and no decision has yet been reached. If that is indeed the case, it would be one more difficulty for Japan. If things were a bit more peaceful at home and we had the energy to extend ourselves overseas, the field training [i.e., dispatch of troops to Korea] would strengthen our military. With the temporizing, irresolute government that we have now, we cannot even think of foreign involvements. Indeed, our northern gateway, which we must protect at all costs, is about to be wrested from us by a foreign power!"[49] In short, Tsuda proposed coming to the "assistance" of Korea because he thought such action would provide a valuable opportunity to build up the Japanese army. The "rich country, strong army" argument he developed in this letter was consistent with Sassa's statist advocacy of national expansion. Indeed, to some extent it was more pragmatic and concrete than Sassa's views.

Tsuda unconditionally approved of the reforms initiated by the Practical Learning regime, including the plan to tear down Kumamoto Castle, which he viewed as a pioneering effort worthy of emulation throughout the country. (Sassa and company, on the other hand, were hostile to those reforms.) "Politics has changed completely," Tsuda wrote his father. "No one argues in favor of temporizing. High and low support our local government, and all of Japan's three hundred other domains are paying close attention to us in considering what direction they should take. I am deeply impressed and happy for the sake of the entire country." In the same letter, Tsuda worried about difficulties in finding foreign instructors for the domain's new School of Western Studies. "We cannot put this matter off," he insisted. "The times require that talent be nurtured. Something must be done about this as soon as possible."[50] Unlike Sassa, Tsuda went so far as to offer concrete assistance to the Practical Learning administration. To be sure, he opposed the central government's all-out Europeanization on the same premises as did the Sassa group.

Only from the standpoint of combining "Japanese spirit and Western expertise" *(wakon yōsai)* did Tsuda approve of Europeanization. He adamantly opposed the introduction of Western values, especially the propagation of Christianity in Japan; hence he was suspicious about such suggestions as adopting the Western alphabet. The central government was about to make a decision on that question, he worried. Would it be mindful of the historical fact that the writing system has an intimate connection with the life of the nation? "If the writing system is changed, before long Western religion will enter the country. If we adopt their religion, our national principles will deteriorate. Then the long-hallowed Way of the Sages will be lost and our realm plunged into darkness." Tsuda persisted in his traditional beliefs, claiming that the way taught by Confucius was nothing less than the path of universal justice. Following that path through international affairs, Japan would "thwart the arrogance of the Europeans and spread the Way of the Sages to the four corners of the earth."[51]

While in America, Tsuda thus remained faithful to the ideals of the Practical Learning party while at the same time developing the vision of a Japanese military strengthened through colonial development and the dispatch of troops to Korea. He insisted that Europeanization be limited. He was intellectually in tune with Sassa's statism. We can see elements of the subsequent political ideology of the Shimeikai in Tsuda's thinking. What we do *not* see in Tsuda's thought are the *sonnō* ideas of Sassa and colleagues, that is, the view of the emperor as the absolute embodiment of national sovereignty.

After the Practical Learning regime abolished the domain school, Sassa, Takahashi, and Tsuda took the paths described above. The end of the traditional education provided by the Jishūkan was a major cause of their ideological awakening, but the school's closure did not affect them alone. It unexpectedly influenced many young members of the ward-affiliated groups; indeed, it significantly affected the character of Kumamoto's traditional *ren*, which had originally been ward alliances. Their affiliations had been local, not ideological; all members of one *ren* were not necessarily part of a single political faction. After the Jishūkan was closed and ward schools were introduced, however, *ren* began to change and gradually turned into groups that subscribed to a particular ideology. That is, they ceased being local alliances and turned into groups with shared intellectual or political interests. There were hints of this change even before the abolition of the domain school; as early as the autumn of 1868, there was unrest within the Uchi-Tsuboi *ren*.

Many adult men of the old Uchi-Tsuboi ward belonged to Tsuboi Practical Learning or to the Loyalists. Their sons were united by the local affiliations of the *ren*. After the Jishūkan was closed, however, the young came to be influenced by the intellectual positions of their elders and began to act on the basis of party affiliations. The youths of the *ren* divided into two factions, the cultural nationalists *(kokusui-ha)* and the Westernizers *(kyoyō-ha)*. After heated arguments, the cultural nationalist faction of Nakayama Heitarō, Andō Kenta, and Sassa Kanjō, Tomofusa's elder brother, declared a complete severing of relations with Sawamura Daihachi's Westernizer group and organized a new Young Men's Tsuboi Association (Seinengumi Tsuboi Ren). Sixteen-year-old Sassa

Tomofusa and his friend Takashima Yoshitaka joined this new kind of *ren,* which was built on an intellectual foundation not inconsistent with the traditionalist position of the Academy party.

Jishūkan teachers appealed for a vindication of their refusal to permit Western learning entry to their school. In a memorial to domain authorities, they wrote that "to use letters running sideways and have students intone Western words at a school where the Way of the Sages is taught is tantamount to sacrificing that school's character. To allow that would arouse passions and invite disturbances. An even greater danger lies in succumbing to the artifice of Western machines. That would inevitably mean looking up to Westerners as superiors and even lead to adopting their religion."[52] The Young Men's Tsuboi Association advocated the same rejectionist ideas—as, indeed, did the Academy party. It must be pointed out, however, that the association which Sassa and the others had joined cannot yet be called a statist party. It was nothing more than a cultural nationalist group.

After the 1870 reforms initiated by the Practical Learning party, the *ren* lost their educational organs and were obliged to seek instruction from elders whom they respected and who in turn became increasingly active in teaching youth. Intellectual exchange was intensified and cultural awareness heightened among youth. Uno Harukaze described the new private schools as the "result of a spirit of sacrifice" on the part of district elders. "Fine homes" were leased in various districts for the schools, "but the owners refused to accept rent. Instructors took no payment; students were not charged tuition." Those who gave and those who received guidance "were devoted to each other with the closeness of father and child. Such relationships cannot be found in the schools of today." The knowledge that they were assisting in "the cultivation of the up-and-coming sons of their ward groups" was recompense enough for the elders, according to Uno.[53] The educational reforms of the Practical Learning party unexpectedly fostered the spirit of fellowship in the new private schools. They became fertile ground for the growth of new, oppositional political forces, but the standard of education in them was not high. Those who wanted more serious academic training went off to the private schools of former Jishūkan scholars, such as the one Kunitomo Shigemasa opened in Uchi-Tsuboi, responding to the demands for higher standards of scholarship.

The political consciousness of Sassa, Takahashi, and others of the Young Men's Tsuboi Association who were deeply influenced by the Loyalist party was raised in this situation. They moved from cultural nationalism to statism. Transcending their *ren,* they overcame traditional lineages and sought like-minded comrades in a broader framework. As a result, they became dissatisfied with the simplistic cultural nationalism and traditionalism of seniors like Nakayama and Andō and broke off relations with these men. In the spring of 1871 they formed a new faction; Sassa Tomofusa became its leader. Although only thirteen or fourteen at the time, Takahashi Nagaaki and Uno Harukaze joined Sassa's group. Thus the *ren* lost its traditional character. Geographical divisions broke down. "Little by little, people crossed ward boundaries and began to associate with like-minded individuals. Even those who had been enemies gradually became good friends."[54]

Kunitomo Shigemasa refused to get involved in the youths' conflicts. He closed his private school, the highest-ranking educational facility of the Uchi-Tsuboi ward. Thus the young men once again lost an opportunity for the pursuit of education. Sassa's group invited the father of one of their colleagues to teach them. Not satisfied with his lessons, they wanted to set up a school on their own. Under the Practical Learning administration, however, this was difficult to do.

In the autumn of 1872, the Ministry of Education enacted the Education Order (Gakusei) and declared that all existing educational institutions in the prefectures be dissolved. Following this policy faithfully, the prefectural government ordered all Kumamoto schools—public and private—to close. In May 1873, in accordance with the Education Order, the administration divided the prefecture into seven middle school districts and requested the central government's approval to begin establishing new schools. Upon receiving it, administrators set about implementing their plan. Sassa and his group, however, criticized the Gakusei, saying that it was form without substance, "a dining table without food."[55] In June 1873 the bureaucrat Yasuoka Ryōsuke was sent from Tokyo to be governor of Kumamoto. Since the members of the Practical Learning party had now lost their power, the Sassa group requested and received permission to found a school in the name of Sassa Kanjō. That institution, called the Sekiinsha (Time Flies School), was set up in the Uchi-Tsuboi ward in November 1873. A Confucian scholar named Ōki Hidenori was engaged as an instructor; Sassa and Takashima became assistant teachers. They sought to familiarize their followers with the political perspectives of their party while maintaining high standards of scholarship. In the second objective they failed, and the Sekiinsha remained an instrument for welding solidarity and inculcating a militant spirit among the young men enrolled there. One of them, Uno Harukaze, recollected that it was a school "in name only. There was no scholarly spirit, no sense of valuing time set apart for diligent study. Rather, our seniors loudly related stories of martyrs, told rousing tales, recited poems, and sang songs composed by stalwarts of the Meiji Restoration. And they had us read important works of the Mito School to elevate our morale."[56] According to Takahashi Nagaaki, "The ironclad rule at the school was unconditional solidarity." In describing the kind of education Sassa carried out there, he emphasizes the inculcation of a strong spirit that "burned like fire."[57]

What brought Sassa's thought to the level of full-fledged statism was his sojourn in Tokyo and his trip to Mito between 1874 and 1876. According to Uno Harukaze, while "mixing with loyalists in Mito," Sassa came to have a high regard for the legacy of Fujita Tōko and Aizawa Yasushi (Aizawa Seishisai; 1781–1863). "His desire to contribute to the nation became all the more keen. He said that if government policies were bad—as indeed they were—the independence of the country would be threatened. Hence it was urgently necessary to reform the administration." Certain powerful ministers must be displaced because "the self-seeking and boastful cannot be trusted." Were there, then, no models of statesmanship left? "Only Saigō Nanshū [Takamori], a man of great intellect and clear vision, remained aloof in Kyushu. Though he drove dogs to hunt in the mountains, was he a man to die of old age on the forest slopes?" What of Sassa himself, however? "Rather than stay confined within the dusty walls of the capital like everyone else, was it not better to remain in obscurity, nurturing one's vigor in the countryside, waiting for the ripe moment?"[58] Such meditations moved Sassa to return to Kumamoto in 1876.

Sassa's stay in the capital and his trip to Mito had convinced him that the Meiji government must be restructured if state power was to be established firmly. Europeanization must be opposed. Sassa made up his mind to engage in secret political activities with Saigō. Letters that Sassa wrote from Tokyo to colleagues back home and his "Opinions Expressed to Colleagues" *(Dōshi ni tei-suru shoken)* directly supplement the view that Uno provides of Sassa's intellectual and political development in those interim years. On 1 August 1874, for instance, he enthusiastically approves of the "argument recently advanced in Chōshū for invading Korea." In Tokyo, he complains, "not even great men can do anything," and he concludes that "there is no other way to reform Japan but to invade Korea and shock the country."[59] In another letter, written on 1 September 1875, he severely criticizes the unfavorable trade balance and other undesirable effects of international commerce. He cites British newspapers to the effect that in the one month of May alone, a single country, England, gained a profit of about 50,000 gold ryō from Japan. "Imagine how serious the situation will become, now that we are dealing more and more freely every month with all the other countries also! Our country, new to the competition, has followed the fashion and has produced 100,000,000 units of paper money. Ah! Unless we stop, either our territory will be divided up or we will become half servants and half masters in our own country." It may become impossible to maintain Japan's independence, Sassa feared. "We must use all our wits and do something!" Again, the "do something" that Sassa proposed as a resolution to Japan's difficulties was to invade Korea.[60]

What he expected from the Time Flies School was that it should prepare young men to be ready and able to break the nation's political deadlock. It was fortunate, he continued in the same letter, that "wise men have taken on the students' education. We can now ignore the ignorant and hold our own counsel." To seize the opportunity when it comes is unquestionably a good rule, but chance is just that: it does not come all the time. Hence one must carefully and constantly observe the situation. "Men with even a little pluck seem to be just waiting for an incident to happen, while neglecting their daily duties. That is a mistake, but it is precisely what we ourselves have done. We must not let our brave young people repeat the same mistake. . . . In the art of war, one who knows the enemy and knows himself need not fear a hundred battles; for one who fights without knowing his enemy, defeat is certain. The wise will follow that strategy. The first thing I want them to teach their students is the necessity of understanding conditions in the world." In demanding that students learn to know "the world," Sassa recognizes a need for knowledge both of the institutions of government—from the top bureaucracy to the local offices—and of the personalities of individual officials. What he is doing is calling for a study of the targets to be attacked.

Sassa's consciousness of political crisis appears even more concretely in his "Opinions Expressed to Colleagues." Aware of the republican aspects of the popular-rights movement, he worries that the situation in Japan is similar to conditions in France, where "royalists and republicans annihilated each other," as he has heard from scholars of Western learning. "They say that down to the present day, the bloodbath has not stopped," he reports, referring presumably to events associated with the Paris Commune, only three or four years in the past. Will Japan, Sassa asks, suffer the same fate in the next few years? The task at hand is to "master the people's hearts," for "if it comes to that, we have no other choice but to make a fierce attack on the so-called republican party and wipe it out. Thus shall the imperial line be preserved forever and the realm be made as solid and secure as Mount Fuji." Toward that end, the students in the ward groups must be inspired to expand their scholarly knowledge and develop a sense of valor. Hence Sassa wants teachers to be active in affairs and cognizant of the state of the world. They should "examine the situation in the realm, associate with the paragons of the realm, and become familiar in depth and detail with conditions overseas, so that they can repay part of their obligation to their country." Japan is imperiled, and the foreign threat is the greatest danger it faces. How can it be saved? "Internal settlement first, expansion abroad second is the usual sequence, but great heroes cannot be expected to follow a pedestrian path in conducting the affairs of the realm." Korea, Sassa notes, "has recently affronted us gravely, making a fool of our envoy." Considering that insult as well as conditions within Japan, he concludes that "even if we lose, we benefit [if we fight]. Since we benefit, we must attack."[61] Korea was surely as good a target as any.

Sassa's sense of crisis was deeply felt. He blamed the doctrines of the popular-rights movement (a product, according to him, of the government's Europeanization policy) for what he saw as a threat to the imperial line. He linked the country's economic crisis to foreign trade and extravagant lifestyles. An invasion of Korea, he thought, would renew the people's spirit, and this spirit was to be fortified by education. Sassa realized that he could accomplish nothing in Tokyo and returned to Kumamoto to bide his time, following Saigō's example. There he was able to influence the likes of Ikebe Kichijūrō, the head of the Academy party, to adopt a similar orientation.

Like Sassa's, the thought of his disciple Takahashi Nagaaki developed pragmatically, revealing a clear subordination of education to politics. In January 1874 Takahashi, responding to Sassa's wishes, transferred from the Sekiinsha to a school opened by Ikebe Kichijūrō after the Practical Learning party took over the government of Kumamoto in 1870 and drove Ikebe from his position of leadership in the administration. Ikebe's school, which was at Yokoshima in Tamana County, became a focus of opposition to Practical Learning and to the central government's policies, which were accepted by that party. In particular, the school was against Europeanization. Naturally, Sassa concluded that Ikebe was "operating on the same principles as we are." He delegated Takahashi to scout out the school with an eye to forming an alliance with Ikebe.[62] Takahashi was warmly welcomed by Ikebe, whose character he admired, and studied with him for a year. This prepared the way for Ikebe's staunch friendship with the Sassa faction.

We have seen Sassa and Takahashi formulating political goals, but what about Tsuda Seiichi? The policy Tsuda wanted to promote, if one may judge from the letters he sent his father from America, was "adopt the best, supplement deficiencies" *(saichō hotan)*. The best way for Japan to become the leader of Asia, he suggested, was to adopt America's mechanized culture. Japan, he thought, was capable of asserting its independence, despite the pressures to which it was subjected by foreign nations; the mission headed by Iwakura Tomomi and sent to Europe and the United States could be expected to hold its own against the foreign powers. Tsuda expressed confidence in Japan's future, while stressing the immediate necessity of sending talented people overseas to study. He wished that "the wise men who go abroad would direct their eyes to the customs and manners, the machines and techniques of the West and alert their ears to the politics and ethics, the strengths and weaknesses of various countries; that they would consider the history of those countries' past and present prosperity or decline and form an estimate of the truth or falsity of their political methods and ethical doctrines, of the benefit or harm of their technology. They should then adopt what is worth adopting and reject what ought to be rejected." Solving Japan's most pressing needs was not the only aim. "If the Land of the Gods develops into a land of civilization and enlightenment, that will not be a blessing for us alone. It will awaken ancient countries around us—China, Korea, Annam—from millennia of sleep," and they will follow Japan. Western technology was far ahead of Asia's, and the need to apply it to Japan's benefit patent. "Human mental faculties, however, are limited, while the things we must learn are limitless. If even the wholehearted cooperation of many could not apprehend them all, much less could one person do it, even in a lifetime of trying. I am therefore waiting for comrades of like mind to come here to study."[63]

In another letter Tsuda advocates the suppression of Christianity, both because of Japan's domestic situation and because resistance to unreasonable foreign pressures is imperative: "International law gives every country the right to self-determination. Domestic affairs should be dealt with by a country according to time and circumstance, and it is wrong for foreign countries to interfere in them. Such is the case with the foreigners' incessant evangelism, which ignores Japanese actualities and is an affront to our nation. We must prohibit it decisively and show them that we have our own Way." Because Confucianism, the doctrine of humanity and righteousness, informs their cultures, Japan and China surpass all other nations. "If we permit this religion of deceit [Christianity] into our country, however, the Way of the Sages will perish, false doctrines will appear, simple and honest customs will vanish, and frivolous habits will flourish." Once the Way is lost, good people will become extinct, and the Land of the Gods will turn into a realm of beasts—a prospect too sad to contemplate.[64]

As his letters show, Tsuda's Yale education failed to undermine the framework he had gained from Tsuboi Practical Learning. On the contrary, it cultivated in him a reverence for national independence while reinforcing his view that to "adopt the best and supplement deficiencies" was essential for the welfare of Japan. Unlike Sassa's and Takahashi's, Tsuda's political vision was extensive; his statism was not a form of reverence for the emperor but derived from Confucian political morality.

After returning to Japan from the United States in August 1873, Tsuda produced an "Atlas of the Eighteen Provinces of Ch'ing China" (*Shin jūhasshō yochizu*), published in March 1875, which was based on a world atlas drawn up by the Englishman Wilde. Tsuda's posting to Peking as understudy to the Japanese embassy's first secretary in May of that year demonstrated his great interest in Chinese affairs. But he certainly had no intention of becoming a career bureaucrat. He gained some knowledge of China, but in September 1876 he resigned his post there and returned to Japan. In October of the following year he was invited to enter the bureaucracy again, this time as a secretary and instructor at the training center of the Finance Ministry's Paper Note Bureau. This situation did not last long, either. As a member of the Practical Learning party, Tsuda did not oppose the Meiji government's internal policy of Europeanization, but he could not approve of its conduct of foreign affairs. Not interested in living out his life as a petty official, he resigned in September 1878 and returned to Kumamoto in March 1880.

In October 1876, just after Tsuda had returned to Tokyo after quitting his post in China, the Shinpūren Revolt erupted in Kumamoto. As we have seen, the Confederates of the Divine Wind—members of the "God-Revering" Keishintō—were direct disciples of Sassa's teacher Hayashi Ōen. They appealed to the Time Flies School to join their rising, but to no avail. The statism of Sassa, in particular, was too pragmatic and political for him to be attracted by the religiosity and fanaticism of the "God Reverers." In a letter that he wrote from Mito to a friend in 1874, he ridiculed their sacred inspiration: "So they are elated to be given positions as Shinto priests, are they? Have they really wound up waving the sacred staff and streamers, and distributing amulets? Now that is some diminution of the scale of their ambitions—laughable! The Land of the Gods is sure to be restored to its pristine condition thanks to characters like these."[65]

Not only did Sassa fail to join the uprising, he led members of the Time Flies School in defending the residence of the Hosokawa family to protect his former lord from being used by the Shinpūren. Thus he made the Confederates his enemies. This was the same Sassa who the following year entrusted Saigō Takamori, the leader of the Satsuma

Rebellion, with the dream he had cherished since his Mito days, reform-ing the government. With the help of Ikebe Kichijūrō, he organized a Kumamoto company and threw in his lot with Saigō's army in February 1877. It goes without saying that Takahashi Nagaaki and Uno Haru-kaze followed where Sassa led.

In the "Discourse on the Current Situation" *(Jiseiron),* which he wrote as an appeal to Ikebe, Sassa lays out the reasons for his decision to turn against the government:[66]

> The sovereign's authority shrinks, the law declines, honor is swept in the dust. The treasury grows ever emptier, but an ever greater flood of cur-rency is issued. Taxes are heavy, and the fields resound with lamentations. And what is the approach to foreign countries? Crimes committed by for-eigners are not tried; the right to levy maritime customs has been aban-doned, and no duties are collected. In the worst cases, what is taking place in the name of trade is the carving up of the territory of our impe-rial ancestors and sage rulers of the past without reflection. . . . Ah! Where-in do we deserve the name of an independent empire? Wherein reposes the security of our people? What steps is the government taking to save us? The realm cracks; soon it shall be clawed apart.

What this plaint, written in florid Chinese classical style, seems to be saying is that the main cause of the nation's downfall is the European-ization pursued in an authoritarian manner by a government that acts tough toward its subjects but is weak and powerless toward foreigners. Such an impotent government must be reformed before national sover-eignty can be restored and secured.

Ikebe responded to Sassa's appeal by observing that those who are envious of European and American wealth and power condemn them-selves to copy Western culture and institutions, part and parcel. "Thus there are those who advocate republican politics, those who are seduced by Christianity, and those who ape Westerners in their manners, their costume, and their eating habits." Surely, this would lead to endless assimilation, a prospect that Ikebe dreaded. "Those who yearn after Western customs excuse themselves by claiming that they are 'adopting the best and supplementing deficiencies.' They will bewitch the people, and the Japanese will end up adoring foreign novelties while disdaining the precious heritage of their native country." Ikebe joined Sassa in censuring the government's lack of autonomy in its dealings with for-eigners. He determined to take action: "I, too, am a Japanese and a man. Since the day of my birth, I have been the beneficiary of the em-peror's blessings. Now my country faces danger. Am I to overlook what is happening and do nothing?"[67]

Leading their respective followers, Sassa and Ikebe took their stand with Saigō. Ikebe died in battle, and Sassa became a captive. Only Tsuda, just back from China, took a different path. Fearing the spread of civil war, he went to Kagoshima to try to persuade Saigō to end his revolt. Since it was too late for that, he joined the government army. His political thought evidently embraced a broader statist thesis than that of Sassa and company.

From his experience in the Satsuma Rebellion, Sassa came to realize that military opposition to the government was futile. He retained his commitment to correcting misrule but gave up all thought of engaging in armed conflict. With Takahashi, Uno, and others, he turned instead to educating a new generation. The fighting of 1877 had affected the politics of Kumamoto gravely, but its effect on education was even more profound. Elementary education, which had developed so rapidly in the decade's middle years, suffered heavily when the conflict temporarily closed all schools. A school examiner's report from the year 1878 asserts that since the promulgation of the Education Order of 1872, more than seven hundred elementary schools had been built in Kumamoto Prefecture. After the outbreak of the Satsuma Rebellion in February 1877, however, thirty-seven of those schools were razed in the course of the fighting, six were destroyed by insurgent violence, eleven others perished in flames, thirty-seven were brought down by typhoons, and fifty-seven suffered other major injuries. The others escaped harm from storm or fire, but they, too, were closed. "The damage to the movement for literacy in the prefecture has been ruinous."[68]

Not only elementary education had suffered. All kinds of public and private schools were closed, including teacher-training institutions and middle schools. Uno Harukaze claims that almost all the houses in the vicinity of Kumamoto Castle were burned to the ground and "all the schools destroyed" during the Satsuma Rebellion. When it ended, "the people who had been dispersed in all directions gradually returned to the castle town. Those who had funds built houses on some parts of the scorched plain, but most people rented houses in the outlying districts. Kumamoto looked like a wasteland. Since most people were busy trying to eke out a living, education was completely abandoned."[69] The sons of samurai lost their educational facilities along with everyone else.

Facing this scene of devastation, Sassa, Tsuda, and other statists moved toward the formation of a conservative alliance. In the political realm, the core of that coalition would be the Shimeikai; in the educational, the School of Kindred Spirits would be its center. Sassa and company, who had joined the Satsuma Rebellion, fought in a militant movement for political reform, and failed at armed force, discovered a new arena for their activities. Henceforth, the main action would take place in the educational sphere. That is where they would exert themselves in the effort to unite popular sentiment by the dissemination of their nationalistic, statist ideology.

Three conclusions may be drawn from an inquiry into the statists of Kumamoto and their educational activities. First, the statist thought of people like Sassa Tomofusa, Tsuda Seiichi, and Takahashi Nagaaki was notable for its claim to being an oppositionist, antigovernment political philosophy. They continually engaged in confrontations with established leaders and official dogma. In short, an outsider mentality vividly colored their ideology. Second, that ideology was nurtured in the matrix of traditional Kumamoto political thought, but it did not remain traditional. In the hands of the younger generation of various factions, it changed markedly, to be recast in the form of statism as it adjusted to new conditions. Finally, and most important, since its development was closely related to the independent political consciousness of people formerly of samurai status, it was an autonomous ideology developed outside the corridors of state power. That is why the educational endeavors of Sassa and company attracted the sons of the local samurai of Kumamoto and why their thought could function as an ideology which actively supported the Meiji state's nationalism at its base.

In a sense, the School of Proliferating Talent was the fountainhead of the Meiji government's educational method. Even so, the school's educational policies had developed in concert with an oppositionist political movement, and its educational goals remained exclusively under the cultivation of men who sought to realize the political goals of the Shimeikai. The Seiseikō sought to cultivate the talents of men who would bring nationalistic programs to the fore through the political process. This type of education differed distinctly from what the central government compassed in its plans, and in particular from the policies of Mori Arinori, who sought to rear apolitical Japanese to support the state. How did these two thoroughly different educational approaches become one?

In 1881 the Meiji government purged its administration of bureaucrats of the school of enlightenment associated with Fukuzawa Yukichi (1835–1901), from Ōkuma Shigenobu (1838–1922) on down. Their advocacy of English-style constitutionalism was the sin held against them, for Itō Hirobumi had decided to bring a governmental system anchored in a Prussian-style bureaucracy into being. Itō's constitutional choice, featuring as it did the authority of the emperor as the nation's ideological foundation, coincided precisely with the political goal of Sassa and company—the realization of a state based on the emperor system. Since the government's design of a national political structure incorporated their statist ideal, their cherished plans were fulfilled. Their educational efforts had come to fruition, and the success of their political movement had been adequately demonstrated in their own eyes.

In March 1884 they therefore transformed the Shimeikai into the Shimei Study Association (Shimei Gakkai), removing from it all traces of its former political character. As a natural consequence, the educational goals of the School of Proliferating Talent were radically changed; more precisely put, they were aligned with the central government's objectives and integrated into its national educational program. For Sassa and his comrades, this was an enormous political achievement; they no longer felt the need for partisan activities. For the Meiji government, it was a sign that a clear pathway to the rapid realization of its educational plans was opening throughout the country.

Among statist samurai outside the corridors of power, the Meiji government found people who were willing to shoulder the burden of its nationalist educational program. These outsiders and their followers assured the government's educational policy of active support at the grass roots.

7

The Spirit of Political Opposition in the Meiji Period
The Academic Style of the
Tōkyō Senmon Gakkō

Translated by I. J. McMullen

Political opposition in the Meiji period seems to have derived from two main intellectual sources: traditional Confucianism and English thought. The former provided a conservative foundation, on which Confucian humanism, with its stress on government by virtue, confronted bureaucratic authoritarianism and the legal system that underpinned it. The latter opposed the German statism appropriated by the Meiji bureaucracy as its model, pitting against it English individualism and liberalism. It pursued a basically individualistic concept of the modernization of state and society and sought to realize values that it identified as English in Japan.

The spirit of opposition in the Tōkyō Senmon Gakkō (Tokyo Specialist School), the subject of this chapter, drew its inspiration from English thought. By the end of the nineteenth century, the association between the school and the English tradition had become established in the minds of Japanese. When the school was refounded and expanded as Waseda University in 1902, the contemporary press offered its congratulations. The *Niroku shinpō* identified Waseda's president, Takata Sanae, as a champion of English values, and urged him to adopt a more conspicuous role on the national stage. Further, it explicitly contrasted the "English constitutional values that flow in the blood of the great majority of our people, with the apparent exception of a few brash young men freshly emerged from the gates of the Imperial University" with the officially sanctioned Prussian philosophy of the state, which it condemned as the "emasculated constitutional theory of Hozumi Yatsuka."

Here was a clear recognition of the connection between the Tokyo Specialist School, the English tradition in politics, and the intellectual basis of political opposition.[1]

English thought, however, had not been consistently identified with political opposition from the beginning of the Meiji period. During the epoch of "civilization and enlightenment" *(bunmei kaika)* that followed the Meiji Restoration, both the government itself and intellectuals outside officialdom had striven to vanquish feudal social attitudes with English empiricism and utilitarian ethics. English political theory had exerted a major influence on the constitutional drafts prepared by the Sain (Chamber of the Left) and the Genrōin (Chamber of Elder Statesmen) between 1871 and 1880.[2] And in the faculties of Law and Letters of the Tōkyō Kaisei Gakkō, at the time the state's highest educational institution, almost exclusively English learning had been purveyed by English teachers. Thus English thought was initially not associated with political opposition; on the contrary, it had constituted an important source of officially approved "enlightenment" in the early years of Meiji.

It was only after the Political Crisis of 1881 that English thought became a conscious inspiration for political opposition. In that year, the bureaucrats of the Satsuma-Chōshū clique purged the anglophile faction of Ōkuma Shigenobu from the government and made the deliberate choice of the German—in particular, the Prussian—constitutional system as the model for a modern Japanese state and style of governance. Inoue Kowashi spelled out this decision in a memorandum to fellow oligarch Itō Hirobumi in June 1881: "Delegation of the control of the executive primarily to popular deliberation is [the procedure to be found in] England. Not to delegate in this way is the procedure of Prussia. In establishing its polity, our country should emulate Prussia; it should not model itself on England."[3]

From this time on, English thought provided an important inspiration for criticism of and vigilance toward bureaucratic policies. It appealed to opponents of the penetration of state control and to supporters of the expansion of individual freedom and initiative in both the political and the economic spheres. The critical spirit inspired by the English tradition gradually spread among the middle strata of the population. Vigorous political, journalistic, and economic activity in both metropolis and provinces progressively established it as an accepted attitude among Meiji Japanese, even though it had to labor to fulfill its promise within the constraints of an authoritarian state structure. English thought also encouraged the growth of the modern bourgeois consciousness that developed among Japanese in the late Meiji decades and the Taishō era. And it was the Tokyo Specialist School that served as an important conduit for systematically disseminating the English tradition nationwide among the middle strata, even after English thought had been officially eliminated from the government and the bureaucracy.

The Independence of Learning

The Tōkyō Senmon Gakkō was founded by Ōkuma Shigenobu (1838–1922) in October 1882, a year after he had been purged from the government and six months after he had formed the Constitutional Reform party (Rikken Kaishintō). Those personally involved in making arrangements for the new school, however, were Ono Azusa (1852–1886) and his pupils, the young men of the Ōtokai. This association was a political study group set up by students of the faculties of Law and Letters of the University of Tokyo. It was centered on Ono Azusa, and its members, who shared a respect for Ono's personality and ideas, included Takata Sanae (family name sometimes read as Takada; 1860–1938), Amano Tameyuki (1859–1938), Ichishima Kenkichi (1860–1944), Okayama Kenkichi (1854–1894), Sunakawa Katsutoshi (1860–1933), Yamada Ichirō (1860–1905), and Yamada Kinosuke (1859–1913). These men, who aspired to become politicians dedicated to establishing a constitutional state, joined the new Reform party immediately after being graduated from the University of Tokyo in July 1882. Under Ono's guidance, they participated in the establishment of the Specialist School with the intention, as they saw it, of educating a constitutional citizenry.[4]

The Specialist School was founded, it needs hardly be said, on the ideal of "the independence of learning." This ideal was professed by Ōkuma himself and, with a somewhat different nuance, also by the youths of the Ōtokai, for whom it symbolized nothing less than their spirit of political opposition. As Takata later described it, their very enrollment in the Reform party was an act of defiance in the face of the government-supported university's attempts to discourage them. "At that time, university graduates were in extremely short supply. Not only were they lionized in society, even within the university there was a reluctance to let them join political parties. Accordingly, students were urged, through Professor Toyama [Masakazu] among others, to enter government service. I was even urged to become an official of the Ministry of Education. The monthly stipend was the huge sum of 50 yen, very favorable treatment at the time. But ours was a swollen-headed group, and we declined."[5] There is evidence, however, that among the seven members of the Ōtokai, at least Takata and Amano had been fostered in an antigovernment atmosphere before their exposure to English thought and had a strong antagonism to governmental power even before this experience.

Takata was the son of a lumber merchant who had failed at the time of the Meiji Restoration. His family had been Edoites for generations, and his antipathy to the so–called Government Forces, drawn from western Japan, that invaded Edo at the time of the restoration, was profound: he had "not the slightest idea," he says in his reminiscences, what the term meant, but imagined in his "childish way" that they were "like villains, or at least like bullies, in every respect."[6] Takata, who had the gallant frame of mind and the refined artistic taste of the Edoite, continued to nurse an aversion toward the country samurai of the domain clique *(hanbatsu)* that ran the Meiji government. In this respect, he bore a close resemblance to Tsubouchi Yūzō (Tsubouchi Shōyō; 1859–1935)—not, it is true, a member of the Ōtokai, but a man who was to hold a full-time post at the Specialist School from 1883 and was later to be called, in company with Takata and Amano, one of "Waseda's Holy Triad." Tsubouchi was from a Nagoya background, but he had been familiar with the arts, letters, and theater of Edo from childhood and had developed the sensibility characteristic of the latter city. During his student days, his love of the Edoite character had inspired him to affect a pure Edo dialect in his speech. He recollected how their shared tastes—their fondness for novels and the kabuki theater, their fascination with the ripe Edo culture of the Bunka-Bunsei epoch—had occasioned his friendship with Takata, "an Edoite through and through," with whom he had "associated quickest and with least reserve" among his friends.[7]

These two were at the heart of a student literary group that was joined by Ichishima Kenkichi and Yamada Ichirō of the Ōtokai. All these literary enthusiasts felt resentment at the military manner of the samurai students from large feudal domain backgrounds; they demonstrated their own Edoite loyalties by wearing white socks, in contrast to the dark blue of the scions of samurai. "Most of the Hitotsubashi students," Takata recollects, "preserved the rough style that had prevailed at the restoration, and tended to be Bohemian. Among the elite students from Satsuma, Tosa, or Kaga, a startling number cultivated exotically heroic postures, flaunted sexual perversions, twirled thick walking sticks, and blustered around ostentatiously. We conceived a strong aversion to this and reacted by pushing a literary taste whenever there was the opportunity."[8] The urbane contempt for physical strength exhibited here by Takata alienated him and his friends from the Party of Liberty (Jiyūtō), which glorified opposition to the despotism of the domain clique and espoused a destructive revolutionary philosophy. Takata identified, rather, with the Reform party, which had an overwhelmingly urban constituency.

Amano Tameyuki was the son of a Karatsu domain doctor. His father had been personal physician to Ogasawara Nagamichi (1822–1891), the domain's heir presumptive, and had served in Edo. Nagamichi had occupied high civil and military positions in the Tokugawa shogunate at the time of the restoration and remained a shogunal loyalist to the end. As a consequence of his recalcitrant failure to adhere to the imperial court, the samurai in his service suffered grave political and economic adversities. The Amano household accepted the hospitality of a servant in a village in Chiba Prefecture, and the father had the misfortune to die there. The family then returned to Karatsu, where it lived under difficult circumstances; Tameyuki began his studies at the age of ten at the local English School. With the abolition of feudal domains in 1871, this school, too, declined. Tameyuki, however, responded to his mother's earnest hope that "she might somehow launch her children on careers, both to comfort her dead husband's spirit and to revive the house of Amano."[9] He went to the capital, enrolling first in the Tōkyō Gaikokugo Gakkō and subsequently in the Tōkyō Kaisei Gakkō.

These youthful experiences drew Amano to opposition to the *hanbatsu* regime. On graduation from university, he entered the Reform party with naive and idealistic ambitions to become a constitutional politician and do away with the domination exercised over Japan by the domain clique. "I had the notion," he states, "that if a national assembly were to be convened, I would become a minister at a single bound and come to manage the country's administration. Thus I preserved my integrity and abstained from all aspects of government."[10]

The young men of the Ōtokai thus forswore the glories of the official world and chose true constitutional politics as their way of life. A reaction against power, rooted in their biographical circumstances, was certainly one reason for this choice. Another may have been the conceit to which Takata confessed. Yet neither a simple dissatisfaction with power nor political ambition accounts entirely for their attitude of opposition to the contemporary regime. Rather, this attitude was an intellectually grounded phenomenon. It was based on a specific political philosophy formed by the English values that they studied in the Kaisei Gakkō and the University of Tokyo. Furthermore, it was precisely these values that were to form the link between themselves and Ono.

It is well known that Ono Azusa's political thought was the product of his studies in America and England between 1871 and 1874. Those studies led him to reject both the conservative and the radical forces in the Meiji political world. He committed himself instead to a gradual and realistic political reform aimed at the achievement of a constitutional state, and he came to regard English parliamentary politics as the model for the modernization of Japan—also, like England, a monarchy. His treatise "On Imperial Loyalism" contains a remarkable exposition of why he thought that England most merited emulation:[11]

> Gentlemen, of the large number of royal nations in the world at present, which royal family is the most glorified and which people enjoys the most complete happiness? On these two points, I would suggest, it would be first and foremost England. Why, in my view, is the English royal house so glorified? Why does the English people enjoy complete happiness in this way? For no other reason than this—the English have, through orderly means and sound methods, reformed and advanced their politics. They have done this without cleaving to the old or rushing to adopt the radical. Therefore, if the nations of the world that are under the rule of sovereigns wish to achieve the glorification of their royal families and fulfill the happiness of their people, they should alike model themselves on the example of England and share in the benefits that she offers.

How did the young men of the Ōtokai absorb English thought? What was the nature of their education? The years in which they attended the Kaisei Gakkō and the University of Tokyo were special ones in the history of those establishments. They were enrolled in the Kaisei Gakkō in July 1876, and in September of the next year they were transferred, because of a reform of the school system, to the most advanced class of the Preparatory School (Yobimon) for the University of Tokyo. During this period, English alone was prescribed as the language of instruction at both the Kaisei Gakkō[12] and the Preparatory School; English, accordingly, was the medium through which new ideas were transmitted to these young men. Most influential in the formation of their political attitudes were the English teacher Edward W. Syle and, among the Japanese, Toyama Masakazu (1848–1900; given name sometimes read as Shōichi), an alumnus of the University of Michigan. Miyake Setsurei (1860–1945), a school year junior to the young men of the Ōtokai, remembered of Toyama that he "raised his voice from time to time" in lecturing on Chambers' history of the French Revolution, "seeming to express sympathy with those events." After that first text, Toyama proceeded to such works as Herbert Spencer's *Philosophy of Style* and *Representative Government* as well as Thomas Macaulay's *Hallam's Constitutional History* and his essays on Robert Clive and Warren Hastings.[13] Takata, too, recorded his impressions of Syle's instruction: "One fact which I remembered from being taught by Professor Syle was that the promulgation of the Magna Carta was forced on

King John by an alliance of the aristocracy and people of England. This was the beginning of constitutions in the world. At the same time, however, the Englishmen of that period had a thoroughly conservative spirit and proclaimed, 'Nolums legas Anglia mutari [sic]—we do not wish to alter the established laws of England.' In other words, it was not that the people of England desired new laws, but that they wished to be governed in perpetuity by the old, free system."[14]

In September 1878, these young men entered the Main Division (Honka) of the University of Tokyo, where they would be assigned between the Faculty of Law and the Faculty of Letters. Takata, Amano, Ichishima, and Yamada Ichirō chose Letters, while the remaining three Ōtokai men—Yamada Kinosuke, Okayama, and Sunakawa—selected Law. They did not, however, go on to their elected specializations until their second year; as freshmen, they attended classes common to both faculties. During their first year in the Main Division, they studied the history of England and of Europe under the English professors Syle and Charles James Cooper, as well as various works of Spencer under Toyama, thus deepening their familiarity with English constitutional history and constitutional thought. It was, however, their freshman-year experience of lectures on English literature given by William A. Houghton (1852–1917) that particularly seems to have intensified their interest in the literary tradition of Great Britain.

Many students considered Houghton's lectures difficult and onerous, but those who had a good command of the English language, such as Takata of the Faculty of Letters and Tan Itsuma of the Faculty of Law, were stimulated by his "minute and scrupulous" exposition of literary works.[15] Through Takata and Tan, enthusiasm for English literature spread also to Tsubouchi and among the members of the Ōtokai such as Yamada, Ichishima, and others. The interest in foreign letters sparked by Houghton was linked to the thorough grounding that men like Takata and Tsubouchi already possessed in the culture of the Edo period; indeed, their knowledge of Japanese literature served to confer depth and authority on their new studies. These studies, in turn, created an intensely emotional dimension to their relationship with England. Their anglophile views were further developed and deepened academically from 1879, their second year as university students, when they were divided between the two faculties of Law and of Letters and began their specialist studies of English law, politics, and economics.

The Faculty of Letters in this period offered courses in philosophy, politics, and political economy. Among the four members of the Ōtokai who entered this faculty, Amano selected political economy; the others specialized in politics. It was in this year that Ernest Fenollosa joined the professorial staff and took charge of the teaching of philosophy, politics, and political economy. Syle had retired, and Cooper taught history and ethics. Houghton continued to be responsible for English literature.

The textbooks employed by these teachers have been documented, thus making it possible to reconstruct the curriculum pursued by these young men.[16] For his philosophy course, Fenollosa employed Francis Bowen's *Modern Philosophy from Descartes to Schopenhauer and Hartmann* and Albert Schwegler's *Handbook of the History of Philosophy*; in political economy, he used John Stuart Mill's *Principles of Political Economy* and John Elliott Cairnes' *Some Leading Principles of Political Economy Newly Expounded*; in politics, essays by Herbert Spencer together with Walter Bagehot's *Physics and Politics*. In ethics, Cooper used George Payne's *Elements of Mental and Moral Science* as well as Spencer's *Principles of Ethics,* Jeremy Bentham's *Introduction to the Principles of Morals and Legislation,* and Mill's *Utilitarianism.* Cooper lectured on English constitutional history and the philosophy of history; in ancient history, he used textbooks prepared for English-speaking students. This range of material demonstrates how English-centered the studies of these young men were at the University of Tokyo.

That they digested their English learning is attested by the praise accorded them by Cooper in a report to the university's president: "Mr. Takata gives me much satisfaction by the attention and diligence of his studies. Mr. Amano excels in every examination and greatly exceeds my expectations in his regular class work." On this class of students as a whole, Cooper wrote with evident satisfaction: "I observe particularly good results in my class on the history of English prose. . . . I set fortnightly essays for the students. Their compositions are all elegant and free of faults. Truly, this is the first time I have had such good students as these."[17] Thus the education offered by the Faculty of Letters was English in emphasis and was to remain so until these men entered their fourth year of studies in 1881. From that year, Germany was gradually accorded greater emphasis.

The Faculty of Law, similarly, was English-centered, despite the fact that the formal curriculum published at its inauguration in 1877 stipulated French law as the major object of study.[18] The second-year curriculum in 1878 covered English law (summary outline; immovable property law; movable property law; contract law; criminal law), the French language, current Japanese law, and the history of Japanese criminal law. For the third year, along with ancient and current Japanese law, the curriculum was devoted to English law (law of evidence; administrative

law; procedural law; criminal procedural law; tort), the English constitution, and the French language. In actuality, French law was only
introduced in the fourth year, with the essentials of French civil law.
There were some modifications to the course in 1879–1880, but these
only involved moving English constitutional law from the third year of
studies forward to the second and teaching French criminal law in the
third year. In 1881, however, the course was reorganized with German
law at its heart. In the radical restructuring that took place the following year, even English constitutional law was dropped, ending the special emphasis on matters English that had been a feature of study at the
University of Tokyo while these young men were enrolled there.

Such, in sum, were the academic circumstances under which the
members of the Ōtokai were familiarized with English thought. Their
experience suggests that their spirit of political opposition was a self-
conscious one, inspired by the English values that they absorbed both
intellectually and emotionally during their student years. As Yamada
Ichirō expressed it in eulogizing Okayama Kenkichi, "The members of
the Ōtokai were not drawn together as a group by any personal attrac-
tion; they formed an alliance because they shared the same intellectual
beliefs."[19] Behind those beliefs—and at the core of the Ōtokai—lay
English values.

These young men's familiarity with matters English from constitutional history to literature developed further into a positive evaluation
of the English national character. "Long ago, while at the University,"
Yamada said, they had held discussions on what caused nations to prosper and had concluded that while many examples could be adduced
"among the old, civilized states," the only ones "worth emulating by
the developing countries in the nineteenth century" were England,
France, Germany, and Russia. They recognized that "the characters of
these four peoples were not the same. Each had excellencies and deficiencies. You could not generalize about them." Nevertheless, if one
model had to be chosen, it was clear that it must be England:[20]

> It is the disposition of the English alone that is self-denying yet persever-
> ing, steady yet progressive, self-respecting yet without vanity. In respond-
> ing to events, they seem slow, yet they can be relied upon to attain
> success. The French, despite their lack of courage, have powers of endur-
> ance that compensate for their deficiency. The Germans, despite their lack
> of wisdom, are highly self-disciplined, and can thus overcome their fail-
> ing. The conduct of the English is not without its shortcomings, but those
> are publicly admitted. Their behavior is not free from misdeeds, but it is
> scrutinized by the entire people. [Englishmen] swagger in crowded public

places, and, striding to the four corners of the earth, never exhibit fear or vacillation. A people of this quality is worthy to be made a pattern for our developing nation.

The Ōtokai neither lavished uncritical praise on England nor indulged in unqualified admiration of the English. Rather, its members considered the actualities of Japan—a monarchy—and examined the national characteristics of various peoples of the world. On the basis of this comparative investigation, they decided that England was Japan's proper model, thus rejecting the government's pro-German position.

Such was the intellectual background to the ideal of the "independence of learning" at the Tokyo Specialist School. Its upholders struggled to realize this ideal in education and in society against official opposition. In the course of time, after the school was refounded in 1902 as Waseda University, the ideal was to lose all but a symbolic significance, as we shall see. During this early period of the institution, however, commitment to the "independence of learning" not only expressed the political position of its founder Ōkuma, the leader of the Constitutional Reform party, but also epitomized the spirit of opposition of the young men of the Ōtokai, imbued as they all were with antagonism toward state control.

There were, historically, two meanings to the expression "the independence of learning." The first, which had a nationalist dimension, is reflected in the speech Ono Azusa gave at the Specialist School's opening ceremony in October 1882: "If we do not foster the well-being of our populace, develop its independent spirit, and take responsibility for it, we cannot expect to preserve the independence of our Imperial Land. Quite a few ways exist by which these ends may be sought. But the means of laying an enduring basis and constructing a permanent foundation are to be found only in the achievement of the independence of learning."[21] Here, forcefully expressed, was "the independence of learning" in the sense of the independence of the Japanese intellectual world from foreign countries—in short, as a premise for Japanese national independence.

In later years, Ōkuma was to summarize "the independence of learning" in this sense as "a progressive evolutionary stage of antiforeignism *(shinka shita jōi),*" a force that opposed "the tendency, as Western learning gained ascendency, for men to become intoxicated by foreign lands and become subject, one after the other, to spiritual conquest."[22] In this first sense, therefore, the concept reflects the nationalist side of Ōkuma and the Ōtokai group. This nationalism, however, was also at the same time an expression of these men's spirit of political opposition. Thus in his opening-day speech, Ono criticized the lack of autonomy in the government's cultural and educational policies, noting that "we have never yet observed any so-called Japanese learning to have existed or to have been taught to our students." From the past, he alleged, governments had paid respect to Chinese learning; since the restoration, Japanese had learned sometimes from England and America, at other times from France; now they were attempting to copy from Germany. "This is how we become dependent on foreign countries and fail to control matters ourselves."[23]

The second sense of "the independence of learning" expresses these men's spirit of opposition even more clearly. If the first meaning of the term referred to independence from external, international pressures, this second sense is internal and domestic. It denotes independence from political control and especially from the power of the state. In his speech at the Specialist School's foundation ceremony in 1882, Ono had touched on this topic, declaring that it was his hope to make the institution independent, outside the political parties. Nonetheless, this connotation of freedom from the interference of the state had been largely suppressed until Waseda's opening ceremony twenty years later, when it featured in several retrospective speeches. Ōkuma, for instance, cited his own experience of being purged in the Political Crisis of 1881: "Once I left the government and took a detached view of its power, the unacceptability of its operations became obvious. Thus my attention was drawn for the first time to the great danger of placing our sacred learning under its autocratic control."[24] Here again, belief in the ideal of "the independence of learning" is traced back to the seminal opposition to state control espoused by Ōkuma and those associated with him in the foundation of the Specialist School.

In 1886, the University of Tokyo was renamed the Imperial University, accepted the government official Watanabe Kōki (1848–1901) as its president, and proclaimed its educational function to be the training of bureaucrats for the state. Not surprisingly, this institution became a target of the Ōtokai group's critical spirit. As Takata Sanae put it, Watanabe Kōki "was no more than a bureaucrat who bowed to the wishes of the domain clique's elder statesmen." Assigned the mission of "making the university the claws and teeth of their interests," he was determined, "by promoting German and bureaucratic principles," to steer the university's graduates to the cause of *hanbatsu* politics. "This much was patently clear not only to Mr. Ōkuma and Mr. Ono, but to the rest of us as well. For this reason, the separation of politics and learning—that is, the principle that learning must be divorced from politics—became clearly implicit in the expression 'the independence of learning.' "[25]

That expression manifested the objective of the Tokyo Specialist School at the time of its foundation. The goal envisioned by the school was educating a citizenry that would possess a spirit of independence from foreign influence and from the power of the state; would autonomously, rather than under coercion, contribute to the well-being of the nation; and would be imbued with a spirit of opposition to governmental interference. Such were the ideals of the Ōtokai.

The Tokyo Specialist School and Meiji Society

The development achieved by the Tokyo Specialist School within a mere two decades was spectacular. By the time of the school's reconstitution as Waseda Daigaku in October 1902, it had grown from an institution of "a mere seventy or eighty students" to one of three thousand, an expansion without parallel (it was claimed) even in the West.[26] Various reasons, including the great efforts of the school authorities, can be adduced for this growth. Most salient, however, is that the school's mode of intensive specialist courses and instruction in Japanese effectively met the educational needs of the time. This point had been emphasized in the advertisement inserted in the *Yūbin hōchi* of 22 September 1882 to announce the institution's opening:[27]

> *Item.* This school is dedicated to intensive course work and offers instruction in politics, economics, law, science, and the English language.
> *Item.* Politics, economics, law, and science are to be taught entirely in Japanese, and the students will take written notes in this language.
> *Item.* The course will be three years in duration, with each year divided into two semesters. There will be a division into classes. Each of the three classes will require one year to complete.

As suggested previously, the immediate aim of the Specialist School's intensive education was to dispatch into the world bearers of the spirit of opposition inspired by English thought, and to do so as fast and in as large numbers as possible. These men were to serve in building a new Japan. Hence the school's educational policy placed special emphasis on adapting the new learning to contemporary realities and sought the unity of theory and practice. This attitude contrasted with that of the Imperial University, which may have taught the "principles of politics" but was by no means free—so the Specialist School's partisans alleged—from the "tendency to indulge in empty theorizing." In their school, by contrast, "importance was attached, in the English manner, to a combination of experience and theory; attention was directed to reality as well as to study; and efforts were made to avoid indulging in abstraction."[28]

That the educational policy of the school responded to the needs of the day was a prominent theme in the speeches made at its opening ceremony on 15 October 1882. In taking up this theme, the school's principal, Ōkuma Hidemaro, proclaimed that "the realm has been transformed anew, and a new kind of learning is about to arise."[29] Ono Azusa elaborated on this slogan:[30]

> There is a partisan point of view that deplores the clamor of political dis-
> cussion in metropolis and provinces and chastises students for indulging
> in political and legal studies and failing to pursue science. To make these
> accusations, however, is to be guilty of a failure to understand the circum-
> stances of today. . . . As I see it, the areas of politics that need reform and
> of law that need progress in our country are not isolated but pervasive; it
> is almost as though everything needs to be changed. That is why there is
> such a demand for "political science" and "jurisprudence." Students flock
> to these two disciplines simply because they want to respond to those
> pressing needs. Those who question this have only a superficial grasp of
> the situation; hence they blame the students. I do not understand their
> grounds for so doing.

Ono advocated the priority of intensive education in politics and law over a scientific education for two practical reasons. One had to do with the government's pledge, proclaimed in an imperial rescript in October 1881, that a national assembly would be convened in 1890. There was a real need, Ono thought, for a philosophy of constitutional government and a knowledge of the law to be disseminated among the people by that time. The second reason related to his perception that "unless we reform politics now and make progress in law, we will lack the wherewithal to guide the students of our realm toward progress in science."[31] It was Ono's view, in other words, that the establishment of a modern state and society was itself a prerequisite for effective educa-tion in science; accordingly, to advocate the primacy of scientific over political education was a reversal of the proper priorities. In putting forward such educational proposals, the government was engaged, Ono believed, in a political maneuver designed to suppress social demands and depoliticize intellectuals.

The target of this criticism is clear. In 1879, Itō Hirobumi (1841–1909) had come out against the scheme proposed by the Meiji em-peror's Confucian adviser, Motoda Nagazane (1818–1891; given name often read as Eifu), for the implementation of a National Doctrine based on "the fostering of virtue" and had presented his own counter-proposal "On Education" to the emperor. Here he laid down the basic line that was to be followed by the bureaucratic government toward higher education: "The training of advanced students should direct them toward science; it should not incite them to political discussion."[32] It was precisely this "partisan point of view" that was the object of Ono's attack.

Itō's dictum reflected a policy that served the interests of state power, one that was indeed designed to depoliticize intellectuals and transform them into technicians. It must be viewed against the background of the national growth of the popular-rights movement *(jiyū minken undō)*. In contrast, the Tokyo Specialist School's belief in the primacy of the study of politics and law envisaged an education that responded to the demands of Meiji society. For all its florid rhetoric, the speech made at the school's opening by the young lecturer Amano Tameyuki nicely illustrates that vision:[33]

> What sort of person would launch himself onto the ocean of learning? There are two kinds. One is the person who liberates himself beyond the blue clouds and brown dust of the world, who has ears and eyes—though not for worldly currents, for he seeks the truth. The second is the person who gives back to the world what he acquires from his studies, who regards learning as a vessel with talent as its helm and virtue as its rudder, who braves the perils of the mountainous seas, who rides their crests and strives to rescue the people from drowning. The first kind is essential; but is not the second kind even more indispensable, given the circumstances of our nation today? Consider the state of the law. The most marvelous of golden rules and jeweled precepts have been selected from among the various nations of the West; good attorneys and good judges, however, seem to be as scarce as stars in the morning sky. Under these circumstances, if those who can purvey the truth of the law do not come forth in large numbers, what will befall the lives, property, and honor of our more than thirty million people?

The intensive education pursued in the Specialist School thus aimed at the training of men who would protect the interests of the populace and at the reform of what was perceived by the school's founders to be the backward politics and law of the Meiji state. As we have already seen, those who established these priorities had the example of England in their minds. It was, therefore, natural that they should recognize the necessity to study English alongside the major course work in politics and economics, law, and science (all taught in Japanese) and that they should establish a special course for that purpose. Ono Azusa argued at the opening ceremony that learning foreign languages was indispensable to anyone who wished to acquire more than a superficial knowledge of the "new kind of learning" or, indeed, "to perfect the independence of learning in our country." One who wished to acquire knowledge of developments abroad had to be able to read foreign books in the original. The school's choice of English—rather than German or French—for teaching original texts was not accidental. As Ono saw it, German scholarship did not lack profundity, nor was French learning deficient in breadth. "Where the fostering of a spirit of self-governance among the people and the enhancement of a lively disposition are concerned, however, one cannot but press the spirit of the English race." The matter, he said, had been "given the most thorough consideration."[34] True to its name, the Specialist School stood for intensive education in the form of specialized courses, using Japanese as the medium of instruction. At the same time, it emphasized the acquisition of the English language as a means for absorbing English civilization, the fountainhead of the attitude of political opposition that characterized the school; it rejected the pro-German posture of the Meiji state and fostered the realization of English values in Meiji society; and it sought to nurture talent that would disseminate those values.

The path forward, however, was not smooth. It was obstructed by various pressures from the state, which directed coercive measures against the school itself and at the political position of its founder, Ōkuma. "In the eyes of the government, this school was a cradle of revolt," Ōkuma complains in his recollections. "It was constantly harassed by the attentions of investigators." When these "spies" failed to turn in reports satisfactory to their employers, the government sought to sabotage the institution by secretly directing provincial officials to discourage enrollment in it. "Wherever there were provincials who considered entering this school, the local officials exerted pressure on their close relatives to restrain them, with the result that there were very few actual entrants. Three courses—politics, law, and science—were opened, and students were recruited for them, but the total for the three amounted to no more than eighty."[35]

The provost of the Tōkyō Senmon Gakkō in its early years, Hideshima Ieyoshi (1852–1912), charges that agents provocateurs "were infiltrated into both classroom and dormitory" not only by the government but also by political parties opposed to the school's founder and its founding principle. These enemies of "the independence of learning" ignored the school's "unambiguous declaration that it had no connection with political parties or political establishments" and "exhausted every possible means to obstruct us." Indeed, "when the opportunity presented itself, they provoked riots" among the students. "Things reached such a pass that in the year immediately after our foundation, for instance, we were forced to order the expulsion of the majority of the 128 students."[36]

In addition, Hideshima pointed to the institution of an extension course in law at the University of Tokyo's Faculty of Law as indirect state obstruction of enrollment in the Tokyo Specialist School. This extension course was started on 5 July 1883, on the proposal of Hozumi Nobushige (1856–1926) and four other professors of the Faculty of Law, with the clear intention of controlling and suppressing private law schools. In 1885, recruitment for the extension course was stopped, and it was amalgamated with the law school of the Ministry of Justice. During the two years of its existence, however, it offered a three-year program with Japanese as the medium of instruction, a format similar to that of the Specialist School. Because the graduates, like those of the major course in the Faculty of Law, were offered the privilege of becoming attorneys without examination, the extension course proved attractive to young aspiring lawyers and had an enrollment of eighty-five students while it lasted.

What was the thinking of the University of Tokyo professors who proposed this course? Their premise was that Meiji society was already advanced, not backward, and that the intensive education of lawyers to respond to the needs of society was essential. As they put it, "The relationship between law and society is, in our respectful opinion, truly an essential one. Therefore, progress in the law must constantly be adjusted to the progress of society."[37] The clear underlying assumption is that law was subordinate to the policies of the Meiji state and to social realities. This opinion contrasts with that held in the Specialist School, where the primacy attached to politics and law was associated with the notion of progress and reform in these fields, with the forthcoming constitution in mind. Meiji society was still backward, not advanced, was the view there; it was, however, hoped idealistically that its condition could be improved, so that the Japanese state and society should not be the occasion of embarrassment in the company of constitutional countries. In short, there was a great contrast of attitudes between the two institutions.

Recall that after 1881, the Faculty of Law of the University of Tokyo abandoned its previous English orientation and assumed a German coloring. Naturally, the kind of legal thought favored by the state would be taught in that university's extension course in law. The professors who proposed that course attempted to use the Faculty of Law to impose uniformity on legal thought among the Japanese people and to institute an official Meiji state legal system, arguing that only a unified law could serve the national interest. They deplored the lack of "an academy that would unify the standard and measure of learning and knowledge," regretted the proliferation of private schools, and even lamented the condition of their own faculty, "which is by no means free of symptoms of decline." Noting the existence of the Senmon Gakkō and Senshū Gakkō in Tokyo,[38] they suggested that Japan's abundance of private schools offering instruction in law was unrivaled in foreign countries. "These private schools, however, are all deficient in endowment and small in scale. They cannot possibly satisfy the realm's expectations."[39]

These were the major forms of pressure exerted by the state on the Tōkyō Senmon Gakkō during its early years, but there were other kinds of interference as well. Ōkuma mentions in his reminiscences, for example, that attempts were made to keep financiers from making loans to Ōkuma himself and to prevent part-time lecturers from giving classes at his school. The law course is said to have suffered most from the latter form of obstruction. Such interventions, however, could be counterproductive. As Ōkuma put it, "Human psychology is interesting. In a way, this kind of pressure had the effect of increasing the number of people who, out of curiosity, wanted to enter Ōkuma's school to see what it was like."[40] Thus interest in the school, rather than decreasing as a result of state pressure, actually continued to rise.

This trend is demonstrated not only by an increase in student numbers but also by the nationwide distribution of their origins. Further, it is attested by the success of the Specialist School's correspondence course, the first of its kind to be attempted in Japan. Let us first look at the increase in students in residence and in graduates between the years 1883 and 1902, when the institution was renamed Waseda University.

Year	Students	Graduates
1883	127	
1884	179	12
1885	190	67
1886	372	54
1887	386	65
1888	538	55
1889	663	165
1890	744	244
1891	517	183
1892	639	157
1893	615	183

continued

Year	Students	Graduates
1894	640	150
1895	658	163
1896	707	135
1897	736	156
1898	812	124
1899	846	166
1900	1,020	148
1901	1,547	240
1902	2,367	196

If one keeps in mind that the school began with eighty charter members this list demonstrates an almost fivefold increase in the number of students five years from the school's foundation (1887); an eightfold increase by the tenth year (1892); more than a ninefold increase by the fifteenth year (1897); and nearly a thirtyfold increase by the twentieth year (1902).[41] One cause that can be suggested for the rising interest in the school is the inauguration of a literature course centered on Tsubouchi Yūzō in September 1890. The youth of the second decade of Meiji had been captivated by politics, but that political ardor had cooled off. The new, mid-Meiji generation evidently sought their raison d'être not so much in political as in cultural values.

Since the school's foundation, its students' provenance had been characterized by nationwide diffusion, another proof of popular interest. On 27 July 1885, for example, the *Tōkyō Nichinichi shinbun* reported that the origins of the sixty-seven members of the second graduating class extended right across the nation to include Akita, Iwate, Niigata, Ishikawa, Toyama, Tokyo, Saitama, Chiba, Ibaraki, Tochigi, Aichi, Gifu, Shizuoka, Nagano, Osaka, Mie, Hiroshima, Yamaguchi, Okayama, Tottori, Ehime, Kōchi, Fukuoka, Nagasaki, Ōita, Kumamoto, and Kagoshima. The "Chart of Graduates by Metropolitan District and Prefecture" of 1901 reveals that their origins had spread by then beyond Japan's main islands to include Hokkaidō in the north and Okinawa in the south, a total of three metropolitan districts and forty-four prefectures.[42]

The consistently broad diffusion of the origins of its students is of great significance in understanding the Specialist School's character. It suggests that, unlike the Tōō Gijuku of Hirosaki or the school of the Risshisha in Tosa, this was not an institution founded on the anti-*hanbatsu* resentments of the old feudal domains that had lost out in the political struggles of the Bakumatsu and Restoration epoch. Nor was it like Keiō Gijuku, a school founded by Fukuzawa Yukichi (1835–1901) and committed to "enlightenment." Fukuzawa's school tried to nurture leaders for the new Japan regardless of political divisions and sought to transcend the dichotomy between governmental "ins" and private, out-of-power "outs" in the Meiji period, as it had that between "imperial loyalists" and "proshogunalists" during the Bakumatsu era. Rather, this broad geographical diffusion of its students suggests that the Tokyo Specialist School, as the rallying point of a nationwide political senti-ment, was a true product of the Meiji period itself. The bureaucratic government's antagonism to the rising popular-rights movement of the second decade of Meiji had forced the regime to make a decision over the appropriate form that Japan, as a modern polity, should adopt. The choice, as already indicated, was the German model. Among the great number of people who were dissatisfied with the German state system, many gave their support to the Tōkyō Senmon Gakkō.

The success of its correspondence course may be cited as a third piece of evidence that the Specialist School responded to the nationwide aspi-rations of Meiji society. This project originated from an idea of Tsuji Takayuki (d. 1887), the founder of the important periodical *Kyōiku jiron* (Educational Review). Takata Sanae kept a written record of his lectures on politics, and Tsuji suggested that Takata edit these class notes with a view to publishing them several times a month in the form of a journal. "External students will be recruited and the journal dis-tributed among them. Questions will be permitted and replies made in spaces left between the abstracts of lectures. If this were done, then the education given in the school would reach beyond its walls, and a highly acceptable state of affairs would result."[43]

The project began in 1886. Initially, it was managed in the name of the school by Yokota Keita, one of Takata's friends, and involved the publication of lectures on political economy, law, and administration. Yokota withdrew within three or four years, however, and from 1888 the correspondence course came under the school's direct management. From 1895, lectures of the course in literature were also published. Fig-ures for external students first become available in 1890, and it is un-known how many made use of this arrangement before then. The totals, combining the political economy and administration courses from 1890 to 1901 and adding the literature course from 1895, are as follows:

Year	Students
1890	1,922
1891	1,115
1892	1,286

continued

Year	Students
1893	1,780
1894	2,057
1895	2,991
1896	4,588
1897	6,260
1898	7,715
1899	10,213
1900	12,556
1901	11,784

The large numbers of students attested by these figures were "predominantly aspirants to study from remote areas, or people who were unable to attend school during the day because of their work"—in other words, working youths from cities and agricultural areas.[44] That this project succeeded in reaching a total of more than 64,200 people within a dozen years vividly demonstrates Meiji society's interest in the Tokyo Specialist School. At the same time, it also suggests that antibureaucratic sentiments were widely harbored by Meiji Japanese.

Education at the Tokyo Specialist School

The Tokyo Specialist School developed so spectacularly in so short a time because its early educational activities responded to the political sentiments prevalent among the youth of the second decade of Meiji and because its basic orientation reflected the social needs of the period. To be sure, the course in physics and chemistry that was Ōkuma Hidemaro's pet project had to be abandoned because of lack of interest after struggling on for a year and a half. Despite the first principal's painstaking efforts, no more than seven or eight students could be attracted to the course, which proved to be financially impracticable before it had produced even a single class of graduates. Evidently, "those were still the days when only the theoretical disciplines of politics and law were popular, and practical disciplines such as physics and chemistry considered remote subjects to which society paid little serious attention."[45]

In this early phase of the school's history, most of the students attempted to build careers in politics and law. Many of them were older men with some experience of the world. It is, moreover, incontrovertible that a good number were attracted by the fact that the Tōkyō Senmon Gakkō was Ōkuma Shigenobu's school and was thus identified with the opposition to the bureaucratic regime. Students were also drawn to the school by its educational aims and special pedagogical methods, most notably the intensive course-work and the use of Japanese as the medium of instruction.

Until the late 1880s, the typical student had no time to spare for a leisurely or extended student life and no choice but to seek the most rapid completion of his course of studies. Tanaka Tadaichirō (1867–1921), who matriculated in 1886, recollected that down to his time "men who were supposedly students were apt to have a wife back in the country, or to be engaged in some job and be studying law or doing economics on the side; for them, study was, so to speak, a sideline. So there were many students who were older than their teachers. . . . Only around the time when I was about to graduate [1889] did the students truly become scholars, devoting themselves fully to learning and study without any outside distractions."[46]

It was, however, not only the older men intent on finishing their studies quickly who benefited from the Specialist School's use of Japanese as the medium of instruction. This instructional method, peculiar to the institution, compensated for the inadequate linguistic skills and the limited financial means of provincial middle school graduates. In effect, it provided the opportunity for the provincials to satisfy their fascination with Tokyo and at the same time their appetite for learning. Not only was English language instruction weak in the provincial middle schools of the early 1880s, but the pupils considered having to study English a detour to learning. Few did it with any enthusiasm. For instance, we are told that "a sullen, resentful mood prevailed around that time" at Shibata Middle School in Niigata Prefecture, which sent a number of students including Ueno Kieiji and the future industrialist Konda Bunjirō (1862–1927) to the Specialist School's first entering class. "The pupils were nurtured in Chinese literary studies. There was a tendency to neglect the study of English, more because it was bothersome than because it was particularly difficult. Then, through the instigation of Mr. Ueno and others, a debate took place over whether we should study English or abandon books in the English language. In the end, representations were even made to the provincial governor."[47] In the case of the well-known publicist and politician Hayami Seiji (1868–1926), too, the motive for enrolling was the accessible, Japanese-language-based education offered by the Specialist School. In the summer of 1883, Hayami left the middle school of Hiroshima, his hometown, and went to the metropolis, where he became a member of the second entering class on the advice of a certain Morikawa, his countryman. "For me, the Tokyo Specialist School is the most congenial," Morikawa told him. "Even if you can't read the original texts, the teacher uses translations, and you can use them to study from."[48]

The practical attractions exerted by the institution on provincial youths did not pale after its early days but continued into 1884, when the course in physics and chemistry was abandoned and English converted from a supplementary into a major course, and persisted even after 1888, when the school initiated specialist education in politics and economics, law, and administration using the English language. A comparison of the totals of graduates from the English- and Japanese-based courses between the years 1886 (when the former produced its first graduates) and 1902 demonstrates this fact. The graduates of the Japanese-language course during these seventeen years number 1,837, more than double the 887 of the English course. "That the Tokyo Specialist School took the lead in using the Japanese language to transplant the difficult new knowledge and had the students study [through that medium] was a response to the requirements of our world of learning of the time. As a result, the numbers of young students coming from all parts of the country to study increased as day succeeded day, and the school precincts were suddenly filled."[49]

Indeed, the Specialist School did attract many provincial youths of an ambitious bent who wished to put their education into practice in society with the least possible delay. The use of Japanese as the medium of instruction was not, however, adopted initially for the convenience of provincial youth. Rather, the school's founders chose this method as the best way to achieve their objective of "the independence of learning." It was an epoch-making experiment in the world of Japanese higher education, and it may indeed be said to have responded to the needs of mid-Meiji society. Ōkuma's theory of the "progressive evolutionary stage of antiforeignism" was being put into practice by this method. Behind its adoption was undoubtedly a genuine pedagogical concern, broached by Ono Azusa at the school's foundation ceremony: "When foreign languages and texts are used in teaching, as they have been until now," a dichotomy is produced, because a portion of "the intellectual energies used by the students to approach the substance of their studies" must be diverted to the onerous effort to master foreign languages. Such a wasteful practice, if continued, would in the end "arrest the students' faculties to plumb the depths of learning."[50] Perhaps more to the point, however, the Tokyo Specialist School's use of Japanese was intended to contrast directly with the University of Tokyo's employment of foreign languages as the medium of instruction. Hence the method itself can be described as an expression of the Specialist School's spirit of opposition. Its early use, carried out as it was in an atmosphere of blatant state intervention, had the effect of inculcating antiregime sentiments among the students, whatever their initial motives for enrolling may have been.

Yet another profound influence on the students, one that became part of the school's tradition, was the personal inspiration of Ono Azusa. Ono died in 1886, after only a short involvement with the Tōkyō Senmon Gakkō, but he left a strong impression on it. Saitō Kazutarō, a member of the first entering class, remarks that Ono was neither the school's principal nor even a regular member of its faculty; his teaching activities there in 1882–1883 (Saitō's first year) were limited to a class in the theory of Japanese financial administration, together with extracurricular lectures on the constitution; he nonetheless "took the greatest trouble over nurturing the spirit of the students and fostering their attitude of independence." As a result, Saitō concludes, "the academic style of Waseda and the temper of its students originate entirely from [Ono's] influence. They have been passed down to today, twenty years on, and they pervade the entire nation. That is why the school is as prosperous as it is today." According to this devoted admirer, Ono had a good knowledge not only of politics, economics, and law, but also of literature. "His fondness for learning and his affection for his students surely were matchless. Especially his lofty and open-hearted disposition was, I feel, highly suited to a scholar. Thus the students' respect for him was truly quite out of the ordinary."[51]

Saitō's classmate, the Niigata entrepreneur Hiroi Hajime (1865–1934), recalls in particular the effect of Ono's extracurricular lectures on "his magnum opus," the "Outline of National Constitutions" *(Kokken hanron)*. "Such an extraordinary inspiration emanated from him that especially when he reached his conclusion, tying together loyalty to the emperor and constitutional politics, both the students and he himself would weep." Yaguchi Nuitarō also refers to the great debt he owed to Ono's "Outline": "My sole motive for deciding to enter the Tokyo Specialist School was this single book. When I read it, the school was brought to my attention for the first time, and I was unable to suppress the ambition to study politics and become a politician." Having been received by Ono with much "personal kindness," Yaguchi continues, he "became fervently involved in political debate."[52] Just as Ono's personality and thought had inspired the youths of the Ōtokai, so he continued to exert a strong influence among his students in the early years of the Specialist School.

The Ōtokai group that had joined forces with Ono at the school sought to perpetuate his ideals even after he himself had passed from the scene. Among them were three men who continued to play a vital role in the institution's history for decades after its foundation: Takata Sanae in politics and constitutional studies; Amano Tameyuki, the transmitter of Mill's economics; and the literary scholar Tsubouchi Shōyō. In offering congratulations on the opening of Waseda University in October 1902, the *Rikugō zasshi* (Cosmos) singled out these three for praise as the "animating spirits" who guaranteed "the unity among the teachers that is clearly the major element in any school's development." Hence the journal had "no hesitation in affirming that these three gentlemen have determined the school's fortunes." During its early years, however, these men were anything but blessed with financial rewards. For five or six years after the foundation of the school, Takata recollected, "I never once used cash to have a new set of clothes made, but used to wear items of dress bequeathed to me by my mother." Amano, according to Takata, was in similarly straitened circumstances: "He used always to be wearing a black silk garment, one inherited from his parents, that glistened with dirt round the collar." Nonetheless, these men pursued an energetic rivalry with the University of Tokyo. "No doubt we were pretty feckless," Amano recalled with a sense of wonder in later years. "When we came to this school and began to teach here, even Mr. Takata was only about twenty-three. We were like children. Even so, we endeavored to challenge the Imperial University."[53]

The young lecturers' educational ardor and contentment with honorable poverty captivated the hearts of their students and formed the basis for excellent teacher-pupil relationships. That such relationships were not limited to the school's early years may be deduced from a reflective passage included in *Joranshū,* an anthology of memoirs of this period. The distinguished literary critic Hasegawa Tenkei (1876–1940) recalls his own graduation from the literary course in September 1897: "So-called teachers the world over are mostly constrained by trifling regulations and ignorant of the methods of living education. So their pupils' attitude toward them, like that of peasants to officials, is usually one of outward submission and inward mockery. This is not the case with the education in our school." According to Hasegawa, his instructors' learning was distinguished by "extensive citation of facts and penetrating criticism," and "minute and painstaking explanation" was the hallmark of their teaching. "What greater good fortune could we have had? But this great good fortune was not ours alone. Ought it not be described as pedagogy's great good fortune in our nation?"[54]

A free educational atmosphere pervaded the school, its classrooms, and its dormitories. Indeed, the newspaperman and Tokyo municipal official Miyagawa Tetsujirō (1868–1919) went so far as to describe it as "freedom of a type beyond freedom itself, education that was indulgent almost to the point of selfishness and willfulness."[55] The students, however, considered this freedom to be the precondition for "the independence of learning." The personal and intellectual influence of Ono Azusa, no less than the feelings of trust inspired by the young lecturers in their students, had imbued those enrolled in the school with the spirit of opposition. These men were keenly sensitive to the antagonism between their school and the power of the state, as Miyagawa testifies:[56]

> The Tōkyō Senmon Gakkō was hated by the government of the time. It was loathed by the world of academic cliques. It was shunned by the world of political parties of a different direction. From whatever angle one looked, as much as setting foot in that school appeared to be unhelpful to [a man's] interests. There were quite a few scholars [in Japan] at the time; as a result of such considerations, however, that species naturally wouldn't think of coming here. Such were the times in which we were nourished. . . . We finished our studies, after a fashion, but we were in constant opposition to the adverse tide of society and naturally conceived the notion that we were incompatible with the style of the times. Consequently, in everything that we did, revolutionary ideas came first, and we constantly fantasized on the kind of success gained by those who, when confronted with Fortune, manage to vault in a single bound from student to minister or councillor.

According to the reminiscences of other graduates from these early years, the intensity of their political consciousness was constantly manifested in critical speeches at oratorical and athletic meetings and frequently led to skirmishes with the police. Nor was it only the students of the politics course who felt this way. Even among the specialists in jurisprudence, many were more interested in politics than in the study of law.[57]

The prevalence of these attitudes among the students reflected their acceptance of their school's ideal, "the independence of learning." It was natural, therefore, that they should adopt a strongly hostile posture to government interference in learning when the Ministry of Education sought to impose its fiat on their institution.

We have already encountered evidence of that ministry's view that private law schools must be put under control; recall the extramural law course established at the University of Tokyo. In August 1886, immediately after this extramural course had been transferred to the administration of the Ministry of Justice, the Ministry of Education promulgated the "Regulations for the Special Direction of Private Law Schools," designed for the oversight of all such schools in the Tokyo Metropolitan District. Specifically, they placed the private law schools under the direction of the president of the Imperial University, prescribing that he "shall select a delegate from the staff of the Imperial University's College of Law and have him supervise the said schools both in ordinary times and during examinations" (Article 3). As a result, the Tokyo Specialist School was placed under the supervision of Assistant Professor Hijikata Yasushi (1859–1939) of the College of Law. The regulations further stipulated censorship of the content of instruction, prescribing that "the heads of the said private law schools must send the monthly class schedule to the president of the Imperial University by the third day of every month" (Article 4). The president had the right to "advise the heads of the said private law schools regarding the revision of their curricula and methods of instruction on the basis of the report submitted by his delegate" (Article 8).[58]

The object of these controls was the law schools. For the time being, there was felt to be no need, even in the case of the Specialist School, for direction to be imposed on the course in politics and economics. In May 1888, however, the Ministry of Education abandoned this system and promulgated new "Regulations for Special Authorized Schools," placing them under its own immediate supervision. Not only law but the politics and economics course, too, henceforward required approval. The former applied. So did the course in administration that was newly instituted in June of that year, which was duly granted approval under the revised name of the Second Course in Law.[59] Politics and economics, however, held out against the new regulations.

The latter course attempted to preserve the freedom of education in political science, even to the point of sacrificing the privilege of draft exemption for its students. Its tough stand is to be attributed to a broad movement of opposition among the students. The school authorities were receptive to this movement, reflecting as it did their institution's traditional spirit of opposition to government interference. Namiki Kakutarō, the student at the center of the movement against authorization, recalls the incident thus:[60]

> I was in No. 18 of the Second Dormitory of the Tōkyō Senmon Gakkō, had just finished reading my textbook, and was about to extinguish the light when the late Mr. Itō Chōroku came into my room. He had heard, he said, that in May 1888 the Ministry of Education had drawn up Regulation No. 3, something called "Regulations for Special Authorized Schools," to the effect that all law schools were to vie for authorized status, and that our Tōkyō Senmon Gakkō, too, would be under the control of these regulations. If indeed the situation was as he said, I told him, the purpose of our school's foundation would be utterly vitiated. Ours may be a relatively new school; since it has virtually assumed for itself the functions of a private university, however, it would be quite unacceptable for it to submit to official direction and become a "cradle for bureau-

crats" or anything of the sort. We should therefore consult further on this matter, et cetera. The next day, after the end of classes, Horigoe Kansuke, Tanaka Tadaichirō, . . . and other gentlemen met in the reception room of the dormitory, and the upshot after a very thorough discussion was, first, that we selected a representative and stated our sentiments to the school authorities and, second, that we elected a committee and embarked on a course of calling on all the newspapers and journals and the members of the School Council to enlist their aid.

It would appear that the school's educational activities and its teachers' combative attitude raised the students' political awareness. For a while, as Miyagawa Tetsujirō noted, that awareness produced among them the ambition to become creative politicians aspiring to high office. A national assembly was about to be established. Facing that prospect, and deeply influenced by English political thought as they were, they chose the path of debate concerning constitutional issues, rather than radical or revolutionary political action.

According to the alumni association's register for 1890, the careers chosen by graduates of the Specialist School in its early years were as follows: 50 newspaper or journal reporters; 30 company employees; 30 teachers; about 20 higher officials; more than 10 members of metropolitan or prefectural assemblies; more than 10 attorneys or notaries public; and several members of the Diet. The total of some 160 represents roughly 40 percent of the total of 418 graduates until 1889. The remaining 60 percent most likely followed their family occupations. This evidence shows that most graduates found their way into life outside officialdom, with the press as their most popular choice. Furthermore, the majority seem to have taken work in the provinces or to have returned to their villages and to agriculture. That they went into lay rather than official life no doubt followed naturally from the spirit of opposition with which they had been imbued at the school, and that more of them went to the provinces than stayed in the metropolis was surely a consequence of the positive career guidance they received from the school authorities. The advice Takata Sanae gave to the graduates in his valedictory speech of July 1891 is typical: "First, at all costs avoid becoming officials. There is an overabundance of talent in officialdom; should a reform of the administrative system be carried out, you will find yourselves unable to make careers there. In private life, however, there is plenty of room for achievement. Second, by all means go to the provinces. As a result of the centralization of knowledge that we see before us in our country, we are at risk of contracting a national congestion of the brain. Hence newcomers should fan out into all the provinces, settle down, and make it their business to disseminate knowledge there."[61]

This pattern of provincial careers became well established. As the Specialist School observed its fifteenth anniversary in 1897, Provost Ichishima Kenkichi found eminent cause for self-congratulation in the nationwide distribution of the alumni. The school had produced a total of 1,771 graduates since awarding its first diplomas in 1884, and they had spread all over Japan, "from the corners of Hokkaidō in the north to the tip of Kyushu in the south." Even the neighbor country, Korea, was represented by a member of the current graduating class. Ichishima did not have information regarding the careers chosen by each and every one of the graduates, but his partial list accounted for 134 bank employees; 125 journalists; 95 judicial officials and attorneys; 77 administrative officials; and 55 educators. Beyond that, he could not be specific, save for noting that there were "quite a few" members of the two houses of the Diet, graduates of the Imperial University, and alumni of foreign universities. "The careers of our graduates are varied and multifarious," Ichishima concluded. "It would not be idle self-praise on the part of this school to say that they have become a major force in the middle ranks of society everywhere they are to be found. It is a reality recognized by everyone who travels over the country."[62]

In Ichishima's summary, nonofficial continue to predominate over official careers. It is important to note, however, that the number of those going into the business world has overtaken that of entrants into journalism. Why were the positions of the press and business reversed? This development may be interpreted to reflect the development of domestic capitalism after the Sino-Japanese War of 1894–1895. The explanation may also be that concern with economic and cultural activities increased in general from the middle 1890s and that the attitude of overt, direct political opposition found among the graduates of the early years was filtered through a broader spectrum of values and transformed into less explicitly political forms of opposition. The establishment of a literature course in 1890 offered talented men new access to careers in education (hence the evident increase of graduates going into that field). That the establishment of a commerce course should have been placed on the agenda of the school authorities in 1891—though nothing came of the proposal just then—seems further to have intensified this general trend.

Above all, however, this phenomenon reflects the efficacy of an education that sought to "unite theory and practice." The Specialist School's teachers had striven to exemplify this ideal, one of their institution's principal educational goals since its foundation, by engaging themselves in various endeavors beyond the campus walls. Takata and Amano, for instance, had undertaken such activities as editing and publishing the *Chūō gakujutsu zasshi* (Central Learned Journal; started in February 1886) and the *Nihon rizai zasshi* (Economic Journal of Japan; started in February 1890); they had involved themselves with the *Yomiuri shinbun* and the *Chōya shinbun*; when the national assembly was convened, they became members. In a speech he gave at the opening ceremony of Waseda University, Amano explained his motivation by stressing his lifelong effort to stay abreast of Japanese actualities. That, he maintained, was the reason he entered the Diet and took employment with the *Chōya shinbun*; he had no intention of becoming a politician or a newspaper man. "I did these things in order to expose myself to social realities."[63] In due time, the teachers' endeavors influenced the students in the same direction, and the ideal of the unity of theory and practice came to have a real effect even in the economic sphere.

Students were encouraged in the pursuit of economic objectives; they were freed of the hold of narrowly political values that had gripped them in the second decade of Meiji. Miura Tetsutarō, a student of the politics and economics course who attended Amano's lectures in 1902, notes how stimulated he was "as the lectures proceeded and the theories of private profit and free competition were gradually elucidated. As one who had started his studies in an academy of Chinese learning that stressed 'putting the Way into practice and bequeathing a name to posterity,' I was filled with wonder at the scope of the argument." Miura's previous interest in constitutional theory vanished; he became "dedicated to emulating Professor Amano."[64] Miura was not alone in setting aside his original ambitions for the sake of "private profit and free competition." Business was the most popular career among the Specialist School's graduates in 1897; in 1901 it was again first, with 97 entrants as against 28 for the press. The popularity of business remained preeminent into the 1900s, and the stability of this pattern of career selection underlay the establishment of the long-pending commerce course in April 1903.

According to a chart included in a volume commemorating the thirtieth anniversary of Waseda University's foundation, the total number of graduates from the commerce course between 1907 (when the first class obtained their degrees) and 1913 was 2,222. The comparative figures for graduates from other courses during the same period are 804 from literature, 733 from politics and economics, and 238 from law.[65] The overwhelming numerical superiority of commerce clearly reveals the direction in which the Tokyo Specialist School and Waseda University steered most of their talent. Because of the relative brevity of the school's history, however, most of the graduates who went into the business world—unlike their counterparts with Keiō or Hitotsubashi backgrounds—had, as of that time, been unable to achieve positions of leadership or power and had had to content themselves with the status of middle-ranking salaried employees. Masuda Giichi (1869–1949), a 1895 graduate, confessed in 1902 that "we Waseda graduates . . . are not yet as successful in establishing influence in the business world as we have been in the world of the press." Only twenty years had passed from the school's foundation. "Our graduates are still young. It is not easy to enter the world of business and attain a pivotal position at a single jump."[66]

Masuda found consolation, however, in the "truly remarkable fact" that his fellow alumni had established themselves firmly in positions of influence in the economic sections of journals and newspapers. Evidently, the shift in values within the school that encouraged men to enter the business world also exerted an important influence on those who entered the press. From the late 1890s onward, journalists of Specialist School origin drifted away from political commentary and came to criticize state economic policy from the point of view of the liberal economics taught by Amano. "There is scarcely one among the Tokyo metropolitan and national newspaper companies that does not have an old boy of our school on its staff," Masuda noted, "and these old boys put forward economic theories of a particular character." As for journals, the *Tōyō Keizai shinpō* (Oriental Economist), *Tōkyō Keizai zasshi* (Tokyo Economic Journal), *Taiyō* (Sun), *Taiheiyō* (Pacific), *Ginkō tsūshinroku* (Bank Correspondent), and *Jitsugyō no Nihon* (Business Japan) "are all mainly produced by Waseda old boys." In short, "all the journals viewed in the economic world as trustworthy and valuable are, it is no exaggeration to say, managed by Waseda men."[67]

In the middle of the 1890s, therefore, student interests shifted from political to economic priorities. The business world and the economic press became popular career choices. This tendency grew increasingly stronger with the establishment of the Japanese capitalist system after the Sino-Japanese War. Certainly, the tense antagonism toward state control that had characterized the school's early years was no longer conspicuous. This does not, however, signify the decline of attitudes of opposition. On the contrary, state economic policy came to be criticized from the point of view of English liberal economic theory, something that was surely appropriate for a period that witnessed the rise of capitalism. Attitudes of opposition continued to be supported by English values, which were invoked to protect autonomy and freedom and to plead their superiority over state control. Masuda Giichi rejoiced at the

consistency of Waseda men's views: "They are always demolishing interventionist policies and promoting independent, autonomous approaches.
. . . Waseda alumni do not advocate an extreme free trade theory, but
they believe nonetheless that it is a misguided policy for the state to
adopt a recklessly interventionist and protectionist trade policy, crush-
ing the spirit of freedom and autonomy. . . . I do not know how you
gentlemen may feel, but Waseda men are indifferent to personal considerations. They do not play sycophant to men of influence. They strive to
keep their arguments impartial."[68]

To be sure, the attitude of antagonism to state power that had prevailed in the early years of the Tokyo Specialist School was diluted in
the 1890s. The spirit of opposition assumed an economic rather than a
political coloring. Finally, from around 1897, that spirit became linked
to a new educational objective, the ideal of a "model citizenry." This
ideal was to be given a special emphasis after the school was reconstituted as Waseda University in 1902. In this development it is possible to
see how the original spirit of opposition lost something of its explicitly
political orientation and became linked to a more generalized, autonomous moral awareness. This attitude achieved ascendency among the
middle classes charged with the development of the modern elements in
the Meiji state, that is, its constitutional and capitalist economic systems. In its turn, it confronted the nonmodern or bureaucratic values
that inhered in the Meiji state. Hence the ideal of the model citizenry
deserves some additional discussion.

Waseda University and the Model Citizenry

In both the political and the educational fields, a relaxation may be
observed in the relationship between the Tokyo Specialist School and
the regime from the middle of the 1890s. On the educational side, the
problematic "Regulations for Special Authorized Schools" that had
provoked a student opposition movement were abandoned in November 1893, and students in the politics and economics course became eli-
gible for draft deferments. In December of the same year, the school
gained the justice minister's accreditation under the "Regulations for
the Selection of Judges and Public Prosecutors." The literary course was
modified in accordance with the "Regulations for Licensing Teachers in
Private Schools" in 1898. This modification led to official approval,
granted on 7 July that year, of the Specialist School's qualifications to
train middle school teachers, a privilege previously extended only to
governmental higher institutes for teacher training. Particularly symbolic was the introduction of German law, previously rejected as the

fountainhead of bureaucratic absolutism. It was adopted into the law curriculum simultaneously with the school's change to university status in 1902. "It was recognized that the legal system of our country was chiefly adapted from the German tradition. Hence the study of German law was perceived to be a necessity, and courses in the study of German law in the original texts were established."[69]

On the political side, Ōkuma became foreign minister in the Matsu-kata cabinet of 1896, thus becoming identified with the regime whose influence on education he had earlier been so eager to repudiate. The Specialist School used his position as an opportunity to formulate plans for expansion. Then, in September 1898, the Constitutional party (Kenseitō) cabinet was set up with Ōkuma as its prime minister. Once more, the Specialist School used its founder's rise to political promi-nence as the opportunity for further expansion. As is well known, the Ōkuma-Itagaki cabinet was short-lived because of dissension between elements of the former Reform and Liberal parties in its ranks. None-theless, the very fact of the cabinet's formation encouraged the school authorities in the belief that as long as political conditions were favor-able, the possibility of establishing permanent constitutional govern-ment within the Meiji state was within reach. Even after Ōkuma was relieved of his premiership in November 1898, he was permitted to retain the ceremonial privileges of his former office, and this gesture contributed to the rapid dissolution of the antagonism between the school and the regime.

As though to underline the disappearance of this traditional antago-nism, none other than Itō Hirobumi, Ōkuma's former adversary in the Political Crisis of 1881, on the day of the festive opening of the new Waseda University guaranteed the school's political neutrality:[70]

> Many adopt the mistaken view that attempts are being made to make the Tōkyō Senmon Gakkō into an instrument for the expansion of the politi-cal parties. I judge this to be an underestimation of Count Ōkuma's com-petence. Count Ōkuma is enthusiastic about both politics and education, but he is of course mindful of the separation between them. He places the tasks of school education outside politics. It is to be clearly recognized that he has emphatically rejected the device of abusing educational insti-tutions as tools for the expansion of party power. Discerning people in society may understand this, but most others have failed to do so. I am an outsider. An outsider may be unprejudiced, which compels me to make this unequivocal statement to the world.

How did the recognition of the school's neutrality affect the "indepen-dence of learning"—the founding ideal of the school—and the spirit of opposition that informed it? Two points are to be made. First, as the antagonism between the school and the regime vanished, the spirit of opposition was diluted and lost its formerly pronounced political coloration. Second, there resulted an intensified moral consciousness among those who studied at the school.

The first point is illustrated by the fact that the raison d'être of this school, now restyled Waseda University, was no longer, as formerly, to "challenge the Imperial University" and thus implicitly to oppose state education. Rather, a symbiotic relationship would be sought. The rationale presented by Takata at Waseda's opening ceremony was that "arrangements for the state institutions of higher learning have, for various reasons, remained incomplete." In this situation, "albeit a private university, we would like to make an effort to render a little assistance to state education." Despite this offer of assistance, the school was too proud to attempt to replicate the bureaucratic values of the Imperial University within its own walls. Rather, Takata took the position that "we see no reason why newly founded schools should necessarily be on the same scale or share the same organization as established ones."[71]

Consistently with this declaration, Waseda exhibited three characteristics not to be found in the Imperial University. First, Waseda inherited the Specialist School's principle of intensive education and made the preparatory course for university a year and a half shorter than was the case in government high schools. Second, it adhered to the Specialist School's educational policy of the "unity of theory and practice," taking the view that "we should like, as far as possible, to make this a practical university."[72] Third, it avowed that humanistic education—which was considered, along with specialist education, to be the school's objective—should envisage what Takata referred to as a "model citizenry."

These characteristics all reflected Waseda's critical attitude toward the bureaucratic values of official learning. Takata put it as follows in the opening ceremony: "I wonder if, after all, it is not appropriate for a university to pursue the general policy of avoiding so-called examination-based education as far as possible, and rather to build a model citizenry. I feel particularly that the concept of building a model citizenry implies that the object of a university is to nurture human beings."[73] That concept was patterned after the gentleman's education of England, which was founded, as Takata saw it, on "the principle that education is for self-discipline, for self-mastery. It is for producing gentlemen, for giving birth to patriots."[74] Takata was critical of the examination-centered Meiji state education system, in which middle and higher education were ultimately linked to the recruitment of bureaucrats. Education, as he expressed it on another occasion, concerned itself rather with "those who would lead the ordinary people." The "model citizenry," therefore, was clearly not made up of bureaucrats who controlled the people by power. Rather, they were outstandingly well-educated human beings who constituted models for the guidance of the populace. The moral basis at the center of their personalities, furthermore, was to be sought in a spirit of independence, and latent in it was precisely that spirit of opposition which had previously had a political dimension. Moreover, the education of this model citizenry was not a conventional one, for it emphasized civic values that enabled men to "discharge their duties as citizens in today's complicated constitutional polity."[75]

Tsubouchi Shōyō expounded the model citizenry from the point of view of the individual student's character formation. In October 1899 he addressed freshmen on the subject of "the academic style of the Tokyo Specialist School." Takata's notion of the education of a model citizenry was, Tsubouchi said, certainly what the school aspired to achieve. He, however, would like to elaborate on its significance in his own fashion, and his starting point was the school's founding ideal, "the independence of learning." As Tsubouchi saw it, this ideal was the moral foundation for the establishment of the individual student's autonomy: "Because ours is a school born with an emphasis on independence, it seems that even if no one teaches it, the spirit of independence in thought and action has come to be permanently imbued in our students and everyone connected with the school. It would appear that it has become an ideal [among us] to proceed through life with this kind of independence."[76]

In the Waseda academic style described by Tsubouchi, the tone of "the independence of learning" was no longer political. Instead of a spirit of political opposition, a spirit of "independence in thought and action" was posited as the basic principle of conduct. A number of virtues associated with this principle were emphasized as contributing to the personality formation of those who studied at the school. Among them were "self-reliance and self-confidence," defined as "the so-called self-help that places its reliance in the self and does not borrow the strength of others"; "introspection and self-reproach," the mental function that "reflects on oneself, censures oneself, and reproaches oneself first"; and "self-regulation and self-cultivation," the moral quality that "regulates first the self and nourishes one's own strength." These virtues in turn produced an attitude that "honored spirit more than ceremony," an "egalitarianism" or "democracy" that emphasized a universal spiritual equality, and "world-encompassing vision" that extended the principle of equality internationally. As a result, so Tsubouchi claimed, "progressive, idealistic" mores were engendered naturally. Most important were "self-reliance and self-confidence" and their reverse side, "introspection and self-reproach."

The mood produced in the Specialist School by these values was not at all a "passing fancy" or an "affectation," Tsubouchi asserted. "It has penetrated more deeply than one might think into the minds of the leading men connected with this school." He believed that it "must stem entirely from an attitude of self-reliance, self-reproach, and autonomy in all things." In other schools, Tsubouchi thought, "there may exist some students who possess splendid ideas, but many of them are apt to collapse or come to grief halfway. Ultimately, this is because they lack autonomy. If they had an attitude of self-reproach, even if they suffered a thousand reverses, they would never bear resentment against others, since they would attribute those setbacks to their own personal inadequacies." Those associated with "this school," however, formed a distinct contrast. "As befits men who reproach themselves, they do not indulge in resenting the world or blaming others. Their disposition is such that if they once blunder over something, their mood is of ever greater vigor."[77]

Thus Tsubouchi identified the model citizenry as individuals possessed of strong, introspective, and autonomous personalities who would not flinch even in the face of overwhelming adversity. He perpetuated the spirit of opposition that had originally lain at the root of this school's ideal of the "independence of learning," but did so in the altered form of the individual autonomy of a modern citizenry.

If Tsubouchi's model citizenry was defined in terms of the development of individual character, Takata Sanae visualized his model Waseda student as a "superior citizen," that is, as a leader in society. "Superior citizens," in Takata's view, were "political animals by natural disposition" and possessed an awareness that they were not simply individuals but "members of a polity along with bearing personal and domestic duties."[78] In other words, they were none other than cultivated modern citizens with a grasp of constitutional values, personages whose mission it was to secure the accurate reflection of the citizens' political will in elections. This objective, however, was no longer to be pursued through confrontations with the regime. On the contrary, it was to be attained through an understanding of the harmony between "individualism and statism." Takata believed that "if the nation's politics are sound, one's own business will prosper. If they are unsound, the business will decline and one's profits will diminish. The spread of the view that there is no conflict of interest between the state and oneself is, I believe, an excellent thing. If this idea continues developing gradually, it will naturally be followed by the notion that the country is one's own property and consequently deserves one's utmost devotion. This is the true spirit of constitutional politics."[79] Takata further wrote, " 'When the politics of the country are in confusion, the individual's circumstances deteriorate' and 'When the state is unstable, the individual's family is no longer safe.' I should like everyone to become aware of these [maxims] and at least manage to vote seriously. If the populace does not take its electoral duties seriously, constitutional politics are doomed."[80]

Takata remained true to the English beliefs that he had earlier espoused. His ideal polity was one where constitutional politics were implemented on the basis of proper elections. The antagonism between citizenry and state should be resolved and harmony between the two achieved thereby. Any such antagonism, together with any irrational politics that did not reflect the popular will, should accordingly have become morally unacceptable and disappeared, once a constitution had been promulgated and a national assembly convened in Japan.

Notwithstanding, nearly twenty years after the promulgation of the constitution, Takata was obliged to concede that "there persist many unconstitutional phenomena too offensive to behold with one's eyes," of which "the rampancy of *genrō* (elder statesmen) politicians and the corruption of the Imperial Diet" were prime examples. The prevalence of such abuses was "needless to say caused by deficiencies in the constitutional thinking of the Japanese," that is, in the people's political consciousness. Hence Takata looked to the effective education of a model citizenry in constitutional values. That citizenry, and especially the graduates of Waseda, would play a role in bringing enlightenment and progress to a political consciousness still so backward as to deserve being called a hotbed of unconstitutional phenomena. "When a country has a model and exemplary citizenry, possesses healthy political thought, and accumulates a constitutional spirit to guide its populace, that country prospers. If it lacks these things, it declines. This is an inevitable state of affairs. I am hoping beyond hope that the eight thousand students of Waseda Academy, when they take their places in the world on completion of their studies, will make [constituting] this model and exemplary citizenry their responsibility."[81]

Takata's model citizenry was thus premised on an anticipated harmony between the individual and the state within the framework of a constitutional polity. We witness here the fading away of the antagonism against the regime that had been so much a part of the Specialist School's earlier spirit of opposition. Instead, Takata posited an intimate and harmonious relationship between the life of individuals and the politics of the state. The model citizenry was to teach the populace political responsibility and inform it of the correct approach to elections. It was to be nothing less than the people's political teachers.

The Tokyo Specialist School's political posture of opposition had been transmuted over time into an educational concern. The spirit of independence invoked by Tsubouchi now formed the spiritual backbone that supported the individual within his harmonious relationship with the state. Thus the tension that had characterized the institution's early years was resolved. Moreover, a positive value was now attributed to private, individual, and free economic activity. Waseda had turned its energies to educating a model citizenry that was to enlighten the populace concerning the legal and ethical basis of a private, individual, and free citizen's life.

Waseda's ideal of a model citizenry was founded on the pattern of the English gentleman and embodied English values. Its moral basis, as Tsubouchi indicated, was sought in the autonomous individual's consciousness of moral responsibility, his "independence of thought and action," and his "introspection and self-examination." Its legal basis rested in the harmony between the individual and a state that accepted the legitimacy of private, individual interests, a position consonant with English constitutional thought. Having identified for itself a mission not discharged by its old state-sponsored competitor—to educate teachers of the populace—Waseda in the late Meiji era attained an eminence that rivaled that of the Imperial University.

8
Thought and Education in the Late Meiji Era

Translated by J. Dusenbury

Ever since Minister of Education Mori Arinori fashioned its institutional and intellectual foundations in 1886, Meiji education moved steadfastly from a nationalistic position toward twin goals—the development of national self-consciousness among the populace and the fostering of talent to serve the nation. For the rest of the Meiji era, no other educational viewpoint developed that might have presented a fundamental challenge to this orientation, and no political or social forces arose that might have supported such a challenge. The uncontested dominance of this nationalistic perspective owed little to the Imperial Rescript on Education. Rather, it rested on the widely held perception of Japan's precarious position in international society. Diverse political and social interests expressed their approval of this orientation, but their assent did not go beyond agreement with the basic aims of the government's educational policy. It indicated neither a willingness to hew to the line of the Education Ministry's particular policies nor an unconditional acceptance of the existing educational system.

Indeed, the development of education in the latter part of the Meiji era can in large part be understood in terms of the interplay between popular educational movements and government educational policy. Supported by prevailing currents of social thought, those movements produced critiques both of the substantive content of public education and of specific educational initiatives pursued by the government. Revisions were gradually made in response to these criticisms. This evolution was related to broader movements in the intellectual world. Changes occurred in the meaning of concepts that were important in the formation of images of state and society—concepts such as nationalism, globalism, and individualism. This chapter will explore those changes through the course of the Sino-Japanese and the Russo-Japanese wars and will examine how they affected attitudes toward education.

From the Promulgation of the Constitution to the Sino-Japanese War

The Imperial Constitution, promulgated in 1889, created for Japan a legal order appropriate to a modern state. Japan's awareness of itself as a nation had yet to mature, however, making the preservation of its dignity problematic both at home and abroad. Almost from the beginning of its existence, the Meiji government, moved by righteous indignation, had been engaged in mapping out plans for the revision of the unequal treaties that had been foisted upon Japan by foreign powers. By the end of 1878, it had unveiled a policy of Europeanization that sought to resolve this problem by making those powers aware of the degree to which Japan was becoming Westernized. Internally, the government anticipated the confusion that the import of foreign culture and the introduction of parliamentary politics would bring to the social order and sought to reduce the potential adverse effect of those changes by promulgating the Imperial Rescript on Education in 1890. The rescript's authoritative aura and all-embracing character, the government hoped, would create a national ideal for education and unify the people's hearts and minds. Because it was too abstract, however, the rescript was inherently unable to bring meaningful, internal unity to educational thought. Not only did it draw the intellectual world into a disruptive dispute with Christians, but it also brought on an abuse of authority, as the government could exercise control over education formally and externally by the mere fact of invoking the rescript's imperial aura.

What were the major intellectual influences on the world of education during the third decade of the Meiji era (1868–1912)? The most important were the doctrine of a citizen-centered society built upon the common man *(heiminshugi)*, which was propounded by Tokutomi Sohō (1863–1957); the cultural nationalism *(kokusuishugi)* of Kuga Katsunan (1857–1907) and Miyake Setsurei (1860–1945); and a conservative, traditional style of thought that sought its foundations in the imperial rescript and opposed both Christianity and the "democratic" orientation of Tokutomi. These schools of thought appeared at the end of the 1880s, galvanized by distaste for the Europeanization promoted by the government as a means of bringing about treaty revision. Their objective was to develop an alternative ideal for state and people, one grounded in Japanese history and directed toward the realities of the international situation in which Japan found itself. They sought to overcome the tendency toward utilitarianism that had been conspicuous ever since the epoch of "civilization and enlightenment" *(bunmei kaika)* of the early Meiji era, and they opposed the universalistic, rationalistic tendencies of the schools that advocated the adoption of Western cultural norms *(keimō).*

Tokutomi Sohō made his entry on the intellectual scene with his essay "The Future Japan" *(Shōrai no Nihon)* in 1886. The following year, in continued pursuit of his vision of a national state that rested on the strength of the common people, he ushered in the third decade of Meiji thought with the publication of the journal *Kokumin no tomo* (The Nation's Friend). The first issue of this magazine sold thousands of copies overnight. In the making of the new Japan, Tokutomi expected much from the dynamism of youth. At the same time, following Spencer's evolutionary theory of social development and the economics of the Manchester school, he discovered the emergence of industrial society —a society upheld by the common people *(heimin),* that is, the citizens *(shimin).* What Tokutomi had in mind when he spoke of the common people was nothing less than a new nation *(kokumin).* At this time, however, his thought had a radical element that was not necessarily compatible with "the nation" as envisaged by authoritarian nationalism *(kokkashugi)* or those who saw it in terms of a unique Japanese cultural essence.

The radical character of Tokutomi's thought, however, was not of the abstract, "enlightenment" variety. True to its period, it had its origins in the hard realities of Japan's predicament and in a concrete appreciation of history. Tokutomi recognized only too well the pressure that Western powers were bringing to bear on Asia. "What lies ahead for us," he asked, "in a world where enlightened peoples use violence and tyranny to destroy barbarians?"[1] Moreover, he had a keen perception of changes in Japanese society, one that indicates he was not simply merchandising Spencerian ideas.[2] For instance, he fully understood the leadership role played by a group of wealthy farmers and local officials (including his father) in his native Kumamoto. This group, known under the name of the Practical Learning party (Jitsugakutō), were students of Yokoi Shōnan (1809–1869) who put their personal experience in local government to use in the postrestoration administration of Kumamoto Prefecture. They provided a major part of the inspiration for Tokutomi's idea of the common man.

Tokutomi's thought, relying as it did on Spencer and the Manchester school, provided a global perspective on the course of human development. At the same time, his writings presented the Japanese experience as a concrete basis for that development. This gave them a freshness born of anticipating the Japan of the future and helps explain why Tokutomi appealed to so many people.

Tokutomi played no small role in the realm of education during this period. He was critical both of the revival of Confucianism advocated by contemporary traditionalists and of syncretistic approaches to Eastern and Western morality. He also rejected the program laid down by the Education Order (Gakusei) of 1872, considering it to be one-sided, overly intellectualized, and focused simply on interpreting the new civilization of the West. Sohō believed that compulsory education was the foundation of constitutional government. It should accordingly be rooted in the nature of humanity itself, in what he called human education *(ningen kyōiku),* because the elementary school was "a model for the society of the common man *(heimin shakai)."*[3] To this end, moral education should "extract a unified set of moral concepts from the world's ethical systems and adapt them to the sensibilities of our country."[4] The goal was to "create a people with fidelity to principle, full of the spirit of independence and self-respect, a bold, diligent, straightforward, tenacious people that holds its ground and does not readily submit to others." The proper means to that end was learning by doing *(rōsaku kyōiku),* which taught "self-reliance and self-sufficiency" through "unstinting application of mind and body" to specific projects. Learning by doing lay at the heart of Tokutomi's educational theory. It was education for the whole person. It had "unlimited potential for the mental, moral, and physical development of the child."[5] This theory, aiming as it did at nurturing a constitutional people, won the support of progressive intellectuals after the Sino-Japanese War of 1894–1895. It was an intellectual harbinger, one that stimulated social criticism of the increasing uniformity, rigidity, and formality of Japanese education as it was developing under bureaucratic leadership.

Miyake Setsurei and Kuga Katsunan were, like Tokutomi Sohō, both members of the younger generation. They understood Western thought and were familiar with world affairs. Their doctrine of cultural nationalism focused on the Japanese people as the autonomous bearers of a unique and relatively homogenous culture. Setsurei's thought took its departure from the notion that "a nation must develop its own positions in both foreign and domestic affairs,"[6] while Katsunan's doctrine of "bringing the liberty and happiness of the Japanese people to fruition" originated in the "principle of nationality." Each sought to rediscover the peculiar worth of the Japanese people and find a new course to Japan's future. As Katsunan put it, "We are not conservatives; we are progressives."[7] Kuga Katsunan, the political theorist, sought to link the moral authority of the emperor with constitutional government to check the pursuit of private interests by the bureaucracy and the political parties. Miyake Setsurei spoke of rediscovering the cultural creativity of the Japanese people.

This is not the place for a detailed discussion of these two men and their writings. Since Miyake Setsurei continued to be a critic of education throughout the Meiji and Taishō periods, however, attention ought to be directed to his theory of the preservation of the national essence *(kokusui hozon ron)*. It would be a mistake to assume that this doctrine amounted to hidebound traditionalism. On the contrary, it presupposed a global field of vision. Miyake stressed the interrelationship between the nation and the world, as befitted a man trained in Western philosophy. "To devote oneself to one's country is to devote oneself to the world," he maintained. "To exalt the special characteristics of one's people is to nurture the human race."[8] His thought was directed toward the realization of the universal human ideals of truth, goodness, and beauty. Its distinctive feature was its emphasis on the unique activities of each individual and nation as a means of accomplishing this goal. This idea was undergirt by nothing less than an organic theory of the cosmos, which he set forth in "My View of the World" *(Gakan shōkei)* in 1892 and "The Universe" *(Uchū)* in 1909.

In Setsurei's view, the world, the nation, and the individual were all cells in the great organism that was the universe. Just as every one of the cells that make up an organism has its own individual role, Setsurei maintained, each of the individuals that constitute the nation and each of the nations that form the world has a particular function and capacity. The free development of the capacities of these national and individual cells promotes the evolution of world culture and leads toward the future realization of truth, goodness, and beauty. His call for the freedom of individuals and nations as a means of furthering human capacities made Setsurei an effective critic of the Japanese educational system's growing rigidity, a trend that began to manifest itself with the Sino-Japanese War and the fixing of the organizational patterns of state and society that accompanied Japan's modernization.

The schools of conservative, traditionalist thought arose chiefly in reaction to the revival of Christianity that accompanied the Europeanization policy adopted by the government at the end of the 1870s. As the assassination of Mori Arinori (b. 1847) in 1889 suggests, the traditionalists saw themselves as being engaged in a struggle to destroy evil in the name of righteousness. The Kokkyō Daidōsha (Great Way of National Teaching Society) of Torio Koyata (1847–1905) and Kawai Kiyomaru (1848–1917) may be mentioned as a prime example of this reactionary phenomenon, as can the Yuishin Gakkai (Society for the Study of the Divine Will) associated with Shinto priests. But even the kinder and gentler conservatism of the Nihon Kōdōkai, the Japanese Association for Spreading the Way that Nishimura Shigeki (1828–1902) brought into being in 1887, sought the wellspring of traditional moral values in Shinto, Buddhism, and Confucianism and brandished the slogan of Japan's national polity *(kokutai)* to challenge the proponents of Europeanization.

The Shinto traditionalists were known as the Takamagahara-ha (Abode of the Gods faction), and the younger generation of intellectuals who had grown up breathing the fresh air of Meiji would have nothing to do with them.[9] The traditionalists attacked Uchimura Kanzō (1861–1930), a Christian teacher at the First Higher Middle School in Tokyo, for his alleged show of disrespect toward the emperor in 1891, and they denounced Professor Kume Kunitake (1839–1931) of the Imperial University for daring to suggest that "Shinto Is an Outmoded Custom of Worshiping Heaven" in the title of a historical study that he had published that same year.[10] They did so in the name of the Imperial Rescript on Education and the cause of unifying the nation's morals. Taking the opportunity afforded by the so-called Clash between Religion and Education—the controversy between the conservative philosopher Inoue Tetsujirō (1855–1944) and proponents of Christianity, named after the title of a polemic discourse he published in early 1893—the Takamagahara-ha persecuted Christianity without reason and sought to incite public opinion to purge progressives from the world of education.[11] This anti-Western, anti-Christian stream of thought persisted throughout the Meiji era. Conservatives in the House of Peers kept traditionalist issues alive, continuing to portray Western values as a threat to the national polity.

Within and without the government, educational activities before the Sino-Japanese War took place against the background of these intellectual currents and in the climate created by their configurations. Let us turn now to a discussion of these activities, beginning with the initiatives of those outside the seats and the structures of power.

The world of education in general and teachers in particular supported Mori Arinori's nationalistic educational policy. Teachers were more than willing to applaud an educational program designed to inculcate students with essentially Japanese virtues. Having listened to a discussion of nationalistic versus individualistic education, the 880 educators who participated in the first All-Japan Educators General Assembly (Zenkoku Kyōikusha Daishūkai) "all raised their hands and shouted en masse, 'The state, banzai!' "—or so the *Tōkyō Nichinichi shinbun* reported on 27 May 1890, three days after the assembly was convened. Not surprisingly, the proposal made by the assembly's chairman, Isawa Shūji (1851–1917), to create a National Education Society (Kokka Kyōikusha) immediately garnered more than 300 members. By May 1891 membership in this society, whose stated tenets included "fostering the vitality of love of country and enhancing loyalty to the emperor" as well as "expounding the essentials of national education and carrying out its basic principles," reached 5,650, and by August of the following year it had grown to 7,000 people. The society continued to expand in such a way that Minister of Education Inoue Kowashi (1843–1895) felt compelled to regulate its activities by issuing the so-called gag ordinance *(kenkō kunrei)* of 28 October 1893.

Again, it was teachers who first proposed that the state designate the morals texts to be used in elementary schools. A resolution favoring this proposal was initially approved at the April 1891 meeting of the All-Japan Education Association (Zenkoku Kyōiku Rengōkai) and submitted to the minister of education; it was later introduced into both the upper and lower houses of the Imperial Diet. The association also approved an item requesting that a photograph of the emperor and empress be "bestowed on" each elementary school. Teachers were quite receptive to treatises that promoted the militaristic spirit in education, such as "A National Education Policy" by Kusakabe Sannosuke (1856–1925), an Education Ministry official under Mori, and "On National Education, or A Strategy for Military Education" by education scholar Yunome Horyū.[12] The two new education magazines that joined the *Dai Nihon Kyōikukai zasshi* (Great Japan Education Association Magazine) in the second half of the 1880s, namely, *Kyōiku jiron* (Educational Review) and Kusakabe's *Kyōiku hōchi* (Educational News), were both strongly nationalistic in flavor.

In explaining the teachers' nationalistic tendencies, Tokutomi Sohō cited their authoritarian mentality: "Especially surprising is the way in which teachers in the provinces look upon the Ministry of Education as a kind of Head Temple" or "a morals factory."[13] Nevertheless, the teachers' movement for state-supported education, led by Isawa Shūji, should not necessarily be viewed as conservative or reactionary. In question here, to be more precise, is the political movement of the Association for the Realization of State-Supported Education (Kokuritsu Kyōiku Kisei Dōmeikai), a group that was organized as an independent unit of the National Education Society on the occasion of its second general meeting, at Sendai in August 1892. This group came into being in response to Isawa's call, before the seven thousand assembled, for financial assistance to be rendered elementary education from the national treasury. As the association was created for the purpose of putting pressure on the government to make that assistance a reality, it was naturally opposed to the provisions of Mori's Elementary School Ordinance, according to which schools were, in principle, to be operated with funds from tuition. Instead, the "Covenant" adopted at the meeting demanded "the use of public expenditures to ensure that the general populace receive the necessary education." It stated candidly that the association's political aim was to get the Imperial Diet to pass legislation "providing for the disbursement of financial aid to elementary schools from the national treasury as a first step toward the goal of state-supported education."[14]

Teachers were strictly prohibited by Education Minister Inoue Kowashi from engaging in political activities, and this movement was accordingly suppressed by the gag ordinance of October 1893. Isawa, however, gathered support from a broad supraparty group of Diet members from both houses and from influential educators outside the government, such as Yumoto Takehiko (1857–1925), and was eventually able to revive the movement in the form of the Educational Policy Research Society (Gakusei Kenkyūkai). Founded in June 1894 with Konoe Atsumaro (1863–1904) as its chairman, this society aimed at reforming the school system, improving school administration, securing funds for education, and increasing teachers' salaries. Until the last years of the Meiji era, it continued its efforts to sway public opinion, influence the Diet, and pressure the government for action on these problems.

The movement for state-supported education was led by private educators and politicians. It was critical of the Ministry of Education. All the same, its aim was to obtain financial backing for the nationalistic educational system organizationally framed and ideologically formulated by Mori Arinori. In other words, it sought to perfect that system and to make nationalistic education truly encompass the whole nation. Its conflict with the Ministry of Education was not over ideology but over the means of making nationalistic education a reality.

The immediate conditions for this movement were created by the implementation of the self-government system in April 1888. This system gave local government bodies real power in educational administration and finance. Teachers in the provinces, dissatisfied with the policies of municipal and village councils—educational budget cuts, worsening compensation, and the inadequacy of measures taken to ensure that all children be enrolled in school—developed a strong desire for public education to be guaranteed by the state, that is, the national government. In proposing his National Education Society, Isawa was seeking to create the organizational power that would make the realization of their demands possible.

To what kind of nationalism did Isawa himself subscribe? On 1 June 1890, a few days after making the proposal that led to the founding of the National Education Society, he addressed a social gathering of the society on the topic "Our Essential Purpose." In this speech he revealed the gist of the nationalistic thought that would support his subsequent actions. Explaining his view of the state, he observed that "our nation possesses an eternal, unchanging, imperishable vitality made up of the four elements of land, people, society, and economy. One scholar compares this great dynamic organism to a living person. This doctrine is truly apt and has easily won our heart."[15] Isawa linked this organic theory of the state to a German-style construct in which the head of state is the self; the legislature, the will; and the administration, the act. States, he argued, have individuality just like people. Japan's individuality—that is, its national essence *(kokusui)*—he sought in its unbroken line of imperial sovereigns, thus transforming a theory of the national essence into a theory of the national polity.

Now that he had elucidated the meaning of the state, Isawa turned to a discussion of national education: "Should we or should we not recognize education as a fundamental activity of the state? Insofar as the state is a great active being, it clearly must take responsibility for its spiritual no less than for its physical growth. Spiritual growth can only be ensured through education."[16] Isawa's use of an organic theory of the state enabled him to locate education unequivocally within the scope of the state's responsibility. In pursuing the implications of that responsibility, he legitimized the demands of contemporary educational circles and attempted to fashion "the state" into an ideological weapon that would permit the government to fulfill its natural obligation to guarantee education to all its people. Isawa succeeded in utilizing this theory to appeal to members of the National Education Society and rationalize their demands for state funding of compulsory education because teachers were already familiar with the idea of the state as an organism through Miyake Setsurei's journal *Nihonjin* and similar sources. Moreover, the call for state-supported education involved such real problems as the economic position of teachers and the difficulty of getting the boys and girls of the poor enrolled in school; hence it was not unrelated to Sohō's focus on the common man. Although it was promoted under the name of "nationalism," this movement actually asserted itself on behalf of something more. Influenced by multiple intellectual currents, it envisioned real progress in education.

Nationalism was pervasive, but it had various shadings. Undeniably, the progressive nationalism *(kokuminshugi)* of Tokutomi Sohō and the ethnic nationalism *(minzokushugi)* preached by Miyake Setsurei and Kuga Katsunan contributed much to modern educational practice, as the Ministry of Education keenly felt their intellectual influence in formulating its policies. For example, the revised Elementary School Ordinance of October 1890 is widely interpreted as having highlighted the nationalistic character of elementary school education. To be sure, in contrast to the 1886 ordinance, which referred to the elementary school simply as the place where compulsory education was to be conducted, the revision specified that the basic purposes of schooling were "to be attentive to the physical development of the child, to impart the foundations of moral and national education, and to teach the ordinary knowledge and skills necessary to daily life." Yet when one looks at the explanation provided by Egi Kazuyuki (1853–1932), the drafter of these regulations, one cannot continue to ignore their relationship to the thought of Sohō and Setsurei. Whereas moral education, according to Egi, sought to produce "the circumstances for making good men," the foundations of national education were taught with the aim of creating "the circumstances appropriate to the forming of a nation." The nations of the world (Egi continued in the same vein as Setsurei) are too numerous to count but each has its special character. Adapting the people who represent the constitutive elements of a nation to this special character is therefore the logical objective of national education *(kokumin kyōiku)*.[17]

It is clear that as far as Egi was concerned, universalistic human education and particularistic national education were both proper concerns of the elementary schools. In him there is no evidence of the parochialism that equates morality with national morality. Egi agreed with Tokutomi Sohō's notion that moral education in the elementary school was nothing else than "equipping our people with the qualifications that would make them a nation and fostering the morality necessary for men as men."[18] The most important thing to note, however, is that Egi did not assume a reactionary stance; he did not dwell in Takamagahara, the "Abode of the Gods." Of course his morality, in contrast to that of Sohō, did have a strong conservative character, for he regarded loyalty and filial piety as universal human virtues. Nevertheless, inasmuch as Egi envisaged national and human education being carried on together, one detects in him a type of progressivism. He was prepared to consider a harmonious relationship between the state and the individual.

This contemplation of how to reconcile the state and the individual can be seen more clearly in the thinking of the oligarch-turned-party-politician Itō Hirobumi (1841–1909). In a speech delivered before members of the Kyoto Prefectural Assembly on 25 March 1889, he explained the significance of establishing a national assembly by noting that both the "doctrine that the state is the standard" and the "doctrine that each individual is the axis" were one-sided. "The individual and the state must go forward hand in hand. We must see to it that the interests of the state and the rights and well-being of each individual are advanced," Itō insisted. The chief aim in setting up the Diet, he asserted, was "to devise a mechanism for bringing the two into harmony so that they may develop together."[19]

It is opportune to return at this point to the policies of Inoue Kowashi, who worked under Itō on the preparation of the constitution and became minister of education in March 1893. His educational policies vigorously propagated nationalism, but they concealed progressive tendencies. Surprisingly enough, they received the support of Tokutomi Sohō:[20]

> To be frank, I was one of those who did not expect much from Mr. Inoue Kowashi as minister of education or from his "bureaucratization of learning." He has, however, accomplished much more than I had expected, and it appears that if public opinion were to come to his aid, he would like to do many more things. . . . He removed extreme scenarios from morals texts and took up the question of popular morals, believing that the lessons of the classics should be put into practice in daily life. Previous ministers of education never dreamt of such things. . . . His desire for the creation of a national literature in the vernacular, his plans for expanding the availability of vocational education—although he may have simply taken these ideas from ordinary public discussion, one should appreciate his will to reform and be grateful for his willingness to take up his pen and write biographies of filial sons and faithful wives in newspapers and magazines. At a time when elder statesman cabinets and their political abuse of reform bring us to despair of this temporizing, vacillating world, the Ministry of Education alone moves forward energetically and decisively.

Inoue had also been quick to recognize Sohō's abilities. He gave Sohō's first book, "The Youth of Nineteenth-Century Japan and Their Education" *(Dai jūkyūseiki Nihon no seinen oyobi sono kyōiku)*, high marks when it appeared in 1886. When Sohō wrote in 1887 that "the dangers of our foreign policy lie not without but within," attacking officials who had turned their backs on the domestic scene in their preoccupation with what was happening abroad (and criticizing the activities of the cultural reactionaries of the "national essence" school in the process),[21] Inoue bestowed his approval. Generally viewed as a nationalist bureaucrat, Inoue had more in common intellectually with progressive nationalism than one might expect. For instance, in a cautionary note written to his fellow oligarch Yamagata Aritomo (1838–1922) during the drafting of the Imperial Rescript on Education, he observed, "If we follow the present doctrine of constitutional polity, the ruler does not interfere with his subjects' free exercise of their minds."[22]

The promotion of vocational education may well be Inoue's most important achievement in educational policy. From the late 1870s, Inoue had looked to the German model. He adopted a rationalistic perspective, rid himself of narrow-minded traditional thought, and devoted his energies to building the essential structures of the state. Now, as minister of education, he became keenly interested in the role that education ought to assume in the development of the economy on which the state rested. Inoue viewed the contemporary world as an arena of competition among production technologies and concluded that vocational education was necessary if Japan was to survive that competition. Hence Inoue introduced a bill calling for state assistance to vocational education before the Fifth and again before the Sixth Diet, explaining his reasons as follows: "Today the world is in a state of peace, but this peace is a matter of form. In reality we do not have a conflict of swords and guns, but a contest of business and practical skills. Every country on the surface of the globe is engaged in combat in the realms of business, practical arts, manufacturing, and trade. Every day we neglect this conflict affects the wealth and power, indeed the fate of the country."[23]

Inoue, the rationalist, noted that the progress of industry in the West was closely linked to the development of science. He made this point in a directive issued on 26 November 1893, after his bill providing state assistance to vocational education had become law. Traditionally, he pointed out, "education and manual labor have stood in distinct spheres," but modern needs dictated their reconciliation. "If we would increase the future wealth of the state, we must endeavor to present our children with an education in which science and technology are harmoniously combined with industry."[24] Vocational training, a global trend that was linked to Tokutomi Sohō's vision of a society built upon the common man, was thus camouflaged in Inoue Kowashi's policies under the name of nationalistic education.

During the third decade of the Meiji era, the Ministry of Education developed policies that were very sensitive to trends among progressive intellectuals. Inoue in particular evinced a willingness to accept as his own the demands and challenges of the times that were articulated by young leaders of the intellectual world. He sought practical solutions to those challenges, albeit from a different standpoint than theirs. This sensitivity alone explains why, when illness forced the retirement of this author of the infamous gag ordinance in August 1894, a large number of newspapers and magazines lamented his passing from the scene.

In the years immediately before the Sino-Japanese War, traditionalist thought acquired new and powerful protection in the Imperial Rescript on Education. Traditionalists advocated purging Japan of the Christian peril and fostered the rise of the ideology of Japan's unique national polity. Yet other modes of thought—the popular nationalism of the Min'yūsha, the cultural nationalism of the Seikyōsha (Society for Political Education)—pointed toward a vision of the state's and the people's future from a global perspective. In striving to overcome the realities that stood in the way of the achievement of their visions, these intellectual movements had a progressive character. Even as authoritarian nationalism was becoming an ever more imposing façade for the Ministry of Education and for educators outside the government, the ideal of a citizen-centered society mediated by nationalism—and nationalism mediated by that ideal—continued to take care of the business of modernizing education.

From the Sino-Japanese War to the Russo-Japanese War

During the Sino-Japanese War popular hostility toward China rose, and the people's awareness of themselves as a nation deepened. There were no antiwar voices such as those that would be heard a decade later at the time of the Russo-Japanese War, and the people displayed the wartime patriotism demanded of them without reservation. In an article that bore the English subtitle "Justification of the Corean War" and another that discussed "The Purpose of the Sino-Japanese War" (both published in the autumn of 1894), even Uchimura Kanzō, destined to become a strong advocate of antiwar views in the future, appealed to the world to see the war as a conflict between progressive Japan and the conservative Ch'ing Empire. The purpose of this conflict, he maintained, was to awaken China.[25] The varieties of thought that had appeared in the third decade of the Meiji era also sought national unity, putting themselves behind the war effort. Differences were set aside, and for the time being the intellectual world was united in its nationalism.

So was the world of education. The Educational Policy Research Society, which constituted itself anew in June 1894, temporarily halted its drive for the reform of the school system to concentrate on such issues as winning tuition exemptions for the children of men in military service or those who had died in the war. It conducted a petition drive for assistance with educational expenditures in an effort to ease the anxieties of soldiers at the front. Isawa's National Education Society also cooperated with the war effort. At its Fourth General Meeting in November 1894, members resolved "to sacrifice ourselves courageously, wholeheartedly, and single-mindedly in carrying out the Imperial Will." They also took a "wartime oath," pledging that besides fulfilling their "obvious obligation" to work hard at their jobs, they would cut their daily expenses and save what funds they could to help educate the children of men who were serving in the armed forces and of those who had fallen for their country.[26]

Among teachers, who were already deeply imbued with nationalism, extreme antiforeign patriotism and the adulation of men in uniform built to a fever pitch during and immediately after the war, culminating at the time of the Tripartite Intervention of April 1895. Not a few sought to instill these attitudes in their charges, as may be deduced from a letter to the editor of *Kyōiku jiron* sent in by an Akita teacher who wrote, "Since the beginning of the Sino-Japanese War, morals instruction in the schools has changed radically. Teachers dwell only on the exploits of heroes and paragons of courage, rambling on at will about heaven-shaking, earth-moving events. In time, will they not lead education itself astray?"[27]

Although it was not uncommon in the classroom, this type of jingoism was neither incited by Ministry of Education directives nor instigated by education leaders outside the government or by leading educational journals. Prominent educators, both in and out of government, did cooperate fully with the war effort, but their activities were by no means extremist. Maintaining an eminently cool and rational attitude, they admonished the teachers in the schools for their frenzy. War, as far as they were concerned, was less an occasion for wild enthusiasm than for fear that basic educational activities would be slighted or ignored.

The vehement nationalist Isawa Shūji was no exception. He and his fellow members of the National Education Society hoped to minimize the sacrifices education would be asked to make for the war effort. In the "wartime oath" that has just been mentioned, they swore not to discontinue educational activities unless mandated by law, "no matter what untoward event should occur." They also pledged to see to it that funds for education were not reduced. Addressing the meeting on the relationship between war and education, Isawa defined the Sino-Japanese conflict as a struggle between nationalisms, which Japan was winning without really fighting because the Ch'ing Empire, while it possessed territory, did not constitute a nation-state. Here were the fruits of education, he observed, going on to stress that educational objectives should not be shaken by the war.[28]

Kyōiku jiron, the leading education magazine of the time, also dealt appropriately with the way schooling should be conducted under wartime conditions. Those who were attempting to reduce educational expenditures in the name of the war were "truly enemies of education who would lead the nation to its demise," it said, urging its readers "to resist them to the bitter end." Concerning the way the war should be explained to children, the magazine counseled that conditions in Japan and in China should be taught in a calm, disinterested, and unbiased way and warned that anyone who led the younger generation to assume that "Japan alone is worthy of respect while foreign countries may be viewed as barbarous, savage, and beastlike" must be reprimanded.[29]

The same journal also expressed concern about the rapidly growing tendency for children to be fascinated with soldiers and poured cold water on teachers' hymns of praise to martial valor: "Children love action, and they take the stories of their elders at face value. . . . Thus when schoolteachers talk about the achievements of gallant, dashing, fierce generals and brave soldiers, children are aroused without realizing it and come to believe that to become a military man is the most honorable thing one can do in life and that other callings are base and unworthy. Eventually, they aspire to become soldiers. This would seem to be a truly felicitous phenomenon, but in reality it is something that we should be very concerned about, because a nation requires persons in all walks of life. It cannot be preserved by soldiers alone."[30]

This, in a word, healthy attitude among educational leaders in private life had its counterpart in the Ministry of Education. Saionji Kinmochi (1849–1940), known as the most liberal of the bureaucrats, was installed as Inoue Kowashi's successor at the ministry in October 1894. Generally viewed as a globalist both by those who supported and those who disapproved of his persuasion, Saionji fashioned a progressive educational policy that reflected a broad vision undistorted by the war.

Saionji's first expression of his views as minister of education came in an address at the Tokyo Higher Normal School on 19 October 1894. Noting the truly amazing advance of civilization in Western countries, he averred that "in the East, Japan alone can rank with them in enlightenment and progress." Educators, he stressed, were the "driving force" behind that progress, and he lauded them for "accepting the responsibility of leadership." He hoped that the future teachers in his audience would be ever more intent upon devoting themselves to the nation.[31]

Some weeks later Saionji talked about educational policy in a New Year's interview with the *Kyōiku jiron*. His aim, he said, was "to provide the nation with a complete education worthy of a civilized people." Conversely put, the goal of education was to enable Japan to attain world standards in civilization. In particular, there was a need to promote scientific education, because "in the years to come, the prosperity of science will greatly affect the fate of human life, the rise and fall of nations, and the interests of individuals." Education in foreign languages was also highly important, as it was obvious that "Western civilization cannot be imported unless we become familiar with the languages and literatures of the West." Finally, women's education must not be slighted: "The higher the level of a nation's enlightenment, the higher the position of its women."

For Saionji, who had set his sights on making the civilization of the world Japan's own, what needed to be repudiated first of all was a narrow-minded emphasis on the uniqueness of the Japanese spirit. He stated his view categorically: "I have never liked the way obstinate religionists do things. Therefore I do not believe it desirable for education to be conducted solely in a religious spirit. I do not refer to religion in the narrow sense—say, Christianity or Buddhism. I speak in a much broader sense. For instance, I do not disagree with the assertion that for Japanese, education means nurturing the Japanese spirit. To stress the necessity of such nurture in a religious fashion, however, and to maintain that nothing else needs to be taught—this is something I do not care for."[32] This was the Saionji to whom the Ministry of Education turned for the correction of patriotic excesses as the war proceeded and a group of conservative nationalists and extremist teachers assumed greater prominence in political and intellectual circles.

The Sino-Japanese War was followed by the rapid rise of national consciousness among the people, and nationalism of various stripes spread among intellectuals and educators. But the Tripartite Intervention that came on the heels of military triumph awakened a people drunk with victory to the harsh reality of international pressures on their country and to the gravity of the international competition into which Japan had been drawn. Popular interest in the outside world rose accordingly. Alongside the nationalistic position that viewed the world from a Japanese angle, there appeared its antithesis—a globalist position that looked at Japan from the standpoint of the world. Hence the postwar intellectual realm assumed a complex configuration that turned around what might be called a Japan axis.

The first problem that postwar intellectual and education circles had to deal with was Saionji's view of education. As Japan's victory became more certain, his progressive position grew more distinct. In March 1895 he revealed his convictions at a public ceremony. "Now is a time to enhance national glory, to exalt civilization," he said at the Tokyo Higher Normal School's graduation exercises. "In contemporary society, however, many are still in love with the mean customs of the East and are afraid to change them. They preach loyalty and filial piety from a narrow-minded, servile point of view. Or else they are fascinated by the eccentric behavior of the ancients and wish to make them models of human life. These attitudes present not a few obstacles to the advance of civilization."[33] On 24 May, shortly after the war's conclusion,[34] Saionji invited the heads of the higher schools and normal schools to his official residence and informed them of his ministry's future goals. After speaking of the need for instruction in science, physical education, schooling for women, and foreign-language training, he touched upon the mental preparation required of educators, once again publicly challenging the conservatives. "To train twentieth-century men and women is our responsibility as educators, something we must be fully prepared to do from now on. If we are content with what we are and look no more at the outside world, if we simply cry, '*Yamato-damashii,* Japanese spirit!' as though we did not understand that we are at the mercy of the currents of world civilization—I cannot approve of this attitude."[35]

Strong opposition arose immediately against Saionji's progressive educational policy or, rather, against Saionji the public figure and minister of education who had disavowed the "Japanese spirit." This opposition first made its appearance among parochial politicians and nationalistic teachers, but soon thereafter publicists and intellectuals found themselves engaged in a lively debate about Saionji's view of civilization, a debate that focused on the question of globalism versus Japanism.

Newspapers that joined the opposition to Saionji included *Nihon,* the *Hinode shinbun,* the *Kokkai shinbun,* and the *Asahi shinbun.* They had two objections. First, considering his standpoint "globalistic," they argued that to advocate globalism at a time when the fundamental guidelines for education had already been laid down by the Imperial Rescript was to throw educational policy objectives into confusion. Second, they maintained that Saionji's slight of *Yamato-damashii* represented an attempt to revive the Europeanization of the past, ignored national character, and vitiated national self-awareness.

Supporters of Saionji's views included *Kokumin no tomo,* the *Jiji shinpō,* and the *Chōya shinbun.* They viewed his position as the right one at the right time, offering as it did a correction to Inoue Kowashi's policies and their tendency to emphasize the principle of nationality. They observed, furthermore, that Saionji's orientation was global, modern, and democratic compared to Inoue's, but that he was by no means antinationalistic. Rather, they called Saionji's approach rational. It was aimed, they noted, at preventing a reactionary turn in the direction of educational policy, one that would surely affect the very future of the nation.[36]

Reflecting on this period later, Saionji commented that the Imperial Rescript on Education alone was an "inadequate" basis for the formulation of educational policy. Japan, he felt, ought to "move in a more liberal direction."[37] The controversy that surrounded his tenure as minister of education had led Saionji to consider the promulgation of a new educational rescript. He had learned by experience that if progressive educational policies were to be implemented, the document from which reactionary forces drew their intellectual authority must first be revised.

Thus a parting of the ways occurred in the postwar intellectual world over Saionji's views on education. The vehement dispute finally ended in a victory for the globalists. Conservative schools of thought obstinately resisted, but on the surface, at least, they lost their intellectual dominance as the nineteenth century came to a close. Among those who were considered globalists during these years were Saionji's direct intellectual descendant Takegoshi Yosaburō (also known as Takegoshi Sansa; 1865–1950), as well as Tokutomi Sohō and Fukuzawa Yukichi (1835–1901) with his group of followers. In addition there was the Christian camp, including Uchimura Kanzō and Kutsumi Kesson (Yasutada; 1860–1925). In July 1896 Takegoshi, one of Saionji's ardent devotees, launched a new magazine, *Sekai no Nihon*. He explained his reasons for the venture in an editorial in the journal's first issue: "Eight or nine years ago the loudest cry to be heard among the Japanese people was 'Japan for the Japanese!' In the last three or four years this has changed to 'Japan for the Orient!' Now we would change it once again to 'Japan for the World—*Sekai no Nihon!*' Of course force has made it so, but there must also be a reason. Our determination to publish this journal springs from our desire to take advantage of that ineluctable force and to bring about the acceptance of necessary reason." The ineluctable force was the growing power of Japan itself; the necessary reason was the great law of "common existence and common order in the life of humanity." The position that most correctly conformed to the thrust of Japan's development and the laws of mankind was none other than globalism, *Sekai no Nihon* maintained: "We must become aware of ourselves as being 'for the world,' enter onto the world stage, reinvent debate on affairs of state from a global perspective, and mediate among the powers with a global heart and mind." The journal did not presume to tell the Japanese to create such a tide but simply to move forward with it.

This editorial demonstrates eloquently that *Sekai no Nihon* had no other objective than to expel the parochial, bigoted notions of Japan's uniqueness from national life and to impress the idea of "Japan for the World" on the hearts of the Japanese people. This journal ceased publication in 1900, but while it was in circulation it introduced a fresh element to postwar intellectual life, lending its pages to progressive thinkers such as Uchimura Kanzō and Ume Kenjirō (1860–1910) as well as to proponents of Japanism such as Takayama Chogyū (1871–1902), Masaoka Shiki (1867–1902), and Ōmachi Keigetsu (1869–1925).

Takegoshi and other globalists who made their debut after the Sino-Japanese War were no longer preoccupied with Japan's "backwardness." Even for men of earlier generations, such as Fukuzawa Yukichi and Tokutomi Sohō, this sense had grown much weaker. They no longer thought of Western civilization as the ideal or as a model for their country because, they felt, Japan had already become a member of world civilization. Hence they sought to nurture a national spirit appropriate for a civilized people. They criticized the narrow-minded doctrines of Japan's unique national essence not so much for creating an obstacle to the realization of that goal as for being a spiritually pathological phenomenon in the civilized society of contemporary Japan. This was the basis of Takegoshi's strong plea for his "ineluctable force" and "necessary reason," and it explains why these publicists, believing as they did that culture and social institutions were destined to undergo a transformation, were such forceful advocates of a healthy globalization of the Japanese mind.

Nationalism and ideologies of Japan's unique national character that sought to resist globalism could not be persuasive in this intellectual climate as long as they based their arguments solely and simply on tradition. Consequently, postwar nationalism did not intrinsically exclude globalist thinking. Nor did nationalism any longer concern itself with concepts of state power, as it had done in the days of the popular-rights movement *(jiyū minken undō)*. It focused rather on the question of the posture Japan should take toward the outside world as it confronted international competition.

To be sure, it was not only the feeling of tension toward the outside that stimulated the rise of globalist thought and brought an element of the modern to nationalism. Society's rapid modernization in the years after the war was also a major factor. Commerce and industry developed rapidly as the capitalist economy got on track, stimulating individual economic activity and heightening the demand for freedom to seek the satisfaction of material desires. The conviction that free competition was the road to economic growth grew stronger. In politics, the first party cabinet, headed by Ōkuma Shigenobu (1838–1922) and Itagaki Taisuke (1837–1919), made its appearance in June 1898. Popular understanding of the constitution grew. Moreover, the promulgation of the Civil Code in the same year brought family relationships under the control of the law, although it incorporated many of their traditional aspects. Even so, the Civil Code made existing social relationships subject to reflection, creating the possibility that what had heretofore been habitual, emotional ties might come to be understood in terms of modern rights and obligations. In 1899 the revision of the unequal treaties, something that had been on the national agenda since the Meiji Restoration, finally restored Japan's full sovereignty. "Mixed residence" also began, enlarging opportunities for popular contact with Europeans and Americans and opening a way to personal awareness of the wider world.

The wartime growth in information services and popular education campaigns continued in peacetime, as the publishing industry grew by leaps and bounds. In the several years following the war, literary and intellectual magazines representing a wide variety of viewpoints came into being. The general magazine *Taiyō* (1895); Takegoshi's *Sekai no Nihon* and Mitsuoka Shin'ichirō's *Jitsugyō no Nihon*, both started in 1896; *Rōdō sekai*, edited by Katayama Sen (1897); Takayama Chogyū's *Nihonshugi* (1897); and the *Chūō kōron* (1899; its direct predecessor, *Hanseikai zasshi*, dates back to 1887)—these and other publications played a major role in creating a free and progressive intellectual atmosphere.

The strain of nationalism that had the greatest effect on the popular mind and became the major rival of globalism in the postwar milieu was the Japanism *(Nihonshugi)* of Takayama Chogyū. Chogyū placed more emphasis on the significance of the Tripartite Intervention than on Japan's military victory. He explained his reasons for becoming a publicist in the following terms: "No matter how much Japan's victory has increased the suspicion of foreign countries, no matter how much steeper it has made our nation's climb, the people, still drunk from the victory banquet, shudder in fear and look back enraged. In these circumstances the idea of Japan's position in the world has been placed before the people as a sharp doubt. Japanism has arisen to respond to this doubt."[38] What Chogyū meant by Japanism was "a practical morality grounded in the national character of the people *(kokutai minsei)* and an experiential understanding of the grand design of the Imperial Ancestors, an ethic concerned with the realization of the great ideal of the state and the great aspirations of the people."³⁹ Even so, Chogyū's thought bore a resemblance to globalism in several respects. The standard of his "practical morality" was not measured by traditional values; it was, rather, a progressive criterion that granted freedom of choice to the people. "Even something that has existed in our country for a long time or is peculiar to our country must be removed without delay, should it bring on the slightest damage to the state and to the people."⁴⁰ Chogyū's view of the state was not inconsistent with the interests of the individual. On the contrary, it showed a healthy balance between the state and the individual: "After all, the state was established so that the purpose of human existence, that is, happiness, might be peacefully attained. It is not as if there were, from the beginning, some form apart from the individual, called the state, that restricted our free activity."⁴¹ Finally, he did not believe his Japanism to be incompatible with globalism: "Indeed, they should perhaps be considered the same, insofar as both consider the ultimate goal of human life to be the realization of complete and equal happiness. Thus the point at issue between them is merely the method by which this ultimate goal is to be realized."⁴²

While it was founded upon the people's national character, Chogyū's Japanism maintained a link with new, nontraditional values such as liberty, the individual, and the world. As such it can be described as a progressive nationalism, an attempt to look out upon the world from a Japanese perspective. However, Chogyū's days as a publicist for Japanism ended in 1900. Thereafter he moved from the hedonistic individualism that can be seen in his "Doctrine of the Aesthetic Life" *(Biteki seikatsuron)* to Nietzschean individualism and then to Nichiren Buddhism.

At just about the time Takayama Chogyū cast aside his Japanism, in May 1900, the Boxer Rebellion that shook the Ch'ing Empire entered a critical phase. The Russian occupation of Manchuria and the dispatch of Japanese troops to Peking followed. At this juncture, in September 1900, the Kokumin Dōmeikai was formed. This People's Alliance was a political organization that pressed the government for an independent solution to the Korean and Manchurian problems. Hailing this opposition group for its hard-line posture, Tomizu Hirondo (1861–1935) and six others from among the best and the brightest of Japan's academia clamored for war with Russia, advocating naked aggression. Imperialism had made its appearance in the intellectual world. Employing as its theoretical weapon a Social Darwinism that rationalized the "survival of the fittest" in international society, it replaced Japanism as the most popular form of nationalism. Still, through the efforts of Yumoto Take-hiko and the philosopher Inoue Tetsujirō, who had joined Chogyū in forming the Greater Japan Association (Dai Nihon Kyōkai) in May 1897, Japanism managed to stay alive throughout the next decade without falling into extreme imperialism. Indeed, it remained a major influence on educators through Yumoto's *Kyōiku jiron* and other journals.

On 23 May 1895, the first postwar general meeting of the Imperial Education Society opened in Kyoto. During this three-day conference, participants heard lectures by personages such as Inoue Tetsujirō, Kusa-kabe Sannosuke, Kanō Jigorō (1860–1938), Maeda Masana (1850–1921), Taguchi Ukichi (1855–1905), and Tsuji Shinji (1842–1915). Each set forth the direction that he believed postwar education should take. Maeda spoke of developing the people's capacity for cooperation, while Kanō advocated promoting study abroad, both to inform the world of Japan's worth and to train Japanese who should develop into pioneers of world civilization. Kusakabe stressed the desirability of training in the martial arts. Inoue pointed to the urgent need to unify the people ideologically, while even the liberal Taguchi spoke both of patriotism and the need to nurture love for the Japanese race. The concerns of these speakers afford us some insight into the general tendency of educational opinion after the war against China.[43] And yet the transformation of nationalist thought was the most distinctive feature of the postwar educational world. In opposing Saionji's policies, nationalistic educators spread the perception that "national education" had been the cause of victory. What kind of education would truly strengthen the nation, however? What should it consist of? Not only did nationalists no longer find it possible to ignore the "global"—just as has been noted in the case of Japanism—but aggressive criticism from the globalist perspective prompted them to reconsider their views. As they confronted and, indeed, assimilated globalism, they began to think of how to modernize education.

Consideration of this question took the form of a discussion of the substance of education. The *Kyōiku jiron* of this period repeatedly took up this issue. According to that journal, the basic evil of the Japanese educational system was that from the beginning it had not looked beyond the formal and the superficial and had ignored what surely ought to be the chief aim of education—"the nurture of active, progressive men who can get things done."[44] Among the many who addressed the subject of educational substance, Takata Sanae (family name sometimes read Takada; 1860–1938) insisted that national education should seek to disseminate constitutionalism and globalism.[45] An editorial in the *Rikugō zasshi* (Cosmos) urged that the school be made into a place for the education of good citizens and advocated student self-government toward that end.[46] And Taguchi Ukichi argued that sheltering the student has no place in education. If independence and self-reliance are to be the goal, he concluded, that education is best which interferes least.[47] The majority promoted the objective of human character formation from a globalist and progressive point of view.

Most notable of all is perhaps the opinion expressed in Kutsumi Kesson's "View of Education and the Times" *(Kyōiku jidaikan)*. "If education misunderstands the spirit of the times," he wrote, "the people will lose their future. If a generation employs the wrong kind of education, the state will lose its future."[48] Contemporary education had falsely understood its relationship to the times and was leaning toward nationalism, he observed. "The inspiration of our times is not the same nationalistic spirit as that of ancient [*sic*] Europe," Kesson insisted. "We must recognize that this spirit is here, but that is only half the picture. On the other side I perceive the brilliant advance of the global and cosmic. For education to forget this and run exclusively to nationalism is a terrible error that will eventually result in the people's falling into a perverse bigotry."[49] Japan was in the constitutional age, he asserted, and therefore "we must not employ education appropriate to the age of despotism. Old ideals are useless; a new spirit must be adopted." Kesson wanted "an education that brings together the spirit and thought of liberty and rights, the highest ideals and morals known to man, and the science and practical arts common to the world"—in short, "an education that can fashion a complete human being."[50] Even Inoue Tetsujirō, who stressed national unity and Japanism, could not ignore globalism and came to advocate a reconciliation between national and humanitarian education. The individual was not only a member of the Japanese nation but also of world society, Inoue reasoned; hence education should adopt a course that would lead Japan to take the initiative in putting humanitarianism into practice in the world.[51]

Against this background of intellectual concern with the modernization of educational objectives, the Educational Policy Research Society emerged as the focus of nongovernmental action on education's behalf. In this regard, it succeeded the movement for state-supported education. This society was chaired by Konoe Atsumaro, and its members included the influential political figures Ebara Soroku (1842–1922), Shimada Saburō (1852–1923), Kudō Yukimoto (1841–1904), Hatano Denzaburō (1856–1907), Kusumoto Masataka (1838–1902), and Kikuchi Kurō (1847–1926), as well as Yumoto Takehiko and Kusakabe Sannosuke, who had seats in the House of Peers. Takata Sanae, Isawa Shūji, and Kubota Yuzuru (1847–1936) were among the educational leaders who were prominent in the organization. As its members brought the issues discussed in their circle to the Imperial Diet, the society exercised a considerable influence on the Ministry of Education's policy decisions.

The chief issues raised by the Educational Policy Research Society—the endowment of education, establishment of a Higher Education Council, reform of the educational system, improvement in teachers' salaries, abolition of the gag ordinance—were linked by a common intellectual perspective, the demand for a fully modern education. The first of these issues is particularly important, as it indicates the character of the nationalism that was prevalent among educators during this period. This issue involved a proposal to take a portion of the reparations obtained from the Ch'ing Empire and set it aside as an endowment for compulsory education. Those who emphasized the role of education in winning the war saw such an endowment as a fitting victory memorial, a way of acknowledging that education was no less important to the nation than military preparedness. Indeed, the reasoning at work here placed education ahead of armaments as an immediate priority of the state.

This point of view persisted throughout the latter part of the Meiji era. When a wave of extreme imperialism and militarism swept political and intellectual circles in the aftermath of the Boxer Rebellion and the Manchurian question in 1901, leaving educational concerns in limbo, Kubota Yuzuru rose in the upper house of the Fifteenth Diet to interrogate the government concerning school policy. Speaking for educational interests, he criticized the government for expanding armaments at the cost of educational expenditures.[52] Independent-minded educators joined with concerned political figures to encourage the weakest department of the government, the Ministry of Education. They did all they could to secure its budget, which was again in danger of being sacrificed. They not only demanded an expansion of compulsory schooling, but worked for the augmentation of higher and vocational education. It is apparent that the nationalism common in postwar educational circles was not necessarily militaristic. On the contrary, it sought to restrain militarism and criticized efforts to increase armaments that disregarded the need for a balanced strength.

Reform of the educational system remained unresolved until the Extraordinary Conference on Education (Rinji Kyōiku Kaigi) was convened in 1917, but solutions to the other major issues, imperfect though they were, were put into effect during this interwar period. Regulations providing for a Higher Education Council were issued in December 1896. The Education Endowment Ordinance was promulgated in November 1899. The Law to Provide National Assistance to

Elementary Education of March 1900 dealt with the problem of teachers' salaries, as did the Law on Additional Allowances for Elementary Teachers in Cities, Towns, and Villages. Moreover, the gag ordinance and similar ordinances that had existed since the late 1870s were all abolished in 1898, during the tenure of Ozaki Yukio (1859–1954) as minister of education.

How is it that independent educational movements could, in a matter of a few short years, see their demands for the modernization of schooling enacted into law and put into effect? Their success would be inexplicable were we to overlook the fact that Ministry of Education officials continued to hold progressive educational objectives. The progressive orientation of the first postwar minister of education, Saionji Kinmochi, has already been noted. In January 1898 Saionji reassumed that office in the third Itō cabinet and resumed pursuit of his goals for education. Prime Minister Itō Hirobumi shared Saionji's views. On various occasions beginning about 1897, Itō developed the theme that social progress should be promoted through world civilization. Otherwise, he argued, a dynamic nation could not be built. In a conversation recorded during his next stint as prime minister (12 January–24 June 1898), Itō addressed his call for progressive education directly to educational circles. Talk of *Yamato-damashii* and patriotism in the "repel the barbarians" spirit had no place in the education of children at this late date, Itō observed. He urged the rejection of narrow-minded patriotism, maintaining that it was wrong to "lean one-sidedly toward spiritual education while failing to support the specialized sciences of practical use to the nation."[53]

To Itō's successor as premier, Ōkuma Shigenobu, the nation's progress was a gift of the spread of education, and its further dissemination was the most urgent policy matter of all.[54] The Ōkuma cabinet collapsed, however, on 31 October 1898 after only four months in office. It was followed by the administration of the military elder statesman General Yamagata Aritomo, who assigned the Ministry of Education to Admiral Kabayama Sukenori (1837–1922). Selected by Kabayama to head the ministry's various bureaus were young, progressive bureaucrats, including such products of the Imperial University's Faculty of Letters as Sawayanagi Masatarō (1865–1927), Ueda Kazutoshi (1867–1937), and Okada Ryōhei (1864–1934). Kabayama turned over the formation of policy to these men, and the result was a set of policies that were surely somewhat radical for a cabinet and a ministry headed by military men. These policies were embodied in the Revised Elementary School Ordinance of August 1900 and included a one-year extension of compulsory education, the abolition in principle of elementary school tuition, the reduction of weekly hours of instruction, the adoption of the use of the

Japanese syllabary to aid pronunciation, the abolition of the examination system, and the limitation of the number of Chinese characters to be taught.

Kikuchi Dairoku (1855–1917), the minister of education in the Katsura cabinet (June 1901–December 1905), maintained a similar course. During his tenure he made almost a hundred speeches at schools and educational meetings throughout the country, consistently enunciating a policy that looked forward to the growth of an entrepreneurial spirit among the people. Kikuchi sought the advancement of industrial education and rejected the militaristic spiritualism that impeded the development of ways of thinking conducive to appreciating the importance of economic matters. In a commencement address at the Tokyo Higher Normal School in March 1902, he declared, "Our schools give plenty of weight to nurturing loyalty and patriotism and cultivating nationalistic concepts. But there is much more to be done regarding the means of expressing these ideals. A nation does not rest on government and military affairs alone. We must not forget that agriculture, industry, and commerce are essential elements of a wealthy nation. To become a government official or a soldier is not the only way to be loyal and patriotic. I believe it is of utmost importance to inculcate economic thinking, to arouse an entrepreneurial spirit, and to foster a creative climate among the people."[55]

Toward the end of 1902, while Kikuchi was still minister of education, public concern was raised by a graft case that would eventually involve more than two hundred officials accused of accepting bribes from publishers interested in securing governmental approval of their privately compiled textbooks. As a result of this Textbook Scandal (Kyō-kasho Gigoku), the government assumed the responsibility for compiling elementary school texts. The first state textbooks in morals became mandatory in April 1904. Interestingly enough, their content reveals the progressive character of turn-of-the-century Ministry of Education officials.

The demand for "state textbooks" originated not so much from the ministry as from opposition political and educational circles. The first formal call for their compilation came at the ninth session of the House of Peers in February 1896, and frequent petitions in support of this proposal were subsequently produced in both houses of the legislature and the Higher Education Council. There were two main reasons for these demands. The first, advanced by the council and by members of the House of Representatives who had ties to the Educational Policy Research Society, was that producing low-cost textbooks at government expense would reduce the cost of compulsory education, at the same time eliminating the bribery associated with obtaining textbook approval. The other had its origins in the demand for national unity regarding popular morals that was put forward by conservatives in politics and education and by their spokesmen in the House of Peers. From about the time Takayama Chogyū abandoned Japanism, this group began to see a threat in the spread of individualism and the rise of capitalism. According to them, these developments in the world of letters and in the economy, compounded with the egoistic and libertarian attitudes that permeated society, represented a degeneration of national morality. They feared that the degenerate trend would be reflected in compulsory education.

It is true that the Sino-Japanese War had not only aroused a deeper awareness of Japan as a state and a nation vis-à-vis the outside world but had stimulated youth to go one step further—to an inward search for the self and individual self-awareness vis-à-vis the state. The ethic of self-realization propounded by Chogyū's "Doctrine of the Aesthetic Life" captured the hearts of those not satisfied with nationalism and globalism. The age of anguish and doubt had begun. *Seishinkai* (The Spiritual World), a journal started by the Buddhist priest Kiyozawa Manshi (1863–1903) in 1901, and the mystical religious thought of the belletrist Tsunajima Ryōsen (1873–1907) spurred on these anxious and skeptical youths as they confronted religion. Although their longing for individualism did not represent a positive denial of the state, they moved away from a concern with the affairs of the nation, cultivating a studied apathy.

As early-twentieth-century youth became more involved with personal concerns and interests, one observer detected two distinct orientations: materialistic individualism and spiritual individualism. "When contemporary youth acquire individual self-awareness, they seem to lose national self-awareness or at least a part of it. Those who lean toward materialistic concerns become 'worshipers of Mammon.' The comparatively healthy among them are spoken of as being 'hell-bent on success.' Those who lean toward the spiritual become the party of disappointment, agony, despondence, and pessimism. The comparatively healthy among them become students of the problem of human existence or conceited daydreamers."[56]

Conservative educators and politicians, anxious lest this intellectual climate reach the classroom, in February 1899 submitted to the Thirteenth Diet a proposal in support of state ethics textbooks. Their stated purpose was to "nourish the virtue of all the nation's schoolchildren under the same principles, developing a spirit of loyalty and patriotism." The following year, the Fourteenth Diet petitioned the government to disseminate the Imperial Rescript on Education, asserting that to be "the only way" to redeem a situation in which "public morals were endangered." In February 1902 the Confucianist Shionoya Isotari introduced before the lower house of the Sixteenth Diet a bill to add a Faculty of Ethics to the Imperial University, as he perceived an urgent need to train a cadre of teachers of morals. "Another long-winded discussion of the present decline of morals is unnecessary," Shionoya observed. "Suffice it to say, to leave things as they are portends national ruin."[57]

In April 1900 the Ministry of Education responded to the demands of these conservative nationalists by forming an Ethics Texts Survey Committee headed by Katō Hiroyuki (1836–1916), an establishment scholar and notorious opponent of the popular-rights movement, who had abjured the liberal views of his youth.[58] By December 1903 the committee had completed its task. Its conservative origins notwithstanding, the texts that resulted were written from a globalist perspective. They dealt with individual ethics, social ethics, the ethics of the workplace, and so forth—in other words, with the ethics of modern civil society. At the same time, they explained things one needed to be aware of in dealing with foreigners and took great pains to admonish against antiforeign conceits. As for the traditional values of loyalty, filial piety, and the obligations of subjects, anticipated by those who had sought state compilation of ethics texts—there is no indication that they received particular emphasis.

The progressive atmosphere that prevailed in educational circles both in and out of government even found its way into that citadel of nationalistic education, the normal school. In May 1900 Education Minister Kabayama, speaking at the National Conference of Normal School Presidents, criticized the militaristic and formalistic education that prevailed in their schools and pointed to the need for an infusion of fresh air that would foster self-government, autonomy, and respect for individuality. As if in response to the minister's call, Noguchi Entarō (1868–1941), the first head of the Himeji Normal School, which opened in October 1901, introduced there a liberal education, something entirely absent heretofore from the Japanese normal school. Treating every student like a gentleman was Noguchi's avowed educational principle. He abolished the examination system, permitted self-government in student dormitories, and worked to establish a cheerful and open-minded atmosphere in his school.

Noguchi's aims are clearly set forth in an exhortation on the theme of the "ideal educator" that he issued in September 1903. The first of his three main principles explains the human qualities essential to becoming a good teacher: "Enjoy nature, love mankind, be aware of your natural place in society and your duties toward the nation; acquire sublime and gentle sentiments toward the universe; revere and rejoice in these feelings, knowing that education is the most effective way to bring them to fruition." The third principle stresses the independent and autonomous spirit appropriate to the teacher: "Do not neglect the fine points of appearance in speech and conduct; put your economic house in order; esteem integrity and honor; hold fast to your principles; respect your own independence; do not be addicted to fame or fawn on power and status; be courteous and sincere, accessible but not excessively familiar."[59]

As these progressive tendencies began to emerge, a large number of normal schools came to permit the reading of literature—something discountenanced previously. About 1900 or 1901, students at Tokyo Normal School who shared an interest in fiction formed a creative writing group called the Ibunkai (Society to Apply the Written Word). The reminiscences of graduates from other regions—Okayama, Kumamoto, Akita—suggest that authors such as Ōmachi Keigetsu, Tokutomi Roka (1868–1927), Kuroiwa Ruikō (1862–1920), Kōda Rohan (1867–1947), Ozaki Kōyō (1867–1903), and Natsume Sōseki (1867–1916) were eagerly read among normal-school students. As teachers became familiar with literature, they grew more aware of themselves as individuals; as a progressive educational policy came to be implemented, their new self-awareness led to the gradual diffusion of a liberal consciousness. The old virtues of dignity, obedience, and fraternity gave way to the groping toward a new vision—that of the teacher as a human being.

Change was occurring in the realm of educational theory as well. The doctrines of Johann Herbart (1776–1841), which focused on moral education, had been adopted in Japan and had already become formalized in the third decade of Meiji. They were supplanted by the discussion of such ideas as learning by doing, natural education, vocational education, and creative education. Teachers enthusiastically greeted the appearance of Higuchi Kanjirō's "New Integrated Teaching Method" *(Tōgōshugi shin kyōjuhō),* which focused not on the needs of the nation-state but on the development of skills the individual needed to adapt to life in society. First published in 1899, this work advocated child-centered education. "Self-activity" was its prescription. Higuchi wanted teachers to encourage children's spontaneity, thereby enabling them to carry on a full life.[60]

From the Russo-Japanese War to the Last Years of Meiji

Education was not asked to make major sacrifices at the time of the Sino-Japanese War, but the Russo-Japanese War dealt it a significant blow. On 20 February 1904, ten days after the war's outbreak, the Ministry of Education issued a directive on educational policy in wartime to local school administrators. The need to supply funds for military expenditures would affect education adversely, the ministry feared, and it sought to prepare school authorities for what was to come. Retrenchment, it warned, was unavoidable both in activities and in facilities. Every effort must, however, be made to avoid reduced enrollments, cuts in teachers' salaries, and anything else that might diminish the effectiveness of education—"for that would impair the foundations of national power."[61]

The minister of education during the war was Kubota Yuzuru. An influential member of the Educational Policy Research Society, he entered the cabinet as the bearer of the long-cherished desires of educational circles—state support of education and school system reform. Kubota was more conservative and bureaucratic than Saionji. He preached the need for nationalism in the realm of moral education. For all that, he consistently called for improvement and enrichment of the educational system and insisted that education be given priority over military affairs.

Under Kubota, the Ministry of Education was intent on protecting the health of wartime education. Circumstances, however, did not favor that effort. In April 1904 the increased military expenditures required by the war forced the government to promulgate the Extraordinary Special Tax Law. Because this law limited the amount of additional land tax that could be levied by local governments to 30 percent, its practical effect was to reduce the operating budgets of towns and villages. A curtailment of funds for compulsory education was the inevitable consequence, and educational activities were constricted. The promulgation of this tax law was attended, in the same month, by the Education Ministry's issuing a "Communiqué concerning School Expenditures." This communiqué proposed countermeasures aimed at maintaining educational standards within the limits of local budgets even as the number of schoolchildren increased. Teachers, it suggested, could hold night classes; grades could be combined. To reduce expenditures, it was also permissible (where unavoidable) to dismiss substitute teachers, teachers of special courses, and older teachers, in that order.

While school enrollments increased by about seventy thousand in 1904 from the previous year, the number of teachers declined by 3,108 and the number of classes by 1,576. This diminution in staff and facilities led to a sudden increase in work load for individual teachers.[62] The cut in expenditures was, however, not the only reason for teachers' excessive work loads. Another was the sudden increase in the general demand for education among a populace eager to read communications from the front and newspaper reports of the military situation; night schools and youth associations sprang up throughout the country. In short, the teachers' time came to be divided between the regular school system and extramural demands. More and more of them began to use "answer books" to get ready for class. Contrary to the Ministry of Education's best intentions, it consequently became impossible to avert a decline in the quality of education. The Educational Policy Research Society's response to these conditions was a manifesto, issued on 20 April 1904, that warned against the deleterious effects of educational decline. This document, which was sent to the Ministry of Education as well as to local officials in cities, towns, and villages throughout the country, asserted that since talent cannot be nurtured and developed in a day, education was basic among all productive activities. Win or lose, it continued, Japan must maintain a thriving educational system.[63]

It was not that the government had no qualms about sacrificing education because the nation was on a wartime footing. Indeed, an imperial edict of July 1904 expressly stated that "education must not be neglected, even though a nation at war faces momentous times. Let those charged with this task be diligent."[64] This was a last resort, an exhortation by which a government in want of other resources sought to encourage local authorities to promote education in spite of their economic difficulties.

Meanwhile, the upsurge in popular hostility toward the enemy was much greater than it had been during the Sino-Japanese War. Teachers, who had been in general quite taken with the military during the previous conflict, became even more emotionally caught up in the new one. They addressed their classes on the purpose of the war and told tales of combat, seeking to inspire their pupils with militaristic enthusiasm and animosity toward the enemy. Even during the struggle with Russia, however, educational leaders in and out of government assumed a dispassionate attitude, just as they had during the war with the Ch'ing Empire.

Minister of Education Kubota was concerned lest the outbreak of hostilities lead to the spread of irrational antiforeignism in the schools. On 10 February 1904, the day the war began, he therefore issued an ad hoc directive to local government officials. "Although we are now poised for a conflict with Russia, students must not be carried away with youthful ardor and hurl insults at the Russian people," the directive cautioned. "This war's true purpose is winning a lasting peace."[65] In September, the Ministry of Education addressed the question of war songs by cautioning that "the enemy should be treated with due propriety and without so much as a hint of slander or ridicule."[66] Educational leaders outside the government also criticized teachers who exercised a "baleful influence" on education by an excess of patriotic zeal. "Taking up the entire morals instruction period with war stories," for instance, was going too far.[67] The educational world as a whole, both government and private, maintained its progressive tendencies during the war.

During and after the Russo-Japanese War, national self-awareness among the populace was much stronger than it had been after the previous conflict. At the time of the war with China, Japan was under strong pressure from the Powers, as was evidenced by the Tripartite Intervention, and was not fully able to feel itself a member of the world community. After the Russo-Japanese War, however, the Japanese people were seized with a sense of pride, convinced that Japan was not inferior to the civilized nations. Casting aside their long-standing passive attitude, the Japanese quickly prepared themselves to play an active role in the world. This new self-confidence made popular expectations of a favorable postwar settlement all the stronger. Surely, people thought, the real stature of Japan, the victorious nation, would be reflected in the peace treaty.

In one segment of the postwar intellectual world, naked imperialism gathered strength. Flying high on the wings of victory, its proponents advocated further conquest. Among the most articulate advocates of war were the "Seven Savants" (Shichi-Hakase) led by Tokyo Imperial University law professor Tomizu Hirondo. At educational gatherings throughout the land, they clamored for territorial expansion, advocating aggrandizement as the way to Japan's modernization. Annexation, in their view, was the only way to expand Japanese markets and make the growth of Japanese domestic industry possible.[68] Dissatisfied with the terms of the Portsmouth Treaty, they fanned the flames of public opinion against the government, which had, in their eyes, agreed too readily to a humiliating peace. When the Ministry of Education suspended Tomizu from his post on the grounds that these activities exceeded the proper limits of a university professor's behavior, the controversy was destined to be enveloped in wider unrest.

The Portsmouth Treaty had, in fact, betrayed popular expectations, touching off an explosion of antigovernment dissatisfaction. A large popular demonstration that was held in Hibiya on 5 September 1905 attacked the government with the slogans "Revoke the treaty!" "Continue the war!" and "Impeach the government!" provoking a confrontation with the police and the tragic spilling of blood. Coinciding as it did with such an outburst of agitated public opinion, the action taken against Tomizu became good material for further attacks on the government, and the professor's suspension became a major issue in intellectual circles.

Society in general and intellectual circles in particular opposed a government that had hurried to end the war. The imperialistic mentality that called for a continuation of the war and the expansion of Japanese territory showed great strength on the surface. Once popular agitation over the peace treaty quieted down, however, globalism again became the dominant intellectual current. Attention was redirected to the modern development of state and people as a way of maintaining and advancing the international position to which military victory had suddenly elevated Japan. Miyake Setsurei put this trend into focus: "Victory raised national prestige, allowing us to become one of the Powers and elevating us, as a nation-state, to a position of which we should be very proud. At the same time, the world replaced a single country as the standard, giving rise among us to a tendency to think about ourselves and our happiness as members of the whole human race. This was not a sudden change. The term *globalism* came into use around the time Saionji was minister of education. He himself is said to have been one of its promoters. But the experience of going to war against one of the world's most powerful nations and winning has suddenly broadened our perspectives, so that it often seems as if we can see north, south, east, and west in one glance."[69]

No doubt many supported Tomizu Hirondo for his patriotic opposition to a humiliating peace, but the biggest reason public opinion no less than university professors came to Tomizu's aid and confronted the Ministry of Education was the desire to protect university autonomy and academic freedom from government oppression. "Professorial speech should be free," the constitutional scholar Minobe Tatsukichi (1873–1948) maintained. "To restrict it by means of state power is outrageous. To seek to close a person's mouth because what he says just happens to run counter to one's own policies is an abuse of power—an abuse of law and an abuse of power. How can we abandon Tomizu in silence?"[70]

Globalist thought became more common in society at large as a result of the Hibiya and Tomizu incidents. It gained further strength as the Katsura cabinet, which had been at the helm during the Russo-Japanese War, gave way in January 1906 to more liberal leadership. Its successor, the Saionji cabinet (which was backed by the Seiyūkai party) displayed a more tolerant attitude toward the socialist movement. Thus in February 1906, not quite five years after the Social Democratic party (Shakai Minshutō) was founded in May 1901—only to be banned immediately—the Japan Socialist party (Nihon Shakaitō) formed by Katayama Sen (1859–1933), Nishikawa Kōjirō (1876–1940), and Sakai Kosen (Toshihiko; 1870–1933) among others was officially recognized.

Against the backdrop of this popularization of globalist thought, educational debate increasingly came to focus on the question of modern character formation. Without "modern men," so the thinking went, Japan would be unable to engage successfully in international competition. Immediately after the Sino-Japanese War, Saionji's globalism had received a mixed reaction among educators. After the Russo-Japanese War, however, it met with little resistance. Even the *Kyōiku jiron*—by no means an all-out supporter of globalism in the late 1890s—concluded 1907 with an appeal for the recognition of the vital need for globalistic education. At a meeting of local officials the previous April, Saionji had made comments to the effect that education was the wellspring of a nation's development, that it "set the standards for the light of culture to be ordered in the realm," and that its very essence was "to seek knowledge broadly throughout the world." The *Kyōiku jiron* expressed its approval of these sentiments: "Today, when our country needs specialized global education much more urgently than a structure of national unity, the time has come to add our support to Marquis Saionji's views."[71]

Takata Sanae played a major role in the spread of globalistic thinking in educational circles. Takata had not only been a member of the Educational Policy Research Society, he had also served under Minister of Education Ozaki Yukio in the Ōkuma cabinet as head of the Higher Education Bureau. Subsequently, he came to have great influence in nongovernmental educational circles as the president of Waseda University. After the Russo-Japanese War, he availed himself of frequent public-speaking opportunities at the Imperial Education Association, Waseda University, and similar forums to set forth his progressive educational views. Postwar education, he argued, confronted the urgent need to nurture men endowed with the constitutional spirit and a global perspective. Japan must adopt a global policy and act on the world stage in a peaceful manner. To do so successfully, it needed men willing and able to venture into global activities on the basis of an understanding of the harmony between individualism and statism. To work for the good of one's self benefits the state, Takata believed. Conversely, when the state prospers, the individuals who are its citizens benefit. In short, there was no conflict between the state and the individual. "With the steady growth of this idea, there naturally will appear the notion that the country is one's own and that since it is one's own country, one must devote one's self to it. This is the true constitutional spirit."[72]

The appearance of "Lectures on the New Education" *(Shin kyōiku kōgi)* by Tanimoto Tomeri (1867–1946) in November 1906 ushered in a new phase in Japanese educational thought. Tanimoto, who had attracted attention immediately after the Sino-Japanese War with his espousal of a somewhat novel form of nationalistic education, had returned to Japan from study in Europe just before the Russo-Japanese War. Reflection on his experiences abroad convinced him that the enhancement of national fortunes required the type of education that emphasized the individual, and the aim of the "new education" he preached was the expansion of each individual's unique capabilities. This individualistic education was necessary, Tanimoto asserted, because of two shortcomings concealed beneath the sense of national unity that was commonly assumed to be a strong point of the Japanese people. These two shortcomings—"uniformity without respect for individuality" and the lack of an independent mind or a spirit of self-reliance—made the Japanese people incapable of a true, self-conscious national solidarity, Tanimoto feared. Victory may have been achieved with the aid of a "unity of ignorance," but "would that be sufficient when it came to creating a flourishing commerce and industry after the war?"[73]

To overcome these shortcomings, Tanimoto's "new education" sought to avoid making too much of loyalty and patriotism. Instead, it focused on instilling the concept of rights and obligations in the people. Nurturing this concept, Tanimoto believed, would help to create a nation capable of making constitutionalism and self-government work. It would develop men who eagerly sought fellowship with people from all over the world, men imbued with the recognition that people everywhere are the same—that is, with what Tanimoto called "globalism" or "humanitarianism." Together, these attitudes should produce a democratic, modern, active, and high-spirited personality. The method Tanimoto proposed for developing such a personality was called "dynamic education" or "education for self-development," an approach that accommodated itself to nature as it sought to cultivate the child's talents. Only through this kind of education, Tanimoto maintained, would it be possible to nurture a constitutional people who understood that "to seek the interests of the state was to benefit oneself" and that, conversely, "what was good for oneself would benefit the state."[74] That both Tanimoto and Takata should have sought their image of the ideal citizen in the reconciliation of individualism and nationalism is extremely interesting, as it is indicative of the character and direction of progressive educational thought after the Russo-Japanese War.

This type of progressive educational theory prospered for several years after the war. As Takata had said, however, to reconcile individualism and nationalism, maintaining harmony between private interests and those of the state, it was vitally important to train the people in constitutional thought. This was the linchpin that held everything together: without it, the balance between private and public interests would be destroyed, the individual and the government be wrenched apart. For all that, as Miyake Setsurei pointed out, the dignitaries of the Meiji government shared an ingrained habit with officials of the old shogunate: they regarded the people with ambivalence. "On the one hand, they have sought to keep the people removed from politics; on the other, they have been unable to do without the people in the pursuit of their own fame and fortunes. . . . All who hold government posts must share the blame for this climate, but it is the elder statesmen and education officials who are the most responsible."[75] In short, efforts to foster constitutional thought among the people lagged in Meiji Japan, both in intellectual circles and in the realm of education. The resulting dissociation of the individual from the state, feared by Takata, was described by the poet and social critic Ishikawa Takuboku (1885–1912) in a manner that allows us a real glimpse of the mind-set of postwar youth: " 'A state must be powerful. We have no reason to stand in the way of the growth of a powerful state. But please excuse us from lending a hand.' The patriotism of almost all the comparatively well-educated young people of today consists of just that. They treat the state as a remote entity, one that bears no relation to them."[76]

During the early years of the twentieth century, social pedagogy rose quickly to prominence in the persons of such young education scholars as Yoshida Kumaji (1874–1964) and Ōse Jintarō (1865–1944). They were concerned about youth's psychological and moral separation from the body politic, a phenomenon that had grown steadily since the Sino-Japanese War. Making use of the concept of the state as a social organism, they endeavored to lay the foundations for a harmonious relationship between the individual and society, the individual and the state. Yet the development of individualism in the postwar period had sufficient momentum to overcome pedagogical theories of this holistic vein and to facilitate the spread of distinctly individualistic approaches, such as those of Takata and Tanimoto.

As has been noted, materialistic and spiritualistic individualism were both fairly common among young people even before the war. Postwar social and cultural developments exacerbated these trends and reshaped their expression. The development of a full-blown capitalistic economy obviously provided an ever-increasing stimulus to materialistic individualism in society at large. But society began to rigidify. The political as well as the bureaucratic system solidified, limiting mobility. The *Kyōiku jiron* described the consequences for society in general and the bureaucratic world in particular: "Ten or fifteen years ago, those with an ordinary education all got good jobs. Those with higher education were much in demand, welcome wherever they wished to go. Today it is not so. Whether great or small, positions are filled. There are almost no openings."[77] Graduates of the law department of Tokyo Imperial University might still look forward to successful careers with little anxiety. Large numbers of students of private schools, however, were robbed of their hopes for making a career through diligence. They were driven instead to abandon themselves to lives of pleasure or to the pursuit of their material desires.

Spiritual individualism also developed in a climate that differed from that of the prewar period. This climate was defined chiefly by the rise of naturalism in literature. Prewar spiritual individualism reflected the struggle of anxious young people to resolve their doubts about the meaning of human life and the nature of the self in religious or idealistic terms. In contrast, postwar naturalism professed to be without ideals, without solutions. Spurning views of human life that were not based on "reality" and seeking to break down traditional authority and social norms, it turned youth's earnest quest for "the true" toward a concern with the truth of the self and an affirmative exploration of the passions as naturally human. An editorial in the *Yomiuri shinbun* of 22 November 1910 suggests that toward the end of the Meiji era, the influence of naturalism came to extend beyond student circles and penetrated the ranks of young teachers: "One of the most regrettable things we have noted in observing elementary and middle school teachers is that a decadent view of human life has long since become prevalent among them. If we are not mistaken in our observations, the most avid readers of naturalistic novels and the like are not young students but schoolteachers."

In May 1906, at a time when this sort of individualism—one that could find no way to reconcile itself with the state—was popular, the Japan Socialist party organized mass protests against a fare increase on the Tokyo streetcars. Antigovernment feelings rose among the populace. The Socialist party organs *Chokugen* (Straight Talk) and *Hikari* (Light) stepped up educational activities to a level not seen since the days of the old *Heimin shinbun* (Commoner's News).[78] Even under the Katsura cabinet's policy of oppressing socialism, students and teachers had constituted the major readership group of socialist publications. Now, under the relatively liberal Saionji cabinet, the party endeavored to win over large numbers of them to the socialist cause.

Once globalism was transformed into an individualism indifferent to the state or a socialism antagonistic to it, the government—which had originally encouraged globalism as a means of national development—could not but feel that it had become a dangerous mode of thought. This was true even of the Saionji cabinet. Instead of promoting the development of constitutional thought and the spirit of autonomy of which Takata and Tanimoto had spoken, the government sought to prevent the spread of socialism and naturalism through an educational program that emphasized "boosting morale and tightening public morals" and through increased supervision of student activities in the schools. This was the goal of the "Directive concerning Control of Student Thought and Morals" issued by Minister of Education Makino Nobuaki (1869–1949) in June 1906—the first reactionary step in postwar educational policy and the first policy to give rise to reactionary developments in the educational world.

Upon receiving this directive, educators acted "as if they had been given the revealed gospel. Observing a youth deep in thought, they would scold, 'You are depressed!' and yell at him to 'become familiar with wholesome thinking.' Spotting others who were reading new publications, newspapers, or magazines, they would tear into them, 'You do not have permission! Why are you reading something other than your textbook?' "[79] In April 1907 Makino followed up the control directive by issuing new "Regulations for Normal Schools." The first article insisted that "being filled with the spirit of loyalty and patriotism" was especially important for teachers, because they were regularly called upon "to arouse in their pupils a constancy of purpose as members of the nation."[80]

Middle- and upper-level teachers generally welcomed Makino's directive on the control of thought and morals. In it they saw an effective pretext for regimenting students who were developing a relativistic attitude toward school authorities under the influence of naturalism. Not all publicists and intellectuals, however, were won over, and public comment was mixed. Most pleased with the directive were conservative politicians of the House of Peers and the Privy Council, men such as Kaeda Nobuyoshi (1832–1906), Higashikuze Michitomi (1833–1912), Tanaka Fujimaro (1845–1909), and Nomura Yasushi (1842–1909). In the spring of 1904, this group had already presented Minister of Education Kubota with a written statement critical of the progressive content of the ministry's morals texts. In these texts, they observed, "the part that deals with the doctrine of the subjects' duties toward the state is rather undistinguished." Specifically, they noted, "it seems a trifle negligent in teaching pupils to understand their obligations as subjects of the state and as members of a family."[81] The ministry, however, rebuffed their complaint, finding no need to revise the texts. Makino's directive gave them another opportunity to push for more conservative morals education.

Conditional approval was also voiced by the *Yomiuri shinbun*, by

Yorozu chōhō, and by *Nihon.* The *Yomiuri,* however, expressed concern lest this directive become a pretext for restrictions on the press and on intellectual life. *Yorozu chōhō* feared that national morality might run to the extremes of Confucian morality, while *Nihon* observed that circumspection among the upper echelons of society was essential in implementing the directive. The majority of publicists and intellectuals, however, took a critical stance. According to the *Mainichi shinbun,* the directive's result was sure to be the type of expedient education that hindered children's free development; this was not the way to nurture the growth of a great nation. "Minister of Education Makino's educational policy might not be reactionary, but it is conservative," observed the *Mainichi;* hence it would "interfere with the Japanese people's great leap forward." The critical *Jiji shinpō* thought that "if students who have a sense of despair in their hearts embrace skepticism and anguish, that should not be seen as a pathological phenomenon." To Shimamura Hōgetsu (1871–1918), writing in the *Tōkyō Nichinichi shinbun,* it seemed that "student skepticism is part of a kind of revolutionary movement in the realm of the spirit, an inevitable and unavoidable general tendency that had its origins in the assimilation of Western civilization. This directive runs against that natural tendency."[82] Finally, it was posited in the *Kyōiku jiron* that being troubled over utopian ideas was part and parcel of the quest for truth, goodness, and beauty. "Since pursuing ideals is the way in which students fulfill their obligations as students, should not the minister of education do everything he can to encourage it?"[83]

On 13 September 1906, Ebina Danjō (1856–1937), Abe Isoo (1865–1949), Ukita Kazutami (1859–1945), and Ebara Soroku invited Makino to a meeting of their National Renewal Society (Kokumin Sakushinkai) and asked him to explain the purpose of his directive. Ukita remarked, "The transmission of socialism is a reality, but involves only a very small number of people; the vast majority are peaceful progressives. It is also a fact that the people possess the spirit of liberty. While we can certainly appreciate why you would want to propagate conservatism, we hope that it will not lead to the rejection of the spirit of liberty."[84] In sum, they asked Makino to exercise restraint in implementing the government's conservative educational policy.

The strength of this criticism notwithstanding, it had little effect on the Ministry of Education's policy. The Saionji cabinet resigned—amid allegations that it was soft on socialism—immediately following the Red Flag Incident (Akahata Jiken)[85] in June 1908 and was replaced by the second Katsura cabinet. The government grew more and more reactionary. An item in the internal affairs section of the Katsura cabinet's platform noted that as a result of mechanized production and free competition, the discrepancy between rich and poor had grown and the unity and order of society had been disrupted. These phenomena may be insignificant at present, the document stated, but they should not be ignored, because they encouraged socialism, which would eventually "develop the force of a wildfire, one that cannot be contained. Therefore, the need for nurturing national morality through education is obvious."[86] In short, the Katsura cabinet took upon itself the task of checking the social contradictions that were intensifying as a result of the development of capitalism. To this end, it sought to devise a solid triangular structure of domestic political controls—education, social policy, and police power.

The imperial rescript of 13 October 1908 (known as the Boshin Rescript) was emblematic of the Katsura cabinet's program: "Be faithful in your work and frugal in managing your wealth. Trust one another and deal justly with each other. Create good customs."[87] That Komatsubara Eitarō (1852–1919), a Home Ministry bureaucrat with ties to Yamagata, should have been Katsura's minister of education is also suggestive. It has been observed that Komatsubara was not simply a minister in the Katsura cabinet but was representative of it.[88] Komatsubara joined hands with Home Minister Hirata Tōsuke (1849–1925) to reverse the tide of progressive thought that had spread through the postwar educational world. Embracing the views of traditionalists who dominated the House of Peers, he proceeded to develop a conservative educational policy on the basis of the notion that Japan had a unique national polity.

Under Komatsubara's stewardship, the Ministry of Education yielded before the criticism of the Higashikuze group and the Kōdōkai—which found the morals texts lacking in the virtues of familism, respect for the gods, and reverence for the emperor—and undertook their wholesale revision. The head of the editorial committee charged with compiling the new texts was Hozumi Yatsuka (1860–1912), a conservative legal scholar who had consistently advocated ancestor worship and a familial view of the state since 1891, when he had opposed head on the modernization of the social compact that he thought he detected in the Civil Code. Not surprisingly, this second set of state-compiled textbooks, completed in 1911, aimed at inculcating all the traditional, familistic virtues—loyalty, filial piety, respect for the gods, and ancestor worship. The ministry's pursuit of conservative goals was reinforced by a variety of initiatives.

In September 1909 a directive on the encouragement of moral education in the curriculum went out to principals of schools under the Ministry of Education's direct control. In 1910 and 1911 the ministry made an effort to see that its interpretation of familistic morality was disseminated to every corner of the country by holding a series of lectures for instructors at normal schools and boys' and girls' middle schools; Hozumi Yatsuka was the lecturer. A ministerial ordinance of September 1908 abolished the limitations on the number of Chinese characters taught in the schools. Here the ministry took into account the criticism of the Higashikuze group, which had argued that limitations prescribed by the Revised Elementary School Ordinance of 1900 might create a nation of people who could not even read the rescripts of its emperors. The surveillance of students was intensified under the Supervision of Student and Pupil Activities Ordinance of January 1909, which was directed at events previously organized by the students on their own— lectures, commemorative gatherings, field days, and so forth. Adult education also played a part in the government's plans. Acting in concert with the local improvement movement of the Hōtokukai (Repaying Kindness Society), the Home Ministry sought to disseminate and develop community education programs aimed at purifying social morals, fostering good customs, and banishing "unwholesome thought."

In May 1910, at the start of the notorious Lese-Majesty Incident (Taigyaku Jiken; also called the Kōtoku Incident),[89] Katsura's Home Ministry intensified its efforts to suppress socialism, and the Ministry of Education reinforced its attempt to control popular thought, employing a morality based on what it termed Japan's unique national polity. About this time traditionalism reemerged conspicuously even among the political opposition and independent educators. In October 1910, Yumoto Takehiko—an early nationalist—urged teachers in a *Kyōiku jiron* editorial to promote "healthy thought" among the young people of the provinces and to keep them from coming into contact with "scandalous ideas."[90] In another *Kyōiku jiron* editorial in January 1911, he proposed the establishment of a "national education religion" that would make respect for the gods the principal object of *kokutai*-based education.[91] The following month Arakawa Gorō, a member of the House of Representatives, proposed an intellectual closure of the country to prevent the influx of "dangerous thought" from overseas. Should that prove impractical, Arakawa continued, then there at least ought to be a fundamental reform that would make loyalty and filial piety the sum and substance of education.[92] Also in February, a "Draft Bill for the Advancement of National Moral Education" was introduced in the House of Peers. This bill called for an education filled with the spirit of the Imperial Rescript on Education and the Boshin Rescript so that the ideas of loyalty and filial piety would not be shaken by progress in material civilization.

The reactionary atmosphere that enveloped educational circles both in and out of government also impinged on the student world. In May

1901 it was reported that traditional Chinese learning was all the rage in middle and normal schools and that the *Analects* of Confucius were being read extensively. By April 1911, the *Jiji shinpō* was observing that issuing new editions of the classics was the current fashion in the publishing world and concluded that students and young people no longer sought new knowledge from the West—that they seemed instead to be vainly yearning for old-fashioned ideals.

Among teachers, too, "national polity" theorists became a powerful force. The revised Japanese history texts edited by the ministry, which appeared in 1910, took the position that the Japanese imperial court had once split into Northern and Southern factions, which had co-existed for the better part of the fourteenth century. This interpretation, however, was attacked on the basis of the doctrine developed in *Dai Nihonshi* (a monumental history of Japan compiled largely by Edo-period Confucians of the Mito School),[93] which stressed the sole legitimacy of the Southern Court. For a time it appeared that objective historical fact would be sacrificed on the altar of the *kokutai*. The first to take up this question and criticize the government on this issue was a group of schoolteachers led by Minema Kasui (1873–1949).[94] The theory of two parallel courts had caused no problems when it was adopted in history texts before the 1904 revision. Now, however, it struck terror in the hearts of Prime Minister Katsura and Education Minister Komatsubara, who had themselves brandished the sword of the unique, unchanging, and sempiternal national polity. Opposition parties used the issue in the Diet to attack the government. That is the sort of political and educational climate that prevailed at the time of the Lese-Majesty Incident.

Even amid this extreme nationalistic stirring in political and educational circles, however—even when it seemed that education would be thrust into a wholly reactionary role as a weapon to protect the national polity—the Katsura cabinet's educational policies did not fail to draw criticism from a progressive, globalist position. For example, the *Kyō-iku jiron* commented in regard to the Ministry of Education's training sessions for morals teachers: "The weakness of morals teachers is not that they do not know that the family comes first but that not knowing the morality of individualism, they are totally unable to conceive of a morality in which character is the first principle."[95] True individualism, it argued, was precisely what was required to cure the abuses of the times. Again, at a training institute for citizens' education sponsored by Ōkuma Shigenobu in December 1910, Ukita Kazutami sought to explain why familistic morality was not what Japan needed: "Morality should have society's welfare in view. It should adapt to the times. In a constitutional world, the moral position is one that regards all segments of society as equals. Here the standard of morality lies in an inner consciousness, in the character of the individual. In the feudal age we honored our ancestors. Henceforth let us place the development of our descendants first."⁹⁶ Tanimoto Tomeri, too, stuck to his guns and continued to espouse his "new education" on the lecture circuit. In a talk he gave in Himeji in 1910, he took an oblique swipe at the Education Ministry's moral education, which he found to be in the grip of traditionalistic values. Education had traditionally sought models in the past, he said, but the "new education" took a different approach. Its model was a man who, "unfettered by old habits and outmoded customs, purposes greatness, expects to launch bold undertakings, and is independent and self-sustaining."⁹⁷

The liberal education movement enjoyed an upsurge, and modernization proceeded rapidly in the educational realm once the Meiji era gave way to Taishō (1912–1926). Evidently, the globalism that had exerted such a great influence on Meiji education was not so weak as to be destroyed by the reaction initiated by Katsura and Komatsubara. In the end, it would appear that the second Katsura cabinet's educational policy was no more than a temporary manifestation of political impoverishment—a case of the government's failing to take appropriate measures to deal with the social contradictions that inevitably appear in the modern development of a nation-state.

Conclusion

Nationalism was the ideal that guided education in the Meiji era. That much is beyond dispute. One should not, however, be misled by the conventional portrayal, which holds that Meiji nationalism, a doctrine undergirt ideologically by loyalty and patriotism, served the needs of militarism and imperialism only. In particular, the belief that this sort of nationalism became conspicuous in education after the Sino-Japanese War fails to do justice either to the aims of Ministry of Education officials or to the substance of education in the late Meiji era.

This study has attempted to reevaluate that widely held view and, at the same time, to shed some light on what kinds of ideal images of the nation the leading schools of late Meiji thought sought to construct. Particular attention was directed to examining the degree to which war brought about the infiltration of militarism and imperialism into education and led to a revival of traditional moral education as the intellectual basis for national unity.

The findings were rather unexpected. Few ideological movements or schools of thought looked to public education to fuel the growth of national power that occurred as a result of the Sino-Japanese and the

Russo-Japanese wars. Nor do the wars seem to have had a major influence on the formation of educational goals. To be sure, there were those who sought to couple war and education and argued for the indispensability of militaristic schooling. Some voices insisted that national unity required the establishment and dissemination of a moral code for subjects. These opinions were widespread in political and educational circles and even more deeply ingrained in the conservative sensibilities of the people. It would be fair to say, however, that the leading schools of thought of the late Meiji era found their primary mission in restraining this deep, conservative current of thought.

In line with Japan's capitalistic development and together with the elevation of its international status through war, these schools of thought challenged their countrymen to enlarge their global vision. They appealed for individual self-awareness as a necessary basis for national consciousness. They taught that free economic growth, rather than military expansion, was the appropriate course for a nation that would conduct itself properly in the world. To this end, they continually endeavored to persuade Ministry of Education authorities that the goal of public education should be to reconcile individualism, nationalism, and globalism. Those who advanced these notions did not, however, acknowledge ideologies disruptive of the social order.

During the fourth decade of the Meiji era, Ministry of Education officials tended to respect intellectual currents that conformed to the course of capitalistic development rather than listen to the voices of conservatives. While continuing to hold fast to nationalism as a basic policy, those officials endeavored to incorporate as much of the global, universal, and rational as they could into their educational goals. Those, they believed, were the true means of national development.

In the next decade, however, the question of how to deal with socialism arose, and the Home Ministry began to interfere more obtrusively in school and community education. The Home Ministry had of course meddled in education before. This time, however, its intervention was spearheaded by a powerful bureaucracy and police; moreover, it was backed by prominent local families. Perhaps for the first time, local school administrators actually came to have more respect for its views than for those of the Ministry of Education. Consequently, it is more accurate to think of the conservatism encountered in local schools as the result of the Home Ministry's manipulation behind the scenes than as a product of the Education Ministry's leadership. The truth is that in the late Meiji era the role of the progressive schools of thought was less that of attacking a weakened Ministry of Education than of supporting its independence against pressures applied by the Home Ministry.

Notes

INTRODUCTION

1. Bernard Bailyn, *Education in the Forming of American Society* (New York: Vintage Books, 1960), p. 9.

2. Ronald P. Dore, *Education in Tokugawa Japan* (Berkeley: University of California Press, 1965; also London: Athlone Press and Ann Arbor: Center for Japanese Studies, University of Michigan, 1984 reprint ed.); Herbert Passin, *Society and Education in Japan* (New York: Teachers College Press, 1965; Tokyo and New York: Kodansha International, 1983 reprint ed.); John Whitney Hall, "Education and Modern National Development," in *Twelve Doors to Japan,* ed. Hall and Richard K. Beardsley (New York: McGraw-Hill, 1965), pp. 384–426. Also of interest is an even earlier study by Hall, "The Confucian Teacher in Tokugawa Japan," in *Confucianism in Action,* ed. David S. Nivison and Arthur F. Wright (Stanford: Stanford University Press, 1959), pp. 268–301.

3. Henry DeWitt Smith II, *Japan's First Student Radicals* (Cambridge, Mass.: Harvard University Press, 1972); Ivan Parker Hall, *Mori Arinori* (Cambridge: Harvard University Press, 1973); Carol Gluck, *Japan's Modern Myths: Ideology in the Late Meiji Period* (Princeton: Princeton University Press, 1985); Earl H. Kinmonth, *The Self-Made Man in Meiji Japanese Thought: From Samurai to Salary Man* (Berkeley: University of California Press, 1981); Donald T. Roden, *Schooldays in Imperial Japan: A Study in the Culture of a Student Elite* (Berkeley: University of California Press, 1980).

4. Tetsuo Najita, *Visions of Virtue in Tokugawa Japan: The Kaitokudō Merchant Academy of Osaka* (Chicago: University of Chicago Press, 1987); Peter

Nosco, *Remembering Paradise: Nativism and Nostalgia in Eighteenth-Century Japan* (Cambridge, Mass.: Council on East Asian Studies, Harvard University, 1990); Mary Evelyn Tucker, *Moral and Spiritual Cultivation in Japanese Neo-Confucianism: The Life and Thought of Kaibara Ekken, 1630–1714* (Albany: State University of New York Press, 1989); Janine Anderson Sawada, *Confucian Values and Popular Zen: Sekimon Shingaku in Eighteenth-Century Japan* (Honolulu: University of Hawai'i Press, 1993).

5. Donald R. Thurston, *Teachers and Politics in Japan* (Princeton: Princeton University Press, 1973); Benjamin C. Duke, *Japan's Militant Teachers: A History of the Left-Wing Teachers' Movement* (Honolulu: University Press of Hawai'i, 1973); Horio Teruhisa, *Educational Thought and Ideology in Modern Japan: State Authority and Intellectual Freedom,* ed. and trans. Steven Platzer (Tokyo: University of Tokyo Press, 1988); Byron K. Marshall, *Academic Freedom and the Japanese Imperial University, 1868–1939* (Berkeley: University of California Press, 1992), and *Learning to Be Modern: Japanese Political Discourse on Education* (Boulder, Colo.: Westview Press, 1994); Leonard J. Schoppa, *Education Reform in Japan: A Case of Immobilist Politics* (London: Routledge, 1991); Mark E. Lincicome, *Principle, Praxis, and the Politics of Educational Reform in Meiji Japan* (Honolulu: University of Hawai'i Press, 1995).

6. E.g., Aoki Michio, *Bunka-Bunsei no minshū to bunka* (Bunka Shobō Hakubunsha, 1985); Fukawa Kiyoshi, *Kinsei minshū no kurashi to gakushū* (Kōbe Shinbun Shuppan Sentā, 1988); Takahashi Satoshi, *Minshū to gōnō: Bakumatsu-Meiji no sonraku shakai* (Miraisha, 1985); and Tsukamoto Manabu, *Tokai to inaka: Nihon bunka gaishi* (Heibonsha, 1991).

7. Terasaki Masao, "The Study of Japanese Educational History: A Brief History and Related Problems," *Acta Asiatica* 54:113 (1988).

8. *Kindai Nihon kyōiku seido shiryō,* ed. Kindai Nihon Kyōiku Seido Shiryō Hensankai (Dai Nihon Yūbenkai Kōdansha, 1956–1959).

9. *Aichi-ken kyōikushi,* ed. Aichi-ken Kyōiku Iinkai (Aichi-ken Kyōiku Iinkai, 1972–1975); *Nagano-ken kyōikushi,* gen. ed. Kaigo Tokiomi, ed. Nagano-ken Kyōikushi Kankōkai (Nagano-ken Kyōikushi Kankōkai, 1972–1983).

10. Among the most important of the numerous publications of Ishikawa Ken are *Nihon shomin kyōikushi* (Tōkō Shoten, 1929); *Gakkō no hattatsu* (Iwasaki Shoten, 1953); *Nihon gakkōshi no kenkyū* (Shōgakkan, 1960); and a 14-volume compilation of the content of textbooks from Tokugawa times into the postwar period, *Nihon kyōkasho taikei* (Kōdansha, 1968). The most important studies of Kaigo Tokiomi include *Meiji shonen no kyōiku* (Hyōron-sha, 1973), and *Kyōiku chokugo no seiritsushi* (published by author, available through Tōkyō Daigaku Shuppankai, 1965). There is a 10-volume collection of his major works: *Kaigo Tokiomi chosakushū* (Tōkyō Shoseki, 1981).

11. Informal conversational comment of Rai Kiichi, professor of history at Hiroshima University.

12. Chapters 2, 3, 6, 7, and 8 are from Motoyama Yukihiko, *Kindai Nihon no seiji to kyōiku* (Mineruva Shobō, 1972).

13. Motoyama, "Bakumatsu-ishinki ni okeru shomin no ishiki to kōdō," in *Meiji ishinshi no mondaiten,* ed. Sakata Yoshio (Miraisha, 1962), pp. 241–306.

14. On education in the Taishō period, see especially his "Meiji kokka no kyōiku shisō: Taishō kyōiku to no kanren o chūshin ni," in *Taishō no kyōiku,* ed. Motoyama (Daiichi Hōki Shuppan, 1978), pp. 39–162. On the media and public opinion, see "Meiji shonen no kyōiku ikken: Kyōiku yoron zenshi no kōsatsu," in *Meiji kyōiku yoron no kenkyū,* ed. Motoyama (Fukumura Shuppan, 1969), 1:1–67. On political assemblies and educational policy, see "Teikoku gikai ni okeru kyōiku giji no hensen," in *Teikoku gikai to kyōiku seisaku,* ed. Motoyama (Shibunkaku, 1981), pp. 3–68, and "Kyōto fukai to kyōiku mondai," in *Kyōto fukai to kyōiku seisaku,* ed. Motoyama (Nihon Tosho Sentā, 1990), pp. 3–56. On the history of political parties, see *Seitō seiji no shidō: Seiji shisōshiteki kōsatsu* (Mineruva Shobō, 1978). Motoyama's work on nativist thought includes *Motoori Norinaga* (Shimizu Shoin, 1978).

15. See Carol Gluck, "The People in History: Recent Trends in Japanese Historiography," *Journal of Asian Studies* 38.1:25–50 (November 1978).

16. Translated from "Jukyōteki tokuchishugi no rinen to kokumin seiji no keisei: Tani Tateki no seiji shisō," in Motoyama, *Meiji shisō no keisei* (Fukumura Shuppan, 1969), pp. 148–200; first appeared as "Tani Tateki no seiji shisō ni tsuite" in *Jinbun gakuhō* 6:87–114 (March 1956).

17. Translated from "Meiji shoki keimōka no shisō: Meirokusha no hitobito o chūshin to shite," in *Meiji shisō no keisei,* pp. 68–120; first appeared as "Bunmei kaika-ki ni okeru shin chishikijin no shisō" in *Jinbun gakuhō* 4:45–84 (February 1954).

18. Translated from "Meiji kōki no shisō to kyōiku," in *Kindai Nihon no seiji to kyōiku,* pp. 260–308; first appeared under the same title in *Kyōto Daigaku Kyōikugakubu kiyō* 11:1–33 (March 1965).

19. Motoyama, "Meiji shoki no kyōiku seisaku to sono seijiteki haikei: Chūō seifu no baai," in *Kindai Nihon no seiji to kyōiku,* pp. 1–70.

20. Translated from "Meiji zenki no chihō seiji to chūtō kyōiku no tenkai: Kōchi-ken no baai," in *Kindai Nihon no seiji to kyōiku,* pp. 71–119; first appeared under the title "Kōchi-ken no chūtō kyōiku" in *Meiji zenki no gakkō seiritsushi* (Miraisha, 1965), pp. 49–99, a volume edited by Motoyama and devoted to the subject of middle schools.

21. Translated from "Kokkenshugi undō to kyōiku katsudō: Kumamoto no Shimeikai to Seiseikō no kankei o megutte," in *Kindai Nihon no seiji to kyōiku,* pp. 120–173; first published as "Meiji jidai ni okeru kokkashugi kyōiku no ichi genryū," in *Kyōto Daigaku Kyōikugakubu kiyō* 6:30–65 (September 1960).

22. Translated from "Meiji ni okeru zaiya seishin no keisei: Tōkyō Senmon Gakkō o chūshin ni mitaru," in *Kindai Nihon no seiji to kyōiku,* pp. 213–259;

first published as "Meiji no Nihonjin ni okeru zaiya seishin no keisei," in *Jinbun gakuhō* 24:34–63 (March 1967).

23. See Bailyn, p. 14.

CHAPTER 1: *Patterns of Thought and Action of the Common People during the Bakumatsu and Restoration Epoch*

1. See "Hyakushō ikki nenpyō," compiled, edited, and published by Kyōto Daigaku Nōgakubu Nōrin Keizai Gakka Nōshi Kenkyūshitsu (3 September 1959), pp. 316–328. This chronological table is a substantial revision of Kokushō Iwao, "Hyakushō ikki nendaihyō," *Hyakushō ikki gaikan oyobi nenpyō, Keizaishi kenkyū* 17.3 (1937). The two incidents attributed to unspecified years of the Kaei era (1848–1853) have been ignored in the calculations.

Neither 1860 nor 1864 is an accidental datum point in the comparison presented here. The Bakumatsu and Restoration epoch entered on an independent historical path both politically and economically in 1860. After 1864 the Tokugawa shogunate confronted its feudatories not once but twice with demands for vast expenditures to help support its punitive campaigns against the Chōshū domain.

2. On the third day of the Twelfth Month of the fifth year of the Meiji period (1872), Japan switched from its traditional calendar to the Gregorian calendar. That day became 1 January of the sixth year of Meiji (1873). Before that day, dates are given according to the old calendar; from it, by the new. Thus 1858.6.19, the date on which the U.S.-Japan Treaty of Friendship and Commerce was signed, is the nineteenth day of the Sixth Month of Ansei 5 (1858), 1868.2 is the Second Month of Keiō 4 (1868), and so forth. Dates are fully converted in cases where the traditional calendar's lag behind the Western calendar would cause a discrepancy in the year of the occurrence. Thus Ansei 1 (1854).11.27, the first day of the Ansei era, is converted to 15 January 1855; the date of Tokugawa Yoshinobu's ascension to the shogunate, Keiō 2 (1866).12.5, is given as 10 January 1867, and so forth.

3. *Tōkyō Shōhō Kaigijo yōkenroku gōgai* (1880), cited in Yamaguchi Kazuo, *Bakumatsu bōekishi* (Chūō Kōron-sha, 1943), pp. 239–240.

4. *Jinpū shūran*, comp. Hiratsuka Seikei (1867), cited in Yamaguchi, pp. 234–236.

5. *Kyōto-fu kyōikushi*, ed. Kyōto-fu Kyōikukai (Daiichi Shobō, 1983 reprint ed.), p. 514. One *koku* = 180.4 liters (47.7 gallons) or 5.1 bushels.

6. See Yamaguchi, pp. 237–238.

7. Tōyama Shigeki, *Meiji ishin* (Iwanami Shoten, 1951), appended chart.

8. See Yamaguchi, p. 259.

9. Ibid., p. 4.

10. Ibid., p. 12.

11. Ibid., pp. 217–218.

12. The ambitious scheme of the Hiroshima domain included militias in Aki County (on the islands Kurahashijima, Shimokamagarijima, and Setojima), Saeki County (in Hatsukaichi and Nōmijima), Toyota County (in Tadanoumi and Mitarai), and Mitsugi County (on Innoshima and Mukaishima).

13. Horie Hideichi, "Bakumatsu ni okeru kaikyū tōsō," in *Kindai Nihon no keisei,* ed. Rekishi Gakkai (Iwanami Shoten, 1953), pp. 1–21.

14. Naitō Seichū, "Bakusei kaikaku no shakaiteki kiban—Bitchū tenryō Kurashiki-mura," in *Hansei kaikaku no kenkyū,* ed. Horie Hideichi (Ochanomizu Shobō, 1955), pp. 281–340.

15. Wakita Osamu, "Bakusei kaikaku no shakaiteki kiban—Settsu mensaku chitai," ibid., pp. 237–280.

16. Naramoto Tatsuya, "Meiji Ishin to nashonarizumu," in *Nihon no nashonarizumu,* ed. Maruyama Masao (Kawade Shobō, 1953), pp. 53–85.

17. *Takai Kōzan shōden,* ed. Kami Takai Kyōikukai (Kami Takai Kyōikukai, 1933), p. 27.

18. *Seien kaikōroku,* comp. Seien Kaikōroku Kankōkai (Seien Kaikōroku Kankōkai, 1927), 1:34, 42, 32.

19. *Hara Rokurō-ō den,* ed. Hara Kunizō (Hara Kunizō, 1937), 2:297.

20. Miyaoi Yasuo, *Minka yōjutsu,* cited in Itō Tasaburō, *Sōmō no Kokugaku* (Masago Shobō, 1966), pp. 7–8.

21. Miyaoi Yasuo, *Nōgyō yōshū,* cited ibid., p. 21.

22. "Dōmei danwa no jōjō," cited in Hirao Michio, *Yoshimura Toratarō* (Daidō Shobō, 1941), p. 22. The *Nihongi* passage to which the compact refers is *Kamiyo, kami no maki* 1:28; see *Teihon Nihon shoki,* ed. Maruyama Rinpei (Kōdansha, 1966), 1:20. The five grains are millet, panic grass, wheat, beans, and rice.

23. See Hirao, p. 70. Hanawa Jirō (also known as Hanawa Tadatomi; 1808–1863) succeeded his father Hanawa Hokiichi (1746–1821), the compiler of the monumental *Gunsho ruijū* (Classified Collection of Japanese Classics), as the head of the shogunate's Institute for the Interpretation of Japanology (Wagaku Kōdansho Goyōgakari) in 1822. During the Bakumatsu crisis, he had the ill luck of being ordered to conduct research into the procedures that governed the treatment of foreigners in Japan prior to the adoption of the closed-country policy in the 1630s. The false rumor that he was actually investigating the precedents for dethroning an emperor infuriated the superpatriots, and Hanawa was cut down by *shishi* swordsmen—none other than the future pillars of the Meiji state, Yamao Yōzō (1837–1917) and his fellow Chōshū man Itō Hirobumi (1841–1909).

The imperial princess Kazu no Miya Chikako (1846–1877), who had been betrothed to Prince Arisugawa no Miya Taruhito (1835–1895) since 1851, was married to Shogun Tokugawa Iemochi (1846–1866; r. 1858–1866) on 1862.2.11

over the imperial loyalist zealots' violent opposition (see p. 69). The imperial court extracted the promise to reinstitute the Closed Country policy from the shogunate before agreeing to this political marriage importunately sought by Edo.

24. *Hara Rokurō-ō den,* 1:30–38.

25. Katsura Takashige, *Yotsugigusa tsumiwake,* cited in Itō, pp. 115–116. Cf. Suzuki Shigetane, *Yotsugigusa,* in *Kokugaku undō no shisō,* ed. Haga Noboru and Matsumoto Sannosuke, Nihon Shisō Taikei 51 (Iwanami Shoten, 1974 second printing), pp. 231–243. The Divine Grandson (Sume-Mima no Mikoto) is Ninigi no Mikoto. The Heavenly Progenitors (Amatsu Mioyagami) are Ame no Minakanushi no Kami, Taka-Mimusubi no Kami, and Kami-Musubi no Kami. On the key terms Produce *(tsukuru),* Fulfill *(osamu),* Adhere *(katamu),* and Execute *(nasu),* see pp. 242–243; also see the supplementary notes s.v. *shurikosei,* pp. 601–602.

26. Hattori Shisō, *Kindai Nihon no naritachi* (Sōgensha, 1953), p. 149.

27. Naramoto Tatsuya, "Kinsei hōken shakai ni okeru shōgyō shihon no mondai," in *Kinsei hōken shakaishi ron* (Takagiri Shoin, 1948), pp. 3–61.

28. Umeda Unpin to Kasa Hayata, Ansei 2 (1855); in Saeki Chūzō, *Umeda Unpin ikō narabi ni den* (Yūhōdō Shoten, 1929), p. 71.

29. The author is indebted to Professor Taniguchi Sumio of Okayama University, who kindly arranged for him to borrow the manuscript of "Miyake Takayuki den" by a certain Tsurajima author, on which much of the foregoing treatment of Miyake Jōtarō is based.

30. Cited in Ogawa Gorō, "Chōshū-han ni okeru shomin kinnō undō no tenkai to sono shisōteki haikei," in *Onoda Kōkō kenkyū ronsō* (Onoda Kōtō Gakkō, Yamaguchi Prefecture, n.d.).

31. See *Shiraishi Shōichirō nikki,* entries for Bunkyū 2.10.26–27 and 12.17 (17–18 December 1862 and 15 February 1863), in *Ishin nichijō sanshū,* ed. Nihon Shiseki Kyōkai, Nihon Shiseki Kyōkai Sōsho 10 (Tōkyō Daigaku Shuppankai, 1969 reprint ed.), 1:35 and 38.

32. Naramoto, "Kinsei hōken shakai ni okeru shōgyō shihon no mondai," p. 58.

33. See *Shiraishi Shōichirō nikki,* pp. 49–52, 58, 62–63, and 71 respectively.

34. *Tōkō Sensei ibun,* ed. Tōkō Sensei Gojūnensai Kinenkai (Min'yūsha, 1916), p. 169.

35. Kokushō Iwao, *Hyakushō ikki no kenkyū* (Iwanami Shoten, 1928), pp. 38–39.

36. Motoori Norinaga, *Hihon tamakushige, Motoori Norinaga zenshū,* ed. Ōkubo Tadashi (Chikuma Shobō, 1972), 8:341–342.

37. Buyō Inshi, *Seji kenbunroku* (Kaizōsha, 1930), p. 93.

38. Yanagita Kunio, *Kyōdo seikatsu kenkyūhō,* Chikuma Sōsho 79 (Chikuma Shobō, 1967), p. 19.

39. *Seien kaikōroku,* 1:55.

40. Sawa Nobutada and Mochizuki Shigeru, *Ikuno gikyo to sono dōshi* (Tōkyōdō, 1932), p. 289. Nishimura Shōbei (1814–1883) was a merchánt.

41. "Atarashi Heita no oboegaki," cited ibid., p. 288.

42. "Tanshū sōjō shimatsu," in *Kanbu tsūki,* comp. Tamamushi Sadayū, ed. Nihon Shiseki Kyōkai, Zoku Nihon Shiseki Kyōkai Sōsho (Tōkyō Daigaku Shuppankai, 1976 reprint ed.), 2:125.

43. *Hara Rokurō-ō den,* 1:78.

44. Tamura Yoshinaga, *Tenchūgumi no kenkyū* (Nakagawa Shoten, 1920), p. 69.

45. "Kaei 6 ushidoshi Tochio-gumi hyakushō sōdō ryakki," in *Echigo Sado nōmin sōdō* (Niigata-ken Naimubu, 1930), pp. 431–432. *Tsumugi* is a kind of silk fabric.

46. See Kobayashi Shigeru, "Meiji henkaku-ki ni okeru nōmin tōsō," in *Hisutoriya* 12:1–23 (1955).

47. "Keiō 4-nen Nishi Kanbara-gun Yoshida maki-chihō no uchikowashi sōdō kiroku" (oral report of the Yoshida township official Kobayashi Tokutarō and Kimura Ginzō), *Echigo Sado nōmin sōdō,* pp. 453–458.

48. Tsukiguro Masuji, *Hōraku,* cited in *Echigo Sado nōmin sōdō,* pp. 464–465.

49. "Meiji gannen Minami Kanbara-gun Shitada-gō sōdō," *Echigo Sado nōmin sōdō,* p. 465.

50. Yura Nisshō, "Gōso nikki," *Bizen Bitchū Mimasaka Hyakushō ikki shiryō,* ed. Nagamitsu Norikazu (Kokusho Kankōkai, 1978), 3:970–973. The Miuchi uprising began on 3 January 1867 (Keiō 2.11.28).

51. Ibid., p. 978.

52. Ibid., pp. 973, 985.

53. Ibid., p. 997.

54. Tamura Eitarō, *Yonaoshi* (Yūzankaku, 1960), p. 95; 1 gō = 0.18 liter.

55. Fukuchi Gen'ichirō, *Kaiō jidan,* Ōzora-sha Denki Sōsho 110 (Ōzora-sha, 1993), p. 161.

56. "Muryo zasshū," in *Kanbu tsūki,* 2:519–520.

57. Report compiled by Katsu Awa no Kami, 1866.8; in *Renjō manpitsu,* ed. Nihon Shiseki Kyōkai, Nihon Shiseki Kyōkai Sōsho 192 (1974), 2:304–305.

58. "Edo ryoshi," Keiō 2 (1866).8; in *Shinbun kaisō,* ed. Osatake Takeki (Iwanami Shoten, 1934), p. 269.

59. *Matsumoto shishi,* ed. Matsumoto Shiyakusho (Matsumoto Shiyakusho, 1933), 2:88.

60. Tsuchiya Takao and Ono Michio, ed., *Meiji shonen nōmin sōjōroku* (Keisō Shobō, 1953), pp. 658–659.

61. Ono Takeo, ed., *Ishin nōmin hōkidan* (Tōkō Shoin, 1965), p. 168.

62. Ibid., p. 164. As the term *ryōten* usually signifies two noble personages

who are father and son, "Their Two Lordships" (Goryōten-sama) would logically appear to be a reference to the twelfth daimyo of Kōchi or Tosa *han,* Yamanouchi Toyosuke (1794–1872; r. 1809–1843), and to his son, the fifteenth daimyo Yamanouchi Toyoshige (also known as Yōdō; 1827–1872; r. from January 1849), whom the shogunate had forced into retirement in 1859. "His Honor the Governor" (Ochiji-sama) was Toyoshige's cousin Yamanouchi Toyonori (1846–1886; r. from 1859), the sixteenth daimyo of Kōchi, who held the position of domanial governor from the time of the rendition of the domanial registers to the throne in 1869.6 to the abolition of domains and the establishment of prefectures in 1871.7. (Note, however, that Toyonori was also Toyoshige's adopted son.) Also see Tsuchiya and Ono Michio, *Meiji shonen nōmin sōjōroku,* p. 503.

63. "Shinsen naeuri," in Sakuragi Akira, *Sokumenkan Bakumatsu shi* (Maekawa Shoten, 1905), p. 85.

64. Ibid.

65. Sakuragi, p. 56.

66. Ibid., p. 109.

67. "Naeuri," ibid., pp. 238–239.

68. Sakuragi, pp. 234–235. The ostensible "trial of strength" in this song is a sumo tournament, in which the wrestlers are divided between two sides, the East and the West. Here, East refers to the shogunate in its eastern capital of Edo, and West is a synonym for the imperial court in the western city of Kyoto.

69. Ibid., p. 255.

70. "Yo no naka iizukushi," ibid., pp. 264–265.

71. Sakuragi, pp. 309–310.

72. Ibid., p. 302.

73. See *Tōzai hyōrin,* ed. Nihon Shiseki Kyōkai, Nihon Shiseki Kyōkai Sōsho 145 (1973), 2:24–27.

74. "Onshoshidai shimatsu," in *Kanbu tsūki,* 1:231.

75. "Sasshū shimatsu," pt. 1, ibid., p. 147.

76. Sakuragi, p. 387.

77. Ibid. The reference is to the popular belief that propping a broom business-end up against the wall of the house will ensure the early departure of an unwanted guest.

78. "Rōshi shūkai shimatsu," pt. 2, *Kanbu tsūki,* 1:228.

79. Ibid., p. 227.

80. Information supplied by the money changer Iseya Tōbei, Fuyachō Sanjō-agaru, Kyoto, in 1862.7; *Tōzai hyōrin,* 2:70.

81. Extract from a letter dated [Bunkyū 3 (1863)].6.28; *Tōzai kibun,* ed. Nihon Shiseki Kyōkai, Nihon Shiseki Kyōkai Sōsho 142 (1968), 1:632.

82. Letter dated [Bunkyū 3].8.6; ibid., p. 776.

83. Secret report on the situation in Kyoto, 1863.10.4–8; in *Tōzai kibun,* Nihon Shiseki Kyōkai Sōsho 143 (1968), 2:424.

84. Letter from Kyoto, dated [Genji 1 (1864)].2.26; in *Kasshi zatsuroku,* comp. Kodera Gyokuchō, ed. Nihon Shiseki Kyōkai, Nihon Shiseki Kyōkai Sōsho 52 (1970), 1:106.

85. Letter from Kyoto, dated [1864].4.1; ibid., pp. 302–303.

86. "Kekka sōjō shimatsu," *Kanbu tsūki,* 2:34–35.

87. Ibid., pp. 535–536.

88. Sakuragi, p. 408.

89. Letter dated [Bunkyū 2 (1862)]. intercalary 8.28; in *Tōzai hyōrin,* Nihon Shiseki Kyōkai Sōsho 144 (1973), 1:380–381.

90. Extract from a letter dated [1862].9.4; ibid., p. 433.

91. Extract from a letter dated [1862].10.12; in *Tōzai hyōrin,* 2:139. The first of the two comic poems—*Shungaku no / yama ga kuzurete / kado ga tsuku*—involves a visual pun, as the character for "summit," read *gaku* or *take,* is made up of two written components, *yama* or "mountain" and *goku* or "prison." If *yama* is stripped away and the character for "gate," pronounced either *kado* or *mon,* is added to the remnant, the result is *gokumon,* the prison gate where Shungaku's head will presumably be put on exhibition.

92. Letter dated [1863].3.10; in *Tōzai kibun,* 1:269.

93. *Kaei Meiji nenkanroku* (Kosho Hozon Shooku, n.d.), fasc. 12, f. 13.

94. Letter from Edo, dated [1863].3.6; in *Tōzai kibun,* 1:272.

95. Letter dated [1863].4; ibid., p. 405.

96. Sakuragi, p. 408.

97. Letter dated [1863].4.9; in *Tōzai kibun,* 1:415.

98. *Kasshi zatsuroku,* 1:214.

99. "Yobokure bushi," ibid., Nihon Shiseki Kyōkai Sōsho 53 (1970), 2:623.

100. "Kenjō-taru tai," ibid., p. 8. The author, who signs with the pen name Chiharu, is identified in the text as Isomura Tetsuya, a member of the shogunate's reserve force *(yoriai),* that is, a bannerman with a putative income of more than 3,000 *koku.*

101. "Yobokure bushi," ibid., p. 625.

102. Sakuragi, pp. 641–642.

103. Copy of official notice to commoners' townships, dated [1865].5; in *Renjō kibun,* ed. Nihon Shiseki Kyōkai, Nihon Shiseki Kyōkai Sōsho 189 (1974), 1:382.

104. Letter dated [1865].6.2; ibid., p. 465.

105. Sakuragi, p. 662.

106. Ibid., p. 664.

107. Cited in *Shinbun kaisō,* pp. 60–61.

108. *Renjō manpitsu,* 2:95. The writer notes that palanquins are called *hoi-kago* because of the rhythmic "hoi! hoi!" the bearers yell to pace themselves.

109. Letter dated [1867].6; in *Teiu zasshūroku,* ed. Nihon Shiseki Kyōkai, Nihon Shiseki Kyōkai Sōsho 140 (1972), 1:133.

110. *Renjō kibun,* Nihon Shiseki Kyōkai Sōsho 140 (1968), 2:352.

111. Ibid., p. 47.

112. Sakuragi, p. 746. This *kyōka* parodies the celebrated lines from the *Terakoya* scene of the *jōruri* and kabuki play by Takeda Izumo et al., *Sugawara denju tenarai kagami* (first performed 1746): *Ume wa tobi / sakura wa karuru / yo no naka ni / nani tote matsu no / tsurenakaruran.* These lines in turn cite a poem by Minamoto no Shitagō (911–983).

CHAPTER 2: *The Political Background of Early Meiji Educational Policy*

1. On the third day of the Twelfth Month of the fifth year of the Meiji period (1872), Japan switched from its traditional calendar to the Gregorian calendar. That day became 1 January of the sixth year of Meiji (1873). Before that day, dates are given according to the old calendar; from it, by the new. Thus 1871.7.14 is the fourteenth day of the Seventh Month of Meiji 4 (1871), 1868.2 is the Second Month of Keiō 4 (1868), and so forth. Dates are fully converted in cases where the traditional calendar's lag behind the Western calendar would cause a discrepancy in the year of the occurrence. Thus Keiō 3 (1867).12.9 is given as 3 January 1868; the date of Tokugawa Yoshinobu's ascension to the shogunate, Keiō 2 (1866).12.5, is converted to 10 January 1867, and so forth.

2. See Kyōikushi Hensankai, *Meiji ikō kyōiku seido hattatsushi* [hereafter: *Hattatsushi*] (Kyōiku Shiryō Chōsakai, 1964 second printing), 1:87.

3. Ōkubo Toshiaki, *Nihon no daigaku* (Sōgensha, 1943), p. 209.

4. Ōkubo, Kido, and Gotō represented Satsuma, Chōshū, and Tosa, respectively, and acted as advisers to the government's chief executive officer *(sōsai)*, the imperial prince Arisugawa no Miya Taruhito, and to his two deputies, Iwakura and Sanjō Sanetomi.

5. "Dōjō shokei o imashimuru ikensho," *Iwakura Tomomi kankei monjo*, ed. Nihon Shiseki Kyōkai (Nihon Shiseki Kyōkai, 1927), 1:224–225.

6. *Iwakura Kō jikki*, ed. Tada Kōmon (Hara Shobō, 1968 reprint ed.; Meiji Hyakunenshi Sōsho 66), 1:1009.

7. Ōkubo to Kido, 1868.intercalary 4.3; *Ōkubo Toshimichi monjo*, ed. Nihon Shiseki Kyōkai (Nihon Shiseki Kyōkai, 1927), vol. 2, no. 202, p. 260.

8. Ōkubo to Iwakura, Meiji 1.12.25 (6 February 1869); ibid., no. 284, pp. 493–494.

9. *Iwakura Tomomi kankei monjo* (1929), 2:128–129.

10. *Hattatsushi*, 1:87.

11. On the *sonnō jōi* movement in Totsugawa, see chap. 1, "Patterns of Thought and Action of the Common People during the Bakumatsu and Restoration Epoch," pp. 41–43, 52.

12. *Fukkoki*, ed. Dajōkan (Naigai Shoseki K.K., 1930), 1:155.

13. Nukina to Iwakura, n.d.; "Kazoku Kaikan Gakushūin shiryō," *Iwakura Tomomi kankei monjo* (1935), 8:399.

14. *Gakushasei,* in *Hattatsushi,* 1:88–92.

15. Ibid., pp. 90–91.

16. "Ozaka sento no kenpakusho," *Ōkubo Toshimichi monjo,* vol. 2, no. 179, pp. 192–193.

17. Kido to Itō, 1868.1.27; *Kido Takayoshi monjo,* ed. Kido Kō Denki Hensanjo (Kido Kō Denki Hensanjo, 1930), vol. 3, no. 8.5, p. 9.

18. Ōkubo to Kido, 1868.intercalary 4.2; *Ōkubo Toshimichi monjo,* vol. 2, no. 202, pp. 260–261. The Tokugawa shogunate's institute of Western studies, called Kaiseisho from 1863, was renamed Kaisei Gakkō by the Meiji government and eventually turned into the Daigaku Nankō (South University College); see pp. 143 and 145–146.

19. Kido to Itō, 1869.3.11; *Kido Takayoshi monjo,* vol. 3, no. 9.37, p. 282. The two Kyushu domains, Kurume *han* and Higo *han* (also known as Kumamoto *han*), were notorious areas of resistance to the early Meiji government. They were havens for disaffected samurai from Chōshū and elsewhere until the spring of 1871, when the antigovernment activists were suppressed.

20. Tokutomi Iichirō, *Kinsei Nihon kokuminshi,* vol. 69: *Meiji Tennō gyou shi* (Jiji Tsūshinsha Shuppankyoku-nai Kinsei Nihon Kokuminshi Kankōkai, 1963), 8:360.

21. Text in *Hōrei zensho,* ed. Naikaku Kanpōkyoku (Hara Shobō, 1974 reprint ed.), Meiji 1:331, 1:137–146. The document was issued on 1868.intercalary 4.21 and publicly distributed on the twenty-seventh.

22. Memorandum to Iwakura, 1868.intercalary 4; *Ōkubo Toshimichi monjo,* vol. 2, no. 208, p. 279.

23. "Suishi jōhyō," 1868.6; *Iwakura Tomomi kankei monjo,* 1:310–311.

24. *Hōrei zensho,* Meiji 1:332, 1:146.

25. Ibid., Meiji 1:337, p. 147.

26. Iwakura to Sanjō, 1868. 5.13; *Iwakura Kō jikki* (Meiji Hyakunenshi Sōsho 67), 2:451.

27. *Hōrei zensho,* Meiji 1:593, 1:237.

28. Tamamatsu to Iwakura, 1868.7; *Iwakura Tomomi kankei monjo* (1930), 4:66.

29. Tamamatsu, Hirata, and Yano to Iwakura's secretariat, 1868.7; ibid., pp. 67–69.

30. Ogawa to Iwakura, 1868.8.13; ibid., pp. 77–78.

31. Ōkubo to Iwakura, Meiji 1.12.25 (6 February 1869); *Ōkubo Toshimichi monjo,* vol. 2, no. 284, p. 494.

32. Hasegawa Akimichi, "Kōdō jutsugi," in *Hasegawa Akimichi zenshū,* ed. Shinano Kyōikukai (Shinano Mainichi Shinbun-sha, 1935), 2:445–446.

33. Hasegawa, "Kōdō Kōgaku zatsuroku," ibid., p. 423.

34. Hasegawa, "Kōdō jutsugi," ibid., p. 447.

35. Hasegawa, "Meiji gannen shichigatsu kengensho," ibid., p. 160.

36. *Ōkubo Toshimichi nikki,* ed. Nihon Shiseki Kyōkai (Nihon Shiseki Kyōkai, 1927), 2:31–32; entry for 1869.4.1.

37. *Hattatsushi,* 1:94–95.

38. Ibid., pp. 95–96.

39. Ibid., p. 99; Meiji 1.12.10.

40. Ibid., pp. 101–102.

41. "Shōdō jiko rirekisho," *Hasegawa Akimichi zenshū,* 2:628.

42. Quoted in Ōkubo Toshiaki, *Nihon no daigaku,* p. 216.

43. *Ōkubo Toshimichi nikki,* 1:463; entry for 1868.5.24.

44. Kido remarks that he found this "a very heavy responsibility." *Kido Takayoshi nikki,* ed. Nihon Shiseki Kyōkai (Nihon Shiseki Kyōkai, 1932), 1:53; entry for 1868.6.12.

45. *Iwakura Kō jikki,* 2:504.

46. *Kido Takayoshi nikki,* 1:77; entry for 1868.8.3.

47. *Iwakura Kō jikki,* 2:550.

48. Ibid., pp. 556–557.

49. Cited in Matono Hansuke, *Etō Nanpaku* (Hara Shobō, 1968 reprint ed.; Meiji Hyakunenshi Sōsho 79), 1:363.

50. *Iwakura Kō jikki,* 2:552.

51. Ōkubo to Kido, 1868.9.6; *Ōkubo Toshimichi monjo,* vol. 2, no. 255, p. 399.

52. *Ōkubo Toshimichi nikki,* 1:487; entry for 1868.10.13. Ōu is another name for Mutsu and Dewa, the northernmost provinces of Honshu.

53. *Iwakura Kō jikki,* 2:598.

54. *Hattatsushi,* 1:93.

55. "Kanshokumon 14," *Hōki bunrui taizen,* ed. Naikaku Kirokukyoku (Naikaku Kirokukyoku, 1891), 1:1.

56. *Hattatsushi,* 1:93.

57. *Fukkoki,* 6:536.

58. Ibid., p. 537.

59. Ibid.

60. *Iwakura Kō jikki,* 2:602–603.

61. "Futsū kyōiku no shinkō o kyūmu to subeki kengensho" (draft), Meiji 1.12.2 (14 January 1869); *Kido Takayoshi monjo* (1933), vol. 8, no. 19.23, pp. 78–79.

62. "Kokuze kōmoku," 1869.1; *Itō Hirobumi den,* ed. Shunpo Kō Tsuishōkai (Hara Shobō, 1970 reprint ed.; Meiji Hyakunenshi Sōsho 144), 1:423.

63. Ibid., p. 422.

64. Under this table of organization, instituted on Meiji 1.12.10, the principals *(tōdori)* of the Shōhei Gakkō and of the Kaisei Gakkō were officials of grade five, as were professors of the second rank (there were no professors of the first rank); professors of the third rank were officials of grade six; probationary junior professors were grade seven officials, as were administrators

below the rank of principal; subchiefs were grade eight officials; and ordinary clerks were in grade nine.

65. *Hōki bunrui taizen*, p. 4.

66. *Hattatsushi*, 1:106–107.

67. Naitō Meisetsu, *Meisetsu jiden* (Okamura Shoten, 1922), p. 42.

68. Kido to Suzuki Naoe, 1869.2.17; *Kido Takayoshi monjo*, vol. 3, no. 9.28, p. 264.

69. "Gigyō ryōkan kisoku," *Hōrei zensho*, Meiji 2:54, 2:18–19, and "Gisan benkan bunka," ibid., Meiji 2:55, pp. 19–22.

70. Ōkubo to Komatsu Genba no Kami, Ijichi Sō no Jō, and Yoshii Kōsuke, 1869.1.10; *Ōkubo Toshimichi monjo*, vol. 3, no. 292, p. 17.

71. "Seifu no teisai ni kansuru kengensho," 1869.1; ibid., no. 290, pp. 9–10.

72. Iwakura to Ōkubo, 1869.1.14; ibid., no. 294 supp., p. 27.

73. Agenda for debate, minuted with endorsements from Ōkubo et al., 1869.1.24; ibid., no. 299, item [17], pp. 56–57.

74. "Matsuoka Tokitoshi monjo," quoted in Ōkubo Toshiaki, *Nihon no daigaku*, p. 218.

75. "Hanji shokusei," in Sashihara Yasuzō, *Meiji seishi*, 1 (1892), *Meiji bunka zenshū*, gen. ed. Yoshino Sakuzō, vol. 2: *Seishi-hen* (Nihon Hyōronsha, 1928), pp. 53–54.

76. *Ōkubo Toshimichi nikki*, 2, 22–23; entry for 1869.2.16.

77. Tanaka Sōgorō, *Meiji Ishin taiseishi* (Chikura Shobō, 1941), pp. 241–242.

78. Kido to Ōmura, first part of 1869.1; *Kido Takayoshi monjo*, vol. 3, no. 9.10, p. 231.

79. Kido to Ōmura, 1869.1.30; ibid., no. 9.9, p. 229.

80. "Hanseki hōkan ni kansuru kengensho" (draft), 1868.2; ibid., vol. 8, no. 19.9, p. 26.

81. *Kido Takayoshi nikki*, 1:99–100.

82. Ōkubo to Iwakura, 1869.1.14; *Ōkubo Toshimichi monjo*, vol. 3, no. 294, p. 25.

83. Ōkubo to Iwakura, 1869.4.26; ibid., no. 330, pp. 161–162.

84. "Shokuinrei narabini kan'i sōtōhyō," 1869.7.8, *Hōrei zensho*, Meiji 2:622, 2:249–264.

85. Ibid., pp. 256–258; *Hattatsushi*, 1:124–126.

86. Iwakura's proposal at the Dajōkan conference of 1869.1.25 that the superintendents of schools be sent from Kyoto to Tokyo to set up uniform university rules for eastern and western Japan was made just after the four major domains had volunteered to surrender their registers. The Kyoto superintendents, orders from Iwakura in hand, cooperated with their Tokyo counterparts in the task of establishing university procedures. That task was accomplished on 1869.6.15, two days before the registers were rendered to the throne.

87. *Hattatsushi*, 1:117.

88. Ibid. The Three Principal Relationships are those between ruler and subject, father and son, and husband and wife. The Five Abiding Virtues are humanity, duty, ritual propriety, knowledge of right and wrong, and trustworthiness.

89. Ōkubo Toshiaki, *Nihon no daigaku*, pp. 227–231.

90. Text in *Shūgiin nisshi, Meiji bunka zenshū*, vol. 4: *Kensei-hen*, pp. 169–170; record of discussion (1869.9.17), ibid., pp. 170–172.

91. Katō Yūrin, *Daishōgakkō kengi, Meiji bunka zenshū*, vol. 10: *Kyōiku-hen*, pp. 29–36.

92. *Hattatsushi*, 1:134; Meiji 2.12.14.

93. Ibid.; Meiji 2.12.17.

94. *Daigaku kisoku oyobi chūshōgaku kisoku*, ibid., pp. 139–142.

95. "Fuken shisei junjo," *Hōrei zensho*, Meiji 2:117, 2:60.

96. *Hattatsushi*, 1:142.

97. "Yano-ke monjo," quoted in Ōkubo Toshiaki, *Nihon no daigaku*, p. 243.

98. *Tōkyō Teikoku Daigaku gojūnenshi*, ed. Tōkyō Teikoku Daigaku (Tōkyō Teikoku Daigaku, 1932), 1:75–82.

99. *Hattatsushi*, 1:156.

100. Ōkubo Toshiaki, *Nihon no daigaku*, pp. 235–236.

101. "Kenkokusaku," in *Iwakura Kō jikki*, 2:826–836.

102. Saigō Kichinosuke to Ōkubo, 1870.3.23; *Ōkubo Toshimichi monjo*, vol. 3, no. 437 supp., p. 421.

103. Ōkubo to Soejima, 1870.1.6; ibid., no. 420, p. 376.

104. "Seifu no shisetsu ni kansuru ikensho," 1870.3.19; ibid., no. 430, p. 399.

105. *Iwakura Kō jikki*, 2:830.

106. Ibid., p. 835.

107. *Hattatsushi*, 1:166, 167.

108. *Tōkyō Teikoku Daigaku gojūnenshi*, 1:192.

109. Ibid., p. 188.

CHAPTER 3: *Local Politics and the Development of Secondary Education in the Early Meiji Period*

1. That was the case apart from the brief period between August 1876 and March 1880, when Kōchi Prefecture temporarily assumed jurisdiction over the former Awa *han* (the present Tokushima Prefecture).

2. On the third day of the Twelfth Month of the fifth year of the Meiji period (1872), Japan switched from its traditional calendar to the Gregorian calendar. That day became 1 January of the sixth year of Meiji (1873). Before that day, dates are given according to the old calendar; from it, by the new. Thus 1853.6 is the Sixth Month of the sixth year of Kaei (1853), 1862.4.5 is

the fifth day of the Fourth Month of Bunkyū 2 (1862), and so forth. Dates are fully converted where the traditional calendar's lag behind the Western calendar would cause a discrepancy in the year of the occurrence. Thus the Twelfth Month of Meiji 2 (2 January–31 January 1870) is converted to January 1870, and so forth.

3. Kaei 6.12, that is, from 30 December 1853 to 28 January 1854.

4. *Kōchi-han kyōiku enkaku torishirabe,* ed. Seifūkai (Seifūkai, 1932), p. 129.

5. Hirao Michio, *Yōdō Kō kiden* (Hōbunsō, 1943), p. 9.

6. *Kōchi-han kyōiku enkaku torishirabe,* p. 10.

7. Hirao Michio, *Yoshida Tōyō,* Jinbutsu Sōsho 26 (Yoshikawa Kōbunkan, 1959), pp. 127–132.

8. *Kōchi-han kyōiku enkaku torishirabe,* p. 22.

9. Fukushima Nariyuki, "Kōchi-han hankō no hensen," in *Tosa shidan,* no. 36 (September 1931), p. 15.

10. See Tani Tateki, "Ishinzen ni okeru Tosa seitō no shōchō," *Tani Tateki ikō,* ed. Nihon Shiseki Kyōkai (Tōkyō Daigaku Shuppankai, 1975 reprint ed.; Zoku Nihon Shiseki Kyōkai Sōsho, 1st ser., no. 6), 1:248–268.

11. "Seikyō itchi no gi ketsudan no gi," in *Kōchi-han kyōiku enkaku torishirabe,* p. 70.

12. Hirao Michio, "Kaiseikan sōritsu kō," *Tosa shidan,* no. 84 (October 1954), pp. 1–3.

13. Hirao, *Yōdō Kō kiden,* pp. 197–198.

14. *Kōchi-han kyōiku enkaku torishirabe,* p. 124.

15. Fukushima, p. 15.

16. *Kōchi-han kyōiku enkaku torishirabe,* pp. 78–79.

17. Tani Tateki, *Waizan taibōroku, Tani Tateki ikō,* 1:174.

18. *Kōchi kenshi,* ed. Nagase Kiyoshi (Kōchi Kenshi Kankōkai, 1933), p. 78.

19. *Kōchi-han kyōiku enkaku torishirabe,* p. 93.

20. Inoue Kiyoshi, *Nihon no gunkokushugi* (Gendai Hyōronsha, 1975), p. 167.

21. See Tani, *Waizan taibōroku,* pp. 215–216.

22. *Kōchi-ken gikaishi,* ed. Kōchi-ken Gikaishi Hensan Iinkai (Kōchi-ken Gikai, 1962), 1:12–13.

23. *Kōchi-han kyōiku enkaku torishirabe,* p. 15.

24. Ibid., p. 13.

25. Ibid., p. 85.

26. Ienaga Saburō, *Ueki Emori kenkyū* (Iwanami Shoten, 1960), p. 54.

27. *Kōchi-han kyōiku enkaku torishirabe,* p. 72.

28. Fukushima, pp. 18–19.

29. Uzaki Kumakichi, *Toyokawa Ryōhei* (Toyokawa Ryōhei Denki Hensankai, 1922), p. 66.

30. *Kōchi-han kyōiku enkaku torishirabe,* p. 85.

31. Fukushima, p. 19.

32. Ibid.

33. Etō Shinpei, a samurai of Saga *han* who had been put under house arrest by his domain for his involvement with *sonnō jōi* zealots during the Bakumatsu period, became a co-opted official *(chōshi)* of the central government when the Meiji state was established. From 1868 on, he occupied a series of important positions; in 1871, for instance, he became the first incumbent of the post of vice-minister *(taifu)* in the newly created Ministry of Education. He headed the Ministry of Judicial Affairs as its first lord *(shihōkyō)* between April 1872 and April 1873, and was made imperial adviser *(sangi)* on leaving that post. In October 1873, however, Etō—the advocate of an aggressive policy—found himself on the side of the losers at the forceful conclusion of the oligarchs' dispute over whether Japan should invade Korea. He left the central government and returned to Saga, where he placed himself at the head of a group of disgruntled former samurai called the Conquer Korea party (Seikantō) and allied himself with another, similarly disaffected group of *shizoku* who advocated a return to the old regime and called themselves the Patriotic party (Yūkokutō). They rose in arms, occupied Saga Castle, attacked prefectural offices, and issued calls for like-minded groups in Satsuma and Tosa to join them. The Saga Rebellion (Saga no Ran) was quickly suppressed by a government force commanded by Ōkubo Toshimichi; Etō was arrested in Tosa and was executed.

34. Hirao Michio, *Risshisha to minken undō* (Kōchi Shiritsu Shimin Toshokan, 1965), p. 13.

35. *Jiyūtō shi,* gen. ed. Itagaki Taisuke (Aoki Shoten, 1955), 1:131, 137–138.

36. *Monbushō daini nenpō* [1874] (Senbundō Shoten, 1964 reprint ed.), p. 14.

37. *Monbushō daisan nenpō* [1875], p. 605.

38. Hirao, *Risshisha to minken undō,* pp. 20–21.

39. These English instructors from Keiō included Yano Zenzō, Nagata Kazumi, Kira Tōru, Kadono Ikunoshin, and Jō Sentarō.

40. Shimazaki Isoma, *Kyū kakusha jiseki* (Jiyū Minken Hyakunen Kōchi-ken Kinen Jigyō Jikkō Iinkai, 1981), p. 37.

41. Ienaga, p. 138.

42. Shimazaki, p. 37.

43. *Yokoyama Matakichi Sensei den,* ed. Chōno Harunobu (Chōno Harunobu, 1941), p. 82.

44. Shimazaki, p. 1.

45. Aki Kiyoka, "Tosa Jiyūtō jidai seinen kessha dan," in *Tosa shidan,* no. 1 (September 1912), pp. 19–20.

46. *Yokoyama Matakichi Sensei den,* p. 74.

47. Shimazaki, p. 9.

48. Ibid., pp. 10–11.

49. *Monbushō daini nenpō*, p. 13; *Monbushō daisan nenpō*, p. 605.

50. Mori Matakichirō and Kondō Arata, "Ishin zengo Tosa kakuha no shōchō," *Tosa shidan*, no. 3 (October 1918), p. 15.

51. *Yoshida Kazuma Sensei*, ed. Kainan Gakkō Dōsōkai (Isobe Kōyōdō, 1917), p. 46.

52. Ibid., p. 43.

53. Ibid., p. 65.

54. See Hirao Michio, *Shishaku Tani Tateki den* (Fuzanbō, 1935), p. 405. The Akizuki and Hagi rebellions of October and November 1876 were abortive antigovernment uprisings of disgruntled former samurai; for details, see chap. 6, n. 41.

55. Tani to Sasaki, 22 December 1876; *Tani Tateki ikō* (1976; Zoku Nihon Shiseki Kyōkai Sōsho, 1st ser., no. 8), 3:419.

56. Teraishi Masamichi, *Nangakushi* (Fuzanbō, 1934), p. 897.

57. *Kindai Kōchi-ken kyōiku-shi, Shiryō-hen* (Kōchi-ken Kyōiku Iinkai, 1964), pp. 429, 430.

58. Fukushima, p. 19.

59. *Kindai Kōchi-ken kyōiku-shi, Shiryō-hen*, p. 491.

60. *Kōchi Kenritsu Daiichi Chūgakkō Dōsōkai shi*, no. 12 (January 1909), p. 34.

61. *Kindai Kōchi-ken kyōikushi, Shiryō-hen*, p. 493.

62. Ibid., p. 498.

63. Kataoka Naoharu, *Kaisōroku* (Hyakushikyo Bunko, 1933), pp. 12–14.

64. Shimazaki, p. 1. The other associations mentioned in this text are the Kaiunsha, Jidōsha, Junminsha, Kyōkyōsha, Heikensha, Rokubakukai, Sansankai, Shōdōsha, Kyōshisha, Byōdōkai, Jirikisha, Rikieki Jiyūtō, Uemachi Jiyūtō, Kitamachi Jiyūtō, and Minamimachi Jiyūtō in Kōchi City; on the city outskirts, there were the Seitōsha in Kuman and the Funkisha in Nakasuka.

65. *Monbushō daishichi nenpō* [1879], p. 298.

66. *Monbushō daikyū nenpō* [1881] (1966), pp. 596–597.

67. *Kōchi shinbun*, 4 June 1881, editorial by Sakamoto Namio.

68. *Doyō shinbun*, 21 June 1883.

69. Kataoka Naoharu to Imahashi Iwao, cited in Hirao, *Risshisha to minken undō*, p. 172.

70. Kataoka, *Kaisōroku*, p. 16.

71. *Kōchi Kenritsu Daiichi Chūgakkō Dōsōkai shi*, no. 12, p. 34.

72. Aki, pp. 19–20.

73. Kataoka, *Kaisōroku*, pp. 18–19.

74. *Doyō shinbun*, 23 January 1883; 1 February 1883.

75. Ibid., 21 June 1883.

76. *Monbushō daijū nenpō* [1882] (1966), p. 710.

77. *Kindai Kōchi-ken kyōikushi, Shiryō-hen*, p. 47.

78. *Isawa Shūji senshū*, ed. Shinano Kyōikukai (Shinano Kyōikukai, 1958), p. 19.

79. Ibid., p. 8.

80. *Aki kyōdo-shi*, comp. Aki-chō Yakuba (MS in Kōchi Kenritsu Toshokan).

81. Teraishi, p. 896.

82. "Reinansha Kachō Gakusha ryakureki," *Tosa shidan*, no. 48 (August 1934), p. 170.

83. *Isawa Shūji senshū*, p. 15.

84. *Nakamura chōshi*, ed. Nakamura-chō Yakuba (Nakamura-chō Yakuba, 1950), p. 149. The Meidō Gakusha's founders included the old Imperial Loyalists Kuwabara Masaatsu, Miyazaki Yoshimichi, and Miyagawa Tadataka. Its staff included Morisawa Tan and Tominaga Tadashi, who taught the Chinese classics.

85. Tosa Joshi Kōtō Jogakkō and Tosa Joshi Chūgakkō, eds., *Gojūnen no ayumi* (Tosa Joshi Kōtō Jogakkō and Tosa Joshi Chūgakkō, 1952), pp. 8–13.

86. Glennan and MacAlpin would appear to be the most likely equivalents of names known only by their *katakana* phonetic approximations, "Gurinan" and "Makuarubin."

87. *Ōishi Tamotsu-kun den oyobi ikō*, ed. Miyamoto Eisaku (Dōjinsha, 1925), p. 10.

88. Ienaga, pp. 316–317.

89. Shimazaki, p. 4.

90. Others were the Taihei Gakkō, founded in 1888 by Itagaki Taisuke's son Hokotarō, and a number of similar institutions, such as the Eigakkai (1887), Seika Gakkai (1889), Kyūyō Gakkan (1889), and the Kōtō Eiwa Gakkō (1889). See *Kindai Kōchi-ken kyōikushi*, passim.

CHAPTER 4: *The Confucian Ideal of Rule by Virtue and the Creation of National Politics*

1. "Shin Hoshutō," *Kokumin no tomo*, no. 11 (4 November 1887), p. 12; facsimile ed., *Kokumin no tomo*, ed. Fujiwara Masato (Meiji Bunken Shiryō Kankōkai, 1982 second printing), 1:139.

2. The name of this society derives from the date of its foundation, the sixth year of Meiji, i.e., 1873. On its character and activities, see chap. 5, "Meirokusha Thinkers and Early Meiji Enlightenment Thought."

3. Nishimura Shigeki, *Hakuō shigen*, in *Hakuō sōsho*, ed. Nihon Kōdōkai (Nihon Kōdōkai and Hakubunkan, 1909), 1:513.

4. Ibid., p. 502.

5. Yamaji Aizan, *Gendai Nihon kyōkaishi ron*, in *Nihon no meicho*, vol. 40:

Tokutomi Sohō, Yamaji Aizan, ed. Sumiya Mikio (Chūō Kōron-sha, 1971), pp. 382–384.

6. *Hakuō Nishimura Shigeki den,* ed. Nishimura Sensei Denki Hensankai (Nihon Kōdōkai, 1933), 1:436.

7. Office established in December 1878 and abolished in May 1885. There were three "area armies" (Eastern, Middle, and Western). The three appointees were directly responsible to the emperor and held equal rank with the first lord (i.e., minister) of the army *(rikugunkyō)* and the head of the General Staff.

8. Tani Tateki, "Rikugun onkyūrei kaisei no iken," in *Tani Tateki ikō* (hereafter: *Ikō),* ed. Nihon Shiseki Kyōkai (Tōkyō Daigaku Shuppankai, 1976 reprint ed.; Zoku Nihon Shiseki Kyōkai Sōsho, 1st ser., no. 8), 3:76–77.

9. Miyake Setsurei, *Dōjidaishi* (Iwanami Shoten, 1950), 2:77.

10. *Iwakura Kō jikki,* ed. Tada Kōmon (Hara Shobō, 1968 reprint ed.; Meiji Hyakunenshi Sōsho 68), 3:655.

11. Osatake Takeki, *Nihon kenseishi taikō* (Nihon Hyōronsha, 1939), 2:566.

12. Kuroda was at the time in question the head of the government's Land Development Bureau (Kaitakushi), an office charged with boosting the resources of Hokkaidō. Properties acquired by that office at a cost of more than 14,000,000 yen in public funds would have been transferred under that scheme to Godai and his associates for a mere 380,000 yen, interest free, payable over thirty years.

13. Tani et al., "Kokken sōritsu gikai kaisetsu no kenpaku," *Ikō,* 3:87–89.

14. Hirao Michio, *Shishaku Tani Tateki den* (Fuzanbō, 1935), p. 507.

15. Uematsu Kōshō, *Meiji shiden* (Tōkaidō Shoten, 1912), p. 82. The Kaishintō (more properly, Rikken Kaishintō [Constitutional Reform party]) was founded by Ōkuma in April 1882. Uematsu worked for the Kaishintō-affiliated Tōyō Keizai Shinpōsha.

16. Undated draft, text in Ōkubo Toshiaki, "Meiji jūyonen seihen to Inoue Kowashi," in *Kaikoku hyakunen kinen Meiji bunkashi ronshū,* ed. Kaikoku Hyakunen Kinen Bunka Jigyōkai (Kengensha, 1952), p. 635.

17. *Segai Inoue Kō den,* ed. Inoue Kaoru Kō Denki Hensankai (Naigai Shoseki K.K., 1934), 3:913–914.

18. Draft of 22 April 1887; ibid., p. 881.

19. Sashihara Yasuzō, *Meiji seishi,* 1 (1892), *Meiji bunka zenshū,* gen. ed. Yoshino Sakuzō, vol. 2: *Seishi-hen* (Nihon Hyōronsha, 1928), pp. 526–527.

20. "Gaikō no urei wa soto ni arazu shite uchi ni ari," *Kokumin no tomo,* no. 2 (15 March 1887), p. 10; facsimile ed., 1:18.

21. Nishimura Shigeki, *Nihon dōtoku ron* (originally a lecture given in 1886; published as a book in 1887), in *Hakuō sōsho,* 1:5–94.

22. "Hoshuteki handō no taisei," *Kokumin no tomo,* no. 10 (21 October 1887), pp. 3–5; facsimile ed., 1:123–124.

23. The term used in Japanese is *minponshugi*. For the reasons stated in Ryusaku Tsunoda et al., *Sources of Japanese Tradition*, 6th ed. (New York and London: Columbia University Press, 1964), 2:221–222, it is usually translated as "democracy." Contrary to the compilers of *Sources of Japanese Tradition*, however, I prefer to translate *minshushugi* as "democracy," which means that for the translation of *minponshugi* I am reduced to an unwieldy but nonetheless accurate paraphrase, inspired by Yoshino Sakuzō's authoritative interpretation of the term (ibid., p. 221): "In politics the fundamental end of the exercise of the nation's sovereignty should be the people." (Translator's note.)

24. *Itō Hirobumi den*, ed. Shunpo Kō Tsuishōkai (Hara Shobō, 1970 reprint ed.; Meiji Hyakunenshi Sōsho 144), 2:540.

25. I.e., the fighting in the north of Japan between the imperial forces and pro-Tokugawa domains that lasted from the Fourth until the Ninth Month of 1868.

26. Hirao, p. 271, glosses this as a reference to Yamanouchi Yōdō (Yamanouchi Toyoshige; 1827–1872), the fifteenth daimyo of the Tosa domain, even though his father Yamanouchi Toyosuke (1794–1872), the twelfth daimyo, would appear to be the more likely candidate for the adjective "aged."

27. Tani, *Waizan taibōroku*, *Ikō* (1975; Zoku Nihon Shiseki Kyōkai Sōsho, 1st ser., no. 6), 1:179–180. Nitta Yoshisada (1301–1338) and Kusunoki Masashige (d. 1336) were warriors famous for their loyalty to the imperial cause. In 1332, Kusunoki held out in Chihaya Castle (situated in what is now the southeastern corner of Osaka Prefecture) against a shogunal army described in the military romance *Taiheiki*, 8, as one million strong. Nitta seized the shogunate's headquarters city, Kamakura, and slaughtered its garrison in 1333. Funada Yoshimasa was Nitta's resourceful vassal; Onchi Sakon Mitsukazu, a semilegendary figure, is famed as a loyal retainer of Kusunoki.

28. Tani, "Gunkenron ni tsuki kengi," *Ikō*, 3:39.

29. Tani, *Waizan taibōroku*, *Ikō*, 1:178–179.

30. Ibid., p. 227.

31. Ibid., p. 239.

32. *Ikō*, 3:49.

33. This expedition, ostensibly a punitive mission against a tribe of Paiwan aborigines called the Baujanhsia [J: Botansha], who had killed fifty-four Ryūkyū castaways in early 1872, was at the same time an effort to demonstrate that Japan exercised sovereignty over the Ryūkyū Islands and an attempt to test whether the Ch'ing empire exercised sovereignty over Taiwan, with a view to possible Japanese expansion there. (Ryūkyū was in an ambiguous position under international law: exploited as a colony by Satsuma since 1609, it had been in fact a Japanese dependency throughout the Edo period, although the fiction that it was a vassal "kingdom" of China was maintained for commercial purposes). The main body of the expeditionary force, commanded by Saigō

Tsugumichi (1843–1902), landed at Sheliao-kang [J: Sharyōkan] on the south-western coast of Taiwan on 22 May 1874 and had overrun the Baujanhsia territory by 3 June. Its official mission was completed in July, when the tribe formally submitted to the Japanese. To exert pressure on China, however, the Japanese government kept the force on Taiwan and made no move to withdraw it until the very end of October 1874, when a face-saving agreement was reached through British diplomatic intervention: the Ch'ing empire would pay Japan an indemnity amounting to 750,000 yen, but China's sovereignty over Taiwan was acknowledged. This was modern Japan's first overseas military adventure. It cost the lives of twelve soldiers killed in action, one who drowned, and no fewer than 525 who died of malaria and other diseases—not to mention the 9,550,000 yen expended on mounting the expedition.

34. *Ikō,* 3:497.

35. Tani, "Yōkō nikki," *Ikō* (1976; Zoku Nihon Shoseki Kyōkai Sōsho, 1st ser., no. 7), 2:441–670.

36. In his entry for 22 March 1886, Tani writes, "Hong Kong is only one part of the English possessions in the Far East, yet its defenses are like this. They do have a reason for looking down on us. How could I not lament this?" Ibid., p. 446.

37. Ibid., p. 450. Tani refers to the battle of Tell El-Kabīr (13 July 1883), where the Egyptian army was defeated by the English. ʿUrābī Pasha, at the time minister of war, was taken prisoner and after a trial (and the reprieve of his death sentence) was banished to Ceylon. See Alexander Schölch, *Ägypten den Ägyptern! Die politische und gesellschaftliche Krise der Jahre 1878–1882 in Ägypten* (Zürich/Freiburg, 1972), translated as *Egypt for the Egyptians! The Socio-Political Crisis in Egypt, 1878–1882,* St. Antony's Middle East Monographs 14 (London and Oxford: Ithaca Press, 1981).

38. Tani, "Yōkō nikki," *Ikō,* 2:461.

39. Ibid., p. 494.

40. Ibid., pp. 496, 497–498.

41. Ibid., pp. 508–509.

42. Tani to "someone in [his] home province," 1889; *Ikō,* 3:554.

43. Ibid., p. 550.

44. Shimamura to Tani in Paris, 18 September 1886; *Ikō,* 3:509.

45. Tani, "Yōkō nikki," *Ikō,* 2:534–535.

46. *Ikō,* 3:551.

47. Tani, "Yōkō nikki," *Ikō,* 2:535.

48. *Ikō,* 2:587–588.

49. Tani to Soga, 23 January [1887]; *Ikō,* 3:520. Here Tani noted that military preparations, too, would be completed as a consequence. This was of crucial importance, because "the only instrument with which we can enforce the maintenance of our sovereignty is the army."

50. The members of this group included Sugiura Jūgō (1855–1924), Chigami Kiyoomi (1856–1916), Hasegawa Yoshinosuke (1855–1912), Furushō Kamon (1840–1915), Takahashi Kenzō (1855–1898), and Fukutomi Takasue.

51. Sashihara, pp. 528–529. The chief promoter of this "Convention" was Hayashi Kaneaki (1852–1920), a sometime member of the Jiyūtō.

52. Tani, "Kokka taiyō," *Ikō*, 3:99.

53. Ibid., p. 101.

54. Ibid., p. 103.

55. Ibid., p. 105.

56. Ibid., p. 109.

57. Ibid., p. 112.

58. Ibid., pp. 113–114.

59. Ibid., p. 116.

60. Tani, diary entry for 22 January 1889; *Ikō*, 2:683.

61. *Ikō*, 3:90–91.

62. Ibid., pp. 95–96.

63. Itō to Kuroda, 5 July [1887]; text in Hirao, pp. 582–583.

64. Quoted in Suzuki Yasuzō, *Jiyū minken undō shi* (Kōbunsha, 1947), p. 192.

65. Quoted ibid., p. 187, as commentary reprinted in the *Doyō shinbun* from the *Mezamashi shinbun*.

66. Shiga was a geographer who had recently returned from a journey to Australia and the South Seas. He and Miyake collaborated in the journal *Nihonjin*, founded in April 1888. Sometime later, in February 1889, Kuga started the newspaper *Nihon* with Tani's financial assistance. These were the leading proponents of cultural nationalism in the public opinion of the 1890s.

67. The name of this club is written with the two cyclical characters that together stand for the year 1887.

68. "Shin Hoshutō," *Kokumin no tomo*, 11:9–10 and 11:14; facsimile ed., 1:138–139, 140.

69. This party lasted from 1882 to 1883. Tani was among its supporters.

70. Kuga Katsunan, *Kinji seiron kō* (1891), in *Nihon no meicho*, vol. 37: *Kuga Katsunan, Miyake Setsurei*, ed. Kano Masanao (1971), p. 120.

71. Miyake Setsurei, *Shinzenbi Nihonjin* (1891), ibid., p. 286.

72. Yamaji, pp. 410–411.

73. "Shin Hoshutō," *Kokumin no tomo*, 11:11; facsimile ed., 1:139.

74. Tani, diary entry for 14 June 1889; *Ikō*, 2:775.

75. Tani to Hirota Masao, 1892; *Ikō*, 3:571.

76. The Jiyūtō mentioned here is the Liberal party organized in January 1890 by Ōi Kentarō. It should be distinguished from its namesake, the Jiyūtō (Party of Liberty) formed in 1881 by Itagaki Taisuke and dissolved in 1884.

CHAPTER 5: *Meirokusha Thinkers and Early Meiji Enlightenment Thought*

1. Ōkuma Shigenobu, comp., *Fifty Years of New Japan,* ed. Marcus B. Huish (London: Smith, Elder, 1909), 2:555.

2. Fukuzawa Yukichi, *Minjō isshin* (1879), in *Meiji bungaku zenshū,* vol. 8: *Fukuzawa Yukichi shū,* ed. Tomita Masafumi (Chikuma Shobō, 1966), p. 62.

3. Fukuzawa Yukichi, "Gakusha no shokubun o ron-zu," *Gakumon no susume* 4 (1874), in *Fukuzawa Yukichi zenshū* [hereafter: FYZ], ed. Keiō Gijuku (Iwanami Shoten, 1959), 3:48–54. *Gakumon no susume* is available in English translation by David A. Dilworth and Umeyo Hirano, *An Encouragement of Learning,* Monumenta Nipponica Monograph (Tokyo: Sophia University, 1969); the essay on the duty of a scholar appears on pp. 21–28; it is also available in *Fukuzawa Yukichi on Education: Selected Works,* trans. and ed. Eiichi Kiyooka (Tokyo: University of Tokyo Press, 1985), pp. 85–92. Concentrating on the controversy that arose over this essay unfortunately means that other important Meirokusha thinkers, such as Nakamura Masanao (Nakamura Keiu; 1832–1891) and the Mitsukuri brothers, Shūhei (1825–1886) and Rinshō (1846–1897), must be omitted from consideration here.

Note that "Meiroku" (Meiji Six) indicates 1873, the sixth year of the Meiji era, when the society was founded.

4. Fukuzawa, *Gakumon no susume* 1 (1872), FYZ, 3:29.

5. Seki Shingo, "Jōyoku o moppara ni subeki no ron," in *Zokumu keidan,* ed. Nakajima Katsuyoshi (1876), *Meiji bunka zenshū,* gen. ed. Yoshino Sakuzō, vol. 5: *Jiyū minken-hen* (Nihon Hyōronsha, 1927), p. 142.

6. Katō Yūichi, "Bunmei kaika," pt. 1 (1873), *Meiji bunka zenshū,* vol. 20: *Bunmei kaika-hen* (1929), p. 10.

7. Kyokkōken Shujin, "Kaika no hanashi" (1872?), ibid., p. 73.

8. *Meiroku zasshi* was published between the spring of 1874 and the fall of 1875; a total of forty-three issues appeared. They are included in their entirety in *Meiji bunka zenshū,* vol. 18: *Zasshi-hen* (1928), pp. 43–265. There is a complete English translation by William R. Braisted, *Meiroku Zasshi: Journal of the Japanese Enlightenment* (Tokyo: University of Tokyo Press, 1976).

Meiroku zasshi will hereafter be cited as *MZ,* with page numbers understood to refer to volume 18 of the prewar edition of *Meiji bunka zenshū.* The statement by Nishimura Shigeki that is quoted here appears in his "Shūshin chikoku nito ni arazaru no ron," *MZ,* no. 31 (March 1875), p. 204.

9. Torio Koyata, "Kokusei inga ron," in *Tokuan zensho* (Torio Mitsu, 1911), 1:587.

10. As reported in *Soyo fuku kaze,* 1868.5.16, in *Bakumatsu Meiji shinbun zenshū* (Sekai Bunko, 1961), 3:400.

11. Kido Takayoshi to Ōmura Masujirō, first part of 1869.1; *Kido Taka-*

yoshi monjo, ed. Kido Kō Denki Hensanjo (Kido Kō Denki Hensanjo, 1930), vol. 3, no. 9.10, pp. 231–232.

12. The transfer of the capital is discussed in detail in chap. 2, "The Political Background of Early Meiji Educational Policy."

13. Ōkuma, *Ōkuma Haku sekijitsu dan,* ed. Nihon Shiseki Kyōkai (Tōkyō Daigaku Shuppankai, 1980), p. 321.

14. Hagiwara Otohiko, *Tōkyō kaika hanjō shi* (1874), *Meiji bunka zenshū,* vol. 19: *Fūzoku-hen* (1928), p. 183.

15. Takamizawa Shigeru, *Tōkyō kaika hanjō shi* (1874), ibid., p. 244. Note that while bearing the same title, this is a different work from Hagiwara's.

16. Miyake Setsurei, *Dōjidai shi* (Iwanami Shoten, 1947), p. 253.

17. Takamizawa, p. 261. "Crabby script" refers to letters that run sideways like crabs, that is, Western writing.

18. Nishimura, "Shūshin chikoku," *MZ,* p. 204.

19. Fukuzawa, *Bunmeiron no gairyaku* (1875), *FYZ,* 4:185. This work is available in English translation by David A. Dilworth and G. Cameron Hurst, *An Outline of a Theory of Civilization* (Tokyo: Sophia University, 1973).

20. Kido to Kawakita Shunsuke (Gijirō), 1872.2.1; *Kido Takayoshi monjo,* vol. 4, no. 12.3, p. 337.

21. Fukuzawa, *Bunmeiron no gairyaku, FYZ,* 4:146.

22. Fukuzawa, "Teichū kōron" (1877), in *Fukuzawa Yukichi shū,* p. 247.

23. Fukuzawa, *Gakumon no susume* 5 (1874), *FYZ,* 3:60.

24. Fukuzawa, *Bunmeiron no gairyaku, FYZ,* 4:209.

25. Nishimura, *Ōjiroku* (1906), excerpt in *Meiji bungaku zenshū,* vol. 3: *Meiji keimō shisō shū,* ed. Ōkubo Toshiaki (1967), p. 412.

26. Nishimura, "Kaika no do ni yorite kaimoji o hassubeki no ron," *MZ,* no. 1 (undated), p. 58.

27. Asō Yoshiteru, *Kinsei Nihon tetsugaku shi* (Kondō Shoten, 1942), p. 269.

28. Fukuzawa, "Fukuzawa zenshū shogen" (1897), *FYZ,* 1:23.

29. Torio, *Tokuan zensho,* 1:585.

30. Sashihara Yasuzō, *Meiji seishi,* 1 (1892), *Meiji bunka zenshū,* vol. 2: *Seishi-hen* (1928), pp. 526–527.

31. Mori Arinori, "Meirokusha daiichi-nenkai yakuin kaisen ni tsuki enzetsu," *MZ,* no. 30 (February 1875), p. 199.

32. Suehiro Tetchō, *Shinbun keireki dan,* ed. Muramatsu Ryūkō (1900), *Meiji bunka zenshū,* vol. 17: *Shinbun-hen* (1928), p. 53.

The Osarizawa copper mine in Akita Prefecture was operated as a domain enterprise by Nanbu *han* until 1868, when it passed into the hands of a Morioka merchant named Kagiya Mohei. In 1871, however, it was confiscated from him by the Ministry of Finance, only to be sold to another private entrepreneur —a procedure that scandalized the public. Prominently implicated in this scandal was Inoue Kaoru (1836–1915), a Chōshū man who was vice-minister of finance between 1871 and 1873. Inoue's close ties with commercial capital were notorious; Saigō Takamori is said to have called him "Mitsui's chief clerk." Subjected to a judicial investigation, Inoue was forced to leave his government position, but he regained favor and occupied important posts later. In 1885, he was appointed foreign minister in the first Itō cabinet.

33. "Count Ito on the Constitution (A Speech at Ōtsu, 1889)," *Transactions of the Asiatic Society of Japan*, 1st ser., vol. 42, pt. 1: *Japanese Government Documents*, ed. W. W. McLaren (1914), p. 617.

34. Fukuzawa, *Gakumon no susume* 3 (1873), FYZ, 3:43.

35. Katō Hiroyuki, *Kokutai shinron* (1875), in *Nihon no meicho*, vol. 34: *Nishi Amane, Katō Hiroyuki*, ed. Uete Michiari (Chūō Kōron-sha, 1972), p. 404.

36. Nishi Amane, "Kokumin kifū ron *(Nashionaru kerekutoru),*" MZ, no. 32 (March 1875), p. 208.

37. Tsuda Mamichi, "Gakusha shokubunron no hyō," MZ, no. 2 (undated), pp. 59–60; Braisted, pp. 24–25.

38. Nishimura, "Chingen issoku," MZ, no. 3 (undated), p. 62.

39. Nishimura, "Shūshin chikoku," MZ, p. 204.

40. Nishimura, "Seifu to jinmin to rigai o koto ni suru ron," MZ, no. 39 (June 1875), pp. 244–245.

41. Fukuzawa's article, which prompted the symposium, did not appear in *Meiroku zasshi*. The four Meirokusha responses to Fukuzawa (by Katō Hiroyuki, Mori Arinori, Tsuda Mamichi, and Nishi Amane), making up the symposium, were published together in MZ, no. 2, pp. 58–61; Braisted, pp. 21–28.

42. Fukuzawa, "Gakusha no shokubun o ron-zu," FYZ, 3:48–49.

43. Fukuzawa, "Gakusha anshin ron" (1876), FYZ, 4:216–218.

44. Fukuzawa, *Bunmeiron no gairyaku*, FYZ, 4:32–33.

45. Ibid., p. 23.

46. Ibid., pp. 16–17, 23.

47. Fukuzawa, *Gakumon no susume* 15 (1876), FYZ, 3:123, 125.

48. Fukuzawa, *Gakumon no susume* 5, ibid., p. 61.

49. Fukuzawa, "Gakusha no shokubun o ron-zu," ibid., p. 52.

50. Ibid., p. 49.

51. Ibid., pp. 49–50.

52. Fukuzawa, *Gakumon no susume* 5, ibid., p. 60.

53. Fukuzawa, "Gakusha no shokubun o ron-zu," ibid., pp. 50–51, 52–53.

54. Ibid., pp. 53–54.

55. Fukuzawa, *Gakumon no susume* 3, ibid., p. 44.

56. Fukuzawa, "Gakusha anshin ron," FYZ, 4:219.

57. Fukuzawa, "Oboegaki" (1875–1881), in *Fukuzawa Yukichi senshū*, ed. Fukuzawa Yukichi Chosaku Hensankai (Iwanami Shoten, 1951), 1:247.

58. Fukuzawa Yukichi to Baba Tatsui, 12 October 1874; in *Kindai Nihon shisō taikei*, vol. 2: *Fukuzawa Yukichi shū*, ed. Ishida Takeshi (Chikuma Shobō, 1975), p. 552.

59. Fukuzawa, *Gakumon no susume* 2 (1873), *FYZ*, 3:38.

60. Katō Hiroyuki, "Fukuzawa-sensei no ron ni kotau," *MZ*, no. 2, p. 58; Braisted, pp. 21–22.

61. Ibid.

62. J. K. Bluntschli, *Allgemeines Staatsrecht*, trans. Katō Hiroyuki: *Kokuhō hanron* (1872–1874), *Meiji bunka zenshū*, supp. vol. 2 (Nihon Hyōron Shinsha, 1971), pp. 31–32.

63. Katō Hiroyuki, *Tonarigusa* (preface dated Bunkyū 1.12.7 [6 January 1862]), in *Nihon no meicho*, 34:313–316.

64. Katō Hiroyuki, *Seiyō kakkoku seisui kyōjaku ichiranhyō*, in *Nihon kindai shisō taikei*, vol. 13: *Rekishi ninshiki*, ed. Tanaka Akira and Miyachi Masato (Iwanami Shoten, 1991), pp. 67–68.

65. *Taiyō* (June 1899), p. 68. *Rikken seitai ryaku* (1868) is included in *Nihon no meicho*, 34:329–343.

66. Katō Hiroyuki, *Shinsei taii*, ibid., pp. 347–348.

67. Ibid., pp. 349–351.

68. Ibid., pp. 356–357.

69. Katō Hiroyuki, *Kokutai shinron*, ibid., p. 384.

70. Ibid., pp. 404–405. Monarchic rule is praiseworthy if it exercises self-restraint. In this regard Katō found a model in the enlightened despotism of Frederick the Great and a countermodel in the self-deifying presumption of Louis XIV; ibid., pp. 390–391.

71. Ibid., pp. 400–401. Katō notes ibid. that even in "civilized and enlightened" countries with constitutional systems, the right to a voice in government is "of course not granted to women, minors, idiots, criminals, and indigents on welfare; nor to those who lack adequate property"—these last because they are uneducated, hence "ignorant and incapable of reason," that is, insensible of state concerns and incompetent to participate in plans for the public welfare. The radical elements that caused so much harm to France, he notes, came mostly from among the poor. To be sure, Katō also quotes J. S. Mill to the effect that women do not necessarily have intellects inferior to men's and so deserve the suffrage; he himself professes insufficient knowledge to decide the matter and defers judgment to others on some future day.

72. Tsuda Shin'ichirō Mamichi, *Taisei kokuhōron* (explanatory remarks dated Keiō 2 [1866], Ninth Month; first published Edo: Kaiseisho, Keiō 4 [1868]), *Meiji bunka zenshū*, vol. 8: *Hōritsu-hen* (1928), pp. 65–104.

Vissering was a professor of law at Leiden University, but Tsuda and his fellow stipendiary of the shogunate, Nishi Amane, were no more than Vissering's private students. Contrary to the common assumption, they were not enrolled in the university. The *kokuhō* of Tsuda's title is a translation of Vissering's Dutch term *staatsregt*.

73. Tsuda, "Gakusha shokubunron no hyō," *MZ*, p. 59.

74. Tsuda, "Seiron," pt. 2, *MZ*, no. 11 (June 1874), p. 108.

75. Tsuda, "Jōyoku ron," *MZ*, no. 34 (April 1875), pp. 221–222.

76. Tsuda, "Gakusha shokubunron no hyō," *MZ*, p. 60.

77. Tsuda, "Seiron," pt. 3, *MZ*, no. 12 (June 1874), p. 116.

78. Tsuda, "Kaika o susumuru hōhō o ron-zu," *MZ*, no. 3, p. 65.

79. Tsuda, "Hogozei o hi to suru setsu," *MZ*, no. 5 (undated), p. 73.

80. Tsuda, "Naichi ryokō ron," *MZ*, no. 24 (December 1874), pp. 171–172.

81. Tsuda, "Gakusha shokubunron no hyō," *MZ*, p. 60.

82. Nishi Amane, "Gakusha shokubun o hi to suru ron," *MZ*, no. 2, pp. 60–61; Braisted, pp. 25–28.

83. Nishi Shūsuke (Amane) to Matsuoka Rinjirō, [Bunkyū 2 (1862)].5.15, *Nishi Amane zenshū*, ed. Ōkubo Toshiaki (Munetaka Shobō, 1962), 1:8; quoted in Mori Rintarō, *Nishi Amane den* (1898), in *Ōgai zenshū: chosaku hen* (Iwanami Shoten, 1953), 11:39.

84. Nishi, "Kaidaimon" (1870?), *Nishi Amane zenshū*, 1:19.

85. Nishi, *Seisei hatsuun* (1873), ibid., p. 36.

86. Nishi, *Hyakuichi shinron* (1874), ibid., pp. 282–286.

87. Nishi, "Shōhaku sakki" (1882), ibid., p. 165. The allusion is to Mencius, IA:3; see *The Works of Mencius*, tr. James Legge (New York: Dover, 1970 reprint ed.), p. 131: "When the grain and fish and turtles are more than can be eaten, and there is more wood than can be used, this enables the people to nourish their living and mourn for their dead, without any feeling against any. This condition, in which the people nourish their living and bury their dead without any feeling against any, is the first step of royal government."

88. Nishi, *Hyakuichi shinron*, ibid., p. 267.

CHAPTER 6: *The Statist Movement and Its Educational Activities*

1. The name "Shimeikai" is written with three characters that respectively mean "purple"; "dark," "gloomy," "profound," or "the sea"; and "society." Hence its literal sense is "Purple Depths Society" or "Deep-Red Sea Society." One of its founders notes that Shimeikai was chosen as the society's name "because it was the creation of men of Tsukushi"—an ancient name for Kyushu that also includes the character for "purple"; see Tsuda Seiichi, *Baikei Tsuda Sensei densan*, ed. Yoshida Masataka (Tsuda Seiichi Sensei Nijūgokaiki Tsuitō-kai, 1933), p. 121. There was the obvious intention to invoke the memory of the noted Kumamoto scholar Ri Shimei (pseud. of Harada Jun; 1738–1814).

The descriptive element *seisei* in the name "Seiseikō" occurs in various Chinese classics in a fairly wide range of meanings (see Morohashi, 18498:59–61), but is in this case undoubtedly an abbreviation of the well-known phrase *seisei taru tashi* (Chinese: *chi-chi tuo-shih;* see the Book of Songs, *Ta-ya: Wen Wang;* Mao 235), "many gentlemen of eminent worth." Early in the history of the Chou kingdom (the ideal realm of Confucian philosophers) such talented gentlemen stood as the pillars of the state, the poem goes on to say. Hence "Seiseikō" suggests a School of Proliferating Talent that will contribute to the state's proper governance.

2. The Kainan Shijuku and the Risshi Gakusha are discussed in chap. 2, the Tokyo Specialist School (Tōkyō Senmon Gakkō) in chap. 7.

3. Sassa Tomofusa, "Seiseikō rekishi," in *Kokudō Sassa Sensei ikō* [hereafter: *Ikō*], ed. Sassa Kokudō Sensei Ikō Kankōkai (Kaizōsha, 1936), p. 158.

4. Ibid., p. 160.

5. *Ikō*, p. 557; retrospective of Uno Harukaze.

6. Sassa, "Seiseikō rekishi," p. 159. Cf. Samuel Smiles, *Self-Help: With Illustrations of Character and Conduct* (Boston: Ticknor and Fields, 1864), pp. iii–iv.

7. Tokutomi Sohō, *Sohō jiden* (Chūō Kōron-sha, 1935), p. 155.

8. See Tsuda, *Baikei Tsuda Sensei densan,* pp. 119–121.

9. The Imperial Edict (Seishō) of 14 April 1875 proclaimed that a constitutional system of government would be instituted gradually and provided for the establishment of a deliberative Chamber of Elder Statesmen (Genrōin), a Court of Cassation (Daishin'in), and an assembly of regional administrators.

10. *Ikō*, p. 20.

11. Ibid., p. 25.

12. Ibid., p. 24.

13. Tsuda, *Baikei Tsuda Sensei densan,* p. 129.

14. *Ikō*, pp. 24–25.

15. Ibid., p. 24.

16. Ibid., p. 165.

17. Ibid., p. 148.

18. Ibid.

19. Ibid., p. 168.

20. According to a teacher at the Seiseikō, Uno Harukaze, the Three Main Principles, which comprehended the school's unique character, were all the more exemplary because "few among the population live upright lives, carrying out duties and responsibilities, showing a sense of honor and displaying vigor. Few raise the flag on national commemoration days; on memorial days few visit the graves of their parents." Strict observance of all such duties was, of course, the hallmark of the School of Proliferating Talent. *Kumamoto-ken kyōikushi,* ed. Kumamoto-ken Kyōikukai (Rinsen Shobō, 1975 reprint ed.), 1:690.

21. *Ikō*, p. 505.

22. Sassa, "Seiseikō rekishi," pp. 163, 169.

23. *Ikō*, p. 17.

24. Ibid., p. 215.

25. Ibid., p. 418.

26. Ibid., p. 16.

27. Ibid.

28. Ibid., pp. 181, 506.

29. Ōkubo Toshiaki, *Mori Arinori* (Bunkyō Shoin, 1944), p. 4. Prince Kanenaga (name also read as Kaneyoshi; 1329–1383), a son of Emperor Go-Daigo, was appointed generalissimo of the west *(seisei taishōgun)* in 1336 and in that capacity exerted power over a great part of Kyushu in behalf of the Southern Court until the 1370s, when forces loyal to the Muromachi shogunate reduced him to impotence. Also see n. 36 below.

30. Sassa, "Nihon kyōiku no shugi," *Ikō*, p. 218.

31. *Kumamoto-ken kyōikushi*, 1:40.

32. Uno Harukaze, *Gakan Kumamoto kyōiku no hensen* (Daidōkan Shoten, 1931), p. 8. Evidently, there were *ren* throughout the samurai wards of the castle town Kumamoto: Yamazaki-ren, Tōrichō-ren, Suidōchō-ren, Sendanbata-ren, Takebe-ren, Kyōmachi-ren, Akaoguchi-ren, Furukyōmachi-ren, Kōraimon-ren, and Motoyama-ren.

33. *Kumamoto-ken kyōikushi*, 1:320.

34. Uno, p. 18.

35. Ibid., p. 72.

36. Go-Daigo, who ascended the throne in 1318, was a visionary who sought to restore direct imperial rule over Japan and plotted the overthrow of the Kamakura shogunate. The shogunate discovered his plans to raise forces toward that end in 1324 and punished his co-conspirators but accepted the sovereign's protestations of lack of evil intent. On discovering a similar conspiracy in 1331, the shogunate banished Go-Daigo to the island province of Oki and installed a rival as Emperor Kōgon (1313–1364). This event marked the inception of an imperial schism; Kōgon became the first ruler of the so-called Northern Court. He was, however, forced to abdicate in 1333, when Go-Daigo escaped from his island exile and returned to the throne in Kyoto after generals ostensibly acting in his cause overthrew the Kamakura regime. The principal of those ambitious generals, Ashikaga Takauji (1305–1358), in 1335 turned against Go-Daigo. In 1336, Takauji elevated another prince of the "Northern" lineage to the throne as Emperor Kōmyō (1321–1380; r. 1336–1348) and proclaimed the beginning of the Muromachi shogunate; Go-Daigo, who refused to disavow his sovereignty, fled to Yoshino, a mountainous region south of Kyoto, where he established a rival court early in 1337. The imperial schism continued after his death two and a half years later and was not resolved until 1398. Super-loyalists of the late Edo period and thereafter considered the "Southern" to be the sole legitimate lineage.

37. See *Kōhon Higo bunkyōshi,* ed. Shimoda Kazuyoshi (Kyōtōsha, 1923), p. 426.

38. *Kumamoto-ken kyōikushi,* 1:129.

39. Sassa, "Kumamoto kakutō enkaku ippan," *Ikō,* p. 6.

40. Ibid.

41. The Hagi Uprising (October–6 November 1876; Yamaguchi Prefecture) was an antigovernment disturbance led by Maebara Issei (1834–1876), a former imperial adviser *(sangi),* and joined by disgruntled former samurai of the Chō-shū domain. When troops of the government's Hiroshima garrison moved to suppress the rebels, they sought to flee but were captured; Maebara and a number of his followers were executed. The Akizuki Uprising (26 October–3 November 1876; Fukuoka Prefecture) was another abortive rebellion of former samurai dissatisfied with the Meiji government's progressive policies. Some 210 former retainers of the Akizuki domain marched to join the Shinpūren of Kumamoto but were intercepted by troops of the Kokura garrison. Their leader Miyazaki Kurumanosuke committed suicide; the majority of the others were arrested.

42. Sassa, "Kumamoto kakutō enkaku ippan," pp. 7–8. Sassa also draws attention to Motoda Nagazane, who "stood conspicuously between the Komeda and Yokoi factions, on very friendly terms with both. His followers can be called the Yamazaki Practical Learning group."

43. The group's founders included Miyazaki Shinkei, Sakimura Tsuneo, Hirakawa Korekazu, Matsuyama Moriyoshi, and Arima Gennai.

44. See *Kumamoto-ken kyōikushi,* 1:211–219 and 300–307 on writing schools and private academies, respectively.

45. See Tokutomi Sohō, *Sohō jiden,* pp. 142–143.

46. Uno, p. 45.

47. Ibid., p. 43.

48. *Ikō,* p. 573.

49. Letter dated 6.18 in the Japanese and 16 July [1870] in the Western calendar; Tsuda, *Baikei Tsuda Sensei densan,* p. 48.

50. Letter dated 20 March 1871; ibid., p. 52.

51. Letter dated 20 September 1871; ibid., pp. 55–56.

52. Uno, p. 39.

53. Ibid., p. 80.

54. Ibid., p. 93.

55. Ibid.

56. *Kumamoto-ken kyōikushi,* 1:501. Among the "important works" cited are Aizawa Yasushi's *Shinron* (New Proposals; 1825) as well as two works by Fujita Tōko, *Kōdōkanki* (Record of the Kōdōkan; 1838) and *Kaiten shishi* (Turn Heaven Round: A Poetical History; 1844).

57. Chiba Eijirō, *Takahashi Nagaaki den* (Nagasaki Jirō Shoten, 1938), p. 11.

58. *Ikō,* p. 3.

59. Letter addressed to Fukano Ichizō; *Ikō*, p. 420.

60. Letter addressed to Fukano, Matsuzaki, Tomonari, and others; *Ikō*, pp. 423–424.

61. Ibid., p. 428.

62. See Chiba, p. 11.

63. Letter dated 13 January 1872; Tsuda, *Baikei Tsuda Sensei densan*, p. 60.

64. Letter dated Meiji 5 (1872).3.13; ibid., p. 61.

65. *Ikō*, p. 421. He had written to some old acquaintances who were now God Reverers, Sassa says, but his letters went unanswered. Could it be, he wonders, that they were left unopened because he had used Western-style—not Japanese—envelopes?

66. Ibid., p. 233.

67. Ibid., pp. 234–235.

68. *Kumamoto-ken kyōikushi*, 1:409.

69. *Ikō*, p. 553.

CHAPTER 7: *The Spirit of Political Opposition in the Meiji Period*

1. *Waseda Daigaku kaikō Tōkyō Senmon Gakkō sōritsu nijūnen Kinenroku* [hereafter: *Kinenroku*], ed. Yamamoto Rikio (Waseda Gakkai, 1903), p. 108. Hozumi Yatsuka (1860–1912), who had studied at the University of Heidelberg, was professor of constitutional law at the University of Tokyo. Associated with the imperial household in important advisory positions, he is best known for his controversialist advocacy of a Japanese variant of the divine right of kings. The legal scholar Hozumi Nobushige, another professor at the University of Tokyo, was his elder brother; see p. 332 herein.

2. The Sain, founded in 1871, was a quasi-legislative body of the central government. It was abolished in 1875, when the newly established Genrōin took over its activities. The Genrōin was in turn abolished in October 1890, just prior to the convocation of the first Imperial Diet.

3. Text in Ōkubo Toshiaki, "Meiji jūyonen seihen to Inoue Kowashi," *Kaikoku hyakunen kinen Meiji bunkashi ronshū*, ed. Kaikoku Hyakunen Kinen Bunka Jigyōkai (Kengensha, 1952), p. 630.

4. The Tokyo Specialist School had originally been planned, in accordance with the wishes of Ōkuma's adopted son, Ōkuma Hidemaro (1856–1910; family name Nanbu before adoption), as an institution devoted mainly to the kind of education in the natural sciences that he had received in the United States. The involvement of the young men of the Ōtokai resulted, however, in a shift of aim, so that the school would instead offer three courses of instruction—law, politics and economics, and science—together with English language training.

5. *Hanpō mukashibanashi*, narrated by Takata Sanae, comp. Susukida Sadataka (Waseda Daigaku Shuppanbu, 1927), p. 78.

6. Ibid., p. 16.

7. Ibid., pp. 48–49.

8. Ibid., pp. 60–61. The Tōkyō Kaisei Gakkō was in Hitotsubashi.

9. Asano Eijirō and Nishida Chōju, *Amano Tameyuki* (Jitsugyō no Nihon-sha, 1950), p. 11.

10. Ibid., pp. 40–41 (from a speech given at Waseda in 1909 in commemorating the anniversary of the Meiji Constitution).

11. Ono Azusa, "Kinnōron," cited in Nagata Shinnosuke, *Ono Azusa* (Fuzanbō, 1897), p. 158.

12. The Tōkyō Kaisei Gakkō was the successor to an institution called the Daigaku Nankō; see chap. 2. In April 1873, it abandoned the threefold system of English, French, and German as the languages of instruction and adopted English exclusively for its specialist disciplines.

13. Miyake Setsurei, *Jibun o kataru* (Asahi Shinbun-sha, 1950), p. 96. Meant by Chambers' history of the French Revolution is *France: Its History and Revolutions* (Edinburgh: W. R. Chambers, 1871).

14. *Hanpō mukashibanashi*, p. 33. "Nolumus leges Angliae mutare" is the correct form of the citation; see *Bracton's Note Book*, ed. F. W. Maitland (London: C. J. Clay and Sons, 1887), 1:104. The phrase occurs in the context of a debate between bishops and barons in the great council in 1236; the latter were not prepared to see a change in the law governing bastards' (lack of) inheritance rights. Thanks for supplying this reference are due to Dr. John R. L. Maddicott, Fellow of Exeter College, Oxford. (Translator's note.)

15. *Hanpō mukashibanashi*, p. 51.

16. See Yanagida Izumi, *Wakaki hi no Tsubouchi Shōyō*, Meiji Bunka Kenkyū 1 (Shunjūsha, 1960), pp. 81–134.

17. Ibid., p. 93.

18. See *Tōkyō Teikoku Daigaku gojūnenshi*, ed. Tōkyō Teikoku Daigaku (Tōkyō Teikoku Daigaku, 1932), 1:566–581.

19. Yamada Ichirō, "Okayama Kenkichi tsuitōroku," in *Godō genkōroku*, ed. Okayama Dōsōkai (Suzuki Minato, 1895), p. 92.

20. See Nagata, pp. 148–149.

21. *Kinenroku*, appendix, pp. 3–4.

22. Ibid., p. 224.

23. Ibid., appendix, p. 4.

24. Ibid., p. 287.

25. *Hanpō mukashibanashi*, pp. 107–108.

26. *Rikugō zasshi*, quoted in *Kinenroku*, p. 127.

27. *Hanseiki no Waseda*, ed. Waseda Daigaku (Waseda Daigaku Shuppan-bu, 1932), p. 32.

28. *Ōkuma Kō hachijūgonenshi*, ed. Ōkuma Kō Hachijūgonenshi Kai, Meiji Hyakunenshi Sōsho (Hara Shobō, 1970 reprint ed.), p. 41.

29. *Hanseiki no Waseda*, p. 35.

30. *Kinenroku,* appendix, pp. 6–7.

31. Ibid., appendix, p. 7.

32. Itō Hirobumi, "Kyōikugi," *Kyōiku chokugo kanpatsu kankei shiryō,* Kokumin Seishin Bunka Bunken 22 (Kokumin Seishin Bunka Kenkyūjo, 1940 second printing), 1:8–9.

33. Asano and Nishida, pp. 51–52.

34. *Kinenroku,* appendix, p. 8.

35. *Hanseiki no Waseda,* p. 89.

36. Ibid., p. 304.

37. "Tōkyō Daigaku Hōgakubu-nai ni bekka setsuritsu no gi ni tsuki kengi," *Tōkyō Teikoku Daigaku gojūnenshi,* 1:595.

38. The Senshū Gakkō was founded in 1880 as a night school for working youth. It had a two-year program of instruction in law and economics; classes were taught in Japanese. In 1913 it was renamed Senshū Daigaku.

39. *Tōkyō Teikoku Daigaku gojūnenshi,* 1:598–599.

40. *Hanseiki no Waseda,* p. 89.

41. "Gakusei-sū tokugyōsei-sū ichiran hyō," *Sōritsu sanjūnen kinen Waseda Daigaku sōgyōroku,* ed. Waseda Daigaku Henshūbu (Waseda Daigaku Shuppanbu, 1913), chart inserted between pp. 198 and 199.

42. "Tokugyōsei fuken-betsu hyō," *Kinenroku,* pp. 169–172.

43. *Hanpō mukashibanashi,* p. 192.

44. "Kōgaisei nenbetsu hyō," *Kinenroku,* appendix, pp. 166–167.

45. Ibid., pp. 290–291.

46. Ibid., p. 337. Tanaka became an important Waseda administrator.

47. Susukida Sadataka, ed., *Konda Bunjirō-kun no shōgai* (Kōkonkai, 1929), p. 618.

48. Minato Kunizō, ed., *Hayami Seiji den* (Hayami Chiyono, 1932), p. 31.

49. *Kinenroku,* p. 138.

50. Ibid., appendix, p. 5.

51. Ibid., pp. 328–330.

52. Quoted in Kimura Takeshi, *Waseda gaishi* (Kōdansha, 1964), p. 137.

53. *Kinenroku,* pp. 129, 295–296, 300.

54. *Hanseiki no Waseda,* p. 123.

55. *Kinenroku,* pp. 348–349.

56. Ibid., pp. 350–351.

57. According to the law student Ueno Kieiji, in this respect "there was no sharp distinction between the courses in law and in politics." Susukida Sadataka, ed., *Konda Bunjirō-kun no shōgai,* p. 46.

58. "Shiritsu hōritsu gakkō tokubetsu kantoku jōki," *Tōkyō Teikoku Daigaku gojūnenshi,* 1:1097–1098.

59. *Kinenroku,* p. 324.

60. Ibid., pp. 344–345.

61. *Hanseiki no Waseda,* pp. 125–126.

62. Nagata, p. 215.

63. *Kinenroku,* pp. 74–75.

64. Asano and Nishida, p. 157.

65. *Sōritsu sanjūnen kinen Waseda Daigaku sōgyōroku,* pp. 180–181.

66. From a speech Masuda gave at the anniversary ceremony of 21 October 1902; *Kinenroku,* pp. 364–365. Masuda, who is perhaps known best as the founder of the publishing firm Jitsugyō no Nihon-sha, was himself highly influential in the world of the press.

67. Ibid., p. 360.

68. Ibid., p. 366.

69. *Sōritsu sanjūnen kinen Waseda Daigaku sōgyōroku,* pp. 145–146.

70. *Kinenroku,* p. 51.

71. Ibid., pp. 17–20.

72. Ibid., pp. 60–61.

73. Ibid., p. 20.

74. Takata Sanae, "Kagakuteki kyōiku no hei," *Kyōiku jigen* (Kōbundō Shoten and Ishikawa Bun'eidō, 1908), p. 262.

75. Takata, "Waga daigaku no hōfu to kyōshi," ibid., pp. 191–193.

76. *Kinenroku,* appendix, p. 43.

77. Ibid., appendix, pp. 56–57.

78. Takata, "Waga daigaku no hōfu to kyōshi," p. 194.

79. Takata, "Sengo Nihon wa ika naru jinbutsu o yō-suru ka," *Kyōiku jigen,* p. 59.

80. Takata, "Kensei no konjaku," ibid., pp. 102–103.

81. Ibid., pp. 98, 102–103.

CHAPTER 8: *Thought and Education in the Late Meiji Era*

1. Tokutomi Sohō, *Shōrai no Nihon,* in *Meiji bungaku zenshū,* vol. 34: *Tokutomi Sohō shū,* ed. Uete Michiari (Chikuma Shobō, 1974), p. 57.

2. See, for instance, "Onmitsu naru seijijō no hensen," *Kokumin no tomo,* no. 17 (2 March 1888), p. 2; facsimile ed., *Kokumin no tomo,* ed. Fujiwara Masato (Meiji Bunken Shiryō Kankōkai, 1982 second printing), 2:45. In evidence of the rise of the commoner class, Tokutomi offers here the observation that the ratio of commoners to students of samurai provenance at Keiō Academy is inverted after 1880, and that by 1882 commoners represented 57 percent of the student body.

3. Tokutomi, "Shōgakkō oyobi shōgakkō kyōiku," ibid., no. 96 (3 October 1890), p. 2; facsimile ed., 7:168.

4. Tokutomi, "Shōgakkō no tokuiku," ibid., no. 84 (3 June 1890), p. 5; facsimile ed., 6:269.

5. Tokutomi, "Rōsaku kyōiku," ibid., no. 133 (13 October 1891), p. 6; facsimile ed., 9:189.

6. Miyake Setsurei, *Meiji shisō shōshi* (Heiko Shuppansha, 1913), p. 44.

7. Kuga Katsunan, *Kinji seiron kō* (1891), *Kuga Katsunan shū*, ed. Uete Michiari, Kindai Nihon Shisō Taikei 4 (Chikuma Shobō, 1987), p. 44.

8. Miyake Setsurei, *Shinzenbi Nihonjin* (1891), in *Meiji bungaku zenshū,* vol. 33: *Miyake Setsurei shū,* ed. Yanagida Izumi (1967), p. 200.

9. Hasegawa Nyozekan, *Aru kokoro no jijoden,* Denki Sōsho 87 (Ōzorasha, 1991), p. 198.

10. Kume Kunitake, "Shintō wa saiten no kozoku," in *Shigakkai zasshi,* 23:1–15 (October 1891), 24:25–40 (November 1891), and 25:12–24 (December 1891); bound volume, *Shigakkai zasshi* (Taiseikan, 1891), 2:636–650, 728–742, and 799–811 respectively. Kume recanted his thesis, but was nonetheless forced to resign from the Imperial University in 1892. Ōkuma Shigenobu gave Kume a part-time position as a lecturer at the Tōkyō Senmon Gakkō in 1893; in 1899 he joined the Waseda faculty as a regular member.

11. Inoue Tetsujirō had established himself as a nationalist stalwart in 1891 with his exegesis of the Imperial Rescript on Education, *Chokugo engi;* in *Kyōiku chokugo kanpatsu kankei shiryōshū,* ed. Kokumin Seishin Bunka Kenkyūjo (Kokumin Seishin Bunka Kenkyūjo, 1939), 3:227–235. He initiated the controversy by denouncing Christianity as an unnationalistic doctrine of undifferentiated universal brotherhood in "Shūkyō to kyōiku to no kankei ni tsuki Inoue Tetsujirō-shi no danwa," *Kyōiku jiron,* no. 272 (5 November 1892), pp. 24–26. Inoue elaborated on this theme in "Kyōiku to shūkyō no shōtotsu," serialized ibid., no. 279 (15 January 1893), pp. 14–19; no. 280 (25 January 1893), pp. 17–24; no. 281 (5 February 1893), pp. 11–17; and no. 283 (25 February 1893), pp. 12–19. Uchimura Kanzō took up the challenge with his famous rejoinder, "Bungaku Hakushi Inoue Tetsujirō-kun ni tei-suru kōkaijō," ibid., no. 285 (15 March 1893), pp. 16–19. A good number of other authors also exerted themselves in the defense of Christianity, but it would be fair to say that in the end the controversy revealed that Japanese Christians were willing to compromise with the dogmas of nationalism.

12. Kusakabe Sannosuke, *Kokka kyōikusaku* (Tōkyō Kyōikusha, 1888); Yunome Horyū, *Kokka kyōikuron, ichimei Shōbu zōshi saku* (Yunome Horyū, 1890).

13. Tokutomi, "Shōgakkō no tokuiku," p. 5; facsimile ed., 6:268.

14. Kaminuma Hachirō, *Isawa Shūji* (Yoshikawa Kōbunkan, 1962), p. 179.

15. Shinano Kyōikukai, ed., *Isawa Shūji senshū* (Shinano Kyōikukai, 1958), p. 444.

16. Ibid., p. 446.

17. Kokumin Kyōiku Shōreikai, ed., *Kyōiku gojūnenshi* (Min'yūsha, 1922), p. 125.

18. Tokutomi, "Shōgakkō no tokuiku," p. 4; facsimile ed., 6:269.

19. Sashihara Yasuzō, *Meiji seishi,* 2 (1893), *Meiji bunka zenshū,* gen. ed. Yoshino Sakuzō, vol. 3: *Seishi-hen* (Nihon Hyōronsha, 1929), p. 55.

20. Tokutomi, "Bunkyō wa daiji nari," *Kokumin no tomo,* no. 204 (3 October 1893), p. 8; facsimile ed., 13:186.

21. Tokutomi, "Gaikō no urei wa soto ni arazu shite uchi ni ari," *Kokumin no tomo,* no. 2 (15 March 1887), pp. 1–12; facsimile ed., 1:15–18.

22. Kaigo Tokiomi, *Kyōiku chokugo seiritsushi no kenkyū* (Kaigo Tokiomi, 1965), p. 251.

23. *Teikoku Gikai kyōiku giji sōran,* ed. Abe Isoo (Rinsen Shoten, 1971 reprint ed.), 1:112.

24. *Jitsugyō kyōiku gojūnenshi,* ed. Monbushō Jitsugyō Gakumukyoku (Jitsugyō Kyōiku Gojūshūnen Kinenkai, 1936), p. 229.

25. Uchimura Kanzō, "Nisshin sensō no gi (Justification of the Corean War)," originally in *Kokumin no tomo,* 3 September 1894; "Nisshin sensō no mokuteki ikan," originally ibid., 3 October 1894; in *Uchimura Kanzō chosakushū* (Iwanami Shoten, 1953), 2:23–33 and 42–51 respectively.

26. Kaminuma, p. 203.

27. *Kyōiku jiron,* no. 367 (25 June 1895), p. 36.

28. Kaminuma, pp. 203–204.

29. *Kyōiku jiron,* no. 336 (15 August 1894), p. 28.

30. Ibid., no. 357 (15 March 1895), p. 10.

31. Ibid., no. 343 (25 October 1894), p. 32.

32. Ibid., no. 350 (1 January 1895), p. 15.

33. Ibid., no. 361 (25 April 1895), p. 8.

34. An armistice was concluded between Japan and the Ch'ing Empire on 30 March 1895, and representatives of the two countries signed the Shimonoseki Peace Treaty on 17 April. Included in the treaty's terms was the cession of the Liaotung Peninsula to Japan, a provision that became the object of the Tripartite Intervention of 23 April. On 5 June Japan agreed to the Russo-Franco-German demand that it abandon its claims to Liaotung, and the exchange of ratifications took place three days later.

35. *Kyōiku jiron,* no. 365 (5 June 1895), p. 28.

36. See the column "Naigai zassan," in *Kyōiku jiron,* nos. 367 (25 June), 368 (5 July), and 369 (15 July 1895).

37. *Saionji Kinmochi jiden,* ed. Kimura Ki (Dai Nihon Yūbenkai Kōdansha, 1949), p. 114.

38. Takayama Chogyū, "Kokusui hozon to Nihonshugi," *Chogyū zenshū,* ed. Anesaki Masaharu et al. (Hakubunkan, 1915), 4:378.

39. Takayama, "Meiji shisō no hensen," ibid., p. 254.

40. Ibid., p. 253.

41. Takayama, "Sekaishugi to kokkashugi," ibid., pp. 307–308.

42. Takayama, "Kako ichinen no kokumin shisō," ibid., p. 268.

43. See *Kyōiku jiron*, no. 365 (25 May 1895), pp. 28–38.

44. Ibid., no. 580 (25 May 1901), p. 44.

45. Takata Sanae is treated at length in chap. 7, "The Spirit of Political Opposition in the Meiji Period." Constitutionalism and globalism were two of his lasting, reiterated concerns; see, for instance, his disquisition on the course that national education should take, "Kokumin kyōiku no hōshin," Takata, *Kyōiku jigen* (Kōbundō Shoten and Ishikawa Bun'eidō, 1908), p. 7.

46. "Ika ni shite shimin kyōiku o nasubeki ka," *Rikugō zasshi*, no. 233 (15 May 1900), p. 7.

47. *Kyōiku jiron*, no. 602 (5 January 1902), pp. 31–32.

48. Kutsumi Yasutada, *Kyōiku jidaikan* (Yūbunsha, 1899), preface, pp. 1–2.

49. Ibid., pp. 4–5.

50. Kutsumi, "Rikken jidai no kyōiku," ibid., p. 3.

51. *Kyōiku jiron*, no. 630 (15 October 1902), pp. 4–7.

52. *Teikoku Gikai kyōiku giji sōran*, 2:185.

53. *Kyōiku jiron*, no. 484 (25 September 1898), p. 24.

54. Ōkuma stated these convictions in a speech given at Tōkyō Senmon Gakkō shortly after he was installed as prime minister of the first party cabinet. See ibid., no. 479 (5 August 1898), pp. 19–20.

55. Tadokoro Yoshiji, comp., *Kikuchi Zen-Bunshō enjutsu Kutsumoshū* (Dai Nihon Tosho K.K., 1903), pp. 326–327.

56. An unnamed "correspondent of the *Kokumin shinbun*" writing "in the middle of the Russo-Japanese War," quoted in Yamaji Aizan, *Gendai Nihon kyōkaishi ron*, in *Nihon no meicho*, vol. 40: *Tokutomi Sohō, Yamaji Aizan*, ed. Sumiya Mikio (Chūō Kōron-sha, 1971), p. 423.

57. *Teikoku Gikai kyōiku giji sōran*, 2:81, 90, 214.

58. Among the committee's members were Inoue Tetsujirō, Sawayanagi Masatarō, Takamine Hideo (1854–1910), and Education Ministry Councillor Koba Sadatake (1859–1944). Yoshida Kumaji, Ototake Iwazō (1875–1953), Hirade Kōjirō (1869–1911), and other rising young educators staffed its drafting subcommittee.

59. *Himeji Shihan Gakkō no kyōiku*, ed. Hyōgo-ken Himeji Shihan Gakkō (Hyōgo-ken Himeji Shihan Gakkō Kōyūkai, 1936), frontispiece.

60. Higuchi Kanjirō, *Tōgōshugi shin kyōjuhō*, Kyōiku Meicho Sōsho 6 (Nihon Tosho Sentā, 1982); in particular, see chap. 5, "Katsudōshugi: Kyōju wa seito no jihatsu katsudō o omon-zubeshi," pp. 47–59.

61. Ishitoya Tetsuo, *Nihon kyōinshi kenkyū* (Noma Kyōiku Kenkyūjo, 1958), p. 243.

62. Ibid., p. 245.

63. *Kyōiku jiron*, no. 686 (5 May 1904), p. 46.

64. Ibid., no. 694 (25 July 1904), p. 1.

65. Ibid., no. 678 (15 February 1904), p. 37.

66. Ibid., no. 698 (5 September 1904), p. 37.

67. Ibid., no. 679 (25 February 1904), p. 44.

68. Tomizu Hirondo, *Kaikoroku* (Tomizu Hirondo, 1904), p. 281.

69. Miyake, *Meiji shisō shōshi*, p. 67. To be sure, globalist thought had already become an active force immediately before and during the Russo-Japanese War. A pacifist doctrine strong enough to rival the excessive nationalism of the "Seven Savants" was set forth by Christian intellectuals such as Uchimura Kanzō, Nishikawa Kōjirō, and Kinoshita Naoe (1869–1937) and by the socialists Sakai Kosen and Kōtoku Shūsui (Denjirō; 1871–1911).

70. *Kokka Gakkai zasshi*, 19.10 (October 1905).

71. *Kyōiku jiron*, no. 781 (25 December 1906), pp. 1–2.

72. See Takata, "Sengo Nihon wa ika naru jinbutsu o yō-suru ka," *Kyōiku jigen*, p. 59, and cf. chap. 7, pp. 351–352 herein.

73. Tanimoto Tomeri, *Shin kyōiku kōgi* (Rokumeikan, 1906), p. 51.

74. Ibid., p. 152.

75. Miyake, *Sōkon* (Shiseidō, 1915), pp. 605–606.

76. Ishikawa Takuboku, *Jidai heisoku no genjō*, in *Takuboku zenshū* (Iwanami Shoten, 1961), 10:25.

77. *Kyōiku jiron*, no. 765 (15 July 1906), p. 45.

78. Meant by the "old" *Heimin shinbun* is the weekly newspaper founded by Kōtoku Shūsui and Sakai Kosen in November 1903. Pacifism was one of the policies advocated by this periodical, which was vigorously against the Russo-Japanese War. It was ordered to cease publication as a result of including Kōtoku's translation of the *Communist Manifesto* in its anniversary issue, and no. 64, published on 29 January 1905, was its last issue to appear. *Chokugen* then took its place. The weekly *Heimin shinbun* is to be distinguished from its namesake, a socialist daily newspaper published between January and April 1907.

79. Fujiwara Kiyozō, *Meiji kyōiku shisōshi* (Fuzanbō, 1909), p. 687.

80. *Meiji ikō kyōiku seido hattatsushi,* ed. Kyōikushi Hensankai Kyōiku Shiryō Chōsakai (Kyōikushi Hensankai Kyōiku Shiryō Chōsakai, 1939), 5:552.

81. Tanimoto, *Shin kyōiku kōgi*, p. 202.

82. These opinions are surveyed in the "Jibun issoku" column of *Kyōiku jiron*, no. 763 (25 June 1906), pp. 32–34.

83. *Kyōiku jiron*, no. 777 (15 November 1906), pp. 4–6.

84. Ibid., no. 772 (25 September 1906), p. 35.

85. This incident had its issue in a meeting convened by socialists at a Tokyo public hall called the Kinkikan (hence it is also known as the Kinkikan Incident). Members of the anarchist faction, namely Ōsugi Sakae (1885–1923) and Arahata Kanson (1887–1981), unfurled a red flag inscribed with the characters

museifu kyōsan (anarchist communism). The government used this as a pretext for arresting fourteen leading socialists, including Sakai Kosen.

86. Tokutomi Iichirō, *Kōshaku Katsura Tarō den* (Kō Katsura Kōshaku Kinen Jigyōkai, 1917), 2:348–349.

87. "Boshin shōsho," *Kanpō*, no. 7,592 (14 October 1908), p. 1.

88. Yokoyama Tatsuzō, *Monbudaijin o chūshin to shite hyōron seru Nihon kyōiku no hensen* (Rinsen Shoten, 1964 reprint ed.), p. 221.

89. The Kōtoku Incident was a purge of Japanese socialists and anarchists, twenty-six of whom—most prominently Kōtoku Shūsui—were prosecuted for allegedly plotting the assassination of the Meiji emperor. After a secret trial, twenty-four of the alleged conspirators were sentenced to death and the remaining two to imprisonment. Twelve of the former were reprieved; the rest, including Kōtoku, were executed on 24 January 1911.

90. *Kyōiku jiron*, no. 917 (5 October 1910), p. 1.

91. Ibid., no. 927 (15 January 1911), pp. 2–4.

92. Ibid., no. 931 (25 February 1911), pp. 2–4.

93. The compilation of *Dai Nihonshi*, ordered by the celebrated lord of Mito, Tokugawa Mitsukuni (1628–1700), in 1657, was not completed until 1906. A work in 397 volumes, it covers Japanese history from its legendary beginnings under Jinmu Tennō to the reign of Go-Komatsu Tennō (1377–1433; r. [1382] 1392–1412), an emperor who first ascended the throne in 1382 as the ruler of the Northern Court but ten years later also received the insignia of sovereignty from the Southern Court, thereby presiding over the end of the imperial schism.

94. See *Minema Kasui den,* ed. Yokoyama Kendō (Minema-shi Kanreki Shukugakai Kinen Kankōkai, 1933), pp. 217–231.

95. *Kyōiku jiron,* no. 921 (15 November 1910), p. 41.

96. Ibid., no. 927, p. 42.

97. Ibid., no. 904 (25 May 1910), pp. 4–5.

GLOSSARY

Abe Isoo　安倍磯雄
Abe Masahiro　阿部正弘
Abekawa mochi　安倍川餅
Aburatori　脂取
Adachi Kenzō　安達謙蔵
Agawa　吾川
Aichi　愛知
Aikoku Kōtō　愛国公党
Aizawa Yasushi (Seishisai)
　会沢安（正志斉）
Aizu　会津
Ajiro Hironori　足代弘訓
Akahata Jiken　赤旗事件
Akama　赤間
Akaoguchi-ren　赤尾口連
Akaoka　赤岡
Aki　安芸
Akita　秋田
Akiyama Gyokuzan　秋山玉山
Akizuki　秋月
Akizuki Tanetatsu　秋月種樹
Amano Tameyuki　天野為之
Amaterasu Ōmikami　天照皇神
Amatsu Mioyagami　皇祖天神
Ame no Minakanushi no Kami
　天御中主神
Ame no Muragimi　天邑君

Andō Kenta　安藤健太
Andō Nobumasa　安藤信正
Anegakōji Kintomo　姉小路公知
Annam　安南
Ansei　安政
An'yōin　安養院
Aoki Yoshimasa　青木義正
Arahata Kanson　荒畑寒村
Arakawa Gorō　荒川五郎
Arima Gennai　有馬源内
Arisugawa no Miya Taruhito
　有栖川宮熾仁
Asago　朝来
Asahi shinbun　『朝日新聞』
Asakusa　浅草
Ashikaga　足利
Ashikaga Takauji　足利高氏（尊氏）
Awa　阿波
Baba Tatsui　馬場辰猪
bakuhan　幕藩
Bakumatsu　幕末
Bankoku gaishi　『万国概誌』
Baujanhsia [Botansha]　牡丹社
bettō　別当
Bitchū　備中
Biteki seikatsuron　『美的生活論』
Bōgokai　忘吾会

439

Boshin [1868]　戊辰
Boshin [1908]　戊申
bu　武
bugyōshoku　奉行職
bun　文
Bunbukan　文武館
Bunka　文化
Bunka-Bunsei　文化文政
Bunkyū　文久
bunmei kaika　文明開化
bunmeikoku　文明国
bushi　武士
butsuri　物理
Buyō Inshi　武陽隱士
Byōdōkai　平等会
Chiaraijima　血洗島
Chiba　千葉
Chichibu　秩父
Chidōkan　致道館
chigakuji　知学事
Chigami Kiyoomi　千頭清臣
chihanji　知藩事
Chiharu　千春
Chihaya　千剣破
chihō　治法
Chijifu　知事府
chijutsu　治術
Chikuzen　筑前
Chindai　鎮台
Ch'ing　清
Chinshōfu　鎮将府
chō　町
chobokure　チョボクレ
Chokugen　『直言』
chōshi　徵士
Chōshū　長州
Chou　周
Chōya shinbun　『朝野新聞』
Chu Hsi　朱熹
chūdaifu　中大夫
Chūgoku　中国
Chūhōkyoku　鋳砲局
chūnōsōteki kaikakuha　中農層的
　改革派
Chūō gakujutsu zasshi　『中央学術
　雑誌』
Chūō kōron　『中央公論』

Chūritsu　中立
Chūritsu Gakusha　中立学舎
Chūritsuha　中立派
Chūritsusha　中立社
Chūseitō　中正党
Chūsenkyoku　鋳銭局
*Dai jūkyūseiki Nihon no seinen oyobi
　sono kyōiku*　『第一九世紀日本の
　青年及其教育』
dai kansatsushi　大監察使
Dai Nihon Kyōikukai zasshi　『大日本
　教育会雑誌』
Dai Nihon Kyōkai　大日本協会
Dai Nihonshi　『大日本史』
daiben　大弁
Daidō Danketsu Undō　大同団結運動
Daigakkan　大学官
Daigakkō　大学校
daigakkō goyōgakari　大学校御用掛
Daigakkō kisoku　『大学校規則』
Daigaku　大学
Daigaku Honkō　大学本校
*Daigaku kisoku oyobi chūshōgaku
　kisoku*　『大学規則及中小学規則』
Daigaku Nankō　大学南校
Daigaku Tōkō　大学東校
Daigakuryō　大学寮
Daigakuryō-dai　大学寮代
daigunkan　大軍監
daikan　代官
dainagon　大納言
daisanji　大参事
Daishin'in　大審院
Dajōkan　太政官
Danjō no shōchū　弾正少忠
Danjōdai　弾正台
Dewa　出羽
Dōjima　堂島
Dōshi ni tei-suru shoken　「呈同志
　所見」
Dōshin Gakusha　同心学舎
Doyō shinbun　『土陽新聞』
Ebara Soroku　江原素六
Ebihara Boku　海老原穆
Ebina Danjō　海老名弾正
Echigo　越後
Echizen　越前

Edo　江戸

Edo-fu　江戸府

Egi Kazuyuki　江木千之

Eguchi Takakuni　江口高邦

Ehime　愛媛

Eigakkai　英学会

Ee ja nai ka　エエジャナイカ

Eishi　『英史』

Endō Shichirō　遠藤七郎

Enkakushi ryaku　『沿革史略』

Enomoto Takeaki　榎本武揚

eta　穢多

Etō Shinpei　江藤新平

Ezo　蝦夷

fu　府

Fuchū　府中

fudai　譜代

Fuji　富士

Fujii Ryōsetsu　藤井良節

Fujino Kainan　藤野海南

Fujita Tōko　藤田東湖

Fukagawa　深川

Fukagawa Harumichi　深川治道

Fukakado Fuchimoto　深門淵基

Fukano Ichizō　深野一三

Fukao Shigeyuki　深尾重行

Fukao Tanba　深尾丹波

fukoku kyōhei　富国強兵

fuku-sōsai　副総裁

Fukuchi Gen'ichirō　福地源一郎

Fukuhara Echigo　福原越後

Fukui　福井

Fukui Jun'ichirō　福井純一郎

Fukuoka　福岡

Fukuoka Seima　福岡精馬

Fukuoka Takachika　福岡孝弟

Fukutomi Takasue　福富孝季

Fukuzawa Yukichi　福沢諭吉

Funada Yoshimasa　船田義昌

Funkisha　憤起社

Furukyōmachi-ren　古京町連

Furushō Kamon　古荘嘉門

Fushimi　伏見

Fuyachō Sanjō-agaru　麩屋町三條
　上ル

Fuzoku Hensoku Chūgakkō　附属変則
　中學校

gaibangaku　外蕃学

Gaimushō　外務省

Gakan shōkei　『我観小景』

Gakkakyoku　学課局

gakkō-gakari　学校掛

gakkō goyōgakari　学校御用掛

Gakkō Torishirabe Goyōgakari
　学校取調御用掛

Gakkōkan　学校官

Gakkōtō　学校党

gaku　嶽

Gakumon no susume　『学問のすすめ』

Gakusei　学制

Gakusei Kenkyūkai　学政研究会

Gakushasei　「学舎制」

Gakushūin　学習院

gakutai　学体

Gakuyōsha　嶽洋社

gedaifu　下大夫

Geiyō Gakusha　芸陽学舎

Genji　元治

Genkō　元弘

genrō　元老

Genrōin　元老院

Gen'yōsha　玄洋社

Gifu　岐阜

gijō　議定

Gikyoku　議局

Ginkō tsūshinroku　『銀行通信録』

Giseikan　議政官

gō　合

Go-Daigo　後醍醐

Go-Komatsu Tennō　後小松天皇

Godai Tomoatsu　五代友厚

gōgakkō　郷学校

Gōgaku no shigi　「郷学私議」

gōhei　郷兵

Gohin Edo Mawashi Rei　五品江戸廻
　し令

Gojō　五条

gojū　郷中

Gokajō no Seimon　五ケ条の誓文

gokenin　御家人

gōkō　郷校

goku　獄

gokumon　獄門

gon no daijō　権大丞

gonrei 権令

Goryōkaku 五稜郭

Goryōten-sama 御両天様

gosaikaku-kin 御才覚金

gōshi 郷士

Gōso nikki 『強訴日記』

Gotō Shōjirō 後藤象二郎

Gunkankyoku 軍艦局

Gunma 群馬

Gunmukyoku 軍務局

Gunsho ruijū 『群書類従』

Gyōbushō 刑部省

Gyōseikan 行政官

Gyōyosha 行余社

Gyūkō 吸江

Gyūkō Gakkō 吸江学校

Gyūkō Yōgakkō 吸江洋学校

Hachi Gakkō 蜂学校

Hachiōji 八王子

Hagi 萩

Hagiwara Otohiko 萩原乙彦

hakama 袴

hakase 博士

Hakata 博多

hakkyokusei 八局制

Hakodate 函館

Hakura Azumamaro (Kada no Azumamaro) 羽倉東麿 (荷田春満)

Hamaguri Gomon no Hen 蛤御門 の変

han 藩

Hanawa Hokiichi 塙保己一

Hanawa Jirō (Tadatomi) 塙次郎 (忠宝)

hanbatsu 藩閥

Hani Gorō 羽仁五郎

hanji 判事

hankai 半開

hannin 判任

Hanseikai zasshi 『反省会雑誌』

hanseki hōkan 版籍奉還

haori 羽織

Hara Rokurō 原六郎

Hara Shigetane 原茂胤

Hara Tetsu 原轍

Harada Jun (Ri Shimei) 原田順 (李紫溟)

Harada Sakusuke 原田作助

Harima 播磨

Hasegawa Akimichi 長谷川昭道

Hasegawa Tenkei 長谷川天渓

Hasegawa Yoshinosuke 長谷川芳之助

Hata 幡多

hatamoto 旗本

Hatano Denzaburō 波多野伝三郎

Hatsukaichi 二十日市

Hatsuyōsha 発陽社

Hattori Shisō 服部之総

Hayami Seiji 早速整爾

Hayashi Kaneaki 林包明

Hayashi Ōen 林桜園

Hayashi Yūzō 林有造

Heigakuryō 兵学寮

Heikensha 平権社

heimin 平民

heimin shakai 平民社会

Heimin shinbun 『平民新聞』

heiminshugi 平民主義

hensoku 変則

Hensoku Chūgaku 変則中学

Hibiya 日比谷

Hideshima Ieyoshi 秀島家良

Higashikuze Michitomi 東久世通禧

Higashitani 東谷

Higo 肥後

Higo Kokugaku 肥後国学

Higuchi Kanjirō 樋口勘次郎

Hijikata Hisamoto 土方久元

Hijikata Yasushi 土方寧

Hikari 『光』

Hikawa 氷川

Hikone 彦根

Himeji 姫路

Hina Matsuri 雛祭

hinin 非人

Hinode shinbun 『日出新聞』

Hirade Kōjirō 平出鏗二郎

Hirai Zennojō 平井善之丞

Hirakawa Korekazu 平川惟一

Hirano Kuniomi 平野国臣

Hirao Michio 平尾道雄

Hirata Atsutane 平田篤胤

Hirata Kanetane 平田鉄胤

Hirata Tōsuke 平田東助

Hiroi Hajime　広井一

Hirosaki　弘前

Hirosawa Saneomi　広沢真臣

Hiroshima　広島

hirosohi　ヒロソヒ

Hirota Masao　弘田正郎

Hishida Bunzō　菱田文蔵

Hitotsubashi　一橋

Hitotsubashi Yoshinobu　一橋慶喜

Hizen　肥前

Hoan Jōrei　保安条令

Hōensha　方円社

Hogeikyoku　捕鯨局

hōgigaku　方伎学

hoi-kago　ホイ駕籠

Hōjō　北条

hōki　帚

Hōki　伯耆

Hokkaidō　北海道

Hokuriku　北陸

Hokushintai　北辰隊

Hongaku　本学

Honka　本科

Honkō　本校

Honkyōgaku　本教学

Honshū　本州

Honzankai　本山会

Horie Hideichi　堀江英一

Horigoe Kansuke　堀越寛介

Hōritsu Kenkyūjo　法律研究所

hoshō　輔相

Hoshō Denka　輔相殿下

hoshō-kyō　輔相卿

Hoshu Chūseitō　保守中正党

Hosokawa Junjirō　細川潤次郎

Hosokawa Shigekata　細川重賢

Hōtokukai　報徳会

Hotta Masayoshi　堀田正睦

Hozumi Nobushige　穂積陳重

Hozumi Yatsuka　穂積八束

Hyakuichi shinron　『百一新論』

Hyakusasha　百做社

hyō　俵

Hyōbushō　兵部省

Hyōgo　兵庫

Hyōron shinbun　『評論新聞』

hyōtan no hirakihajime wa hiya de

yari　瓢箪のひらき始めは冷でやり・
兵端のひらき始めは火矢でやり

Hyūga　日向

Ibaraki　茨城

Ibaraki Sadaoki　茨木定興

Ibunkai　以文会

Ichigaya　市ヶ谷

Ichishima Kenkichi　市島謙吉

ichizen　一膳

Igakkō　医学校

Igakusho　医学所

Iguchi Teisuke　井口呈助

Ii Kamon no Kami Naosuke　井伊掃
部頭直弼

Ijichi Sō no Jō　伊知地壮之丞

Ijūin　伊集院

Ijūin Kaneyoshi　伊集院兼善

Ikebe Kichijūrō　池辺吉十郎

Ikeda Ōsuke　池田応助

Ikeda Sōan　池田草庵

Ikeji Taizō　池知退蔵

Ikuno　生野

Ikyoku　医局

Imahashi Iwao　今橋巌

Inhinkan　寅賓館

Innoshima　因島

Inoue Kaoru　井上馨

Inoue Kowashi　井上毅

Inoue Tetsujirō　井上哲次郎

Inoue Ton　井上屯

Irie Bunrō　入江文郎

iru o hakarite idasu o nasu　量入以
為出

Isawa Shūji　伊沢修二

Ise　伊勢

Ise Yamada　伊勢山田

Iseya Tōbei　伊勢屋藤兵衛

Ishikawa　石川

Ishikawa Ken　石川謙

Ishikawa Takuboku　石川啄木

Ishikawajima　石川島

Ishimaru Sanzaburō (Sekisen)
石丸三三郎（石泉）

Isomura Tetsuya　礒邑鐵彌

Itagaki Hokotarō　板垣鉾太郎

Itagaki Taisuke　板垣退助

Itō Chōroku　伊藤長六

Itō Hirobumi　伊藤博文
Itō Tasaburō　伊東多三郎
Iwakura Tomomi　岩倉具視
Iwasaki Nagatake　岩崎長武
Iwashita Masahira　岩下方平
Iwate　岩手
jichiteki kyōiku　自治的教育
Jidōsha　自動社
Jiji shinpō　『時事新報』
Jingikan　神祇官
jinjō chūgakkō　尋常中学校
jinken　人権
jinmin taishū　人民大衆
Jinmu Tennō　神武天皇
jinzai　人材
jirikisha　自力社
Jisei o Ureuru Kai　時勢を憂ふる会
Jiseiron　「時勢論」
Jishūkan　時習館
jitsugaku　実学
Jitsugakuha　実学派
Jitsugakutō　実学党
Jitsugyō no Nihon　『実業之日本』
Jitsugyō no Nihon-sha　実業之日本社
jiyū minken undō　自由民権運動
Jiyūha　自由派
Jiyūtō　自由党
Jō Sentarō　城泉太郎
jōi　攘夷
jokyō　助教
Joranshū　『如蘭集』
jōruri　浄瑠璃
jōshi　上士
juku　塾
Junminsha　純民社
Kabayama Sukenori　樺山資紀
kabuki　歌舞伎
kabunakama　株仲間
Kachō Gakusha　香長学舎
Kada no Azumamaro (Hakura
　Azumamaro)　荷田春満（羽倉東麿）
kado　門
Kadono Ikunoshin　門野幾之進
Kaeda Nobuyoshi　海江田信義
Kaei　嘉永
Kaetsu Ujifusa　嘉悦氏房
Kaga　加賀

Kagami　香美
Kagawa　香川
Kagiya Mohei　鍵屋茂兵衛
Kagoshima　鹿児島
Kaibara Ekken　貝原益軒
Kaigo Tokiomi　海後宗臣
Kaigunkyoku　海軍局
kaikoku　開国
Kaimeiha　開明派
Kainan Gakkō　海南学校
Kainan Gisha　海南義社
Kainan Shijuku　海南私塾
Kaisei Gakkō　開成学校
Kaiseikan　開成館
Kaiseikyoku　改正局
Kaisesho　開成所
Kaishintō　改進党
Kaitakushi　開拓使
Kaiten shishi　『回天詩史』
Kaitensha　回天社
Kaiunsha　開運社
Kajii　梶井
kakushu gakkō　各種学校
Kamada Keisuke　鎌田景弼
Kamakura　鎌倉
Kami-Musubi no Kami　神皇産霊神
Kamo no Mabuchi (Okabe Mabuchi)
　賀茂真淵（岡部真淵）
kan　貫
Kanagawa　神奈川
Kanazawa　金沢
Kanda　神田
Kanda Takahira　神田孝平
Kanenaga [Kaneyoshi]　懐良
Kangakusho　漢学所
Kangyōkyoku　勧業局
Kanō Jigorō　嘉納治五郎
Kansai　関西
kanson minpi　官尊民卑
Kantō　関東
Kan'yō Gakkō　漢洋学校
Karatsu　唐津
Kashokkyoku　貨殖局
Katagiri Seisuke　片桐省介
katamu　固
Kataoka Kenkichi　片岡健吉
Kataoka Naoharu　片岡直温

Katayama Sen　片山潜

Katō Hiroyuki　加藤弘之

Katō Yūrin　加藤有隣

Katōge　鹿峠

Katori　香取

Katsu Awa no Kami Kaishū　勝安房守
海舟

Katsura　桂

Katsura Takahiro　桂誉恕

Katsura Takashige　桂誉重

Katsuragi Hikoichi　葛城彦一

Kawabe　川辺

Kawagoe　川越

Kawai Kiyomaru　川合清丸

Kawakami Hikoji　川上彦次

Kawakatsu Hiromichi　川勝広運

Kawakita Shunsuke (Gijirō)　河北俊弼
（義次郎）

Kawamura　川村

Kawasaki Rosuke　川崎魯輔

Kayakkyoku　火薬局

Kazu no Miya Chikako　和宮親子

Keage　蹴揚

kei　慶

keimō　啓蒙

Keiō　慶応

Keiō Gijuku　慶応義塾

Keishintō　敬神党

ken [prefecture]　県

ken [rights]　権

Ken kōhō　『県公報』

Kenjō-taru tai　「献上樽鯛」

kenkō kunrei　箝口訓令

Kenkonsha　乾坤社

Kenmu　建武

Kenpōkai　憲法会

Kenritsu Chūgakkō　県立中学校

Kenseitō　憲政党

Kensetsu shuisho　「建設趣意書」

Kichibei　吉兵衛

Kido Takayoshi　木戸孝允

kifū　気風

Kiheitai　奇兵隊

Kikuchi Dairoku　菊池大麓

Kikuchi Kurō　菊池九郎

Kikuyabashi　菊屋橋

Kimura Tsuruo　木村絃雄

Kinai　畿内

Kinkikan　錦輝館

Kinnōha　勤王派

Kinnōtō　勤王党

Kinoshita Naoe　木下尚江

kinoto ushi　乙丑

Kira Tōru　吉良亨

Kirino Toshiaki　桐野利秋

Kiryū　桐生

Kita Kanbara　北蒲原

Kitagaki Kunimichi　北垣国道

Kitamachi Jiyūtō　北町自由党

Kitamura Shigeyori　北村重頼

Kiyaku　「規約」

Kiyozawa Manshi　清沢満之

Koba Sadatake　木場貞長

Kōbō　弘法

kōbu gattai　公武合体

Kōchi　高知

Kōchi Chūgakkō　高知中学校

Kōchi-ken Shihan Gakkō　高知県師範
学校

Kōchi-ken Shihan Gakkō Fuzoku
Hensoku Chūgaku　高知県師範学校
附属変則中学

Kōchi Kyōritsu Gakkō　高知共立学校

Kōchi shinbun　『高知新聞』

Kōda Rohan　幸田露伴

Kōdō　皇道

Kōdōkai　弘道会

Kōdōkanki　『弘道館記』

Kōdōsha　公同社

Kogaku　古学

Kōgaku　皇学

Kōgakusho　皇学所

Kōgisho　公議所

Kōgon　光厳

Koike Kunitake　小池国武

Kojima Takanori　児島高徳

Kōjukan　教授館

kōkangaku　皇漢学

kōke　高家

Kokka Kyōikusha　国家教育社

Kokka no Tateki　国家の干城

Kokkai Kisei Dōmei　国会期成同盟

Kokkai shinbun　『国会新聞』

kokkashugi　国家主義

Kokken hanron　『国憲汎論』
Kokkyō Daidōsha　国教大道社
koku　石
Kokugaku　国学
kokuhō　国法
Kokuhō hanron　『国法汎論』
kokuji goyōgakari　国事御用掛
kokumin　国民
Kokumin Dōmeikai　国民同盟会
Kokumin-ha　国民派
kokumin kyōiku　国民教育
Kokumin no tomo　『国民之友』
Kokumin Sakushinkai　国民作新会
Kokumin shinbun　『国民新聞』
kokuminshugi　国民主義
Kokumintō　国民党
Kokura　小倉
Kokuritsu Kyōiku Kisei Dōmeikai　国立教育期成同盟会
Kokushō Iwao　黒正厳
kokusui　国粋
kokusui-ha　国粋派
kokusui hozon ron　国粋保存論
kokusuishugi　国粋主義
kokutai　国体
kokutai minsei　国体民性
Kokutai shinron　『国体新論』
Komatsu Genba no Kami　小松玄蕃頭
Komatsu Tatewaki　小松帯刀
Komatsubara Eitarō　小松原英太郎
Komatsuzaki Bunko　小松崎文庫
Komeda Torao　米田虎雄
Komeda Zeyō　米田是容
kōmei seidai　公明正大
Komukai　小向
Komura Jutarō　小村寿太郎
Kōmyō　光明
Konami Gorō　小南五郎
Konda Bunjirō　昆田文次郎
Kondō Arata　近藤新
Kondō Shitchū　近藤執中
Konoe　近衛
Konoe Atsumaro　近衛篤麿
Konoe Tadahiro　近衛忠煕
Kon'yo zushiki　『坤輿図識』
Kōraimon-ren　高麗門連
kōri bugyō　郡奉行

Koroku-ha　古禄派
Koshi　古志
Koshiji　越路
Kōten Kenkyūjo　皇典研究所
Kōtō Eiwa Gakkō　高等英和学校
Kōtoku Shūsui (Denjirō)　幸徳秋水（伝次郎）
Kōtokuji　広徳寺
Kōyō　向陽
Kōyōkai　高陽会
Kōyōsha　高陽社
koyū　固有
Kōzankyoku　鉱山局
Kōzuke　上野
Kubota Yuzuru　久保田譲
Kudan　九段
Kudō Yukimoto　工藤行幹
Kuga Katsunan　陸羯南
kuge　公卿
Kujō　九条
Kujō Michitaka　九条道孝
Kumagai Renshin　熊谷蓮心
Kumamoto　熊本
Kumamoto Yōgakkō　熊本洋学校
Kuman　久万
Kume Hiroyuki　久米弘行
Kume Kunitake　久米邦武
Kunaishō　宮内省
Kunitokotachi no Mikoto　国常立尊
Kunitomo Shigemasa　国友重昌
Kurahashijima　倉橋島
Kurashiki　倉敷
Kuroda Kiyotaka　黒田清隆
Kurohara　黒原
Kuroiwa Ruikō　黒岩涙香
Kurume　久留米
Kusaka Genzui　久坂玄瑞
Kusakabe Sannosuke　日下部三之介
Kusuda Hideyo　楠田英世
Kusumoto Masataka　楠本正隆
Kusunoki Masashige　楠正成
Kusunose Sachihiko　楠瀬幸彦
Kutsumi Kesson (Yasutada)　久津見蕨村（息忠）
Kuwabara Kaihei　桑原戒平
Kuwabara Masaatsu　桑原正篤
Kuzutsuka　葛塚

kyō 卿

Kyōiku hōchi 『教育報知』

Kyōiku jidaikan 『教育時代観』

Kyōiku jiron 『教育時論』

kyōka 狂歌

Kyōkasho Gigoku 教科書疑獄

Kyōkyōsha 競々社

Kyōmachi-ren 京町連

Kyōritsu Gakkō 共立学校

Kyōritsu Gakusha 共立学舎

Kyōshisha 鏡賜社

kyōtō 郷党

Kyōto Daigakkō 京都大學校

kyōtō kyōiku 郷党教育

Kyōto shugoshoku 京都守護職

kyoyō-ha 許洋派

Kyūyō Gakkan 丘陽学館

Liaotung 遼東

machi bugyō 町奉行

Maebara Issei 前原一誠

Maeda Masana 前田正名

Maeda Mototoshi 前田元敏

Maeda Shigema (Masatane) 前田繁馬
（正種）

Maeshima [Maejima] Hisoka 前島密

Mainichi shinbun 『毎日新聞』

Maki Izumi 真木和泉

Makino Nobuaki 牧野伸顕

Man'en 万延

Maruyama Sakura 丸山作楽

Masaoka Shiki 正岡子規

Masuda Giichi 増田義一

Masuda Uemon no Suke 増田右衛
門介

Matsudaira Hōki no Kami Munehide
松平伯耆守宗秀

Matsudaira Katamori 松平容保

Matsudaira Yoshinaga (Shungaku)
松平慶永（春嶽）

Matsue 松江

Matsugasaki 松ケ崎

Matsukata 松方

Matsumoto 松本

Matsuoka Tokitoshi 松岡時敏

Matsusaka 松坂

Matsushima Gōzō 松島剛三

Matsushiro 松代

Matsuyama Moriyoshi 松山守善

Matsuzaki 松崎

Matsuzawa 松沢

Meidō Gakusha 明道学舎

Meidōkai 明道会

Meiji 明治

Meiji ishin 明治維新

Meiroku zasshi 『明六雑誌』

Meirokusha 明六社

meitoku 明徳

Meitokutō 明徳党

Mezamashi shinbun 『めさまし新聞』

Mie 三重

Mimasaka 美作

min 民

Minami Hachirō 南八郎

Minami Kanbara 南蒲原

Minami Ryōsuke 南亮輔

Minamimachi Jiyūtō 南街自由党

Minamoto no Shitagō 源順

Minbushō 民部省

Minema Kasui 峯間鹿水

Minka yōjutsu 『民家要術』

minken 民権

Minkentō 民権党

Minobe Tatsukichi 美濃部達吉

minponshugi 民本主義

minshushugi 民主主義

Min'yūsha 民友社

minzokushugi 民族主義

Mishima 見島

miso o tsukeru 味噌をつける

Mitarai 御手洗

Mito 水戸

Mitsugi 御調

Mitsui 三井

Mitsukuri Rinshō 箕作麟祥

Mitsukuri Shūhei 箕作秋坪

Mitsuoka Shin'ichirō 光岡辰一郎

Miuchi 海内

Miura Kanju (Gorō) 三浦観樹（梧楼）

Miura Tetsutarō 三浦鉄太郎

Miyagawa Fusayuki 宮川房之

Miyagawa Tadataka 宮川忠敬

Miyagawa Tetsujirō 宮川鉄次郎

Miyake Izaemon 三宅伊左衛門

Miyake Jōtarō 三宅定太郎

Miyake Setsurei　三宅雪嶺
"Miyake Takayuki den"
　「三宅高幸伝」
Miyake Tatsuzō　三宅辰蔵
Miyaoi Yasuo [Miyahiro Sadao]
　宮負定雄
Miyazaki Kurumanosuke　宮崎車之助
Miyazaki Shinkei　宮崎真卿
Miyazaki Yoshimichi　宮崎嘉道
miyosashi　みよさし
mon [gate]　門
mon [unit of currency]　文
Monbushō　文部省
Mooka　真岡
Mori Arinori　森有礼
Mori Matakichirō　森復吉郎
Mori Ōgai　森鴎外
Mori Shintarō　森新太郎
Mori Shunkichi　森春吉
Mōri Tadamasa (Takachika)　毛利忠正
　(敬親)
Morikawa　森川
Morioka　盛岡
Morisawa Tan　森沢胆
Morita Sessai　森田節斉
Motoda Nagazane [Eifu]　元田永孚
Motoori Norinaga　本居宣長
Motoyama-ren　本山連
Motoyama Yukihiko　本山幸彦
Mukaishima　向島
Murata Kiyokaze [Seifū]　村田清風
Muromachi　室町
Musashi　武蔵
museifu kyōsan　無政府共産
Mutsu　陸奥
Myōjin　明神
Myōkenzan　妙見山
Nabeshima Naomasa　鍋島直正
Nagano　長野
Nagaoka　長岡
Nagaoka Moriyoshi　長岡護美
Nagasaki　長崎
Nagasawa　長沢
Nagata Kazumi　永田一三
Naitō Meisetsu　内藤鳴雪
Nakagawa no Miya Asahiko Shinnō
　中川宮朝彦親王

Nakahama Manjirō　中浜万次郎
Nakajima Nobuyuki　中島信行
Nakajima Tarobei　中島太郎兵衛
Nakamikado Tsuneyuki　中御門経之
Nakamura　中村
Nakamura Kōki　中村弘毅
Nakamura Masanao (Keiu)　中村正直
　(敬宇)
Nakanuma Ryōzō (Kien)　中沼了三
　(葵園)
Nakanuma Seizō　中沼清蔵
Nakasuka　中須賀
Nakauchi Genma　中内源馬
Nakayama Heitarō　中山平太郎
Nakayama Tadayasu　中山忠能
Namamugi　生麦
Namiki Kakutarō　並木覚太郎
Nanbu　南部
nanga　南画
Nangaku　南学
Naniwa　浪華
Nankō　南校
Nara　奈良
Naramoto Tatsuya　奈良本辰也
nasu　成
Nasu Shingo　那須信吾
Natsume Sōseki　夏目漱石
Natsushima　夏島
neru　練る
Nichiren　日蓮
Nihon　『日本』
Nihon Kōdōkai [of 1884]　日本講道会
Nihon Kōdōkai [of 1887]　日本弘道会
Nihon Kyōikushi Gakkai　日本教育史
　学会
Nihon Kyōikushi Gakkai kiyō
　『日本教育史学会紀要』
Nihon rizai zasshi　『日本理財雑誌』
Nihon Shakaitō　日本社会党
Nihongi　『日本紀』
Nihonjin　『日本人』
Nihonshugi　日本主義
Niigata　新潟
Niitsu　新津
nikan rokushōsei　二官六省制
Nikkō　日光
ningen kyōiku　人間教育

Ninigi no Mikoto　瓊瓊杵尊
Nippon　日本
Niroku shinpō　『二六新報』
Nishi Amane (Shūsuke)　西周（周助）
Nishi Kanbara　西蒲原
Nishigata Tamezō　西潟為蔵
Nishijin　西陣
Nishikawa Kōjirō　西川光二郎
Nishiki-chō　錦町
Nishimori Shintarō　西森真太郎
Nishimura Shigeki　西村茂樹
Nishimura Shōbei　西村荘兵衛
Nishimura Tsukuda　西村佃
Nishinomiya　西之宮
Nishitani　西谷
Nishō Gakusha　二松学舎
Nitta Yoshisada　新田義貞
Noda Hiroshi　野田寛
Noguchi Entarō　野口援太郎
Nojima Tanzō　野島丹蔵
Nōmijima　能美島
Nomura Morinobu　野村盛陳
Nomura Yasushi　野村靖
Nozu　野津
Nukina Ukon　貫名右近
Numa Morikazu　沼間守一
Numata　沼田
Nuyama　沼山
Nuyama Jitsugaku　沼山実学
Obama　小浜
Ochiji-sama　御チジ様
Odaka Chōshichirō　尾高長七郎
Ōdō kōsui saku　『王道興衰策』
Ōgaki　大垣
Ogasawara Nagamichi　小笠原長行
Ogawa Kazutoshi　小河一敏
Ōgimachi-Sanjō Sanenaru (Saga Sanenaru)　正親町三条実愛（嵯峨実愛）
Ōhara　大原
Ōhara kudari ato ga yokarō　大原下り跡がよかろう・大腹下り後がよかろう
Ōhara Shigetomi　大原重徳
Ōhara Yūgaku　大原幽学
Ōhashi Terutsugu (Masateru)　大橋煮次（正煮）
Ōhashi Totsuan　大橋訥庵

Ōi Kentarō　大井憲太郎
oie sōdō　お家騒動
Ōishi Kanji　大石簡二
Ōishi Madoka　大石円
Ōishi Masami　大石正巳
Ōishi Tamotsu　大石保
Ōita　大分
Oka Jirotarō　岡次郎太郎
Okabe Mabuchi (Kamo no Mabuchi)　岡部真淵（賀茂真淵）
Okada Ryōhei　岡田良平
Okayama　岡山
Okayama Kenkichi　岡山兼吉
Oki　隠岐
Ōki Hidenori　大木淑慎
Ōki Takatō (Minpei)　大木喬任（民平）
Okinawa　沖縄
Ōkubo Toshimichi (Ichizō)　大久保利通（市蔵）
Ōkuma Hidemaro　大隈英麿
Ōkuma Shigenobu　大隈重信
Ōkuni Takamasa　大国隆正
Ōkurashō　大蔵省
Ōmachi Keigetsu　大町桂月
ōmetsuke　大目付
Ōmura Masujirō　大村益次郎
Onarimichi　御成道
Onchi Sakon Mitsukazu　恩地左近満一
Ono　小野
Ono Azusa　小野梓
Ōnogō　多之郷
osamu　理
Osarizawa　尾去沢
Ōse Jintarō　大瀬甚太郎
ōsei fukko　王政復古
Ōsugi Sakae　大杉栄
Otagi Michiteru　愛宕通旭
Ōtokai　鴎渡会
Ototake Iwazō　乙竹岩造
Ōtsuki Hikogorō　大築彦五郎
Ōu　奥羽
Owari　尾張
Ozaki Kōyō　尾崎紅葉
Ozaki Saburō　尾崎三良
Ozaki Yukio　尾崎行雄
Paiwan　排湾

Rai Kiichi　頼祺一
Rai San'yō　頼山陽
Reinansha　嶺南社
ren　連
ri [league]　里
ri [principle]　理
Ri Shimei (Harada Jun)　李紫溟
　（原田順）
Rikieki Jiyūtō　力役自由党
Rikken Kaishintō　立憲改進党
Rikken seitai ryaku　『立憲政体略』
Rikken Teiseitō　立憲帝政党
Rikugō zasshi　『六合雑誌』
Rikugun Shikan Gakkō　陸軍士官
　学校
rikugunkyō　陸軍卿
Rinji Kyōiku Kaigi　臨時教育会議
Risshi Gakusha　立志学舎
Risshisha　立志社
Rōdō sekai　『労働世界』
rōjū　老中
Rokubakukai　六莫会
Rokumeikan　鹿鳴館
rōsaku kyōiku　労作教育
Rusukan　留守官
ryō　両
ryōten　両天
Ryūkyū　琉球
Ryūtei Senka (Tanehiko II)　柳亭仙果
　（二代目種彦）
sabaku　佐幕
Saeki　佐伯
Saga　佐賀
Saga no Ran　佐賀の乱
Saga Sanenaru (Ōgimachi-Sanjō
　Sanenaru)　嵯峨実愛
　（正親町三条実愛）
Sagami　相模
Sagara Fujitsugu　相良藤次
Sagawa　佐川
Sahara Junkichi　佐原純吉
saichō hotan　採長補短
Saigō Takamori (Nanshū)　西郷隆盛
　（南州）
Saigō Tsugumichi　西郷従道
Sain　左院
Sainenji　西念寺

Saionji Kinmochi　西園寺公望
saisei itchi　祭政一致
Saitama　埼玉
Saitō Kazutarō　斉藤和太郎
Sakai　堺
Sakai Kosen (Toshihiko)　堺枯川
　（利彦）
Sakai Tadayoshi　酒井忠義
Sakamoto Namio　坂本南海男
sakangumi　盛組
Sakashita　坂下
Sakazaki Sakan　坂崎賦
Sakimura Tsuneo　崎村常雄
Saku　佐久
Sakuma　佐久間
Sakuma Shōzan [Zōzan]　佐久間象山
Sakurada　桜田
Sakurada Sōshirō　桜田惣四郎
San Daijiken Kenpaku Undō　三大事件
　建白運動
Sanaka　佐中
sangi　参議
sangi shuhan　参議首班
San'in　山陰
sanji　参事
Sanjō　三条
Sanjō Sanetomi　三条実美
sankin kōtai　参勤交替
sansai　三才
Sansankai　三々会
sansei　参政
sanshoku　三職
san'yo　参与
Sanzen'in　三千院
Sasaki Takayuki　佐々木高行
Sassa Junjirō　佐々淳次郎
Sassa Kanjō　佐々干城
Sassa Rikusuke　佐々陸助
Sassa Tomofusa　佐々友房
Sat-Chō　薩長
Sat-Chō-Do　薩長土
Satsuma　薩摩
Sawa　沢
Sawamura Daihachi　沢村大八
Sawamura Katsushi　沢村勝支
Sawayanagi Masatarō　沢柳政太郎
seichūshi　誠忠士

seiji sōsaishoku　政治総裁職

Seika Gakkai　精華学会

Seikantō　征韓党

Seikei Shoin　青谿書院

Seiken Gakusha　静倹学舎

Seikensha　静倹社

Seikyōsha　政教社

Seinengumi Tsuboi Ren　青年組坪井連

seisei　済々

Seisei hatsuun　『生性発蘊』

seisei taishōgun　征西大将軍

seisei taru tashi [chi–chi tuo–shih]
　済済多士

Seiseikō　済々黌

Seishinkai　『精神界』

Seishō　聖詔

seisoku　正則

Seitaisho　「政体書」

Seitetsusho　製鉄所

Seitō Dai-Sōtokufu　征東大総督府

Seitōsha　精到社

Seiyō jijō　『西洋事情』

*Seiyō kakkoku seisui kyōjaku
　ichiranhyō*　『西洋各国盛衰強弱一
　覧表』

Seiyūkai　政友会

Seji kenbunroku　『世事見聞録』

Sekai no Nihon　『世界之日本』

Seki Shingo　関新吾

Sekiinsha　惜陰舎

sekiten　釈奠

Senbon-dōri　千本通

Sendai　仙台

Sendanbata-ren　千段畑連

Sengoku Mitsugu　仙石貢

senmon gakkō　専門学校

senryū　川柳

Senshū Daigaku　専修大学

senshū gakkō　専修学校

Setojima　瀬戸島

Settsu　摂津

sewayaku　世話役

Seyakuin　施薬院

Shakai Minshutō　社会民主党

Sheliao-kang [Sharyōkan]　社寮港

Shiba　芝

Shibata　新発田

Shibata Yūō (Gaiken)　柴田游翁
　（艾軒）

Shibusawa Eiichi　渋沢栄一

Shichi-Hakase　七博士

shichikasei　七科制

Shiga Shigetaka　志賀重昂

Shigakkō　私学校

shigi kenpō　私擬憲法

shihan gakkō　師範学校

shihōkyō　司法卿

Shijō　四条

shijuku　私塾

shiken　私権

Shikoku　四国

Shima Yoshitake　島義勇

Shimada　島田

Shimada Saburō　島田三郎

Shimamura Hayao　島村速雄

Shimamura Hōgetsu　島村抱月

Shimamura Tateo　島村干雄

Shimane　島根

Shimazu Hisamitsu　島津久光

Shimazu Nariakira　島津斉彬

Shimazu Tadayoshi　島津忠義

Shimei Gakkai　紫溟学会

Shimeikai　紫溟会

shimin　市民

Shimizu Koichirō　志水小一郎

Shimokamagarijima　下蒲刈島

Shimomoto Enzō　下元猿蔵

Shimomoto Toshiyoshi　下元敏功

Shimonoseki　下関

Shimōsa　下総

Shimotsuke　下野

Shin Hoshutō　新保守党

Shin jūhasshō yochizu
　『清十八省輿地図』

Shin kyōiku kōgi　『新教育講義』

Shinagawa　品川

Shinano　信濃

shinbunshi jōrei　新聞紙条例

Shindō Shunzaburō　進藤俊三郎

Shingaku　心学

Shinjuku　新宿

shinka shita jōi　進化した攘夷

Shinmachi-dōri　新町通

shinmin　親民

Shinmintō　親民党

Shinpei　親兵

Shinpūren　神風連

shinri　心理

Shinroku-ha　新禄派

Shinron　『新論』

Shinsei taii　『真政大意』

shiokiyaku　仕置役

Shionoya Isotari　塩谷五十足

Shiraishi Rensaku　白石廉作

Shiraishi Shōichirō　白石正一郎

Shirakawa　白川

Shiraki Tamenao　白木為直

shishi　志士

shita kara yomeba　下からよめば

Shitada　下田

Shitaya　下谷

shizoku　士族

Shizuoka　静岡

shō　少輔

Shōdōsha　唱動社

Shōgitai　彰義隊

shōgun kōkenshoku　将軍後見職

Shōhei Gakkō　昌平学校

Shōheikō　昌平黌

shomin　庶民

Shōrai no Nihon　『将来之日本』

Shōren'in　青蓮院

shoshidai　所司代

shotai　諸隊

Shōyōsha　逍遙社

Shūdōsha　修道社

Shūgiin　集議院

Shūkai Jōrei　集会条例

Shukyūha　守旧派

Shun　俊

Shungaku　春嶽

shurikosei　修理固成

Shūritsusha　修立社

Shushi　「主旨」

Sōaisha　相愛社

Soejima Taneomi　副島種臣

Soga Sukenori　曽我祐準

sokkon jōi　即今攘夷

Sōma　相馬

sōmō　草莽

sōmōtai　草莽隊

sonnō　尊王

sonnō jōi　尊王攘夷

sonnō sekiha　尊王斥覇

sōsai　総裁

sōsaikyoku　総裁局

sotsuzoku　卒族

Suehiro Tetchō　末広鉄腸

Sufu Masanosuke　周布政之助

Sugawara denju tenarai kagami
　　　『菅原伝授手習鑑』

Sugiura Jūgō　杉浦重剛

Suidōchō-ren　水道町連

Sume-Mima no Mikoto　皇御孫命

Sumie Jinzaburō　住江甚三郎

Sunakawa Katsutoshi　砂川雄峻

Sunpu　駿府

Suruga　駿河

Suzaka　須坂

Suzaki　須崎

Suzuki Naoe　鈴木直枝

Suzuki Shigetane　鈴木重胤

Tachiuri　立売

Tadanoumi　忠海

Taguchi Ukichi　田口卯吉

taifu　大輔

Taigaku　大学

taigi meibun　大義名分

Taigyaku Jiken　大逆事件

Taihei Gakkō　泰平学校

Taiheiki　『太平記』

Taiheiyō　『太平洋』

Taihō　大宝

Tairō　大老

Taisei kokuhōron　『泰西国法論』

Taishō　大正

Taishōin　待詔院

Taishōkyoku　待詔局

Taiyō　『太陽』

Tajima　但馬

Taka-Mimusubi no Kami　高皇産霊神

Takada　高田

Takahashi Chōkan　高橋長鑑

Takahashi Kenzō　高橋健三

Takahashi Nagaaki　高橋長秋

Takai Kōzan　高井鴻山

Takamagahara-ha　高天原派

Takamine Hideo　高嶺秀夫

Takamizawa Shigeru　高見沢蔵
Takanabe　高鍋
Takanawa　高輪
Takaoka　高岡
Takasegawa　高瀬川
Takashima Yoshitaka　高島義恭
Takasugi Shinsaku　高杉晋作
Takata [Takada] Sanae　高田早苗
Takatori　高取
Takatsukasa Sukehiro　鷹司輔熙
Takayama Chogyū　高山樗牛
Takayama Hikokurō　高山彦九郎
take　嶽
Takebe-ren　竹部連
Takechi Kumakichi　武市熊吉
Takechi Zuizan　武市瑞山
Takeda Izumo　竹田出雲
Takegoshi Yosaburō (Sansa)
　　竹越与三郎（三叉）
Takemoto Chōjūrō　竹本長十郎
Takenouchi Shikibu　竹内式部
Takezaki　竹崎
Takezoe Shin'ichirō　竹添進一郎
Takushikyoku　度支局
Tamamatsu Misao　玉松操
Tamana　玉名
tan　反
Tan Itsuma　丹乙馬
Tanabe Terumi [Teruzane]　田辺輝実
Tanabe Yoshiaki　田辺良顕
Tanaka Fujimaro　田中不二麿
Tanaka Tadaichirō　田中唯一郎
Tanba　丹波
Tango　丹後
Tani Shigeki　谷重喜
Tani Tateki [Kanjō]　谷干城
Taniguchi Sumio　谷口澄夫
Tanimoto Tomeri　谷本富
Tano Gakkō　田野学校
taren　他連
Tategami　立神
Tatsuta　立田
Tayasu Kamenosuke　田安亀之助
Teigai　丁亥
Tekigai chūgi-hen　『敵愾忠義篇』
Tenchūgumi　天誅組
Tenmei　天明

tennō shinsei　天皇親政
Tenpō　天保
tenri　天理
tenryō　天領
terakoya　寺子屋
to　斗
Toba　鳥羽
Tōbu Kangun buchō　東部監軍部長
Tochibori　栃堀
Tochigi　栃木
Tochio　栃尾
tōdori　頭取
Tōgōshugi shin kyōjuhō
　　『統合主義新教授法』
Tōhoku　東北
Tōkaidō　東海道
Toki Yoriyuki　土岐頼行
Tōkō　東校
Tokugawa　徳川
Tokugawa Iemochi　徳川家茂
Tokugawa Iesato　徳川家達
Tokugawa Ieyasu　徳川家康
Tokugawa Mitsukuni　徳川光圀
Tokugawa Yoshinobu　徳川慶喜
Tokushima　徳島
Tokutomi Roka　徳冨蘆花
Tokutomi Sohō　徳富蘇峰
tokuyū　得有
Tōkyō　東京
Tōkyō-fu　東京府
Tōkyō Gaikokugo Gakkō　東京外国
　　語学校
Tōkyō Kaisei Gakkō　東京開成学校
Tōkyō Keizai zasshi　『東京経済雑誌』
Tōkyō Nichinichi shinbun
　　『東京日日新聞』
Tōkyō Senmon Gakkō　東京専門学校
Tōkyō Shōhei Gakkō　東京昌平学校
Tōkyō Shūshin Gakusha　東京修身
　　学社
Tominaga Tadashi　富永直
Tomita Nichigaku　富田日岳
Tomizu Hirondo　戸水寛人
Tomonari　友成
Tonarigusa　『隣草』
Tōō Gijuku　東奥義塾
Tōrichō-ren　通町連

Torio Koyata (Tokuan)　鳥尾小弥太
　（得庵）
Tosa　土佐
Tosa Bunkō　土佐分校
Tosa Heigakkō　土佐兵学校
Tosa Jogakkō　土佐女学校
Tōsandō　東山道
Totsugawa　十津川
Tottori　鳥取
Tōya Gakkō　陶冶学校
Toyama　富山
Toyama Gakkō　外山学校
Toyama Masakazu [Shōichi]　外山正一
Toyama Mitsusuke　外山光輔
Tōyama Shigeki　遠山茂樹
Tōyō dōtoku, Seiyō geijutsu
　東洋道徳、西洋芸術
Tōyō Keizai shinpō　『東洋経済新報』
Tōyō Keizai Shinpōsha
　東洋経済新報社
Toyokawa Ryōhei　豊川良平
Toyooka Ayasuke　豊岡随資
Toyota　豊田
tozama　外様
Tsu　津
Tsuboi　坪井
Tsuboi Jitsugaku　坪井実学
Tsuboi Kuemon　坪井九右衛門
Tsubouchi Yūzō (Shōyō)　坪内雄蔵
　（逍遙）
Tsuchiya Yoshiya　土屋可也
Tsuda Mamichi　津田真道
Tsuda Nobuhiro　津田信弘
Tsuda Seiichi　津田静一
Tsuji Shinji　辻新次
Tsuji Takayuki　辻敬之
Tsukagoshi　塚越
Tsukiji　築地
tsukuru　修
Tsukushi　筑紫
tsumugi　紬
Tsunajima Ryōsen　綱島梁川
Tsurajima　連島
Tsuwano　津和野
Uchi-Tsuboi　内坪井
Uchida Tsunejirō (Masao)　内田恒次郎
　（正雄）

Uchimura Kanzō　内村鑑三
Uchū　『宇宙』
Ueda　上田
Ueda Enzō　上田円増
Ueda Kazutoshi　上田万年
Ueki Emori　植木枝盛
Uemachi Jiyūtō　上町自由党
Uematsu Kōshō　植松考昭
Uemura Kakuzaemon　植村覚左衛門
Ueno　上野
Ueno Hirokōji　上野広小路
Ueno Kieiji　上野喜永次
Ukita Kazutami　浮田和民
Ume Kenjirō　梅謙次郎
Umeda Unpin　梅田雲浜
Uno Harukaze　宇野東風
Uraga　浦賀
Uwajima　宇和島
waboku　和木・和睦
Wagaku　和学
Wagaku Kōdansho Goyōgakari
　和学講談所御用掛
wakadoshiyori　若年寄
Wakasa　若狭
Wakayama　和歌山
wakon yōsai　和魂洋才
Wang Yang-ming　王陽明
Warabi　蕨
Waseda　早稲田
Waseda Daigaku　早稲田大学
Watanabe　渡辺
Watanabe Kōki　渡辺洪基
Watanabe Noboru　渡辺昇
yaban　野蛮
Yabu　養父
Yaguchi Nuitarō　矢口縫太郎
Yakkyoku　訳局
yama　山
Yama no Sachi Ren　山幸連
Yamada Heizaemon　山田平左衛門
Yamada Ichirō　山田一郎
Yamada Kinosuke　山田喜之助
Yamada Takeho　山田武甫
Yamagata Aritomo　山形有朋
Yamaguchi　山口
Yamaji Aizan　山路愛山
Yamaji Motoharu　山地元治

Yamakawa Tomomasu   山川友益
Yamamoto Seishin   山本正心
Yamamoto Yukihiko   山本幸彦
Yamanouchi Toyonobu   山内豊敷
Yamanouchi Toyonori   山内豊範
Yamanouchi Toyosuke   山内豊資
Yamanouchi Toyoyoshi   山内豊栄
Yamanouchi Yōdō (Toyoshige)
   山内容堂（豊信）
Yamao Yōzō   山尾庸三
Yamato   大和
Yamato-damashii   大和魂
Yamazaki   山崎
Yamazaki Ansai   山崎闇斎
Yamazaki-ren   山崎連
Yanagawa Seigan   梁川星巌
Yanagawa Shunsan   柳河春三
Yanagita Kunio   柳田国男
Yano Fumio (Ryūkei)   矢野文雄
   （竜渓）
Yano Harumichi   矢野玄道
Yano Zenzō   矢野善三
Yasuba Yasukazu   安場保和
Yasui Sokken   安井息軒
Yasukuni   靖国
Yasuoka Ryōsuke   安岡良亮
Yatsushiro   八代
Yobimon   予備門
Yochishi ryaku   『輿地誌略』
yōgakkō   洋学校
Yōgakkō   洋学校
yōgaku   洋学
Yōkō nikki   『洋行日記』
Yokoi   横井
Yokoi Shōnan   横井小楠
Yokoshima   横島
Yokosuka   横須賀
Yokota Keita   横田敬太
Yokoyama Kaoru   横山薫
Yokoyama Matakichi   横山又吉
Yōmeigaku   陽明学
Yomiuri shinbun   『読売新聞』

yonaoshi ikki   世直し一揆
yōnenka   幼年課
Yonezawa   米沢
yoriai   寄合
Yorokobi no ō-zuru toshi   慶びの応
   ずるとし
Yorozu chōhō   『万朝報』
Yoshida   吉田
Yoshida Kazuma   吉田数馬
Yoshida Kumaji   吉田熊次
Yoshida Shōin   吉田松陰
Yoshida Tōyō   吉田東洋
Yoshii Kōsuke   吉井幸輔
Yoshimura Toratarō   吉村虎太郎
Yoshino   吉野
Yoshino Kinryō   芳野金陵
Yoshino Sakuzō   吉野作造
Yoshiwara   吉原
Yotsugigusa tsumiwake
   『世継草摘分』
Yūbin hōchi   『郵便報知』
Yuishin Gakkai   惟神学会
Yūkō Gakkō   猶興学校
Yūkō Gakusha   猶興学舎
Yūkokutō   愛国党
Yūkōsha   猶興社
Yumoto Takehiko   湯本武比古
Yunome Horyū   湯目補隆
Yura Nisshō   由良日正
Yuri Kimimasa   由利公正
Yushima   湯島
Yūshinsha   有信社
zaguri   座操
zaigō shōnin   在郷商人
zanbōritsu   讒謗律
Zeikakyoku   税課局
Zenkoku Kyōiku Rengōkai
   全国教育連合会
Zenkoku Kyōikusha Daishūkai
   全国教育者大集会
Zokuron-ha   俗論派
zōsai   雑菜

Index